Level 2

BENCHMARK SERIES

Microsoft® Word 365

2019 Edition

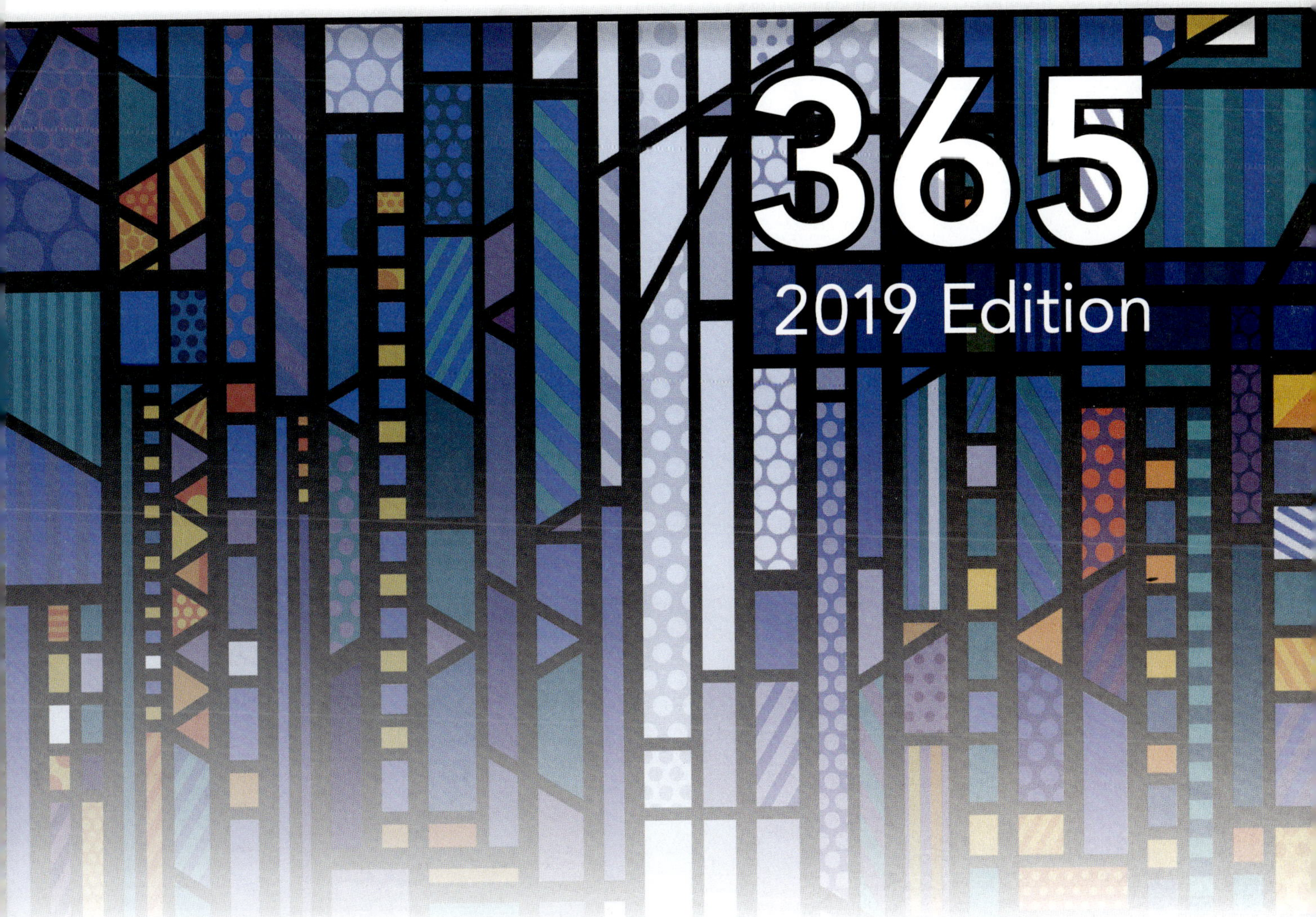

Nita Rutkosky

Audrey Roggenkamp
Pierce College Puyallup
Puyallup, Washington

Ian Rutkosky
Pierce College Puyallup
Puyallup, Washington

PARADIGM
EDUCATION SOLUTIONS

St. Paul

Vice President, Content and Digital Solutions: Christine Hurney
Director of Content Development: Carley Fruzzetti
Developmental Editor: Jennifer Joline Anderson
Director of Production: Timothy W. Larson
Production Editor/Project Manager: Jen Weaverling
Senior Design and Production Specialist: Jack Ross
Cover and Interior Design: Valerie King
Copy Editor: Communicáto, Ltd.
Testers: Janet Blum, Traci Post
Indexer: Terry Casey
Vice President, Director of Digital Products: Chuck Bratton
Digital Projects Manager: Tom Modl
Digital Solutions Manager: Gerry Yumul
Senior Director of Digital Products and Onboarding: Christopher Johnson
Supervisor of Digital Products and Onboarding: Ryan Isdahl
Vice President, Marketing: Lara Weber McLellan
Marketing and Communications Manager: Selena Hicks

Cover Photo Credit: © lowball-jack/GettyImages
Interior Photo Credits: Follow the Index.

ISBN 978-0-76388-718-6 (print)
ISBN 978-0-76388-708-7 (digital)

875 Montreal Way
St. Paul, MN 55102
Email: CustomerService@ParadigmEducation.com
Website: ParadigmEducation.com

Printed in the United States of America

28 27 26 25 24 23 22 21 20 19   1 2 3 4 5 6 7 8 9 10 11 12

Brief Contents

Preface ix

Unit 1
Formatting and Customizing Documents 1

Chapter 1 Applying Advanced Formatting 3

Chapter 2 Proofing Documents 37

Chapter 3 Inserting Headers, Footers, and References 65

Chapter 4 Creating Specialized Tables and Navigating in a Document 99

Unit 2
Editing and Formatting Documents 127

Chapter 5 Customizing Objects and Creating Charts 129

Chapter 6 Merging Documents 163

Chapter 7 Managing Building Blocks and Fields 187

Chapter 8 Managing Shared Documents 211

Index 249

Contents

Preface ix

Microsoft Word Level 2

Unit 1 Formatting and Customizing Documents 1

Chapter 1 Applying Advanced Formatting 3
Applying Character Formatting 4
  Adjusting Character Spacing 4
  Applying OpenType Features 6
  Applying Text Effects 9
  Changing the Default Font 12
Inserting Symbols and Special Characters 13
  Inserting Intellectual Property Symbols 13
  Inserting Hyphens and Dashes 14
  Inserting Nonbreaking Spaces 16
Using Find and Replace Options 17
  Finding and Replacing Font Formatting 17
  Finding and Replacing Paragraph Formatting 17
  Finding and Replacing Special Characters 19
  Finding and Replacing Styles 20
  Finding and Replacing Body and Heading Fonts 21
  Finding and Replacing Using Wildcard Characters 23
Managing Document Properties 25
Inspecting Documents 28
  Using the Document Inspector 28
  Checking the Accessibility of a Document 30
  Checking the Compatibility of a Document 32
Chapter Summary 33

Chapter 2 Proofing Documents 37
Checking Spelling and Grammar 38
  Editing During a Spelling and Grammar Check 38
  Customizing Spell Checking 38
  Using the Editor Task Pane Reading Feature 38
  Changing Grammar Checking Options 41
  Setting the Proofing Language 43
  Displaying Readability Statistics 43
  Creating a Custom Dictionary 45
  Changing the Default Dictionary 45
  Removing a Dictionary 46
Displaying the Word Count 48
Inserting Line Numbers 48
Using the Thesaurus 49
Using Smart Lookup 52
Translating Text to and from Different Languages 55
  Translating Selected Text 55
  Translating a Document 57
  Preparing a Document for Translation 57
Sorting Text 58
  Sorting Text in Paragraphs 58
  Sorting Text in Columns 59
  Sorting on More Than One Field 59
  Sorting Text in a Table 61
Chapter Summary 62

Chapter 3 Inserting Headers, Footers, and References **65**
Inserting Headers and Footers 66
Inserting Elements in Headers and Footers 66
Positioning Headers and Footers 68
Creating a Different First Page Header or Footer 70
Creating Odd and Even Page Headers or Footers 71
Creating Headers and Footers for Different Sections 72
Breaking a Section Link 72
Customizing Page Numbers 74
Printing Sections 75
Keeping Text Together 77
Inserting Footnotes and Endnotes 78
Printing Footnotes and Endnotes 80
Viewing and Editing Footnotes and Endnotes 81
Citing and Editing Sources 83
Formatting a Report Using an Editorial Style 83
Inserting Source Citations 85
Inserting Citation Placeholders 85
Inserting a Citation with an Existing Source 88
Editing a Citation and Source 88
Inserting Page Numbers in a Citation 89
Managing Sources 89
Inserting a Sources List 92
Modifying and Updating a Sources List 93
Formatting a Sources List 94
Choosing a Citation Style 95
Chapter Summary 96

Chapter 4 Creating Specialized Tables and Navigating in a Document **99**
Creating a Table of Contents 100
Applying Styles 100
Inserting a Table of Contents 100
Numbering the Table of Contents Page 100
Navigating Using a Table of Contents 101
Customizing a Table of Contents 103
Updating a Table of Contents 104
Removing a Table of Contents 104
Assigning Levels to Table of Contents Entries 106
Marking Table of Contents Entries as Fields 106
Creating a Table of Figures 110
Creating a Caption 110
Inserting a Table of Figures 111
Updating or Deleting a Table of Figures 113
Customizing a Caption 113
Navigating in a Document 115
Navigating Using the Navigation Pane 115
Inserting and Navigating with Bookmarks 116
Inserting Hyperlinks 118
Editing a Hyperlink 122
Creating a Cross-Reference 123
Chapter Summary 125

Unit 2 Editing and Formatting Documents **127**

Chapter 5 Customizing Objects and Creating Charts **129**
Customizing Objects 130
Customizing Image Layout 130
Applying Formatting at the Format Picture Task Pane 133
Applying Artistic Effects to Images 133
Customizing and Formatting Text Boxes and Shapes 135

Inserting and Customizing Icons 145
Inserting and Customizing 3D Models 147
Creating a Chart 151
Formatting with Chart Buttons 153
Changing the Chart Design 155
Changing Chart Formatting 156
Formatting a Chart with Task Pane Options 158
Chapter Summary 160

Chapter 6 Merging Documents **163**
Completing a Merge 164
Creating a Data Source File 164
Creating a Main Document 166
Previewing a Merge 169
Checking for Errors 169
Merging Documents 169
Merging with Other Main Documents 171
Merging Envelopes 171
Merging Labels 173
Merging a Directory 175
Editing a Data Source File 177
Selecting Specific Records 177
Editing Records 179
Merging Using the Mail Merge Wizard 182
Chapter Summary 184

Chapter 7 Managing Building Blocks and Fields **187**
Managing Building Blocks 188
Inserting a Building Block 188
Sorting Building Blocks 188
Saving Content as a Building Block 191
Editing Building Block Properties 195
Inserting a Custom Building Block 196
Modifying a Custom Building Block 198
Adding a Building Block Gallery as a Button on the Quick Access Toolbar 199
Saving Building Blocks in a Different Template 202
Deleting a Building Block 203
Inserting a Document Property Placeholder 205
Managing Fields 206
Choosing Field Categories 207
Creating Custom Field Formats 207
Updating Fields 207
Chapter Summary 209

Chapter 8 Managing Shared Documents **211**
Inserting and Managing Comments 212
Inserting Comments in the Reviewing Pane 213
Navigating between Comments 215
Editing Comments 215
Showing Comments 215
Replying to Comments 216
Printing Comments 217
Deleting and Resolving Comments 217
Distinguishing Comments from Different Users 217
Tracking Changes in a Document 220
Displaying Changes for Review 220
Showing Markups 220
Displaying Information about Tracked Changes 222
Changing User Information 222
Locking and Unlocking Track Changes 222
Customizing Track Changes Options 222

Printing Markups 223
Customizing Advanced Track Changes Options 225
Navigating to Changes 226
Accepting or Rejecting Changes 226
Restricting a Document 229
Applying Formatting Restrictions 230
Enforcing Protection 232
Applying Editing Restrictions 233
Protecting a Document with a Password 234
Protecting a Document 236
Marking a Document as Final 236
Encrypting a Document 237
Restricting Editing 237
Adding a Digital Signature 237
Opening a Document in Different Views 238
Sharing a Document Electronically 239
Managing Document Versions 241
Chapter Summary 244
Word Level 2 Index **249**

Preface

Achieving Proficiency in Word

The Benchmark Series, *Microsoft® Word 365*, 2019 Edition, is designed for students who want to learn how to use Microsoft's powerful word processing program to create professional-looking documents for school, work, and personal communication needs. After successfully completing a course in Microsoft Word using this courseware, students can expect to be proficient in using Word to do the following:

- Create and edit memos, letters, flyers, announcements, and reports of varying complexity.
- Apply appropriate formatting elements and styles to a range of document types.
- Add graphics and other visual elements to enhance written communication.
- Plan, research, write, revise, design, and publish documents to meet specific information needs.
- Given a workplace scenario requiring a written solution, assess the communication purpose and then prepare materials that achieve the goal efficiently and effectively.

Well-designed pedagogy is important, but students learn technology skills through practice and problem solving. Technology provides opportunities for interactive learning as well as excellent ways to quickly and accurately assess student performance. To this end, this course is supported with Cirrus, Paradigm's cloud-based training and assessment learning management system. Details about Cirrus as well as its integrated student courseware and instructor resources can be found on page xii.

Proven Instructional Design

The Benchmark Series has long served as a standard of excellence in software instruction. Elements of the series function individually and collectively to create an inviting, comprehensive learning environment that leads to full proficiency in computer applications. The following visual tour highlights the structure and features that comprise the highly popular Benchmark model.

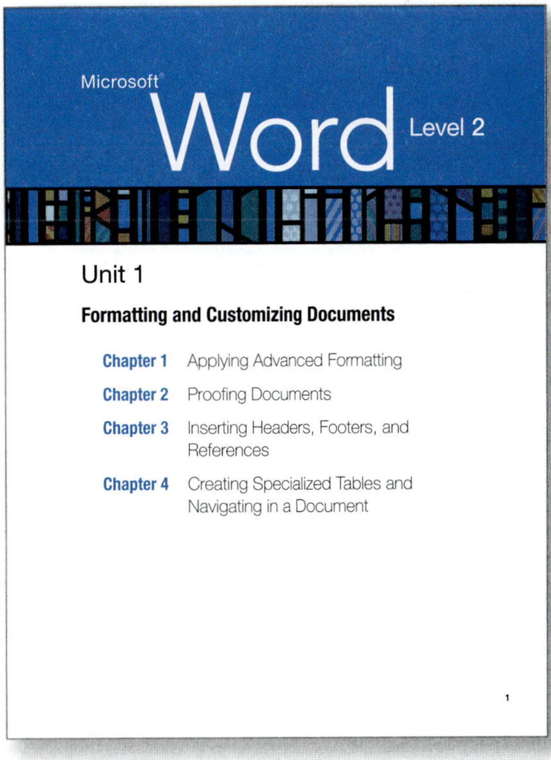
Microsoft® Word Level 2

Unit 1

Formatting and Customizing Documents

Chapter 1 Applying Advanced Formatting

Chapter 2 Proofing Documents

Chapter 3 Inserting Headers, Footers, and References

Chapter 4 Creating Specialized Tables and Navigating in a Document

1

Unit Openers display the unit's four chapter titles. Each level of the course contains two units with four chapters each.

Chapter Openers Present Learning Objectives

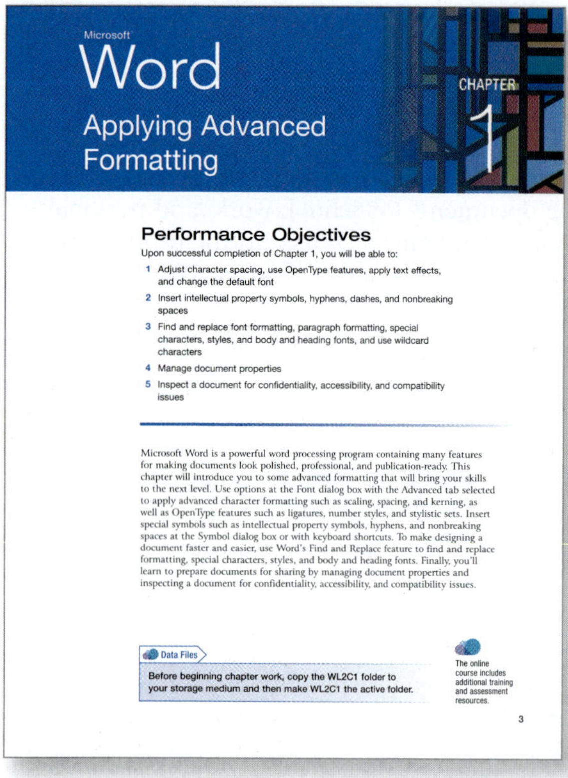

Microsoft

Word

Applying Advanced Formatting

CHAPTER 1

Performance Objectives

Upon successful completion of Chapter 1, you will be able to:

1 Adjust character spacing, use OpenType features, apply text effects, and change the default font
2 Insert intellectual property symbols, hyphens, dashes, and nonbreaking spaces
3 Find and replace font formatting, paragraph formatting, special characters, styles, and body and heading fonts, and use wildcard characters
4 Manage document properties
5 Inspect a document for confidentiality, accessibility, and compatibility issues

Microsoft Word is a powerful word processing program containing many features for making documents look polished, professional, and publication-ready. This chapter will introduce you to some advanced formatting that will bring your skills to the next level. Use options at the Font dialog box with the Advanced tab selected to apply advanced character formatting such as scaling, spacing, and kerning, as well as OpenType features such as ligatures, number styles, and stylistic sets. Insert special symbols such as intellectual property symbols, hyphens, and nonbreaking spaces at the Symbol dialog box or with keyboard shortcuts. To make designing a document faster and easier, use Word's Find and Replace feature to find and replace formatting, special characters, styles, and body and heading fonts. Finally, you'll learn to prepare documents for sharing by managing document properties and inspecting a document for confidentiality, accessibility, and compatibility issues.

Data Files

Before beginning chapter work, copy the WL2C1 folder to your storage medium and then make WL2C1 the active folder.

The online course includes additional training and assessment resources.

3

Chapter Openers present the performance objectives and an overview of the skills taught.

Data Files are provided for each chapter.

Activities Build Skill Mastery within Realistic Context

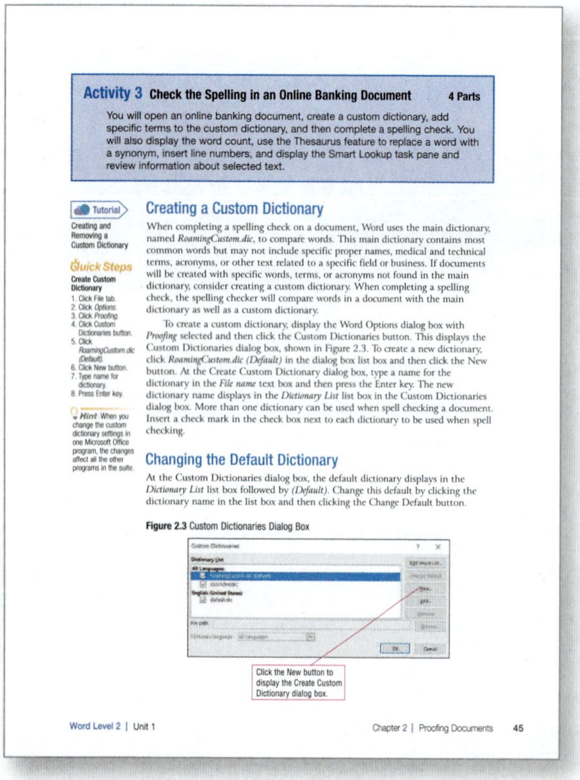

Activity 3 Check the Spelling in an Online Banking Document **4 Parts**

You will open an online banking document, create a custom dictionary, add specific terms to the custom dictionary, and then complete a spelling check. You will also display the word count, use the Thesaurus feature to replace a word with a synonym, insert line numbers, and display the Smart Lookup task pane and review information about selected text.

Tutorial

Creating and Removing a Custom Dictionary

Quick Steps

Create Custom Dictionary

1. Click File tab.
2. Click *Options*.
3. Click *Proofing*.
4. Click Custom Dictionaries button.
5. Click *RoamingCustom.dic (Default)*.
6. Click New button.
7. Type name for dictionary.
8. Press Enter key.

Hint When you change the custom dictionary settings in one Microsoft Office program, the changes affect all the other programs in the suite.

Creating a Custom Dictionary

When completing a spelling check on a document, Word uses the main dictionary, named *RoamingCustom.dic*, to compare words. This main dictionary contains most common words but may not include specific proper names, medical and technical terms, acronyms, or other text related to a specific field or business. If documents will be created with specific words, terms, or acronyms not found in the main dictionary, consider creating a custom dictionary. When completing a spelling check, the spelling checker will compare words in a document with the main dictionary as well as a custom dictionary.

To create a custom dictionary, display the Word Options dialog box with *Proofing* selected and then click the Custom Dictionaries button. This displays the Custom Dictionaries dialog box, shown in Figure 2.3. To create a new dictionary, click *RoamingCustom.dic (Default)* in the dialog box list box and then click the New button. At the Create Custom Dictionary dialog box, type a name for the dictionary in the *File name* text box and then press the Enter key. The new dictionary name displays in the *Dictionary List* list box in the Custom Dictionaries dialog box. More than one dictionary can be used when spell checking a document. Insert a check mark in the check box next to each dictionary to be used when spell checking.

Changing the Default Dictionary

At the Custom Dictionaries dialog box, the default dictionary displays in the *Dictionary List* list box followed by *(Default)*. Change this default by clicking the dictionary name in the list box and then clicking the Change Default button.

Figure 2.3 Custom Dictionaries Dialog Box

Click the New button to display the Create Custom Dictionary dialog box.

Word Level 2 | Unit 1

Chapter 2 | Proofing Documents 45

Multipart Activities provide a framework for instruction and practice on software features. An activity overview identifies tasks to accomplish and key features to use in completing the work.

Typically, a file remains open throughout all parts of the activity. Students save their work incrementally. At the end of the activity, students save, print, and then close the file.

Tutorials provide interactive, guided training and measured practice.

Quick Steps in the margins allow fast reference and review.

Hints offer useful tips on how to use software features efficiently and effectively.

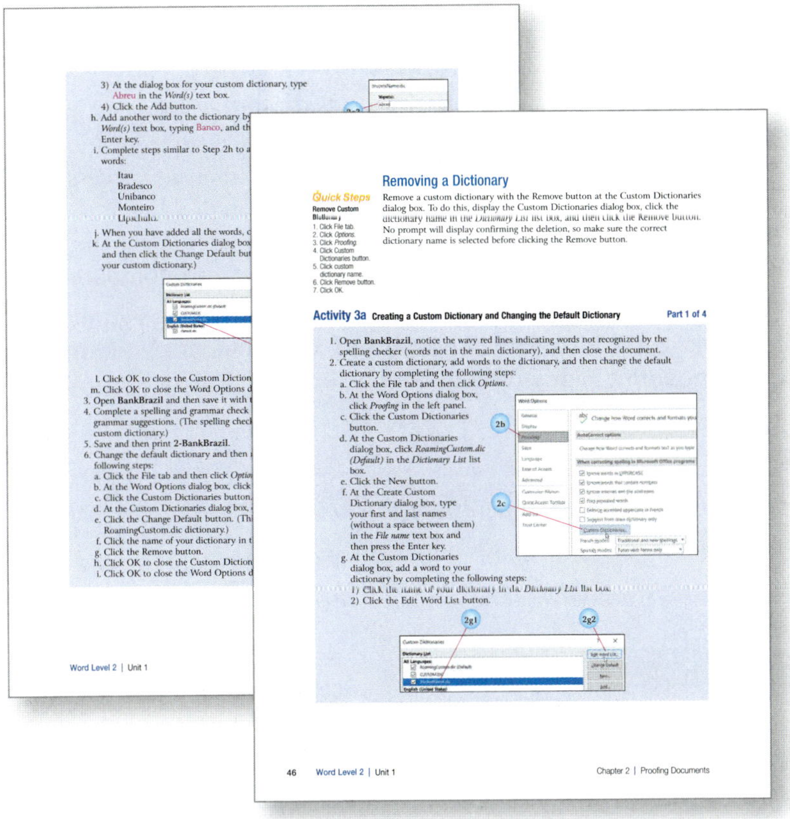

Step-by-Step Instructions guide students to the desired outcome for each activity part. Screen captures illustrate what the screen should look like at key points.

Between activity parts, the text presents instruction on the features and skills necessary to accomplish the next portion of the activity.

Magenta Text identifies material to type.

Check Your Work model answer images are available in the online course, and students can use those images to confirm they have completed the activity correctly.

Chapter Review Tools Reinforce Learning

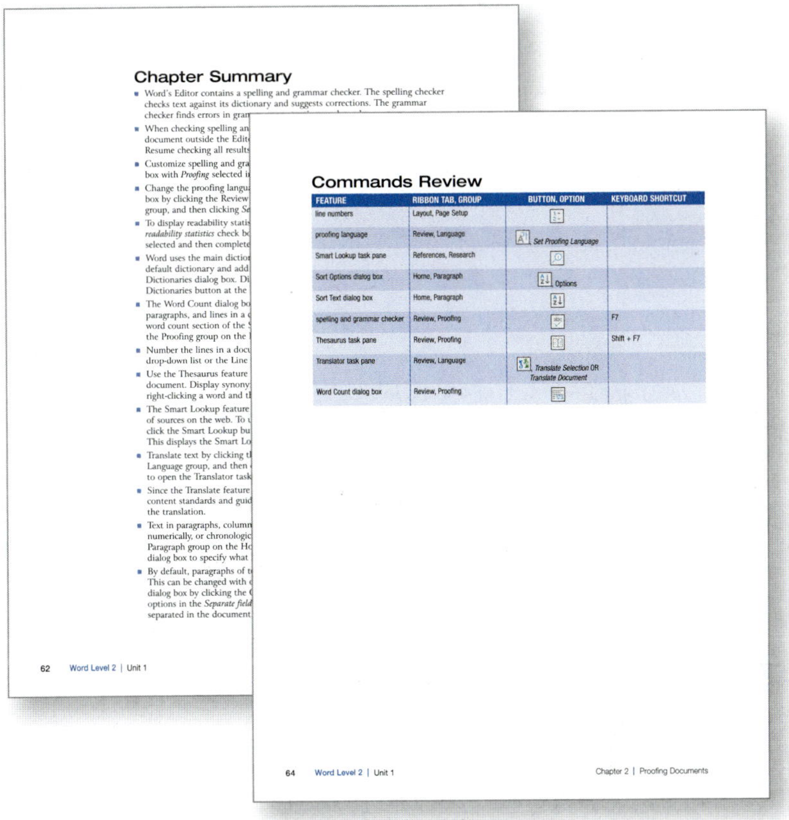

A **Chapter Summary** reviews the purpose and execution of key features.

A **Commands Review** summarizes visually the major software features and alternative methods of access.

The Cirrus Solution

Elevating student success and instructor efficiency

Powered by Paradigm, Cirrus is the next-generation learning solution for developing skills in Microsoft Office. Cirrus seamlessly delivers complete course content in a cloud-based learning environment that puts students on the fast track to success. Students can access their content from any device anywhere, through a live internet connection; plus, Cirrus is platform independent, ensuring that students get the same learning experience whether they are using PCs, Macs, or Chromebook computers.

Cirrus provides Benchmark Series content in a series of scheduled assignments that report to a grade book to track student progress and achievement. Assignments are grouped in modules, providing many options for customizing instruction.

Dynamic Training

The online Benchmark Series courses include interactive resources to support learning.

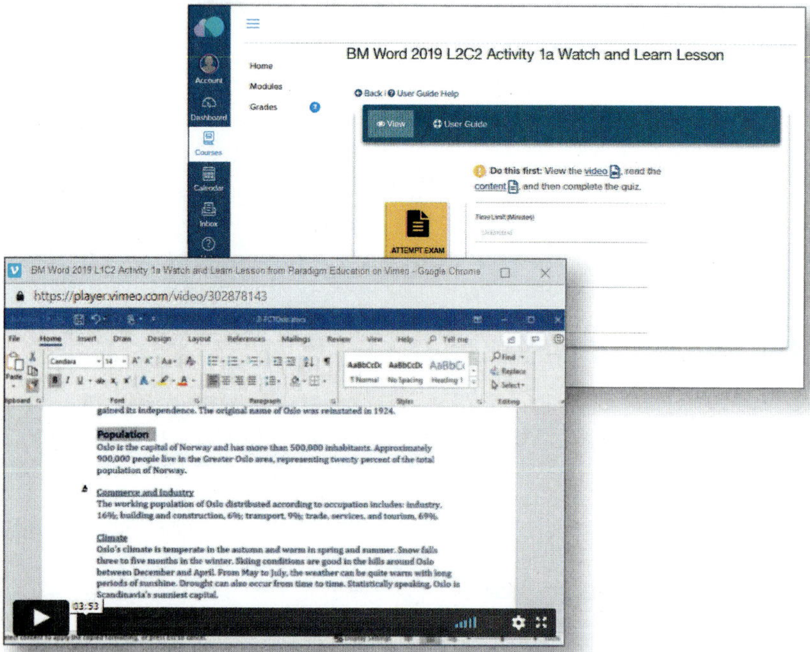

Watch and Learn Lessons include a video demonstrating how to perform the chapter activity, a reading to provide background and context, and a short quiz to check understanding of concepts and skills.

Guide and Practice Tutorials provide interactive, guided training and measured practice.

Hands On Activities enable students to complete chapter activities, compare their solutions against a Check Your Work model answer image, and submit their work for instructor review.

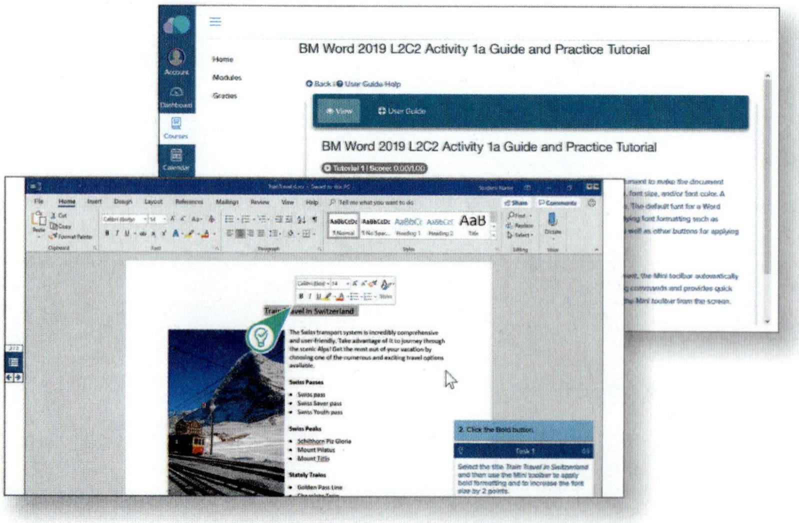

Chapter Review and Assessment

Review and assessment activities for each chapter are available for completion in Cirrus.

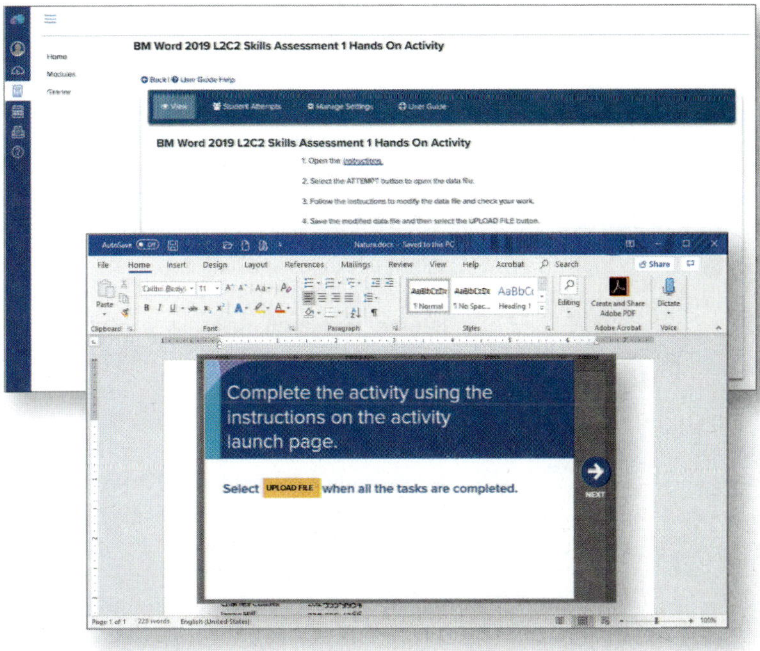

Concepts Check completion exercises assess their comprehension and recall of application features and functions as well as key terminology.

Skills Assessment Hands On Activity exercises evaluate the ability to apply chapter skills and concepts in solving realistic problems. Each is completed live in Word and is uploaded through Cirrus for instructor evaluation.

Visual Benchmark assessments test problem-solving skills and mastery of application features.

A **Case Study** requires analyzing a workplace scenario and then planning and executing a multipart project. Students search the web and/or use the program's Help feature to locate additional information required to complete the Case Study.

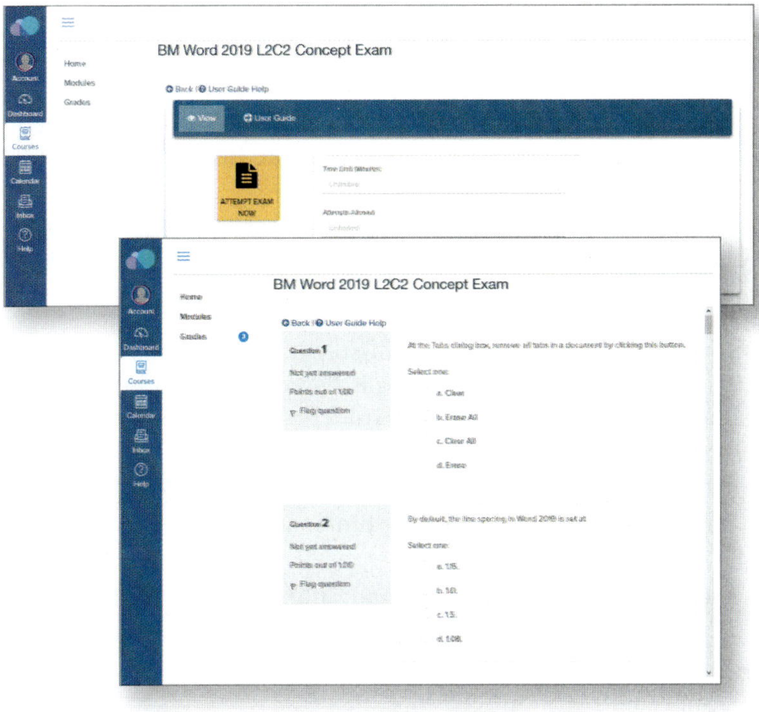

Exercises and **Projects** provide opportunities to develop and demonstrate skills learned in each chapter. Each is completed live in the Office application and is automatically scored by Cirrus. Detailed feedback and how-to videos help students evaluate and improve their performance.

Skills Check Exams evaluate students' ability to complete specific tasks. Skills Check Exams are completed live in the Office application and are scored automatically. Detailed feedback and instructor-controlled how-to videos help student evaluate and improve their performance.

Multiple-choice **Concepts Exams** assess understanding of key commands and concepts presented in each chapter.

Unit Review and Assessment

Review and assessment activities for each unit of each Benchmark course are also available for completion in Cirrus.

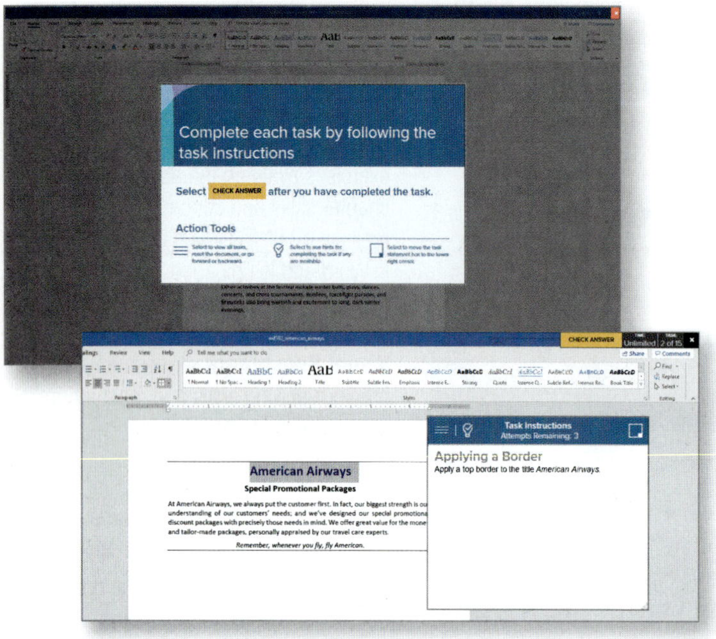

Assessing Proficiency exercises check mastery of software application functions and features.

Writing Activities challenge students to use written communication skills while demonstrating their understanding of important software features and functions.

Internet Research assignments reinforce the importance of research and information processing skills along with proficiency in the Office environment.

A **Job Study** activity at the end of Unit 2 presents a capstone assessment requiring critical thinking and problem solving.

Unit-Level Projects allow students to practice skills learned in the unit. Each is completed live in the Office application and automatically scored by Cirrus. Detailed feedback and how-to videos help students evaluate and improve their performance.

Student eBook

The Student eBook, accessed through the Cirrus online course, can be downloaded to any device (desktop, laptop, tablet, or smartphone) to make Benchmark Series content available anywhere students wish to study.

Instructor eResources

Cirrus tracks students' step-by-step interactions as they move through each activity, giving instructors visibility into their progress and missteps. With Exam Watch, instructors can observe students in a virtual, live, skills-based exam and join remotely as needed—a helpful option for struggling students who need one-to-one coaching, or for distance learners. In addition to these Cirrus-specific tools, the Instructor eResources for the Benchmark Series include the following support:

- Planning resources, such as lesson plans, teaching hints, and sample course syllabi
- Delivery resources, such as discussion questions and online images and templates
- Assessment resources, including live and annotated PDF model answers for chapter work and review and assessment activities, rubrics for evaluating student work, and chapter-based exam banks in RTF format

About the Authors

Nita Rutkosky began her career teaching business education at Pierce College in Puyallup, Washington, in 1978 and holds a master's degree in occupational education. In her years as an instructor, she taught many courses in software applications to students in postsecondary information technology certificate and degree programs. Since 1987, Nita has been a leading author of courseware for computer applications training and instruction. Her current titles include Paradigm's popular Benchmark Series, Marquee Series, and Signature Series. She is a contributor to the Cirrus online content for Office application courses and has also written textbooks for keyboarding, desktop publishing, computing in the medical office, and essential skills for digital literacy.

Audrey Roggenkamp holds a master's degree in adult education and curriculum and has been an adjunct instructor in the Business Information Technology department at Pierce College in Puyallup, Washington, since 2005. Audrey has also been a content provider for Paradigm Education Solutions since 2005. In addition to contributing to the Cirrus online content for Office application courses, Audrey co-authors Paradigm's Benchmark Series, Marquee Series, and Signature Series. Her other available titles include *Keyboarding & Applications I* and *II* and *Using Computers in the Medical Office: Word, PowerPoint®, and Excel®*.

Ian Rutkosky has a master's degree in business administration and has been an adjunct instructor in the Business Information Technology department at Pierce College in Puyallup, Washington, since 2010. In addition to joining the author team for the Benchmark Series and Marquee Series, he has co-authored titles on medical office computing and digital literacy and has served as a co-author and consultant for Paradigm's Cirrus training and assessment software.

Microsoft®

Word Level 2

Unit 1

Formatting and Customizing Documents

Chapter 1 Applying Advanced Formatting

Chapter 2 Proofing Documents

Chapter 3 Inserting Headers, Footers, and References

Chapter 4 Creating Specialized Tables and Navigating in a Document

Microsoft®

Word

Applying Advanced Formatting

CHAPTER 1

Performance Objectives

Upon successful completion of Chapter 1, you will be able to:

1 Adjust character spacing, use OpenType features, apply text effects, and change the default font
2 Insert intellectual property symbols, hyphens, dashes, and nonbreaking spaces
3 Find and replace font formatting, paragraph formatting, special characters, styles, and body and heading fonts, and use wildcard characters
4 Manage document properties
5 Inspect a document for confidentiality, accessibility, and compatibility issues

Microsoft Word is a powerful word processing program containing many features for making documents look polished, professional, and publication-ready. This chapter will introduce you to some advanced formatting that will bring your skills to the next level. Use options at the Font dialog box with the Advanced tab selected to apply advanced character formatting such as scaling, spacing, and kerning, as well as OpenType features such as ligatures, number styles, and stylistic sets. Insert special symbols such as intellectual property symbols, hyphens, and nonbreaking spaces at the Symbol dialog box or with keyboard shortcuts. To make designing a document faster and easier, use Word's Find and Replace feature to find and replace formatting, special characters, styles, and body and heading fonts. Finally, you'll learn to prepare documents for sharing by managing document properties and inspecting a document for confidentiality, accessibility, and compatibility issues.

Data Files

Before beginning chapter work, copy the WL2C1 folder to your storage medium and then make WL2C1 the active folder.

The online course includes additional training and assessment resources.

Activity 1 Apply Advanced Character Formatting to a Letter — 5 Parts

You will open a document containing a donor appreciation letter and then apply advanced character formatting to the text, including character scaling, spacing, and kerning, and apply OpenType features such as ligatures, number styles, and stylistic sets. You will also apply text effects and change the default font for all new documents.

Tutorial

Applying Advanced Character Formatting

Quick Steps

Adjust Character Spacing

1. Click Font group dialog box launcher.
2. Click Advanced tab.
3. Specify scaling, spacing, positioning, and/or kerning.
4. Click OK.

Applying Character Formatting

The Font dialog box with the Advanced tab selected contains a number of options for improving the appearance of text in a document. Use options at the dialog box to adjust character spacing, apply OpenType features, and apply text effects to selected text.

Adjusting Character Spacing

Each typeface is designed with a specific amount of space between characters. This character spacing can be changed with options in the *Character Spacing* section of the Font dialog box with the Advanced tab selected, as shown in Figure 1.1. Display this dialog box by clicking the Font group dialog box launcher on the Home tab and then clicking the Advanced tab at the dialog box.

Choose the *Scale* option to stretch or compress text horizontally as a percentage of the current size from 1% to 600%. Expand or condense the spacing

Figure 1.1 Font Dialog Box with the Advanced Tab Selected

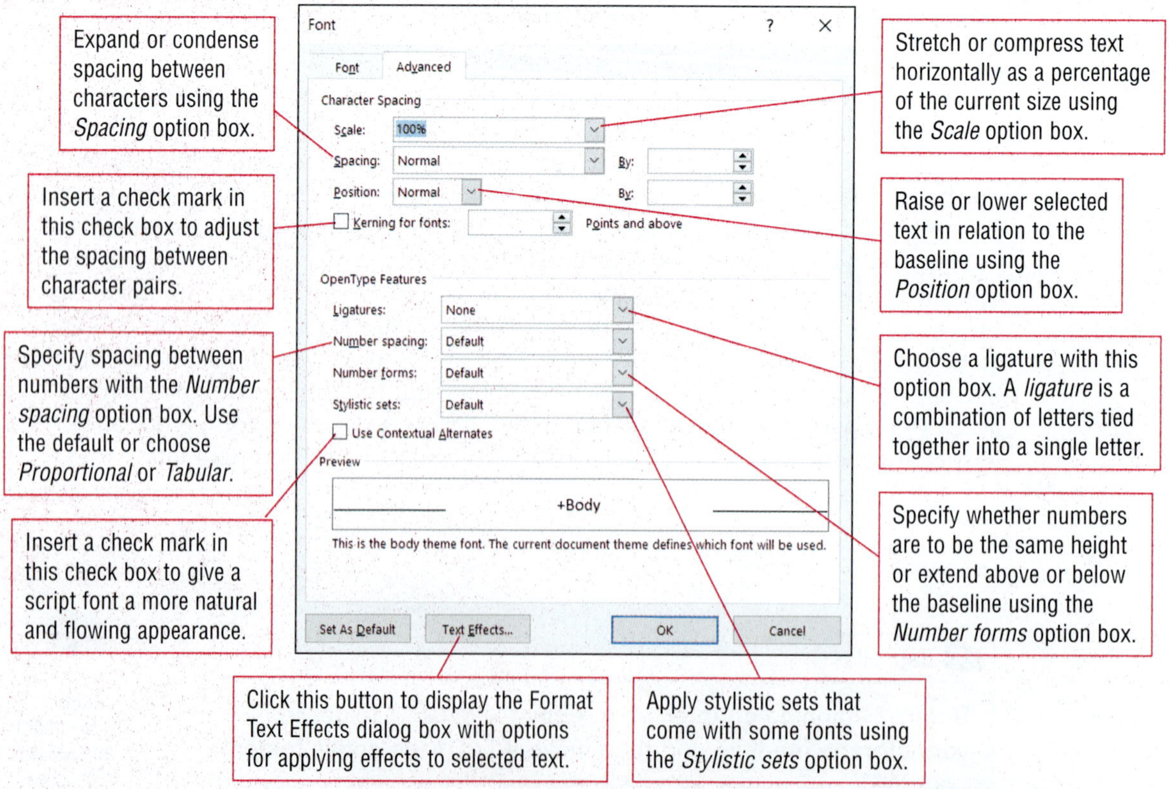

Hint Subtle adjustments to the scaling and spacing of characters can have a big impact on the visual display of text in a document.

Hint Apply kerning for fonts set 14 points or larger or for italic text.

between characters with the *Spacing* option box. Choose the *Expanded* or *Condensed* option and then enter a specific point size in the *By* text box. Raise or lower selected text in relation to the baseline with the *Position* option box. Choose the *Raised* or *Lowered* option and then enter the point size in the *By* text box.

Insert a check mark in the *Kerning for fonts* check box to apply kerning to selected text in a document. Kerning involves adjusting the spacing between certain character combinations by positioning two characters closer together than normal and uses the shapes and slopes of the characters to improve their appearance. Kerning allows more text to fit in a specific amount of space; kerned characters also look more natural and help the eye move along the text when reading. Consider kerning text set in larger font sizes, such as 14 points and larger, and text set in italics. Figure 1.2 displays text with and without kerning applied. Notice how the letters *Te* and *Va* are closer together in the kerned text compared with the text that is not kerned.

Turn on automatic kerning by displaying the Font dialog box with the Advanced tab selected and then inserting a check mark in the *Kerning for fonts* check box. Specify the beginning point size to be kerned in the *Points and above* measurement box.

Figure 1.2 Text with and without Kerning Applied

Tennison Valley (kerned)
Tennison Valley (not kerned)

Activity 1a Adjusting Character Spacing and Kerning Text

Part 1 of 5

1. Open **PRDonorApp** and then save it with the name **1-PRDonorApp**.
2. Select the title *Donor Appreciation*.
3. With the Home tab active, click the Font group dialog box launcher.
4. At the Font dialog box, click the Advanced tab.
5. Click the *Scale* option box arrow and then click *150%* at the drop-down list.
6. Click the *Spacing* option box arrow and then click *Condensed* at the drop-down list.
7. Click the *Kerning for fonts* check box to insert a check mark.
8. Click OK to close the dialog box.
9. Select the text *Enjoy the "flavor of Tanzania" and an evening of cultural entertainment....*
10. Click the Font group dialog box launcher to display the Font dialog box with the Advanced tab selected.
11. Click the *Kerning for fonts* check box to insert a check mark.
12. Click OK to close the dialog box.
13. Save **1-PRDonorApp**.

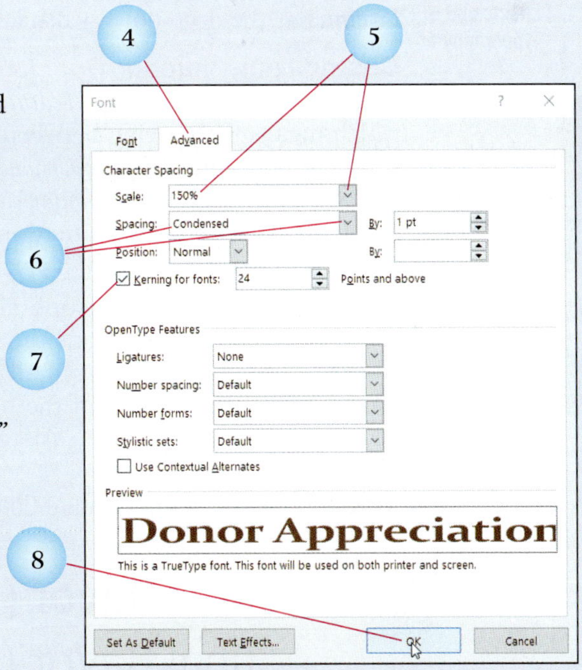

Check Your Work

Tutorial

Applying OpenType Features

Quick Steps

Apply OpenType Features

1. Click Font group dialog box launcher.
2. Click Advanced tab.
3. Specify ligatures, number spacing and forms, and/or stylistic sets.
4. Click OK.

Hint Microsoft and Adobe worked cooperatively to create OpenType fonts, which are scalable fonts based on TrueType fonts.

Text Effects and Typography

Hint Some fonts that use proportional spacing and old style number forms by default include Candara, Constantia, and Corbel.

Hint Some fonts that use tabular spacing and lining number forms include Cambria, Calibri, and Consolas.

Applying OpenType Features

The OpenType font file format was developed by Adobe and Microsoft to work on both Macintosh and Windows computers. The benefits of the OpenType format are cross-platform compatibility, which means font files can be moved between Macintosh and Windows computers; the ability to support expanded character sets and layout figures; and the capability for web page designers to create high-quality fonts for online documents. Microsoft Word offers some advanced OpenType features in the Font dialog box with the Advanced tab selected (refer to Figure 1.1 on page 4) that desktop publishers and web and graphic designers can use to enhance the appearance of text.

Using Ligatures to Combine Characters At the Font dialog box with the Advanced tab selected, *Ligatures* is the first option box in the *OpenType Features* section. A ligature is a combination of characters joined into a single letter. The OpenType standard specifies four categories of ligatures: *Standard Only*, *Standard and Contextual*, *Historical and Discretionary*, and *All*. The font designer decides which category to support and in which group to put combinations of characters.

With the *Standard Only* option selected, the standard set of ligatures that most typographers and font designers determine are appropriate for the font are applied to text. Common ligatures include letter combinations with the letter *f*, as shown in Figure 1.3. Notice how the *fi* and *fl* letter pairs are combined when ligatures are applied.

Use the other ligature options to specify *Contextual* ligatures, which are ligatures that the font designer believes are appropriate for use with the font but are not standard. Choose the option *Historical and Discretionary* to apply ligatures that were once standard but are no longer commonly used; use them to create a historical or "period" effect. The *All* ligatures option applies all the ligature combinations to selected text. Another method for applying ligatures to selected text is to click the Text Effects and Typography button in the Font group on the Home tab, point to *Ligatures* at the drop-down gallery and then click an option at the side menu.

Customizing Number Spacing and Number Forms The *Number spacing* option box in the *OpenType Features* section will automatically display *Default*, which means the spacing between numbers is determined by the font designer. This can be changed to *Proportional*, which adjusts the spacing for numbers with varying widths. Use the *Tabular* option to specify that each number is the same width. This is useful in a situation in which the numbers are set in columns and all the numbers need to align vertically.

Like the *Number spacing* option box, the *Number forms* option box automatically displays *Default*, which means the font designer determines the number form. Change this option to *Lining* if all the numbers should be the same height and not extend below the baseline of the text. Generally, lining numbers are used in tables and forms because they are easier to read. With the *Old-style* option, the lines of

Figure 1.3 Examples of Ligature Combinations

final flavor (using ligatures)
final flavor (not using ligatures)

the numbers can extend above or below the baseline of the text. For some fonts, changing the *Number forms* option to *Old-style* results in numbers such as *3* and *5* extending below the baseline or being centered higher on the line. See Figure 1.4 for examples of number form and spacing.

The spacing and form of numbers can also be adjusted with the Text Effects and Typography button in the Font group. Click the button arrow and then hover the mouse pointer over the *Number Styles* option in the drop-down gallery to display a side menu of options.

Figure 1.4 Number Form and Spacing

Old-style form and proportional spacing (in Candara):

123456789

Lining form and tabular spacing (in Cambria):

123456789

Activity 1b Applying a Ligature and Number Form

Part 2 of 5

1. With **1-PRDonorApp** open, select the text *Enjoy the "flavor of Tanzania" and an evening of cultural entertainment....*
2. Click the Font group dialog box launcher and, if necessary, click the Advanced tab.
3. At the Font dialog box with the Advanced tab selected, click the *Ligatures* option box arrow and then click *Standard and Contextual* at the drop-down list.
4. Click OK to close the dialog box.
5. Select the text *2022 – 2023* and *$3,500,000*.
6. Click the Text Effects and Typography button in the Font group, point to *Number Styles* at the drop-down gallery, and then click *Tabular Old-style* at the side menu.
7. Save **1-PRDonorApp**.

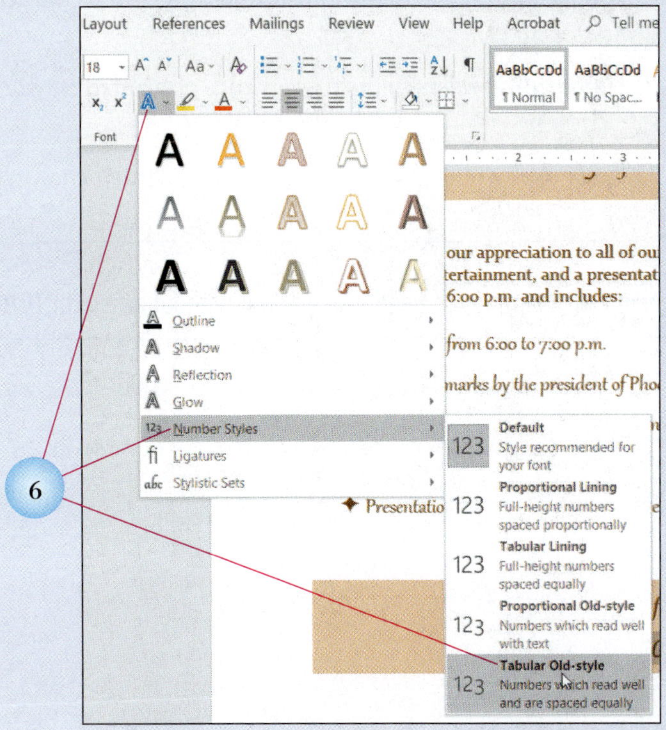

Check Your Work

Applying Stylistic Sets A font designer may include a number of stylistic sets for a specific font. A different stylistic set may apply additional formatting to the characters in a font. For example, the sentences in Figure 1.5 are set in 16-point Gabriola. Notice the slight variations in characters in some of the stylistic sets. Choose a stylistic set and see a visual representation of the characters with the stylistic set applied in the *Preview* section of the dialog box. A stylistic set can also be applied by clicking the Text Effects and Typography button in the Font group, pointing to *Stylistic Sets* at the drop-down gallery, and then clicking the stylistic set at the side menu.

Insert a check mark in the *Use Contextual Alternates* check box in the Font dialog box with the Advanced tab selected to fine-tune letter combinations based on the surrounding characters. Use this feature to give script fonts a more natural and flowing appearance. Figure 1.6 shows text set in 12-point Segoe Script. The first line of text is set with the default setting and the second line of text is set with the *Use Contextual Alternates* option selected. Notice the slight differences in letters such as *t*, *n*, *s*, and *h*.

Not all fonts are developed in the OpenType file format. Experiment with a font using the OpenType features at the Font dialog box with the Advanced tab selected to determine what features are supported by the font.

Figure 1.5 Examples of Gabriola Font Stylistic Sets

Typography refers to the appearance of printed characters on the page. **(Default set)**

Typography refers to the appearance of printed characters on the page. **(Stylistic set 4)**

Typography refers to the appearance of printed characters on the page. **(Stylistic set 5)**

Typography refers to the appearance of printed characters on the page. **(Stylistic set 6)**

Figure 1.6 Examples of Segoe Script Font without and with *Use Contextual Alternates* Selected

A font designer determines the appearance of each character in a font.

A font designer determines the appearance of each character in a font.

Activity 1c Applying a Stylistic Set and Using Contextual Alternates

1. With **1-PRDonorApp** open, select the bulleted text.
2. Display the Font dialog box with the Advanced tab selected.
3. Click the *Stylistic sets* option box arrow and then click *4* at the drop-down list.
4. Click OK to close the dialog box.
5. Select the text *Please call the Phoenix Rising office to let us know if you will be joining us.*
6. Display the Font dialog box with the Advanced tab selected.
7. Click the *Use Contextual Alternates* check box to insert a check mark.

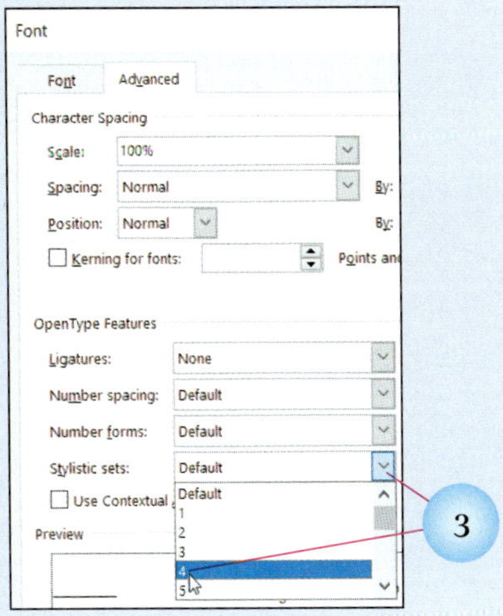

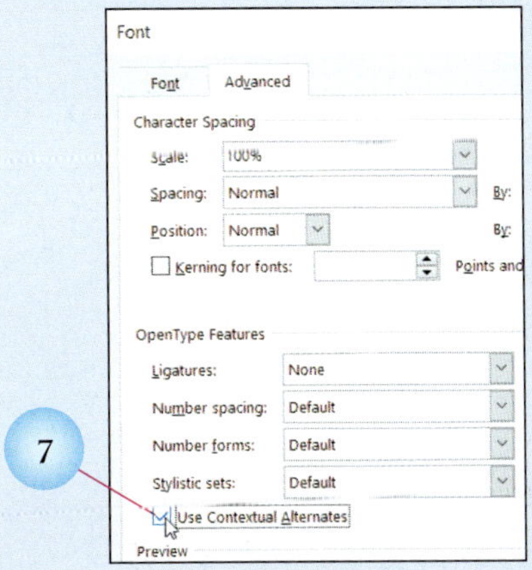

8. Click OK to close the Font dialog box.
9. Save **1-PRDonorApp**.

Check Your Work

Tutorial

Applying Text Effects

Quick Steps

Apply Text Effects

1. Click Font group dialog box launcher.
2. Click Text Effects button.
3. Choose options at Format Text Effects dialog box.
4. Click OK.

Applying Text Effects

Text effects can enhance the look of a document by adding color and interest. Use text effects to create attention-getting flyers and brochures. Or add effects to titles and subtitles to give reports and other documents a more professionally designed look and feel. Click the Text Effects button at the bottom of the Font dialog box with the Advanced tab selected and the Format Text Effects dialog box displays with the Text Fill & Outline icon selected, as shown in Figure 1.7. Click *Text Fill* or *Text Outline* to display the text formatting options. Click the Text Effects icon to display additional effects formatting options. Many of the options available at the dialog box also are available by clicking the Text Effects and Typography button in the Font group on the Home tab.

Figure 1.7 Format Text Effects Dialog Box

Text Fill and *Text Outline* options are available at the dialog box with the Text Fill & Outline icon selected.

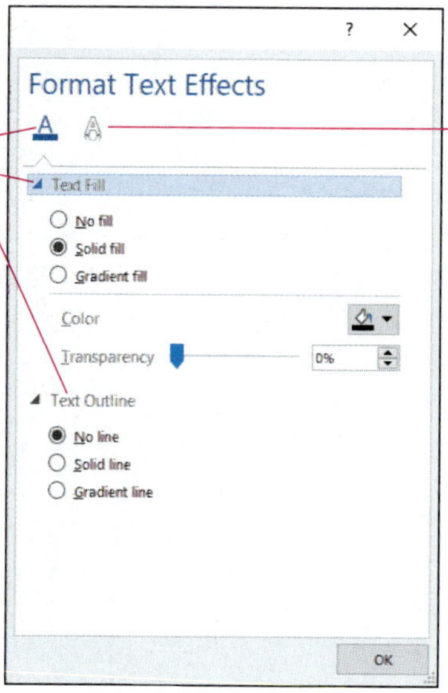

Click the Text Effects icon to display options for applying Shadow, Reflection, Glow, Soft Edges, and 3-D text effects.

Activity 1d Applying Text Effects

Part 4 of 5

1. With **1-PRDonorApp** open, select the title *Donor Appreciation*.
2. Display the Font dialog box.
3. Click the Text Effects button at the bottom of the dialog box.
4. At the Format Text Effects dialog box with the Text Fill & Outline icon selected, click *Text Fill* to expand the options.
5. Click *Gradient fill* to select the option.
6. Click the Preset gradients button and then click the *Medium Gradient - Accent 6* option (last column, third row).

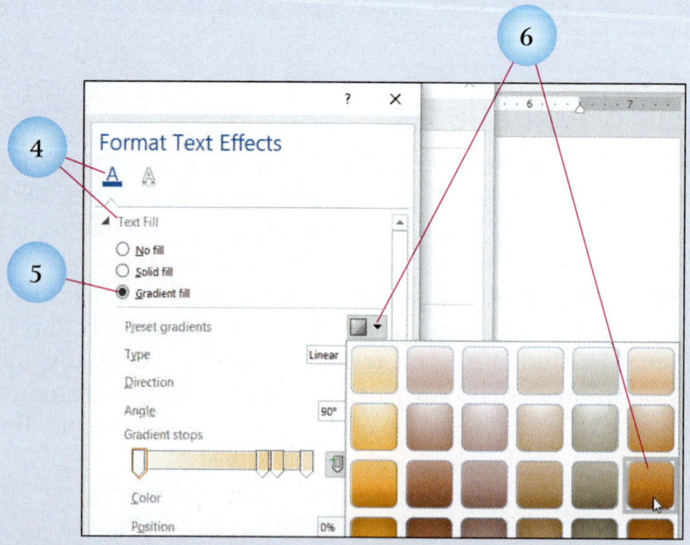

7. Click the Direction button and then click the *Linear Down* option (second column, first row).

8. Scroll down the dialog box and then click *Text Outline* to expand the options.
9. Click *Solid line* to select the option.
10. Click the Color button and then click the *Orange, Accent 6, Darker 50%* option (last column, last row in the *Theme Colors* section).

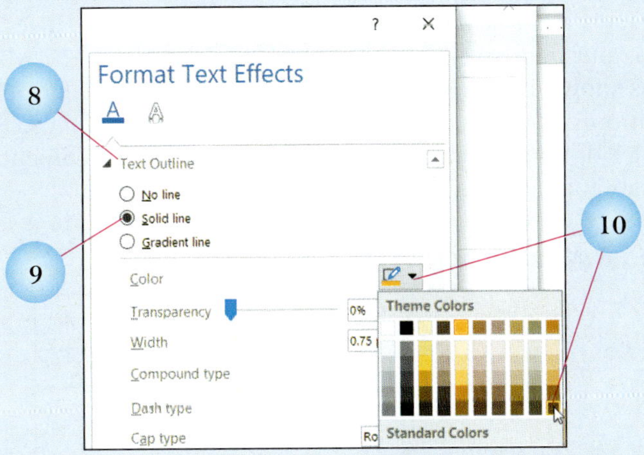

11. Click the Text Effects icon.
12. Click *Shadow* to expand the options.
13. Click the Presets button and then click the *Offset: Left* option (last column, second row in the *Outer* section).

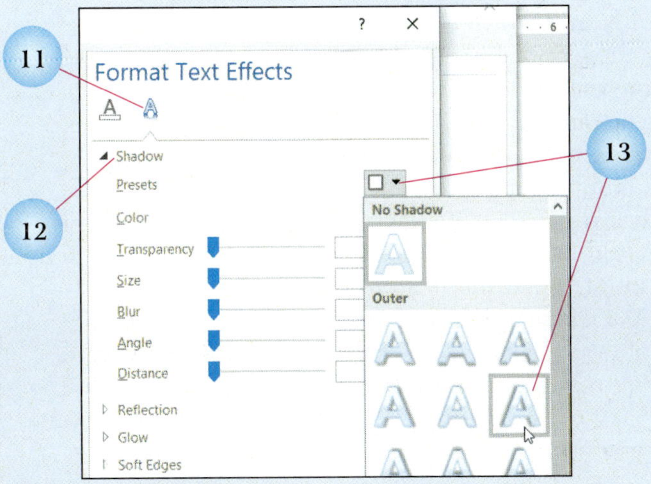

14. Click *Glow* to expand the options.
15. Click the Presets button in the *Glow* section and then click the *Glow: 5 point; Orange, Accent color 6* option (last column, first row in the *Glow Variations* section).
16. Click OK to close the Format Text Effects dialog box.
17. Click OK to close the Font dialog box and then deselect the title.
18. Save **1-PRDonorApp**.

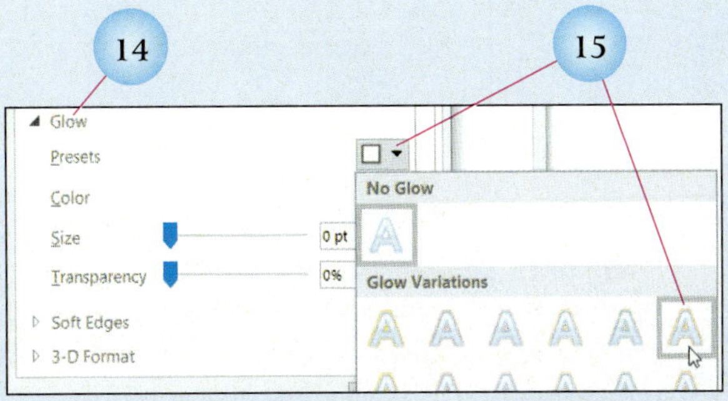

Check Your Work

Tutorial

Changing the Default Font

Quick Steps

Change Default Font

1. Click Font group dialog box launcher.
2. Change font and/or effects.
3. Click Set As Default button.
4. Click *This document only?* or *All documents based on the Normal template?*
5. Click OK.

Changing the Default Font

If documents are generally created with a font other than the default, the default can be changed with the Set As Default button at the Font dialog box. The default font can be changed for the current document or it can be changed in the Normal template, which is the template on which all new documents are based. To change the default font, display the Font dialog box, make changes to the font and/or effects, and then click the Set As Default button. At the Microsoft Word dialog box, as shown in Figure 1.8, click the *This document only?* option to apply the default only to the current document or click the *All documents based on the Normal template?* option to change the default for all new documents based on the default Normal template.

Figure 1.8 Microsoft Word Dialog Box

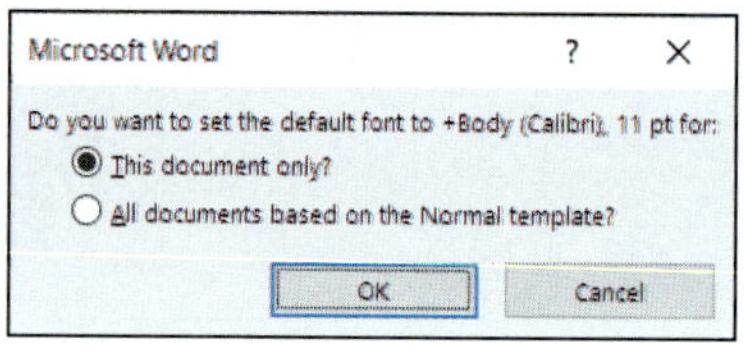

Activity 1e Changing the Default Font

Part 5 of 5

1. For **1-PRDonorApp**, you decide to change the default font to 12-point Constantia in a brown color, since this font is used for most documents created for Phoenix Rising. Change the default font by completing the following steps:
   a. Click in the paragraph of text above the bulleted text. (This text is set in 12-point Constantia and in a brown color.)
   b. Click the Font group dialog box launcher.
   c. If necessary, click the Font tab and then notice that *Constantia* is selected in the *Font* list box, *12* is selected in the *Size* list box, and the *Font color* option box displays a brown color.
   d. Click the Set As Default button.
   e. At the Microsoft Word dialog box, click *All documents based on the Normal template?* to select the option.
   f. Click OK.

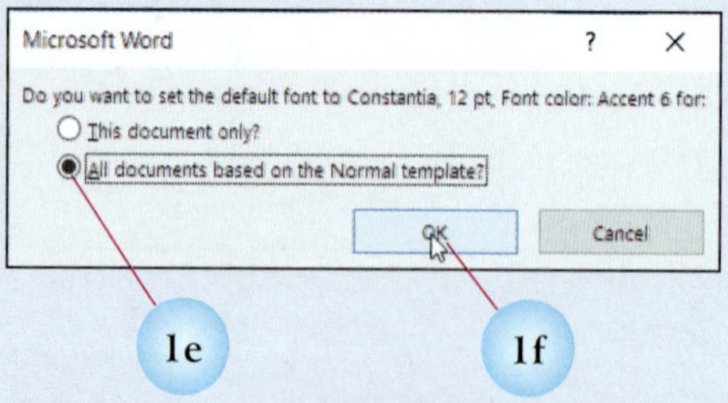

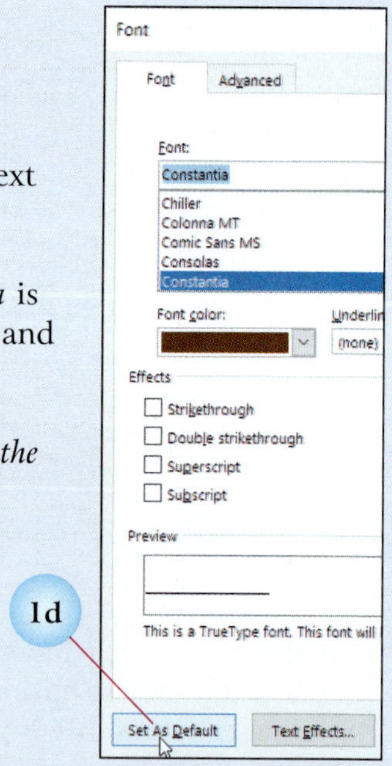

2. Save, print, and then close **1-PRDonorApp**.
3. Press Ctrl + N to open a new blank document based on the Normal template. Notice that *Constantia* displays in the *Font* option box and *12* displays in the *Font Size* option box, indicating that it is the default font.

4. Change the font back to the original default by completing the following steps:
   a. Click the Font group dialog box launcher.
   b. Scroll up the *Font* list box and then click *+Body*. (This is the original default font, which applies the Calibri font to body text in a document.)
   c. Click *11* in the *Size* list box.
   d. Click the *Font color* option box arrow and then click the *Automatic* option at the top of the drop-down list.
   e. Click the Set As Default button.
   f. At the Microsoft Word dialog box, click the *All documents based on the Normal template?* option.
   g. Click OK.
5. Close the blank document without saving changes.

Check Your Work

Activity 2 Create a Document with Symbols and Special Characters **3 Parts**

You will create a document that includes intellectual property symbols; nonbreaking, em dash, and en dash hyphens; and nonbreaking spaces.

Inserting Symbols and Special Characters

Symbols and special characters can be inserted in a document with options at the Symbol dialog box with either the Symbols tab or Special Characters tab selected. Display this dialog box by clicking the Insert tab, clicking the Symbol button, and then clicking the *More Symbols* option. Symbols can also be inserted by typing a sequence of characters or by using keyboard shortcuts. Word creates some special characters automatically as text is typed.

Tutorial

Inserting Intellectual Property Symbols

Inserting Intellectual Property Symbols

Among the symbols that can be inserted in a document are three intellectual property protection symbols: ©, ™, and ®. Insert the © symbol to identify copyrighted intellectual property, use the ™ symbol to identify a trademark, and use the ® symbol to identify a registered trademark.

Insert these symbols with options at the Symbol dialog box with the Special Characters tab selected, by typing a sequence of characters, or by using a keyboard shortcut. Insert a © symbol by typing (c) or pressing Alt + Ctrl + C, insert a ™ symbol by typing (tm) or pressing Alt + Ctrl + T, and insert a ® symbol by typing (r) or pressing Alt + Ctrl + R.

Activity 2a Inserting Intellectual Property Symbols

Part 1 of 3

1. At a blank document, type the text shown in Figure 1.9. Bold and center the title as shown and insert each intellectual property symbol using the appropriate sequence of characters or keyboard shortcut. To insert the sequence of characters for each symbol rather than the actual symbol, type the sequence of characters and then immediately click the Undo button. This changes the symbol back to the sequence of characters. (The text in your document will wrap differently than what is shown in the figure.)
2. Save the document and name it **1-Symbols**.

Check Your Work

Figure 1.9 Activity 2a

INTELLECTUAL PROPERTY PROTECTION

A copyright protects original works in areas such as publishing, music, literature, and drama. Use the © symbol to identify copyrighted intellectual property. Create this symbol by typing (c), by using the keyboard shortcut Alt + Ctrl + C, or by clicking the symbol at the Symbol dialog box with the Special Characters tab selected.

A trademark identifies a word, symbol, device, or name such as a brand name. Use the ™ symbol to identify a trademarked name or product. Create this symbol by typing (tm), by using the keyboard shortcut Alt + Ctrl + T, or by clicking the symbol at the Symbol dialog box with the Special Characters tab selected.

A registered trademark is a trademark that has been registered with the US Patent and Trademark Office. Use the ® symbol to identify a registered trademark. Create this symbol by typing (r), by using the keyboard shortcut Alt + Ctrl + R, or by clicking the symbol at the Symbol dialog box with the Special Characters tab selected.

Tutorial

Inserting Hyphens and Nonbreaking Characters

Inserting Hyphens and Dashes

A hyphen (-) is a punctuation mark used to join compound words, such as *fresh-looking* or *sister-in-law*. Use the hyphen key on the keyboard to insert such hyphens. Hyphens can also be used to divide words that fall at the ends of lines. This can create a more even-looking margin and is especially useful when formatting text in narrow columns.

To hyphenate words that fall at the ends of lines, use the Hyphenation button in the Page Setup group on the Layout tab. This button includes options for automatically or manually hyphenating words that fall at the end of a line. If words are automatically hyphenated, Word inserts an optional hyphen, which displays only when the word is divided across two lines or if the display of nonprinting characters is turned on. If the document is changed so that the word no longer breaks on a line, the hyphen is removed. To control where hyphens appear in words during hyphenation, choose manual rather than automatic hyphenation.

Some text should not be hyphenated and divided across lines. For example, a company name such as *Knowles-Myers Corporation* should not be divided between *Knowles* and *Myers* and set on two lines. To avoid a break like this, insert a nonbreaking hyphen by clicking the *Nonbreaking Hyphen* option at the Symbol dialog box with the Special Characters tab selected or with the keyboard shortcut Ctrl + Shift + -.

An em dash (—) is used to indicate a break in thought or to highlight a term or phrase by separating it from the rest of the sentence. Em dashes are particularly useful in long sentences and sentences with multiple phrases and commas. For example, the sentence "The main focus of this document is on general-purpose, single-user computers—personal computers—that enable users to complete a variety of computing tasks." contains two em dashes: before and after the words *personal computers*.

To create an em dash in a Word document, type a word, type two hyphens, type the next word, and then press the spacebar. When the spacebar is pressed, Word automatically converts the two hyphens to an em dash. If automatic formatting of em dashes is turned off, an em dash can be inserted with the *Em Dash* option at the Symbol dialog box with the Special Characters tab selected or with the keyboard shortcut Alt + Ctrl + - (on the numeric keypad).

Hint An em dash is the width of the capital letter *M* and an en dash is the width of the capital letter *N*.

En dashes (–) are used between inclusive dates, times, and numbers to mean "through." For example, in the text *9:30–11:00 a.m.*, the numbers should be separated by an en dash rather than a regular hyphen. Word does not automatically convert hyphens to en dashes, as it does with em dashes. To create an en dash, click the *En Dash* option at the Symbol dialog box with the Special Characters tab selected or use the keyboard shortcut Ctrl + - (on the numeric keypad).

Activity 2b Inserting Hyphens and Dashes

Part 2 of 3

1. With **1-Symbols** open, press Ctrl + End, press the Enter key, and then type the text shown in Figure 1.9 with the following specifications:
   a. Type an en dash between the times *9:00* and *10:30 a.m.* by pressing Ctrl + - (on the numeric keypad). If you are working on a laptop that does not have a numeric keypad, insert an en dash by clicking the Insert tab, clicking the Symbol button, and then clicking *More Symbols*. At the Symbol dialog box, click the Special Characters tab, click the *En Dash* option, click the Insert button, and then click the Close button.
   b. Create the em dashes before and after the phrase *Excel, PowerPoint, and Access* by typing hyphens (two hyphens for each em dash).
   c. Insert a nonbreaking hyphen within *Tri-State* by pressing Ctrl + Shift + -.
2. Save **1-Symbols**.

Check Your Work

Figure 1.9 Activity 2b

SOFTWARE TRAINING

The Microsoft® Office Word training is scheduled for Thursday, March 11, 2021, from 9:00–10:30 a.m. Additional training for other applications in the Office suite—Excel, PowerPoint, and Access—will be available during the month of April. Contact the Training Department for additional information. All Tri-State employees are eligible for the training.

Inserting Nonbreaking Spaces

As text is typed in a document, Word makes decisions about where to end lines and automatically wraps text to the beginning of new lines. In some situations, a line may break between two words or phrases that should remain together. To control where text breaks across lines, consider inserting nonbreaking spaces between words that should remain together.

Insert a nonbreaking space with the *Nonbreaking Space* option at the Symbol dialog box with the Special Characters tab selected or with the keyboard shortcut Ctrl + Shift + spacebar. If nonprinting characters are turned on, a normal space displays as a dot and a nonbreaking space displays as a degree symbol.

Activity 2c Inserting Nonbreaking Spaces

Part 3 of 3

1. With **1-Symbols** open, click the Show/Hide ¶ button in the Paragraph group on the Home tab.
2. Press Ctrl + End, press the Enter key, and then type the text in Figure 1.10. Insert nonbreaking spaces in the keyboard shortcuts by pressing Ctrl + Shift + spacebar before and after each plus (+) symbol.
3. Turn off the display of nonprinting characters.
4. Save, print, and then close **1-Symbols**.

Check Your Work

Figure 1.10 Activity 2c

KEYBOARD SHORTCUTS

Microsoft Word includes a number of keyboard shortcuts you can use to access features and commands. The ScreenTip for some buttons displays the keyboard shortcut you can use to execute the command. For example, hovering the mouse over the Font button causes the ScreenTip to display Ctrl + Shift + F as the keyboard shortcut. Additional Home tab Font group keyboard shortcuts include Ctrl + B to bold text, Ctrl + I to italicize text, and Ctrl + U to underline text. You can also press Ctrl + Shift + + to turn on superscript and press Ctrl + = to turn on subscript.

Activity 3 Use Find and Replace Options in a Lease Agreement — 5 Parts

You will open a commercial lease agreement; find and replace font formatting, paragraph formatting, special characters, styles, and body and heading fonts; and then find and replace text using a wildcard character.

Using Find and Replace Options

Replace

The Find and Replace dialog box can be used to find and replace fonts, special characters, and body and heading fonts. The expanded Find and Replace dialog box contains a *Use wildcards* option. With this option selected, a wildcard character can be used to find specific text or characters in a document. Display the Find and Replace dialog box by clicking the Replace button in the Editing group on the Home tab.

Tutorial

Finding and Replacing Formatting

Finding and Replacing Font Formatting

Use options at the Find and Replace dialog box with the Replace tab selected to search for characters containing specific font formatting and replace them with other characters or font formatting. With the insertion point positioned in the *Find what* text box, specify the font formatting to be found in the document by clicking the More button to expand the dialog box, clicking the Format button in the lower left corner of the dialog box, and then clicking the *Font* option at the drop-down list. At the Find Font dialog box, specify the formatting to be found and then close the dialog box. Click in the *Replace with* text box and then complete similar steps to specify the replacement font formatting.

Finding and Replacing Paragraph Formatting

The Find and Replace dialog box contains options for searching for and replacing specific paragraph formatting. Identify the paragraph formatting to be found in the document by clicking in the *Find what* text box, clicking the Format button in the lower left corner of the dialog box, and then clicking *Paragraph* at the drop-down list. At the Paragraph dialog box, specify the formatting to be found and then close the dialog box. Click in the *Replace with* text box and then complete similar steps to specify the replacement paragraph formatting.

Activity 3a Finding and Replacing Font and Paragraph Formatting — Part 1 of 5

1. Open **ComLease** and then save it with the name **1-ComLease**.
2. Find text set in the Corbel font with dark red color and replace it with text set in Constantia with automatic color by completing the following steps:
   a. Click the Replace button in the Editing group on the Home tab.
   b. At the Find and Replace dialog box, click the More button to expand the dialog box.

c. Click in the *Find what* text box, click the Format button in the lower left corner of the dialog box, and then click *Font* at the drop-down list.
d. At the Find Font dialog box, scroll down the *Font* list box and then click *Corbel*.
e. Click the *Font color* option box arrow and then click the *Dark Red* color (first color option in the *Standard Colors* section).
f. Click OK to close the dialog box.
g. Click in the *Replace with* text box.
h. Click the Format button in the lower left corner of the dialog box and then click *Font* at the drop-down list.
i. At the Replace Font dialog box, scroll down the *Font* list box and then click *Constantia*.
j. Click the *Font color* option box arrow and then click the *Automatic* option.
k. Click OK to close the dialog box.
l. At the Find and Replace dialog box, click the Replace All button.
m. At the message indicating 40 replacements were made, click OK.

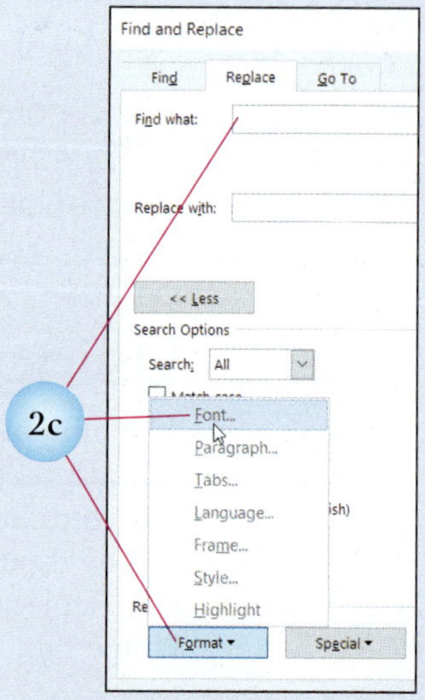

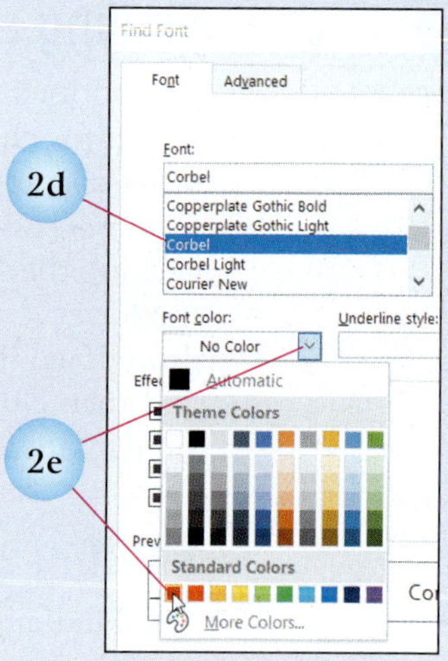

3. With the Find and Replace dialog box open, search for all first-line indents in the document and remove the indents by completing the following steps:
   a. With the insertion point positioned in the *Find what* text box, click the No Formatting button.
   b. Click the Format button and then click *Paragraph* at the drop-down list.
   c. At the Find Paragraph dialog box, click the *Special* option box arrow in the *Indentation* section and then click *First line* at the drop-down list.
   d. Click OK to close the Find Paragraph dialog box.
   e. At the Find and Replace dialog box, click in the *Replace with* text box.
   f. Click the No Formatting button.
   g. Click the Format button and then click *Paragraph* at the drop-down list.
   h. At the Replace Paragraph dialog box, click the *Special* option box arrow in the *Indentation* section and then click *(none)* at the drop-down list.
   i. Click OK to close the Replace Paragraph dialog box.
   j. Click the Replace All button.
   k. At the message indicating 7 replacements were made, click OK.

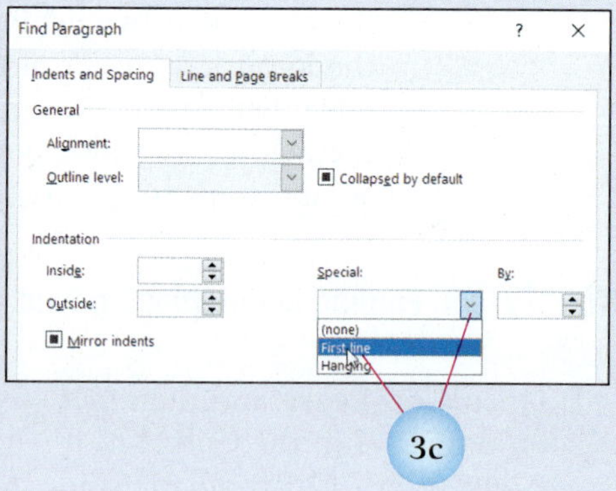

4. Close the Find and Replace dialog box.
5. Save **1-ComLease**.

Check Your Work

Tutorial
Finding and Replacing Special Characters

Quick Steps

Find and Replace Special Character

1. Click Replace button.
2. Click More button.
3. Click Special button.
4. Click character at drop-down list.
5. Click in *Replace with* text box.
6. Insert replacement character.
7. Click Replace All button.
8. Click OK.

Finding and Replacing Special Characters

Find or find and replace special characters with the Special button at the expanded Find and Replace dialog box. Click the Special button and a drop-down list displays similar to the one shown in Figure 1.11. Click a special character in the drop-down list and a code representing the character is inserted in the text box where the insertion point is positioned. For example, with the insertion point positioned in the *Find what* text box, clicking *Paragraph Mark* at the Special button drop-down list inserts the code ^*p* in the text box. If a character code is known, it can be typed directly in the *Find what* or *Replace with* text box

Figure 1.11 Special Button Drop-Down List

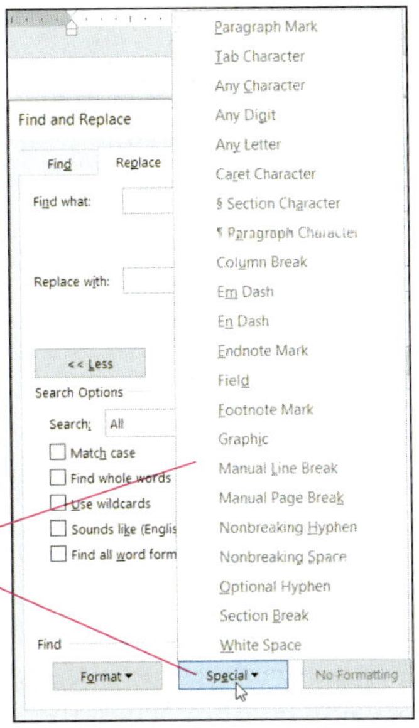

Click the Special button to display a drop-down list of character options. Click an option and a code is inserted in the *Find what* (or *Replace with*) text box.

Activity 3b Finding and Replacing Special Characters

Part 2 of 5

1. With **1-ComLease** open, search for and delete all continuous section breaks by completing the following steps:
   a. Click the Replace button in the Editing group on the Home tab.
   b. If necessary, expand the Find and Replace dialog box.
   c. If formatting information displays below the *Find what* text box, click the No Formatting button.
   d. Click the Special button at the bottom of the dialog box.
   e. Click *Section Break* in the drop-down list. (This inserts ^*b* in the *Find what* text box.)
   f. Click in the *Replace with* text box and make sure the text box is empty. If formatting information displays below the text box, click the No Formatting button.

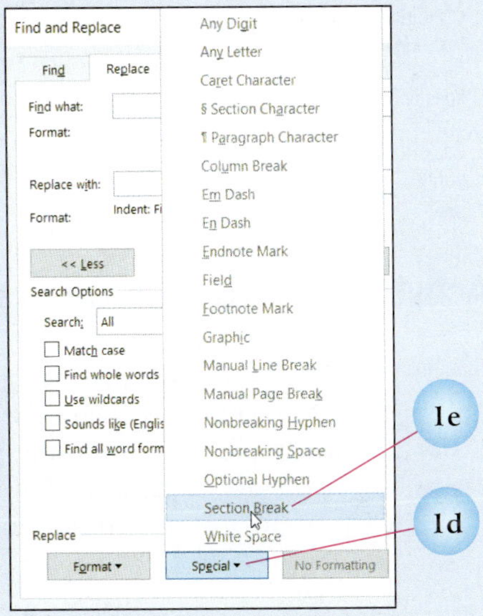

g. Click the Replace All button.
h. At the message indicating 3 replacements were made, click OK.

2. With the expanded Find and Replace dialog box open, find all occurrences of regular hyphens and replace them with nonbreaking hyphens by completing the following steps:
   a. With ^*b* selected in the *Find what* text box, type - (a hyphen).
   b. Press the Tab key to move the insertion point to the *Replace with* text box.
   c. Click the Special button at the bottom of the dialog box.
   d. Click *Nonbreaking Hyphen* at the drop-down list.
   e. Click the Replace All button.
   f. At the message indicating 19 replacements were made, click OK.
   g. Close the Find and Replace dialog box.
3. Save **1-ComLease**.

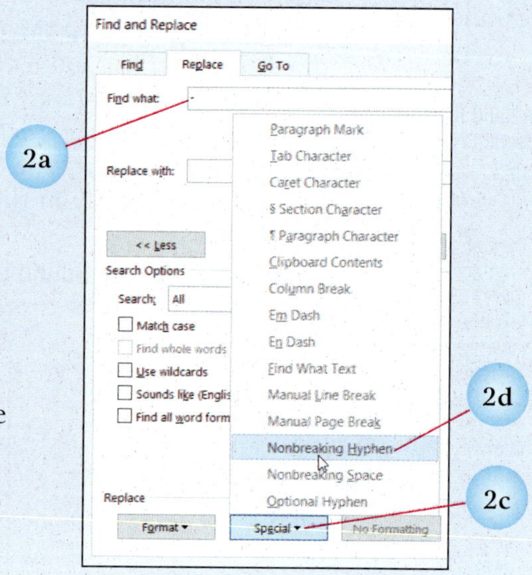

Check Your Work

Tutorial

Finding and Replacing Styles

Finding and Replacing Styles

The Find and Replace dialog box can be used to find specific styles in a document and replace them with other styles. To find styles, display the Find and Replace dialog box and then click the More button. At the expanded Find and Replace dialog box, click the Format button and then click *Style* at the drop-down list. At the Find Style dialog box, click the style in the *Find what style* list box and then click OK. Click in the *Replace with* text box at the Find and Replace dialog box, click the Format button, and then click *Style*. At the Replace Style dialog box, click the replacement style in the *Replace With Style* list box and then click OK.

Quick Steps

Find and Replace Style

1. Click Replace button.
2. Click More button.
3. Click Format button.
4. Click *Style*.
5. Click style.
6. Click OK.
7. Click in *Replace with* text box and then repeat steps 3-6 to specify replacement style.
8. Click Replace All button.
9. Click OK.

Activity 3c Finding and Replacing Styles

Part 3 of 5

1. With **1-ComLease** open, search for Heading 3 styles and replace them with Heading 2 styles by completing the following steps:
   a. Click the Replace button in the Editing group on the Home tab.
   b. If necessary, expand the Find and Replace dialog box.
   c. Clear any text and formatting from the *Find what* and *Replace with* text boxes.

d. With the insertion point positioned in the *Find what* text box, click the Format button and then click *Style* at the drop-down list.
e. At the Find Style dialog box, scroll down the *Find what style* list box and then click *Heading 3*.
f. Click OK to close the Find Style dialog box.

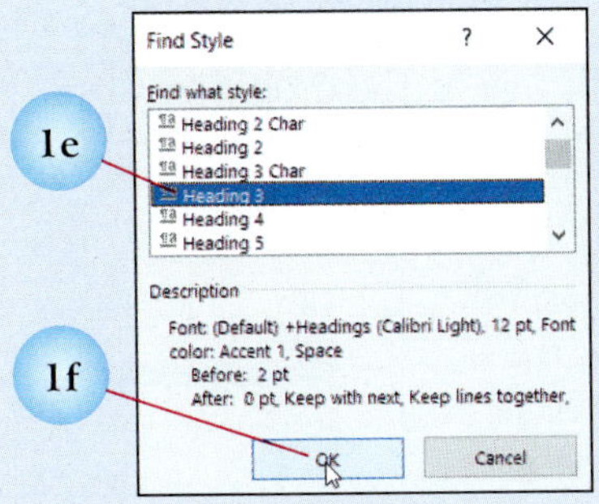

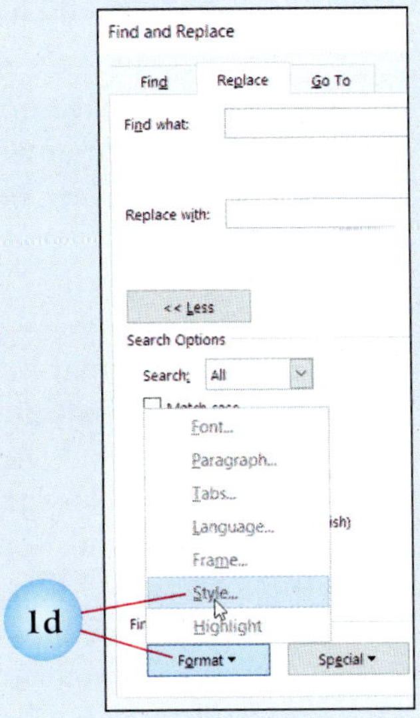

g. At the Find and Replace dialog box, click in the *Replace with* text box.
h. Click the Format button and then click *Style* at the drop-down list.
i. At the Replace Style dialog box, scroll down the *Replace With Style* list box, click *Heading 2*, and then click OK.
j. At the Find and Replace dialog box, click the Replace All button.
k. At the message indicating 6 replacements were made, click OK.
l. Click the Close button to close the Find and Replace dialog box.

2. Save **1-ComLease**.

Check Your Work

Tutorial

Finding and Replacing Body and Heading Fonts

Quick Steps

Find and Replace Body or Heading Font

1. Click Replace button.
2. Click More button.
3. Click Format button.
4. Click *Font*.
5. Click *+Body* or *+Headings* in *Font* list box.
6. Click OK.
7. Click in *Replace with* text box.
8. Insert replacement font.
9. Click Replace All button.
10. Click OK.

Finding and Replacing Body and Heading Fonts

By default, a Word document has the Office theme applied, which applies the Office set of colors, fonts, and effects. The theme fonts include a body font and heading font. The default settings for theme fonts are *Calibri (Body)* and *Calibri Light (Headings)*. These fonts display at the beginning of the *Font* option box drop-down gallery. If a different theme has been applied, other body and heading fonts will be used; they can be viewed at the *Font* option box drop-down gallery.

A document can be searched for one body or heading font and then replaced with a different font. To do this, display the Find and Replace dialog box with the Replace tab selected. Expand the dialog box, click the Format button, and then click *Font* at the drop-down list. At the Find Font dialog box, scroll up the *Font* list box and then click *+Body* if searching for the body font or click *+Headings* if searching for the heading font. Click in the *Replace with* text box and then complete the steps to insert the replacement font.

Activity 3d Finding and Replacing Body and Heading Fonts

Part 4 of 5

1. With **1-ComLease** open, search for the +Body font and replace it with Constantia by completing the following steps:
   a. Click the Replace button in the Editing group on the Home tab.
   b. If necessary, expand the Find and Replace dialog box.
   c. With the insertion point positioned in the *Find what* text box, click the No Formatting button.
   d. Click the Format button and then click *Font* at the drop-down list.
   e. At the Find Font dialog box, scroll up the *Font* list box and then click *+Body*.
   f. Click OK to close the Find Font dialog box.
   g. At the Find and Replace dialog box, click in the *Replace with* text box and then click the No Formatting button.
   h. Click the Format button and then click *Font* at the drop-down list.
   i. At the Replace Font dialog box, scroll down the *Font* list box and then click *Constantia*.
   j. Click OK to close the Replace Font dialog box.
   k. At the Find and Replace dialog box, click the Replace All button.
   l. At the message indicating 43 replacements were made, click OK.

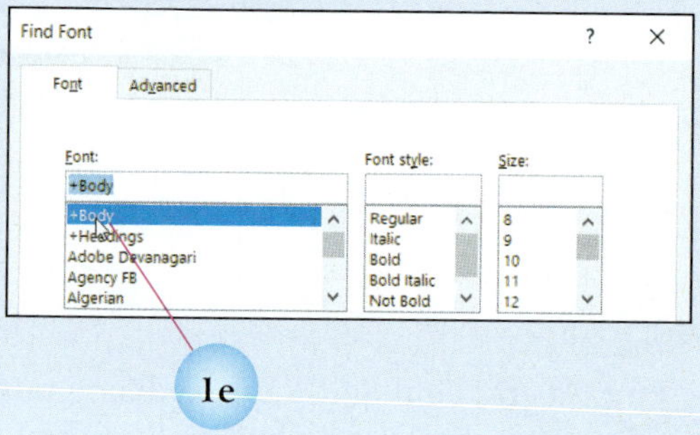

2. With the Find and Replace dialog box open, search for text set in the +Headings font and replace it with text set in 14-point Corbel bold and the standard dark blue color, and then change the paragraph alignment to center alignment by completing the following steps:
   a. With the insertion point positioned in the *Find what* text box, click the No Formatting button.
   b. Click the Format button and then click *Font* at the drop-down list.
   c. At the Find Font dialog box, click *+Headings* in the *Font* list box.
   d. Click OK to close the Find Font dialog box.
   e. At the Find and Replace dialog box, click in the *Replace with* text box.
   f. Click the No Formatting button.
   g. Click the Format button and then click *Font* at the drop-down list.
   h. At the Replace Font dialog box, scroll down and then click *Corbel* in the *Font* list box, click *Bold* in the *Font style* list box, scroll down and then click *14* in the *Size* list box, and click the *Font color* option box arrow and then click the *Dark Blue* option (ninth color option in the *Standard Colors* section).
   i. Click OK to close the Replace Font dialog box.
   j. At the Find and Replace dialog box, click the Format button and then click *Paragraph* at the drop-down list.

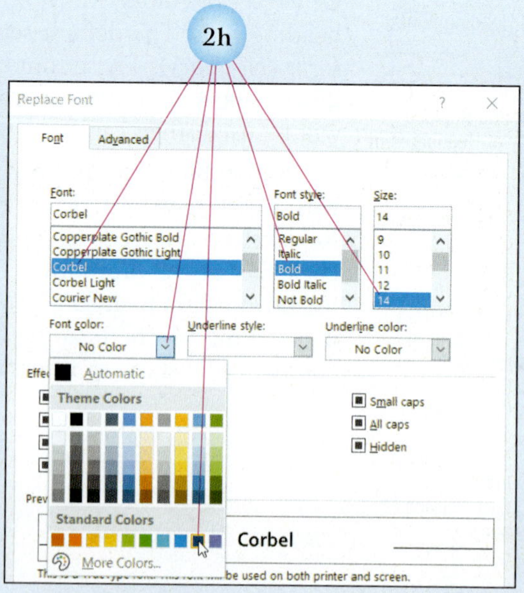

k. At the Replace Paragraph dialog box, click the *Alignment* option box arrow and then click *Centered* at the drop-down list.

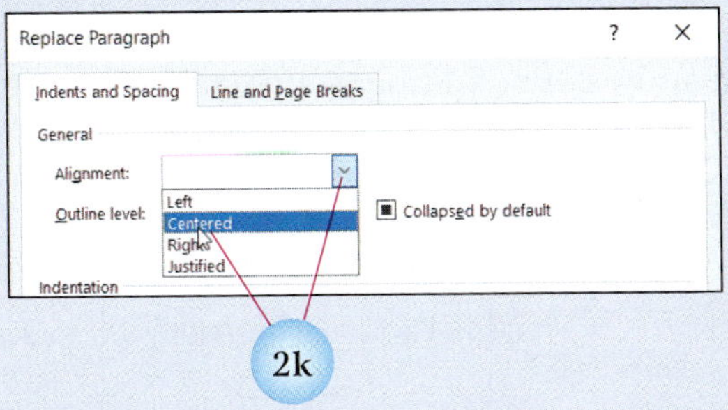

l. Click OK to close the Replace Paragraph dialog box.
m. Click the Replace All button.
n. At the message indicating 7 replacements were made, click OK.
3. Click the Less button and then close the Find and Replace dialog box.
4. Scroll through the document and notice the heading, formatting, and paragraph changes made to the document.
5. Save **1-ComLease**.

Check Your Work

Tutorial

Finding and Replacing Text Using a Wildcard Character

Quick Steps

Find and Replace Text Using Wildcard Character

1. Click Replace button.
2. Click More button.
3. Click *Use wildcards* check box.
4. Click in *Find what* text box.
5. Type find text using wildcard character.
6. Click in *Replace with* text box.
7. Type replacement text.
8. Click Replace All button.
9. Click OK.

Finding and Replacing Using Wildcard Characters

The expanded Find and Replace dialog box contains a *Use wildcards* check box. Insert a check mark in this check box to use wildcard characters in a search to find or find and replace data. For example, suppose the company name *Hansen Products* also mistakenly appears in a document as *Hanson Products*. Both spellings can be found by typing *Hans?n* in the *Find what* text box. Word will find *Hansen* and *Hanson* if the *Use wildcards* check box contains a check mark. If the *Use wildcards* check box does not contain a check mark, Word will try to find the exact spelling *Hans?n* and not find either spelling in the document. Table 1.1 identifies some common wildcard characters along with the functions they perform. For information on additional wildcard characters, use the Help feature.

Table 1.1 Wildcard Characters

Wildcard Character	Function
*	Indicates any characters. For example, type le*s and Word finds *less*, *leases*, and *letters*.
?	Indicates one character. For example, type gr?y and Word finds *gray* and *grey*.
@	Indicates any occurrence of the previous character. For example, type cho@se and Word finds *chose* and *choose*.
<	Indicates the beginning of a word. For example, type <(med) and Word finds *medical*, *medicine*, and *media*.
>	Indicates the ending of a word. For example, type (tion)> and Word finds *election*, *deduction*, and *education*.

Activity 3e Finding and Replacing Using a Wildcard Character

1. With **1-ComLease** open, use a wildcard character to search for words beginning with *leas* by completing the following steps:
   a. Click the Find button arrow in the Editing group on the Home tab and then click *Advanced Find* at the drop-down list.

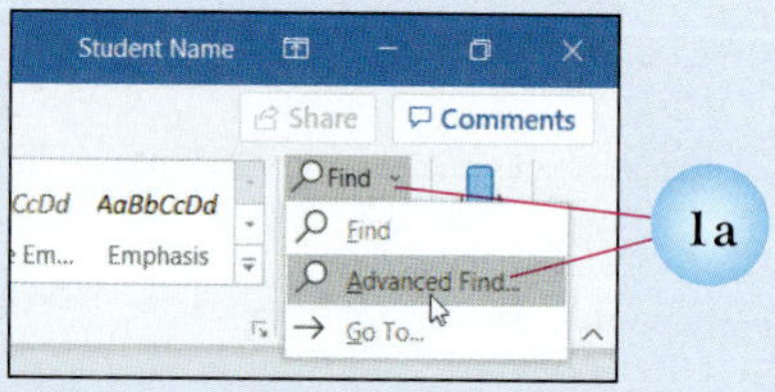

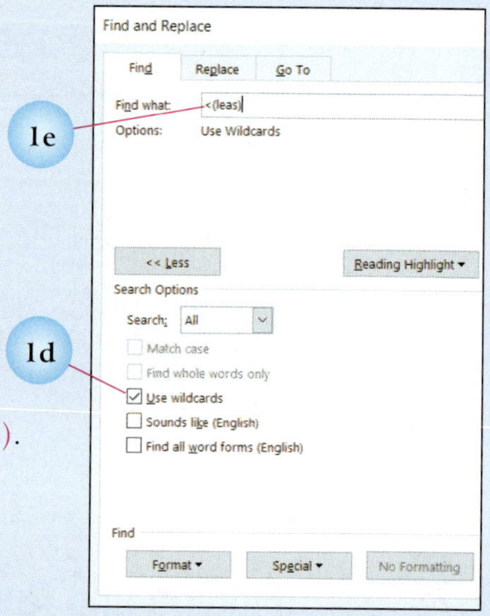

   b. At the Find and Replace dialog box, click the More button.
   c. Click the No Formatting button.
   d. Click the *Use wildcards* check box to insert a check mark.
   e. Click in the *Find what* text box and then type <(leas).
   f. Click the Find Next button to find the first occurrence of a word that begins with *leas*.
   g. Click the Find Next button four more times.
   h. Press the Esc key to end the find and close the Find and Replace dialog box.
2. The name *Arigalason* is spelled a variety of ways in the document. Use a wildcard character to search for all the versions of the name and replace them with the correct spelling by completing the following steps:
   a. Press Ctrl + Home to move the insertion point to the beginning of the document.
   b. Click the Replace button.
   c. At the Find and Replace dialog box, delete the text in the *Find what* text box and then type Ar?galas?n.
   d. Make sure that the dialog box is expanded and that the *Use wildcards* check box contains a check mark.
   e. Press the Tab key.
   f. Click the No Formatting button.
   g. Type Arigalason (the correct spelling) in the *Replace with* text box.
   h. Click the Replace All button.

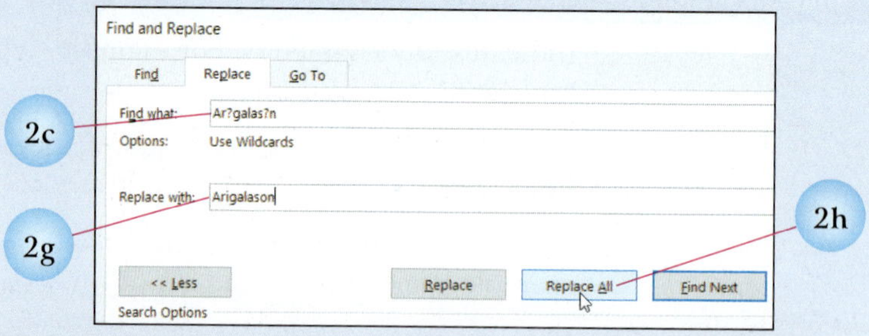

   i. At the message indicating that 23 replacements were made, click OK.
3. Close the Find and Replace dialog box.
4. Save, print, and then close **1-ComLease**.

Check Your Work

Activity 4 Insert Properties and Inspect a Document

4 Parts

You will open a document (an advertising flyer), insert document properties, inspect the document and remove specific elements, and then check the compatibility and accessibility of the document.

Tutorial

Managing Document Properties

Managing Document Properties

Every document has properties associated with it, such as the type of document, the location in which it has been saved, and when it was created, modified, and accessed. Document properties can be viewed and modified at the Info backstage area. To display information about the open document, click the File tab and then click the *Info* option. Document property information displays at the right side of the Info backstage area, as shown in Figure 1.12.

The document property information at the Info backstage area includes the file size, number of pages and words, total editing time, and any tags or comments that have been added. Some properties, such as the title, tags, or comments, may be edited. Hover over the property and a rectangular text box with a light blue border displays. Click inside the text box to type or edit information. In the *Related Dates* section, dates display for when the document was created and when it was last modified and printed. The *Related People* section includes the name of the author of the document and provides options for adding additional author names. Display additional document properties by clicking the Show All Properties hyperlink.

Figure 1.12 Info Backstage Area

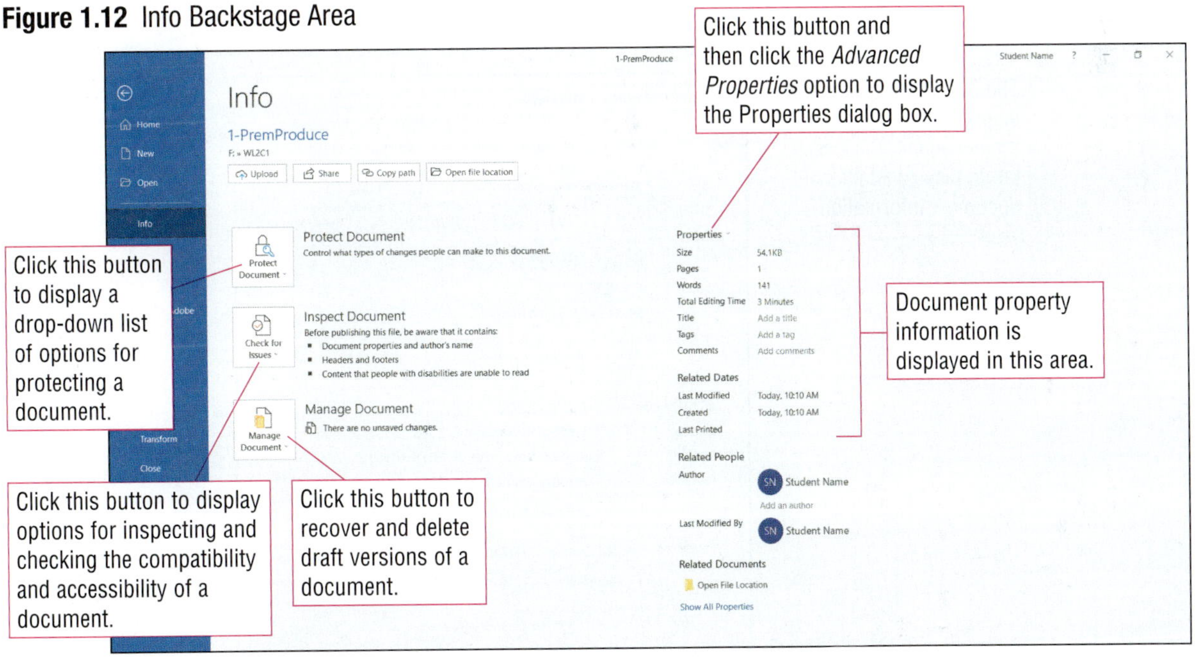

Quick Steps

Display Properties Dialog Box

1. Click File tab.
2. Click *Info* option.
3. Click Properties button.
4. Click *Advanced Properties*.

In addition to adding or updating document property information at the Info backstage area, specific information about a document can be viewed, added, edited, and customized with options at the Properties dialog box, shown in Figure 1.13. (The specific name of the dialog box reflects the currently open document.) Open the dialog box by displaying the Info backstage area, clicking the Properties button, and then clicking *Advanced Properties* at the drop-down list.

The Properties dialog box with the General tab selected displays information about the document type, size, and location. Click the Summary tab to view fields such as *Title*, *Subject*, *Author*, *Company*, *Category*, *Keywords*, and *Comments*. Some fields may contain data and others may be blank. Insert, edit, or delete text in the fields. With the Statistics tab selected, information displays such as the number of pages, paragraphs, lines, words, and characters. With the Contents tab selected, the dialog box displays the document title. Click the Custom tab to add custom properties to the document. For example, a property can be added that displays the date the document was completed, information on the department in which the document was created, and much more.

Another method for displaying document properties is to display the Open dialog box, click the document in the content pane, click the Organize button, and then click *Properties* at the drop-down list. Or right-click the file name in the content pane and then click *Properties* at the shortcut menu. The Properties dialog box that displays contains the tabs General, Security, Details, and Previous Versions. Some of the information in this Properties dialog box is the same as the information in the Properties dialog box that is accessed through the Info backstage area, while some of the information is different. Generally, consider using the Properties dialog box accessed through the Info backstage area to add, edit, and create custom properties and use the Properties dialog box accessed through the Open dialog box to view document properties.

Figure 1.13 Properties Dialog Box with the General Tab Selected

The Properties dialog box displays information about the document. Click each tab to display additional document information.

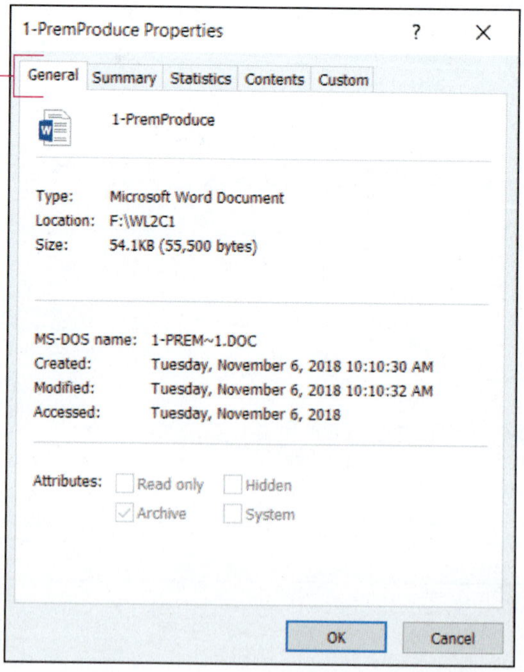

Activity 4a Inserting Document Properties

1. Open **PremProduce** and then save it with the name **1-PremProduce**.
2. Insert document properties by completing the following steps:
   a. Click the File tab and then, if necessary, click the *Info* option.
   b. Hover the mouse pointer over the text *Add a title* at the right of the *Title* document property, click in the text box, and then type Premium Produce.
   c. Display the 1-PremProduce Properties dialog box by clicking the Properties button and then clicking *Advanced Properties* at the drop-down list.

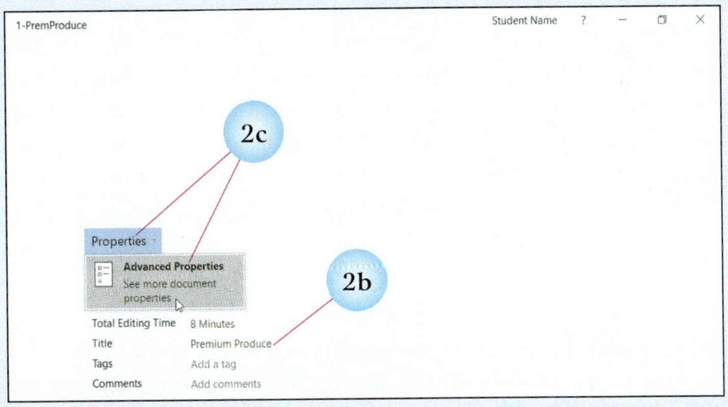

   d. At the 1-PremProduce Properties dialog box with the Summary tab selected, press the Tab key to make the *Subject* text box active and then type Organic produce.
   e. Click in the *Category* text box and then type Premium Produce flyer.
   f. Press the Tab key and then type the following words, separated by commas, in the *Keywords* text box: organic, produce, ordering.
   g. Press the Tab key and then type the following text in the *Comments* text box: This is a flyer about organic produce and the featured produce of the month.
   h. Click OK to close the dialog box.

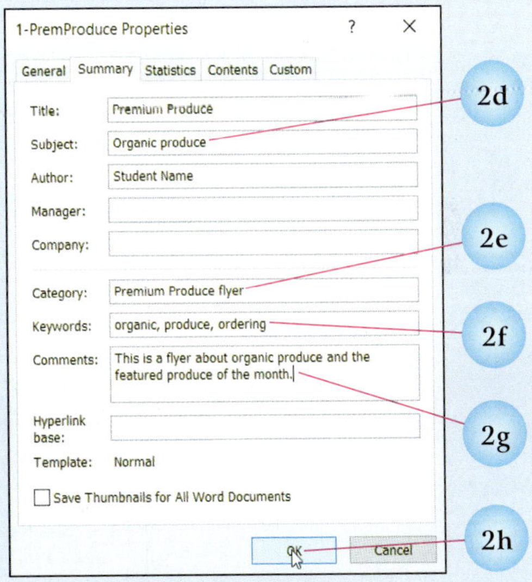

3. Click the Back button to return to the document.
4. Save **1-PremProduce** and then print only the document properties by completing the following steps:
   a. Click the File tab and then click the *Print* option.
   b. At the Print backstage area, click the first gallery in the *Settings* category and then click *Document Info* at the drop-down list.
   c. Click the Print button.
5. Save **1-PremProduce**.

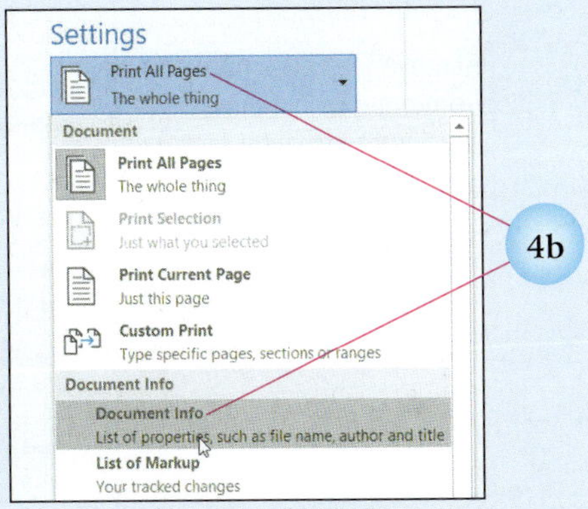

Check Your Work

Tutorial

Inspecting a Document

Inspecting Documents

Use options from the Check for Issues button drop-down list at the Info backstage area to inspect a document for personal and hidden data along with compatibility and accessibility issues. Click the Check for Issues button at the Info backstage area and a drop-down list displays with the options *Inspect Document*, *Check Accessibility*, and *Check Compatibility*.

Using the Document Inspector

Check for Issues

Use Word's Document Inspector to inspect a document for personal data, hidden data, and metadata (data that describes other data, such as document properties). In certain situations, some personal or hidden data may need to be removed before a document is shared with others. To check a document for personal and hidden data, click the File tab, click the Check for Issues button at the Info backstage area, and then click the *Inspect Document* option at the drop-down list. This displays the Document Inspector dialog box, shown in Figure 1.14.

By default, the Document Inspector checks all the items listed in the dialog box. To control what items are inspected in the document, remove the check marks preceding items that should not be checked. For example, if the headers and footers in a document do not need to be checked, click the *Headers, Footers, and Watermarks* check box to remove the check mark. To scan the document to check for the selected items, click the Inspect button at the bottom of the dialog box.

When the inspection is complete, the results display in the Document Inspector dialog box. A check mark before an option indicates that the Document Inspector did not find the specific items. If an exclamation point displays before an option, it means that the items were found and a list of the items displays. To remove the found items, click the Remove All button at the right of the option. Click the Reinspect button to ensure that the specific items were removed and then click the Close button.

Figure 1.14 Document Inspector Dialog Box

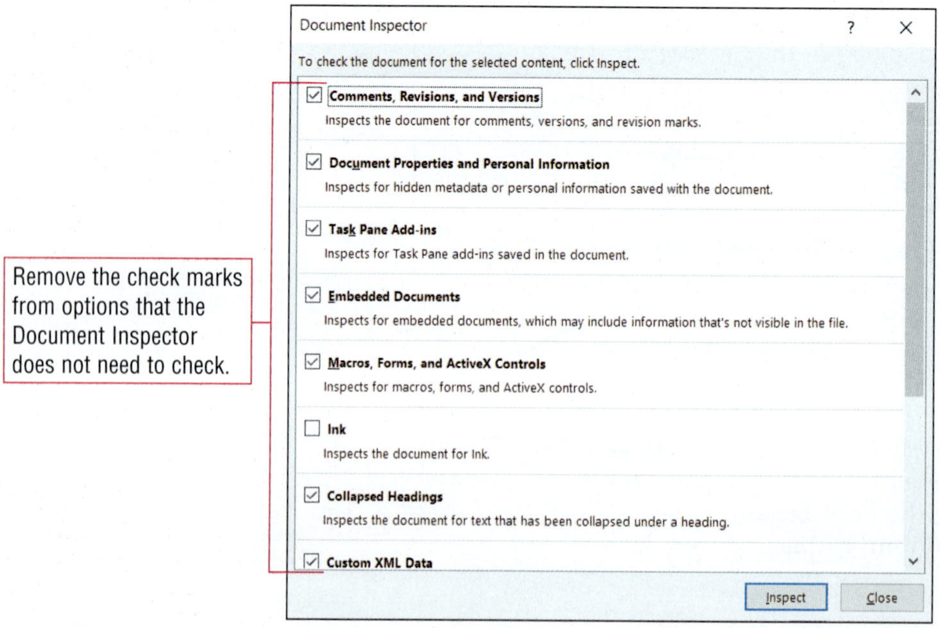

Activity 4b Inspecting a Document

Part 2 of 4

1. With **1-PremProduce** open, type and then hide text by completing the following steps:
   a. Press Ctrl + Home to move the insertion point to the beginning of the document and then type Before distributing the flyer, make sure the Pricing link is active.
   b. Select the text you just typed.
   c. Click the Home tab, if necessary.
   d. Click the Font group dialog box launcher.
   e. At the Font dialog box with the Font tab selected, click the *Hidden* check box in the *Effects* section to insert a check mark.
   f. Click OK to close the dialog box.

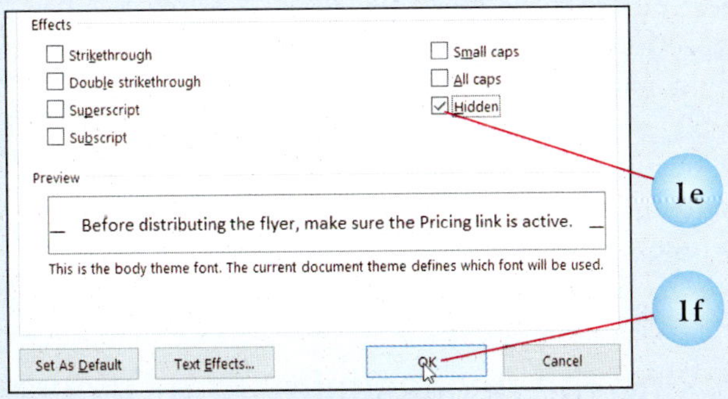

2. Click the Save button on the Quick Access Toolbar.
3. Inspect the document by completing the following steps (this document contains a watermark, a footer, document properties, and hidden text):
   a. Click the File tab and then, if necessary, click the *Info* option.
   b. Click the Check for Issues button at the Info backstage area and then click *Inspect Document* at the drop-down list.
   c. At the Document Inspector dialog box, specify not to check the document for collapsed headings by clicking the *Collapsed Headings* check box to remove the check mark.
   d. Click the Inspect button.

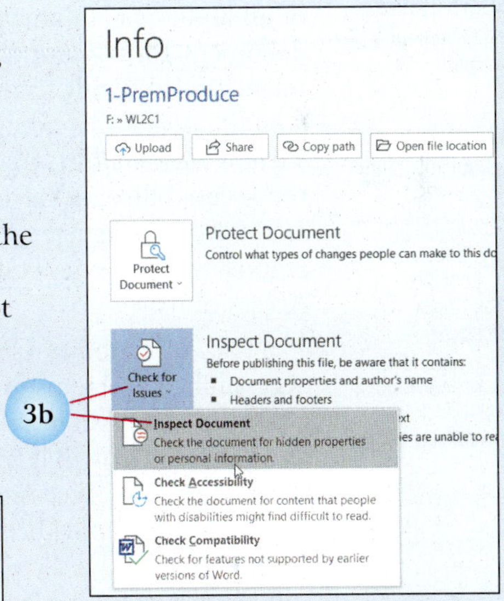

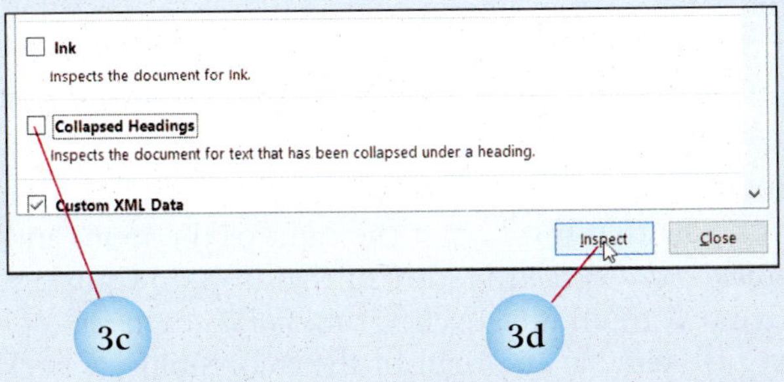

   e. Notice that the results show the document contains document properties and personal information. Scroll down the list box showing the inspection results and notice that the results show that the document also contains a header, a footer, and hidden text.

f. Remove the footer and watermark by clicking the Remove All button at the right of the *Headers, Footers, and Watermarks* section. (Make sure that a message displays below *Headers, Footers, and Watermarks* stating that the text was removed.)

g. Remove the hidden text by clicking the Remove All button at the right of the *Hidden Text* section. (Make sure that a message displays below *Hidden Text* stating that the text was removed.)

h. Click the Reinspect button.

i. Click the Inspect button.

j. Review the inspection results and then click the Close button.

k. Click the Back button to return to the document.

4. Save **1-PremProduce**.

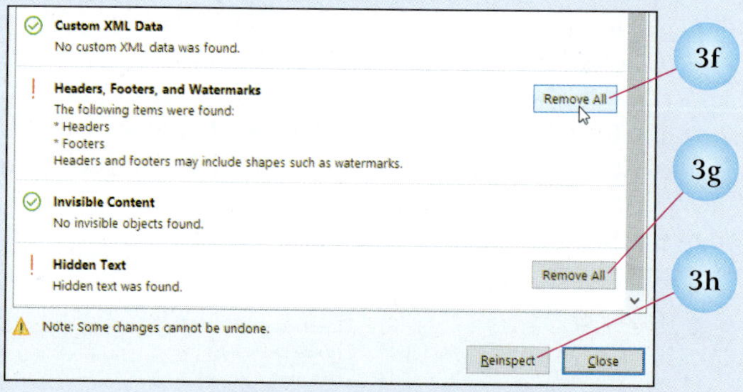

Tutorial

Checking the Accessibility and Compatibility of a Document

Quick Steps

Check Accessibility

1. Click File tab.
2. Click *Info* option.
3. Click Check for Issues button.
4. Click *Check Accessibility*.

OR

1. Click Review tab.
2. Click Check Accessibility button.

Checking the Accessibility of a Document

When preparing a document, making sure the content is accessible to people of all abilities is important. Word provides the Accessibility Checker to check a document for content that a person with disabilities (such as a visual impairment) might find difficult to read or understand using assistive technology. If a document contains a possible accessibility issue, a message will display on the Status bar such as *Accessibiltiy: Investigate*. Check the accessibility of a document by clicking the accessibility message on the Status bar or clicking the Check for Issues button at the Info backstage area and then clicking *Check Accessibility*. Another option is to click the Review tab and then click the Check Accessibility button in the Accessibility group.

The Accessibility Checker examines the document for the most common accessibility problems and sorts them into three categories: errors (content that will not be accessible); warnings (content that may be difficult to understand); and tips (content that may be understood, but can be improved to make it more accessible). The Accessibility Checker examines the document, closes the Info backstage area, and then displays the Accessibility Checker task pane. Select an issue in one of the sections and an explanation of why it is an issue and how it can be corrected displays at the bottom of the task pane.

To correct an accessibility issue, click the item in the Accessibility Checker task pane, click the down arrow that displays at the right of the item, and then click an option in the *Recommended Actions* section of the drop-down list. For example, to add alternative text to an image, click the *Add a description* option. This displays the Alt Text task pane at the right of the Accessibility Checker task pane. Click in the Alt Text task pane text box and then type a description of the item. If a person with a visual impairment uses a screen reader to hear a reading of the document, the screen reader will read the text in the Alt Text text box describing the item.

Activity 4c Checking the Accessibility of a Document

1. With **1-PremProduce** open, conduct an accessibility check by completing the following steps:
   a. Click the File tab and then, if necessary, click the *Info* option.
   b. At the Info backstage area, click the Check for Issues button and then click *Check Accessibility* at the drop-down list.
   c. Notice the Accessibility Checker task pane at the right side of the screen, which contains an *Errors* section. Click *Picture 4* in the *Errors* section and then read the information at the bottom of the task pane describing why the error should be fixed and how to fix it.

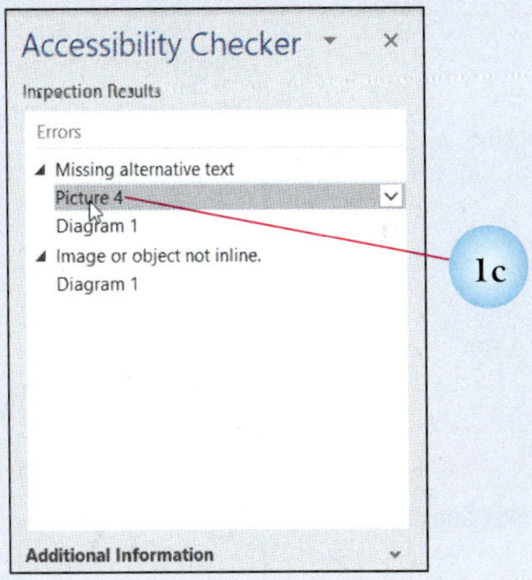

2. Add alternative text (a verbal description of what the image represents) to the image by completing the following steps:
   a. Click the down arrow at the right of *Picture 4*.
   b. Click the *Add a description* option at the drop-down list.
   c. At the Alt Text task pane at the right of the Accessibility Checker task pane, click in the text box and then type Cornucopia of fruits and vegetables representing Premium Produce.

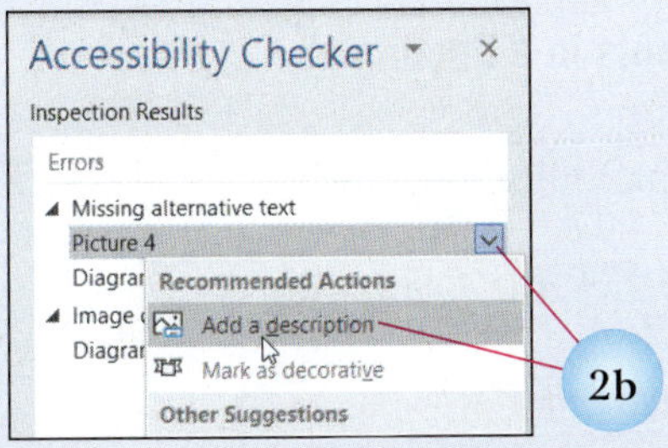

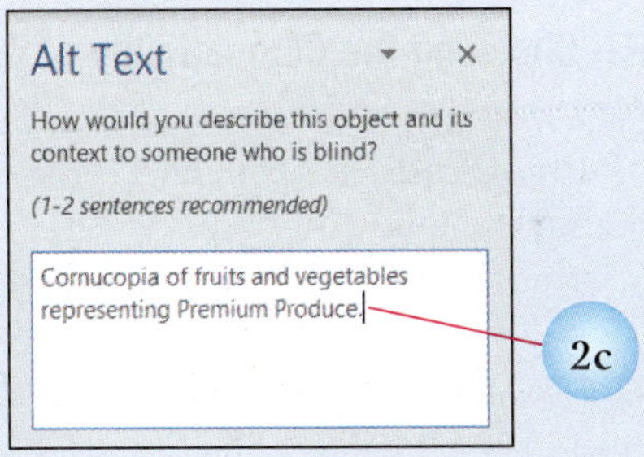

3. Point to *Diagram 1* in the *Errors* section (the *Diagram 1* that displays below the *Missing alternative text* heading), click the down arrow at the right of *Diagram 1*, and then click *Add a description* at the drop-down list.

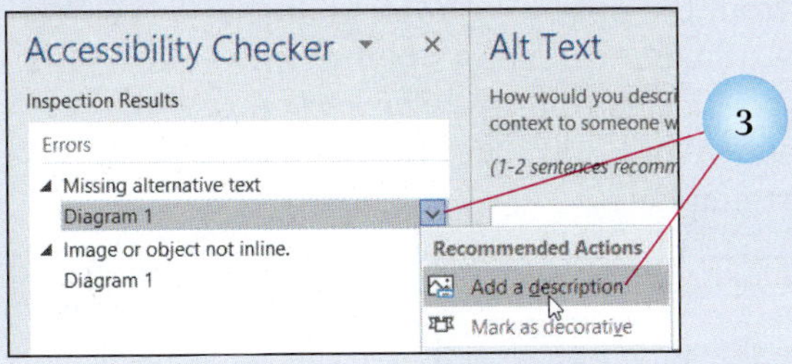

4. Click in the text box in the Alt Text task pane and then type SmartArt graphic indicating no pesticides, no herbicides, and organically grown produce.
5. Close the Alt Text task pane.
6. Click *Diagram 1* in the *Errors* section and then read the information in the task pane about why an image or object should be inline with text.

7. Click the down arrow at the right of *Diagram 1* and then click *Place this inline* at the drop-down list. (This changes the text wrapping of the SmartArt to *In Line with Text*.
8. Close the Accessibility Checker task pane by clicking the Close button in the upper right corner.
9. Save **1-PremProduce**.

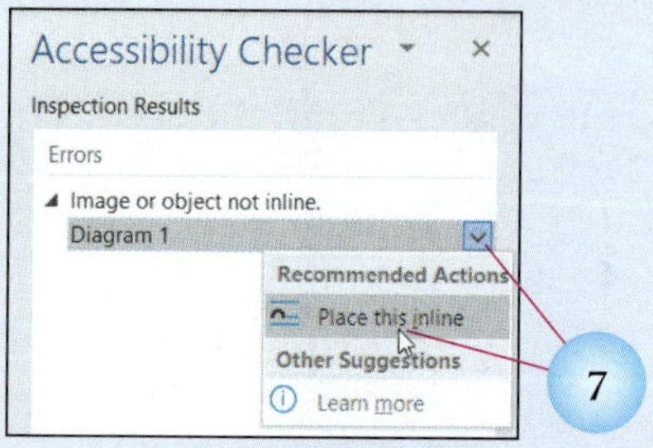

Check Your Work

Checking the Compatibility of a Document

Quick Steps
Check Compatibility
1. Click File tab.
2. Click *Info* option.
3. Click Check for Issues button.
4. Click *Check Compatibility*.
5. Click OK.

The Compatibility Checker will check a document and identify elements that are not supported or will function differently in previous versions of Word, from Word 97 through Word 2010. To run the Compatibility Checker, open a document, click the Check for Issues button at the Info backstage area, and then click *Check Compatibility* at the drop-down list. This displays the Microsoft Word Compatibility Checker dialog box, which includes a summary of the elements in the document that are not compatible with previous versions of Word. This box also indicates what will happen when the document is saved and then opened in a previous version.

Activity 4d Checking the Compatibility of Elements in a Document — Part 4 of 4

1. With **1-PremProduce** open, check the compatibility of elements in the document by completing the following steps:
   a. Click the File tab and then, if necessary, click the *Info* option.
   b. Click the Check for Issues button at the Info backstage area and then click *Check Compatibility* at the drop-down list.
   c. At the Microsoft Word Compatibility Checker dialog box, read the information in the *Summary* text box.
   d. Click the *Select versions to show* option box and then click *Word 97-2003* at the drop-down list. (This removes the check mark from the option.) Notice that the information about SmartArt graphics being converted to static objects disappears from the *Summary* text box. This is because Word 2007 and later versions all support SmartArt graphics.

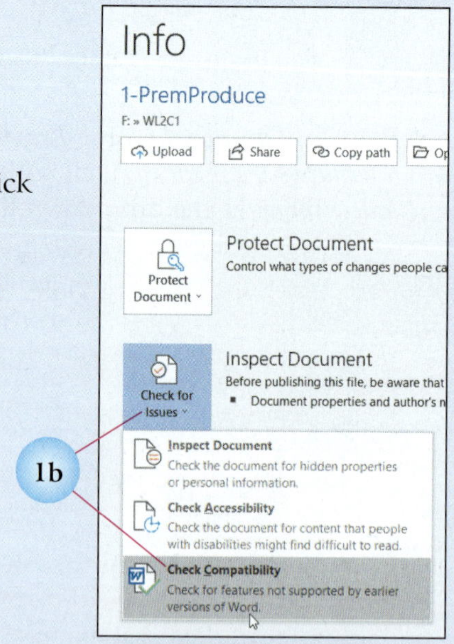

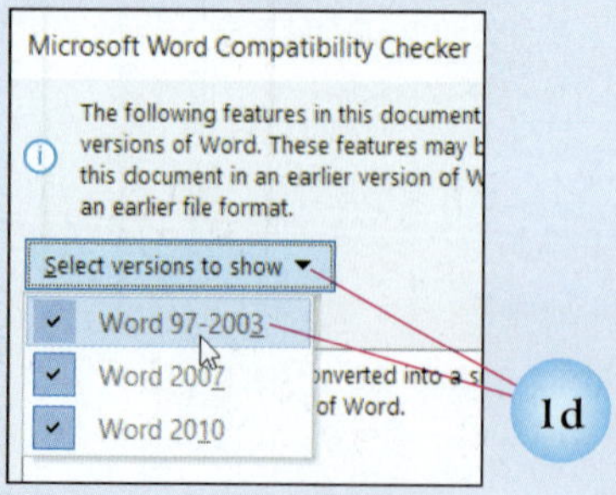

   e. Click OK to close the dialog box.

2. Save the document in Word 2003 format by completing the following steps:
   a. Press the F12 function key to display the Save As dialog box with WL2C1 the active folder.
   b. At the Save As dialog box, click the *Save as type* option box and then click *Word 97-2003 Document* at the drop-down list.
   c. Select the text in the *File name* text box and then type 1-PremProduce-2003format.
   d. Click the Save button.

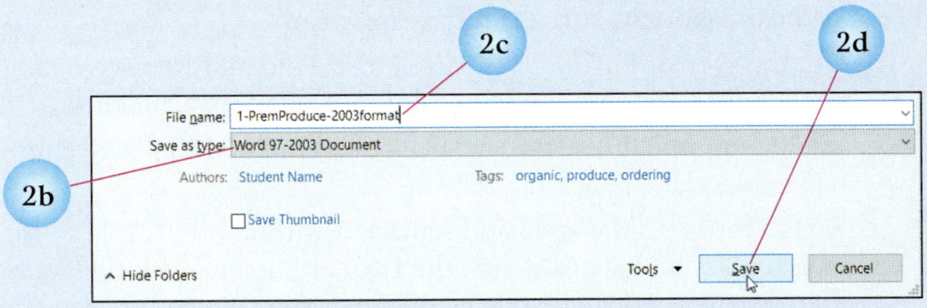

   e. Click the Continue button at the Microsoft Word Compatibility Checker dialog box.
3. Close **1-PremProduce-2003format**.

Check Your Work

Chapter Summary

- Use options in the *Character Spacing* section of the Font dialog box with the Advanced tab selected to adjust character spacing and turn on kerning.
- The OpenType features available at the Font dialog box with the Advanced tab selected include options for choosing a ligature style, specifying number spacing and form, and applying stylistic sets.
- The Text Effects and Typography button in the Font group on the Home tab contains options for applying text effects such as outline, shadow, reflection, and glow effects as well as typography options such as number styles, ligatures, and stylistic sets.
- Click the Text Effects button at the Font dialog box to display the Format Text Effects dialog box. Use options at this dialog box to apply text fill and text outline effects to selected text.
- Change the default font with the Set As Default button at the Font dialog box. The default font can be changed for the current document or all new documents based on the Normal template.
- Use the © symbol to identify copyrighted intellectual property, use the ™ symbol to identify a trademark, and use the ® symbol to identify a registered trademark.
- Insert a nonbreaking hyphen by clicking the *Nonbreaking Hyphen* option at the Symbol dialog box with the Special Characters tab selected or by using the keyboard shortcut Ctrl + Shift + -.
- Use an em dash to indicate a break in thought or to highlight a term or phrase by separating it from the rest of the sentence. Insert an em dash by typing a word, typing two hyphens, typing the next word, and then pressing the spacebar. An em dash can also be inserted with the keyboard shortcut Alt + Ctrl + - (on the numeric keypad) or at the Symbol dialog box with the Special Characters tab selected.

- Use an en dash to indicate inclusive dates, times, and numbers. To insert an en dash, click the *En Dash* option at the Symbol dialog box with the Special Characters tab selected or use the keyboard short Ctrl + - (on the numeric keypad).
- Insert nonbreaking spaces between words that should not be separated across a line break. Insert a nonbreaking space by clicking the *Nonbreaking Space* option at the Symbol dialog box with the Special Characters tab selected or with the keyboard shortcut Ctrl + Shift + spacebar.
- Use the Format button at the expanded Find and Replace dialog box to find and replace character and paragraph formatting in a document.
- Use the Special button at the expanded Find and Replace dialog box to find and replace special characters.
- Search for a specific style and replace it with another style at the expanded Find and Replace dialog box. Click the Format button, click the *Style* option, and then specify the search style at the Find Style dialog box and the replacement style at the Replace Style dialog box.
- A Word document contains a body font and a heading font. A document can be searched to find a body or heading font and replace it with a different font.
- Wildcard characters can be used to find text in a document. To use a wildcard, display the expanded Find and Replace dialog box and then click the *Use wildcards* check box to insert a check mark.
- Document properties can be viewed and modified at the Info backstage area and at the Properties dialog box. Display the Properties dialog box by clicking the Properties button at the Info backstage area and then clicking *Advanced Properties* at the drop-down list.
- Inspect a document for personal data, hidden data, and metadata with options at the Document Inspector dialog box. Display this dialog box by clicking the Check for Issues button at the Info backstage area and then clicking *Inspect Document* at the drop-down list.
- The Accessibility Checker checks a document for content that a person with disabilities might find difficult to read or understand with the use of assistive technology. Run the Accessibility Checker by clicking the Check for Issues button at the Info backstage area and then clicking *Check Accessibility* at the drop-down list, by clicking the accessibility message on the Status bar, or by clicking the Review tab and then clicking the Check Accessibility button.
- Run the Compatibility Checker to check a document and identify elements that are not supported or that will function differently in previous versions of Word. Run the Compatibility Checker by clicking the Check for Issues button at the Info backstage area and then clicking *Check Compatibility* at the drop-down list.

Commands Review

FEATURE	RIBBON TAB, GROUP/OPTION	BUTTON, OPTION	KEYBOARD SHORTCUT
Accessibility Checker	File, *Info*	, *Check Accessibility*	
Compatibility Checker	File, *Info*	, *Check Compatibility*	
copyright symbol	Insert, Symbols	, *More Symbols*	Alt + Ctrl + C
Document Inspector dialog box	File, *Info*	, *Inspect Document*	
em dash	Insert, Symbols	, *More Symbols*	Alt + Ctrl + - (on numeric keypad)
en dash	Insert, Symbols	, *More Symbols*	Ctrl + - (on numeric keypad)
Find and Replace dialog box	Home, Editing	, *Replace*	Ctrl + H
Font dialog box	Home, Font		Ctrl + D
nonbreaking hyphen	Insert, Symbols	, *More Symbols*	Ctrl + Shift + -
nonbreaking space	Insert, Symbols	, *More Symbols*	Ctrl + Shift + spacebar
Properties dialog box	File, *Info*	Properties, *Advanced Properties*	
registered trademark symbol	Insert, Symbols	, *More Symbols*	Alt + Ctrl + R
Symbol dialog box	Insert, Symbols	, *More Symbols*	
Text Effects and Typography button	Home, Font		
trademark symbol	Insert, Symbols	, *More Symbols*	Alt + Ctrl + T

Microsoft®

Word

CHAPTER 2

Proofing Documents

Performance Objectives

Upon successful completion of Chapter 2, you will be able to:

1. Complete a spelling check and a grammar check on text in a document
2. Display readability statistics
3. Create a custom dictionary, change the default dictionary, and remove a dictionary
4. Display document word, paragraph, and character counts
5. Insert line numbers
6. Display synonyms and antonyms for specific words using the thesaurus
7. Use the Smart Lookup feature
8. Translate text to and from different languages
9. Sort text in paragraphs, columns, and tables

Microsoft Word includes proofing tools to help you create well-written, error-free documents. These tools include a spelling checker, grammar checker, and thesaurus. If documents will be created with specific words, terms, or acronyms not found in the main spelling dictionary, a custom dictionary can be created. When completing a spelling check, the spelling checker will compare words in a document with the main dictionary as well as a custom dictionary. Word provides a translation feature for translating text into different languages. In Word, text in paragraphs, columns and tables can be sorted alphabetically or numerically in ascending or descending order. In this chapter, you will learn how to use the proofing tools, create a custom dictionary, translate text to and from different languages, and sort text.

Data Files

Before beginning chapter work, copy the WL2C2 folder to your storage medium and then make WL2C2 the active folder.

The online course includes additional training and assessment resources.

Activity 1 Check Spelling in an Investment Plan Document 1 Part

You will open an investment plan document and then complete a spelling and grammar check.

Checking Spelling and Grammar

Check Document

Quick Steps

Check Spelling and Grammar

1. Click Review tab.
2. Click Check Document button.
   OR
   Press F7.
3. Change or ignore errors.
4. Click OK.

Word contains an Editor feature that checks the spelling and grammar of a document. To check a document for spelling and grammar errors, click the Review tab and then click the Check Document button in the Proofing group or press the F7 function key. When checking the spelling of a document, the Editor flags misspelled words and offers corrections.

The Editor's spell checking feature can find and correct misspelled words, duplicate words, and irregular capitalizations. To check spelling, it compares the words in the document with the words in its dictionary. If it finds a match, it passes over the word. If the word is not found in its dictionary, it offers possible corrections. Following are examples of issues that can be identified by the Editor:

- misspelled words (any words not found in the Editor's dictionary)
- typographical errors (such as transposed letters)
- double occurrences of a word (such as *the the*)
- irregular capitalization
- some proper names
- jargon and some technical terms

The grammar checker searches a document for errors in grammar, punctuation, and word usage. Using the spelling checker and grammar checker can help create well-written documents but does not replace the need for proofreading.

Editing During a Spelling and Grammar Check

When checking the spelling and grammar in a document, edits or corrections can be made in the document. Do this by clicking in the document outside the Editor task pane, making the change or edit, and then clicking the Resume checking all results button in the task pane.

Tutorial

Customizing Spelling and Grammar Checking

Customizing Spell Checking

Customize the spelling checker with options at the Word Options dialog box with the *Proofing* option selected, as shown in Figure 2.1. Display this dialog box by clicking the File tab and then clicking *Options*. At the Word Options dialog box, click *Proofing* in the left panel. Use options at this dialog box to specify what the spelling checker should review or ignore.

Hint Read grammar suggestions carefully. Some may not be valid in a specific context and a problem identified by the grammar checker may not actually be an issue.

Using the Editor Task Pane Reading Feature

The Editor task pane includes a reading feature that will read aloud the sentence that displays in the Editor task pane. To hear a reading of the sentence, click the speaker icon to the right of the sentence. The suggested word and definition that display in the *Suggestions* list box can also be read aloud by clicking the word in the list box and then clicking the *Read Aloud* option at the drop-down list. For the reading feature to work, the computer speakers must be turned on.

Figure 2.1 Word Options Dialog Box with the *Proofing* Option Selected

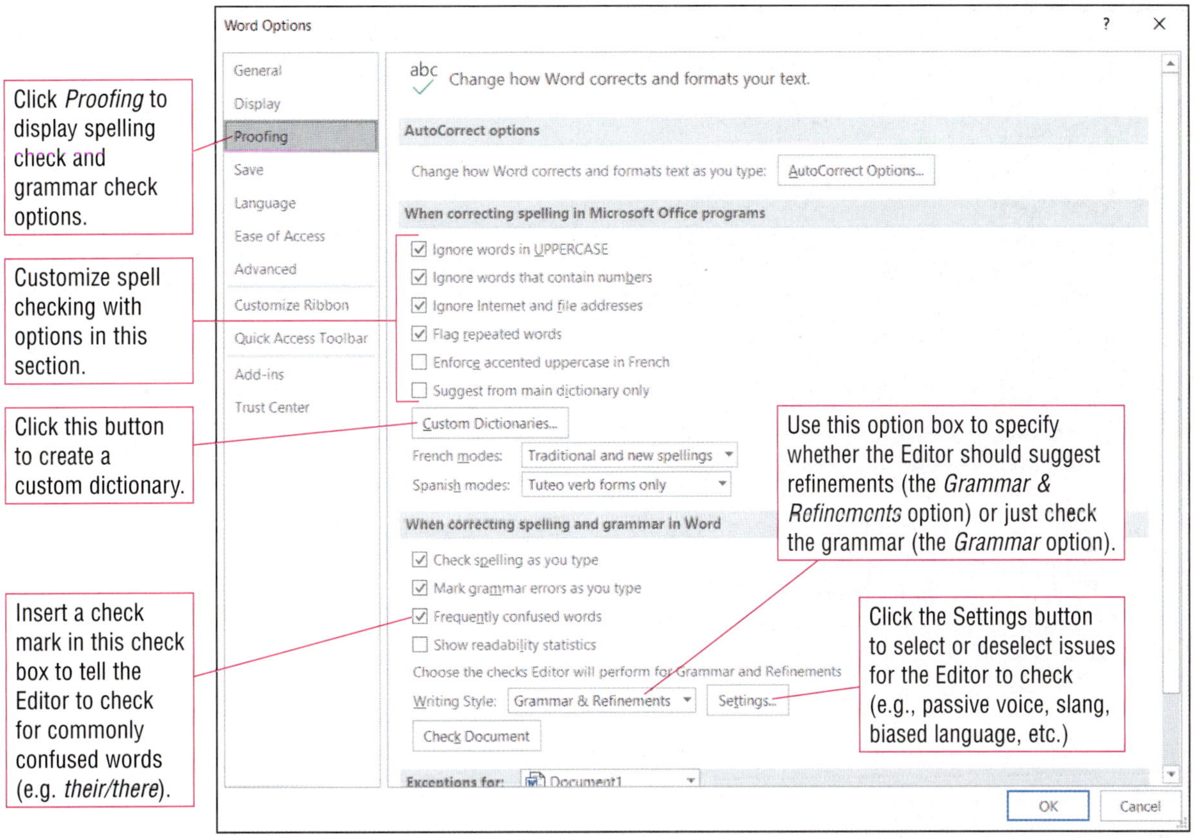

Activity 1 Spell Checking a Document with Uppercase Words

Part 1 of 1

1. Open **PlanDists** and then save it with the name **2-PlanDists**.
2. Change a spell checking option by completing the following steps:
   a. Click the File tab.
   b. Click *Options*.
   c. At the Word Options dialog box, click the *Proofing* option in the left panel.
   d. Click the *Ignore words in UPPERCASE* check box to remove the check mark.
   e. Click OK to close the dialog box.
3. Complete a spelling check on the document by completing the following steps:
   a. Click the Review tab.
   b. Click the Check Document button in the Proofing group.
   c. At the Editor task pane, click the Results button (contains the text *7 Results*) that appears near the top of the task pane.

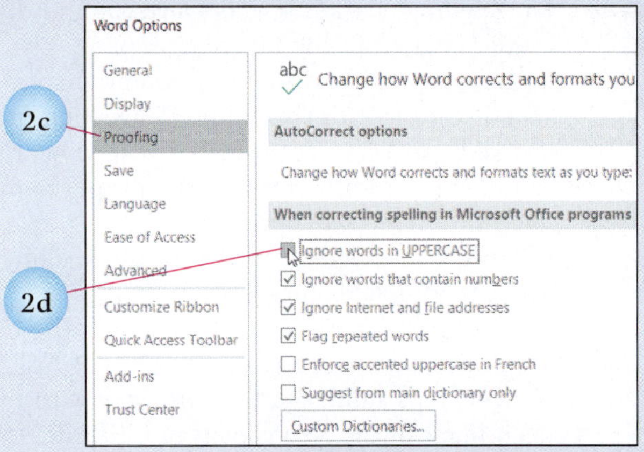

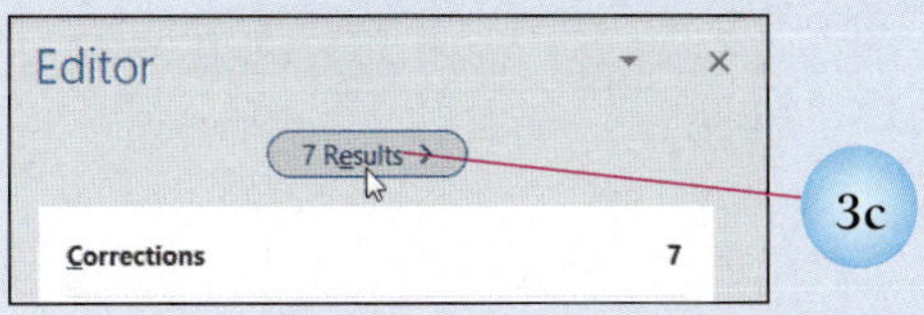

d. The spelling checker displays *ERLY DISTRIBUTIONS* in the Editor task pane and the correct spelling displays in the *Suggestions* list box. Click *EARLY* in the *Suggestions* list box to change the word to the correct spelling.

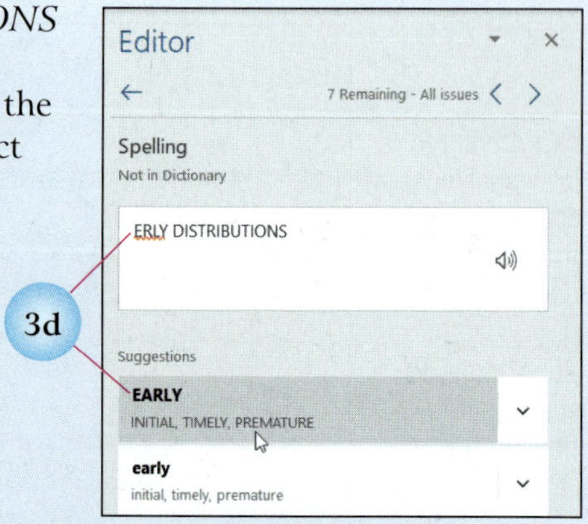

e. The spelling checker selects the word *distributin* and the correct spelling displays in the *Suggestions* list box. Since this word is misspelled in other locations in the document, click the down arrow at the right of *distribution* in the *Suggestions* list box and then click *Change All* at the drop-down list.

f. The spelling checker selects *ftaer*. The proper spelling *after* is not available in the *Suggestions* list box. Double-click *ftaer* in the document and then type after. (This dims the Editor task pane and a Resume checking all results button appears in the task pane.)

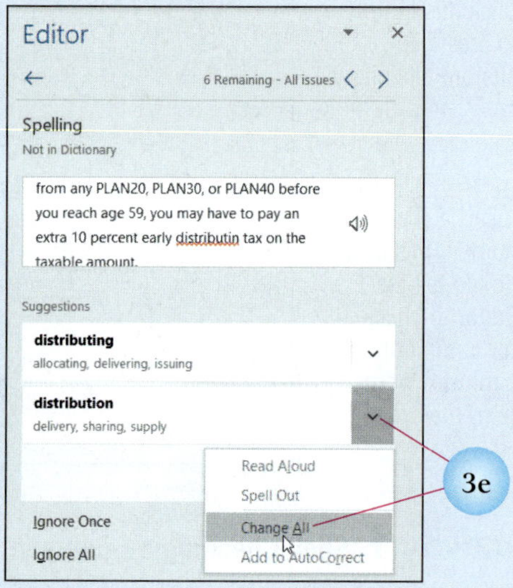

g. Click the Resume checking all results button to continue the spelling check.

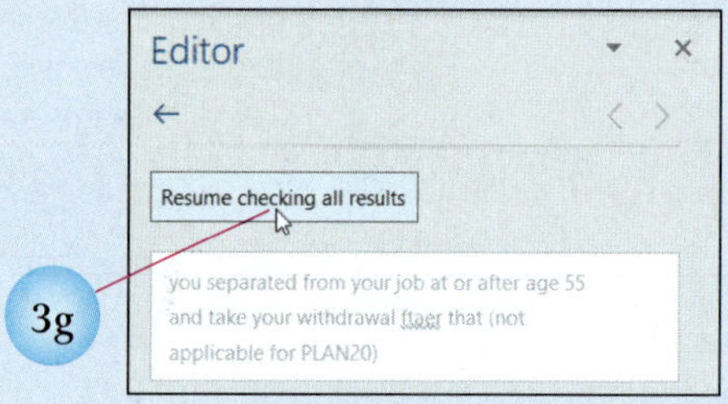

h. The spelling checker selects *to*. (This is a double word occurrence.) Click the *Delete Repeated Word* option to delete the second occurrence of *to*.

i. The spelling checker selects *Haverson* and displays *Logan Haverson* in the Editor task pane. Listen to the name being read by clicking the speaker icon at the right of the name. (Your computer speakers must be turned on for you to hear the name being read.) Haverson is a proper name, so click the *Ignore Once* option.

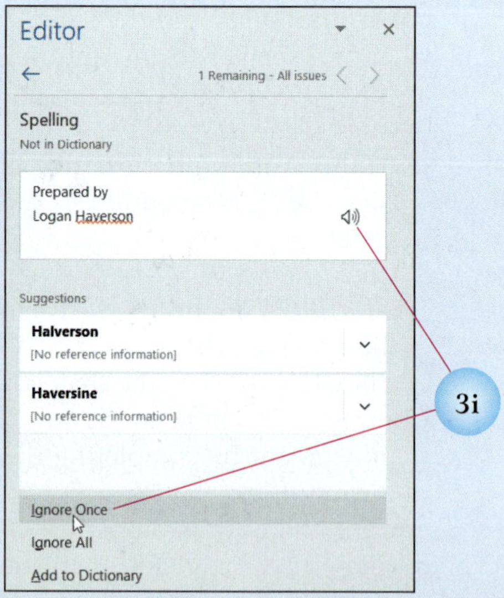

j. When the message displays that the spelling check is complete, click OK.

k. Close the Editor task pane by clicking the Close button in the upper right corner of the task pane.

4. Complete steps similar to those in Step 2 to insert a check mark in the *Ignore words in UPPERCASE* check box.
5. Save, print, and then close **2-PlanDists**.

Check Your Work

Activity 2 Change Grammar Options and Check the Grammar in a Company Letter

2 Parts

You will check the grammar in a company letter, change grammar options, and then check the document for spelling and grammar errors. You will also display readability statistics for the document.

Changing Grammar Checking Options

Quick Steps

Change Grammar Checking Options

1. Click File tab.
2. Click *Options*.
3. Click *Proofing*.
4. Change options in the dialog box.
5. Click OK.

When performing a spelling and grammar check, Word highlights text that may contain grammatical errors and displays the potential errors in the Editor task pane. By default, the grammar checker also looks for ways to refine the writing, such as by eliminating wordiness. To simply check the grammar and not look for refinements, change the option in the Word Options dialog box (see Figure 2.1 on page 39) from *Grammar & Refinements* to *Grammar*.

Click the Settings button at the Word Options dialog box with *Proofing* selected in the left panel and the Grammar Settings dialog box displays with a list of issues the Editor can consider when checking a document (e.g., errors in punctuation, misused words, biased language, and so on). Each option is preceded by a check box. If a check box contains a check mark, the option is active and the Editor will check for the issue. Scroll down the list box to see the issues available for checking in a document. Customize by inserting or removing check marks.

Activity 2a Changing Grammar Options and Checking Grammar

Part 1 of 2

1. Open **MCFLetter** and save it with the name **2-MCFLetter**.
2. Look at the document and notice the dotted line below text in the document indicating a possible grammar error.
3. Change the grammar option by completing the following steps:
   a. Click the File tab and then click *Options*.
   b. Click *Proofing* in the left panel.
   c. Click the *Writing Style* option box arrow and then click *Grammar* at the drop-down list.

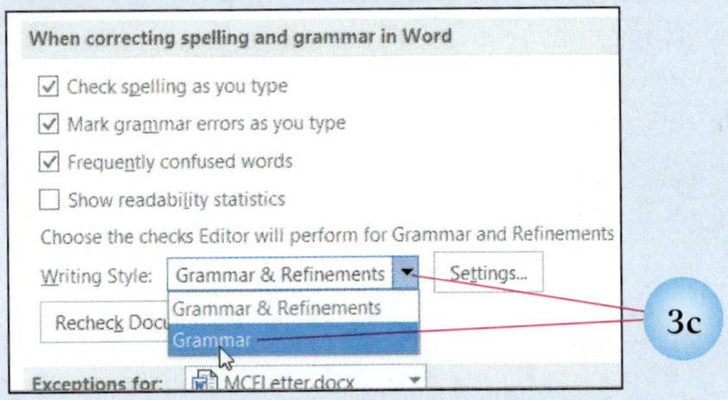

   d. Click OK.
4. At the document, notice that no dotted line displays below text. This is because the *Grammar* option does not check a document for grammar issues such as wordiness and conciseness.

5. Change the grammar option back to the default and specify that the grammar checker is to check for passive voice by completing the following steps:
   a. Click the File tab and then click *Options*.
   b. Click *Proofing* in the left panel.
   c. Click the *Writing Style* option box arrow and then click *Grammar & Refinements* at the drop-down list.
   d. Click the Settings button.
   e. At the Grammar Settings dialog box, scroll down the *Options* list box to the *Clarity and Conciseness* section and then click the *Passive Voice* check box to insert a check mark.
   f. Click OK to close the Grammar Settings dialog box.
   g. Click OK to close the Word Options dialog box.

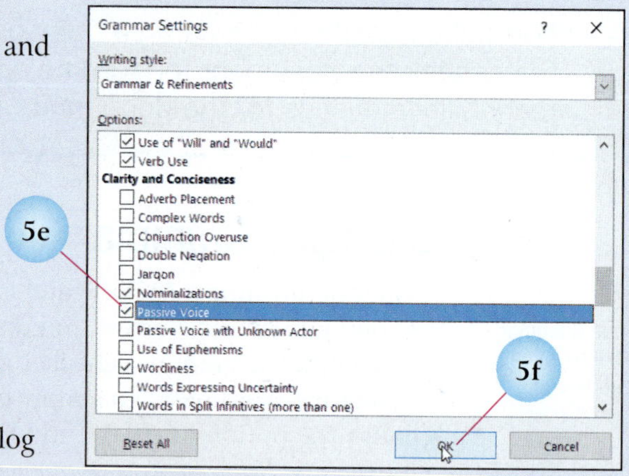

6. Check the spelling and grammar in the document by completing the following steps:
   a. Click the Review tab, if necessary.
   b. Click the Check Document button in the Proofing group.
   c. At the Editor task pane, click the Results button (contains the text *4 Results*).
   d. The grammar checker selects the text *Expense charges are being lowered by McCormack Funds* and does not offer any suggestions in the *Suggestions* list box.
   e. Click the down arrow at the right of the text *Consider using active voice* in the Editor task pane and then read the information that displays below the text about active voice.

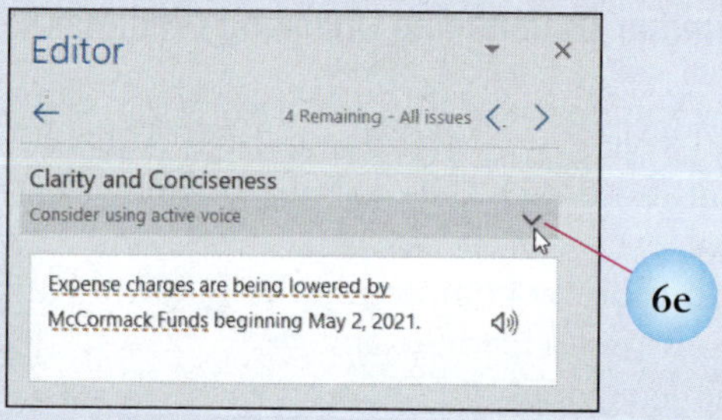

   f. Click in the document and then edit the first sentence in the first paragraph so it reads as *McCormack Funds is lowering expense charges beginning May 2, 2021*.
   g. Click the Resume checking all results button in the Editor task pane.
   h. When the grammar checker selects *all of* in the document, notice the information *Consider using concise language* that displays in the Editor task pane and then click the *all* option in the *Suggestions* list box.
   i. When the grammar checker selects *main focus* in the document, click *focus* in the *Suggestions* list box.
   j. When the spelling checker selects *Langstrom* click the *Ignore All* option in the Editor task pane.
   k. At the message stating that the spelling and grammar check is complete, click OK.
   l. Close the Editor task pane.
7. Remove the check mark from the *Passive Voice* check box by completing the following steps:
   a. Click the File tab and then click *Options*.
   b. Click *Proofing* in the left panel.
   c. Click the Settings button.

d. At the Grammar Settings dialog box, scroll down the *Options* list box to the *Clarity and Conciseness* section and then click the *Passive Voice* check box to remove the check mark.
e. Click OK to close the Grammar Settings dialog box.
f. Click OK to close the Word Options dialog box.
8. Save **2-MCFLetter**.

Check Your Work

Setting the Proofing Language

Language

Quick Steps

Choose Proofing Language

1. Click Review tab.
2. Click Language button.
3. Click *Set Proofing Language*.
4. Click language in list box.
5. Click OK.

Microsoft provides a number of dictionaries for proofing text in various languages. To change the language used for proofing a document, click the Review tab, click the Language button in the Language group, and then click *Set Proofing Language* at the drop-down list. At the Language dialog box, click a language in the *Mark selected text as* list box. To make the selected language the default, click the Set As Default button in the lower left corner of the dialog box. Click OK to close the Language dialog box.

Displaying Readability Statistics

Quick Steps

Show Readability Statistics

1. Click File tab.
2. Click *Options*.
3. Click *Proofing*.
4. Click *Show readability statistics* check box.
5. Click OK.
6. Complete spelling and grammar check.

Readability statistics about a document can be displayed when completing a spelling and grammar check. Figure 2.2 lists the readability statistics for the document used in Activity 2b. The statistics include word, character, paragraph, and sentence counts; average number of sentences per paragraph, words per sentence, and characters per word; and readability information such as the percentage of passive sentences in the document, the Flesch Reading Ease score, and the Flesch-Kincaid Grade Level score. Control the display of readability statistics with the *Show readability statistics* check box in the Word Options dialog box with *Proofing* selected.

The Flesch Reading Ease score is based on the average number of syllables per word and the average number of words per sentence. The higher the score, the greater the number of people who will be able to understand the text in the document. Standard writing generally scores in the 60 to 70 range.

The Flesch-Kincaid Grade Level score is based on the average number of syllables per word and the average number of words per sentence. The score indicates a grade level. Standard writing is generally scored at the seventh or eighth grade level.

Figure 2.2 Readability Statistics Dialog Box

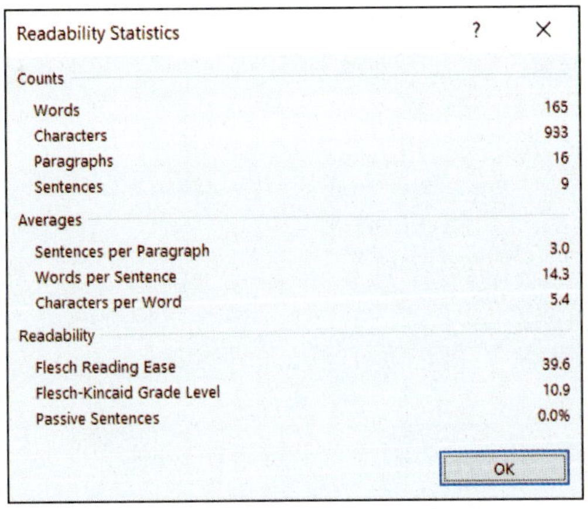

Activity 2b Displaying Readability Statistics

1. With **2-MCFLetter** open, display readability statistics about the document by completing the following steps:
   a. Click the File tab and then click *Options*.
   b. At the Word Options dialog box, click *Proofing* in the left panel.
   c. Click the *Show readability statistics* check box to insert a check mark.

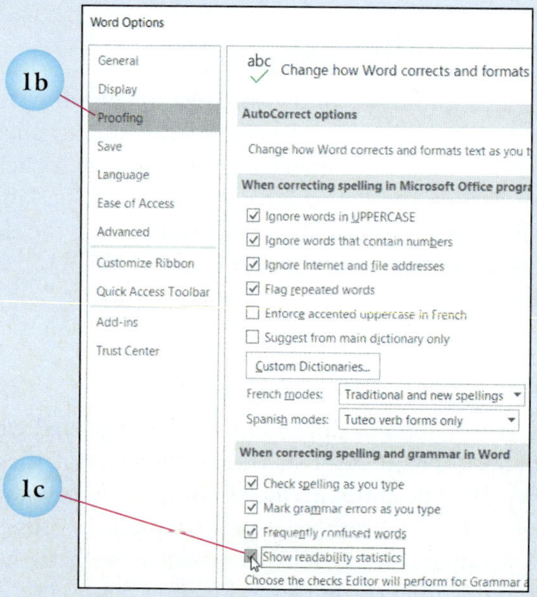

   d. Click OK to close the Word Options dialog box.
   e. At the document, make sure the Review tab is selected and then click the Check Document button.
   f. Look at the readability statistics that display in the Readability Statistics dialog box and then click OK to close the dialog box.
   g. Click OK at the message stating that the spelling and grammar check is complete and then close the Editor task pane.
2. Complete steps similar to those in Steps 1a–1d to remove the check mark from the *Show readability statistics* check box.
3. Save and then close **2-MCFLetter**.

Activity 3 Check the Spelling in an Online Banking Document — 4 Parts

You will open an online banking document, create a custom dictionary, add specific terms to the custom dictionary, and then complete a spelling check. You will also display the word count, use the Thesaurus feature to replace a word with a synonym, insert line numbers, and display the Smart Lookup task pane and review information about selected text.

Tutorial

Creating and Removing a Custom Dictionary

Quick Steps

Create Custom Dictionary

1. Click File tab.
2. Click *Options*.
3. Click *Proofing*.
4. Click Custom Dictionaries button.
5. Click *RoamingCustom.dic (Default)*.
6. Click New button.
7. Type name for dictionary.
8. Press Enter key.

Hint When you change the custom dictionary settings in one Microsoft Office program, the changes affect all the other programs in the suite.

Creating a Custom Dictionary

When completing a spelling check on a document, Word uses the main dictionary, named *RoamingCustom.dic*, to compare words. This main dictionary contains most common words but may not include specific proper names, medical and technical terms, acronyms, or other text related to a specific field or business. If documents will be created with specific words, terms, or acronyms not found in the main dictionary, consider creating a custom dictionary. When completing a spelling check, the spelling checker will compare words in a document with the main dictionary as well as a custom dictionary.

To create a custom dictionary, display the Word Options dialog box with *Proofing* selected and then click the Custom Dictionaries button. This displays the Custom Dictionaries dialog box, shown in Figure 2.3. To create a new dictionary, click *RoamingCustom.dic (Default)* in the dialog box list box and then click the New button. At the Create Custom Dictionary dialog box, type a name for the dictionary in the *File name* text box and then press the Enter key. The new dictionary name displays in the *Dictionary List* list box in the Custom Dictionaries dialog box. More than one dictionary can be used when spell checking a document. Insert a check mark in the check box next to each dictionary to be used when spell checking.

Changing the Default Dictionary

At the Custom Dictionaries dialog box, the default dictionary displays in the *Dictionary List* list box followed by *(Default)*. Change this default by clicking the dictionary name in the list box and then clicking the Change Default button.

Figure 2.3 Custom Dictionaries Dialog Box

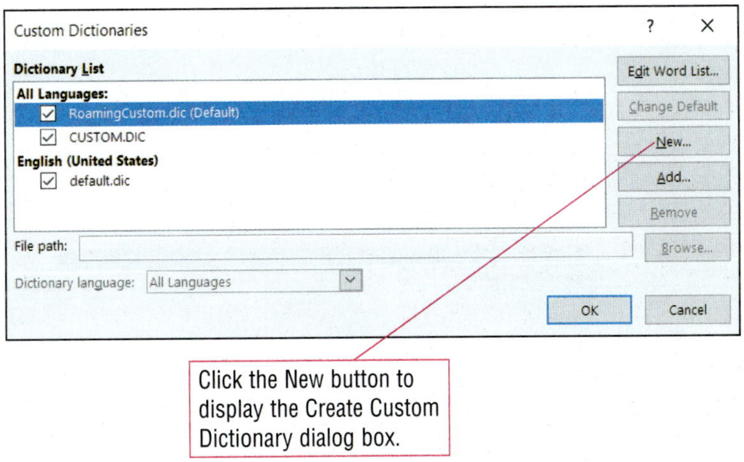

Removing a Dictionary

Quick Steps

Remove Custom Dictionary

1. Click File tab.
2. Click *Options.*
3. Click *Proofing.*
4. Click Custom Dictionaries button.
5. Click custom dictionary name.
6. Click Remove button.
7. Click OK.

Remove a custom dictionary with the Remove button at the Custom Dictionaries dialog box. To do this, display the Custom Dictionaries dialog box, click the dictionary name in the *Dictionary List* list box, and then click the Remove button. No prompt will display confirming the deletion, so make sure the correct dictionary name is selected before clicking the Remove button.

Activity 3a Creating a Custom Dictionary and Changing the Default Dictionary

Part 1 of 4

1. Open **BankBrazil**, notice the wavy red lines indicating words not recognized by the spelling checker (words not in the main dictionary), and then close the document.
2. Create a custom dictionary, add words to the dictionary, and then change the default dictionary by completing the following steps:
   a. Click the File tab and then click *Options*.
   b. At the Word Options dialog box, click *Proofing* in the left panel.
   c. Click the Custom Dictionaries button.
   d. At the Custom Dictionaries dialog box, click *RoamingCustom.dic (Default)* in the *Dictionary List* list box.
   e. Click the New button.
   f. At the Create Custom Dictionary dialog box, type your first and last names (without a space between them) in the *File name* text box and then press the Enter key.
   g. At the Custom Dictionaries dialog box, add a word to your dictionary by completing the following steps:
      1) Click the name of your dictionary in the *Dictionary List* list box.
      2) Click the Edit Word List button.

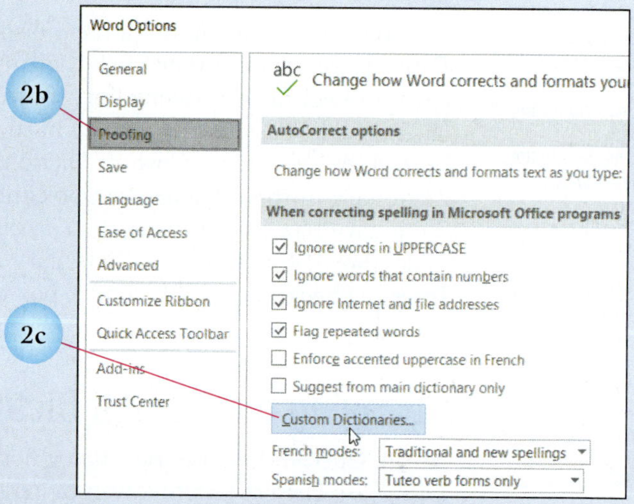

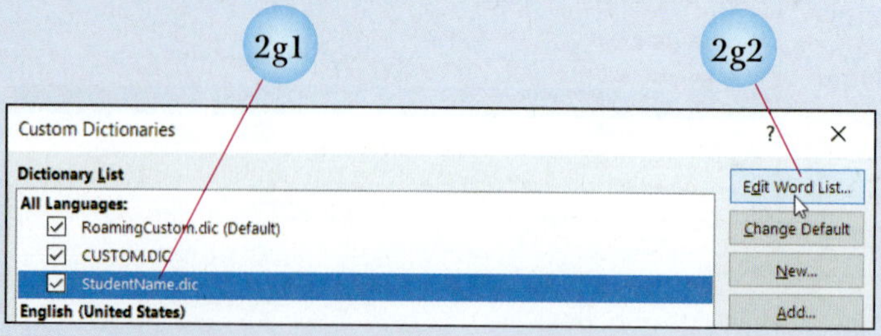

3) At the dialog box for your custom dictionary, type Abreu in the *Word(s)* text box.
4) Click the Add button.

h. Add another word to the dictionary by clicking in the *Word(s)* text box, typing Banco, and then pressing the Enter key.

i. Complete steps similar to Step 2h to add the following words:

Itau
Bradesco
Unibanco
Monteiro
Lipschultz

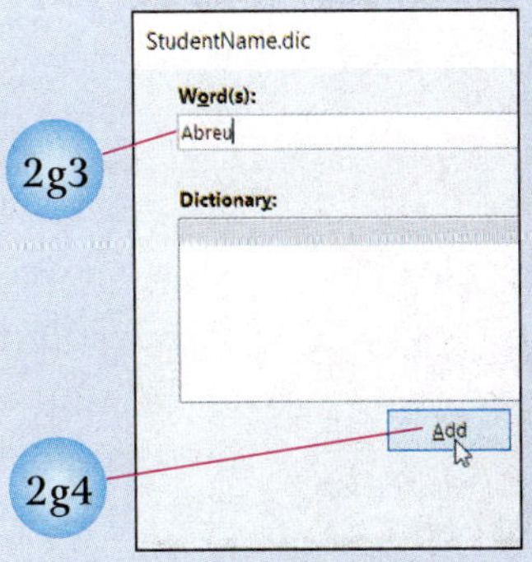

j. When you have added all the words, click OK to close the dialog box.

k. At the Custom Dictionaries dialog box, click the name of your dictionary in the list box and then click the Change Default button. (Notice that the word *(Default)* displays after your custom dictionary.)

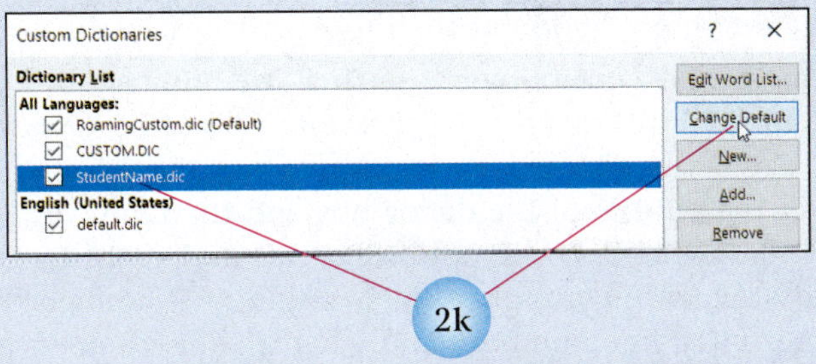

l. Click OK to close the Custom Dictionaries dialog box.

m. Click OK to close the Word Options dialog box.

3. Open **BankBrazil** and then save it with the name **2-BankBrazil**.
4. Complete a spelling and grammar check on the document and accept all spelling and grammar suggestions. (The spelling checker will not stop at the words you added to your custom dictionary.)
5. Save and then print **2-BankBrazil**.
6. Change the default dictionary and then remove your custom dictionary by completing the following steps:
   a. Click the File tab and then click *Options*.
   b. At the Word Options dialog box, click *Proofing* in the left panel.
   c. Click the Custom Dictionaries button.
   d. At the Custom Dictionaries dialog box, click *RoamingCustom.dic* in the *Dictionary List* list box.
   e. Click the Change Default button. (This changes the default back to the RoamingCustom.dic dictionary.)
   f. Click the name of your dictionary in the *Dictionary List* list box.
   g. Click the Remove button.
   h. Click OK to close the Custom Dictionaries dialog box.
   i. Click OK to close the Word Options dialog box.

Check Your Work

Tutorial

Displaying Word Count

Quick Steps

Display Word Count Dialog Box

Click word count section of Status bar.
OR
1. Click Review tab.
2. Click Word Count button.

Word Count

Displaying the Word Count

Words are counted as they are typed in a document and the total number of words in a document is displayed on the Status bar. To display more information—such as the numbers of pages, paragraphs, and lines—display the Word Count dialog box. Display the Word Count dialog box by clicking the word count section of the Status bar or by clicking the Review tab and then clicking the Word Count button in the Proofing group.

Count words in a portion of the document, rather than the entire document, by selecting the portion of text and then displaying the Word Count dialog box. To determine the total word count of several sections throughout a document, select the first section, press and hold down the Ctrl key, and then select the other sections.

Tutorial

Inserting Line Numbers

Line Numbers

Quick Steps

Insert Line Numbers

1. Click Layout tab.
2. Click Line Numbers button.
3. Click line number option.

Inserting Line Numbers

Use the Line Numbers button in the Page Setup group on the Layout tab to insert line numbers in a document. Numbering lines has practical applications for certain legal papers and reference purposes. To number lines in a document, click the Layout tab, click the Line Numbers button in the Page Setup group, and then click a line number option at the drop-down list.

To have more control over inserting line numbers in a document, click the Line Numbers button and then click *Line Numbering Options* at the drop-down list. At the Page Setup dialog box with the Layout tab selected, click the Line Numbers button at the bottom of the dialog box and the Line Numbers dialog box displays, as shown in Figure 2.4. Use options at this dialog box to insert line numbers and to specify the starting number, the location line numbers are printed, the interval between printed line numbers, and whether line numbers are consecutive or start over at the beginning of each page.

Figure 2.4 Line Numbers Dialog Box

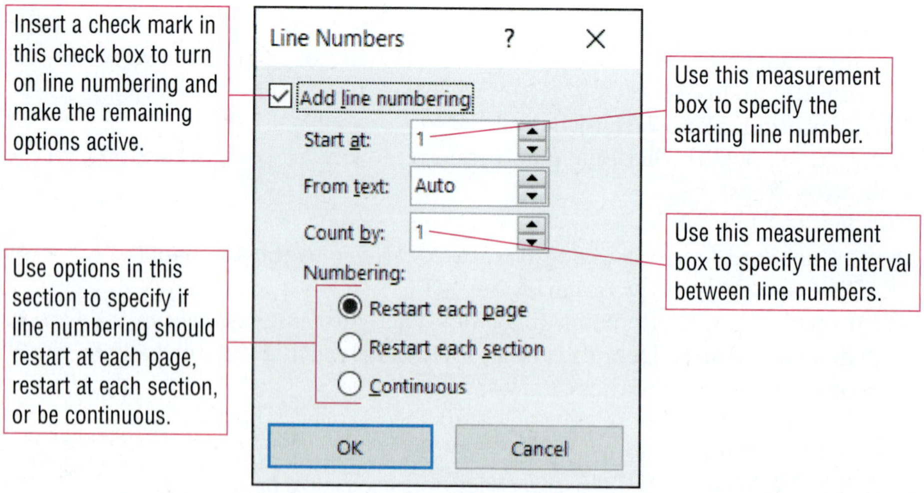

Tutorial

Using the Thesaurus

Thesaurus

Quick Steps

Use Thesaurus

1. Click Review tab.
2. Click Thesaurus button.
3. Type word in search text box.
4. Press Enter key.

Using the Thesaurus

Word offers a Thesaurus feature for finding synonyms, antonyms, and related words for a particular word. Synonyms are words that have the same or nearly the same meaning. When the Thesaurus feature is used, antonyms may display for some words, which are words with opposite meanings.

To use the Thesaurus feature, click the Review tab and then click the Thesaurus button in the Proofing group or use the keyboard shortcut Shift + F7. At the Thesaurus task pane, click in the search text box at the top of the task pane, type a word, and then press the Enter key or click the Start searching button (which contains a magnifying glass icon). A list of synonyms and antonyms for the typed word displays in the task pane list box. Another method for finding synonyms and antonyms is to select a word and then display the Thesaurus task pane. Figure 2.5 shows the Thesaurus task pane with synonyms and antonyms for the word *normally.*

Depending on the word typed in the search text box, words in the Thesaurus task pane list box may appear followed by *(n.)* for *noun*, *(adj.)* for *adjective*, or *(adv.)* for *adverb*. Any antonyms at the end of the list of related synonyms will be followed by *(Antonym)*. If a dictionary is installed on the computer, a definition of the selected word will appear below the task pane list box.

The Thesaurus feature provides synonyms for the selected word as well as a list of related synonyms. For example, in the Thesaurus task pane list box shown in Figure 2.5, the main synonym *usually* displays for *normally* and is preceded by a collapse triangle (a right-and-down-pointing triangle). The collapse triangle indicates that the list of related synonyms is displayed. Click the collapse triangle

Figure 2.5 Thesaurus Task Pane

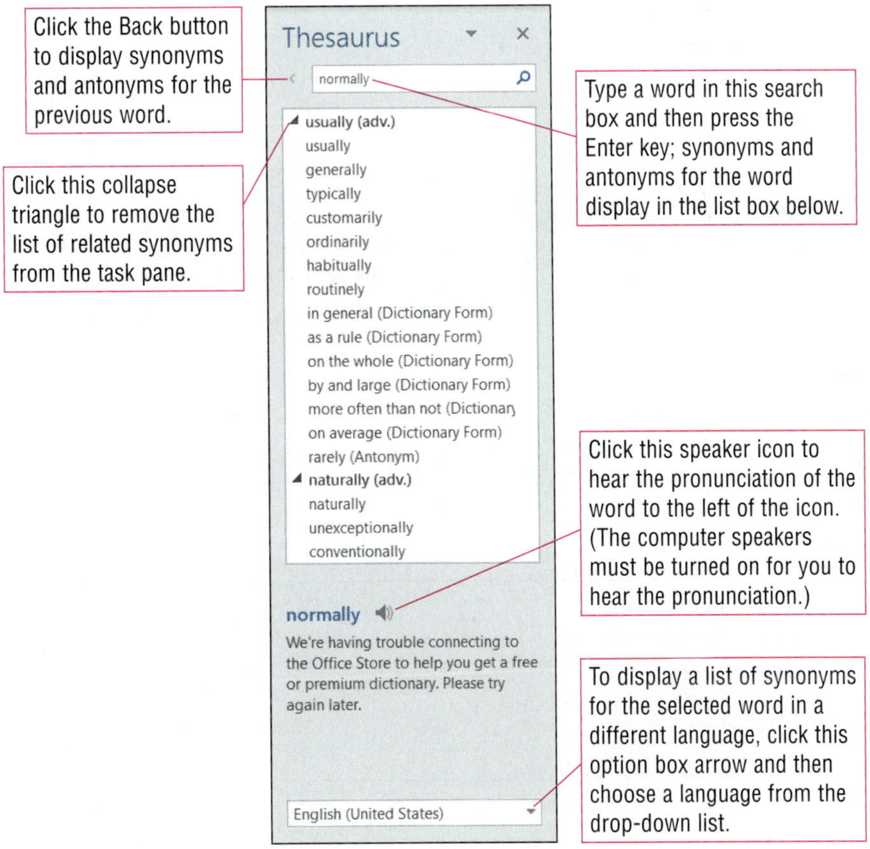

and the list of related synonyms is removed from the task pane list box and the collapse triangle changes to an expand triangle (a right-pointing triangle). Click a word in the Thesaurus task pane list box to see synonyms for it.

When reviewing synonyms and antonyms for words within a document, display the list of synonyms and antonyms for the previous word by clicking the Back button (left-pointing arrow) at the left side of the search text box. Click the down-pointing triangle at the left of the Close button in the upper right corner of the task pane and a drop-down list displays with options for moving, sizing, and closing the task pane.

To replace a selected word in the document with a synonym in the Thesaurus task pane, point to the synonym in the task pane list box using the mouse. This displays a down arrow to the right of the word. Click the down arrow and then click the *Insert* option at the drop-down list.

The Thesaurus task pane, like the Editor task pane, includes a reading feature that will speak the word currently selected in the task pane. To hear the word pronounced, click the speaker icon at the right of the word below the task pane list box. (For this feature to work, the computer speakers must be turned on.)

The Thesaurus task pane also includes a language option for displaying synonyms of the selected word in a different language. To use this feature, click the option box arrow at the bottom of the task pane and then click a language at the drop-down list.

Activity 3b Displaying the Word Count, Inserting Line Numbers, and Using the Thesaurus

Part 2 of 4

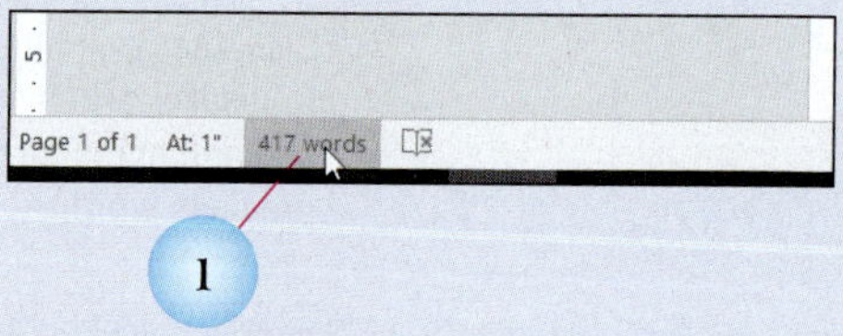

1. With **2-BankBrazil** open, click the word count section of the Status bar.
2. After reading the statistics in the Word Count dialog box, click the Close button.
3. Display the Word Count dialog box by clicking the Review tab and then clicking the Word Count button in the Proofing group.
4. Click the Close button to close the Word Count dialog box.
5. Press Ctrl + A to select the entire document, click the Home tab, click the Line and Paragraph Spacing button in the Paragraph group, and then click *2.0* at the drop-down gallery.
6. Deselect the text and then insert line numbers by completing the following steps:
   a. Click the Layout tab.
   b. Click the Line Numbers button in the Page Setup group and then click *Continuous* at the drop-down list.
   c. Scroll through the document and notice the line numbers that display at the left of the document.
   d. Click the Line Numbers button and then click the *Restart Each Page* option.
   e. Scroll through the document and notice that the line numbers start over again at the beginning of page 2.

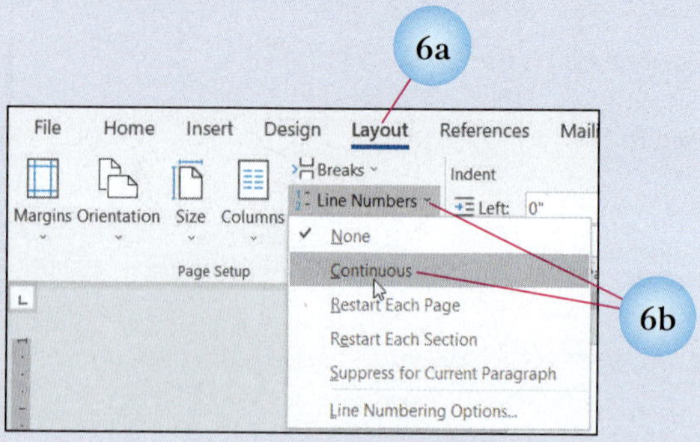

f. Click the Line Numbers button and then click *Line Numbering Options* at the drop-down list.
g. At the Page Setup dialog box, click the Line Numbers button at the bottom of the dialog box.
h. At the Line Numbers dialog box, select the current number in the *Start at* measurement box and then type 30.
i. Click the *Count by* measurement box up arrow. (This displays *2* in the measurement box.)
j. Click the *Continuous* option in the *Numbering* section.
k. Click OK to close the Line Numbers dialog box.

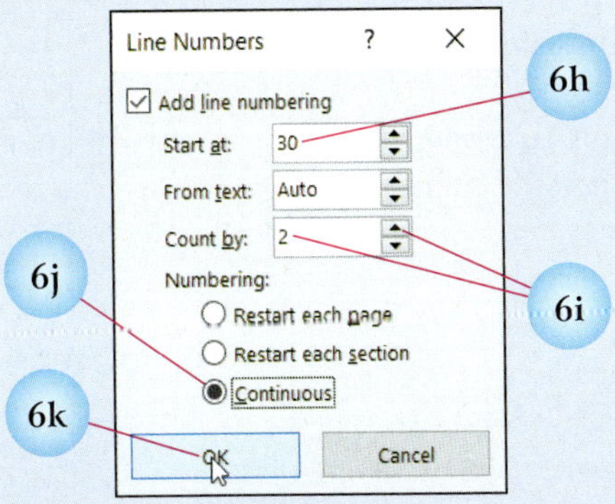

l. Click OK to close the Page Setup dialog box.
m. Scroll through the document and notice the line numbers that display at the left of the document. The numbers start with *30* and increase by intervals of two.
n. Click the Line Numbers button and then click *None* at the drop-down list.
7. Select the document, click the Home tab, click the Line and Paragraph Spacing button in the Paragraph group, and then click *1.0* at the drop-down gallery.
8. Use the Thesaurus feature to change the word *normally* in the first paragraph to *generally* by completing the following steps:
a. Click in the word *normally* in the first paragraph (first word in the seventh line of text).
b. Click the Review tab.
c. Click the Thesaurus button in the Proofing group.
d. At the Thesaurus task pane, point to *generally* in the task pane list box, click the down arrow at the right of the word, and then click *Insert* at the drop-down list.
e. Click the word *generally* in the Thesaurus task pane.
f. If your computer speakers are turned on and a speaker icon displays next to the word below the task pane list box, click the speaker icon to listen to the pronunciation of the word *generally*.
g. Close the Thesaurus task pane.

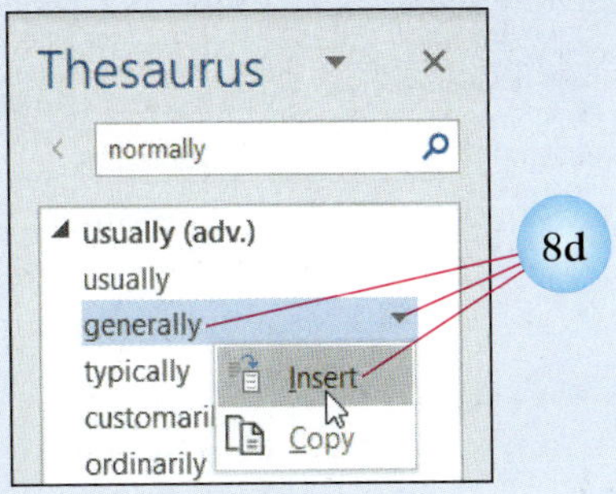

9. Follow steps similar to those in Step 8 to make the following changes using the Thesaurus feature:
a. Change *acquaintances* in the first paragraph to *friends*.
b. Change *combat* in the second paragraph to *battle*.
10. Close the Thesaurus task pane by clicking the Close button in the upper right corner of the task pane.
11. Save **2-BankBrazil**.

Check Your Work

Another method for displaying synonyms of a word is to use a shortcut menu. To do this, position the mouse pointer on the word and then click the right mouse button. At the shortcut menu, point to *Synonyms* and then click the a synonym at the side menu. Click the *Thesaurus* option at the bottom of the side menu to display synonyms and antonyms for the word in the Thesaurus task pane.

Activity 3c Replacing Synonyms Using the Shortcut Menu

Part 3 of 4

1. With **2-BankBrazil** open, position the mouse pointer on the word *vogue* in the second sentence of the third paragraph.
2. Click the right mouse button.
3. At the shortcut menu, point to *Synonyms* and then click *fashion* at the side menu.
4. Save **2-BankBrazil**.

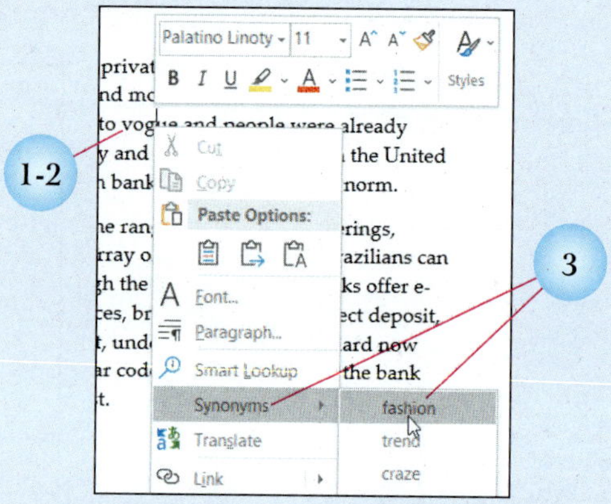

Check Your Work

Tutorial

Using Smart Lookup

Smart Lookup

Using Smart Lookup

The Smart Lookup feature provides information on selected text from a variety of sources on the web. To use the Smart Lookup feature, select text, click the References tab, and then click the Smart Lookup button in the Research group. This opens the Smart Lookup task pane at the right of the screen.

Quick Steps

Use Smart Lookup

1. Select text.
2. Click References tab.
3. Click Smart Lookup Button.

Options and information in the task pane may vary, but typically include a definition of the selected word or phrase and additional information from other sources on the web, as shown in Figure 2.6. Click the *Web* option and a number of websites display with information about the selected text, as shown in Figure 2.7. With the *Pictures* option selected, images related to the selected text display in the task pane.

The Smart Lookup task pane, like the Editor and Thesaurus task panes, includes a reading feature that will read aloud the text in the task pane. To hear the text pronounced, click the speaker icon in the task pane. For this feature to work, the computer speakers must be turned on.

The Smart Lookup feature can also be accessed through the Tell Me feature. To use the Tell Me feature for Smart Lookup, click in the *Tell Me* text box, type text or a function, and then click the last option at the drop-down list (generally displays with the text *See more search results for*).

Figure 2.6 Smart Lookup Task Pane with the *Knowledge* Option Selected

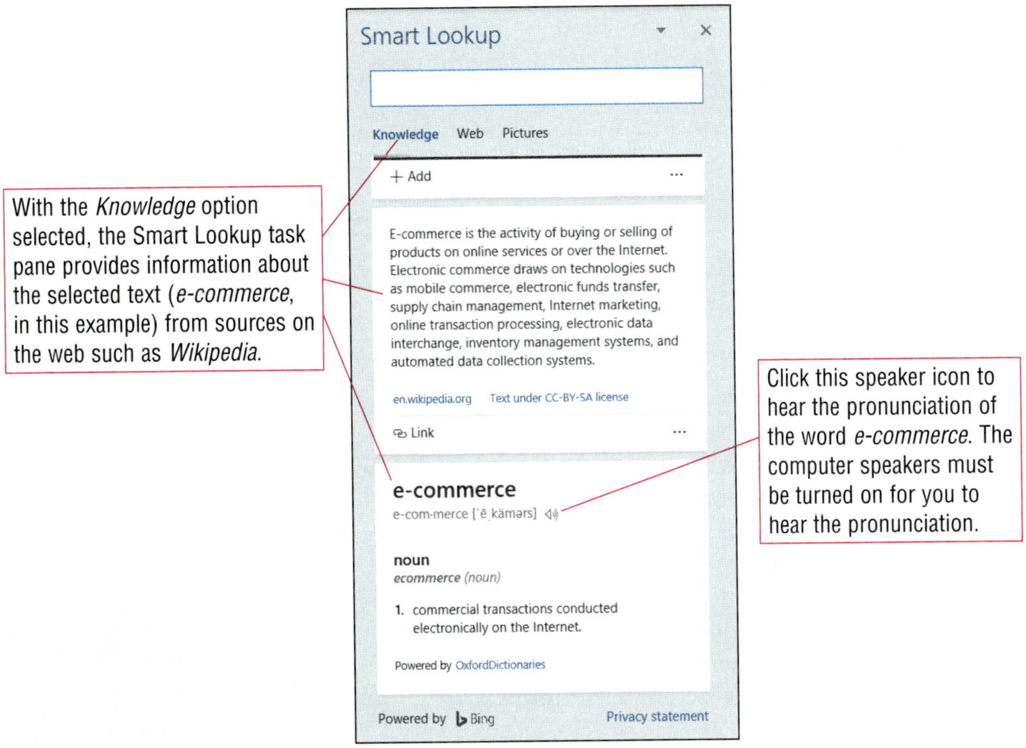

Figure 2.7 Smart Lookup Task Pane with the *Web* Option Selected

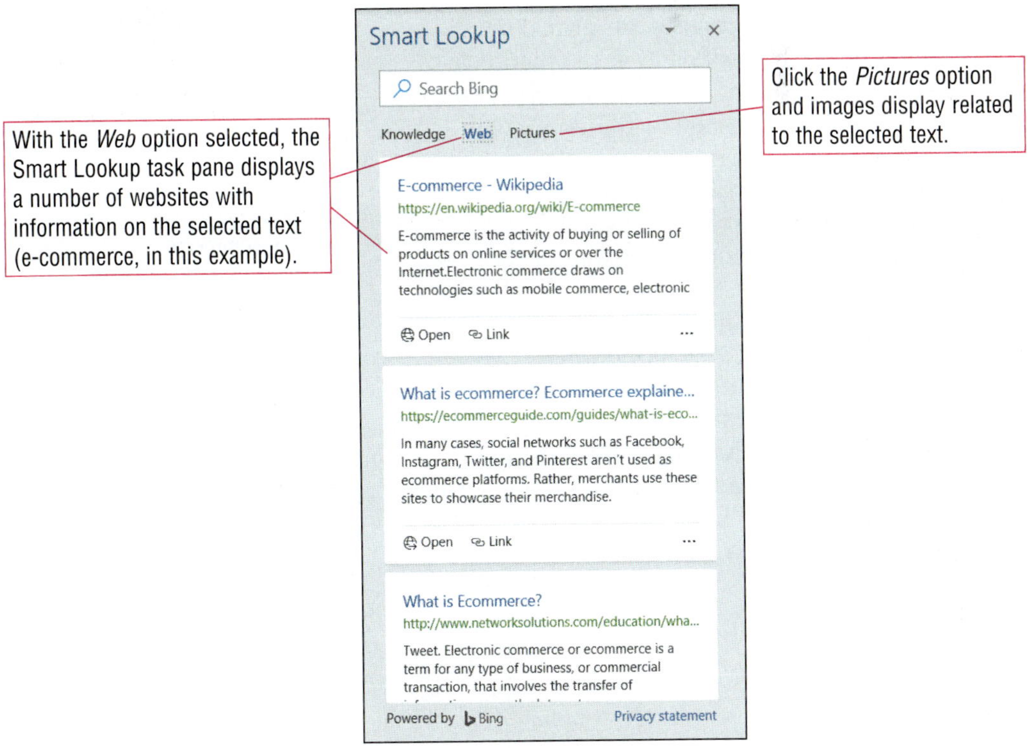

Activity 3d Using the Smart Lookup Feature

Part 4 of 4

1. With **2-BankBrazil** open, display information about and definitions for words by completing the following steps:
   a. Select the word *e-commerce* in the third sentence of the first paragraph.
   b. Click the References tab and then click the Smart Lookup button in the Research group.

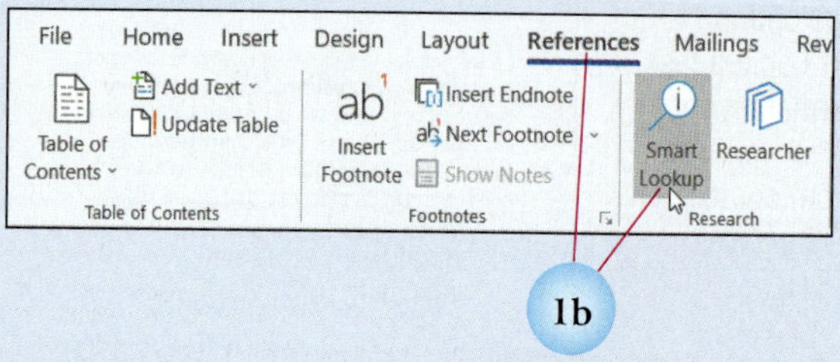

   c. Look at the information about e-commerce in the Smart Lookup task pane with the *Knowledge* option selected. (Note that options in this task pane may vary; if the *Knowledge* option is not available, click the *All* option or explore other options in the pane.) Scroll down the task pane and read the information on e-commerce from *Wikipedia* and read the dictionary definition of e-commerce.
   d. Click the *Web* option.
   e. Scroll down the task pane and read information about e-commerce from various websites.
   f. Click the *Pictures* option and look at the images related to e-commerce.
   g. Click the *Knowledge* option.
   h. If the computer speakers are turned on, scroll down the task pane to the dictionary definition and then click the speaker icon.
   i. Click the Close button in the upper right corner of the task pane.
   j. Select the word *economy* in the second sentence of the second paragraph.
   k. Click the Smart Lookup button on the References tab.
   l. Look at the information in the task pane and then click the *Web* option.
   m. Read the information in the task pane and then click the *Pictures* option.
   n. After looking at the images related to economy, click the Close button to close the task pane.

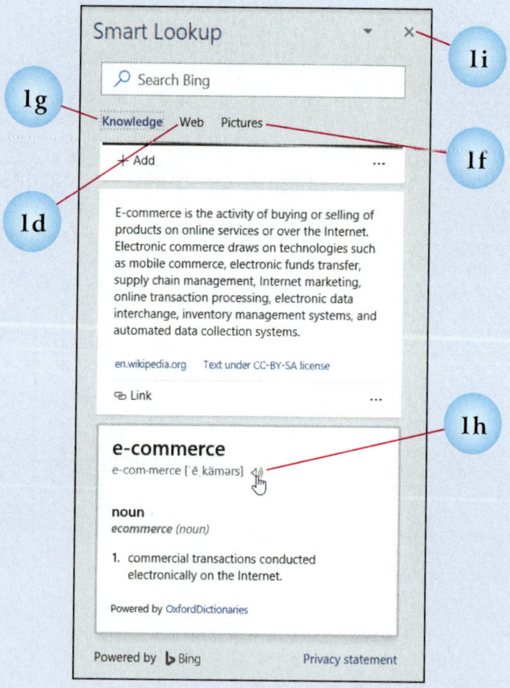

2. Save, print, and then close **2-BankBrazil**.

Check Your Work

Activity 4 Translate Text in Travel Company Documents — 2 Parts

You will use the translation feature to translate selected text from English to Spanish and English to French. You will also translate a document from English to Spanish.

Tutorial
Translating Text to and from Different Languages

Translate

Translating Text to and from Different Languages

Word includes a Translate feature that will translate text to and from different languages. To use the Translate feature, click the Review tab and then click the Translate button in the Language group. At the drop-down list, click the *Translate Selection* option to translate selected text or click the *Translate Document* to translate the contents of the open document.

Translating Selected Text

Quick Steps

Translate Selected Text

1. Click Review tab.
2. Click Translate button.
3. Click *Translate Selection.*

To translate specific text in a document, click the Translate button in the Language group on the Review tab and then click the *Translate Selection* option. This opens the Translator task pane at the right side of the screen with the *Selection* option selected, similar to what is shown in Figure 2.8.

By default, the Translate feature will automatically detect the language in the document and *Auto-detect* will display in the *From* option box. A specific language can be selected by clicking the *From* option box and then clicking the language at the drop-down list. Click the *To* option box and then click the translation language at the drop-down list. Select text in the document and then click the Insert button near the bottom of the task pane. The selected text is replaced by the translated text.

Figure 2.8 Translator Task Pane

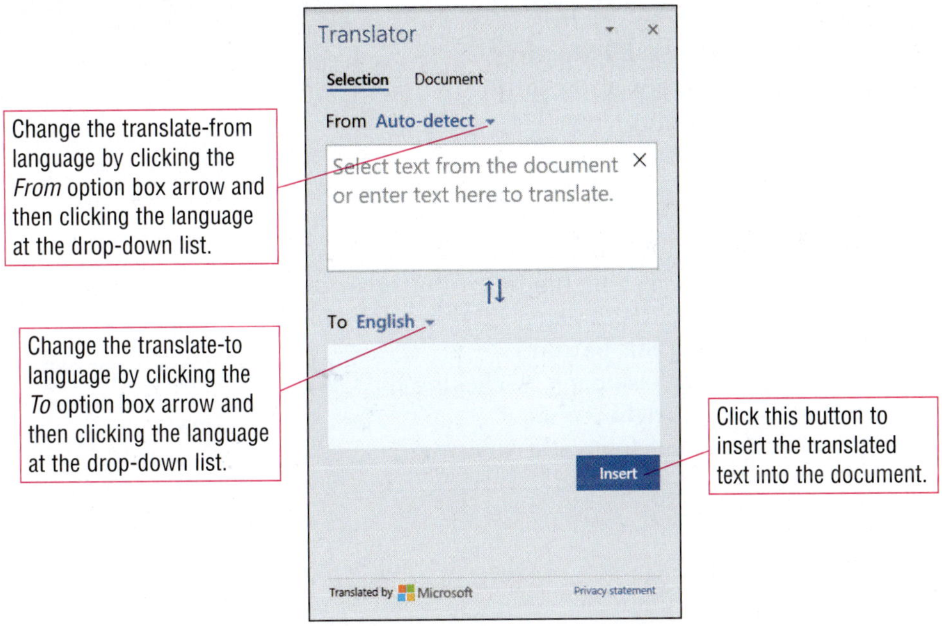

Activity 4a Translating Selected Text

Note: Check with your instructor before completing this activity to make sure you have access to the internet.

1. Open **BTMeeting** and then save it with the name **2-BTMeeting**.
2. Display the Translator task pane by clicking the Review tab, clicking the Translate button in the Language group, and then clicking *Translate Selection* at the drop-down list.

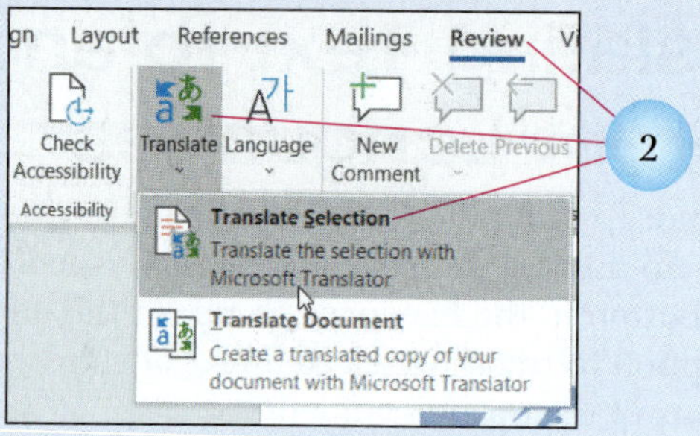

3. At the Translator task pane with the *Selection* option selected, check to make sure the *From* option box displays with *Auto-detect* (or it might also display as *English (detected)*).
4. Click the *To* option box arrow, scroll down the drop-down list, and then click *Spanish*. (The language names display in alphabetical order in the drop-down list.)
5. Click in the document and then press Ctrl + A to select the entire document (except the header and footer). Notice that the translation of the selected text displays below the *To* option box in the Translator task pane.
6. Insert the translated text in the document in place of the selected text by clicking the Insert button at the Translator task pane. (You may need to scroll down the task pane to display this button.)
7. Save and then print **2-BTMeeting**.
8. Click the *To* option box arrow in the Translator task pane, scroll up the drop-down list, and then click *French*.
9. Click in the document and then press Ctrl + A to select the entire document (except the header and footer).
10. Insert the translated text in the document in place of the selected text by clicking the Insert button at the Translator task pane. (You may need to scroll down the task pane to display this button.)
11. Close the Translator task pane by clicking the Close button in the upper right corner.
12. Save, print, and then close **2-BTMeeting**.

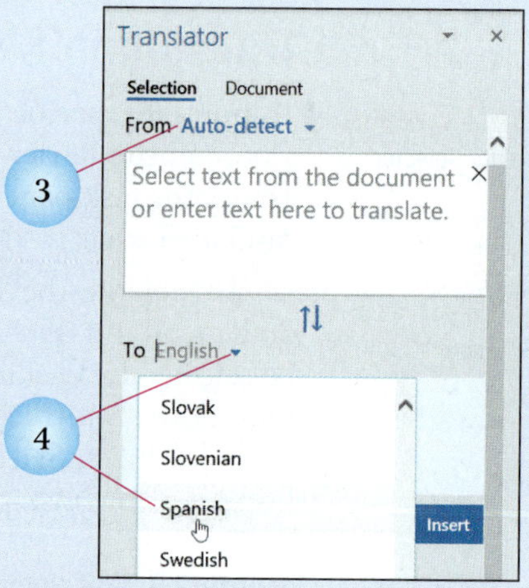

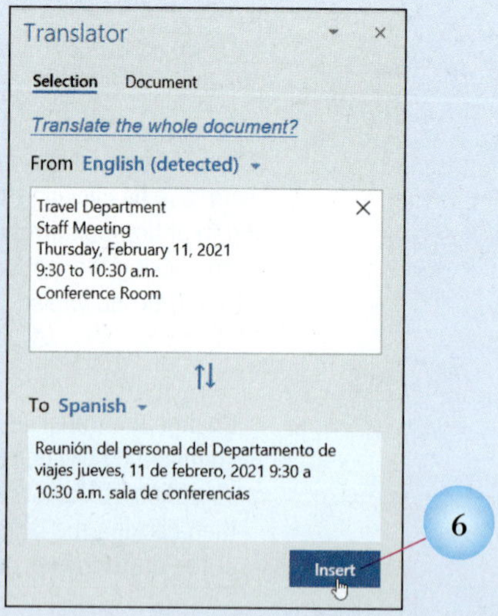

Check Your Work

Translating a Document

Quick Steps

Translate Document

1. Click Review tab.
2. Click Translate button.
3. Click *Translate Document.*

To translate an entire document, click the Translate button in the Language group on the Review tab and then choose the *Translate Document* option. The Translator task pane opens with the *Document* option selected. Select the language to translate from and to and then click the Translate button. A new document opens with the translated text. Click the Translate button and then click the *Translator Preferences* option to narrow the list of languages to be included in the translation list, or click the gear icon in the task pane.

Preparing a Document for Translation

Word's Translate feature is considered a machine translation because a machine, rather than a person, does the translating. While this method is fast and convenient, it is prone to errors. Before sharing a machine-translated document, ask someone familiar with the target language to proofread the text to be sure the information is properly translated. For important or sensitive information to be used in a business context, always rely on a professional translator. To optimize machine translation and reduce errors, follow these guidelines:

- Use standard, formal language. Avoid abbreviations, acronyms, slang, colloquialisms, and idioms, as these may not translate well to a different language.
- Write simple, direct sentences that express only one idea.
- Avoid ambiguities. Use articles (such as *the*) in sentences whenever possible and repeat the noun in a sentence rather than use a pronoun.
- Before translating, run a spelling and grammar check to be sure all words are spelled correctly and that proper punctuation and grammar are used, and apply predesigned heading styles to any headings in the document.

Activity 4b Translating a Document

Part 2 of 2

1. Open **Australia** and then save it with the name **2-Australia**.
2. Display the Translator task pane by clicking the Review tab, clicking the Translate button, and then clicking *Translate Document* at the drop-down list. (If a new document opens with translated text, close the document without saving changes.)
3. At the Translator task pane with the *Document* option selected, make sure that *English* displays in the *From* option box. (If *English* does not display in the *From* option box, click the *From* option box arrow, scroll down the drop-down list, and then click *English*.)
4. Click the *To* option box arrow, scroll down the drop-down list, and then click *Spanish*.
5. Click the Translate button at the Translator task pane. (This opens a new document with the translated document.)
6. Save the document and name it **2-TranslatedDoc**.
7. Print and then close **2-TranslatedDoc**.
8. At the **2-Australia** document, close the Translator task pane and then close the document.

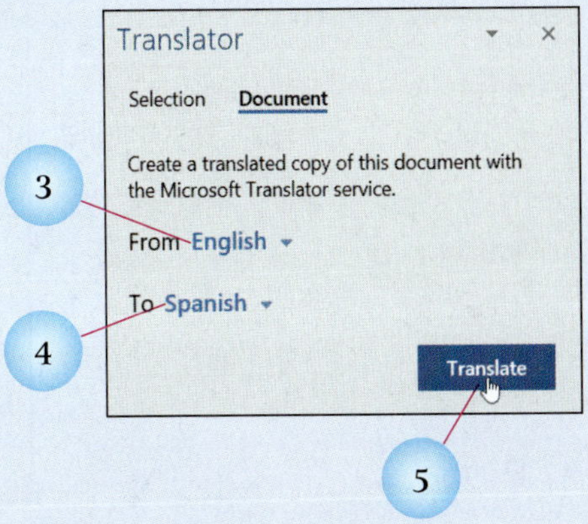

Check Your Work

Activity 5 **Sort Company Information** **3 Parts**

You will open a document containing information on company employees and then sort data in paragraphs, columns, and tables.

Sorting Text

Text in a document can be sorted alphanumerically, numerically, or chronologically. In an alphanumeric sort, punctuation marks and special symbols are sorted first, followed by numbers and then text. Use options at the Sort Text dialog box to specify what is to be sorted. Text in paragraphs, columns, and tables can be sorted.

Tutorial

Sorting Text in Paragraphs

Sort

Quick Steps

Sort Paragraphs of Text

1. Click Sort button.
2. Make changes as needed at Sort Text dialog box.
3. Click OK.

Sorting Text in Paragraphs

To sort paragraphs of text, select the text and then click the Sort button in the Paragraph group on the Home tab. This displays the Sort Text dialog box, which contains sorting options.

The *Type* option at the Sort Text dialog box will display *Text*, *Number*, or *Date* depending on the text selected. Word attempts to determine the data type and chooses one of the three options. For example, if numbers with mathematical values are selected, Word assigns them the *Number* type. However, if a numbered list is selected, Word assigns them the *Text* type since the numbers do not represent mathematical values.

By default, paragraphs of text are sorted by the first word of each paragraph. This can be changed with options at the Sort Options dialog box, shown in Figure 2.9. Display this dialog box by clicking the Options button at the Sort Text dialog box. Use the options in the *Separate fields at* section to specify how text is separated in the document. For example, to sort text by the second word of each paragraph, click the *Other* option box (this moves the insertion point into the text box to the right of the *Other* option box) and then press the spacebar.

Figure 2.9 Sort Options Dialog Box

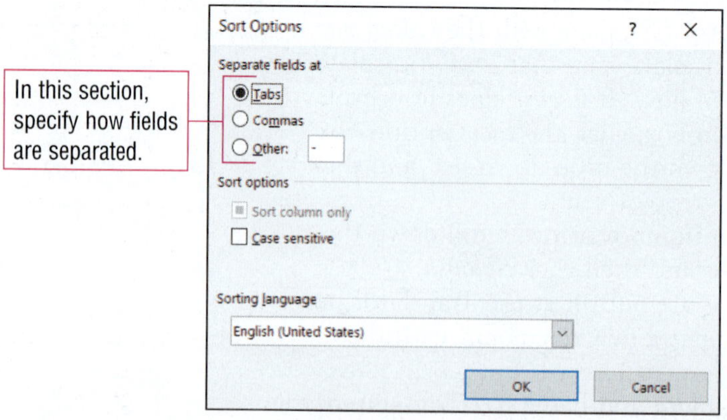

Activity 5a Sorting Text in Paragraphs

Part 1 of 3

1. Open **Sorting** and then save it with the name **2-Sorting**.
2. Sort the text alphabetically by first name by completing the following steps:
   a. Select the seven lines of text at the beginning of the document.
   b. Click the Sort button in the Paragraph group on the Home tab.
   c. At the Sort Text dialog box, click OK.

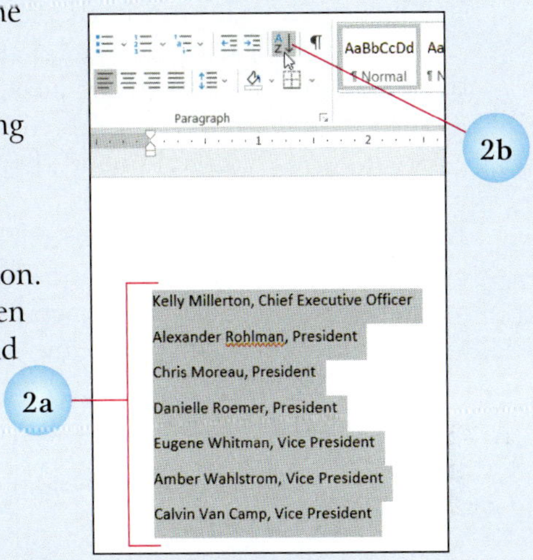

3. Sort the text by last name by completing the following steps:
   a. With the seven lines of text still selected, click the Sort button.
   b. At the Sort Text dialog box, click the Options button.
   c. At the Sort Options dialog box, click *Other* and then press the spacebar. (This indicates that the first and last names are separated by a space.)

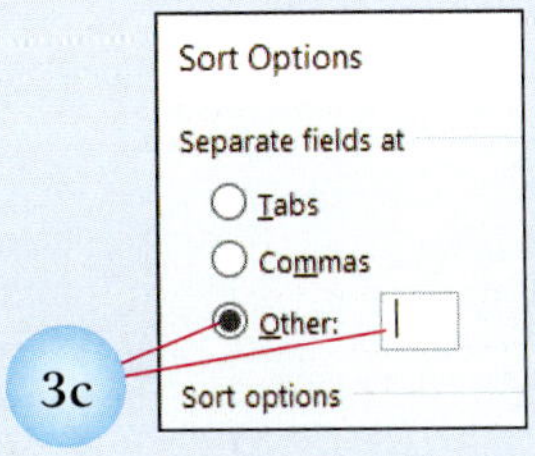

   d. Click OK.
   e. At the Sort Text dialog box, click the *Sort by* option box arrow and then click *Word 2* at the drop-down list.
   f. Click OK.
4. Save **2-Sorting**.

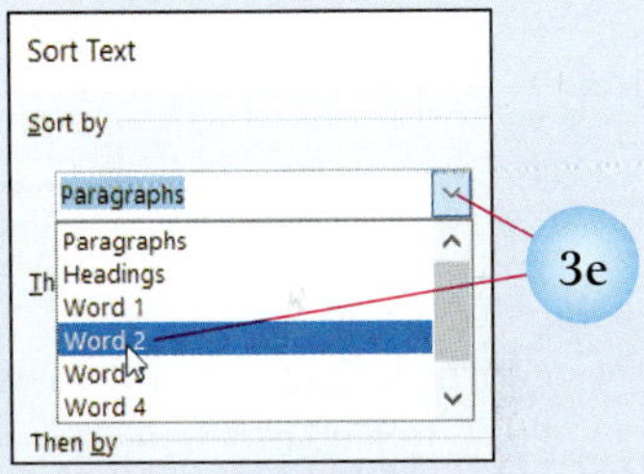

Check Your Work

Tutorial

Sorting Text in Columns

Quick Steps

Sort Text in Columns

1. Select specific text.
2. Click Sort button.
3. Click Options button.
4. Specify *Tabs* as separator.
5. Click OK.
6. Make changes at Sort Text dialog box.
7. Click OK.

Sorting Text in Columns

To sort text set in columns, the text must be separated with tabs. When sorting text in columns, Word considers the left margin *Field 1*, text typed at the first tab *Field 2*, and so on. When sorting text in columns, make sure the columns are separated with only one tab because Word recognizes each tab as beginning a separate column. Thus, using more than one tab may result in field numbers that correspond to empty columns.

Sorting on More Than One Field

Text can be sorted on more than one field. For example, in Activity 5b, Step 3, the department entries will be sorted alphabetically and then the employee names will be sorted alphabetically within the departments. To do this, specify the *Department* column in the *Sort by* option box and then specify the *Employee* column in the *Then by* option box. If a document contains columns with heading text, click the *Header row* option in the *My list has* section.

Activity 5b Sorting Text in Columns

Part 2 of 3

1. With **2-Sorting** open, sort text in columns by completing the following steps:
   a. Select the six lines of text below each of these column headings: *Employee*, *Department*, and *Ext*.
   b. Click the Sort button in the Paragraph group on the Home tab.
   c. At the Sort Text dialog box, click the Options button.
   d. At the Sort Options dialog box, make sure the *Tabs* option is selected in the *Separate fields at* section and then click OK to close the dialog box.
   e. At the Sort Text dialog box, click the *Sort by* option box arrow and then click *Field 2* at the drop-down list. (The left margin is *Field 1* and the first tab is *Field 2*.)

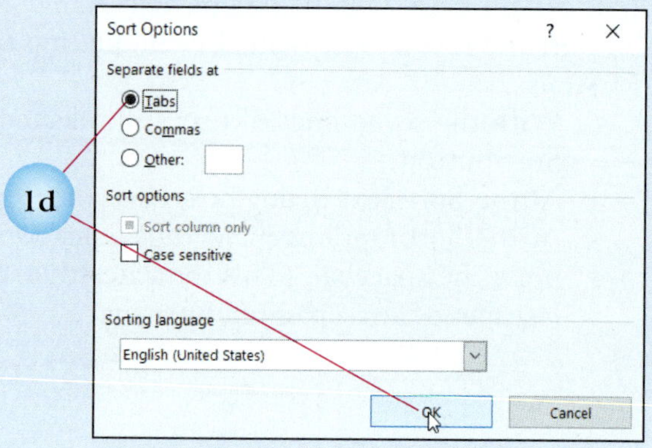

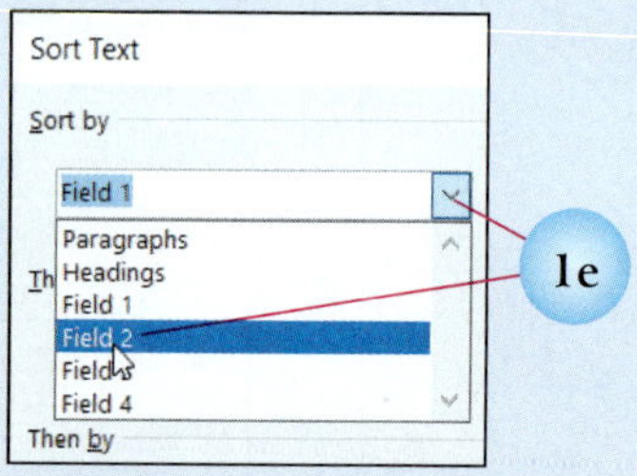

   f. Click OK.
2. With the six lines of text still selected, sort the third column of text numerically by completing the following steps:
   a. Click the Sort button.
   b. Click the *Sort by* option box arrow and then click *Field 4* at the drop-down list.
   c. Click OK.
3. Sort the text in the first two columns by completing the following steps:
   a. Select the seven lines of text set in the columns, including the headings.
   b. Click the Sort button.
   c. At the Sort Text dialog box, click the *Header row* option in the *My list has* section.
   d. If necessary, click the *Sort by* option box arrow and then click *Department*.
   e. Click the *Type* option box arrow in the *Sort by* section and then click *Text*.
   f. Click the *Then by* option box arrow and then click *Employee* at the drop-down list.
   g. Click OK.

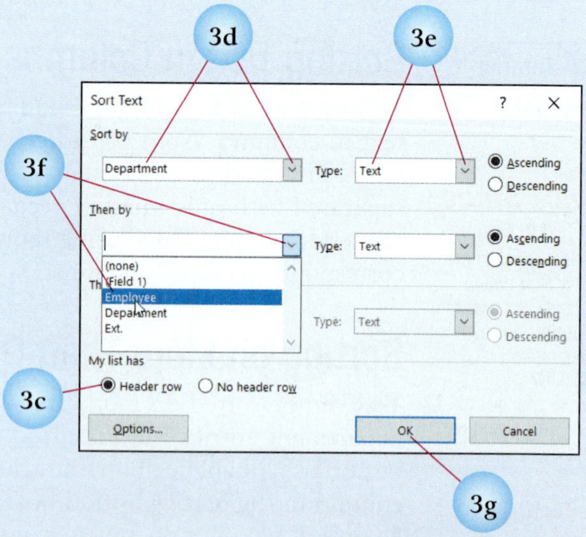

4. Save **2-Sorting**.

Check Your Work

Tutorial

Sorting Text in a Table

Quick Steps

Sort Text in Table

1. Position insertion point in table.
2. Click Sort button.
3. Make changes at Sort dialog box.
4. Click OK.

Sorting Text in a Table

Sorting text in columns within tables is similar to sorting columns of text separated by tabs. When sorting text in a table, the dialog box is named the Sort dialog box rather than the Sort Text dialog box. If a table contains a header, click the *Header row* option in the *My list has* section of the Sort dialog box to tell Word not to include the header row when sorting. To sort only specific cells in a table, select the cells and then complete the sort.

Activity 5c Sorting Text in a Table

Part 3 of 3

1. With **2-Sorting** open, sort the text in the first column of the table by completing the following steps:
   a. Position the insertion point in any cell in the table.
   b. Click the Sort button.
   c. At the Sort dialog box, make sure the *Header row* option is selected in the *My list has* section.
   d. Click the *Sort by* option box arrow and then click *Sales, First Half* at the drop-down list.
   e. Make sure nothing displays in the *Then by* option box. If necessary, click the *Then by* option box arrow and then click *(none)* at the drop-down list.
   f. Click OK.

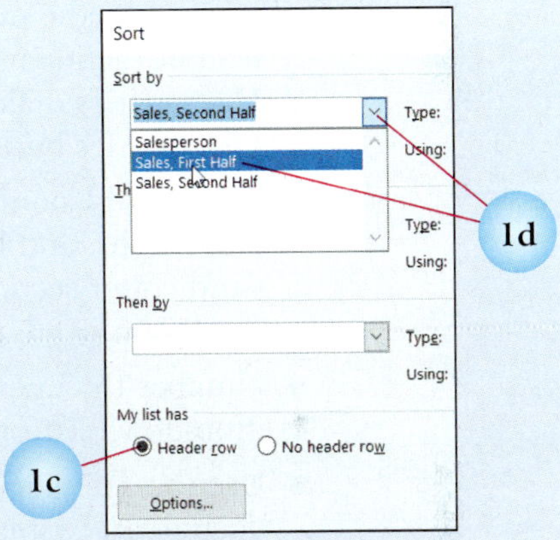

2. Sort the numbers in the third column in descending order by completing the following steps:
   a. Select all the cells in the table except the cells in the first row.
   b. Click the Sort button.
   c. Click the *Sort by* option box arrow and then click *Column 3* at the drop-down list.
   d. Click *Descending*.

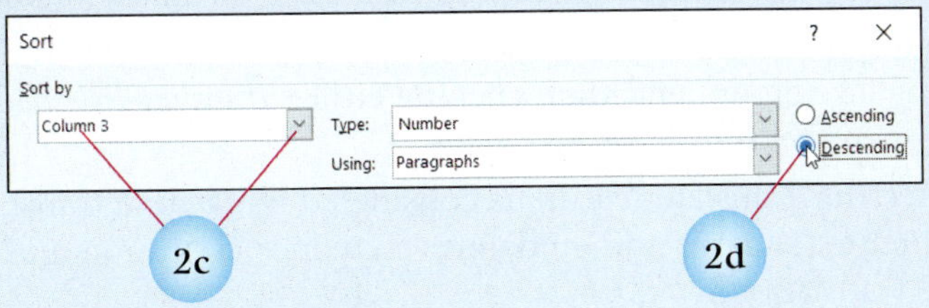

   e. Click OK.
3. Save, print, and then close **2-Sorting**.

Check Your Work

Chapter Summary

- Word's Editor contains a spelling and grammar checker. The spelling checker checks text against its dictionary and suggests corrections. The grammar checker finds errors in grammar, punctuation, and word usage.
- When checking spelling and grammar, make changes by clicking in the document outside the Editor task pane. Make changes and then click the Resume checking all results button in the task pane.
- Customize spelling and grammar checking options at the Word Options dialog box with *Proofing* selected in the left panel.
- Change the proofing language at the Language dialog box. Display this dialog box by clicking the Review tab, clicking the Language button in the Language group, and then clicking *Set Proofing Language*.
- To display readability statistics for a document, insert a check mark in the *Show readability statistics* check box in the Word Options dialog box with *Proofing* selected and then complete a spelling and grammar check.
- Word uses the main dictionary when spell checking a document. Change the default dictionary and add or remove a custom dictionary at the Custom Dictionaries dialog box. Display this dialog box by clicking the Custom Dictionaries button at the Word Options dialog box with *Proofing* selected.
- The Word Count dialog box displays the numbers of pages, words, characters, paragraphs, and lines in a document. Display this dialog box by clicking the word count section of the Status bar or by clicking the Word Count button in the Proofing group on the Review tab.
- Number the lines in a document with options at the Line Numbers button drop-down list or the Line Numbers dialog box.
- Use the Thesaurus feature to find synonyms and antonyms for words in a document. Display synonyms and antonyms at the Thesaurus task pane or by right-clicking a word and then pointing to *Synonyms* at the shortcut menu.
- The Smart Lookup feature provides information on selected text from a variety of sources on the web. To use the Smart Lookup feature, select text and then click the Smart Lookup button in the Research group on the References tab. This displays the Smart Lookup task pane at the right side of the screen.
- Translate text by clicking the Review tab, clicking the Translate button in the Language group, and then clicking either *Translate Selection* or *Translate Document* to open the Translator task pane.
- Since the Translate feature is considered a machine translation, consider content standards and guidelines to reduce confusion and errors and optimize the translation.
- Text in paragraphs, columns, and tables can be sorted alphabetically, numerically, or chronologically. Sort text by clicking the Sort button in the Paragraph group on the Home tab and then using options at the Sort Text dialog box to specify what is to be sorted.
- By default, paragraphs of text are sorted by the first word of each paragraph. This can be changed with options at the Sort Options dialog box. Display the dialog box by clicking the Options button at the Sort Text dialog box. Use the options in the *Separate fields at* section of the dialog box to specify how text is separated in the document.

- When sorting text set in columns, Word considers text typed at the left margin *Field 1*, text typed at the first tab *Field 2*, and so on.
- Sort on more than one field with the *Sort by* and *Then by* options at the Sort dialog box.
- Use the *Header row* option in the *My list has* section in the Sort Text dialog box to sort all the text in rows in a table except the first row.

Commands Review

FEATURE	RIBBON TAB, GROUP	BUTTON, OPTION	KEYBOARD SHORTCUT
line numbers	Layout, Page Setup		
proofing language	Review, Language	, *Set Proofing Language*	
Smart Lookup task pane	References, Research		
Sort Options dialog box	Home, Paragraph	, Options	
Sort Text dialog box	Home, Paragraph		
spelling and grammar checker	Review, Proofing		F7
Thesaurus task pane	Review, Proofing		Shift + F7
Translator task pane	Review, Language	, *Translate Selection* OR *Translate Document*	
Word Count dialog box	Review, Proofing		

Microsoft®

Word

CHAPTER 3

Inserting Headers, Footers, and References

Performance Objectives

Upon successful completion of Chapter 3, you will be able to:

1 Insert headers and footers in documents
2 Format, edit, and remove headers and footers
3 Insert and print sections
4 Keep text together on a page
5 Insert footnotes and endnotes
6 Insert and edit sources and citations
7 Insert, modify, and format sources lists

Word provides a number of predesigned headers (text that displays and prints at the tops of pages) and footers (text that displays and prints at the bottoms of pages) that can be inserted in documents, or custom headers and footers can be created. A document can be divided into sections and different formatting can be applied to each section, such as different headers, footers, and page numbers. In this chapter, you will learn how to create custom headers and footers, how to format and print sections in a document, and how to control soft page breaks within a document. You will also learn how to reference documents and acknowledge sources using footnotes, endnotes, and source lists.

Data Files

Before beginning chapter work, copy the WL2C3 folder to your storage medium and then make WL2C3 the active folder.

The online course includes additional training and assessment resources.

Activity 1 Insert Headers and Footers in a Computer Software Report

8 Parts

You will open a report on computer software and then create, customize, and position headers and footers in the document. You will also create headers and footers for different pages in a document, divide a document into sections, and then create footers for specific sections.

Tutorial

Creating a Custom Header and Footer

Tutorial

Editing a Header and Footer

Header

Footer

Hint One method for formatting a header or footer is to select the header or footer text and then use the options on the Mini toolbar.

Inserting Headers and Footers

Text that appears in the top margin of a page is called a *header* and text that appears in the bottom margin of a page is called a *footer*. Headers and footers are commonly used in manuscripts, textbooks, reports, and other publications to display the page numbers and section or chapter titles. For example, see the footer at the bottom of this page.

Insert a predesigned header by clicking the Insert tab and then clicking the Header button in the Header & Footer group. This displays a drop-down list of header choices. Click the predesigned header and the formatted header is inserted in the document. Complete similar steps to insert a predesigned footer.

If the predesigned headers and footers do not meet specific needs, create a custom header or footer. To create a custom header, click the Insert tab, click the Header button in the Header & Footer group, and then click *Edit Header* at the drop-down list. This displays a Header pane in the document along with the Header & Footer Tools Design tab, as shown in Figure 3.1. Use options on this tab to insert elements such as page numbers, and images; to navigate to other headers and footers in the document; and to position headers and footers on different pages in a document.

Inserting Elements in Headers and Footers

Use buttons in the Insert group on the Header & Footer Tools Design tab to insert elements into the header or footer, such as the date and time, Quick Parts, and images. Click the Date & Time button in the Insert group and the Date and Time dialog box displays. Choose a date and time option in the *Available formats* list box of the dialog box and then click OK.

Click the Document Info button to display a drop-down list of document information fields that can be inserted into the document. Hover the mouse pointer over the *Document Property* option in the Document Info button drop-down list to display a side menu of document properties, such as *Author*, *Comments*, and *Company*, that can be inserted in the header or footer.

Figure 3.1 Header & Footer Tools Design Tab

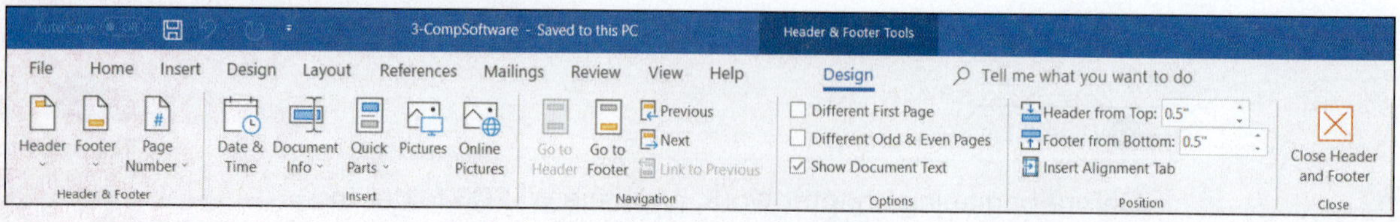

The Quick Parts button in the Insert group on the Header & Footer Tools Design tab contains options for inserting document properties, fields, and other elements. Click the Pictures button to display the Insert Picture dialog box and insert an image from the computer's hard drive or removable drive. Click the Online Pictures button and the Online Pictures window opens with options for searching for and then downloading an image into the header or footer.

Activity 1a Inserting Elements in a Header and Footer

Part 1 of 8

1. Open **CompSoftware** and then save it with the name **3-CompSoftware**.
2. Insert a header by completing the following steps:
   a. Click the Insert tab.
   b. Click the Header button in the Header & Footer group and then click *Edit Header* at the drop-down list.
   c. With the insertion point positioned in the Header pane, click the Pictures button in the Insert group on the Header & Footer Tools Design tab.

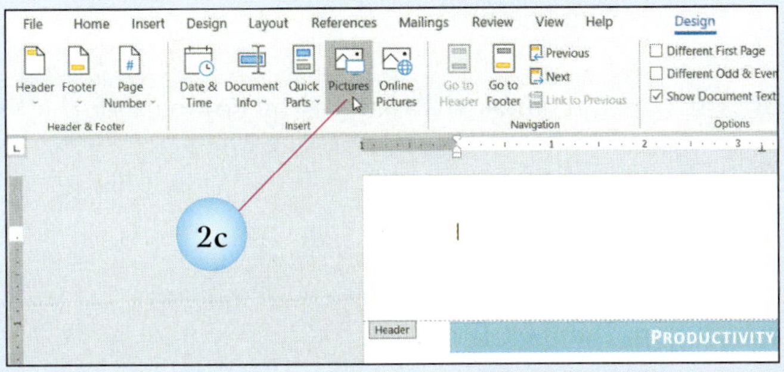

   d. At the Insert Picture dialog box, navigate to your WL2C3 folder and then double-click the ***Worldwide*** image file.
   e. With the image selected, click in the *Shape Height* measurement box in the Size group, type 0.4, and then press the Enter key.
   f. Click the Wrap Text button in the Arrange group and then click *Behind Text* at the drop-down list.
   g. Drag the image up approximately one-third of an inch.
   h. Click outside the image to deselect it.
   i. Press the Tab key two times. (This moves the insertion point to the right margin.)
   j. Click the Header & Footer Tools Design tab and then click the Date & Time button in the Insert group.
   k. At the Date and Time dialog box, click the twelfth option from the top (the option that displays the date in numbers and the time) and then click OK to close the dialog box.
   l. Select the date and time text and then click the Home tab. Click the Bold button, click the *Font Size* option box arrow, and then click *9* at the drop-down gallery.
   m. Double-click in the document to make it active. (The text in the header will display dimmed.)
3. Save **3-CompSoftware**.

Check Your Work

Positioning Headers and Footers

Word inserts a header 0.5 inch from the top of the page and a footer 0.5 inch from the bottom of the page. These default positions can be changed with buttons in the Position group on the Header & Footer Tools Design tab. Use the *Header from Top* and the *Footer from Bottom* measurement boxes to adjust the position of the header and the footer, respectively, on the page.

By default, headers and footers contain two tab settings. A center tab is set at 3.25 inches and a right tab is set at 6.5 inches. If the document contains default left and right margin settings of 1 inch, the center tab set at 3.25 inches is the center of the document and the right tab set at 6.5 inches is at the right margin. If the default margins are changed, the default center tab may need to be changed before inserting header or footer text at the center tab. Position tabs with the Insert Alignment Tab button in the Position group. Click this button and the Alignment Tab dialog box displays. Use options at this dialog box to change tab alignment and set tabs with leaders.

Activity 1b Positioning Headers and Footers — Part 2 of 8

1. With **3-CompSoftware** open, change the margins by completing the following steps:
   a. Click the Layout tab, click the Margins button in the Page Setup group, and then click the *Custom Margins* option at the bottom of the drop-down list.
   b. At the Page Setup dialog box with the Margins tab selected, select the measurement in the *Left* measurement box and then type 1.25.
   c. Select the measurement in the *Right* measurement box and then type 1.25.
   d. Click OK to close the dialog box.
2. Create a footer by completing the following steps:
   a. Click the Insert tab.
   b. Click the Footer button in the Header & Footer group and then click *Edit Footer* at the drop-down list.
   c. With the insertion point positioned in the Footer pane, type your first and last names at the left margin.
   d. Press the Tab key. (This moves the insertion point to the center tab position.)
   e. Click the Page Number button in the Header & Footer group, point to *Current Position*, and then click *Accent Bar 2* at the drop-down list.

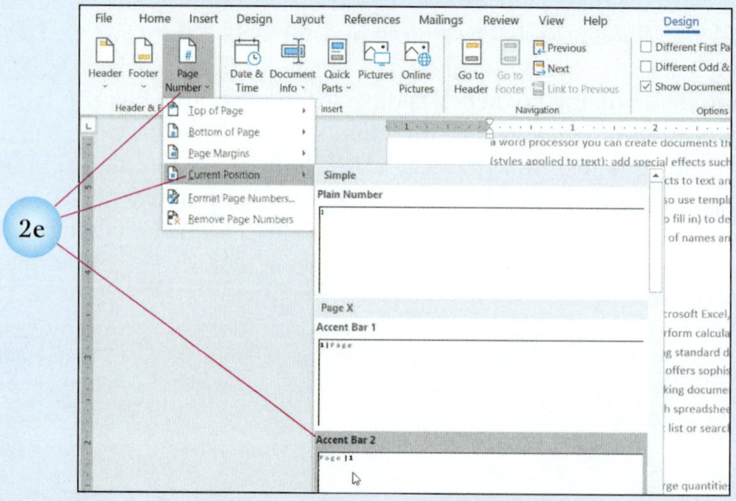

f. Press the Tab key.
g. Click the Document Info button in the Insert group and then click *File Name* at the drop-down list.

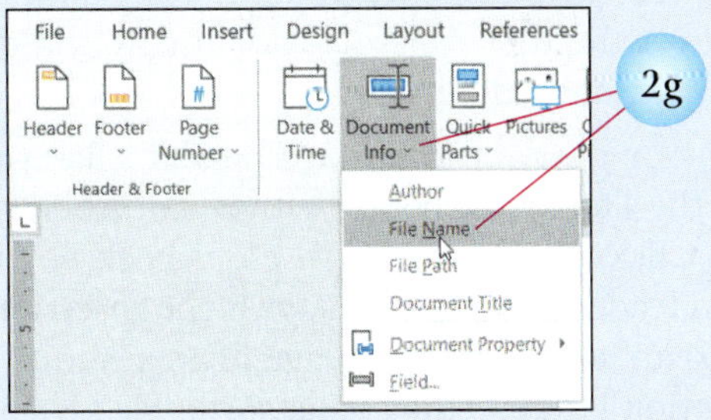

h. You notice that the center tab and right tab are slightly off, because the left and right margins in the document are set at 1.25 inches instead of 1 inch. To align the tabs correctly, drag the center tab marker to the 3-inch mark on the horizontal ruler and drag the right tab marker to the 6-inch mark on the horizontal ruler.

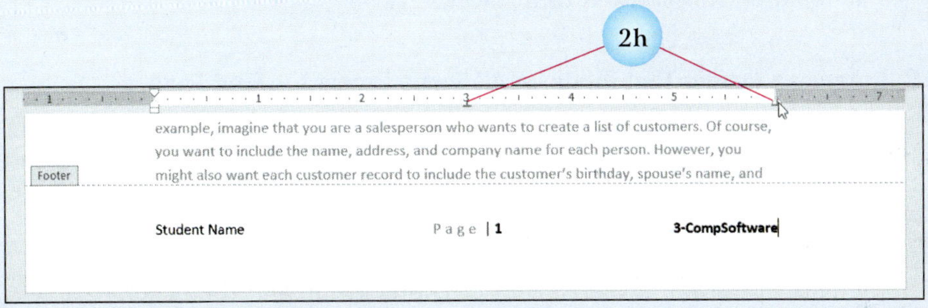

i. Select all the footer text and then change the font size to 9 and apply bold formatting.

3. Change the position of the header and footer by completing the following steps:
   a. Click the Header & Footer Tools Design tab.
   b. Click the Go to Header button in the Navigation group.
   c. Click the *Header from Top* measurement box up arrow until *0.8"* displays.
   d. Click the Go to Footer button in the Navigation group.
   e. Click in the *Footer from Bottom* measurement box, type 0.6, and then press the Enter key.
   f. Click the Close Header and Footer button.

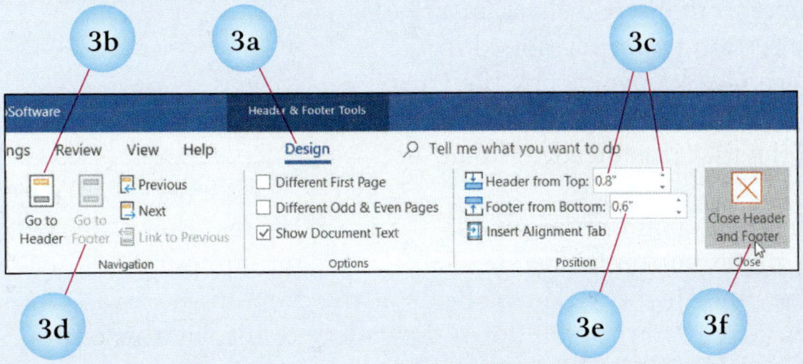

4. Save and then print the first two pages of **3-CompSoftware**.

Check Your Work

Tutorial

Creating a Different First Page Header and Footer

Quick Steps

Create Different First Page Header or Footer

1. Click Insert tab.
2. Click Header or Footer button.
3. Click *Edit Header* or *Edit Footer* at drop-down list.
4. Click *Different First Page* check box.
5. Insert elements and/or text.
6. Click Next button.
7. Insert elements and/or text.

Creating a Different First Page Header or Footer

A header and/or footer inserted in a document will display and print on every page in the document by default. However, different headers and footers can be created within one document. For example, a unique header or footer can be created for the first page of a document and a different header or footer can be created for the subsequent pages.

To create a different first page header, click the Insert tab, click the Header button in the Header & Footer group, and then click *Edit Header* at the drop-down list. Click the *Different First Page* check box to insert a check mark and the First Page Header pane displays with the insertion point inside it. Insert elements or type text to create the first page header and then click the Next button in the Navigation group. This displays the Header pane with the insertion point positioned inside it. Insert elements and/or type text to create the header. Complete similar steps to create a different first page footer.

In some situations, the first page header or footer should be blank. This is particularly useful if a document contains a title page and the header or footer should not display and print on it.

Activity 1c Creating a Header That Prints on All Pages Except the First Page

Part 3 of 8

1. With **3-CompSoftware** open, press Ctrl + A to select the entire document and then press Ctrl + 2 to change to double-line spacing.
2. Remove the header and footer by completing the following steps:
   a. Click the Insert tab.
   b. Click the Header button in the Header & Footer group and then click *Remove Header* at the drop-down list.
   c. Click the Footer button in the Header & Footer group and then click *Remove Footer* at the drop-down list.
3. Press Ctrl + Home and then create a header that prints on all pages except the first page by completing the following steps:
   a. With the Insert tab active, click the Header button in the Header & Footer group.
   b. Click *Edit Header* at the drop-down list.
   c. Click the *Different First Page* check box in the Options group on the Header & Footer Tools Design tab to insert a check mark.
   d. With the insertion point positioned in the First Page Header pane, click the Next button in the Navigation group. (This tells Word that the first page header should be blank.)

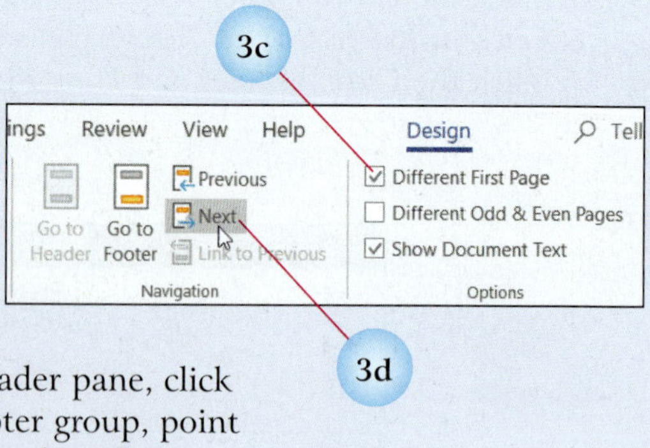

   e. With the insertion point positioned in the Header pane, click the Page Number button in the Header & Footer group, point to *Top of Page*, and then click *Accent Bar 2* at the drop-down gallery. (You may need to scroll down the gallery to display this option.)
   f. Click the Close Header and Footer button.
4. Scroll through the document and notice that the header appears on the second, third, fourth, and fifth pages.
5. Save and then print the first two pages of **3-CompSoftware**.

Check Your Work

Tutorial

Creating Odd Page and Even Page Headers and Footers

Quick Steps

Create Odd and Even Page Headers or Footers

1. Click Insert tab.
2. Click Header or Footer button.
3. Click *Edit Header* or *Edit Footer*.
4. Click *Different Odd & Even Pages* check box.
5. Insert elements and/or text.

Creating Odd and Even Page Headers or Footers

If a document will be read in book form, consider inserting odd and even page headers or footers. When presenting pages in a document in book form with facing pages, the outside margins are the left side of the left page and the right side of the right page. Also, when a document has facing pages, the right-hand page is generally numbered with an odd number and the left-hand page is generally numbered with an even number.

Create even and odd headers or footers to insert this type of page numbering. Use the *Different Odd & Even Pages* check box in the Options group on the Header & Footer Tools Design tab to create odd and even headers and/or footers.

Activity 1d Creating Odd and Even Page Footers

Part 4 of 8

1. With **3-CompSoftware** open, remove the header from the document by completing the following steps:
   a. Click the Insert tab.
   b. Click the Header button in the Header & Footer group and then click *Edit Header* at the drop-down list.
   c. Click the *Different First Page* check box in the Options group to remove the check mark.
   d. Click the Header button in the Header & Footer group and then click *Remove Header* at the drop-down list. (This displays the insertion point in an empty Header pane.)
2. Create one footer that prints on odd pages and another that prints on even pages by completing the following steps:
   a. Click the Go to Footer button in the Navigation group.
   b. Click the *Different Odd & Even Pages* check box in the Options group to insert a check mark. (This displays the Odd Page Footer pane with the insertion point inside it.)
   c. Click the Page Number button in the Header & Footer group, point to *Bottom of Page*, and then click *Plain Number 3* at the drop-down list.

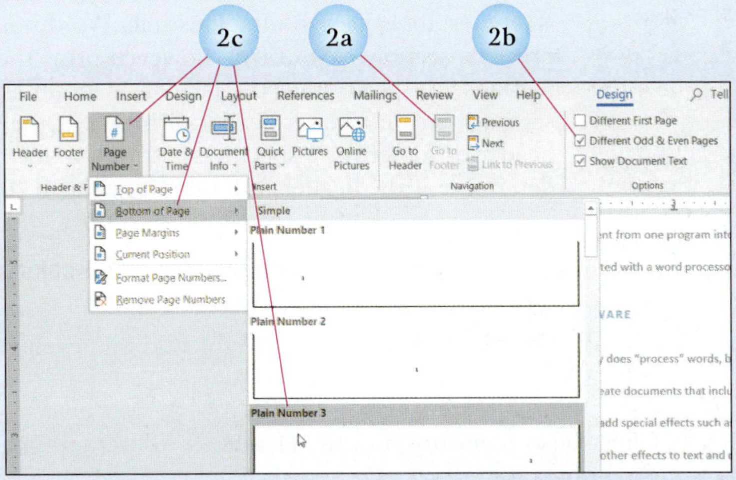

   d. Click the Next button in the Navigation group. (This displays the Even Page Footer pane with the insertion point inside it.)

e. Click the Page Number button, point to *Current Position*, and then click *Plain Number* at the drop-down list.
f. Click the Close Header and Footer button.
3. Scroll through the document and notice the page numbers at the right sides of the odd page footers and the left sides of the even page footers.
4. Save and then print the first two pages of **3-CompSoftware**.

Check Your Work

Creating Headers and Footers for Different Sections

Quick Steps

Create Headers or Footers for Different Sections

1. Insert section break.
2. Click Insert tab.
3. Click Header or Footer button.
4. Click *Edit Header* or *Edit Footer*.
5. Click Link to Previous button to deactivate.
6. Insert elements and/or text.
7. Click Next button.
8. Insert elements and/or text.

A document can be divided into sections by inserting section breaks and then different formatting can be applied to each section. A section break can be inserted that begins a new page or a section break can be inserted that allows the sections to be formatted differently but does not begin a new page. A section break can also be inserted that starts a new section on the next even-numbered page or the next odd-numbered page.

To insert different headers and/or footers on pages in a document, divide the document into sections. For example, if a document contains several chapters, each chapter can be a separate section and a different header and footer can be created for each section. When dividing a document into sections by chapter, insert section breaks that also begin new pages.

Breaking a Section Link

Link to Previous

When a header or footer is created for a specific section in a document, it can be created for all the previous and following sections or only the following sections. By default, each section in a document is linked to the other sections. To print a header or footer only on the pages within a section and not the previous section, deactivate the Link to Previous button in the Navigation group on the Header & Footer Tools Design tab. This tells Word not to print the header or footer on previous sections. Word will, however, print the header or footer on following sections. To specify that the header or footer should not print on following sections, create a blank header or footer at the next section. When creating a header or footer for a specific section in a document, preview the document to determine if the header or footer appears on the correct pages.

Activity 1e Creating Footers for Different Sections and Breaking a Section Link — Part 5 of 8

1. With **3-CompSoftware** open, remove the odd and even page footers by completing the following steps:
   a. Click the Insert tab.
   b. Click the Footer button in the Header & Footer group and then click *Edit Footer* at the drop-down list.
   c. Click the *Different Odd & Even Pages* check box in the Options group to remove the check mark.
   d. Click the Footer button in the Header & Footer group and then click *Remove Footer* at the drop-down list.
   e. Click the Close Header and Footer button.

2. Remove the page break before the second title in the document by completing the following steps:
   a. Move the insertion point immediately right of the period that ends the paragraph in the section *Presentation Software* (near the middle of page 3).
   b. Press the Delete key two times. (The title *Graphics and Multimedia Software* should now display below the paragraph on the third page.)
3. Insert an odd page section break (a section break that starts a section on the next odd page) by completing the following steps:
   a. Position the insertion point at the beginning of the title *Graphics and Multimedia Software*.
   b. Click the Layout tab, click the Breaks button in the Page Setup group, and then click *Odd Page* at the drop-down list.

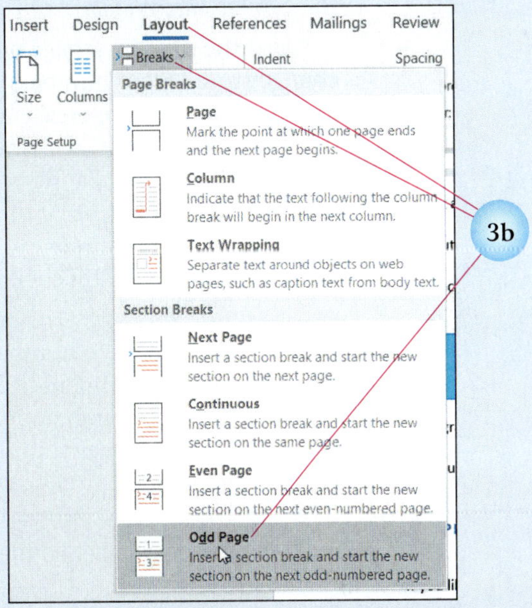

4. Create section titles and footers with page numbers for the two sections by completing the following steps:
   a. Position the insertion point at the beginning of the document.
   b. Click the Insert tab.
   c. Click the Footer button in the Header & Footer group and then click *Edit Footer* at the drop-down list.
   d. At the Footer -Section 1- pane, type Section 1 Productivity Software and then press the Tab key two times. (This moves the insertion point to the right margin.)
   e. Type Page and then press the spacebar.
   f. Click the Page Number button in the Header & Footer group, point to *Current Position*, and then click *Plain Number* at the side menu.
   g. Click the Next button in the Navigation group.
   h. Click the Link to Previous button to deactivate it. (This removes the message *Same as Previous* from the top right side of the footer pane.)

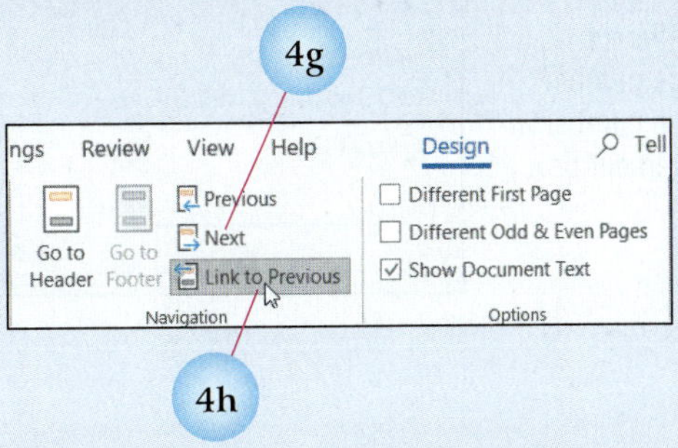

   i. In the footer, change the text *Section 1 Productivity Software* to *Section 2 Graphics and Multimedia Software*.
   j. Click the Close Header and Footer button.
5. Scroll through the document and notice the footers and page numbers in the sections. (Note that due to the section break, there is no page 4 shown in the document.)
6. Save **3-CompSoftware**.

Check Your Work

Tutorial

Customizing Page Numbers

Page Number

Customizing Page Numbers

By default, Word inserts arabic numbers (1, 2, 3, and so on) and numbers pages sequentially beginning with 1. These default settings can be customized with options at the Page Number Format dialog box, shown in Figure 3.2. To display this dialog box, click the Insert tab, click the Page Number button in the Header & Footer group, and then click *Format Page Numbers* at the drop-down list. Another method for displaying the dialog box is to click the Page Number button in the Header & Footer group on the Header & Footer Tools Design tab and then click the *Format Page Numbers* option.

Use the *Number format* option at the Page Number Format dialog box to change from arabic numbers to arabic numbers preceded and followed by hyphens, lowercase letters, uppercase letters, lowercase roman numerals, or uppercase roman numerals. By default, page numbering begins with 1 and continues sequentially through all the pages and sections in a document. Change the beginning page number by clicking the *Start at* option and then typing the beginning page number in the measurement box. The number in the *Start at* measurement box can also be changed by clicking the measurement box up or down arrow.

If section breaks are inserted in a document and then a header and footer are inserted with page numbers for each section, the page numbers are sequential throughout the document. The document used in Activity 1f has a section break but the pages are numbered sequentially. If the page numbering in a section should start with a new number, use the *Start at* option at the Page Number Format dialog box.

Figure 3.2 Page Number Format Dialog Box

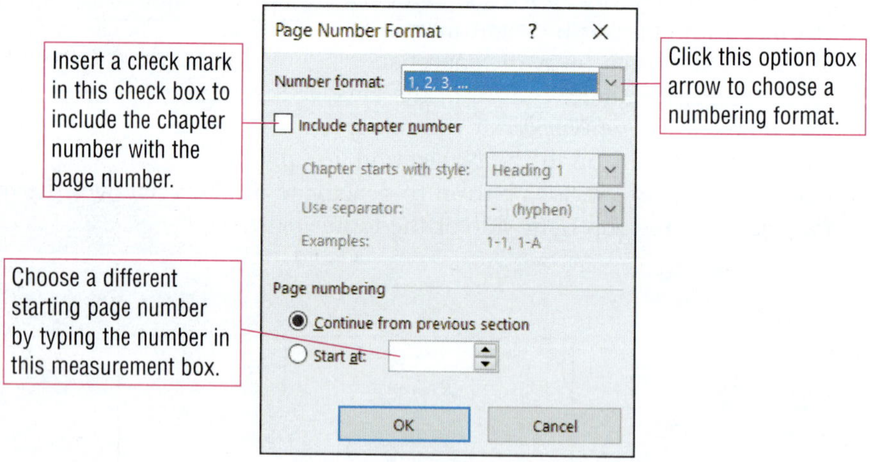

Activity 1f Customizing Page Numbering

Part 6 of 8

1. With **3-CompSoftware** open, change the page numbers to lowercase roman numerals and change the starting page number by completing the following steps:
   a. Press Ctrl + Home.
   b. Click the Insert tab.
   c. Click the Page Number button in the Header & Footer group and then click *Format Page Numbers* at the drop-down list.
   d. At the Page Number Format dialog box, click the *Number format* option box arrow and then click *i, ii, iii, ...* at the drop-down list.
   e. Click the *Start at* option and then type 4.
   f. Click OK to close the dialog box.

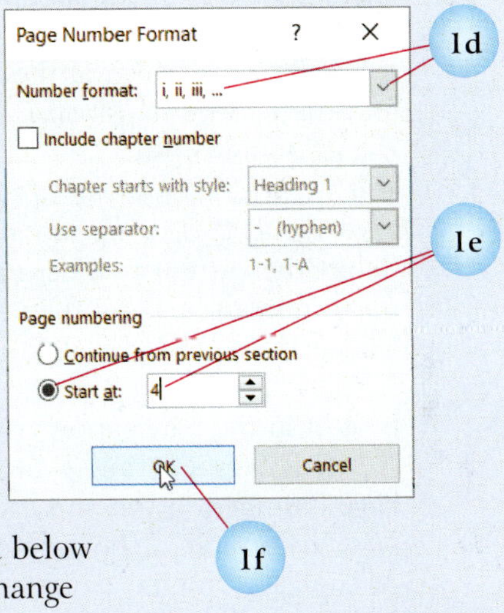

2. Scroll through the document and notice the lowercase roman numeral page numbers (beginning with *iv*) that display at the right margins at the bottoms of the pages.
3. Scroll to the bottom of the page containing the title *GRAPHICS AND MULTIMEDIA SOFTWARE* and notice that the page numbers did not change. (This is because the sections were unlinked.)
4. Position the insertion point in the first paragraph of text below the title *GRAPHICS AND MULTIMEDIA SOFTWARE* and then change the page numbering by completing the following steps:
   a. Click the Page Number button and then click *Format Page Numbers* at the drop-down list.
   b. At the Page Number Format dialog box, click the *Number format* option box arrow and then click *i, ii, iii, ...* at the drop-down list.
   c. Click the *Start at* option and then type 7.
   d. Click OK to close the dialog box.
5. Save **3-CompSoftware** and then print only the first page.

Check Your Work

Tutorial

Printing Sections

Quick Steps

Print Section

1. Click File tab.
2. Click *Print* option.
3. Click in *Pages* text box.
4. Type s followed by section number.
5. Click Print button.

Printing Sections

Print specific pages in a document by inserting page numbers in the *Pages* text box at the Print backstage area. When entering page numbers in this text box, use a hyphen to indicate a range of consecutive pages or a comma to specify nonconsecutive pages.

In a document that contains sections, use the *Pages* text box at the Print backstage area to specify the section and pages within the section to be printed. For example, if a document is divided into three sections, print only section 2 by typing *s2* in the *Pages* text box. If a document contains six sections, print sections 3 through 5 by typing *s3-s5* in the *Pages* text box. Specific pages within or between sections can also be identified for printing. For example, to print pages 2 through 5 of section 4, type p2s4-p5s4; to print from page 3 of section 1 through page 5 of section 4, type p3s1-p5s4; to print page 1 of section 3, page 4 of section 5, and page 6 of section 8, type p1s3,p4s5,p6s8.

Activity 1g Changing Section Page Numbering and Printing Section Pages

Part 7 of 8

1. With **3-CompSoftware** open, press Ctrl + Home to move the insertion point to the beginning of the document.
2. Change the number formats and starting page numbers for sections 1 and 2 by completing the following steps:
   a. Click the Insert tab, click the Footer button in the Header & Footer group, and then click *Edit Footer* at the drop-down list.
   b. At the Footer -Section 1- footer pane, click the Page Number button in the Header & Footer group and then click the *Format Page Numbers* option at the drop-down list.
   c. Click the *Number format* option box arrow and then click the *1, 2, 3, ...* option at the drop-down list.
   d. Select the current number in the *Start at* measurement box and then type 1.
   e. Click OK to close the dialog box.
   f. Display the section 2 footer by clicking the Next button in the Navigation group.
   g. At the Footer -Section 2- footer pane, click the Page Number button and then click the *Format Page Numbers* option at the drop-down list.
   h. At the Page Number Format dialog box, click the *Number format* option box arrow and then click the *1, 2, 3, ...* option at the drop-down list.
   i. Select the current number in the *Start at* measurement box and then type 1.
   j. Click OK to close the dialog box.
   k. Click the Close Header and Footer button.

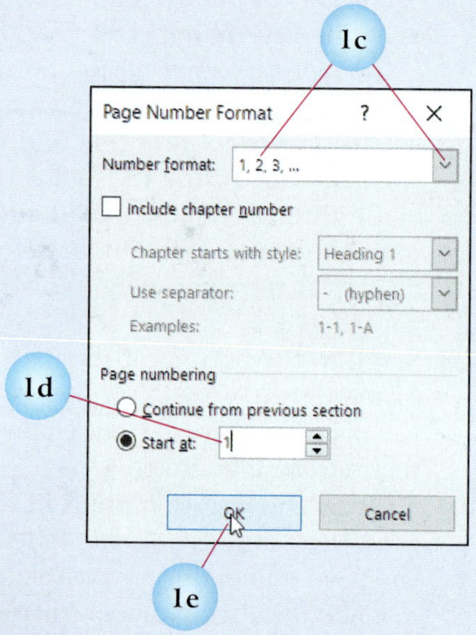

3. Print only page 1 of section 1 and page 1 of section 2 by completing the following steps:
   a. Click the File tab and then click the *Print* option.
   b. At the Print backstage area, click in the *Pages* text box in the *Settings* category and then type p1s1,p1s2.
   c. Click the Print button.
4. Save **3-CompSoftware**.

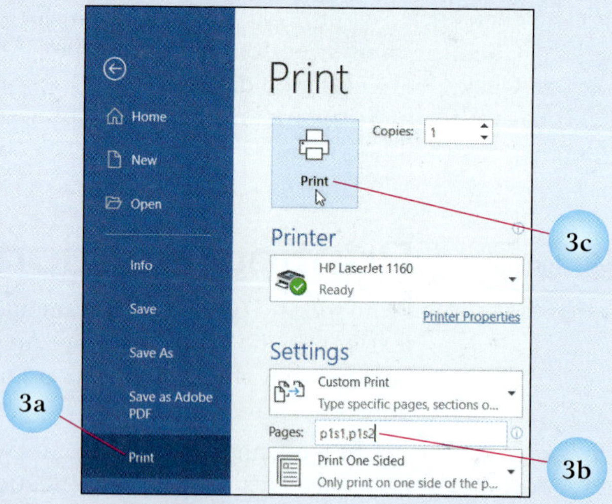

Check Your Work

Tutorial

Keeping Text Together

Quick Steps

Keep Text Together

1. Click Paragraph group dialog box launcher.
2. Click Line and Page Breaks tab.
3. Click *Keep with next*, *Keep lines together*, and/or *Page break before*.
4. Click OK.

Hint Text formatted with the *Keep with next* option applied to it is identified with the nonprinting character ■ in the left margin.

Keeping Text Together

In a multipage document, Word automatically inserts soft page breaks, which are page breaks that adjust when data is added or deleted from the document. However, a soft page break may occur in an undesirable location. For example, a soft page break may cause a heading to display at the bottom of a page while the text related to the heading displays at the top of the next page. A soft page break may also create a widow or orphan. A widow is the last line of text in a paragraph that appears by itself at the top of a page and an orphan is the first line of text in a paragraph that appears by itself at the bottom of a page.

Use options at the Paragraph dialog box with the Line and Page Breaks tab selected, as shown in Figure 3.3, to control widows and orphans and keep a paragraph, group of paragraphs, or group of lines together. Display this dialog box by clicking the Paragraph group dialog box launcher on the Home tab and then clicking the Line and Page Breaks tab at the dialog box.

By default, the *Widow/Orphan control* option is active and Word tries to avoid creating widows and orphans when inserting soft page breaks. The other three options in the *Pagination* section of the dialog box are not active by default. Use the *Keep with next* option to keep a line together with the next line. This is useful for keeping a heading together with the first line of text below it. To keep a group of selected lines together, use the *Keep lines together* option. Use the *Page break before* option to insert a page break before selected text.

Figure 3.3 Paragraph Dialog Box with the Line and Page Breaks Tab Selected

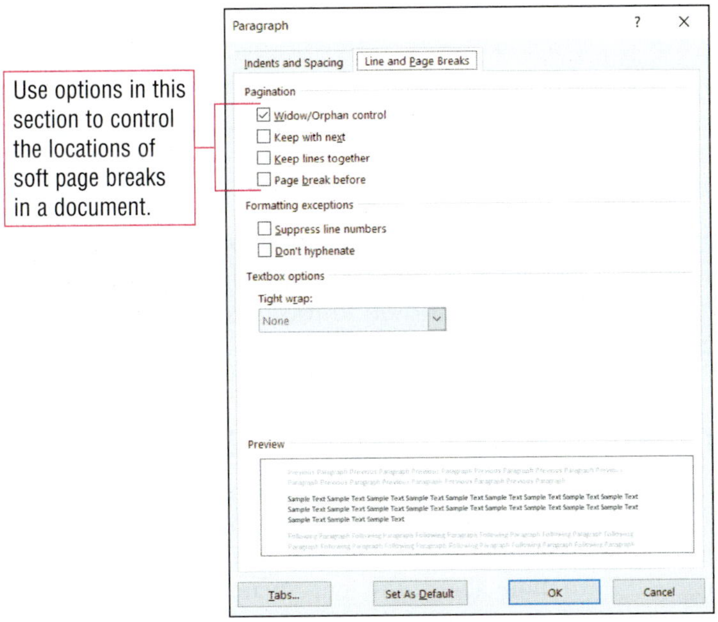

Activity 1h Keeping Text Together

Part 8 of 8

1. With **3-CompSoftware** open, scroll through the document and notice that the heading *SPREADSHEET SOFTWARE* displays at the bottom of page 1 and the paragraph that follows the heading displays at the top of page 2. Keep the heading and paragraph together by completing the following steps:
   a. Position the insertion point in the heading *SPREADSHEET SOFTWARE*.
   b. Make sure the Home tab is active and then click the Paragraph group dialog box launcher.
   c. At the Paragraph dialog box, click the Line and Page Breaks tab.
   d. Click the *Keep with next* check box to insert a check mark.
   e. Click OK to close the dialog box.

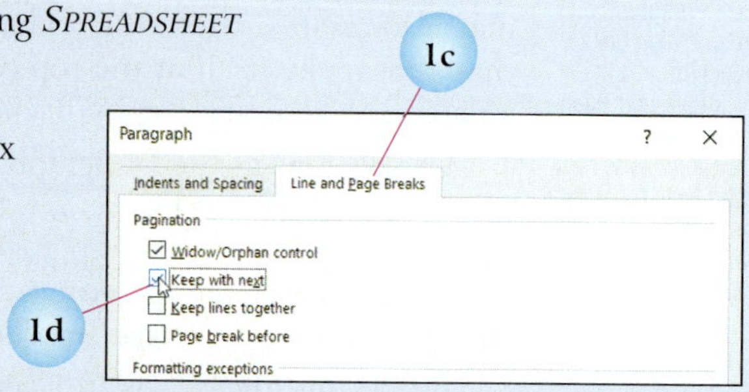

2. Scroll through the document and notice the heading *MULTIMEDIA SOFTWARE* near the end of the document. Insert a soft page break at the beginning of the heading by completing the following steps:
   a. Move the insertion point to the beginning of the heading *MULTIMEDIA SOFTWARE*.
   b. Click the Paragraph group dialog box launcher.
   c. At the Paragraph dialog box with the Line and Page Breaks tab selected, click the *Page break before* check box to insert a check mark.
   d. Click OK to close the dialog box.
3. Save, print, and then close **3-CompSoftware**.

Check Your Work

Activity 2 Insert Footnotes and Endnotes in Reports

3 Parts

You will open a report on pioneers of computing and then insert, format, and modify footnotes. You will also open a report on technology visionaries, insert endnotes, and then convert endnotes to footnotes.

Tutorial

Inserting Footnotes and Endnotes

Hint Ctrl + Alt + F is the keyboard shortcut to insert a footnote and Ctrl + Alt + D is the keyboard shortcut to insert an endnote.

Insert Footnote

Insert Endnote

Inserting Footnotes and Endnotes

A research paper or report contains information from a variety of sources. To give credit to those sources, footnotes or endnotes can be inserted in a document formatted in a specific reference style, such as that of the *Chicago Manual of Style*. (You will learn more about different reference styles in the next activity.) A footnote is an explanatory note or source reference that is printed at the bottom of the page on which the corresponding information appears. An endnote is also an explanatory note or reference but it is printed at the end of the document.

Two steps are involved in creating a footnote or endnote. First, the note reference number is inserted in the document where the corresponding information appears. Second, the note entry text is typed. Footnotes and endnotes are created in a similar manner.

Quick Steps

Insert Footnote

1. Click References tab.
2. Click Insert Footnote button.
3. Type footnote text.

Insert Endnote

1. Click References tab.
2. Click Insert Endnote button.
3. Type endnote text.

To create a footnote, position the insertion point where the reference number is to appear, click the References tab, and then click the Insert Footnote button in the Footnotes group. This inserts a number in the document along with a separator line at the bottom of the page and a superscript number below it. With the insertion point positioned immediately right of the superscript number, type the note entry text. By default, Word numbers footnotes with superscript arabic numbers and endnotes with superscript lowercase roman numerals.

Activity 2a Creating Footnotes

Part 1 of 3

1. Open **CompPioneers** and then save it with the name **3-CompPioneers**.
2. Create the first footnote shown in Figure 3.4 by completing the following steps:
   a. Position the insertion point at the end of the first paragraph of text below the heading *Konrad Zuse* (immediately following the period).
   b. Click the References tab.
   c. Click the Insert Footnote button in the Footnotes group.
   d. With the insertion point positioned at the bottom of the page immediately following the superscript number, type the first footnote shown in Figure 3.4. (Italicize the text as shown in the figure.)

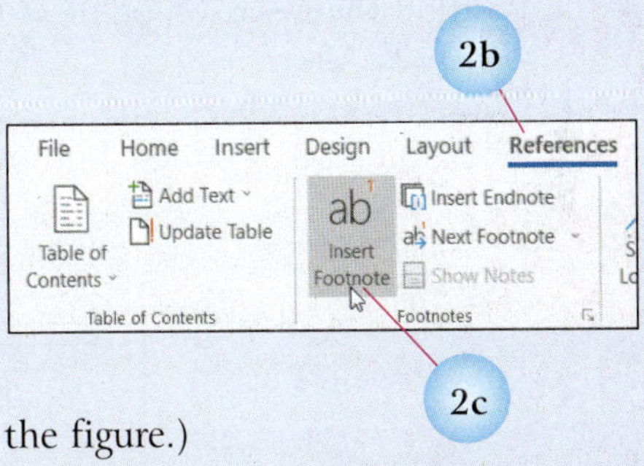

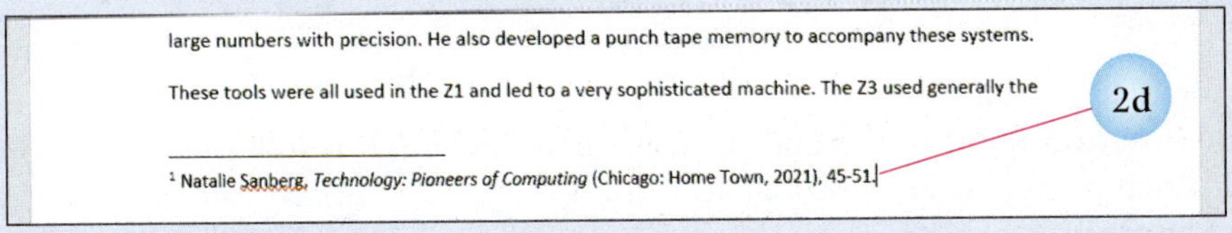

3. Move the insertion point to the end of the third paragraph below the heading *Konrad Zuse*. Using steps similar to those in Steps 2c and 2d, create the second footnote shown in Figure 3.4. (Italicize the text as shown in the figure.)
4. Move the insertion point to the end of the last paragraph below the heading *Konrad Zuse* and then create the third footnote shown in Figure 3.4.
5. Move the insertion point to the end of the third paragraph below the heading *William Hewlett and David Packard* and then create the fourth footnote shown in Figure 3.4.
6. Move the insertion point to the end of the last paragraph in the document and then create the fifth foonote shown in Figure 3.4.
7. Save, print, and then close **3-CompPioneers**.

Check Your Work

Figure 3.4 Activity 2a

Natalie Sanberg, *Technology: Pioneers of Computing* (Chicago: Home Town, 2021), 45-51.

Miguel Whitworth and Danielle Reyes, "Development of Computing," *Design Technologies* (2020): 24-26.

Sam Wells, *Biographies of Computing Pioneers* (San Francisco: Laurelhurst, 2021), 20-23.

Terrell Montgomery, *History of Computers* (Boston: Langley-Paulsen, 2021), 13-15.

Justin Evans, "Hewlett-Packard's Impact on Computing," *Computing Technologies* (2021): 7-12.

Printing Footnotes and Endnotes

When printing a document that contains footnotes, Word automatically reduces the number of text lines on a page to create space for the number of lines in the footnotes and the separator line. If the page does not contain enough space, the footnote number and entry text are moved to the next page. Word separates the footnotes from the text with a 2-inch separator line that begins at the left margin. When endnotes are created in a document, Word prints all the endnotes at the end of the document, separated from the text by a 2-inch line.

Activity 2b Creating Endnotes

Part 2 of 3

1. Open **TechVisionaries** and then save it with the name **3-TechVisionaries**.
2. Create the first endnote shown in Figure 3.5 by completing the following steps:
   a. Position the insertion point at the end of the second paragraph below the heading *Gordon E. Moore*.
   b. Click the References tab.
   c. Click the Insert Endnote button in the Footnotes group.

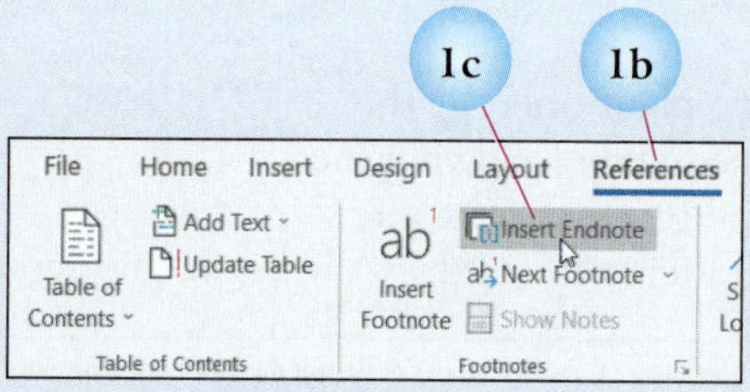

   d. Type the first endnote shown in Figure 3.5.
3. Move the insertion point to the end of the fourth paragraph below the heading *Jack S. Kilby* and then complete steps similar to those in Steps 2c and 2d to create the second endnote shown in Figure 3.5.
4. Move the insertion point to the end of the first paragraph below the heading *Linus Torvalds* and then create the third endnote shown in Figure 3.5.
5. Move the insertion point to the end of the last paragraph in the document and then create the fourth endnote shown in Figure 3.5.
6. Save **3-TechVisionaries**.

Check Your Work

Figure 3.5 Activity 2b

Gina Shaw, *History of Computing Technologies* (Los Angeles: Gleason Rutherford Publishing, 2021): 11-14.

Ellen Littleton, "Jack Kilby: Nobel Prize Winner," *Horizon Computing* (Boston: Robison Publishing House, 2021): 23-51.

Eric Ventrella, "Computer Nerd Hero," *Computing Today* (2021): 5-10.

Joseph Daniels, "Linus Torvalds: Technology Visionary," *Connections* (2021): 13-17.

Tutorial

Viewing and Editing Footnotes and Endnotes

Next Footnote

Show Notes

Hint To view the entry text for a footnote or endnote where the note occurs within the document, position the mouse pointer on the note reference number. The footnote or endnote text displays in a box above the number.

Viewing and Editing Footnotes and Endnotes

To view the footnotes in a document, click the Next Footnote button in the Footnotes group on the References tab. This moves the insertion point to the first footnote reference number following the insertion point. To view the endnotes in a document, click the Next Footnote button arrow and then click *Next Endnote* at the drop-down list. Use other options at the Next Footnote button drop-down list to view the previous footnote, next endnote, or previous endnote. Move the insertion point to specific footnote text with the Show Notes button.

If a footnote or endnote reference number is moved, copied, or deleted, all the remaining footnotes or endnotes automatically renumber. To move a footnote or endnote, select the reference number and then click the Cut button in the Clipboard group on the Home tab. Position the insertion point at the new location and then click the Paste button in the Clipboard group. To delete a footnote or endnote, select the reference number and then press the Delete key. This deletes the reference number as well as the footnote or endnote text.

Click the Footnotes group dialog box launcher and the Footnote and Endnote dialog box displays, as shown in Figure 3.6. Use options at this dialog box to convert footnotes to endnotes and endnotes to footnotes; change the locations of footnotes or endnotes; change the number formatting; start footnote or endnote numbering with a specific number, letter, or symbol; or change numbering within sections in a document.

Figure 3.6 Footnote and Endnote Dialog Box

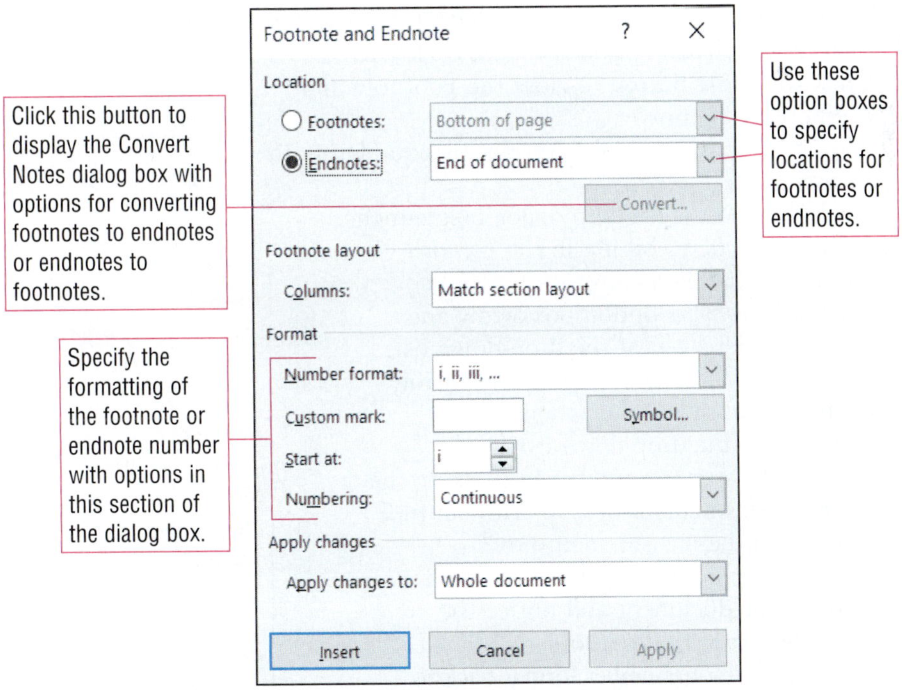

Activity 2c Editing Endnotes, Converting Endnotes to Footnotes, and Editing Footnotes

Part 3 of 3

1. With **3-TechVisionaries** open, press Ctrl + Home to move the insertion point to the beginning of the document and then edit the endnotes by completing the following steps:
   a. If necessary, click the References tab.
   b. Click the Next Footnote button arrow in the Footnotes group and then click *Next Endnote* at the drop-down list.
   c. Click the Show Notes button in the Footnotes group to display the endnote text.
   d. Change the page numbers for the Gina Shaw entry from *11-14* to *6-10*.
   e. Click the Show Notes button again to return to the reference number in the document.

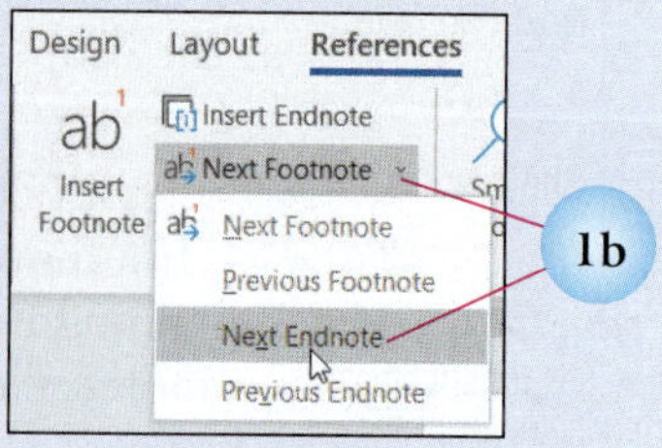

2. Press Ctrl + A to select the document (but not the endnote entry text) and then change the font to Constantia.
3. Change the font for the endnotes by completing the following steps:
   a. Press Ctrl + End to move the insertion point to the end of the document.
   b. Click in any endnote entry and then press Ctrl + A to select all the endnote entries.
   c. Change the font to Constantia.
   d. Press Ctrl + Home.
4. Convert the endnotes to footnotes by completing the following steps:
   a. Click the References tab and then click the Footnotes group dialog box launcher.
   b. At the Footnote and Endnote dialog box, click the Convert button.
   c. At the Convert Notes dialog box with the *Convert all endnotes to footnotes* option selected, click OK.
   d. Click the Close button to close the Footnote and Endnote dialog box.

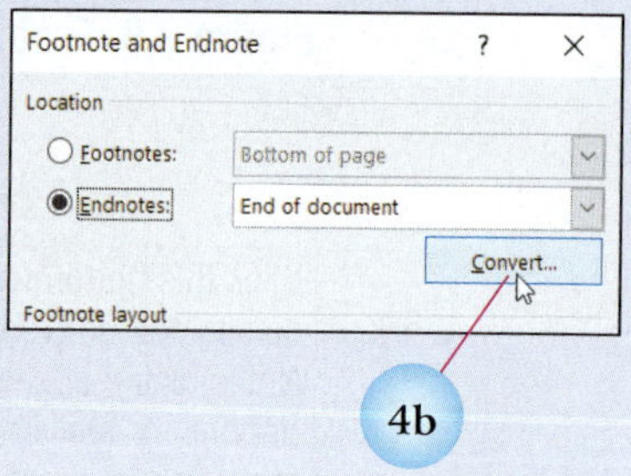

5. Change the footnote number format by completing the following steps:
   a. Click the Footnotes group dialog box launcher.
   b. Click the *Footnotes* option in the *Location* section of the dialog box.
   c. Click the *Footnotes* option box arrow and then click *Below text* at the drop-down list.
   d. Click the *Number format* option box arrow in the *Format* section and then click *a, b, c, …* at the drop-down list.
   e. Change the starting number by clicking the *Start at* measurement box up arrow until *d* displays in the measurement box.
   f. Click the Apply button and then scroll through the document and notice the renumbering of the footnotes.
6. Change the footnote number format back to arabic numbers by completing the following steps:
   a. With the References tab active, click the Footnotes group dialog box launcher.
   b. At the Footnote and Endnote dialog box, click the *Footnotes* option in the *Location* section.

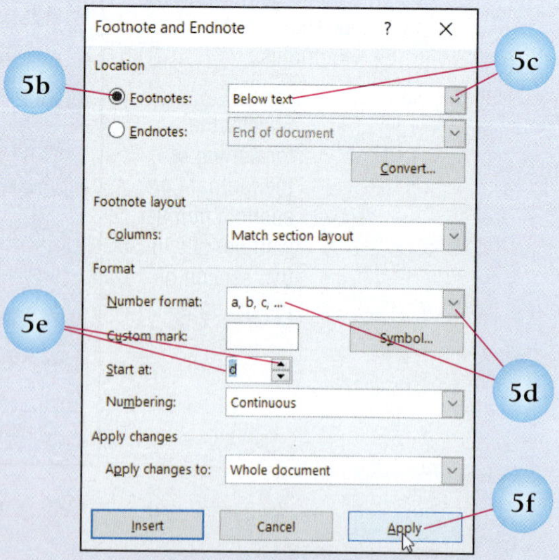

c. Click the *Number format* option box arrow in the *Format* section and then click *1, 2, 3, …* at the drop-down list.
d. Change the starting number back to 1 by clicking the *Start at* measurement box down arrow until *1* displays in the measurement box.
e. Click the Apply button.

7. Delete the third footnote by completing the following steps:
   a. Press Ctrl + Home.
   b. Make sure the References tab is active and then click the Next Footnote button three times.
   c. Select the third footnote reference number (superscript number) and then press the Delete key.
8. Save, print, and then close **3-TechVisionaries**.

Check Your Work

Activity 3 Cite Sources in a Mobile Security Report **8 Parts**

You will open a report on securing mobile devices, add information and insert source citations and a bibliography, and then modify and customize citation styles.

Citing and Editing Sources

In addition to using footnotes and endnotes to credit sources in a research paper or manuscript, consider inserting in-text citations and a sources list to identify sources of quotations, facts, theories, and other borrowed or summarized material. An in-text citation acknowledges that information is being borrowed from a source. Not acknowledging someone else's words or ideas is called *plagiarizing*.

Tutorial
Formatting a Report in MLA Style

Tutorial
Formatting a Report in APA Style

Formatting a Report Using an Editorial Style

Word provides a number of commonly used editorial styles for citing references in research papers and reports, including the American Psychological Association (APA) reference style, which is generally used in the social sciences and research fields; the Modern Language Association (MLA) style, which is generally used in the humanities and English composition; and the *Chicago Manual of Style* (Chicago), which is used both in the humanities and the social sciences and is considered more complex than either APA or MLA style.

To prepare a research paper or report in APA or MLA style, format the document according to the following general guidelines:

- Use standard-sized paper (8.5 × 11 inches)
- Set 1-inch top, bottom, left, and right margins
- Format the text in a 12-point serif typeface (such as Cambria or Times New Roman)
- Double-space text
- Indent the first line of each paragraph 0.5 inch
- Insert page numbers in the header, positioned at the right margin.

When formatting a research paper or report according to MLA or APA style, follow certain guidelines for properly formatting the first page of the document. With MLA style, at the beginning of the first page, at the left margin, insert the author's name (the person writing the report), the instructor's name, the course title, and the current date. Double-space after each of the four lines. After the current date, double-space and then type and center the title of the document. Also double-space between the title and the first line of text. The text should be left-aligned and double-spaced. Finally, insert a header in the upper right corner of the document that includes the author's last name and the page number.

When using APA style, create a title page that is separate from the body of the document. On this page, include the title of the paper, the author's name, and the school's name, all double-spaced, centered, and positioned on the upper half of the page. Also include a header with the text *Running Head:* followed by the title of the paper in uppercase letters at the left margin and the page number at the right margin.

Activity 3a Formatting the First Page of a Research Paper in MLA Style

Part 1 of 8

1. Open **MobileSecurity** and then save it with the name **3-MobileSecurity**.
2. Format the document in MLA style by completing the following steps:
   a. Press Ctrl + A to select the entire document.
   b. Display the Font dialog box with the Font tab selected and change the font to Cambria and the font size to 12 points. Click the Set As Default button in the lower left corner of the dialog box and then click OK at the Microsoft Word dialog box. (This changes the default setting to 12-point Cambria for the current document only.)
   c. Press Ctrl + Home to position the insertion point at the beginning of the document.
   d. Type your first and last names and then press the Enter key.
   e. Type your instructor's name and then press the Enter key.
   f. Type your course title and then press the Enter key.
   g. Type the current date and then press the Enter key.
   h. Type the document title Mobile Security and then center it.

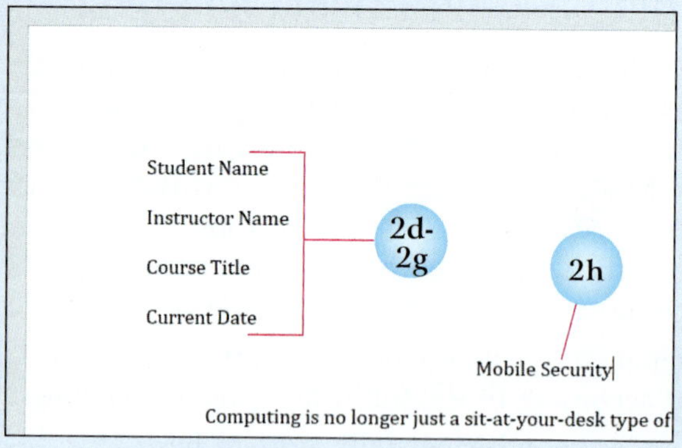

3. Insert a header in the document by completing the following steps:
   a. Click the Insert tab.
   b. Click the Header button in the Header & Footer group and then click *Edit Header* at the drop-down list.
   c. Press the Tab key two times to move the insertion point to the right margin in the Header pane.

d. Type your last name and then press the spacebar.

e. Click the Page Number button in the Header & Footer group on the Header & Footer Tools Design tab, point to *Current Position*, and then click the *Plain Number* option.

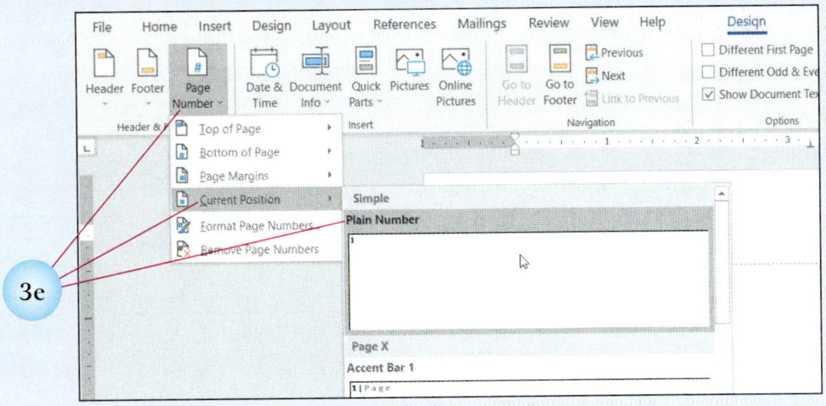

f. Double-click in the body of the document.

4. Save **3-MobileSecurity**.

Check Your Work

Tutorial

Inserting Sources and Citations

Insert Citation

Quick Steps

Insert New Citation

1. Click References tab.
2. Click Insert Citation button.
3. Click *Add New Source*.
4. Type source information.
5. Click OK.

Insert Citation Placeholder

1. Click References tab.
2. Click Insert Citation button.
3. Click *Add New Placeholder*.
4. Type citation name.
5. Click OK.

Inserting Source Citations

When creating an in-text source citation, enter the information about the source in fields at the Create Source dialog box. To insert a citation in a document, click the References tab, click the Insert Citation button in the Citations & Bibliography group, and then click *Add New Source* at the drop-down list. At the Create Source dialog box, shown in Figure 3.7, select the type of source to be cited (such as a book, journal article, or report) and then type the bibliographic information in the required fields. To include more information than required in the displayed fields, click the *Show All Bibliography Fields* check box to insert a check mark and then type the additional bibliographic details in the extra fields. After filling in the necessary source information, click OK. The citation is automatically inserted in the document at the location of the insertion point.

Inserting Citation Placeholders

If information for an in-text source citation will be inserted later, insert a citation placeholder. To do this, click the Insert Citation button in the Citations & Bibliography group and then click *Add New Placeholder* at the drop-down list. At the Placeholder Name dialog box, type a name for the citation placeholder and then press the Enter key or click OK. Insert the citation text later at the Edit Source dialog box, which contains the same options as the Create Source dialog box.

Figure 3.7 Create Source Dialog Box

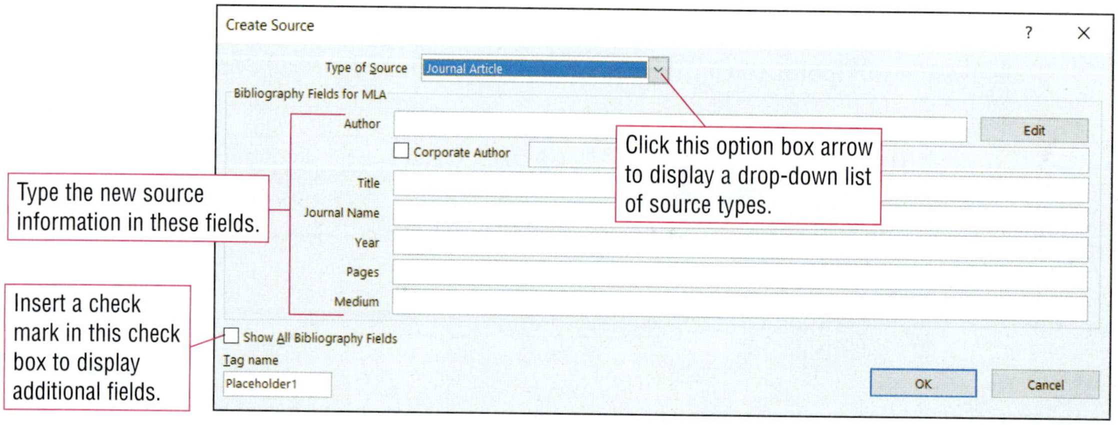

Activity 3b Inserting Sources and a Citation Placeholder

Part 2 of 8

1. With **3-MobileSecurity** open, click the References tab and then check to make sure the *Style* option box in the Citations & Bibliography group is set to *MLA*. If not, click the *Style* option box arrow and then click *MLA* at the drop-down list.

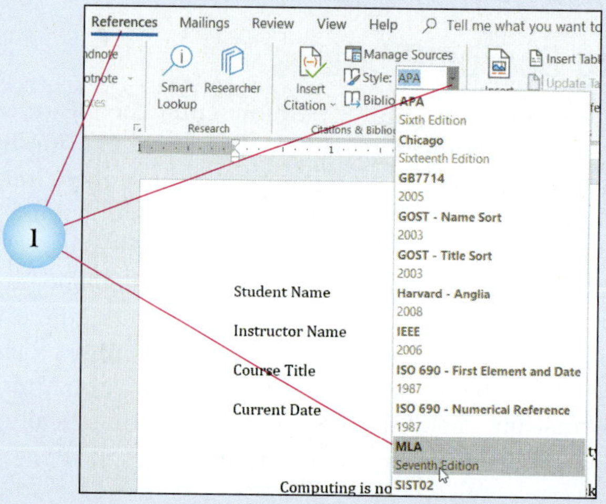

2. Select and then delete the text *(Jefferson)* at the end of the third paragraph of text (before the period that ends the sentence).
3. With the insertion point positioned between the word *laptop* and the period that ends the last sentence in the third paragraph, press the spacebar and then insert a citation by completing the following steps:
   a. Click the Insert Citation button in the Citations & Bibliography group and then click *Add New Source* at the drop-down list.

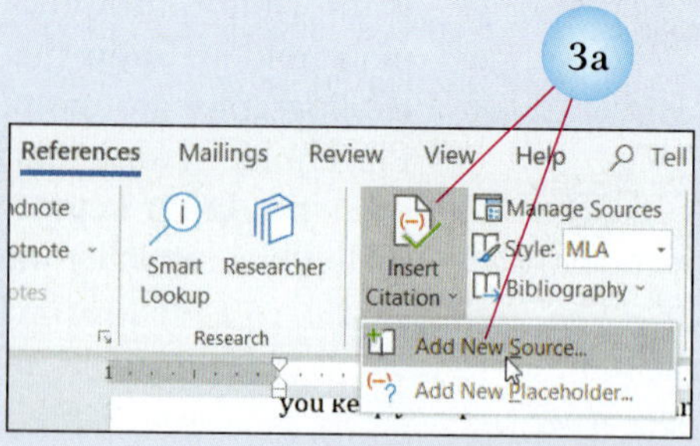

b. At the Create Source dialog box, if necessary, click the *Type of Source* option box arrow and then click *Journal Article* at the drop-down list.
c. In the *Bibliography Fields for MLA* section, click in the *Author* text box, type Gabe Jefferson, and then press the Tab key three times.
d. In the *Title* text box, type Securing Laptops and Mobile Devices and then press the Tab key.
e. In the *Journal Name* text box, type Computing Technologies and then press the Tab key.
f. In the *Year* text box, type 2021 and then press the Tab key.
g. In the *Pages* text box, type 8-10.
h. Click OK.

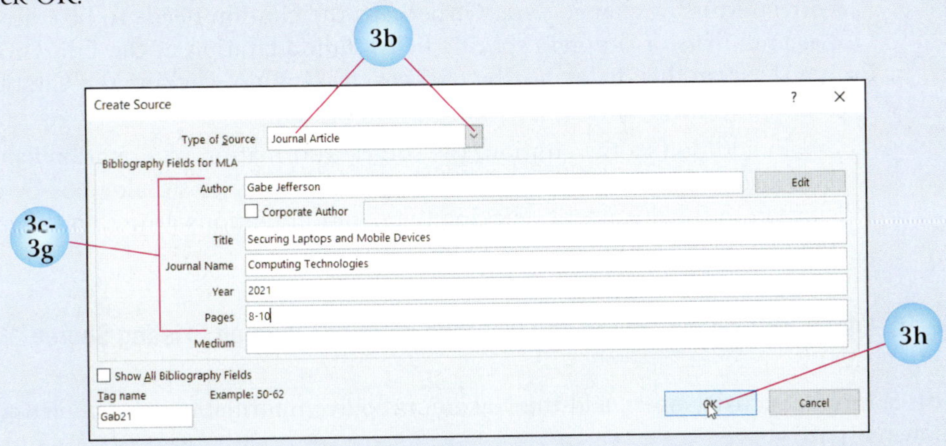

4. Select and then delete the text *(Lopez)* at the end of the fourth paragraph (near the top of the second page).
5. With the insertion point positioned between the word *data* and the period that ends the last sentence in the fourth paragraph, press the spacebar and then insert the following source information for a book. (At the Create Source dialog box, click the *Type of Source* option box arrow and then click *Book* at the drop-down list.)

Author	Rafael Lopez
Title	Technology World
Year	2021
City	Chicago
Publisher	Great Lakes

6. Select and then delete the text *(Nakamura)* in the last paragraph of text.
7. With the insertion point positioned between the word *security* and the period that ends the second sentence in the last paragraph of text, press the spacebar and the insert a citation placeholder by completing the following steps:
   a. Click the Insert Citation button.
   b. Click *Add New Placeholder* at the drop-down list.
   c. At the Placeholder Name dialog box, type Nakamura and then press the Enter key. (You will create the citation and fill in the source information in the next activity.)
8. Save **3-MobileSecurity**.

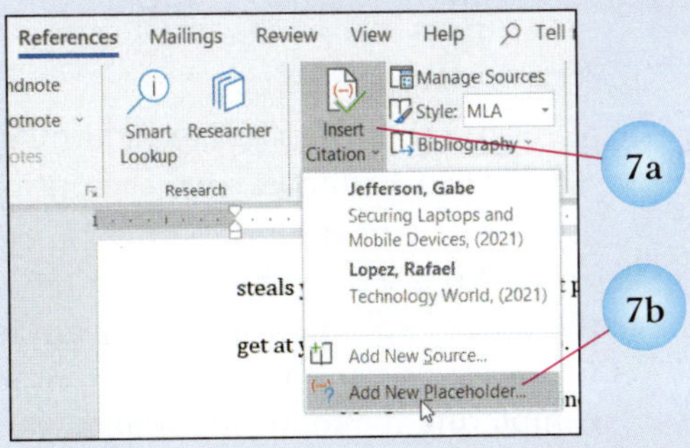

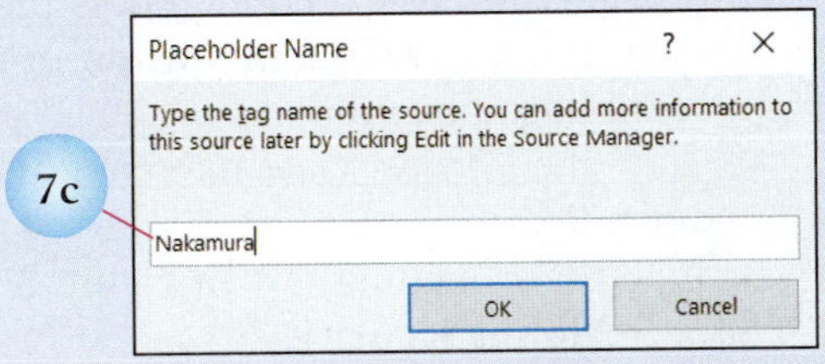

Check Your Work

Quick Steps

Insert Citation with Existing Source

1. Click References tab.
2. Click Insert Citation button.
3. Click source.

Inserting a Citation with an Existing Source

Once source information is inserted at the Create Source dialog box, Word automatically saves it. To insert a citation in a document for source information that has already been saved, click the Insert Citation button in the Citations & Bibliography group and then click the source at the drop-down list.

Tutorial

Editing a Citation and Source

Editing a Citation and Source

After source information is inserted in a document, it may need to be edited to correct errors or change data. Or perhaps the citation needs to be edited to add page numbers or suppress specific fields. Edit a citation at the Edit Citation dialog box. Display this dialog box by clicking the citation, clicking the Citation Options arrow, and then clicking the *Edit Citation* option.

In addition to the citation, the source information of a citation can be edited. Edit a source at the Edit Source dialog box. Display this dialog box by clicking the citation in the document, clicking the Citation Options arrow, and then clicking the *Edit Source* option.

Activity 3c Editing an Existing Source and Inserting a Citation with an Existing Source — Part 3 of 8

1. With **3-MobileSecurity** open, add the Nakamura source information by completing the following steps:
   a. Click the *Nakamura* citation in the document.
   b. Click the Citation Options arrow at the right of the selected citation.
   c. Click *Edit Source* at the drop-down list.
   d. At the Edit Source dialog box, click the *Type of Source* option box arrow and then click *Journal Article*.
   e. Type the following information in the specified text boxes:

Author	Janet Nakamura
Title	Computer Security
Journal Name	Technology Times
Year	2021
Pages	20-28
Volume	6

   (Display the *Volume* field by clicking the *Show All Bibliography Fields* check box and then scrolling down the options list.)
   f. Click OK to close the Edit Source dialog box.

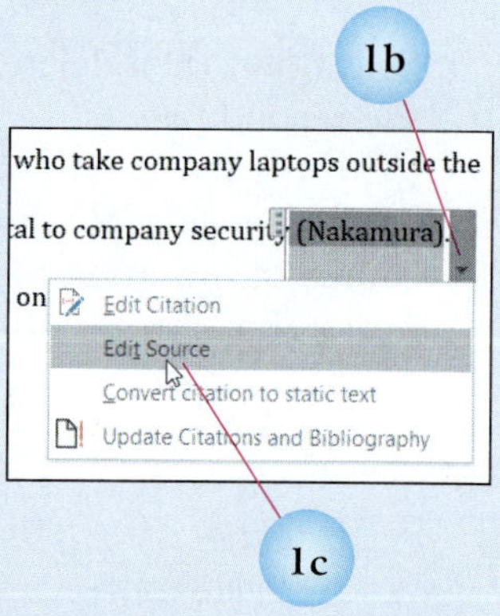

2. Press Ctrl + End to move the insertion point to the end of the document and then press the Enter key. Type the text shown in Figure 3.8 up to the citation text *(Jefferson)* and then insert a citation from an existing source by completing the following steps:
   a. If necessary, click the References tab.
   b. Click the Insert Citation button in the Citations & Bibliography group.
   c. Click the *Jefferson, Gabe* reference at the drop-down list.
   d. Type the remaining text in Figure 3.8.
3. Save **3-MobileSecurity**.

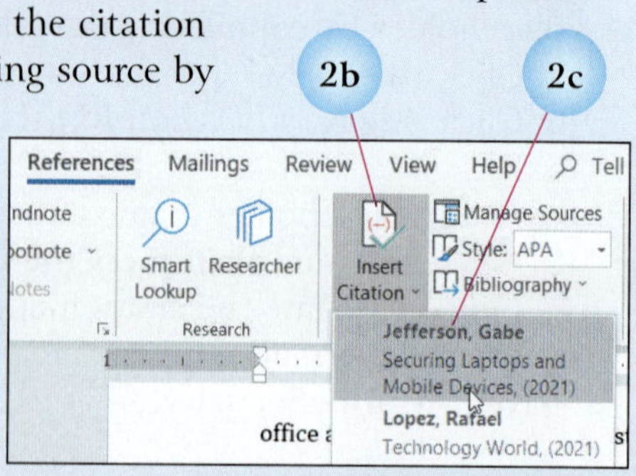

Check Your Work

Figure 3.8 Activity 3c

> If you travel and access the internet using a public location, you must be very careful not to expose private information (Jefferson). Anything you send over a public network can be accessed by malicious hackers and cybercriminals. Limit your use of online accounts to times when it is essential.

Quick Steps

Insert Page Number in Citation

1. Click citation to display placeholder.
2. Click Citation Options arrow.
3. Click *Edit Citation*.
4. Type page number(s).
5. Click OK.

Inserting Page Numbers in a Citation

If a direct quote from a source is included in a report, insert quotation marks around the text used from that source and insert in the citation the page number or numbers of the quoted material. To insert specific page numbers in a citation, click the citation to select the citation placeholder. Click the Citation Options arrow and then click *Edit Citation* at the drop-down list. At the Edit Citation dialog box, type the page number or numbers of the source from which the quote was borrowed and then click OK.

Tutorial

Managing Sources

Manage Sources

Quick Steps

Manage Sources

1. Click References tab.
2. Click Manage Sources button.
3. Edit, add, and/or delete sources.
4. Click Close.

Hint Click the Browse button in the Source Manager dialog box to select another master list.

Managing Sources

All the sources cited in the current document and in previous documents display in the Source Manager dialog box, as shown in Figure 3.9. Display this dialog box by clicking the References tab and then clicking the Manage Sources button in the Citations & Bibliography group. The *Master List* list box in the Source Manager dialog box displays all the sources that have been created in Word. The *Current List* list box displays all the sources used in the currently open document.

Use options at the Source Manager dialog box to copy a source from the master list to the current list, delete a source, edit a source, and create a new source. To copy a source from the master list to the current list, click the source in the *Master List* list box and then click the Copy button between the two list boxes. Click the Delete button to delete a source. Edit a source by clicking the source, clicking the Edit button, and then making changes at the Edit Source dialog box. Click the New button to create a new source at the Create Source dialog box.

If the *Master List* list box contains a large number of sources, search for a specific source by typing keywords in the *Search* text box. As text is typed, the list narrows to sources that match the text. After making all the changes at the Source Manager dialog box, click the Close button.

Figure 3.9 Source Manager Dialog Box

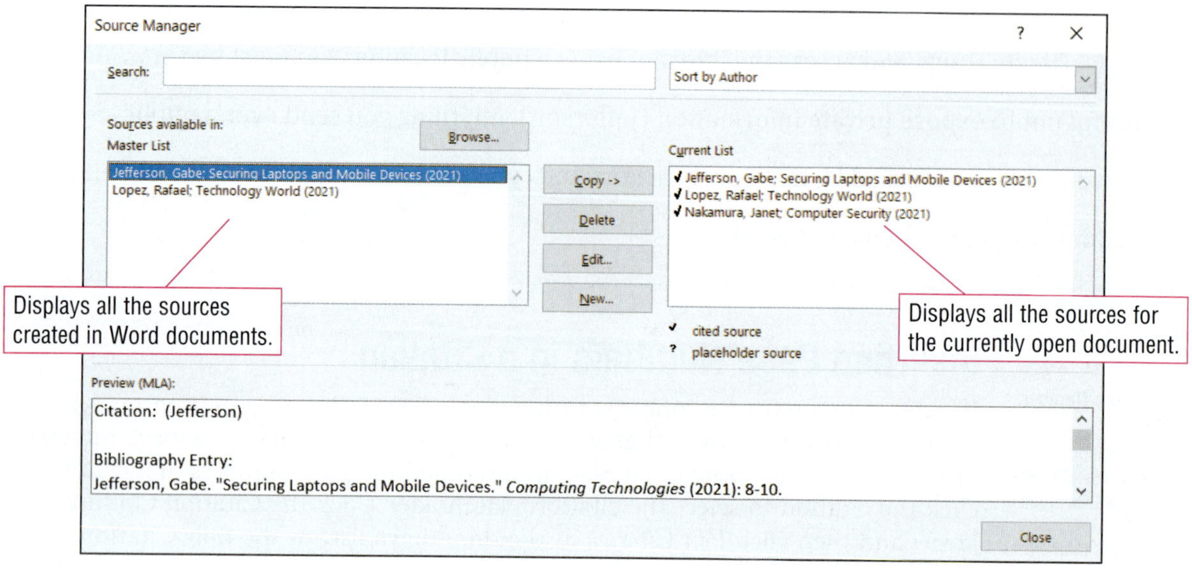

Activity 3d Managing Sources

Part 4 of 8

1. With **3-MobileSecurity** open, edit a source by completing the following steps:
   a. If necessary, click the References tab.
   b. Click the Manage Sources button in the Citations & Bibliography group.
   c. At the Source Manager dialog box, click the *Jefferson, Gabe* source entry in the *Master List* list box.
   d. Click the Edit button.

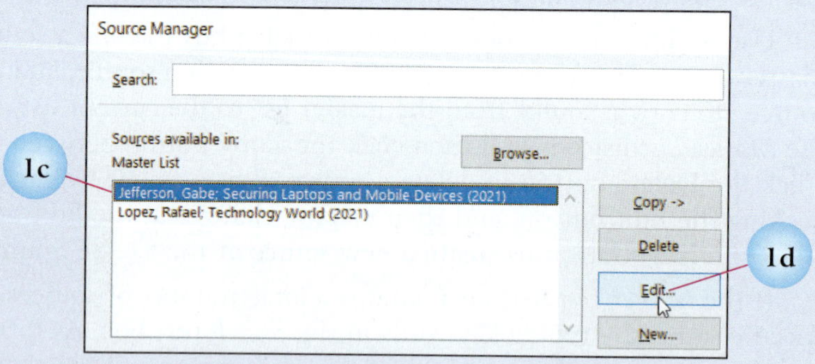

   e. At the Edit Source dialog box, delete the text in the *Author* text box and then type Gabriel Jackson.
   f. Click OK to close the Edit Source dialog box.
   g. At the message asking if you want to update both the master list and current list with the changes, click Yes.
   h. Click the Close button to close the Source Manager dialog box. (Notice that the last name changed in both of the Jefferson citations to reflect the edit.)
2. Delete a source by completing the following steps:
   a. Select and then delete the last sentence in the fourth paragraph in the document (the sentence beginning *If somebody steals your laptop*), including the citation.
   b. Click the Manage Sources button.

c. At the Source Manager dialog box, click the *Lopez, Rafael* entry in the *Current List* list box. (This entry will not contain a check mark because you deleted the citation from the document.)

d. Click the Delete button.

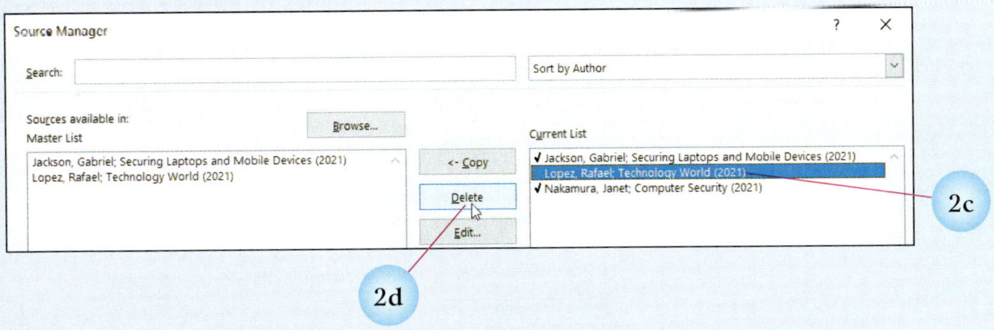

e. Click the Close button to close the Source Manager dialog box.

3. Create and insert a new source in the document by completing the following steps:

a. Click the Manage Sources button.

b. Click the New button in the Source Manager dialog box.

c. Type the following book information in the Create Source dialog box. (Change the *Type of Source* option to *Book*.)

Author	Georgia Miraldi
Title	Evolving Technology
Year	2021
City	Houston
Publisher	Rio Grande

d. Click OK to close the Create Source dialog box.

e. Click the Close button to close the Source Manager dialog box.

f. Position the insertion point one space after the period that ends the last sentence in the document and then type this sentence: "Be especially on guard when accessing your bank accounts, investment accounts, and retail accounts that store your credit card for purchases, and avoid entering your social security number" (Press the spacebar after typing the quotation mark that follows the word *number*.)

g. Insert a citation for Georgia Miraldi at the end of the sentence by clicking the Insert Citation button in the Citations & Bibliography group and then clicking *Miraldi, Georgia* at the drop-down list.

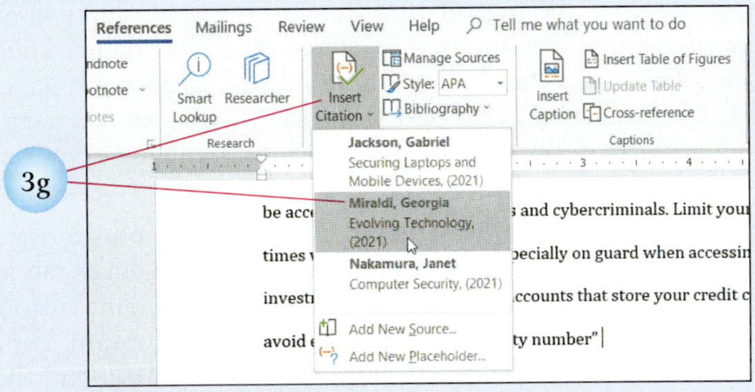

h. Type a period (.) to end the sentence.

4. To correctly acknowledge the direct quote from Georgia Miraldi, the page on which the quote appears in the book needs to be added. Insert the page number in the citation by completing the following steps:
   a. Click the *Miraldi* citation in the document.
   b. Click the Citation Options arrow at the right of the citation placeholder and then click *Edit Citation* at the drop-down list.

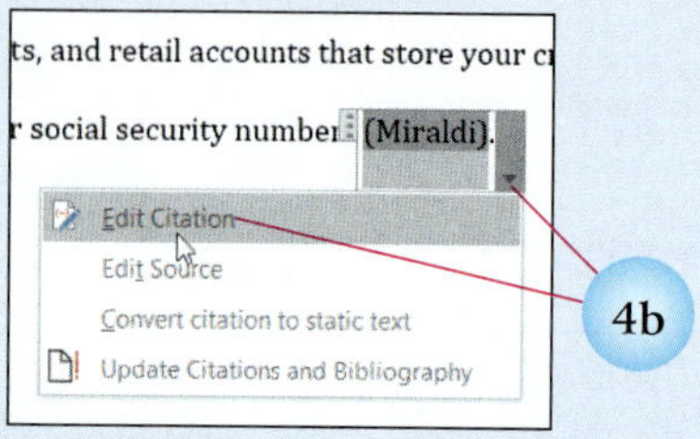

   c. At the Edit Citation dialog box, type 19 in the *Pages* text box.
   d. Click OK.

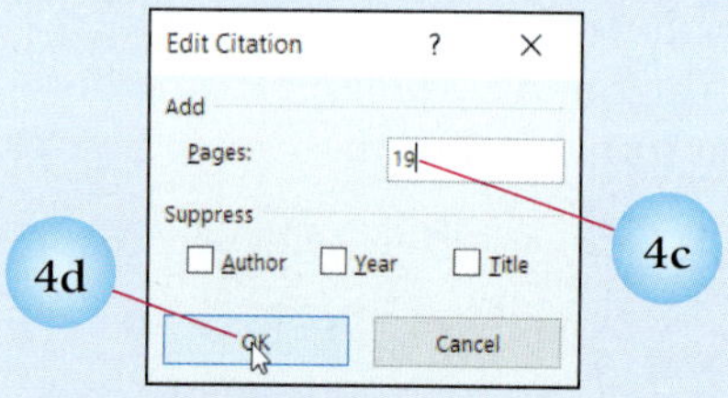

5. Save **3-MobileSecurity**.

Check Your Work

Tutorial

Inserting a Works Cited Page

Quick Steps

Insert Sources List

1. Insert new page at end of document.
2. Click References tab.
3. Click Bibliography button.
4. Click works cited, reference, or bibliography option.

Bibliography

Inserting a Sources List

If citations are included in a report or research paper, a sources list needs to be inserted as a separate page at the end of the document. A sources list is an alphabetical list of the books, journal articles, reports, and other sources referenced in the report or paper. Depending on the reference style applied to the document, the sources list may be a bibliography, a references page, or a works cited page.

When source information for citations is typed in the document, Word automatically saves the information from all the fields and compiles a sources list. The sources are alphabetized by the authors' last names and/or the titles of the works. To include the sources list in a report or research paper, insert a works cited page for a document formatted in MLA style, insert a references page for a document formatted in APA style, and insert a bibliography for a document formatted in Chicago style.

To insert a works cited page, move the insertion point to the end of the document and then insert a new page. Click the References tab and make sure the *Style* option box is set to *MLA*. Click the Bibliography button in the Citations & Bibliography group and then click the *Works Cited* option. For a document formatted in the APA style, click the Bibliography button and then click the *References* option.

Activity 3e Inserting a Works Cited Page

1. With **3-MobileSecurity** open, insert a works cited page at the end of the document by completing these steps:
   a. Press Ctrl + End to move the insertion point to the end of the document.
   b. Press Ctrl + Enter to insert a page break.
   c. If necessary, click the References tab.
   d. Click the Bibliography button in the Citations & Bibliography group.
   e. Click the *Works Cited* option in the *Built-In* section of the drop-down list.

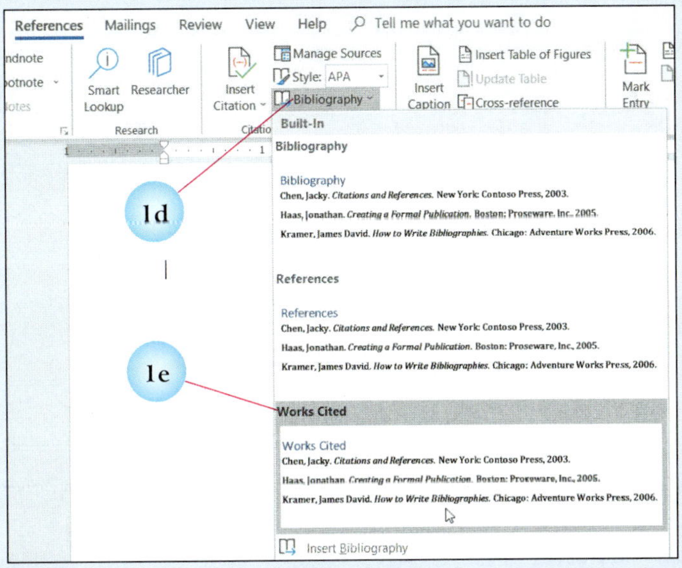

2. Format the works cited page to meet MLA requirements with the following changes:
   a. Select the *Works Cited* heading and all the entries and click the *No Spacing* style in the Styles group on the Home tab.
   b. Change the spacing to 2.0.
   c. Press Ctrl + T to format the works cited entries with a hanging indent.
   d. Center the title *Works Cited*.
3. Save **3-MobileSecurity**.

Check Your Work

Modifying and Updating a Sources List

Quick Steps
Update Sources List
1. Click in sources list.
2. Click Update Citations and Bibliography tab.

If a new source is inserted at the Source Manager dialog box or an existing source is modified, Word automatically inserts the source information in the sources list. If a new citation requires a new source to be added, Word will not automatically update the sources list. To update the sources list, click in the list and then click the Update Citations and Bibliography tab. The updated sources list reflects any changes made to the citations and source information in the document.

Activity 3f Modifying and Updating a Works Cited Page

Part 6 of 8

1. With **3-MobileSecurity** open, create a new source and citation by completing the following steps:
   a. Position the insertion point immediately left of the period that ends the last sentence in the first paragraph of the document (after the word *safer*).
   b. Press the spacebar.
   c. If necessary, click the References tab.
   d. Click the Insert Citation button in the Citations & Bibliography group and then click *Add New Source* at the drop-down list.
   e. At the Create Source dialog box, insert the following source information for a website. (Change the *Type of Source* option to *Web site* and click the *Show All Bibliography Fields* check box to display all the fields.)

Author	Chay Suong
Name of Web Page	Securing and Managing Mobile Devices
Year	2020
Month	April
Day	20
Year Accessed	(type current year in numbers)
Month Accessed	(type current month in letters)
Day Accessed	(type current day in numbers)
URL	https://ppi-edu.net/publishing

   f. Click OK to close the Create Source dialog box.
2. Update the works cited page to include the new source by completing the following steps:
   a. Press Ctrl + End to move the insertion point to the end of the document.
   b. Click in the works cited text.
   c. Click the Update Citations and Bibliography tab above the heading *Works Cited*. (Notice that the updated sources list includes the Suong reference.)
3. Save **3-MobileSecurity**.

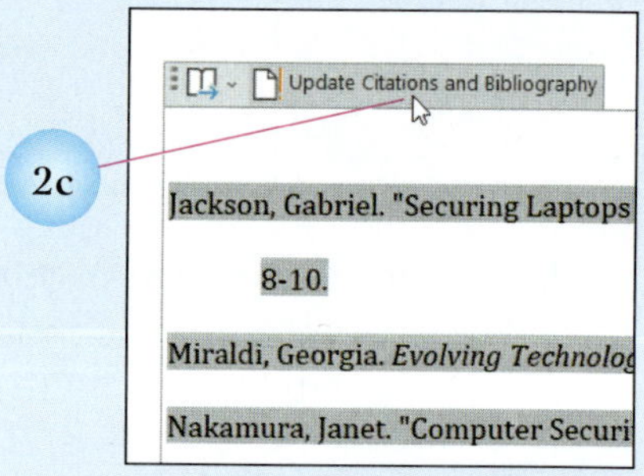

Check Your Work

Formatting a Sources List

The formatting applied by Word to the sources list may need to be changed to meet the specific guidelines of MLA, APA, or Chicago style. For example, MLA and APA styles require the following formats for a sources list:

- Begin the sources list on a separate page after the last page of text in the report.
- Include the title *Works Cited*, *References*, or *Bibliography* at the top of the page and center it on the width of the page.
- Use the same font for the sources list as for the main document.
- Double-space between and within entries.
- Begin each entry at the left margin and format subsequent lines in each entry with a hanging indent.
- Alphabetize the entries.

The general formatting requirements for Chicago style are similar except that single spacing is applied within entries and double spacing is applied between entries.

Activity 3g Formatting a Works Cited Page

Part 7 of 8

1. With **3-MobileSecurity** open, notice that the works cited entries are set in 12-point Cambria and a hanging indent is applied to the entries.
2. Select the four reference entries below the *Works Cited* title, click the Home tab, and then click the *No Spacing* style in the Styles group.
3. With the four entries still selected, press Ctrl + 2 to apply double spacing to the entries and then press Ctrl + T to apply a hanging indent to the entries. (Applying the *No Spacing* style in Step 2 removed the hanging indent.)
4. Save and then print **3-MobileSecurity**.

Check Your Work

Choosing a Citation Style

Quick Steps

Change Citation Style

1. Click References tab.
2. Click *Style* option box arrow.
3. Click a style.

Different subjects and different instructors or professors may require different formats for citing references. The style for reference citations can be changed before beginning a new document or while working in an existing document. To change the style of citations in an existing document, click the References tab, click the *Style* option box arrow, and then click the style at the drop-down list.

Activity 3h Choosing a Citation Style

Part 8 of 8

1. With **3-MobileSecurity** open, change the document and works cited page from MLA style to APA style by completing the following steps:
   a. Click the References tab.
   b. Click the *Style* option box arrow in the Citations & Bibliography group and then click *APA* at the drop-down list.

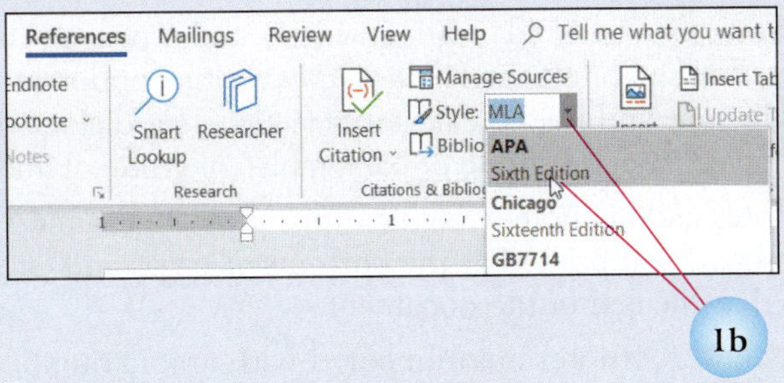

   c. Notice the changes made to the works cited entries.
   d. Scroll up the document and notice the changes to the citations.
   e. Press Ctrl + End to move the insertion point to the end of the document.
   f. Change the title *Works Cited* to *References*.
2. Save the document and then print only the references page.
3. Close **3-MobileSecurity**.
4. Display a blank document, click the References tab, change the style to *MLA*, and then close the document without saving it.

Check Your Work

Chapter Summary

- Text that appears at the top of every page is called a *header*; text that appears at the bottom of every page is called a *footer*. Insert predesigned headers and footers in a document or create custom headers and footers.
- To create a custom header, click the Header button in the Header & Footer group on the Insert tab and then click *Edit Header*. At the Header pane, insert elements or text. Complete similar steps to create a custom footer.
- Use buttons in the Insert group on the Header & Footer Tools Design tab to insert elements such as the date and time, Quick Parts, and images into a header or footer.
- Word inserts headers and footers 0.5 inch from the edge of the page. Reposition a header or footer with buttons in the Position group on the Header & Footer Tools Design tab.
- A unique header or footer can be created on the first page; a header or footer can be omitted on the first page; different headers or footers can be created for odd and even pages; or different headers or footers can be created for sections in a document. Use options in the Options group on the Header & Footer Tools Design tab to specify the type of header or footer to be created.
- Each section in a document is linked to the other sections in the document. To specify that a header or footer prints only on the pages within a section and not the previous sections, click the Link to Previous button in the Navigation group on the Header & Footer Tools Design tab to deactivate the button.
- Insert page numbers in a document in a header or footer or with options at the Page Number button in the Header & Footer group on the Insert tab.
- Format page numbers with options at the Page Number Format dialog box.
- To print sections or specific pages within a section, use the *Pages* text box at the Print backstage area. When specifying sections and pages, use the letter *s* before a section number and the letter *p* before a page number.
- Word attempts to avoid creating widows and orphans when inserting soft page breaks. Turn on or off the *Widow/Orphan control* option at the Paragraph dialog box with the Line and Page Breaks tab selected. This dialog box also contains options for keeping a paragraph, group of paragraphs, or group of lines together.
- Footnotes and endnotes provide explanatory notes and source citations. Footnotes are inserted and printed at the bottoms of pages and endnotes are inserted and printed at the end of the document.
- By default, footnotes are numbered with arabic numbers and endnotes are numbered with lowercase roman numerals.
- Move, copy, or delete a footnote/endnote reference number in a document and all the other footnotes/endnotes automatically renumber.
- Delete a footnote or endnote by selecting the reference number and then pressing the Delete key.
- Consider using in-text citations to acknowledge sources in a paper. Commonly used citation and reference styles include those of the American Psychological Association (APA), Modern Language Association (MLA), and *Chicago Manual of Style* (Chicago).
- Insert a citation using the Insert Citation button in the Citations & Bibliography group on the References tab. Specify source information at the Create Source dialog box.
- Insert a citation placeholder in a document if the source information will be added at a later time.

- Insert a citation in a document for source information that has already been saved by clicking the Insert Citation button in the Citations & Bibliography group and then clicking the source at the drop-down list.
- Edit a source at the Edit Source dialog box. Display this dialog box by clicking the source citation in the document, clicking the Citation Options arrow, and then clicking *Edit Source* at the drop-down list. Another option is to display the Source Manager dialog box, click the source to be edited, and then click the Edit button.
- Copy, delete, and edit sources and create new sources with options at the Source Manager dialog box. Display this dialog box by clicking the Manage Sources button in the Citations & Bibliography group on the References tab.
- Insert a sources list, such as a works cited page, references page, or bibliography, at the end of the document on a separate page. To do so, use the Bibliography button in the Citations & Bibliography group on the References tab.
- To update a sources list, click in the list and then click the Update Citations and Bibliography tab.
- The MLA and APA styles require specific formatting for a list of sources. Refer to page 94 for a list of formatting requirements.
- Change the reference style with the *Style* option box in the Citations & Bibliography group on the References tab.

Commands Review

FEATURE	RIBBON TAB, GROUP	BUTTON, OPTION	KEYBOARD SHORTCUT
bibliography	References, Citations & Bibliography		
create footer	Insert, Header & Footer	, *Edit Footer*	
create header	Insert, Header & Footer	, *Edit Header*	
citation style	References, Citations & Bibliography		
Create Source dialog box	References, Citations & Bibliography	, *Add New Source*	
endnote	References, Footnotes		Alt + Ctrl + D
footer	Insert, Header & Footer		
footnote	References, Footnotes		Alt + Ctrl + F
header	Insert, Header & Footer		
next footnote	References, Footnotes		
page number	Insert, Header & Footer		
show notes	References, Footnotes		
Source Manager dialog box	References, Citations & Bibliography		

Microsoft®

Word

CHAPTER 4

Creating Specialized Tables and Navigating in a Document

Performance Objectives

Upon successful completion of Chapter 4, you will be able to:

1. Insert a table of contents
2. Number the table of contents page
3. Navigate using a table of contents
4. Customize, update, or remove a table of contents
5. Assign levels to table of content entries
6. Mark table of contents entries as fields
7. Insert, update, or delete a table of figures
8. Create and customize captions for figures
9. Navigate in a document using the Navigation pane, bookmarks, hyperlinks, and cross-references
10. Insert hyperlinks to a location in the same document, a different document, a file in another program, or an email address

A book, textbook, report, or manuscript often includes sections such as a table of contents and a table of figures. Creating these sections manually can be tedious. However, using Word's automated features, these sections can be created quickly and easily. In this chapter, you will learn how to mark text for a table of contents and a table of figures and how to insert captions. You will also learn how to insert hyperlinks, bookmarks, and cross-references to allow for more efficient navigation within a document.

Data Files

Before beginning chapter work, copy the WL2C4 folder to your storage medium and then make WL2C4 the active folder.

The online course includes additional training and assessment resources.

Activity 1 Create a Table of Contents for a Computer Interface Report — 2 Parts

You will open a report on computer interfaces, insert a section break, insert the table of contents in the document, and then number the table of contents page. You will also customize and update the table of contents.

Creating a Table of Contents

Table of Contents

A table of contents appears at the beginning of a book, manuscript, report, or other multipage document. It lists chapters, sections, or subsections within a document along with the page numbers where each can be found, and contains headings and subheadings with page numbers. Create a table of contents using the Table of Contents button in the Table of Contents group on the References tab. Identify the text to be included in a table of contents by applying built-in heading styles or custom styles, assigning levels, or marking text.

Applying Styles

Hint If you apply heading styles to the text in a document, you can easily insert a table of contents later.

Word can automatically generate a table of contents using the headings in a document. Before inserting an automatic table of contents, apply styles to the main headings and subheadings in the document using the built-in styles in the Styles group on the Home tab. Text with the Heading 1 style applied will be used for the first level of the table of contents, while text with the Heading 2 style applied will be used for the second level, and so on.

Inserting a Table of Contents

Tutorial

Inserting a Table of Contents

Quick Steps

Insert Table of Contents

1. Apply heading styles.
2. Click References tab.
3. Click Table of Contents button.
4. Click option at drop-down list.

Page Number

Quick Steps

Number Table of Contents Page

1. Click Insert tab.
2. Click Page Number button.
3. Click *Format Page Numbers*.
4. Change number format to lowercase roman numerals.
5. Click OK.

After applying styles to the headings, insert the table of contents in the document. To do this, position the insertion point at the beginning of the document where the table of contents is to appear, click the References tab, click the Table of Contents button, and then click the specific option at the drop-down list.

Numbering the Table of Contents Page

Generally, the page or pages containing the table of contents are numbered with lowercase roman numerals (*i*, *ii*, *iii*). Format the page numbers as lowercase roman numerals at the Page Number Format dialog box, shown in Figure 4.1. Display this dialog box by clicking the Insert tab, clicking the Page Number button in the Header & Footer group, and then clicking *Format Page Numbers* at the drop-down list.

The first page of text in the main document, which usually comes immediately after the table of contents, should begin with arabic number 1. To change from roman to arabic page numbers within the same document, separate the table of contents from the first page of the document with a section break that begins a new page.

Figure 4.1 Page Number Format Dialog Box

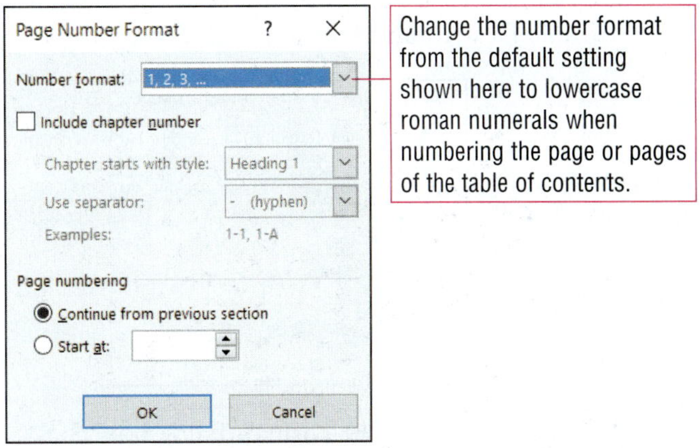

Navigating Using a Table of Contents

Hint You can use a table of contents to navigate quickly in a document and to get an overview of the topics it covers.

When a table of contents is inserted in a document, each entry automatically becomes a hyperlink that can be used to navigate within the document.

To navigate in a document using the table of contents, click in the table of contents to select it. Position the mouse pointer over an entry and a ScreenTip displays with the path and file name as well as the text *Ctrl+Click to follow link*. Press and hold down the Ctrl key, click the left mouse button, and then release the Ctrl key to go directly to the page where the content is located.

Activity 1a Inserting a Table of Contents

Part 1 of 2

1. Open **AIReport** and then save it with the name **4-AIReport**. (This document contains headings with heading styles applied.)
2. Position the insertion point immediately left of the first *N* in *NATURAL INTERFACE APPLICATIONS* and then insert a section break by completing the following steps:
   a. Click the Layout tab.
   b. Click the Breaks button in the Page Setup group.
   c. Click the *Next Page* option in the *Section Breaks* section.
3. With the insertion point positioned below the section break, insert page numbers and change the beginning number to *1* by completing the following steps:
   a. Click the Insert tab.
   b. Click the Page Number button in the Header & Footer group, point to *Bottom of Page*, and then click *Plain Number 2*.

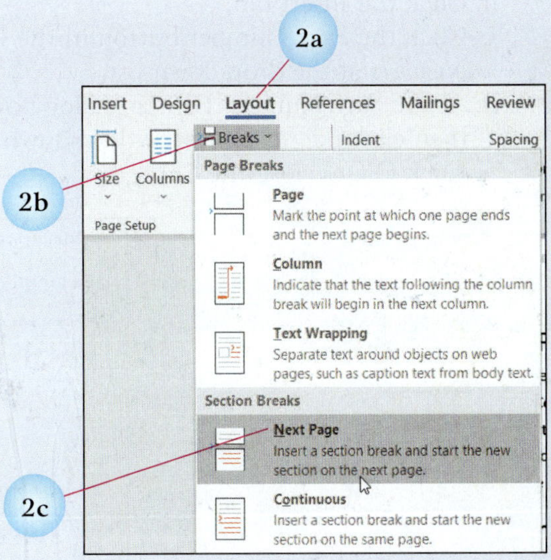

c. Click the Page Number button in the Header & Footer group on the Header & Footer Tools Design tab and then click *Format Page Numbers* at the drop-down list.

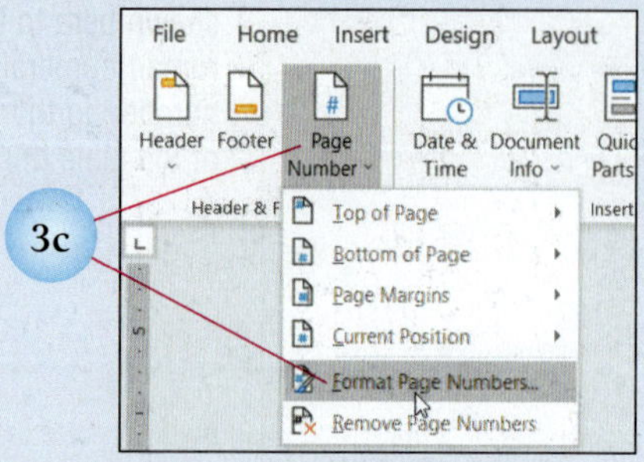

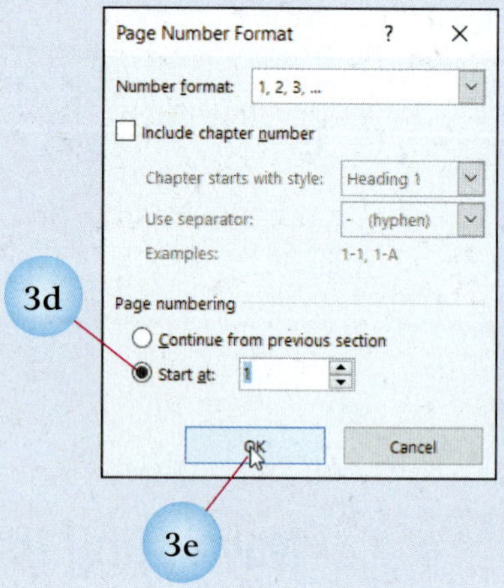

d. At the Page Number Format dialog box, click *Start at* in the *Page numbering* section. (This inserts *1* in the *Start at* measurement box.)
e. Click OK to close the Page Number Format dialog box.
f. Double-click in the document to make it active.

4. Insert a table of contents at the beginning of the document by completing the following steps:
a. Press Ctrl + Home to move the insertion point to the beginning of the document.
b. Click the References tab.
c. Click the Table of Contents button in the Table of Contents group and then click the *Automatic Table 1* option in the *Built-In* section of the drop-down list.

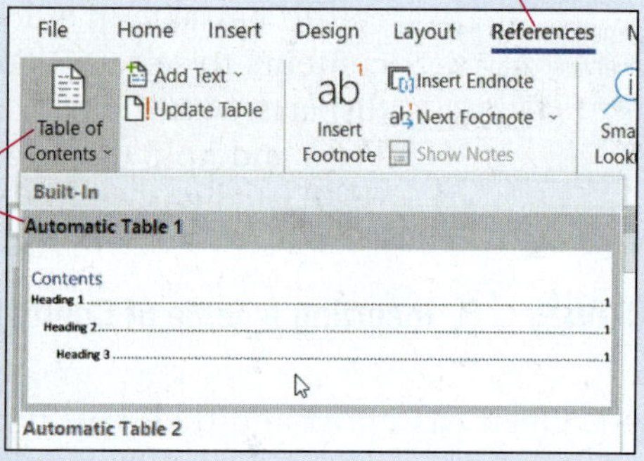

5. Insert a page number on the table of contents page by completing the following steps:
a. Scroll up the document and then click in the heading *Contents*.
b. Click the Insert tab.
c. Click the Page Number button in the Header & Footer group and then click *Format Page Numbers* at the drop-down list.
d. At the Page Number Format dialog box, click the *Number format* option box arrow and then click *i, ii, iii, …* at the drop-down list.
e. Click OK to close the dialog box.

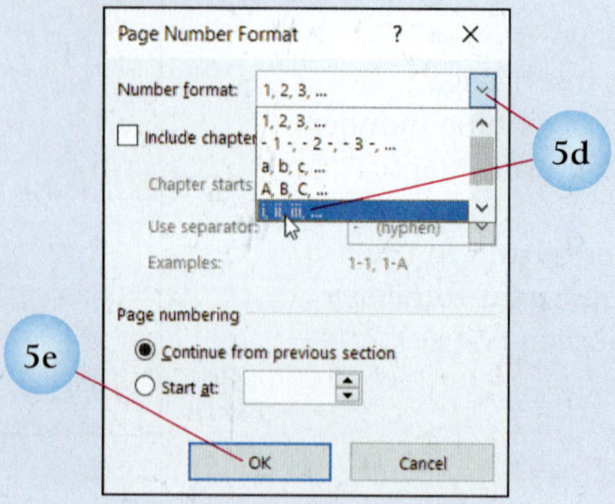

6. Navigate in the document using the table of contents by completing the following steps:
   a. Click in the table of contents.
   b. Position the mouse pointer on the entry *Virtual Reality*, press and hold down the Ctrl key, click the left mouse button, and then release the Ctrl key. (This moves the insertion point to the beginning of the heading *Virtual Reality* in the document.)
   c. Press Ctrl + Home to move the insertion point to the beginning of the document.
7. Save **4-AIReport** and then print only page 1 (the table of contents page).

Check Your Work

Tutorial

Customizing and Updating a Table of Contents

Customizing a Table of Contents

Customize an existing table of contents in a document with options at the Table of Contents dialog box, shown in Figure 4.2. Display this dialog box by clicking the Table of Contents button on the References tab and then clicking *Custom Table of Contents* at the drop-down list.

At the Table of Contents dialog box, a sample table of contents appears in the *Print Preview* section. Change the table of contents format by clicking the *Formats* option box arrow in the *General* section. At the drop-down list, click a format. When a different format is selected, that format displays in the *Print Preview* section.

Page numbers in a table of contents will display after the text or aligned at the right margin, depending on what option is selected. Page number alignment can also be specified with the *Right align page numbers* option. The possible number of levels in the contents list that appears in a table of contents depends on the number of heading levels in the document. Control the number of levels that display with the *Show levels* measurement box in the *General* section. Tab leaders help guide readers' eyes from the table of contents heading to the page number. The default tab leader is a period or dotted line leader. To choose a different leader, click the *Tab leader* option box arrow and then click to select a dotted line, dashed line, or solid underline at the drop-down list.

Figure 4.2 Table of Contents Dialog Box

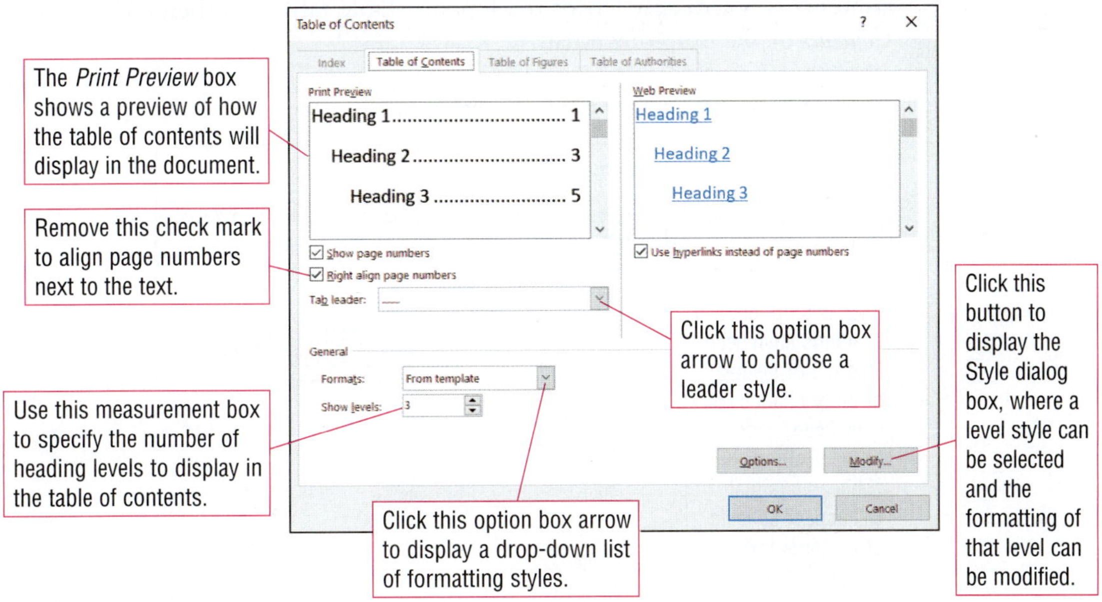

Word automatically formats the entries in a table of contents as hyperlinks and inserts page numbers. Each hyperlink can be used to move to a specific location in the document.

The *Use hyperlinks instead of page numbers* check box in the Web Preview section of the Table of Contents dialog box contains a check mark by default. With this option active, if the document is posted to the web, readers will only need to click the hyperlink to view specific content in the document. If the document is viewed in a web browser or the table of contents is used to navigate in the document, page numbers are not necessary and can be removed from the table of contents by removing the check mark from the *Show page numbers* check box at the Table of Contents dialog box.

If changes are made to the options at the Table of Contents dialog box, clicking OK will cause a message to display asking if the selected table of contents should be replaced. At this message, click Yes.

Updating a Table of Contents

Update Table

Quick Steps

Update Table of Contents

1. Click in table of contents.
2. Click References tab.
3. Click Update Table button, click Update Table tab, or press F9.
4. Click *Update page numbers only* or *Update entire table.*
5. Click OK.

Remove Table of Contents

1. Click References tab.
2. Click Table of Contents button.
3. Click *Remove Table of Contents.*

OR

1. Click in table of contents.
2. Click Table of Contents tab.
3. Click *Remove Table of Contents.*

If headings or other text in a document is deleted, moved, or edited after the table of contents is inserted, the table of contents will need to be updated. To do this, click in the current table of contents and then click the Update Table button in the Table of Contents group, click the Update Table tab, or press the F9 function key (the Update Field key). At the Update Table of Contents dialog box, shown in Figure 4.3, click *Update page numbers only* if changes were made that only affect page numbers or click *Update entire table* if changes were made to the headings or subheadings in the document. Click OK or press the Enter key to close the dialog box.

Removing a Table of Contents

Remove a table of contents from a document by clicking the Table of Contents button on the References tab and then clicking *Remove Table of Contents* at the drop-down list. Another way to remove a table of contents is to click in the table of contents, click the Table of Contents tab in the upper left corner of the table of contents (immediately left of the Update Table tab), and then click *Remove Table of Contents* at the drop-down list.

Figure 4.3 Update Table of Contents Dialog Box

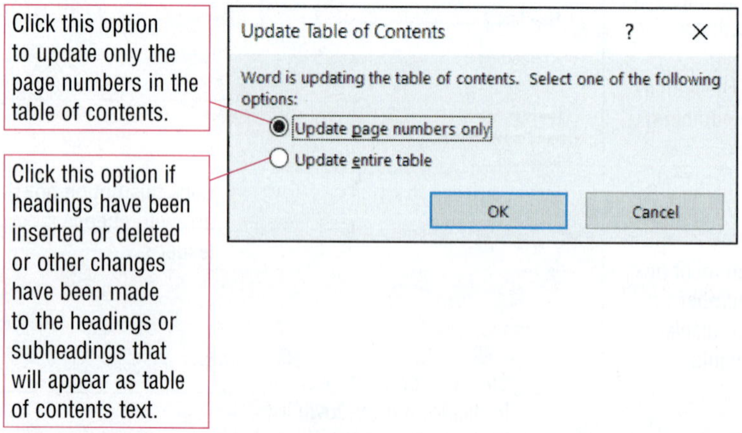

Activity 1b Customizing and Updating a Table of Contents

1. With **4-AIReport** open and the insertion point positioned at the beginning of the document, apply a different formatting style to the table of contents by completing the following steps:
   a. Click the References tab, click the Table of Contents button, and then click *Custom Table of Contents* at the drop-down list.
   b. At the Table of Contents dialog box with the Table of Contents tab selected, click the *Formats* option box arrow in the *General* section and then click *Formal* at the drop-down list.
   c. Click the *Tab leader* option box arrow and then click the solid line option (bottom option) at the drop-down list.
   d. Click the *Show levels* measurement box down arrow to change the number to *2*.
   e. Click OK to close the dialog box.

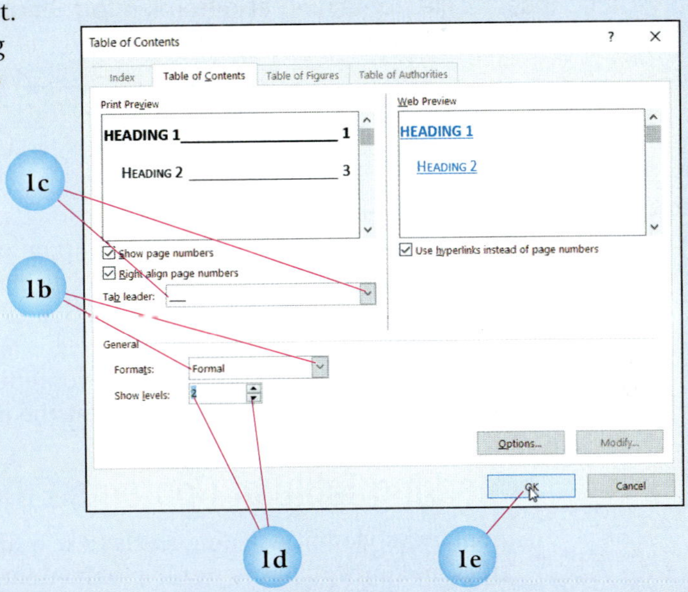

   f. At the message asking if you want to replace the selected table of contents, click the Yes button.
2. Use the table of contents to move the insertion point to the beginning of the heading *Navigation* at the bottom of page 3.
3. Press Ctrl + Enter to insert a page break.
4. Update the table of contents by completing the following steps:
   a. Press Ctrl + Home and then click in the table of contents.
   b. Click the Update Table tab.
   c. At the Update Table of Contents dialog box, make sure *Update page numbers only* is selected and then click OK.

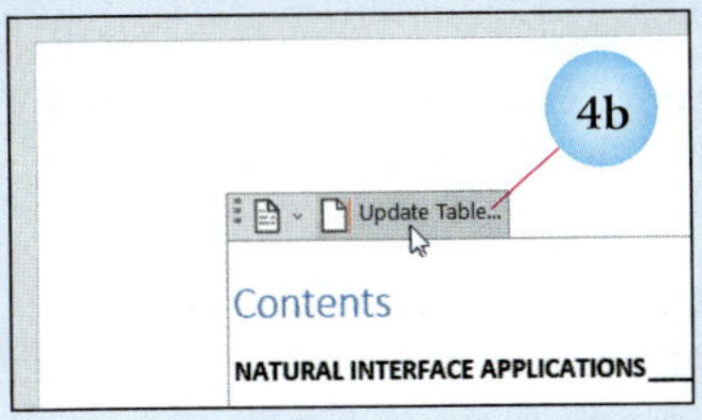

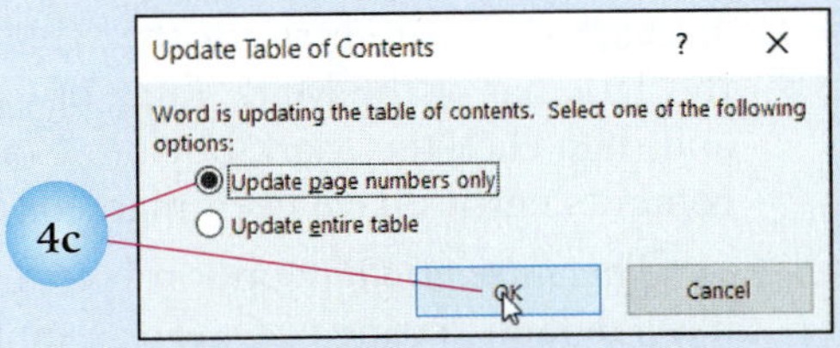

5. Save the document, print only the table of contents page, and then close **4-AIReport**.

Check Your Work

Activity 2 Mark Text for and Insert a Table of Contents in a Company Handbook — 2 Parts

You will open a document that contains employee pay and evaluation information, mark text as table of contents fields, and then insert a table of contents. You will also insert a file containing additional information on employee classifications and then update the table of contents.

Tutorial

Assigning Levels to Table of Contents Entries

Add Text

Assigning Levels to Table of Contents Entries

Another method for identifying text for a table of contents is to use the Add Text button in the Table of Contents group on the References tab. Click this button and a drop-down list of level options displays. Click a level for the currently selected text and a heading style is applied to the text. For example, click the *Level 2* option and the Heading 2 style is applied to the selected text. After specifying levels, insert the table of contents by clicking the Table of Contents button and then clicking an option at the drop-down list.

Marking Table of Contents Entries as Fields

Applying styles or assigning levels to text applies specific formatting. To identify titles and/or headings for a table of contents without applying formatting, mark each title or heading as a field entry. To do this, select the text to be included in the table of contents and then press Alt + Shift + O. This displays the Mark Table of Contents Entry dialog box, shown in Figure 4.4.

In the dialog box, the selected text displays in the *Entry* text box. Specify the text level using the *Level* measurement box and then click the Mark button. This turns on the display of nonprinting characters in the document and also inserts a field code immediately after the selected text.

For example, when the title is selected in Activity 2a, the following code is inserted immediately after the title *COMPENSATION*: { TC "COMPENSATION" \f C \l "1" }. The Mark Table of Contents Entry dialog box also remains open. To mark the next entry for the table of contents, select the text and then click the Title bar of the Mark Table of Contents Entry dialog box. Specify the level and then click the Mark button. Continue in this manner until all the table of contents entries have been marked.

The *Table identifier* option box at the Mark Table of Contents Entry dialog box has a default setting of *C*. (For a table of figures discussed later in this chapter, the table identifier is *F*.) To create more than one table of contents for a document,

Figure 4.4 Mark Table of Contents Entry Dialog Box

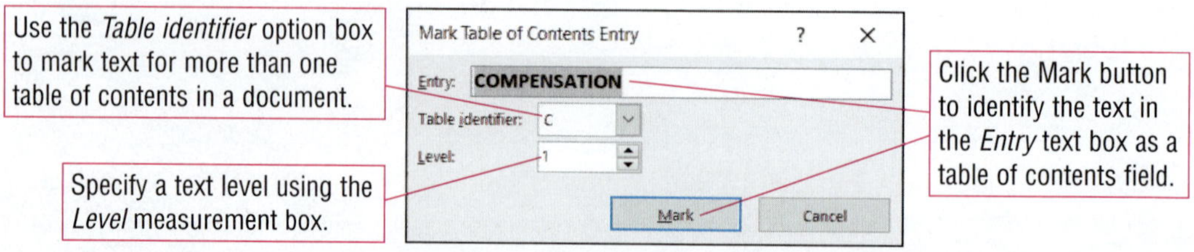

mark text with a specific table identifer and then use that identifer when inserting the table of contents.

If the table of contents entries are marked as fields, the *Table entry fields* option will need to be activated when inserting the table of contents. To do this, display the Table of Contents dialog box and then click the Options button. At the Table of Contents Options dialog box, shown in Figure 4.5, click the *Table entry fields* check box to insert a check mark and then click OK.

Figure 4.5 Table of Contents Options Dialog Box

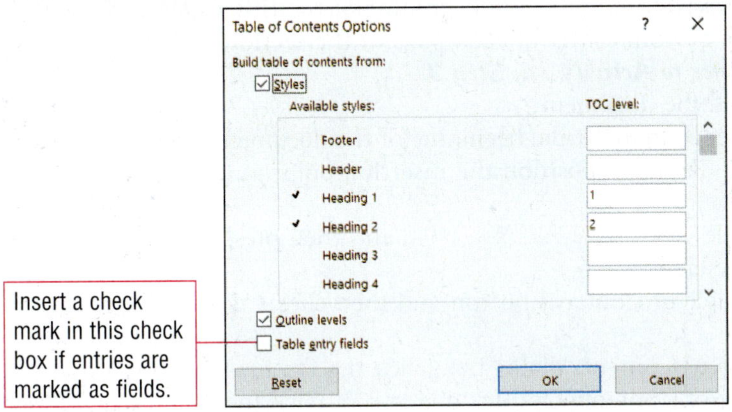

Activity 2a Marking Headings as Fields

Part 1 of 2

1. Open **CompEval** and then save it with the name **4-CompEval**.
2. Position the insertion point immediately left of the *C* in *COMPENSATION* and then insert a section break that begins a new page by clicking the Layout tab, clicking the Breaks button in the Page Setup group, and then clicking the *Next Page* option.
3. Mark the titles and headings as fields for insertion in a table of contents by completing the following steps:
   a. Select the title *COMPENSATION*.
   b. Press Alt + Shift + O.
   c. At the Mark Table of Contents Entry dialog box, make sure the *Level* measurement box is set at *1* and then click the Mark button. (This turns on the display of nonprinting characters.)
   d. Click in the document, scroll down, and then select the title *EVALUATION*.
   e. Click the Mark Table of Contents Entry dialog box Title bar and then click the Mark button.
   f. Click in the document, scroll up, and then select the heading *Rate of Pay*.
   g. Click the dialog box Title bar and then click the *Level* measurement box up arrow in the Mark Table of Contents Entry dialog box to display *2*.
   h. Click the Mark button.

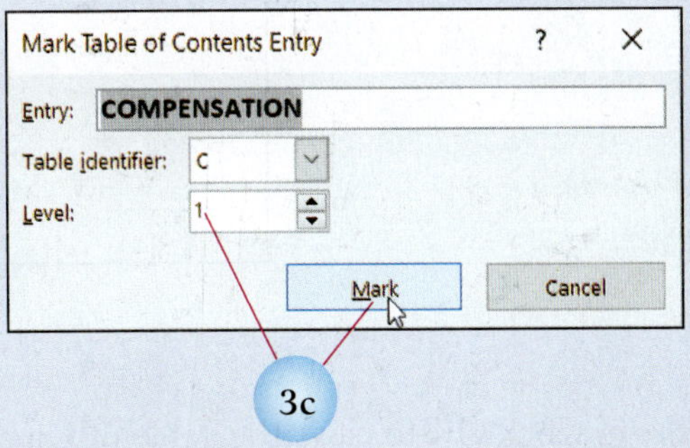

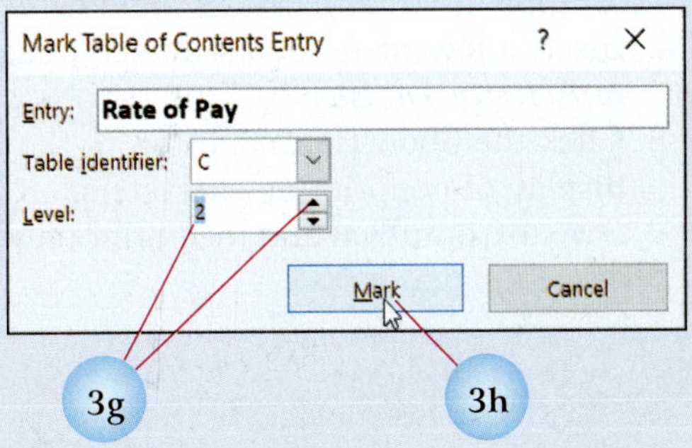

i. Mark the following headings as level 2:

Direct Deposit Option
Pay Progression
Overtime
Work Performance Standards
Performance Evaluation
Employment Records

j. Click the Close button to close the Mark Table of Contents Entry dialog box.

4. Position the insertion point at the beginning of the title *COMPENSATION*. Insert a page number at the bottom center of each page of the section and change the starting number to *1*. ***Hint: Refer to Activity 1a, Step 3.***
5. Double-click in the document.
6. Insert a table of contents at the beginning of the document by completing the following steps:
   a. Press Ctrl + Home to position the insertion point at the beginning of the document (on the new page).
   b. Type the title TABLE OF CONTENTS and then press the Enter key.
   c. Click the References tab.
   d. Click the Table of Contents button and then click *Custom Table of Contents* at the drop-down list.
   e. At the Table of Contents dialog box, click the Options button.
   f. At the Table of Contents Options dialog box, click the *Table entry fields* check box to insert a check mark.
   g. Click OK to close the Table of Contents Options dialog box.

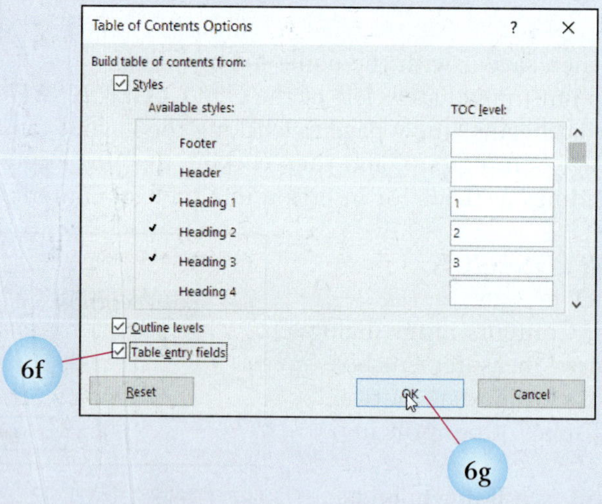

   h. Click OK to close the Table of Contents dialog box.
   i. Apply bold formatting to and center the heading *TABLE OF CONTENTS*.
7. Insert a lowercase roman numeral page number on the table of contents page. ***Hint: Refer to Activity 1a, Step 5.***
8. Click the Show/Hide ¶ button in the Paragraph group on the Home tab to turn off the display of nonprinting characters.
9. Save **4-CompEval** and then print only page 1 (the table of contents page).

Check Your Work

If additional information is inserted in a document with headings marked as fields, the table of contents can be easily updated. To do this, insert the text and then mark the text with options at the Mark Table of Contents Entry dialog box. Click in the table of contents and then click the Update Table tab. At the Update Table of Contents dialog box, click the *Update entire table* option and then click OK.

Activity 2b Updating an Entire Table of Contents

Part 2 of 2

1. With **4-CompEval** open, insert a file into the document by completing the following steps:
   a. Press Ctrl + End to move the insertion point to the end of the document.
   b. Press Ctrl + Enter to insert a page break.
   c. Click the Insert tab.
   d. Click the Object button arrow in the Text group and then click *Text from File* at the drop-down list.
   e. At the Insert File dialog box, navigate to your WL2C4 folder and then double-click ***PosClass***.

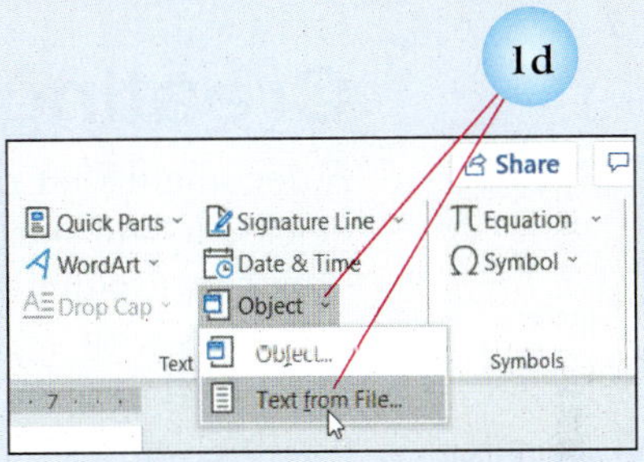

2. Select and then mark text for inclusion in the table of contents by completing the following steps:
   a. Select the title *POSITION CLASSIFICATION*.
   b. Press Alt + Shift + O.
   c. At the Mark Table of Contents Entry dialog box, make sure that *1* displays in the *Level* measurement box and then click the Mark button.
   d. Click the Close button to close the Mark Table of Contents Entry dialog box.
3. Update the table of contents by completing the following steps:
   a. Select the entire table of contents (excluding the title).
   b. Click the References tab.
   c. Click the Update Table button in the Table of Contents group.
   d. At the Update Table of Contents dialog box, click the *Update entire table* option.
   e. Click OK.

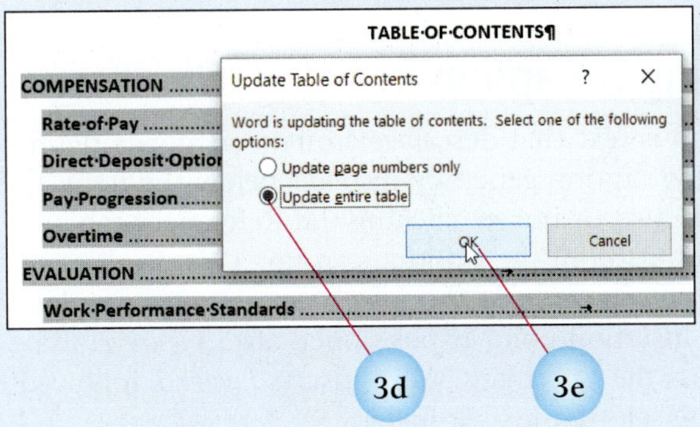

4. Turn off the display of nonprinting characters.
5. Save the document, print only the table of contents page, and then close **4-CompEval**.

Check Your Work

Activity 3 Create a Table of Figures for a Technology Report and a Travel Document — 3 Parts

You will open a report containing information on software, output devices, and the software development cycle, as well as images and a SmartArt diagram; insert captions; and then create a table of figures. You will also create and customize captions and insert a table of figures for an adventure document.

Creating a Table of Figures

Insert Caption

Insert Table of Figures

A document that contains figures should include a table of figures so readers can quickly locate specific figures, images, tables, equations, and charts. Figure 4.6 shows an example of a table of figures. Create a table of figures by marking text or images with captions and then using the caption names to create the table. The Captions group on the References tab includes the Insert Caption button for creating captions and the Insert Table of Figures button for inserting a table of figures in a document.

Figure 4.6 Example of Table of Figures

TABLE OF FIGURES

FIGURE 1 SCANNED LINE ART 3
FIGURE 2 DIGITAL HALFTONE 8
FIGURE 3 BAR CHARTS 12
FIGURE 4 LINE CHARTS 15
FIGURE 5 DETAIL VS. WEIGHT 18

Creating a Caption

Tutorial

Creating and Customizing Captions

Quick Steps

Create Caption

1. Select text or image.
2. Click References tab.
3. Click Insert Caption button.
4. Type caption name.
5. Click OK.

A caption is text that describes an item such as a figure, image, table, equation, or chart. The caption generally displays below the item. Create a caption by selecting the figure text or image, clicking the References tab, and then clicking the Insert Caption button in the Captions group. This displays the Caption dialog box, shown in Figure 4.7. At the dialog box, *Figure 1* displays in the *Caption* text box and the insertion point is positioned after *Figure 1*. Type a name for the figure and then press the Enter key. Word inserts *Figure 1* followed by the typed caption below the selected text or image.

If the insertion point is positioned in a table when the Caption dialog box is displayed, *Table 1* displays in the *Caption* text box instead of *Figure 1*.

Figure 4.7 Caption Dialog Box

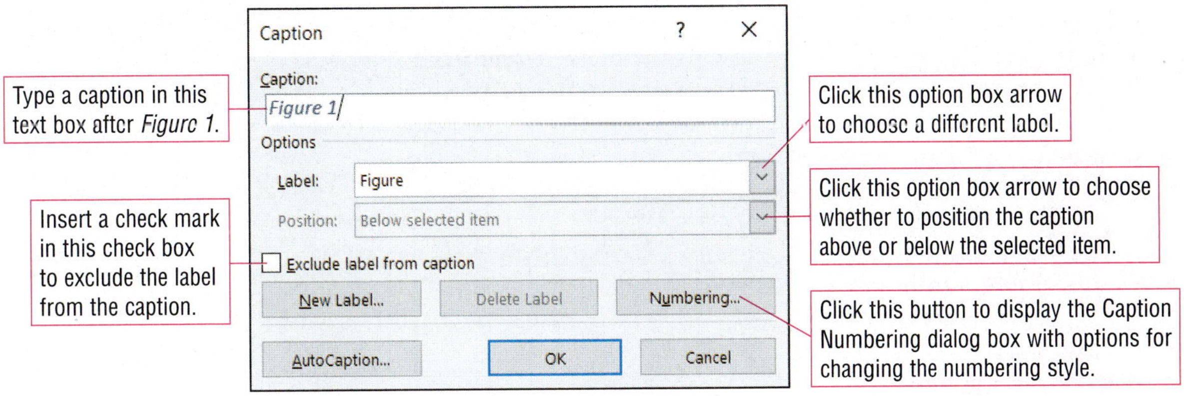

Inserting a Table of Figures

Tutorial

Inserting and Updating a Table of Figures

Quick Steps

Insert Table of Figures

1. Click References tab.
2. Click Insert Table of Figures button.
3. Select format.
4. Click OK.

After marking figures, images, tables, equations, and charts with captions in a document, insert the table of figures. A table of figures generally displays at the beginning of the document after the table of contents and on a separate page. To insert the table of figures, click the Insert Table of Figures button in the Captions group on the References tab. At the Table of Figures dialog box, shown in Figure 4.8, make any necessary changes and then click OK.

The options at the Table of Figures dialog box are similar to the options at the Table of Contents dialog box. They include choosing a format for the table of figures from the *Formats* option box, changing the alignment of the page numbers, and adding leaders before page numbers.

Figure 4.8 Table of Figures Dialog Box

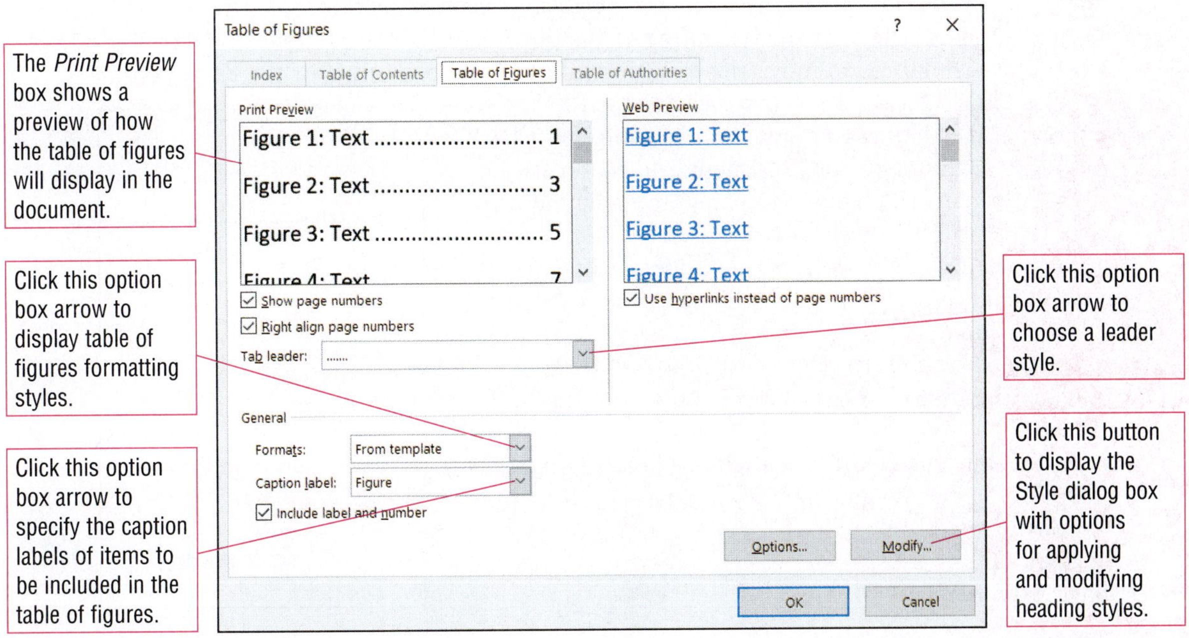

Activity 3a **Creating a Table of Figures** Part 1 of 3

1. Open **TechRpt** and then save it with the name **4-TechRpt**.
2. Add the caption *Figure 1 Word Document* to an image by completing the following steps:
   a. Click the screen image in the *WORD PROCESSING SOFTWARE* section.
   b. Click the References tab.
   c. Click the Insert Caption button in the Captions group.
   d. At the Caption dialog box with the insertion point positioned after *Figure 1* in the *Caption* text box, press the spacebar and then type Word Document.
   e. Click OK or press the Enter key.
   f. Press Ctrl + E to center the caption in the text box.

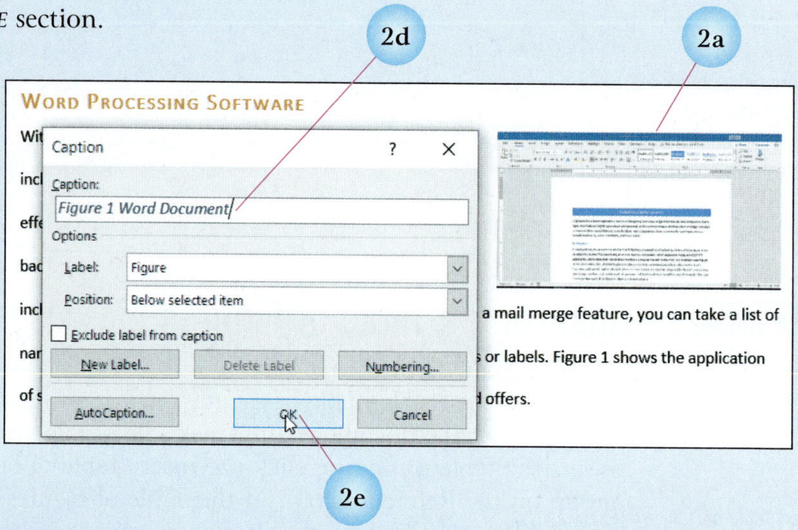

3. Complete steps similar to those in Step 2 to create and center the caption *Figure 2 Excel Worksheet* for the image in the *SPREADSHEET SOFTWARE* section.
4. Complete steps similar to those in Step 2 to create and center the caption *Figure 3 Monitor* for the image in the *MONITOR* section.
5. Complete steps similar to those in Step 2 to create and center the caption *Figure 4 Software Life Cycle* for the SmartArt graphic in the *Developing Software* section.
6. Insert a table of figures at the beginning of the document by completing the following steps:
   a. Press Ctrl + Home to move the insertion point to the beginning of the document.
   b. Press Ctrl + Enter to insert a page break.
   c. Press Ctrl + Home to move the insertion point back to the beginning of the document and then turn on bold formatting, change the paragraph alignment to center, and type the title TABLE OF FIGURES.
   d. Press the Enter key, turn off bold formatting, and then change the paragraph alignment back to left alignment.
   e. If necessary, click the References tab.
   f. Click the Insert Table of Figures button in the Captions group.
   g. At the Table of Figures dialog box, click the *Formats* option box arrow and then click *Formal* at the drop-down list.
   h. Click OK.
7. Save **4-TechRpt**.

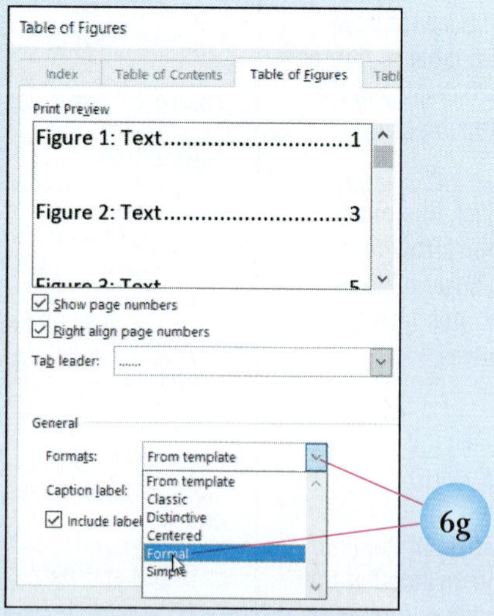

Check Your Work

Updating or Deleting a Table of Figures

Quick Steps

Update Table of Figures
1. Click in table of figures.
2. Click References tab.
3. Click Update Table button or press F9.
4. Click OK.

Delete Table of Figures
1. Select entire table.
2. Press Delete key.

If changes are made to a document after a table of figures is inserted, update the table. To do this, click in the table of figures and then click the Update Table button in the Captions group on the References tab or press the F9 function key. At the Update Table of Figures dialog box, click *Update page numbers only* if changes were made only to the page numbers or click *Update entire table* if changes were made to the caption text. Click OK or press the Enter key to close the dialog box. To delete a table of figures, select the entire table using the mouse or keyboard and then press the Delete key.

Activity 3b **Updating a Table of Figures**

Part 2 of 3

1. With **4-TechRpt** open, insert an image of a laser printer by completing the following steps:
   a. Move the insertion point to the beginning of the second paragraph of text in the *PRINTERS* section.
   b. Click the Insert tab and then click the Pictures button in the Illustrations group.
   c. At the Insert Picture dialog box, navigate to your WL2C4 folder and then double-click the image file ***LaserPrinter***.
   d. Change the height of the image to 1.5".
   e. Change to square text wrapping.
2. Add the caption *Figure 4 Laser Printer* to the printer image and then center the caption.
3. Click in the table of figures.
4. Press the F9 function key.
5. At the Update Table of Figures dialog box, click the *Update entire table* option and then click OK.
6. Save, print, and then close **4-TechRpt**.

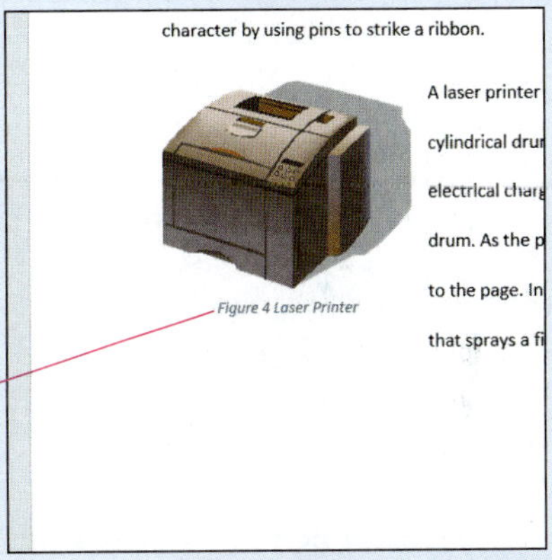

2

Check Your Work

Customizing a Caption

The Caption dialog box contains a number of options for customizing captions. These are shown in Figure 4.7 (on page 110). Click the *Label* option box arrow to specify the caption label. The default is *Figure*; it can be changed to *Equation* or *Table*. The caption is positioned below the selected item by default. Use the *Position* option to change the default position of the caption so it is above the selected item. A caption contains a label, such as *Figure*, *Table*, or *Equation*. To insert only a caption number and not a caption label, insert a check mark in the *Exclude label from caption* check box.

Click the New Label button and the Label dialog box displays. At this dialog box, type a custom label for the caption. Word automatically inserts an arabic number (*1, 2, 3,* and so on) after each caption label. To change the caption numbering style, click the Numbering button. At the Caption Numbering dialog box, click the *Format* option box arrow and then click a numbering style at the drop-down list. For example, caption numbering can be changed to uppercase or lowercase letters or to roman numerals.

If items such as tables are inserted in a document on a regular basis, captions can be inserted automatically with these items. To do this, click the AutoCaption button. At the AutoCaption dialog box, insert a check mark before the item (such as *Microsoft Word Table*) in the *Add caption when inserting* list box and then click OK. Each time a table is inserted in a document, Word inserts a caption above it.

Activity 3c Creating and Customizing Captions and Inserting a Table of Figures

Part 3 of 3

1. Open **TTSAdventures** and then save it with the name **4-TTSAdventures**.
2. Insert a custom caption for the first table by completing the following steps:
   a. Click in any cell in the table.
   b. Click the References tab.
   c. Click the Insert Caption button in the Captions group.
   d. At the Caption dialog box, press the spacebar and then type Antarctic Zenith Adventures in the *Caption* text box.
   e. Remove the label (*Figure*) from the caption by clicking the *Exclude label from caption* check box to insert a check mark.
   f. Click the Numbering button.
   g. At the Caption Numbering dialog box, click the *Format* option box arrow and then click the *A, B, C, …* option at the drop-down list.
   h. Click OK to close the Caption Numbering dialog box.
   i. At the Caption dialog box, click the *Position* option box arrow and then click *Below selected item* at the drop-down list. (Skip this step if *Below selected item* is already selected.)
   j. Click OK to close the Caption dialog box.

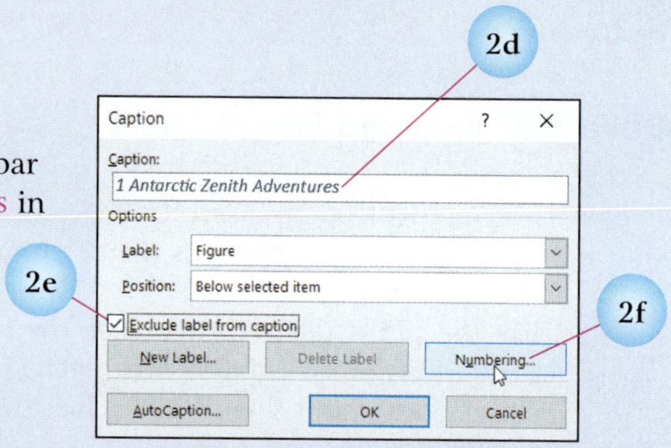

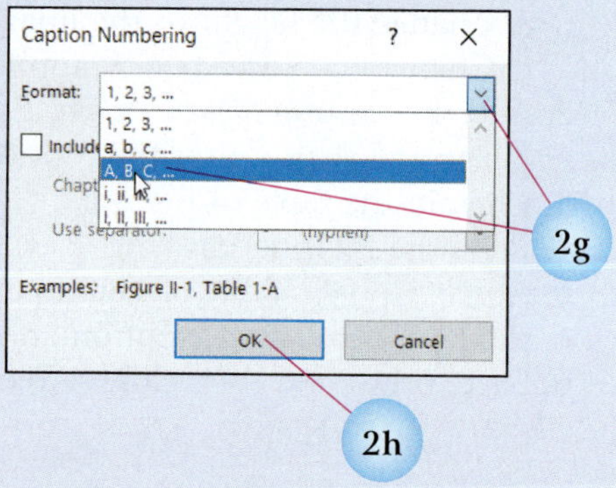

3. After looking at the caption, you decide to add a custom label and change the numbering. Do this by completing the following steps:
   a. Select the caption *A Antarctic Zenith Adventures*.
   b. Click the Insert Caption button.
   c. At the Caption dialog box, click the *Exclude label from caption* check box to remove the check mark.
   d. Click the New Label button.
   e. At the New Label dialog box, type Adventure and then click OK.
   f. Click OK to close the Caption dialog box.

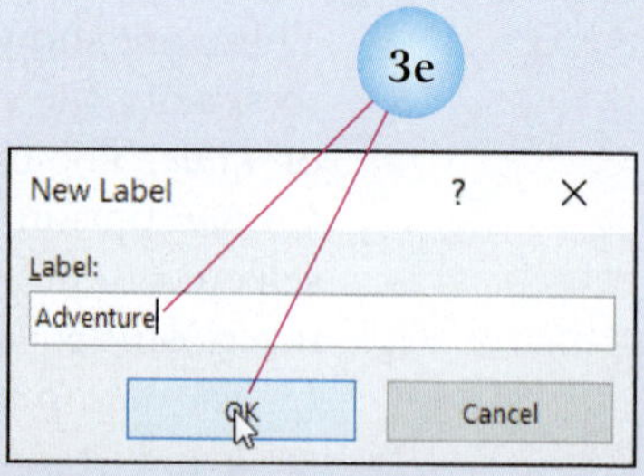

4. Format the caption by completing the following steps:
   a. Select the caption *Adventure 1 Antarctic Zenith Adventures*.
   b. Click the Home tab.
   c. Click the Font Color button arrow.
   d. Click the *Dark Blue* option (ninth color in the *Standard Colors* section).
   e. Click the Bold button.

5. Insert a custom caption for the second table by completing the following steps:
   a. Click in the second table.
   b. Click the References tab and then click the Insert Caption button.
   c. At the Caption dialog box, press the spacebar and then type Tall-Ship Adventures.
   d. Make sure *Below selected item* appears in the *Position* option box and then click OK to close the Caption dialog box.
6. Select the caption *Adventure 2 Tall-Ship Adventures*, apply the Dark Blue font color, and then apply bold formatting.
7. Insert a table of figures by completing the following steps:
   a. Press Ctrl + Home and then press Ctrl + Enter to insert a page break.
   b. Press Ctrl + Home to move the insertion point above the page break.
   c. Turn on bold formatting, type TABLES, turn off bold formatting, and then press the Enter key.
   d. Click the References tab and then click the Insert Table of Figures button in the Captions group.
   e. At the Table of Figures dialog box, click OK.
8. Save, print, and then close **4-TTSAdventures**.

Check Your Work

Activity 4 Navigate in a Computer Viruses and Security Report — 6 Parts

You will open a report on computer viruses and computer security, navigate using the Navigation pane, and then insert and navigate using bookmarks, hyperlinks, and cross-references.

Navigating in a Document

Word provides a number of features for navigating in a document. Navigate in a document using the Navigation pane or using bookmarks, hyperlinks, or cross-references.

Navigating Using the Navigation Pane

Tutorial

Navigating Using the Navigation Pane

Quick Steps

Display Navigation Pane

1. Click View tab.
2. Click *Navigation Pane* check box.

The Navigation pane can be used to navigate in a document by clicking the View tab and then clicking the *Navigation Pane* check box in the Show group to insert a check mark. The Navigation pane displays at the left side of the screen and includes a search text box and a pane with three tabs.

Click the first Navigation pane tab, Headings, and titles and headings with certain styles applied display in the Navigation pane. Click a title or heading and the insertion point moves to it. Click the Pages tab and a thumbnail of each page displays in the pane. Click a thumbnail to move the insertion point to that specific page. Click the Results tab to browse the current search results in the document.

Close the Navigation pane by clicking the *Navigation Pane* check box in the Show group on the View tab to remove the check mark. Another option is to click the Close button in the upper right corner of the pane.

Activity 4a Navigating Using the Navigation Pane

1. Open **Security** and then save it with the name **4-Security**.
2. Since this document has heading styles applied, you can easily navigate in it with the Navigation pane by completing the following steps:
   a. Click the View tab.
   b. Click the *Navigation Pane* check box in the Show group to insert a check mark. (This displays the Navigation pane at the left side of the screen.)
   c. With the Headings tab active, click the heading *CHAPTER 2: INFORMATION THEFT* in the Navigation pane.
   d. Click *CHAPTER 3: COMPUTER VIRUSES* in the Navigation pane.
   e. Click *Systems Failure* in the Navigation pane.

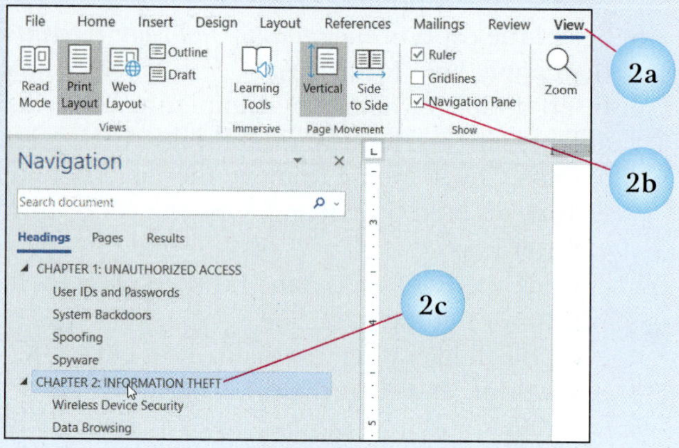

3. Navigate in the document using thumbnails by completing the following steps:
   a. Click the Pages tab in the Navigation pane. (This displays thumbnails of the pages in the pane.)
   b. Click the page 1 thumbnail in the Navigation pane. (You may need to scroll up the Navigation pane to display this thumbnail.)
   c. Click the page 3 thumbnail in the Navigation pane.
4. Close the Navigation pane by clicking the Close button in the upper right corner.
5. Save **4-Security**.

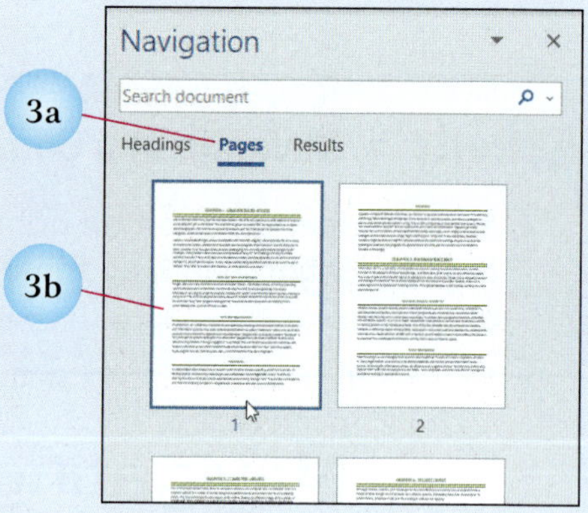

Tutorial

Inserting and Navigating with Bookmarks

Bookmark

Quick Steps

Insert Bookmark

1. Position insertion point at specific location.
2. Click Insert tab.
3. Click Bookmark button.
4. Type name for bookmark.
5. Click Add button.

Inserting and Navigating with Bookmarks

When working in a long document, marking a place in it with a bookmark may be useful for moving the insertion point to that specific location. Create bookmarks for locations in a document at the Bookmark dialog box.

To create a bookmark, position the insertion point at the specific location, click the Insert tab, and then click the Bookmark button in the Links group. This displays the Bookmark dialog box, as shown in Figure 4.9. Type a name for the bookmark in the *Bookmark name* text box and then click the Add button. Repeat these steps as many times as needed to insert additional bookmarks.

Give each bookmark a unique name. A bookmark name must begin with a letter and can contain numbers but not spaces. To separate words in a bookmark name, use the underscore character.

By default, the bookmarks inserted in a document are not visible. Turn on the display of bookmarks at the Word Options dialog box with *Advanced* selected. Display this dialog box by clicking the File tab and then clicking *Options*. At the Word Options dialog box, click *Advanced* in the left panel. Click the *Show bookmarks*

Figure 4.9 Bookmark Dialog Box

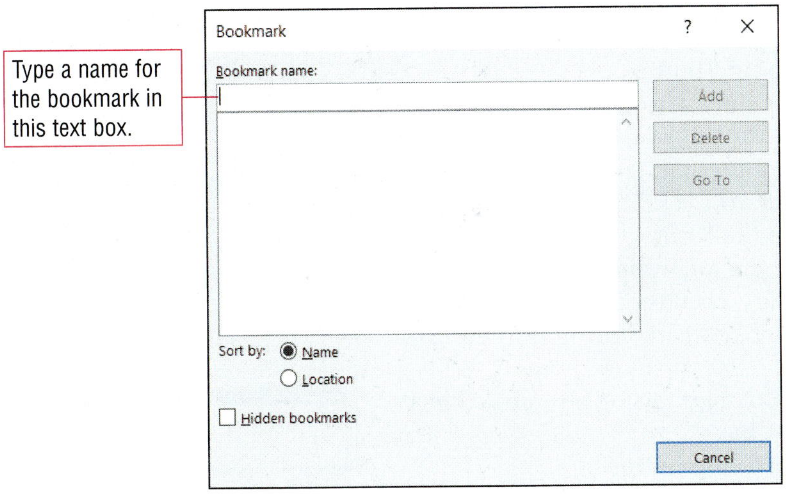

check box in the *Show document content* section to insert a check mark. Complete similar steps to turn off the display of bookmarks. A bookmark displays in the document as an I-beam marker.

Hint Bookmark brackets do not print.

A bookmark can be created for selected text. To do this, first select the text and then complete the steps to create a bookmark. A bookmark created with selected text displays a left bracket ([) indicating the beginning of the selected text and a right bracket (]) indicating the end of the selected text.

Quick Steps

Navigate with Bookmarks

1. Click Insert tab.
2. Click Bookmark button.
3. Double-click bookmark name.

Navigate in a document by moving the insertion point to a specific bookmark. To do this, display the Bookmark dialog box and then double-click the bookmark name or click the bookmark name and then click the Go To button. When Word stops at the location of the bookmark, click the Close button to close the dialog box. When moving to a bookmark created with selected text, Word moves the insertion point to the bookmark and then selects the text. Delete a bookmark in the Bookmark dialog box by clicking the bookmark name in the list box and then clicking the Delete button.

Activity 4b Inserting and Navigating with Bookmarks

Part 2 of 6

1. With **4-Security** open, turn on the display of bookmarks by completing the following steps:
   a. Click the File tab and then click *Options*.
   b. At the Word Options dialog box, click *Advanced* in the left panel.
   c. Scroll down the dialog box and then click the *Show bookmarks* check box in the *Show document content* section to insert a check mark.
   d. Click OK to close the dialog box.
2. Insert a bookmark by completing the following steps:
   a. Move the insertion point to the beginning of the paragraph in the section *TYPES OF VIRUSES* (the paragraph that begins *Viruses can be categorized*).
   b. Click the Insert tab.
   c. Click the Bookmark button in the Links group.

d. At the Bookmark dialog box, type Viruses in the *Bookmark name* text box.
e. Click the Add button.

3. Using steps similar to those in Step 2, insert a bookmark named *Electrical* at the beginning of the paragraph in the section *SYSTEMS FAILURE*.
4. Navigate to the Viruses bookmark by completing the following steps:
   a. If necessary, click the Insert tab.
   b. Click the Bookmark button in the Links group.
   c. At the Bookmark dialog box, click *Viruses* in the list box.
   d. Click the Go To button.
5. With the Bookmark dialog box open, delete the Electrical bookmark by clicking *Electrical* in the list box and then clicking the Delete button.
6. Click the Close button to close the Bookmark dialog box.
7. Save **4-Security**.

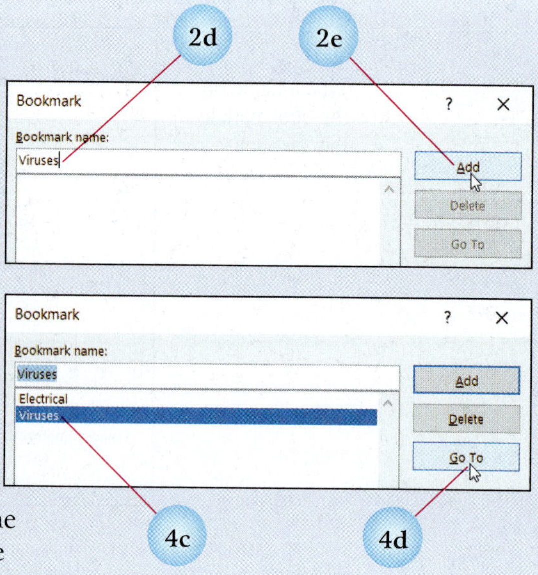

Tutorial

Inserting and Editing a Hyperlink

Link

Quick Steps

Insert Hyperlink

1. Click Insert tab.
2. Click Link button.
3. Make changes at Insert Hyperlink dialog box.
4. Click OK.

Inserting Hyperlinks

Hyperlinks can serve a number of purposes in a document. A hyperlink can be used to navigate to a specific location in a document, to display a different document, to open a file in a different program, to create a new document, and to link to an email address.

Insert a hyperlink by clicking the Link button in the Links group on the Insert tab. This displays the Insert Hyperlink dialog box, as shown in Figure 4.10. This dialog box can also be displayed by pressing Ctrl + K. At the Insert Hyperlink dialog box, identify what to link to and where to find the link. Click the ScreenTip button to customize the ScreenTip for the hyperlink.

Figure 4.10 Insert Hyperlink Dialog Box

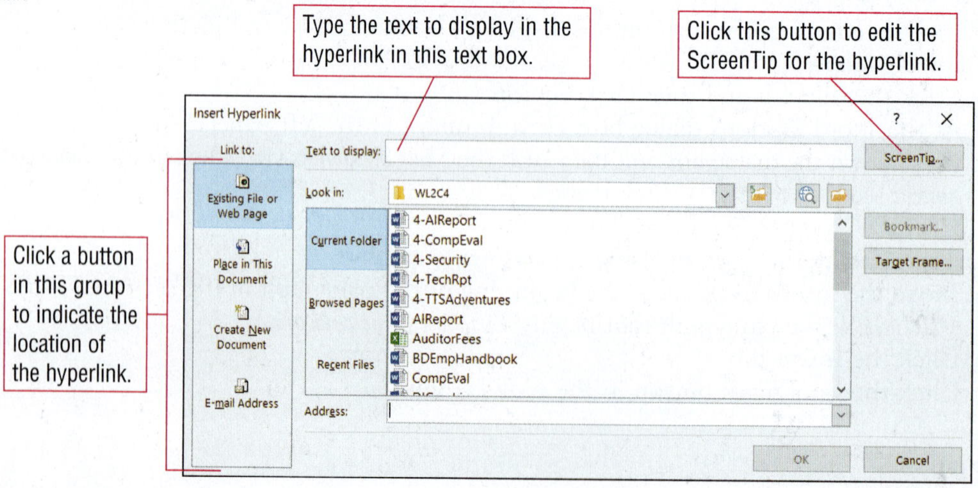

Linking to a Place in the Document To create a hyperlink to another location in the document, first mark the location by applying a heading style to the text or inserting a bookmark. To hyperlink to that heading or bookmark, display the Insert Hyperlink dialog box and then click the Place in This Document button in the *Link to* section. This displays text with heading styles applied and bookmarks in the *Select a place in this document* list box. Click the heading style or bookmark name and the heading or bookmark name displays in the *Text to display* text box. Leave the text as displayed or select the text and then type the text that will appear in the document.

Navigating Using Hyperlinks Navigate to a hyperlink by hovering the mouse pointer over the hyperlink text, pressing and holding down the Ctrl key, clicking the left mouse button, and then releasing the Ctrl key. When hovering the mouse pointer over the hyperlink text, a ScreenTip displays with the name of the heading or bookmark. To display specific information in the ScreenTip, click the ScreenTip button in the Insert Hyperlink dialog box, type the text in the Set Hyperlink ScreenTip dialog box, and then click OK.

Activity 4c Inserting and Navigating with Hyperlinks

Part 3 of 6

1. With **4-Security** open, insert a hyperlink to a bookmark in the document by completing the following steps:
   a. Position the insertion point at the immediate right of the period that ends the first paragraph of text in the section *CHAPTER 4: SECURITY RISKS* (on page 4).
   b. Press the spacebar.
   c. If necessary, click the Insert tab.
   d. Click the Link button in the Links group.
   e. At the Insert Hyperlink dialog box, click the Place in This Document button in the *Link to* section.
   f. Scroll down the *Select a place in this document* list box and then click *Viruses,* which displays below *Bookmarks* in the list box.
   g. Select the text in the *Text to display* text box and then type Click to view types of viruses.
   h. Click the ScreenTip button in the upper right corner of the dialog box.
   i. At the Set Hyperlink ScreenTip dialog box, type View types of viruses and then click OK.
   j. Click OK to close the Insert Hyperlink dialog box.

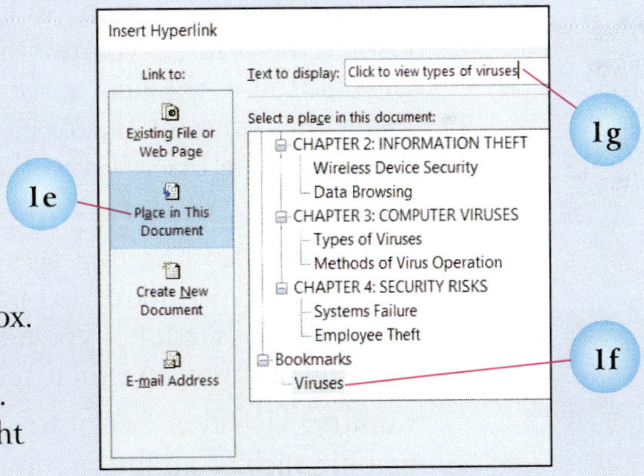

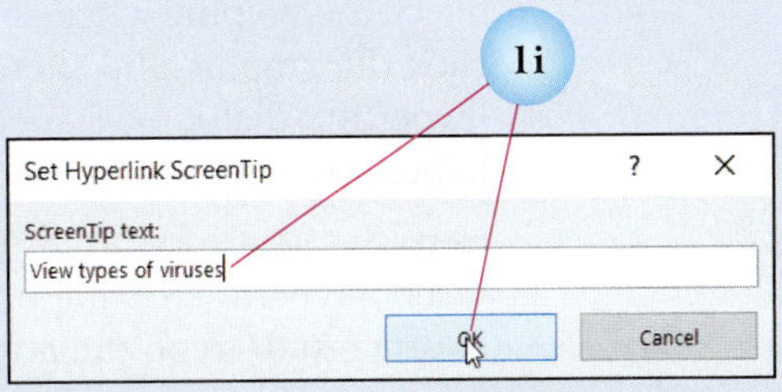

2. Navigate to the hyperlinked location by hovering the mouse pointer over the Click to view types of viruses hyperlink, pressing and holding down the Ctrl key, clicking the left mouse button, and then releasing the Ctrl key.

3. Insert a hyperlink to a heading in the document by completing the following steps:
   a. Press Ctrl + Home to move the insertion point to the beginning of the document.
   b. Move the insertion point to the immediate right of the period that ends the second paragraph in the document and then press the spacebar.
   c. Click the Link button on the Insert tab.
   d. At the Insert Hyperlink dialog box with the Place in This Document button active in the *Link to* section, click the *Methods of Virus Operation* heading in the *Select a place in this document* list box.
   e. Click OK to close the Insert Hyperlink dialog box.

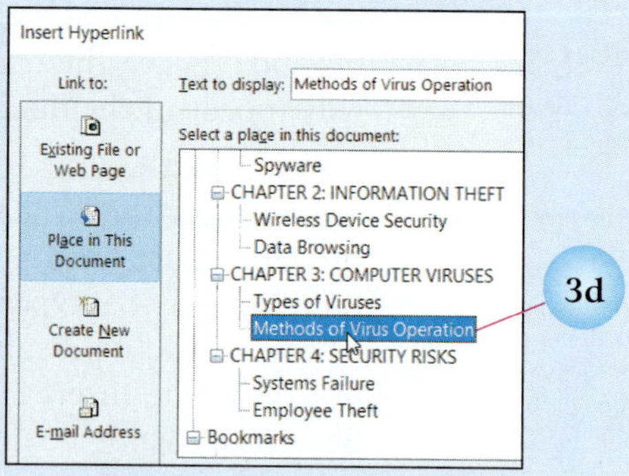

4. Navigate to the hyperlinked heading by hovering the mouse pointer over the Methods of Virus Operation hyperlink, pressing and holding down the Ctrl key, clicking the left mouse button, and then releasing the Ctrl key.
5. Save **4-Security**.

Check Your Work

Linking to a File in Another Application A hyperlink can be inserted in a document that links to another Word document, an Excel worksheet, or a PowerPoint presentation. To link a Word document to a file in another application, display the Insert Hyperlink dialog box and then click the Existing File or Web Page button in the *Link to* section. Use the *Look in* option box to navigate to the folder that contains the specific file and then click the file name. Make other changes in the Insert Hyperlink dialog box as needed and then click OK.

Linking to a New Document In addition to linking to an existing document, a hyperlink can link to a new document. To insert this kind of hyperlink, display the Insert Hyperlink dialog box and then click the Create New Document button in the *Link to* section. Type a name for the new document in the *Name of new document* text box and then specify if the document will be edited now or later.

Linking Using a Graphic A hyperlink to a file or website can be inserted in a graphic such as an image, table, or text box. To create a hyperlink with a graphic, select the graphic, click the Insert tab, and then click the Link button or right-click the graphic and then click *Hyperlink* at the shortcut menu. At the Insert Hyperlink dialog box, specify where to link to and what text to display in the hyperlink.

Linking to an Email Address Insert a hyperlink to an email address at the Insert Hyperlink dialog box. To do this, click the E-Mail Address button in the *Link to* group, type the address in the *E-mail address* text box, and then type a subject for the email in the *Subject* text box. Click in the *Text to display* text box and then type the text to display in the document. To use this feature, the email address must be set up in Outlook.

Activity 4d Inserting a Hyperlink to Another Program, to a New Document, and Using a Graphic

Part 4 of 6

1. The **4-Security** document contains information used by Northland Security Systems. The company also has a PowerPoint presentation that contains similar information. Link the document with the presentation by completing the following steps:
   a. Move the insertion point to the immediate right of the period that ends the first paragraph in the section *CHAPTER 3: COMPUTER VIRUSES* and then press the spacebar.
   b. If necessary, click the Insert tab.
   c. Click the Link button in the Links group.
   d. At the Insert Hyperlink dialog box, click the Existing File or Web Page button in the *Link to* section.
   e. Click the *Look in* option box arrow. At the drop-down list that displays, navigate to your WL2C4 folder and then click the folder.
   f. Click the ***NSSPres*** PowerPoint file in the list box.
   g. Select the text in the *Text to display* text box and then type Computer Virus Presentation.
   h. Click OK to close the Insert Hyperlink dialog box.

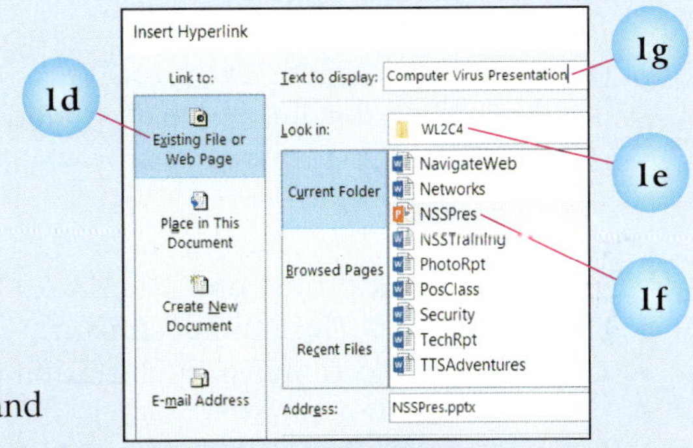

2. View the PowerPoint presentation by completing the following steps:
   a. Position the mouse pointer over the Computer Virus Presentation hyperlink, press and hold down the Ctrl key, click the left mouse button, and then release the Ctrl key.
   b. At the PowerPoint presentation, click the Slide Show button in the view area on the Status bar.
   c. Click the left mouse button to advance each slide.
   d. Click the left mouse button at the black screen that displays the message *End of slide show, click to exit*.
   e. Close the presentation and PowerPoint by clicking the Close button (which contains an *X*) in the upper right corner of the screen.

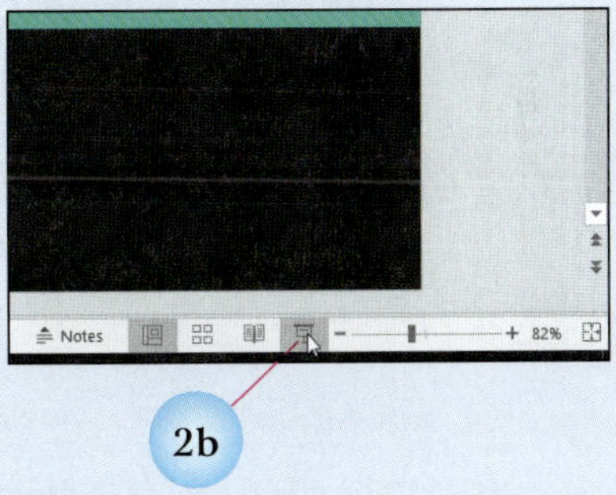

3. Insert a hyperlink with a graphic by completing the following steps:
   a. Press Ctrl + End to move the insertion point to the end of the document.
   b. Click the compass image to select it.
   c. Click the Link button on the Insert tab.
   d. At the Insert Hyperlink dialog box, make sure the Existing File or Web Page button is active in the *Link to* group.
   e. Navigate to your WL2C4 folder and then double-click ***NSSTraining***. (This selects the document name and closes the dialog box.)
   f. Click outside the compass image to deselect it.
4. Navigate to **NSSTraining** by hovering the mouse pointer over the compass image, pressing and holding down the Ctrl key, clicking the left mouse button, and then releasing the Ctrl key.
5. Close the document by clicking the File tab and then clicking the *Close* option.

6. Insert a hyperlink to a new document by completing the following steps:
   a. Move the insertion point to the immediate right of the period that ends the paragraph in the section *USER IDS AND PASSWORDS* and then press the spacebar.
   b. Click the Link button on the Insert tab.
   c. Click the Create New Document button in the *Link to* section.
   d. In the *Name of new document* text box, type 4-PasswordSuggestions.
   e. Edit the text in the *Text to display* text box so it displays as *Password Suggestions*.
   f. Make sure the *Edit the new document now* option is selected.
   g. Click OK.
   h. At the blank document, turn on bold formatting, type Please type any suggestions you have for creating secure passwords:, turn off bold formatting, and then press the Enter key.
   i. Save and then close the document.

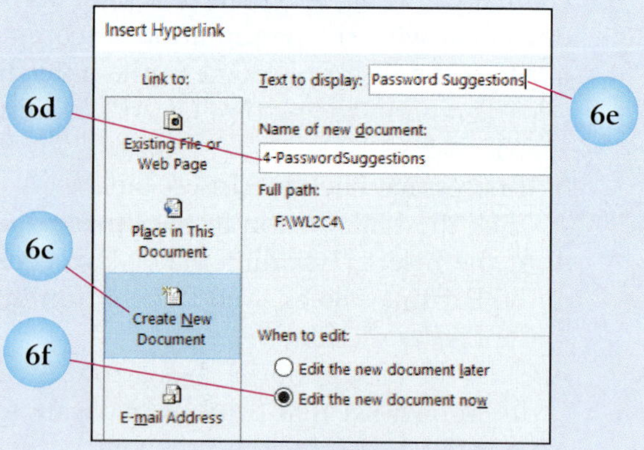

7. Press Ctrl + End to move the insertion point to the end of the document and then press the Enter key four times.
8. Insert a hyperlink to your email address or your instructor's email address by completing the following steps:
   a. Click the Link button.
   b. At the Insert Hyperlink dialog box, click the E-mail Address button in the *Link to* group.
   c. Type your email address or your instructor's email address in the *E-mail address* text box.
   d. Select the current text in the *Text to display* text box and then type Click to send an email.
   e. Click OK to close the dialog box.

   Optional:* *If you have Outlook set up, press and hold down the Ctrl key, click the Click to send an email hyperlink, release the Ctrl key, and then send a message indicating that you have completed inserting hyperlinks in 4-Security.
9. Save **4-Security**.

Check Your Work

Editing a Hyperlink

The hyperlink or the hyperlink destination can be edited with options at the Edit Hyperlink dialog box. The Edit Hyperlink dialog box contains the same options as the Insert Hyperlink dialog box. Display the Edit Hyperlink dialog box by clicking the hyperlinked text and then clicking the Link button on the Insert tab or by right-clicking the hyperlinked text and then clicking *Edit Hyperlink* at the shortcut menu. Like the hyperlink, the hyperlinked text can be edited. For example, a different font, font size, text color, or text effect can be applied to the hyperlinked text. Remove a hyperlink from a document by right-clicking the hyperlinked text and then clicking *Remove Hyperlink* at the shortcut menu.

Activity 4e Editing and Removing a Hyperlink

1. With **4-Security** open, edit a hyperlink by completing the following steps:
   a. Display the hyperlink at the end of the paragraph below the title *CHAPTER 3: COMPUTER VIRUSES*.
   b. Right-click the Computer Virus Presentation hyperlink and then click *Edit Hyperlink* at the shortcut menu.

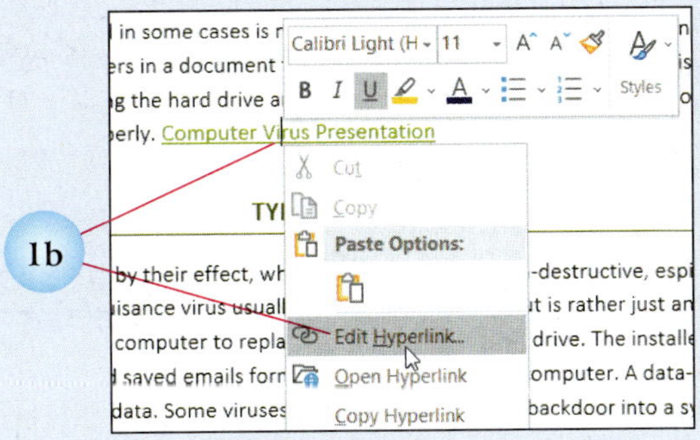

   c. At the Edit Hyperlink dialog box, select the text in the *Text to display* text box and then type Click to view a presentation on computer viruses.
   d. Click the ScreenTip button in the upper right corner of the dialog box.
   e. At the Set Hyperlink ScreenTip dialog box, type View the Computer Viruses PowerPoint presentation and then click OK.
   f. Click OK to close the Edit Hyperlink dialog box.
2. Remove a hyperlink by completing the following steps:
   a. Press Ctrl + Home to move the insertion point to the beginning of the document.
   b. Right-click the Methods of Virus Operation hyperlink at the end of the second paragraph below the title *CHAPTER 1: UNAUTHORIZED ACCESS*.
   c. At the shortcut menu, click the *Remove Hyperlink* option.
   d. Select and then delete the text Methods of Virus Operation.
3. Save **4-Security**.

Check Your Work

Tutorial

Creating a Cross-Reference

Quick Steps

Insert Cross-Reference

1. Type text or position insertion point.
2. Click Insert tab.
3. Click Cross-reference button.
4. Identify reference type, location, and text.
5. Click Insert.
6. Click Close.

Cross-reference

Creating a Cross-Reference

A cross-reference in a Word document refers readers to another location within the document. Providing cross-references is useful in a long document or a document containing related items or sections of information. References to items such as headings, figures, and tables are helpful to readers. For example, a cross-reference can be inserted that refers readers to a location with more information about the topic, to a specific table, or to a specific page. Cross-references are inserted in a document as hyperlinks.

To insert a cross-reference, type introductory text or position the insertion point at a specific location, click the Insert tab, and then click the Cross-reference button in the Links group. This displays the Cross-reference dialog box, similar to the one shown in Figure 4.11. At the Cross-reference dialog box, identify the type of reference, the location to reference, and the specific text to reference.

The reference identified in the Cross-reference dialog box displays immediately after the introductory text. To move to the specified reference, press and hold down the Ctrl key, position the mouse pointer over the text (the pointer turns into a hand), click the left mouse button, and then release the Ctrl key.

Figure 4.11 Cross-Reference Dialog Box

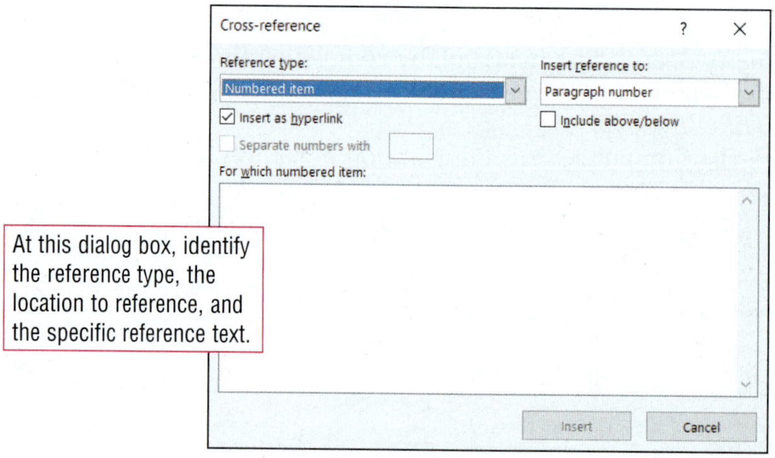

Activity 4f Inserting and Navigating with Cross-References

Part 6 of 6

1. With **4-Security** open, insert a cross-reference in the document by completing the following steps:
   a. Move the insertion point immediately right of the period that ends the paragraph in the section *TYPES OF VIRUSES*.
   b. Press the spacebar and then type (For more information, refer to.
   c. Press the spacebar.
   d. If necessary, click the Insert tab.
   e. Click the Cross-reference button in the Links group.
   f. At the Cross-reference dialog box, click the *Reference type* option box arrow and then click *Heading* at the drop-down list.
   g. Click *Spyware* in the *For which heading* list box.
   h. Click the Insert button.
   i. Click the Close button to close the dialog box.
   j. At the document, type a period followed by a right parenthesis.

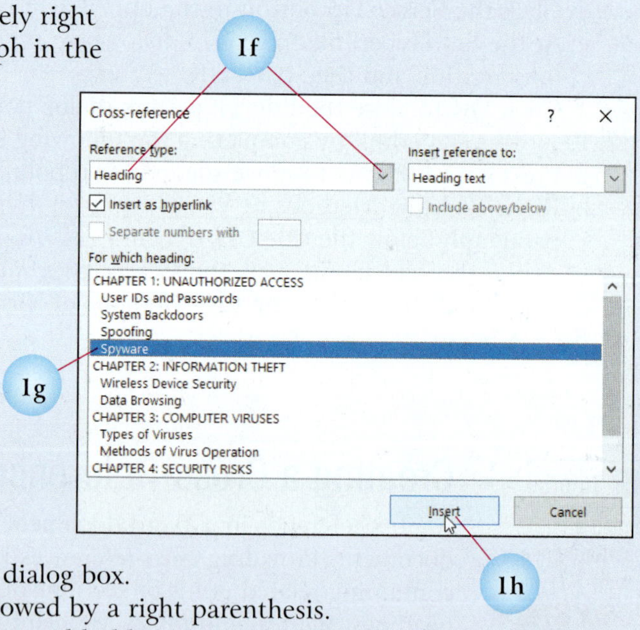

2. Move to the referenced text by pressing and holding down the Ctrl key, positioning the mouse pointer over *Spyware* until the pointer turns into a hand, clicking the left mouse button, and then releasing the Ctrl key.
3. Save and then print **4-Security**.
4. Turn off the display of bookmarks by completing the following steps:
   a. Click the File tab and then click *Options*.
   b. At the Word Options dialog box, click *Advanced* in the left panel.
   c. Click the *Show bookmarks* check box in the *Show document content* section to remove the check mark.
   d. Click OK to close the dialog box.
5. Close **4-Security**.

Check Your Work

Chapter Summary

- Create a table of contents using the Table of Contents button in the Table of Contents group on the References tab. Creating a table of contents involves two steps: applying the appropriate styles to mark text that will be included and inserting the table of contents in the document.
- Identify the text to be included in a table of contents by applying a heading style, assigning a level, or marking text as a field entry.
- To insert a table of contents, position the insertion point where the table is to appear, click the References tab, click the Table of Contents button, and then click an option at the drop-down list.
- Generally, the pages containing the table of contents are numbered with lowercase roman numerals. Change the format of the page number at the Page Number Format dialog box.
- To separate the table of contents from the first page of the document, insert a section break that begins a new page.
- The headings in a table of contents are hyperlinks that connect to the headings where they appear in a document and can be used to navigate in a document.
- Customize a table of contents with options at the Table of Contents dialog box. Display this dialog box by clicking the Table of Contents button on the References tab and then clicking *Custom Table of Contents* at the drop-down list.
- If changes are made to a document after the table of contents is inserted, update the table of contents by clicking in the current table of contents and then clicking the Update Table button in the Table of Contents group on the References tab or by pressing the F9 function key.
- Remove a table of contents by clicking the Table of Contents button on the References tab and then clicking *Remove Table of Contents* at the drop-down list.
- To identify titles and/or headings for a table of contents without applying a style, mark each as a field entry at the Mark Table of Contents Entry dialog box. Display this dialog box by pressing Alt + Shift + O.
- When table of contents entries are marked as fields, the *Table entry fields* option needs to be activated when inserting a table of contents. Do this at the Table of Contents Options dialog box.
- Create a table of figures by marking specific text or images with captions and then using the caption names to create the table. Create a caption by selecting the figure text or image and then clicking the Insert Caption button in the Captions group on the References tab. This displays the Caption dialog box, where the figure name is typed.
- Insert a table of figures in a document by clicking the Insert Table of Figures button in the Captions group on the References tab. A table of figures generally appears at the beginning of the document after the table of contents on a separate page.
- Update a table of figures by clicking in the table of figures and then clicking the Update Table button in the Captions group on the References tab or by pressing the F9 function key. At the Update Table of Figures dialog box, specify if just page numbers are updated or the entire table.

- Customize a caption with options at the Captions dialog box. Display this dialog box by clicking the Insert Caption button in the Captions group on the References tab.
- To navigate in a document using the Navigation pane, click the View tab and then click the *Navigation Pane* check box in the Show group. The Navigation pane includes a search text box and a pane with three tabs: Headings, Pages, and Results.
- Navigate in a document using bookmarks, which move the insertion point to specific locations. Create bookmarks with options at the Bookmark dialog box.
- Insert hyperlinks in a document with options at the Insert Hyperlink dialog box. Insert a hyperlink to a location in the current document, to display a different document, to open a file in a different program, to create a new document, or to link to an email address. A graphic can also be used to link to a file or website. Edit the hyperlink or the hyperlink destination with options at the Edit Hyperlink dialog box.
- Create a cross-reference to another location within the same document with options at the Cross-reference dialog box.

Commands Review

FEATURE	RIBBON TAB, GROUP	BUTTON, OPTION	KEYBOARD SHORTCUT
Bookmark dialog box	Insert, Links		
Caption dialog box	References, Captions		
Cross-reference dialog box	Insert, Links		
Insert Hyperlink dialog box	Insert, Links		Ctrl + K
Mark Table of Contents Entry dialog box			Alt + Shift + O
Navigation pane	View, Show	*Navigation Pane*	
Remove table of contents	References, Table of Contents	, *Remove Table of Contents*	
Table of Contents dialog box	References, Table of Contents	, *Custom Table of Contents*	
Table of Contents Options dialog box	References, Table of Contents	, *Custom Table of Contents,* Options button	
Table of Figures dialog box	References, Captions		
update table of contents	References, Table of Contents		F9

Microsoft®

Word Level 2

Unit 2

Editing and Formatting Documents

Chapter 5 Customizing Objects and Creating Charts

Chapter 6 Merging Documents

Chapter 7 Managing Building Blocks and Fields

Chapter 8 Managing Shared Documents

Microsoft®

Word

CHAPTER 5

Customizing Objects and Creating Charts

Performance Objectives

Upon successful completion of Chapter 5, you will be able to:

1. Insert, format, and customize images and text boxes
2. Group and ungroup objects
3. Edit points and wrap points in a shape
4. Link and unlink text boxes
5. Insert, format, and customize icons
6. Insert, format, and customize 3D models
7. Insert and format charts

Objects such as images, shapes, text boxes, icons, and 3D models can be inserted in a Word document and then formatted with a variety of options. Use buttons on the object format tab and task pane to customize an object. An object can also be formatted with options at the Layout dialog box. In this chapter, you will learn how to customize objects and how to present text visually in a chart and apply formatting to the chart.

Data Files

Before beginning chapter work, copy the WL2C5 folder to your storage medium and then make WL2C5 the active folder.

The online course includes additional training and assessment resources.

Activity 1 Customize the Layout of a Travel Agency Flyer 3 Parts

You will open a travel agency flyer describing sites and activities for tourism in Maui and improve the attractiveness of the layout by inserting and customizing images and a text box.

Customizing Objects

Word provides a number of methods for formatting and customizing objects, such as images, photographs, shapes and text boxes. Format images with buttons on the Picture Tools Format tab and further customize images with options at the Format Picture task pane and the Layout dialog box. Use buttons on the Drawing Tools Format tab to format and customize shapes and text boxes and further customize shapes and text boxes with options at the Format Shape task pane and the Layout dialog box.

Tutorial
Formatting an Image at the Layout Dialog Box

Customizing Image Layout

Customize the layout of images with options at the Layout dialog box. Display the Layout dialog box by clicking the Size group dialog box launcher on the Picture Tools Format tab. The Layout dialog box contains three tabs. Click the Position tab and the dialog box displays as shown in Figure 5.1.

Use options at the Layout dialog box with the Position tab selected to specify horizontal and vertical layout options. In the *Horizontal* section, choose the *Alignment* option to specify left, center, or right alignment relative to the margin, page, column, or character. Choose the *Book layout* option to align the image with

Figure 5.1 Layout Dialog Box with the Position Tab Selected

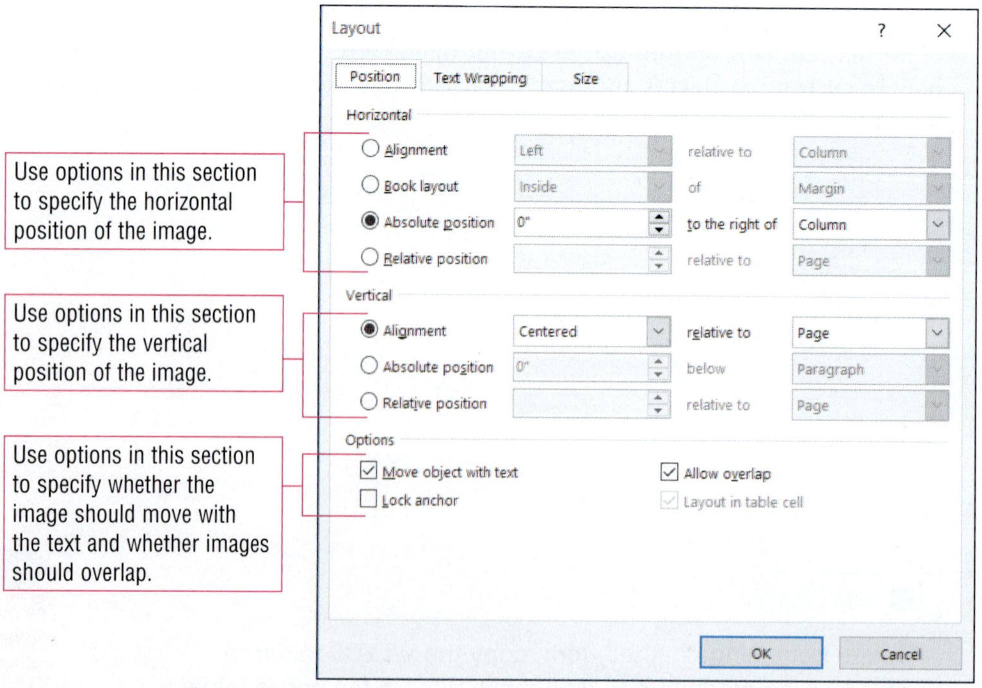

the inside or outside margin of the page. Use the *Absolute position* measurement box to align the image horizontally with the specified amount of space between the left edge of the image and the left edge of the page, column, left margin, or character. The *Relative position* measurement box uses a percentage to position an image relative to a specific location. For example, enter *50%* in the *Relative position* measurement box to align relative to the left margin and the image is positioned half way (50%) between the left edge of the page and the left margin.

In the *Vertical* section of the dialog box, use the *Alignment* option to align the image at the top, bottom, center, inside, or outside relative to the page, margin, or line. Use the *Absolute position* measurement box to align the image vertically with the specified amount of space relative to a specific location and use the *Relative position* measurement box to specify a percentage.

In the *Options* section, attach (anchor) the image to a paragraph so that the image and paragraph move together. Choose the *Move object with text* option to move the image up or down on the page with the paragraph to which it is anchored. Keep the image anchored in the same place on the page by choosing the *Lock anchor* option. Choose the *Allow overlap* option to overlap images with the same wrapping style.

Use options at the Layout dialog box with the Text Wrapping tab selected to specify the wrapping style for the image. Specify which sides of the image the text is to wrap around and the amounts of space between the text and the top, bottom, left, and right edges of the image.

Click the Size tab at the Layout dialog box to display options for specifying the height and width of the image relative to the margin, page, top margin, bottom margin, inside margin, or outside margin. Use the *Rotation* measurement box to rotate the image by degrees and use options in the *Scale* section to change the percentage of the height and width scales. By default, the *Lock aspect ratio* check box contains a check mark, which means that if a change is made to the height measurement of an image, the width measurement automatically changes to maintain the proportional relationship between the height and width. Change the width measurement and the height measurement automatically changes.

To change the height measurement of an image without changing the width or to change the width measurement without changing the height, remove the check mark from the *Lock aspect ratio* check box. To reset the image size, click the Reset button in the lower right corner of the dialog box.

Activity 1a Inserting and Customizing the Layout of an Image

Part 1 of 3

1. Open **TTSMaui** and then save it with the name **5-TTSMaui**.
2. Insert an image by completing the following steps:
   a. Click the Insert tab and then click the Pictures button in the Illustrations group.
   b. At the Insert Picture dialog box, navigate to your WL2C5 folder and then double-click the ***HawaiiBanner*** image file.
3. Select the current measurement in the *Shape Height* measurement box in the Size group on the Picture Tools Format tab, type 2, and then press the Enter key.

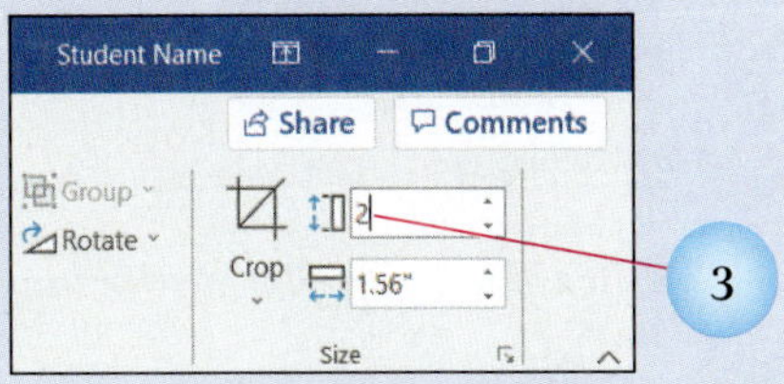

4. Click the *Beveled Matte, White* style in the Picture Styles group (second style from the left).

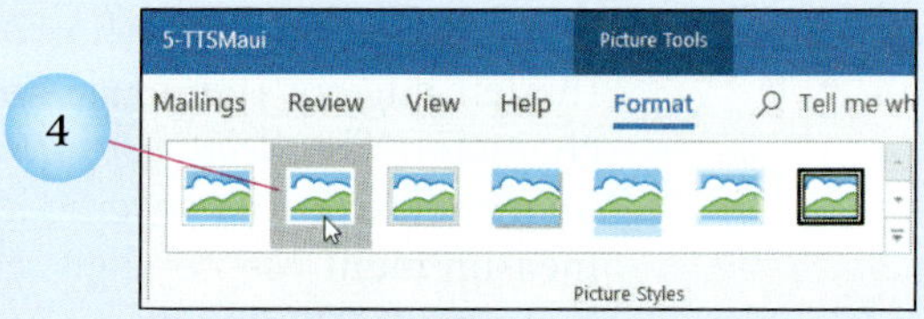

5. Click the Corrections button in the Adjust group and then click the *Brightness: –20% Contrast: +20%* option (second column, fourth row in the *Brightness/Contrast* section).
6. After looking at the image, you decide to reset it. Do this by clicking the Reset Picture button arrow in the Adjust group and then clicking *Reset Picture & Size* at the drop-down list.

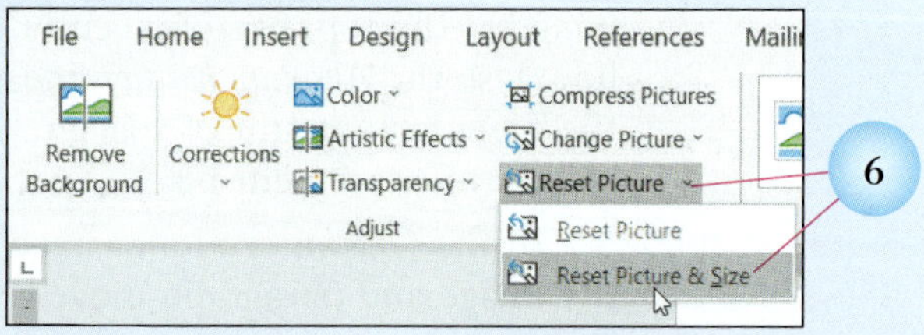

7. Select the current measurement in the *Shape Height* measurement box, type 1.3, and then press the Enter key.
8. Click the Wrap Text button in the Arrange group and then click *In Front of Text* at the drop-down gallery.
9. Position the image precisely on the page by completing the following steps:
   a. With the image selected, click the Size group dialog box launcher.
   b. At the Layout dialog box, click the Position tab.
   c. Make sure the *Absolute position* option in the *Horizontal* section is selected.
   d. Press the Tab key two times and then type 6.2 in the *Absolute position* measurement box.
   e. Click the *to the right of* option box arrow and then click *Page* at the drop-down list.
   f. If necessary, click the *Absolute position* option in the *Vertical* section.
   g. Select the current measurement in the box at the right of the *Absolute position* measurement box and then type 2.
   h. Click the *below* option box arrow and then click *Page* at the drop-down list.
   i. Click OK to close the Layout dialog box.

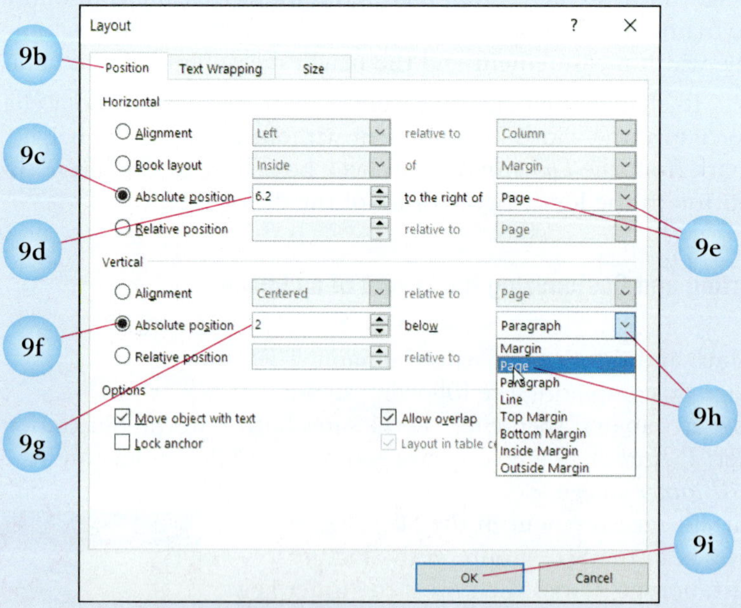

10. Click the *Drop Shadow Rectangle* style in the Picture Styles group (fourth style from the left).

11. Click the Color button in the Adjust group and then click the *Blue, Accent color 1 Light* option (second column, third row in the *Recolor* section).
12. Compress the image by clicking the Compress Pictures button in the Adjust group and then clicking OK at the Compress Pictures dialog box.
13. Click outside the image to deselect it.
14. Save **5-TTSMaui**.

Check Your Work

Tutorial

Formatting an Image at the Format Picture Task Pane

Applying Formatting at the Format Picture Task Pane

Options for formatting an image are available at the Format Picture task pane, shown in Figure 5.2. Display this task pane by clicking the Picture Styles group task pane launcher on the Picture Tools Format tab.

The options in the Format Picture task pane vary depending on the icon selected. The formatting options may need to be expanded within the icons. For example, click *Shadow* in the task pane with the Effects icon selected to display options for applying shadow effects to an image. Many of the options available at the Format Picture task pane are also available on the Picture Tools Format tab. The task pane is a central location for formatting options and also includes some additional advanced formatting options.

Applying Artistic Effects to Images

Artistic Effects

Apply an artistic effect to a selected image with the Artistic Effects button in the Adjust group on the Picture Tools Format tab. Click this button and a drop-down gallery displays with effect options. Hover the mouse pointer over an option in the drop-down gallery to see the effect applied to the selected image. An artistic effect can also be applied to an image with options at the Format Picture task pane with the Effects icon selected.

Figure 5.2 Format Picture Task Pane

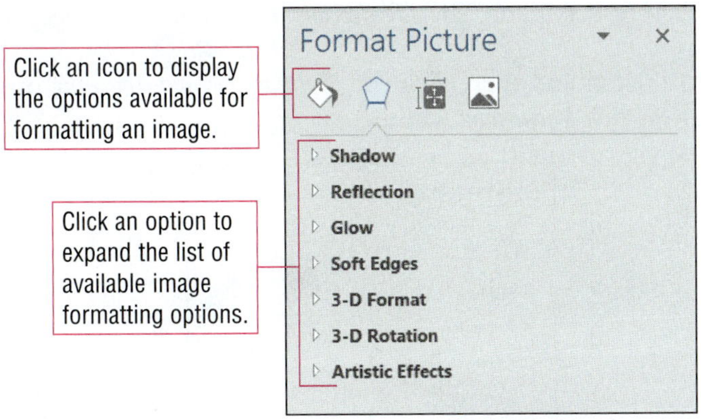

Activity 1b Inserting and Customizing a Photograph

1. With **5-TTSMaui** open, press Ctrl + End to move the insertion point to the end of the document and then insert a photograph by completing the following steps:
   a. Click the Insert tab and then click the Pictures button in the Illustrations group.
   b. At the Insert Picture dialog box, navigate to your WL2C5 folder and then double-click the ***Surfing*** image file.
2. With the surfing photograph selected, click the Picture Effects button in the Picture Styles group, point to *Bevel*, and then click the *Round* option (first column, first row in the *Bevel* section).
3. Click the Artistic Effects button in the Adjust group and then click the *Cutout* option (first column, bottom row).

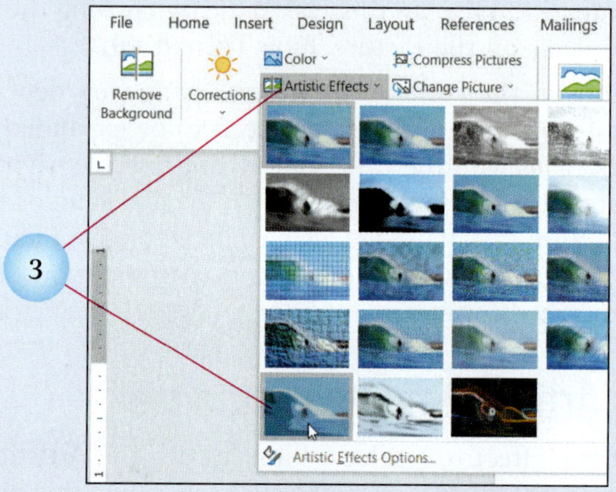

4. After looking at the formatting, you decide to remove it from the image by clicking the Reset Picture button in the Adjust group.
5. Select the current measurement in the *Shape Height* measurement box, type 1.4, and then press the Enter key.
6. Format the photograph by completing the following steps:
   a. Click the Picture Styles group task pane launcher.
   b. At the Format Picture task pane, click *Reflection* to expand the reflection options in the task pane.
   c. Click the Presets button and then click the *Tight Reflection: Touching* option (first column, first row in the *Reflection Variations* section).

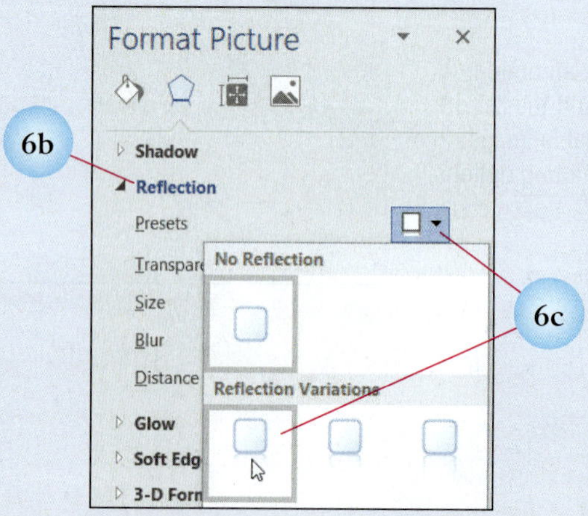

d. Click *Artistic Effects* in the task pane to expand the artistic effect options.
e. Click the Artistic Effects button and then click the *Paint Brush* option (third column, second row).

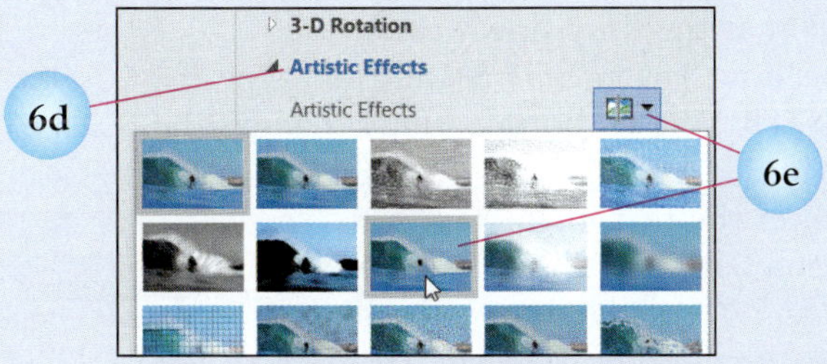

f. Close the task pane by clicking the Close button in the upper right corner.

7. Click the Wrap Text button in the Arrange group on the Picture Tools Format tab and then click *Tight* at the drop-down list.
8. Position the photograph precisely on the page by completing the following steps:
   a. With the photograph selected, click the Position button in the Arrange group and then click *More Layout Options* at the bottom of the drop-down gallery.
   b. At the Layout dialog box with the Position tab selected, select the current measurement in the *Absolute position* measurement box in the *Horizontal* section and then type 5.3.
   c. Click the *to the right of* option box arrow and then click *Page* at the drop-down list.
   d. Select the current measurement in the *Absolute position* measurement box in the *Vertical* section and then type 6.6.
   e. Click the *below* option box arrow and then click *Page* at the drop-down list.
   f. Click OK to close the Layout dialog box.
9. Click outside the photograph to deselect it.
10. Save **5-TTSMaui**.

Check Your Work

Customizing and Formatting Text Boxes and Shapes

When an object such as a text box or shape is inserted in a document, the Drawing Tools Format tab is active. Use options on this tab to format and customize a text box or shape or use options at the Format Shape task pane.

Customizing a Text Box Click the Shape Styles group task pane launcher and the Format Shape task pane displays with three icons: Fill & Line, Effects, and Layout & Properties. Click the WordArt Styles group task pane launcher and the Format Shape task pane displays but with different icons. The task pane displays with *Text Options* selected and with three icons: Text Fill & Outline, Text Effects, and Layout & Properties.

Activity 1c Inserting and Customizing a Text Box

1. With **5-TTSMaui** open, insert a text box by completing the following steps:
   a. Click the Insert tab, click the Text Box button in the Text group, and then click the *Draw Text Box* option at the drop-down list.
   b. Click above the heading *MAUI SITES* and then type Hawaii, the Aloha State.
2. Select the text box by clicking its border. (This changes the text box border from a dashed line to a solid line.)
3. Press Ctrl + E to center the text in the text box.
4. Click the Text Direction button in the Text group and then click *Rotate all text 270°* at the drop-down list.
5. Select the current measurement in the *Shape Height* measurement box, type 6, and then press the Enter key.
6. Select the current measurement in the *Shape Width* measurement box, type 0.8, and then press the Enter key.
7. Format the text box by completing the following steps:
   a. Click the Shape Styles group task pane launcher.
   b. At the Format Shape task pane with the Fill & Line icon selected, click *Fill* to expand the options.
   c. Click the Fill Color button (displays at the right of the *Color* option) and then click the *Blue, Accent 1, Lighter 80%* option (fifth column, second row).
   d. Click the Effects icon and then click *Shadow* to expand the options.
   e. Click the Presets button and then click the *Offset: Bottom* option (second column, first row in the *Outer* section).
   f. Scroll down the task pane and then click *Glow* to expand the options.
   g. Click the Presets button in the *Glow* section and then click the *Glow: 5 point; Blue, Accent color 1* option (first column, first row in the *Glow Variations* section).

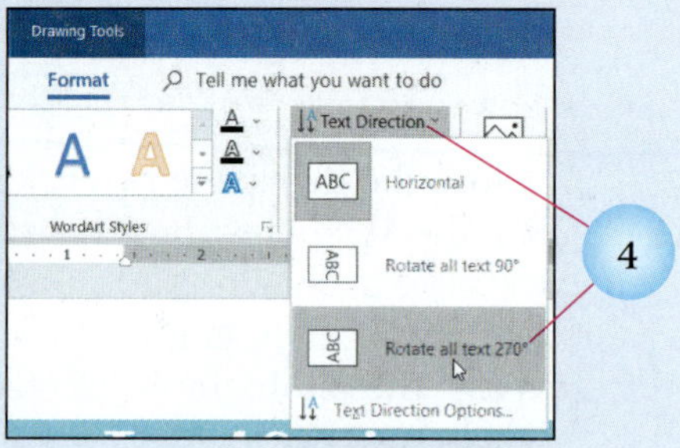

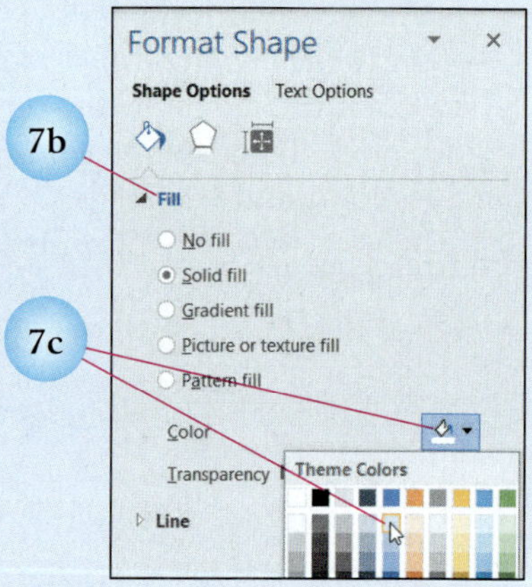

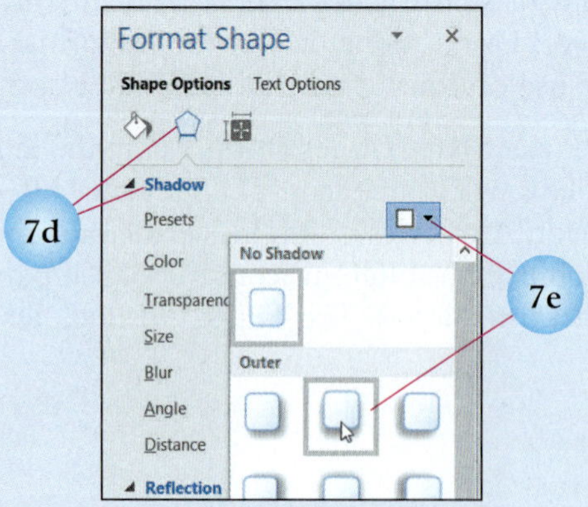

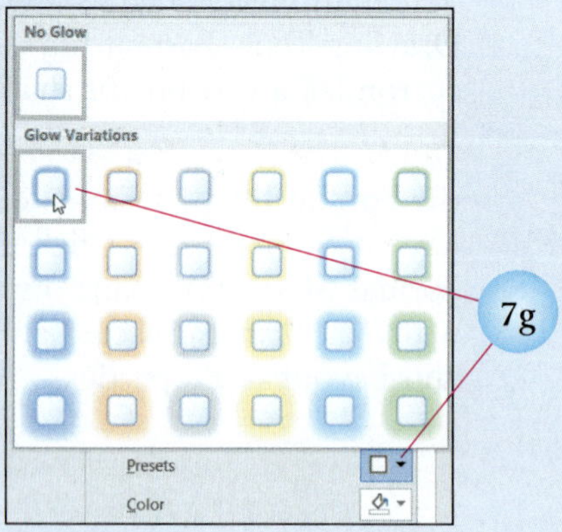

   h. Close the Format Shape task pane by clicking the Close button in the upper right corner.
8. Click the More WordArt Styles button in the WordArt Styles group and then click the option in the fourth column, second row (white fill, blue outline).

9. Position the text box precisely on the page by completing the following steps:
   a. With the text box selected, click the Size group dialog box launcher.
   b. At the Layout dialog box, click the Position tab.
   c. Select the current measurement in the *Absolute position* measurement box in the *Horizontal* section and then type 1.
   d. Click the *to the right of* option box arrow and then click *Page* at the drop-down list.
   e. Select the current measurement in the *Absolute position* measurement box in the *Vertical* section and then type 2.7.
   f. Click the *below* option box arrow and then click *Page* at the drop-down list.
   g. Click OK to close the Layout dialog box.
10. Click the Home tab, click the *Font Size* option arrow, and then click *36* at the drop-down gallery.
11. Click outside the text box to deselect it.
12. Save, print, and then close **5-TTSMaui**.

Check Your Work

Activity 2 Customize Shapes and Link and Unlink Text Boxes in a Financial Services Flyer — 4 Parts

You will open a promotional flyer for a financial services group and customize the design. To do this, you will format, group, customize, ungroup, and edit points of a shape. You will also edit wrap points around an image and link and unlink text boxes.

Customizing Shapes Like a text box, a shape can be customized with buttons and options on the Drawing Tools Format tab or with options at the Format Shape task pane. Customize or format one shape or select multiple shapes and then customize and apply formatting to all the selected shapes. Display the Format Shape task pane for a shape by clicking the Shape Styles group task pane launcher. When a shape is selected, the WordArt Styles group task pane launcher is dimmed and unavailable.

Tutorial

Grouping and Ungrouping Objects

Quick Steps

Group Objects

1. Select objects.
2. Click Picture Tools Format tab (or Drawing Tools Format tab).
3. Click Group button.
4. Click *Group*.

Grouping and Ungrouping Objects Objects in a document, such as images, text boxes, or shapes, can be grouped so that they can be sized, moved, or formatted as one object. Text wrapping other than *In Line with Text* must be applied to each object to be grouped. To group objects, select the objects, click the Picture Tools Format tab (or Drawing Tools Format tab), click the Group button in the Arrange group, and then click *Group* at the drop-down list. With the objects grouped, move, size, or apply formatting to all the objects in the group at once.

To select objects, click the first object, press and hold down the Shift key, click each remaining object to be included in the group, and then release the Shift key. Another method for grouping objects is to click the Select button in the Editing group on the Home tab, click the *Select Objects* option, and then use the mouse to draw a border around all the objects. Turn off selecting objects by clicking the Select button and then clicking the *Select Objects* option.

Hint Group multiple objects to work with them as if they are a single object.

Hint A group can be created within a group.

Grouped objects can be sized, moved, and formatted as one object. However, an object within a group of objects can be sized, moved, or formatted individually. To do this, click the specific object and then make the changes to the individual object.

To ungroup grouped objects, click the group to select it and then click the Picture Tools Format tab (or Drawing Tools Format tab). Click the Group button in the Arrange group and then click the *Ungroup* option at the drop-down list.

Activity 2a Customizing and Formatting Shapes

Part 1 of 4

1. Open **Leland** and then save it with the name **5-Leland**.
2. Rotate the middle arrow shape by completing the following steps:
   a. Scroll down the document and then click the middle arrow shape to select it (on the first page).
   b. Click the Drawing Tools Format tab.
   c. Click the Rotate button in the Arrange group and then click *Flip Horizontal* at the drop-down list.

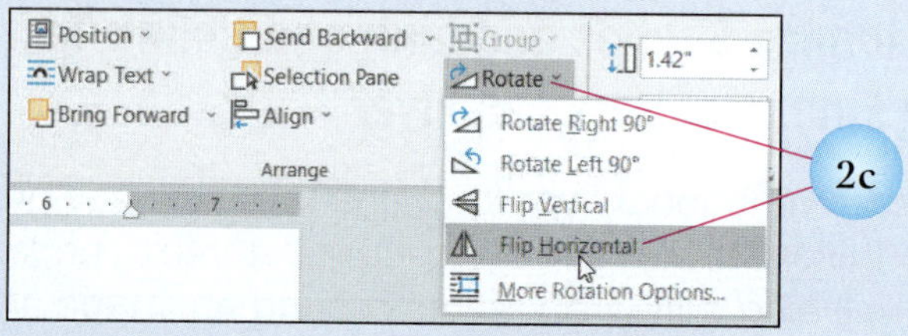

3. Align and format the arrow shapes by completing the following steps:
   a. With the middle arrow shape selected, press and hold down the Shift key.
   b. Click the top arrow shape, click the bottom arrow shape, and then release the Shift key.
   c. With all three arrow shapes selected, click the Align button in the Arrange group and then click *Align Left* at the drop-down list.
   d. Click the Shape Styles group task pane launcher.
   e. At the Format Shape task pane with the Fill & Line icon selected, click *Fill*, if necessary, to expand the fill options.
   f. Click the *Gradient fill* option.
   g. Click the Preset gradients button and then click the *Top Spotlight - Accent 2* option (second column, second row).

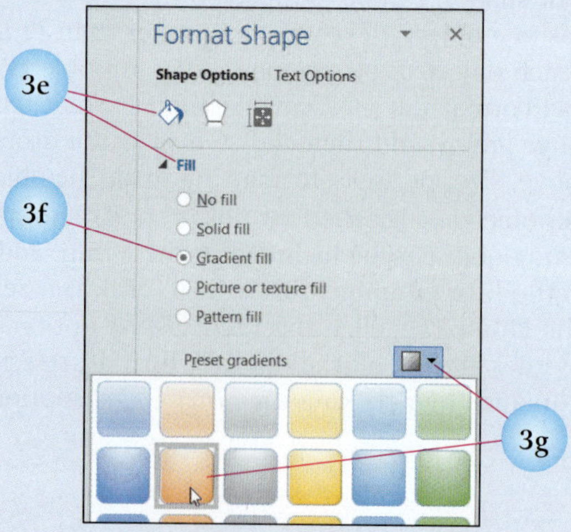

h. Scroll down the task pane and then click *Line* to expand the line options.
i. If necessary, scroll down the task pane and then click the *No line* option.
j. Click the Effects icon (at the top of the task pane).
k. If necessary, click *Shadow* to expand the shadow options.
l. Click the Presets button and then click the *Inside: Top Right* option (third column, first row in the *Inner* section).
m. Close the Format Shape task pane.

4. With the three arrow shapes still selected, group the shapes, size and move the group, and then ungroup the shapes by completing the following steps:
   a. Click the Group button in the Arrange group and then click *Group* at the drop-down list.

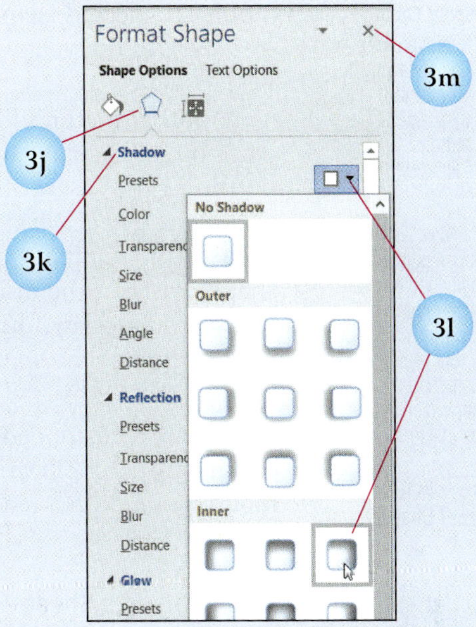

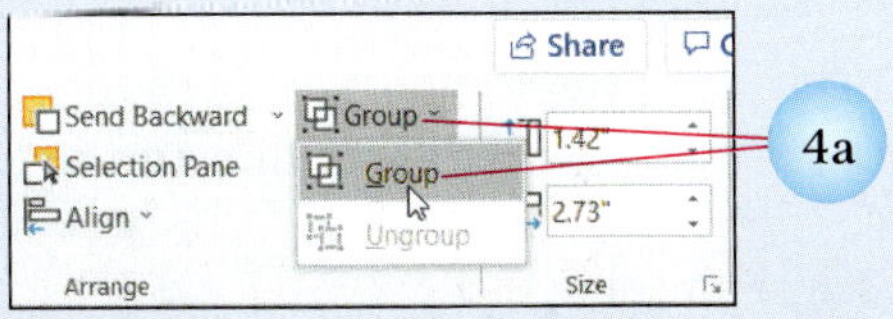

   b. Click in the *Shape Height* measurement box and then type 6 in the Size group.
   c. Click in the *Shape Width* measurement box in the Size group, type 3.7, and then press the Enter key.
   d. Click the Position button in the Arrange group and then click the *Position in Bottom Center with Square Text Wrapping* option (second column, third row in the *With Text Wrapping* section).

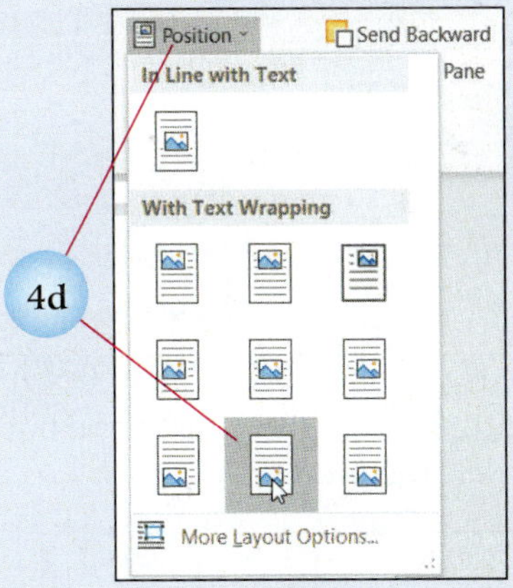

   e. Click the Group button and then click *Ungroup* at the drop-down list.
   f. Click outside the arrow shapes to deselect the shapes.

5. Delete the bottom arrow shape of the three arrow shapes by clicking the shape and then pressing the Delete key.
6. Save **5-Leland**.

Check Your Work

Quick Steps
Display Editing Points
1. Select shape.
2. Click Drawing Tools Format tab.
3. Click Edit Shape button.
4. Click *Edit Points.*

Hint When the mouse pointer is positioned over an editing point, it displays as a box surrounded by four triangles; when positioned over a red line, it displays as a box inside a cross.

Edit Shape

Editing Points in a Shape Sizing handles are small white circles that display around a selected shape. Depending on the shape, small yellow circles might also display. Use the yellow circles to change the width or height of a specific element in the shape.

Another method for customizing specific elements is to display and then use edit points. Display edit points by selecting the shape, clicking the Edit Shape button in the Insert Shapes group on the Drawing Tools Format tab, and then clicking the *Edit Points* option. Edit points display as small black squares at the intersecting points in the shape. A red line also displays between edit points in the shape. Position the mouse pointer on an edit point and the pointer displays as a box surrounded by four triangles ( ). Click and hold down the left mouse button, drag to change the specific element in the shape, and then release the mouse button.

Create a custom editing point by pressing and holding down the Ctrl key, clicking a specific location on a red line, and then releasing the Ctrl key. Position the mouse pointer on a red line and the pointer displays as a box inside a cross ( ).

Activity 2b Editing Points in a Shape

Part 2 of 4

1. With **5-Leland** open, press Ctrl + End to move the insertion point to the end of the document (page 2).
2. Click the shape on the second page to select the shape.
3. With the shape selected, edit points by completing the following steps:
   a. Position the mouse pointer on the top yellow circle, click and hold down the left mouse button, drag to the right approximately one-half inch (use the horizontal ruler as a guide and drag to approximately the 2.5-inch mark on the ruler), and then release the mouse button.

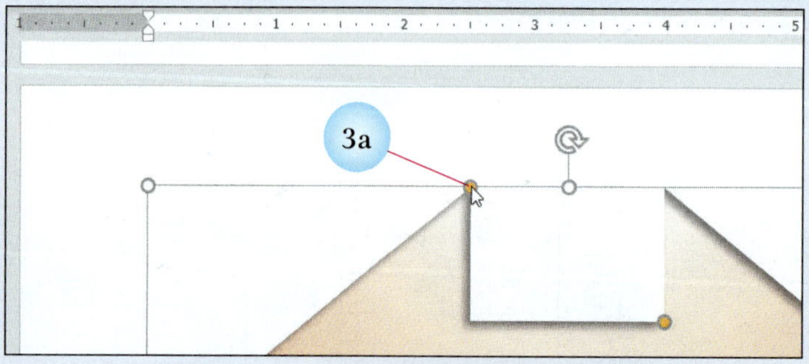

   b. Click the Drawing Tools Format tab, click the Edit Shape button in the Insert Shapes group, and then click *Edit Points* at the drop-down list.

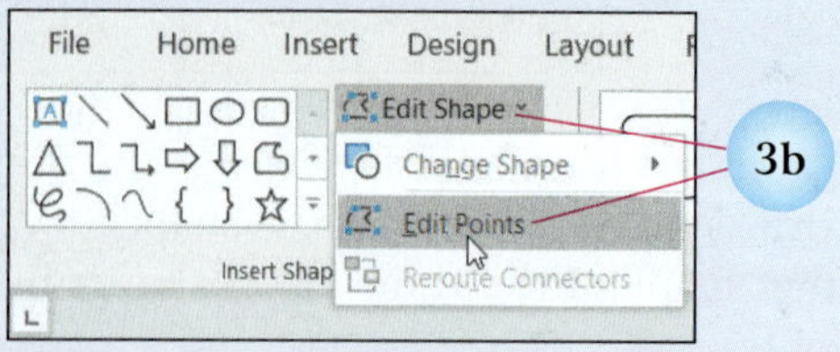

c. Position the mouse pointer on the edit point that displays at the tip of the arrow at the right side of the shape. Click and hold down the left mouse button, drag to the left approximately 1 inch (use the horizontal ruler as a guide), and then release the mouse button. (The shape will move when you release the mouse button.)

d. Position the mouse pointer on the edit point that displays at the tip of the arrow at the left side of the shape. Click and hold down the left mouse button, drag to the right approximately 1 inch (use the horizontal ruler as a guide), and then release the mouse button. (The shape will move when you release the mouse button.)

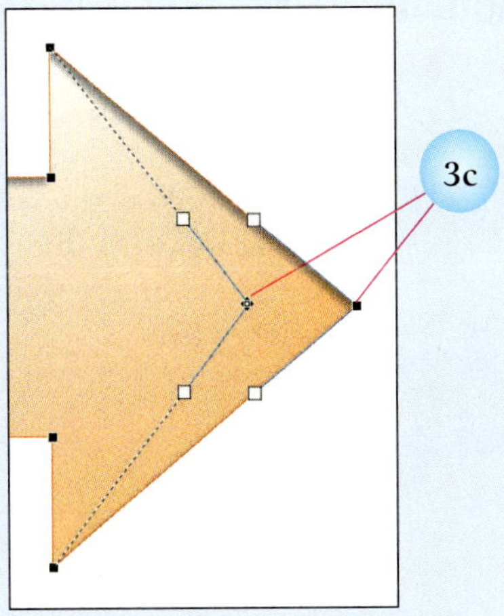

4. Reposition the shape by clicking the Position button in the Arrange group and then clicking the *Position in Top Center with Square Text Wrapping* option (second column, first row in the *With Text Wrapping* section).
5. Insert and format text in the shape by completing the following steps:
   a. With the shape selected, type Free seminar!, press the Enter key, and then type 1-888-555-4588.
   b. Click the border of the shape to change the border to a solid line.
   c. Click the Text Fill button arrow in the WordArt Styles group and then click the *Orange, Accent 2, Darker 50%* color option (sixth column, bottom row in the *Theme Colors* section).
   d. Click the Home tab and then click the Bold button in the Font group.
   e. Click the *Font Size* option box arrow and then click *24* at the drop-down gallery.
6. Press Ctrl + Home to move the insertion point to the beginning of the document.
7. Save **5-Leland**.

Check Your Work

Quick Steps

Display Wrap Points for Object

1. Select object.
2. Click Picture Tools Format tab (or Drawing Tools Format tab).
3. Click Wrap Text button.
4. Click *Edit Wrap Points.*

Hint Remove a wrap point by pressing and holding down the Ctrl key, clicking the wrap point, and then releasing the Ctrl key.

Editing Wrap Points in a Shape When an object such as an image or shape is inserted in a document, a series of wrap points are defined around the object. These wrap points display in a manner similar to the editing points around an object. The difference between editing points and wrap points is that editing points change the shape of specific elements in an object while wrap points wrap text closer to or farther away from an object.

To display wrap points in a shape, select the shape, click the Drawing Tools Format tab, click the Wrap Text button in the Arrange group, and then click the *Edit Wrap Points* option. Display wrap points for an image in a similar manner except click the Wrap Text button on the Picture Tools Format tab. Use wrap points to change how text or other data wraps around an object by dragging specific wrap points.

When wrap points are displayed in an object, red lines appear between wrap points. Create a custom wrap point by clicking and holding down the left mouse pointer on a location on a red line and then dragging to a specific position.

Activity 2c Editing Wrap Points in a Shape

Part 3 of 4

1. With **5-Leland** open, click the border of the banner shape in the paragraph of text below the title.
2. Edit wrap points in the shape by completing the following steps:
   a. Click the Drawing Tools Format tab.
   b. Click the Wrap Text button in the Arrange group and then click *Edit Wrap Points* at the drop-down list.
   c. Drag the wrap point at the left side of the shape into the shape, as shown below.

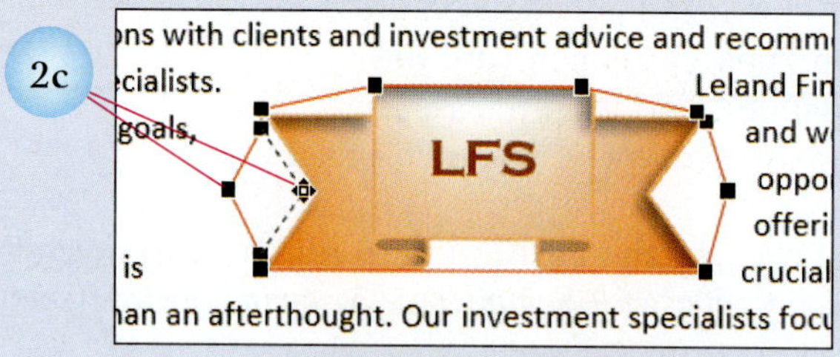

   d. Drag the wrap point at the right side of the shape into the shape, as shown below.

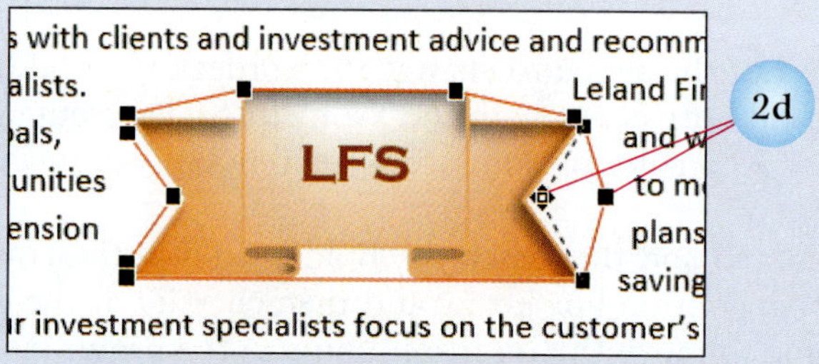

3. Click outside the shape to remove the wrap points.
4. Save **5-Leland**.

Check Your Work

Tutorial
Linking and Unlinking Text Boxes

Create Link

Break Link

Quick Steps
Link Text Boxes
1. Select text box.
2. Click Drawing Tools Format tab.
3. Click Create Link button.
4. Click in another text box.

Hint Link text boxes to flow text in columns across multiple pages.

Inserting a Text Box on a Shape

Not only can text be typed directly in a shape, but a text box can be drawn on a shape. When a text box is drawn on a shape, it is actually added as a layer on top of the shape. To format or move the text box with the shape, select or group the shape with the text box.

Linking and Unlinking Text Boxes

Linking text boxes allows the text in them to flow from one box to another. To do this, draw the text boxes and then click in the first text box. Click the Create Link button in the Text group on the Drawing Tools Format tab and the mouse pointer displays with a pouring jug icon ( ) attached. Click an empty text box to link it with the selected text box. Type text in the first text box and the text will flow to the linked text box.

More than two text boxes can be linked. To link several text boxes, click the first text box, click the Create Link button on the Drawing Tools Format tab, and then click in the second text box. Select the second text box, click the Create Link button, and then click the third text box. Continue in this manner until all the text boxes are linked.

To break a link between two boxes, select the first text box in the link and then click the Break Link button in the Text group. When a link is broken, all the text is placed in the first text box.

Activity 2d Linking and Unlinking Text Boxes

Part 4 of 4

1. With **5-Leland** open, scroll down the document to display the first arrow shape on the first page.
2. Insert, size, and format a text box by completing the following steps:
   a. Click the Insert tab.
   b. Click the Text Box button in the Text group and then click *Draw Text Box* at the drop-down list.
   c. Click in the document near the first shape.
   d. With the text box selected, click in the *Shape Height* measurement box and then type 0.73.
   e. Click in the *Shape Width* measurement box and then type 2.
   f. Click the Shape Fill button arrow in the Shape Styles group and then click *No Fill* at the drop-down list.
   g. Drag the text box so it is positioned on the first arrow (see the image at the right).
   h. Copy the text box to the second arrow shape by pressing and holding down the Ctrl key, clicking the text box border and holding down the left mouse button, dragging the copy of the text box so it is positioned on top of the second arrow shape, and then releasing the mouse button and the Ctrl key.

2g

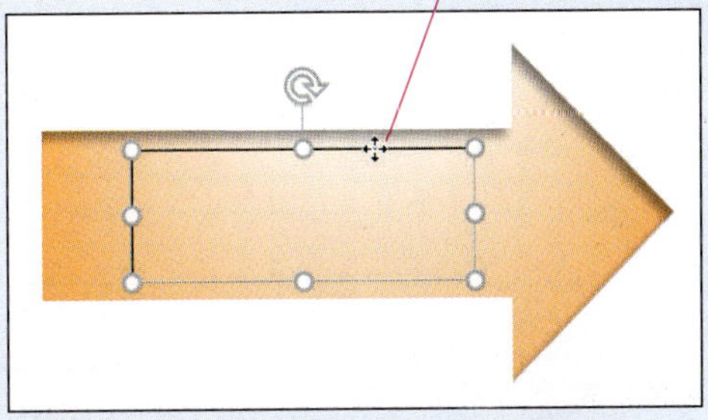

3. Link the text boxes by completing the following steps:
   a. Click the border of the text box on the first arrow shape to select the text box.
   b. Click the Create Link button in the Text group on the Drawing Tools Format tab.
   c. Click in the text box on the second arrow shape.

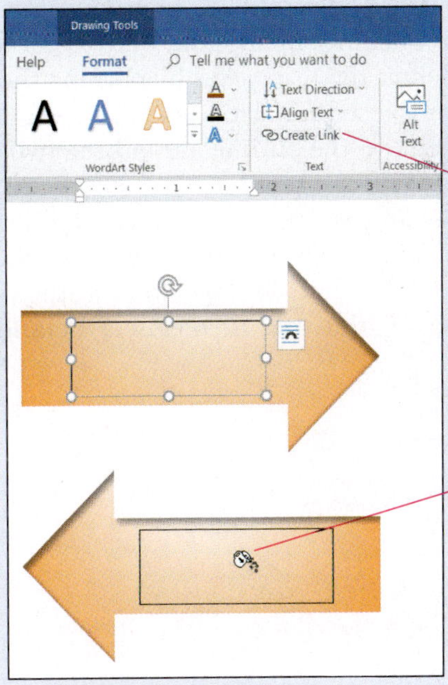

3b

3c

4. Insert text in the text box on the first arrow shape by completing the following steps:
   a. Click in the text box on the first arrow shape.
   b. Click the Home tab, change the font size to 12 points, apply the Orange, Accent 2, Darker 50% font color (sixth column, bottom row in the *Theme Colors* section), and then apply bold formatting.
   c. Click the Center button in the Paragraph group.
   d. Click the Line and Paragraph Spacing button in the Paragraph group and then click *Remove Space After Paragraph*.
   e. Click the Line and Paragraph Spacing button and then click *1.0*.

f. Type Let Leland Financial Services help you plan for retirement and provide you with information to determine your financial direction. (The text will flow to the text box on the second arrow shape.)

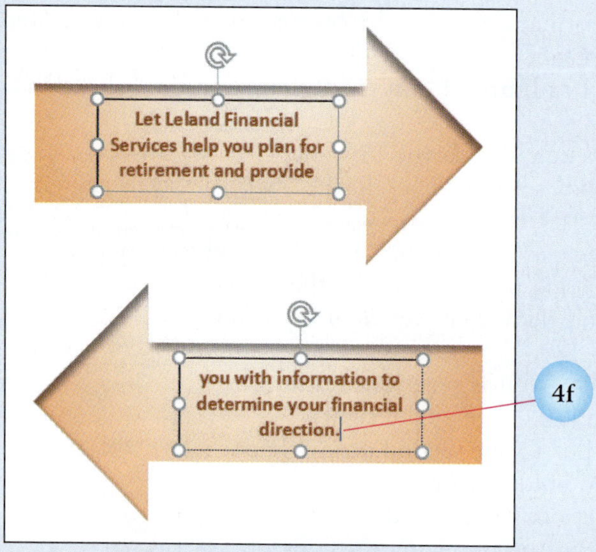

5. Break the link between the text boxes by completing the following steps:
   a. Select the text box on the first arrow shape by clicking the text box border.
   b. Click the Drawing Tools Format tab.
   c. Click the Break Link button in the Text group (previously the Create Link button).
6. Relink the text boxes by clicking the Create Link button and then clicking in the text box on the second arrow shape.
7. Remove the outline around the two text boxes by completing the following steps:
   a. With the text box on the first arrow shape selected, press and hold down the Shift key and then click the text box border of the second arrow shape.
   b. With both text boxes selected, click the Shape Outline button in the Shape Styles group and then click *No Outline* at the drop-down list.
8. Save, print, and then close **5-Leland**.

Check Your Work

Activity 3 Insert an Icon and 3D Model in an Award Certificate — 3 Parts

You will open an award certificate document and then insert and customize a football icon and a 3D model of a lion.

Tutorial
Inserting and Customizing Icons

Icons

Quick Steps
Insert Icon
1. Click Insert tab.
2. Click Icons button.
3. Double-click icon.

Hint Insert multiple icons at the same time by clicking each icon at the Insert Icons window and then clicking the Insert button.

Inserting and Customizing Icons

Use the Icons button in the Illustrations group on the Insert tab to insert an icon in a Word document. An icon is a graphical representation of something, such as an animal, emotion, weather, or an element from nature. Click the Icons button on the Insert tab and the Insert Icons window opens, as shown in Figure 5.3. At this window, scroll down the list box to view the various icons or click a category in the left panel to display a specific category of icons. To insert an icon in a document, double-click the icon in the list box or click the icon and then click the Insert button.

When an icon is inserted and selected in a document, the Graphic Tools Format tab is active, as shown in Figure 5.4. Use options on this tab to apply a graphic style, fill, outline, and effect; type alternate text for the icon; position, align, group, rotate, and size the icon; and apply text wrapping.

Icons, like other images, can be formatted with options at the Layout dialog box and with options at a task pane. Display the Layout dialog box by clicking the Size group dialog box launcher. Click the Graphics Styles group task pane launcher to display the Format Graphic task pane. The task pane contains the Text Fill & Outline icon and the Text Effects icon. Use options at the Format Graphic task pane to format an icon in a manner similar to formatting an image, shape, or text box.

Figure 5.3 Insert Icons Window

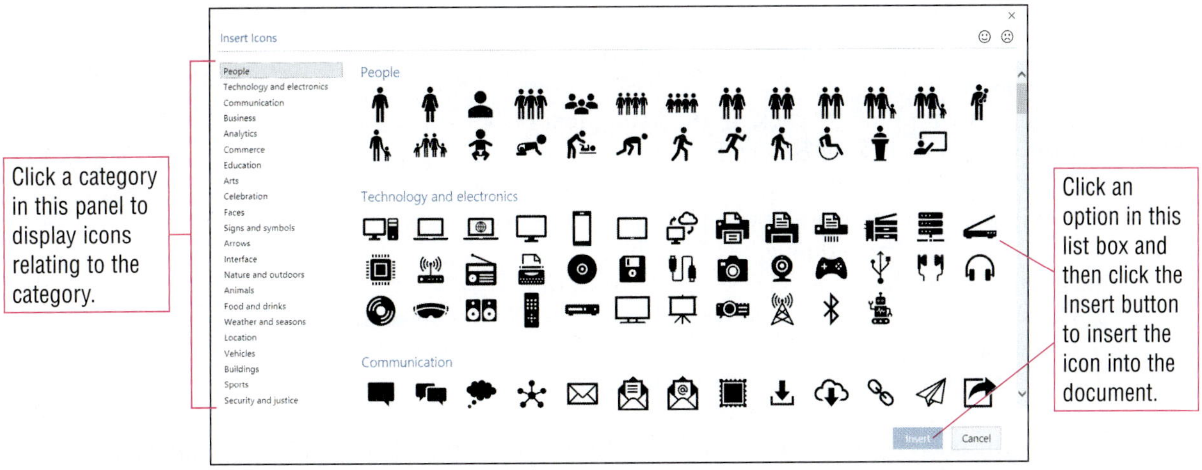

Figure 5.4 Graphic Tools Format Tab

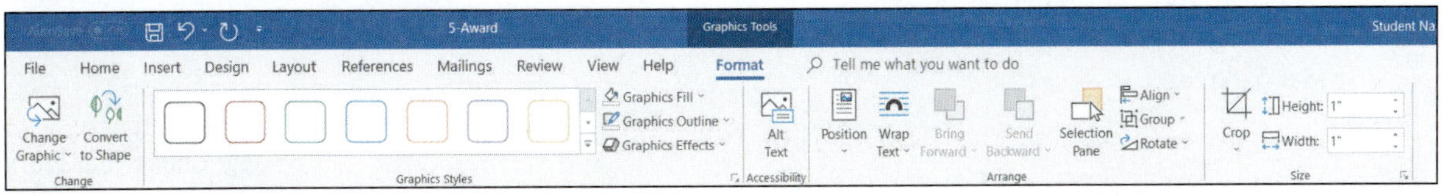

Activity 3a Inserting and Customizing an Icon

1. Open **Award** and then save it with the name **5-Award**.
2. Insert an icon by completing the following steps:
   a. Click the Insert tab.
   b. Click the Icons button in the Illustrations group.
   c. At the Insert Icons window, scroll down the category list box and then click the *Sports* category.
   d. Double-click the football icon (fifth column, second row; location may vary).

3. Increase the height of the football icon by clicking in the *Height* measurement box in the Size group, typing 2.7, and then pressing the Enter key.
4. Apply a style by clicking the *Light 1 Fill, Colored Outline - Accent 4* option (fifth style in the Graphics Styles gallery).

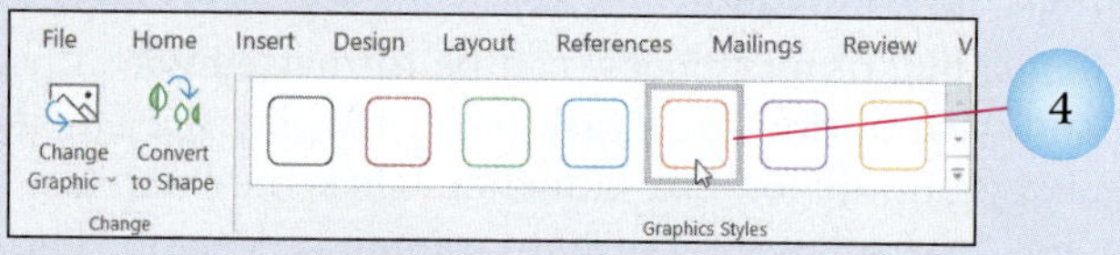

5. Change the width of the icon lines by completing the following steps:
   a. Click the Graphics Styles group task pane launcher.
   b. At the Format Graphic task pane, click *Line*, if necessary, to expand the line options.
   c. Click the *Width* measurement box up arrow two times. (This changes the width to *1.5 pt*.)
   d. Click the Close button in the upper right corner of the task pane.

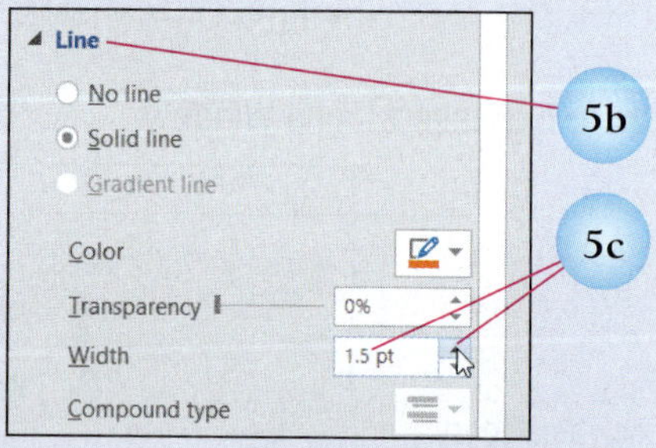

6. Change text wrapping by clicking the Wrap Text button and then clicking *Behind Text* at the drop-down gallery.
7. Precisely position the icon by completing the following steps:
   a. Click the Size group dialog box launcher.
   b. At the Layout dialog box, click the Position tab.
   c. Click the *to the right of* option box arrow in the *Horizontal* section and then click *Left Margin* at the drop-down list.
   d. Select the current measurement in the *Absolute position* measurement box in the *Horizontal* section and then type 4.15.
   e. Click the *below* option box arrow in the *Vertical* section and then click *Top Margin* at the drop-down list.
   f. Select the current measurement in the *Absolute position* measurement box in the *Vertical* section and then type 1.65.
   g. Click OK to close the Layout dialog box.
8. Save **5-Award**.

Check Your Work

Tutorial

Inserting and Customizing 3D Models

3D Models

Quick Steps

Insert 3D Model

1. Click Insert tab.
2. Click 3D Models button.
3. Click 3D model category.
4. Double-click 3D model.

Hint *3D* is an abbreviation for *three-dimensional*. It describes an object that has width, height, and depth.

Pan & Zoom

Inserting and Customizing 3D Models

Word supports inserting 3D models into a document. A 3D model is a graphic file of an image shown in three dimensions. The model can be rotated or tilted to allow viewing from various angles or to display a specific portion or feature. Microsoft's Remix 3D library includes a collection of free 3D models that can be inserted in a document. Access these models by clicking the 3D Models button in the Illustrations group on the Insert tab. At the Online 3D Models window, as shown in Figure 5.5, click a category to view all the 3D models within the category or type one or more keywords in the search text box and then press the Enter key. Some 3D models include animation. These are identified with a "runner" badge (an icon of a runner in the lower left corner of the model). Insert a 3D model in a document by double-clicking the model or clicking the model and then clicking the Insert button.

When a 3D model is inserted in a document, the 3D Model Tools Format tab is active. If the model is animated, the Play 3D group is available on the 3D Model Tools Format tab. Click the Play button to play the animation and click the Scenes button to display a drop-down list of preset animations called *scenes*. Use buttons in the Adjust group to insert a different 3D model or to reset the selected model to its original size and position. The 3D Model Views group includes a gallery of preset views for the model. Click the Alt Text button in the Accessibility group and the Alt Text task pane displays where a description of the model can be added. Use options in the Arrange group to position the model, apply text wrapping, send the model forward or backward, and align the model. Change the height and width of the model with options in the Size group.

The Size group also contains the Pan & Zoom button. Click this button and a button (a magnifying glass with a plus symbol inside) displays at the right of the selected model. Position the mouse pointer on this button, click and hold down the left mouse button, and then drag up to increase the size of the model (pan in) or drag down to decrease the size (pan out). To turn off the pan feature, click the Pan & Zoom button to deactivate it.

When a 3D model is selected, a Layout Options button displays outside the upper right corner. Click the Layout Options button and a side menu displays with text wrapping options. Click a text wrapping option and then click the side menu Close button.

Figure 5.5 Online 3D Models Window

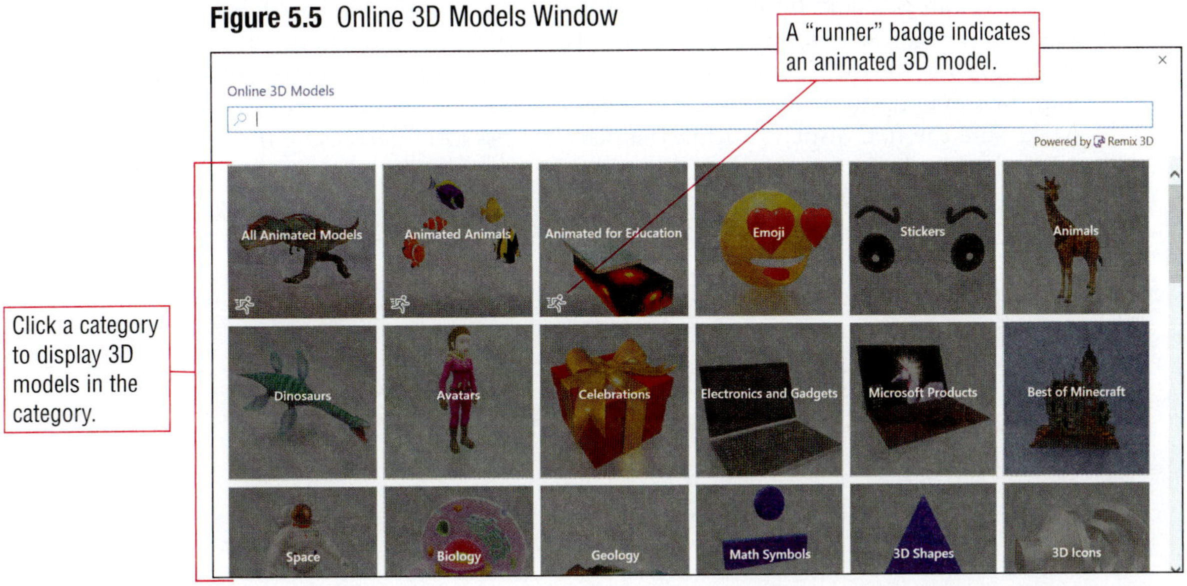

Use the 3D control in the middle of a selected 3D model to rotate or tilt the model. To use the 3D control, position the mouse pointer on the control, click and hold down the left mouse button, and then drag with the mouse to rotate or tilt the model.

Advanced layout options are available at the Layout dialog box. Click the Size group dialog box launcher to display the dialog box. Use options at the Layout dialog box to specify the size, text wrapping, and position of the 3D model.

A 3D model saved to the computer's hard drive can be inserted in a document. Click the 3D Models button arrow and a drop-down list displays with the options *From a File* and *From Online Sources*. Click the *From Online Sources* option and the Online 3D Models window opens. Click the *From a File* option and the 3D Objects folder on the computer's hard drive opens. Insert a 3D model from the folder by double-clicking the model.

Activity 3b Inserting and Customizing a 3D Model

Part 2 of 3

1. With **5-Award** open, press Ctrl + End to move the insertion point to the end of the document.
2. Insert a 3D model from the Remix 3D library by completing the following steps:
   a. Click the Insert tab.
   b. Click the 3D Models button in the Illustrations group.
   c. At the Online 3D Models window, click the *Animals* category.
   d. Double-click the lion model.
   Note: If you do not have access to the Online 3D Models window, open Award3D from your WL2C5 folder. This document contains the 3D lion model.

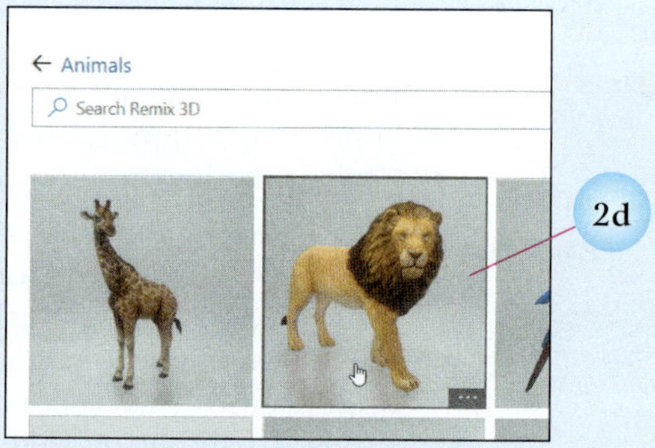

3. Experiment using the 3D control, which displays in the middle of the lion model, by positioning the mouse pointer on the 3D control, clicking and holding down the left mouse button, and then dragging with the mouse to rotate the model.
4. Pan in and out of the model by completing the following steps:
   a. Click the Pan & Zoom button in the Size group on the 3D Model Tools Format tab.
   b. Position the mouse pointer on the button that displays as a magnifying glass with a plus symbol inside (at the right of the model), click and hold down the left mouse button, and then drag up to increase the size of the model and drag down to decrease the size. Make sure the lion displays within the placeholders after decreasing the size.
   c. Click the Pan & Zoom button to deactivate it.
5. Reset the lion model by clicking the Reset 3D Model button in the Adjust group.
6. Change the view of the model by clicking the *Left* view (second option) in the 3D Model Views gallery.

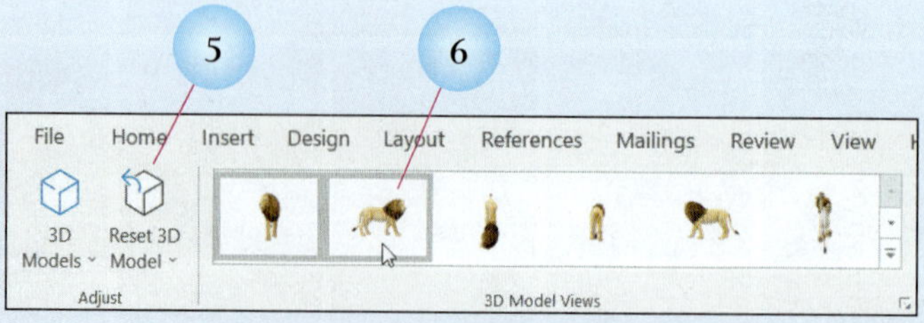

7. Using the 3D control, rotate the model so it displays as shown at the right.
8. Change the height of the model by clicking in the *Height* measurement box, typing 3.7, and then pressing the Enter key.
9. Precisely position the lion model by completing the following steps:
   a. Click the Size group dialog box launcher.
   b. At the Layout dialog box, click the Position tab.
   c. Click the *to the right of* option box arrow in the *Horizontal* section and then click *Left Margin* at the drop-down list.
   d. Select the current measurement in the *Absolute position* measurement box in the *Horizontal* section and then type -0.2. (Hint: Use the hyphen key to create the minus symbol before typing *0.2*.)
   e. Click the *below* option box arrow in the *Vertical* section and then click *Page* at the drop-down list.
   f. Select the current measurement in the *Absolute position* measurement box in the *Vertical* section and then type 4.2.
   g. Click OK to close the Layout dialog box.

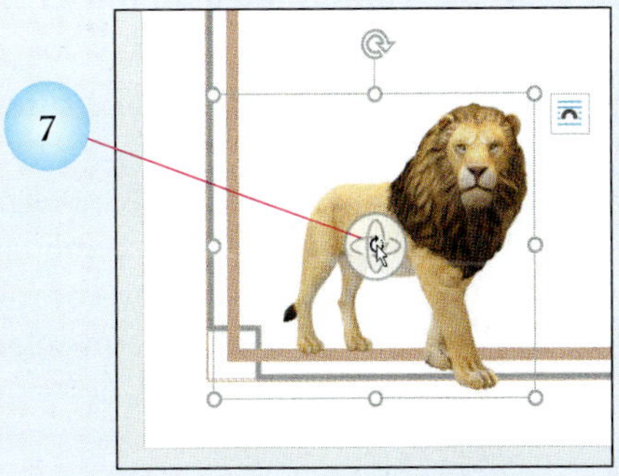

10. Check for alternative text for the lion model by completing the following steps:
    a. Click the Alt Text button in the Accessibility group.
    b. Notice that the description box in the Alt Text task pane contains the word *Lion*.

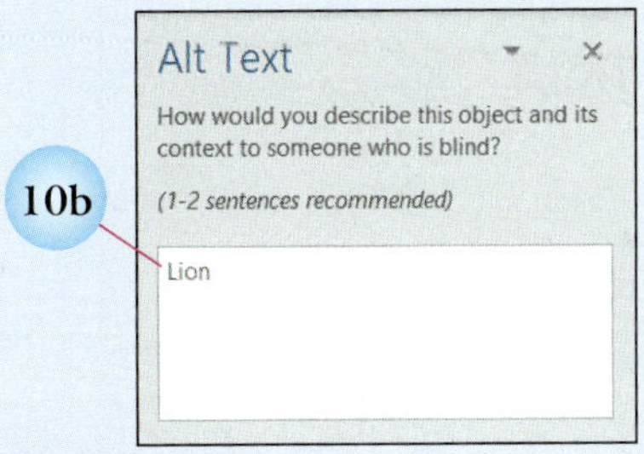

    c. Close the Alt Text task pane.
11. Save **5-Award**.

Check Your Work

Options for formatting and customizing a 3D model are available at the Format 3D Model task pane. Display the task pane by clicking the 3D Model Views group task pane launcher. The task pane displays with four icons: Fill & Line, Effects, Layout & Properties, and 3D Model. The options in the task pane vary depending on the icon selected.

The task pane opens with the 3D Model icon selected and contains options for specifying a rotation and camera view. Click the Fill & Line icon to display options for formatting the border line and fill of the 3D model. Use options at the task pane with the Effects icon selected to apply formatting effects, such as shadow, reflection, glow, and soft edges, and to format and rotate the model. Click the Layout & Properties icon and the options in the task pane are dimmed and unavailable.

Activity 3c Formatting a 3D Model with Task Pane Options

1. With **5-Award** open, make sure the lion model is selected and the 3D Model Tools Format tab is active.
2. Display the Format 3D Model task pane by clicking the 3D Model Views group task pane launcher.
3. Format the lion model by completing the following steps:
   a. With the 3D Model icon selected in the task pane, click *Model Rotation*, if necessary, to expand the options.
   b. Select the current degree measurement in the *X Rotation* measurement box and then type 3.5.
   c. Select the current degree measurement in the *Y Rotation* measurement box and then type 45.
   d. Select the current degree measurement in the *Z Rotation* measurement box and then type 2.7.
   e. Click the Effects icon in the task pane.
   f. Click *Shadow* to expand the shadow options, if necessary.
   g. Click the Presets button and then click the *Offset: Center* option (second column, second row in the *Outer* section).
   h. Close the Format 3D Model task pane.

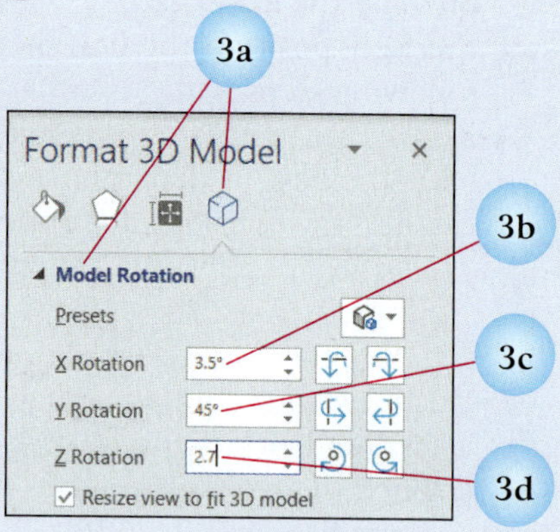

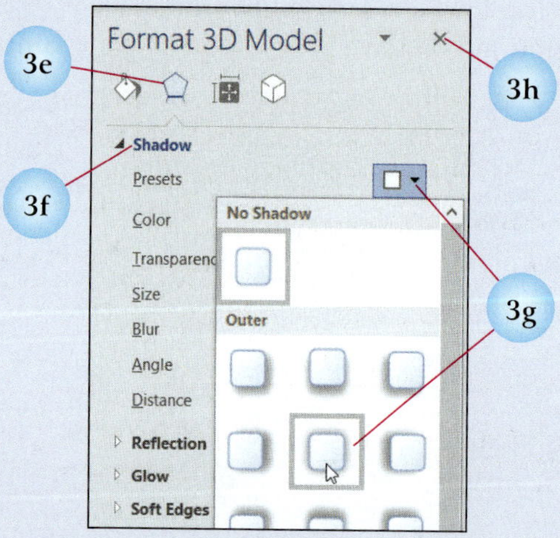

4. Save, print, and then close **5-Award**.

Check Your Work

Activity 4 Create and Format a Column Chart and a Pie Chart

5 Parts

You will use the Chart feature to create and format a column chart and then create and format a pie chart.

Tutorial
Creating a Chart

Chart

Quick Steps

Insert Chart
1. Click Insert tab.
2. Click Chart button.
3. Enter data in worksheet.
4. Close Excel.

Hint You can copy a chart from Excel to Word and embed it as static data or link it to the worksheet.

Creating a Chart

A chart is a visual presentation of data. In Word, a variety of charts can be created, including bar and column charts, pie charts, area charts, and many more. To create a chart, click the Insert tab and then click the Chart button in the Illustrations group. This displays the Insert Chart dialog box, as shown in Figure 5.6. At this dialog box, choose the chart type in the list at the left side, click the chart style, and then click OK.

Click OK at the Insert Chart dialog box and a chart is inserted in the document and a worksheet opens with sample data, as shown in Figure 5.7. Type specific data in the worksheet cells over the existing data. As data is typed in the worksheet, it appears in the chart in the Word document. To type data in the worksheet, click in a cell and type the data; then press the Tab key to make the next cell active, press Shift + Tab to make the previous cell active, or press the Enter key to make the cell below active.

The sample worksheet contains a data range of four columns and five rows and the cells in the data range display with a light fill color. More columns and rows may be added to the range as needed to create the chart. Simply type data in cells outside the data range and the data range expands and incorporates the new data in the chart. This occurs because the table AutoExpansion feature is turned on by default. If data is typed in a cell outside the data range, an AutoCorrect Options button displays in the lower right corner of the cell. Use this button to turn off AutoExpansion.

Figure 5.6 Insert Chart Dialog Box

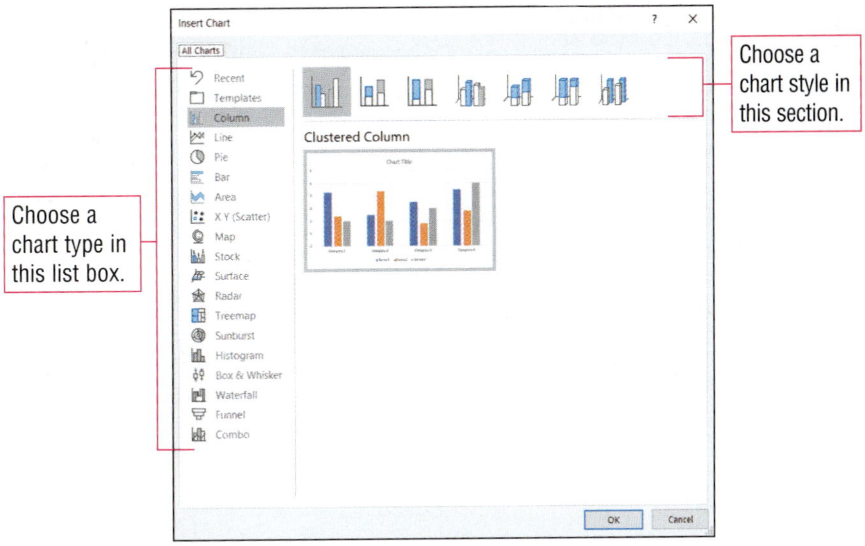

Figure 5.7 Sample Chart

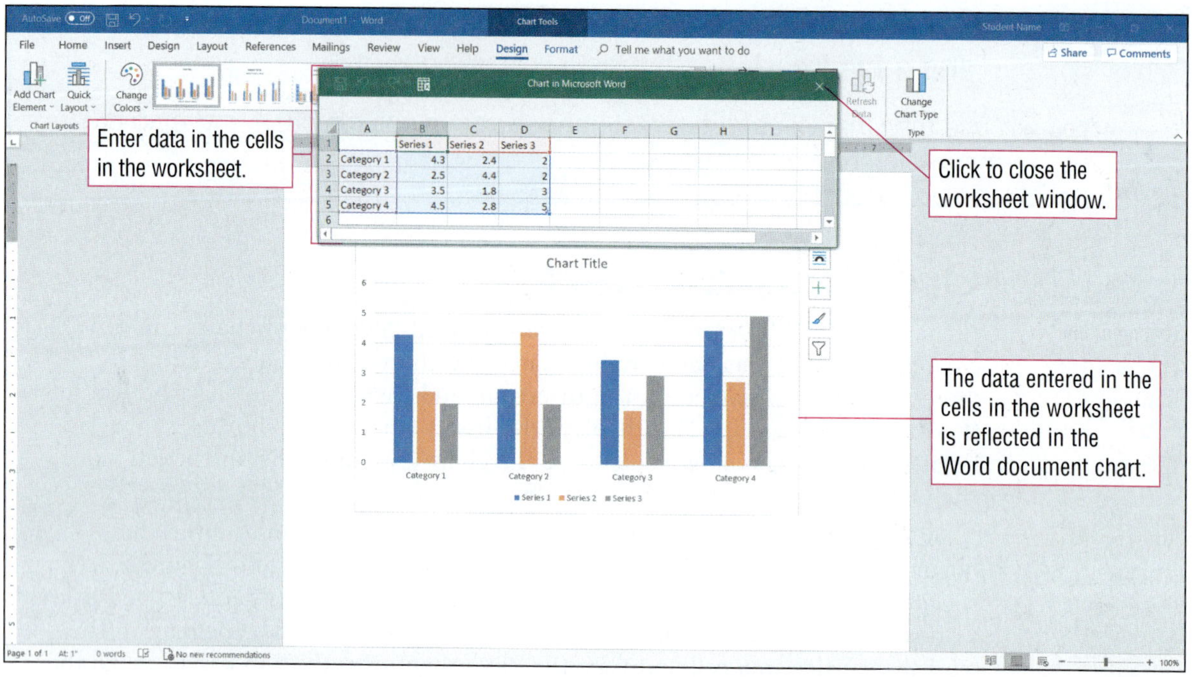

If data is not typed in all four columns and five rows, decrease the size of the data range. To do this, position the mouse pointer on the small blue square icon in the lower right corner of cell E5 until the pointer displays as a diagonally pointing two-headed arrow; then drag up to decrease the number of rows in the range and/or drag left to decrease the number of columns.

Edit Data in Microsoft Excel

Chart data can also be entered in Excel by clicking the Edit Data in Microsoft Excel button that displays in the worksheet window. When all the data is typed, click the Close button in the upper right corner of the worksheet. The worksheet window closes, the Word document window expands, and the chart displays in the document.

Activity 4a Creating a Column Chart

Part 1 of 5

1. At a blank document, click the Insert tab and then click the Chart button in the Illustrations group.
2. At the Insert Chart dialog box, click OK.
3. Type Sales 2019 in cell B1 in the worksheet.
4. Press the Tab key and then type Sales 2020 in cell C1.
5. Press the Tab key and then type Sales 2021 in cell D1.
6. Press the Tab key. (This makes cell A2 active.)
7. Continue typing the remaining data in cells, including dollar signs and commas as shown in Figure 5.8. After typing the last entry, click in cell A1.

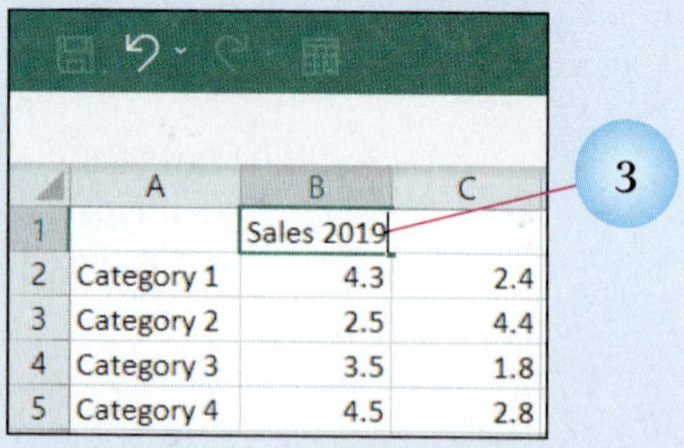

8. Since row 5 does not contain data related to the chart, decrease the size of the data range by completing the following steps:
   a. Position the mouse pointer on the small blue square icon in the lower right corner of cell E5 until the pointer displays as a diagonally pointing two-headed arrow.
   b. Click and hold down the left mouse button, drag up one row, and then release the mouse button. (The data range should contain four columns and four rows.)
9. Click the Close button in the upper right corner of the worksheet window.
10. Save the document and name it **5-Charts**.

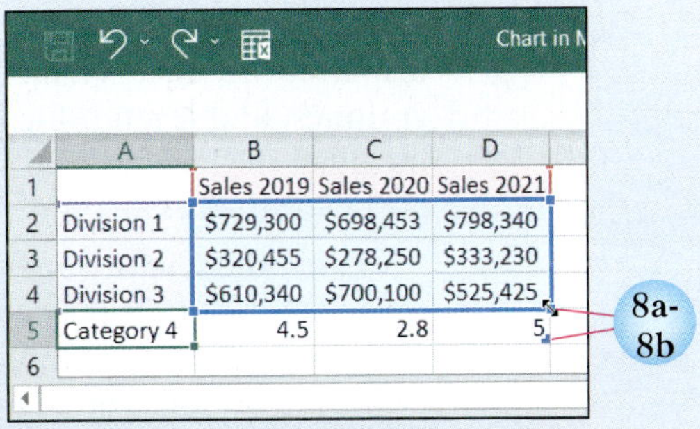

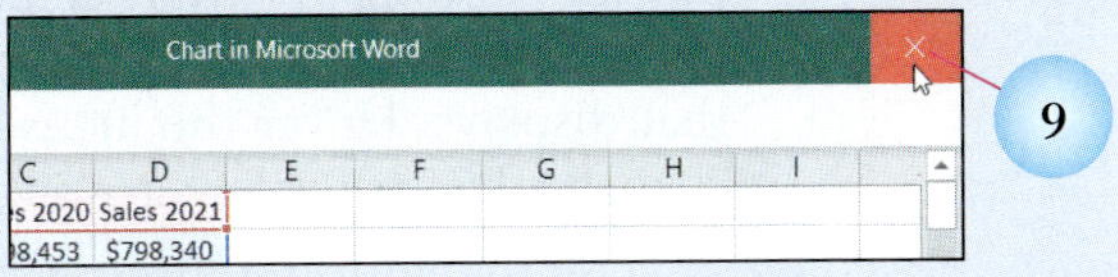

Check Your Work

Figure 5.8 Activity 4a

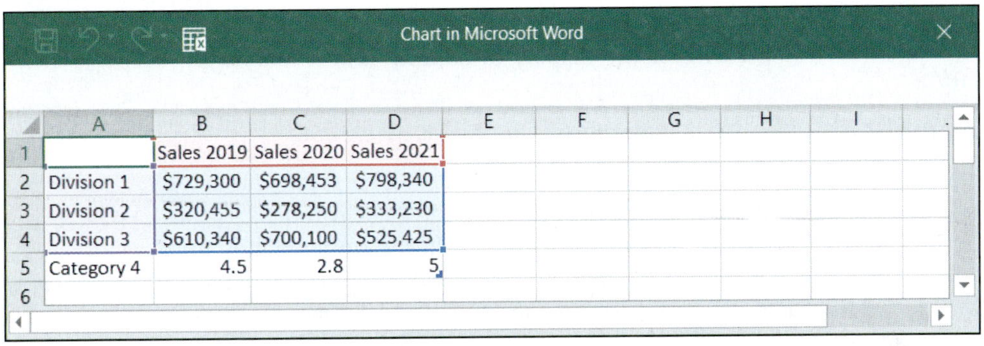

Tutorial

Formatting with Chart Buttons

Formatting with Chart Buttons

When a chart is inserted in a document, four buttons display at the right of the chart border, as shown in Figure 5.9. These buttons contain options for applying formatting to the chart.

Figure 5.9 Chart Buttons

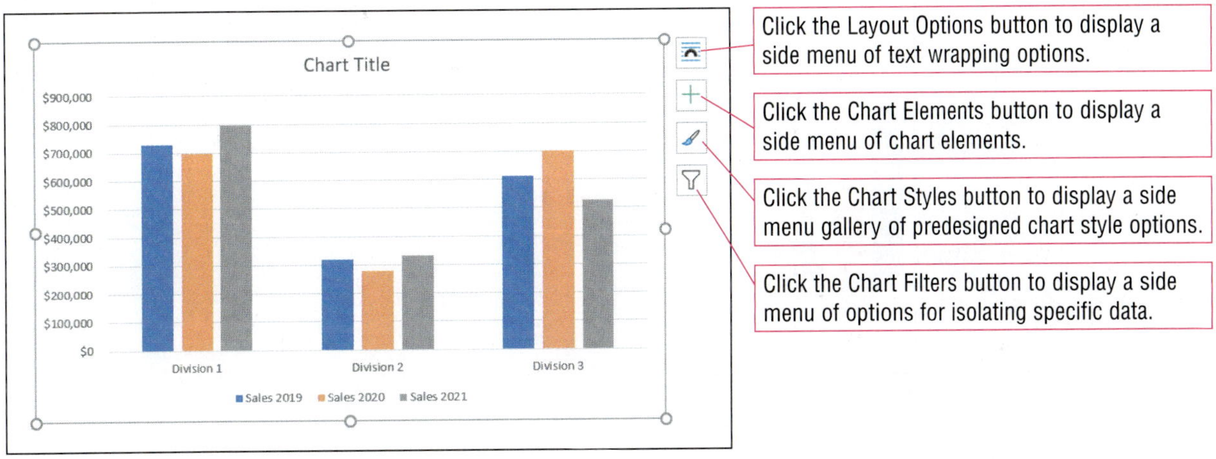

Click the top button, Layout Options, and a side menu displays with text wrapping options. Click the next button, Chart Elements, and a side menu displays with chart elements, such as axis title, chart title, data labels, data table, gridlines, and legend. Elements with check marks inserted in the check boxes are included in the chart. To include other elements, insert check marks in the check boxes for them.

Click the Chart Styles button at the right of the chart and a side menu gallery of styles displays. Scroll down the gallery and hover the mouse pointer over an option and the style formatting is applied to the chart. In addition to providing options for chart styles, the Chart Styles button side menu gallery provides options for chart colors. Click the Chart Styles button, click the Color tab at the right of the Style tab, and then click a color option at the color palette that displays. Hover the mouse pointer over a color option to view how the color change affects the elements in the chart.

Hint Use a pie chart if the data series you want to plot has seven categories or less and the categories represent parts of a whole.

Use the bottom button, Chart Filters, to isolate specific data in the chart. Click the button and a side menu displays. Specify the series or categories to display in the chart. To do this, remove the check marks in the check boxes for those elements that should not appear in the chart. After removing any check marks, click the Apply button in the lower left corner of the side menu. Click the Names tab at the Chart Filters button side menu and options display for turning on and off the display of column and row names.

Activity 4b Formatting with Chart Buttons

Part 2 of 5

1. With **5-Charts** open, make sure the chart is selected.
2. Click the Layout Options button outside the upper right corner of the chart and then click the *Square* option in the side menu (first option in the *With Text Wrapping* section).
3. Remove and add chart elements by completing the following steps:
   a. Click the Chart Elements button below the Layout Options button outside the upper right side of the chart.
   b. At the side menu, click the *Chart Title* check box to remove the check mark.
   c. Click the *Data Table* check box to insert a check mark.

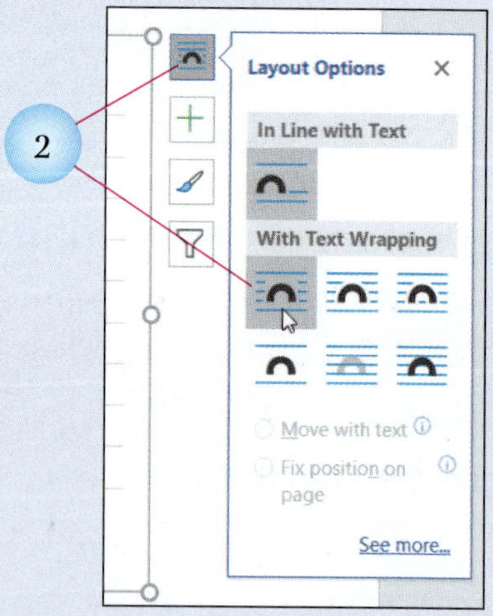

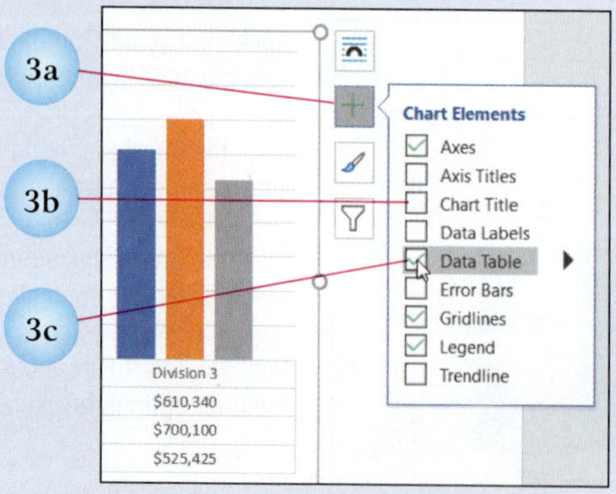

4. Apply a different chart style by completing the following steps:
   a. Click the Chart Styles button below the Chart Elements button.
   b. At the side menu gallery, click the *Style 3* option (third option in the gallery).
   c. Click the Color tab at the top of the side menu and then click the *Colorful Palette 4* option at the drop-down gallery (fourth row in the *Colorful* section).
   d. Click the Chart Styles button to close the side menu.

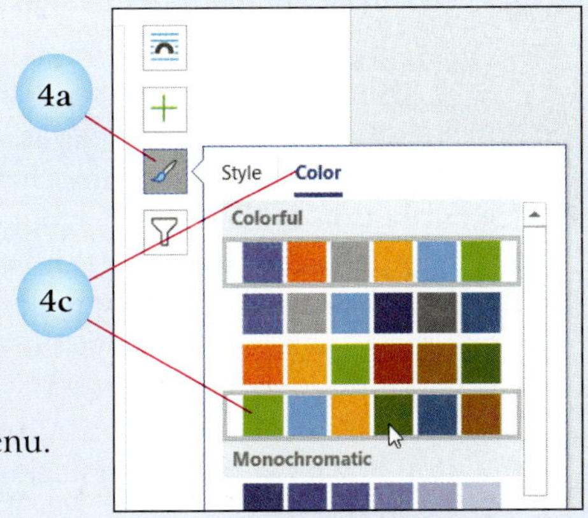

5. Display only Division 1 sales by completing the following steps:
   a. Click the Chart Filters button below the Chart Styles button.
   b. Click the *Division 2* check box in the *Categories* section to remove the check mark.
   c. Click the *Division 3* check box in the *Categories* section to remove the check mark.
   d. Click the Apply button in the lower left corner of the side menu.
   e. Click the Chart Filters button to close the side menu.
   f. After viewing only Division 1 sales, redisplay the other divisions by clicking the Chart Filters button if necessary, clicking the *Division 2* and *Division 3* check boxes to insert check marks, and then clicking the Apply button.
   g. Click the Chart Filters button to close the side menu.
6. Save **5-Charts**.

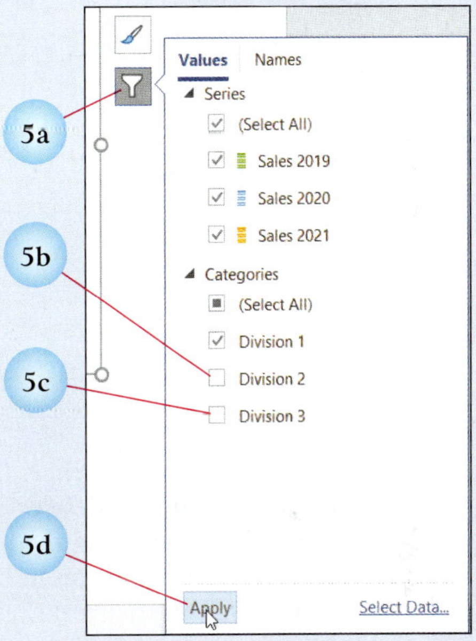

Check Your Work

Tutorial

Changing the Chart Design

Changing the Chart Design

In addition to the buttons that display outside the chart border, options on the Chart Tools Design tab, shown in Figure 5.10, can be used to customize a chart. Use options on this tab to add a chart element, change the chart layout and colors, apply a chart style, select data and switch rows and columns, and change the chart type.

The cells in a worksheet used to create a chart are linked to the chart in the document. To edit the chart data, click the Edit Data button on the Chart Tools Design tab and then make changes to the data in the worksheet.

Figure 5.10 Chart Tools Design Tab

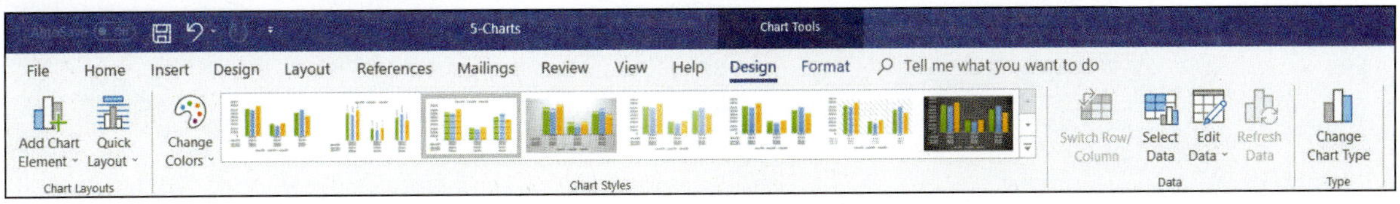

Activity 4c Changing the Chart Design

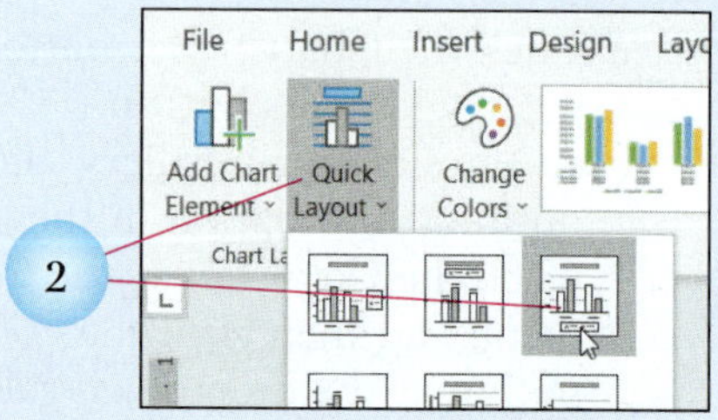

1. With **5-Charts** open, make sure the chart is selected and the Chart Tools Design tab is active.
2. Change to a different layout by clicking the Quick Layout button in the Chart Layouts group and then clicking the *Layout 3* option (third column, first row in the drop-down gallery).
3. Click the *Style 7* chart style in the Chart Styles group (seventh option from the left).
4. Click the Add Chart Element button in the Chart Layouts group, point to *Chart Title* at the drop-down list, and then click *Centered Overlay* at the side menu.

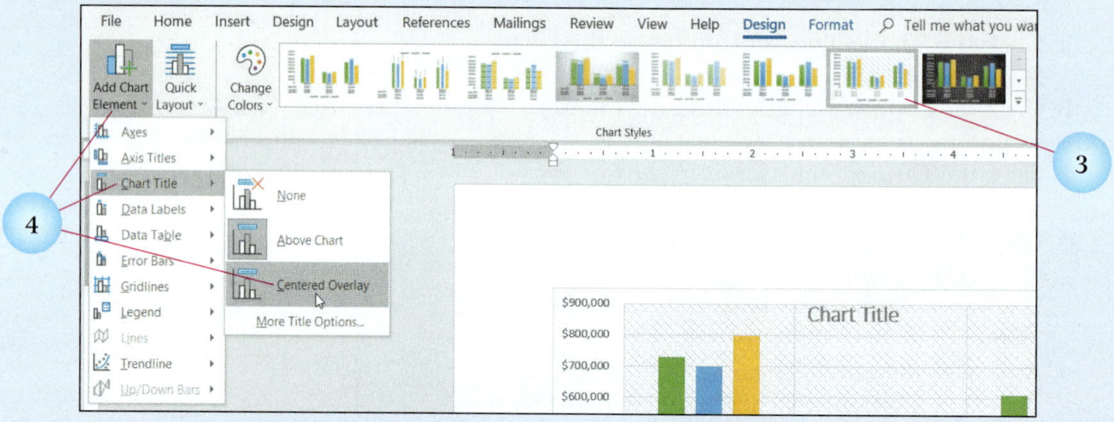

5. Type Regional Sales as the chart title.
6. Click the chart border to deselect the chart title.
7. Edit the data by completing the following steps:
   a. Click the Edit Data button in the Data group.
   b. Click in cell C3 in the worksheet.
   c. Type 375250. (Typing this text replaces the original amount, *$278,250*.)
   d. Click the Close button in the upper right corner of the worksheet.
8. Save **5-Charts**.

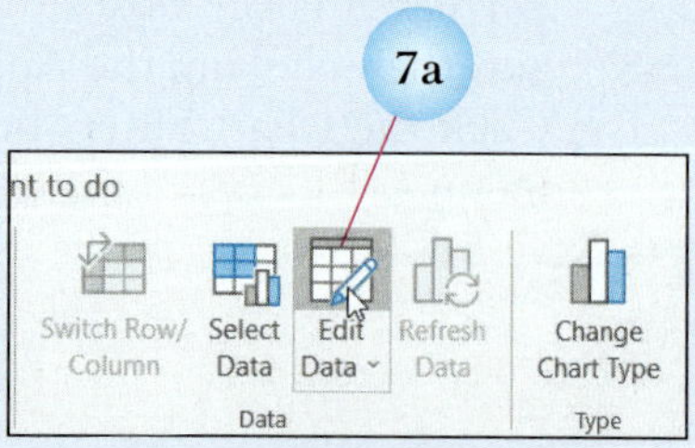

Check Your Work

Tutorial

Changing Chart Formatting

Changing Chart Formatting

Use options and buttons on the Chart Tools Format tab, shown in Figure 5.11, to format and customize a chart and chart elements. To format or modify a specific element in a chart, select the element. Do this by clicking the element or by clicking the *Chart Elements* option box in the Current Selection group and then clicking the element at the drop-down list. Use other options on the Chart Tools Format tab to apply a shape style and WordArt style and to arrange and size the chart or chart element.

Figure 5.11 Chart Tools Format Tab

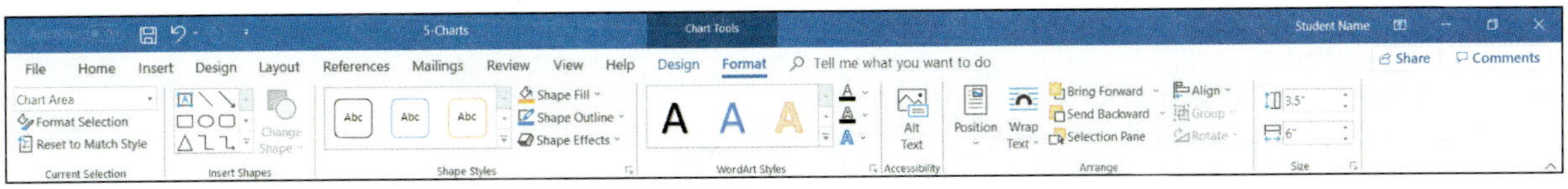

Activity 4d Formatting a Chart and Chart Elements

Part 4 of 5

1. With **5-Charts** open and the chart selected, click the Chart Tools Format tab.
2. Apply a shape style to the chart title by completing the following steps:
   a. Click the *Chart Elements* option box arrow in the Current Selection group and then click *Chart Title* at the drop-down list.
   b. Click the *Colored Outline - Blue, Accent 1* style option (second option in the Shape Styles group).
3. Change the color of the Sales 2021 series by completing the followings steps:
   a. Click the *Chart Elements* option box arrow in the Current Selection group and then click *Series "Sales 2021"* at the drop-down list.
   b. Click the Shape Fill button arrow in the Shape Styles group and then click the *Dark Red* option (first color option in the *Standard Colors* section).

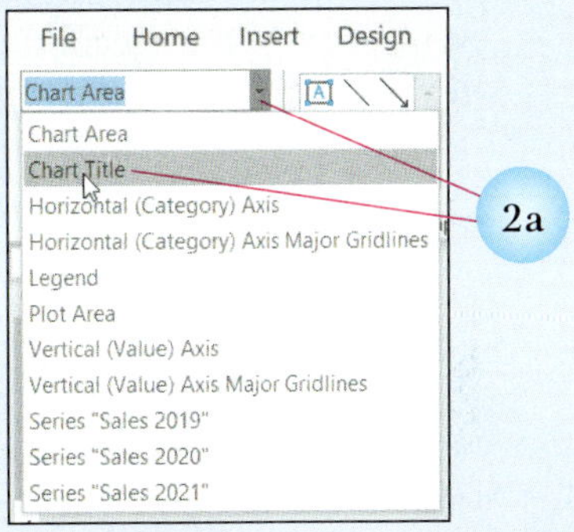

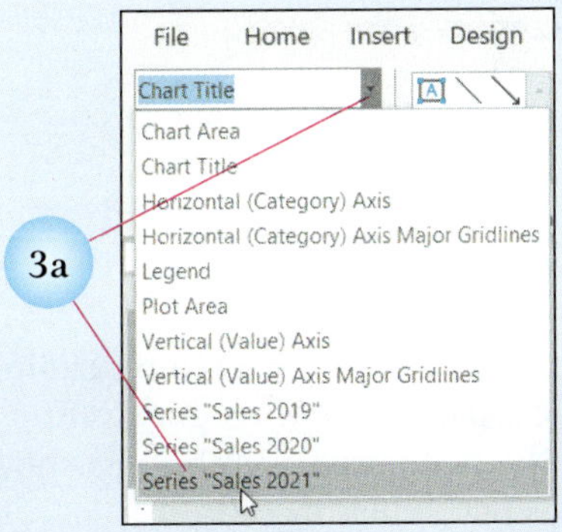

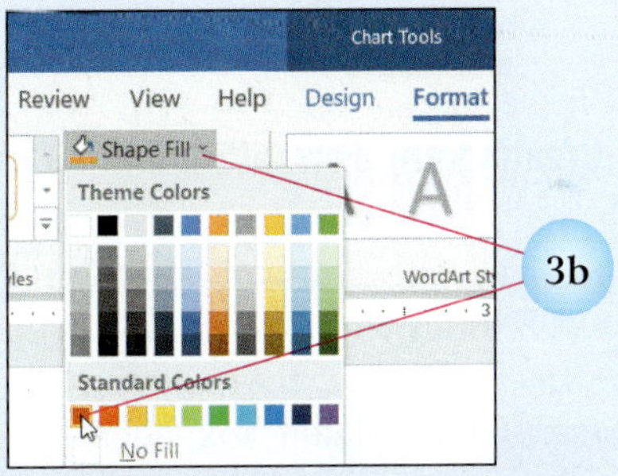

4. Apply a WordArt style to all the text in the chart by completing the following steps:
   a. Click the *Chart Elements* option box arrow.
   b. Click *Chart Area* at the drop-down list.
   c. Click the first WordArt style in the WordArt Styles group (black fill, shadow).

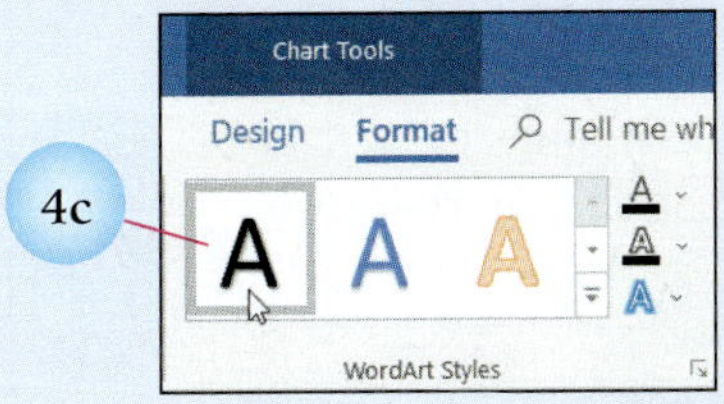

5. Change the size of the chart by completing the following steps:
   a. Click in the *Shape Height* measurement box and then type 3.
   b. Click in the *Shape Width* measurement box, type 5.5, and then press the Enter key.
6. With the chart selected (not a chart element), change its position by clicking the Position button in the Arrange group and then clicking the *Position in Top Center with Square Text Wrapping* option (second column, first row in the *With Text Wrapping* section).
7. Save and then print **5-Charts**.

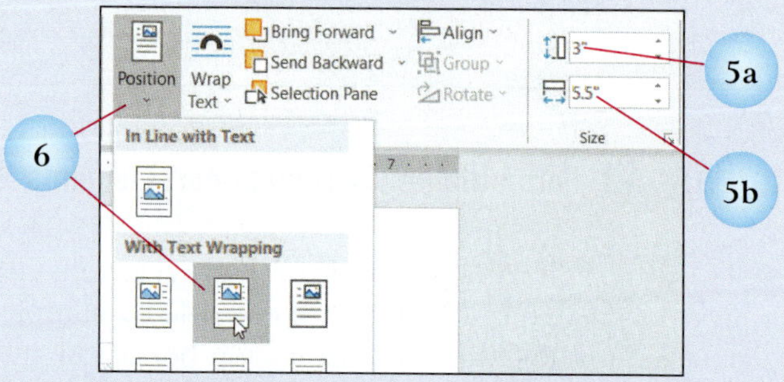

Check Your Work

Formatting a Chart with Task Pane Options

Format Selection

Additional formatting options are available at various task panes. Display a task pane by clicking the Format Selection button in the Current Selection group on the Chart Tools Format tab or a group task pane launcher. The Shape Styles and WordArt Styles groups on the Chart Tools Format tab contain task pane launchers. Which task pane opens at the right side of the screen depends on which chart or chart element is selected.

Activity 4e Creating and Formatting a Pie Chart

Part 5 of 5

1. With **5-Charts** open, press Ctrl + End (which deselects the chart) and then press the Enter key 12 times to move the insertion point below the chart.
2. Click the Insert tab and then click the Chart button in the Illustrations group.
3. At the Insert Chart dialog box, click *Pie* in the left panel and then click OK.
4. Type the data in the worksheet cells, including the percentage symbols as shown in Figure 5.12 (on page 160). After typing the last entry, click in cell A1.
5. Click the Close button in the upper right corner of the worksheet.
6. Click in the title *Percentage* and then type Investments.
7. Add data labels to the pie chart by completing the following steps:
   a. Click the Add Chart Element button in the Chart Layouts group on the Chart Tools Design tab.
   b. Point to *Data Labels* at the drop-down list and then click *Inside End* at the side menu.
8. Click on the chart border to select the chart (not a chart element).
9. Click the Chart Tools Format tab.

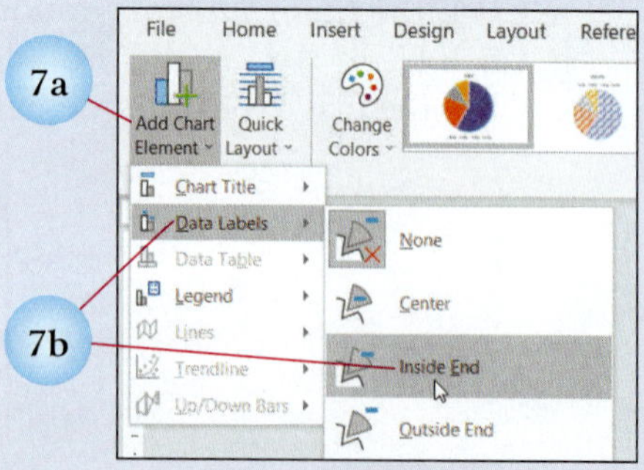

10. Apply formatting to the chart with options at the Format Chart Area task pane by completing the following steps:
   a. With the chart selected, click the Shape Styles group task pane launcher.
   b. At the Format Chart Area task pane with the Fill & Line icon selected, click *Fill* to expand the fill options.
   c. Click the *Gradient fill* option.
   d. Click the Effects icon at the top of the task pane.
   e. Click *Shadow*, if necessary, to expand the shadow options.
   f. Click the Presets button.
   g. Click the *Offset: Bottom* option (second column, first row in the *Outer* section).

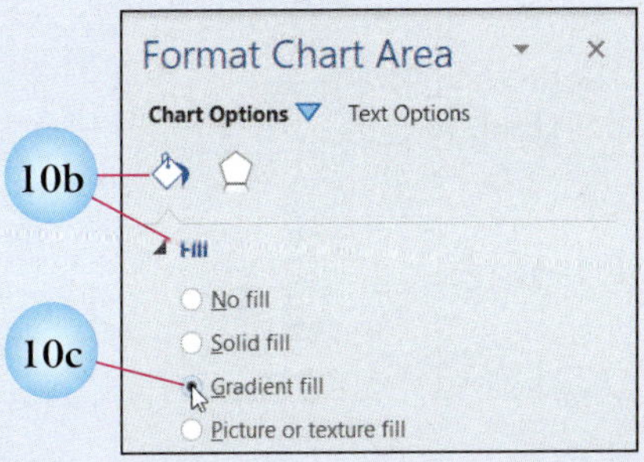

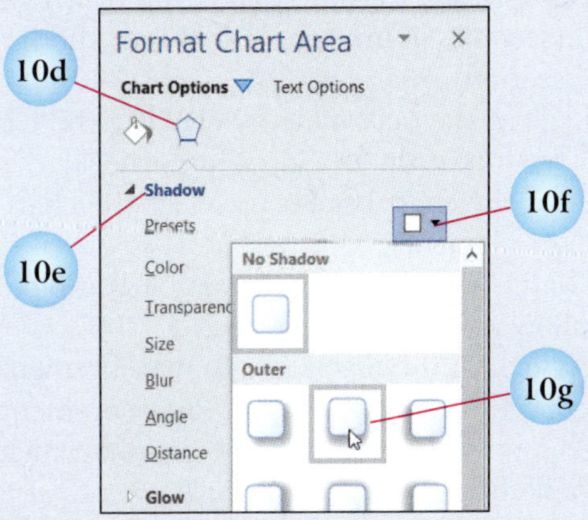

   h. Click the Text Options tab at the top of the task pane.
   i. Click *Text Outline*, if necessary, to expand the options.
   j. Click the *Solid line* option.
   k. Click the Color button and then click the *Blue, Accent 1, Darker 50%* option (fifth column, bottom row in the *Theme Colors* section).

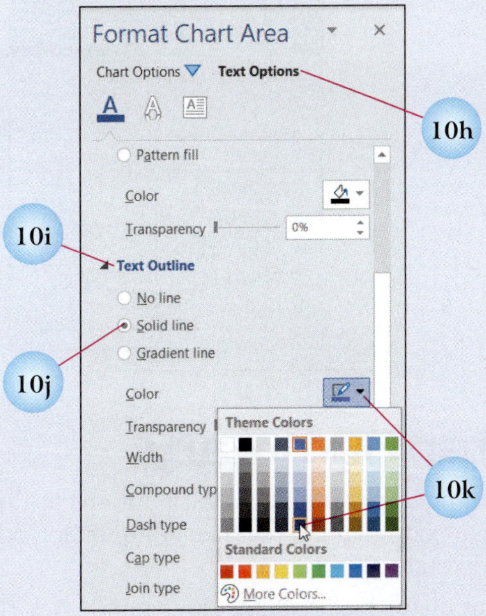

11. Format the pie chart by completing the following steps:
    a. Click in a blank area in any piece of the pie. (This selects all the pieces of the pie. Notice that the name of the task pane has changed to *Format Data Series*.)
    b. Click the Effects icon at the top of the task pane.
    c. Click *3-D Format* to expand the options.
    d. Click the Top bevel button and then click the *Soft Round* option at the drop-down gallery (second column, second row in the *Bevel* section).
    e. Close the task pane by clicking the Close button in the upper right corner.
12. Click the chart border to select the chart (not a chart element).
13. Change the size of the chart by completing the following steps:
    a. Click in the *Shape Height* measurement box and then type 3.
    b. Click in the *Shape Width* measurement box, type 5.5, and then press the Enter key.
14. Change the position of the chart by clicking the Position button in the Arrange group and then clicking the *Position in Bottom Center with Square Text Wrapping* option (second column, third row in the *With Text Wrapping* section).
15. Save, print, and then close **5-Charts**.

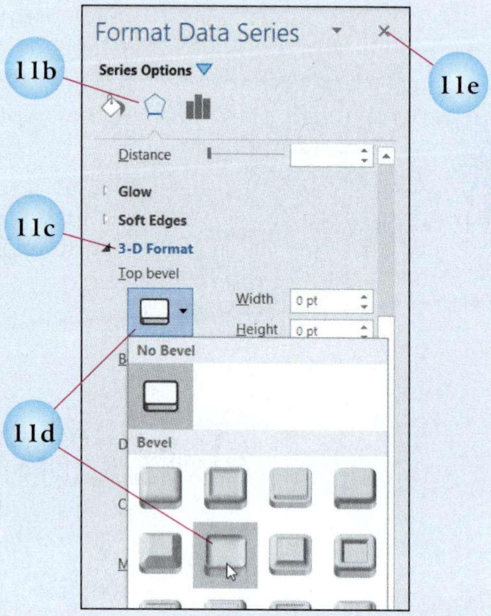

Check Your Work

Figure 5.12 Activity 4e

	A	B
1	Assets	Percentage
2	Loans	34%
3	Bonds	22%
4	Mutuals	20%
5	Stocks	17%
6	Other	7%
7		

Chapter Summary

- Customize the layout of images with options at the Layout dialog box. Display this dialog box by clicking the Size group dialog box launcher on the Picture Tools Format tab.
- The Layout dialog box contains three tabs. Click the Position tab to specify the position of the image in the document, click the Text Wrapping tab to specify a wrapping style for the image, and click the Size tab to display options for specifying the height and width of the image.

- Format an image with options at the Format Picture task pane. Display this task pane by clicking the Picture Styles group task pane launcher on the Picture Tools Format tab.
- Apply artistic effects to a selected image with the Artistic Effects button in the Adjust group on the Picture Tools Format tab or with options at the Format Picture task pane with the Effects icon selected.
- Use the small yellow circles that display around certain selected shapes to change the width and height of a specific element in a shape.
- Use edit points to customize specific elements in a selected shape. Display edit points around a shape by clicking the Edit Shape button in the Insert Shapes group on the Drawing Tools Format tab and then clicking *Edit Points*.
- Display wrap points in a selected shape by clicking the Wrap Text button in the Arrange group on the Picture Tools Format tab or the Drawing Tools Format tab and then clicking *Edit Wrap Points*. Use wrap points to wrap text closer to or father away from an object.
- Link text boxes with the Create Link button in the Text group on the Drawing Tools Format tab. Break a link with the Break Link button in the Text group.
- Insert an icon in a document with the Icons button in the Illustrations group on the Insert tab.
- Use options on the Graphic Tools Format tab to customize an icon. Further customize an icon with options at the Layout dialog box and the Format Graphic task pane.
- Insert a 3D model at the Online 3D Models window. Display the window by clicking the 3D Models button in the Illustrations group on the Insert tab.
- Customize a 3D model with options on the 3D Model Tools Format tab, at the Layout dialog box, and at the Format 3D Model task pane.
- To present data visually, create a chart with the Chart button in the Illustrations group on the Insert tab. Choose a chart type at the Insert Chart dialog box and then enter chart data in a worksheet.
- Four buttons display at the right of a selected chart. Use the Layout Options button to apply text wrapping, the Chart Elements button to add or remove chart elements, the Chart Styles button to apply a predesigned chart style, and the Chart Filters button to isolate specific data in the chart.
- Modify a chart design with options and buttons on the Chart Tools Design tab.
- The cells in a worksheet used to create a chart are linked to the chart in the document. To edit the chart data, click the Edit Data button in the Data group on the Chart Tools Design tab and then make changes to the data in the worksheet.
- Customize the format of a chart and chart elements with options and buttons on the Chart Tools Format tab. Select the chart or a specific chart element and then apply a style to a shape, apply a WordArt style to the text, and arrange and size the chart.
- Apply formatting to a chart with options in task panes. Display a task pane by clicking the Format Selection button in the Current Selection group on the Chart Tools Format tab or a group task pane launcher. The options in the task pane vary depending on the chart or chart element selected.

Commands Review

FEATURE	RIBBON TAB, GROUP/OPTION	BUTTON, OPTION
edit points	Drawing Tools Format, Insert Shapes	, *Edit Points*
Format 3D Model task pane	3D Model Tools Format, 3D Model Views	
Format Graphic task pane	Graphic Tools Format, Graphics Styles	
Format Picture task pane	Picture Tools Format, Picture Styles	
Format Shape task pane	Drawing Tools Format, Shape Styles	
group objects	Picture Tools Format, Arrange OR Drawing Tools Format, Arrange	, *Group*
Insert Chart dialog box	Insert, Illustrations	
Insert Icons window	Insert, Illustrations	
Layout dialog box	3D Model Tools Format, Size OR Drawing Tools Format, Size OR Graphic Tools Format, Size OR Picture Tools Format, Size	
link text boxes	Drawing Tools Format, Text	
Online 3D Models window	Insert, Illustrations	
text box	Insert, Text	, *Draw Text Box*
ungroup objects	Picture Tools Format, Arrange OR Drawing Tools Format, Arrange	, *Ungroup*
unlink text boxes	Drawing Tools Format, Text	
wrap points	Picture Tools Format, Arrange OR Drawing Tools Format, Arrange	, *Edit Wrap Points*

Microsoft®

Word

CHAPTER

6

Merging Documents

Performance Objectives

Upon successful completion of Chapter 6, you will be able to:

1. Create a data source file
2. Create a main document and merge it with a data source file
3. Preview a merge and check for errors before merging documents
4. Create an envelope, a label, and a directory main document and then merge it with a data source file
5. Edit a data source file
6. Select specific records for merging
7. Use the Mail Merge wizard to merge a letter main document with a data source file

Word includes a Mail Merge feature for creating customized letters, envelopes, labels, directories, and email messages. The Mail Merge feature is useful when the same letter is to be sent to a number of people and an envelope needs to be created for each letter. Use Mail Merge to create a main document that contains a letter, an envelope, or other data and then merge it with a data source file. In this chapter, you will use Mail Merge to create letters, envelopes, labels, and directories.

Data Files

Before beginning chapter work, copy the WL2C6 folder to your storage medium and then make WL2C6 the active folder.

The online course includes additional training and assessment resources.

Activity 1 Merge Letters to Customers — 3 Parts

You will create a data source file and a letter document and then merge the main document with the records in the data source file.

Completing a Merge

Use buttons and options on the Mailings tab to complete a merge. A merge generally takes two files: the data source file and the main document. The main document contains the standard text along with fields identifying where variable information is inserted during the merge. The data source file contains the variable information that will be inserted in the main document.

Start Mail Merge

Select Recipients

Use the Start Mail Merge button in the Start Mail Merge group on the Mailings tab to identify the type of main document to be created and use the Select Recipients button to create a data source file or specify an existing data source file. The Mail Merge wizard is also available to provide guidance on the merge process.

Tutorial

Creating a Data Source File

Quick Steps

Create Data Source File

1. Click Mailings tab.
2. Click Select Recipients button.
3. Click *Type a New List* at drop-down list.
4. Type data in predesigned or custom fields.
5. Click OK.

Creating a Data Source File

Before creating a data source file, determine what type of correspondence will be created and what type of information is needed to insert in the correspondence. Word provides predesigned field names when creating the data source file. Use these field names if they represent the specific data. Variable information in a data source file is saved as a record. A record contains all the information for one unit (for example, a person, family, customer, client, or business). A series of fields makes one record and a series of records makes a data source file.

Create a data source file by clicking the Select Recipients button in the Start Mail Merge group on the Mailings tab and then clicking *Type a New List* at the drop-down list. At the New Address List dialog box, shown in Figure 6.1, use the predesigned fields offered by Word or edit the fields by clicking the Customize Columns button. At the Customize Address List dialog box, insert new fields or delete existing fields and then click OK. With the fields established, type the required data. Note that fields in the main document correspond to the column

Figure 6.1 New Address List Dialog Box

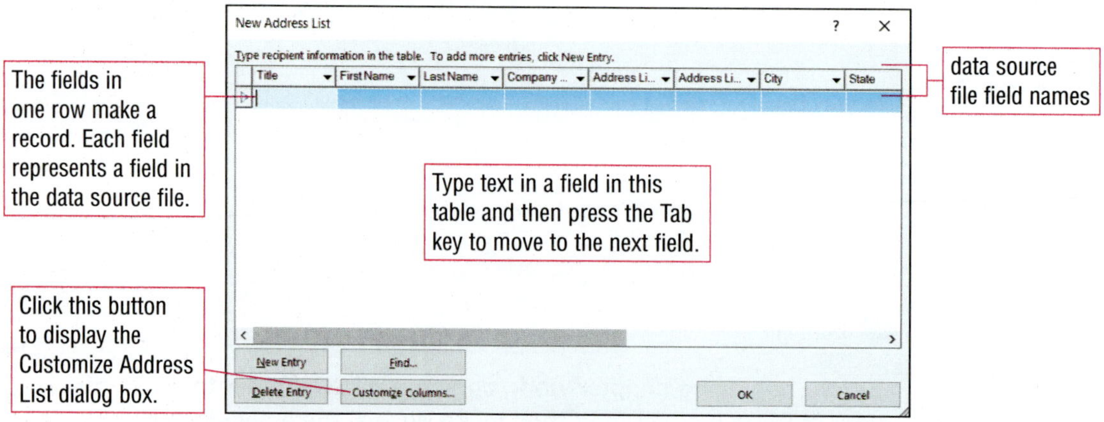

headings in the data source file. When all the records have been entered, click OK. At the Save Address List dialog box, navigate to the desired folder, type a name for the data source file, and then click OK. Word saves a data source file as an Access database. Having Access on the computer is not required to complete a merge with a data source file.

Activity 1a Creating a Data Source File

Part 1 of 3

1. At a blank document, click the Mailings tab.
2. Click the Start Mail Merge button in the Start Mail Merge group and then click *Letters* at the drop-down list.
3. Click the Select Recipients button in the Start Mail Merge group and then click *Type a New List* at the drop-down list.

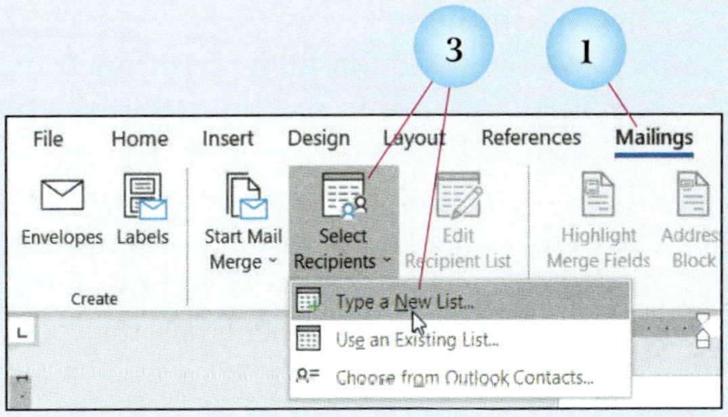

4. At the New Address List dialog box, Word provides a number of predesigned fields. Delete the fields you do not need by completing the following steps:
   a. Click the Customize Columns button.
   b. At the Customize Address List dialog box, click *Company Name* to select it and then click the Delete button.
   c. At the message that displays, click Yes.
   d. Complete steps similar to those in 4b and 4c to delete the following fields:
      Country or Region
      Home Phone
      Work Phone
      E-mail Address

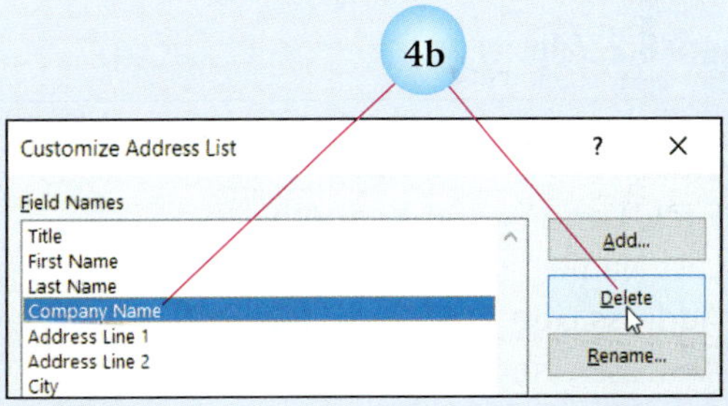

5. Insert a custom field by completing the following steps:
   a. With the *ZIP Code* field selected in the *Field Names* list box in the Customize Address List dialog box, click the Add button.
   b. At the Add Field dialog box, type Fund and then click OK.
   c. Click OK to close the Customize Address List dialog box.

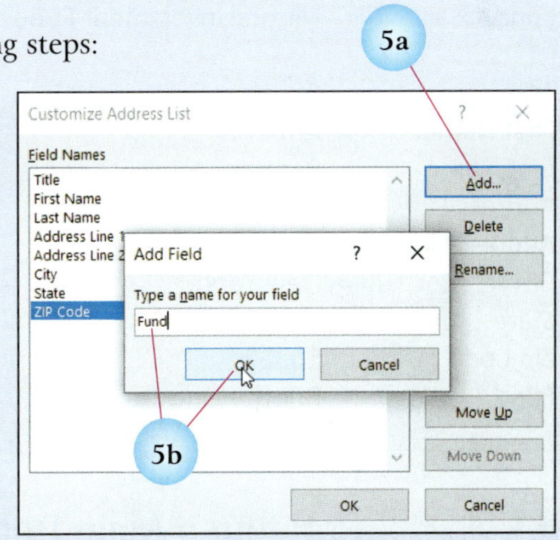

6. At the New Address List dialog box, enter the information for the first client shown in Figure 6.2 by completing the following steps:
   a. Type Mr. in the field in the *Title* column and then press the Tab key. (This moves the insertion point to the field in the *First Name* column. Pressing Shift + Tab will move the insertion point to the previous field. When typing text, do not press the spacebar after the last word in the field, and proofread all the entries to ensure the data is accurate.)
   b. Type Kenneth and then press the Tab key.
   c. Type Porter and then press the Tab key.
   d. Type 7645 Tenth Street and then press the Tab key.
   e. Type Apt. 314 and then press the Tab key.

f. Type New York and then press the Tab key.

g. Type NY and then press the Tab key.

h. Type 10192 and then press the Tab key.

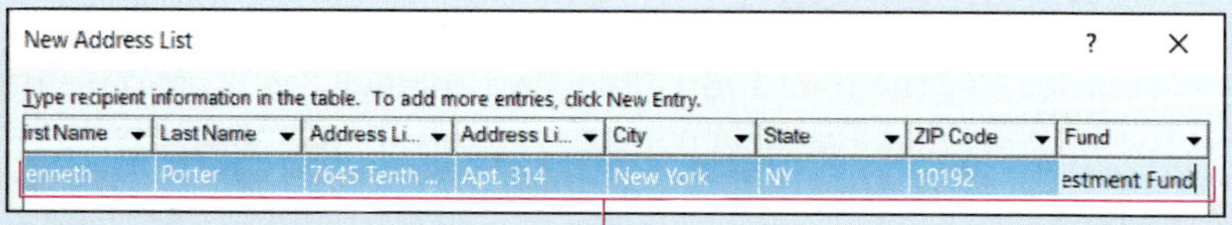

i. Type Mutual Investment Fund and then press the Tab key. (This makes the field in the *Title* column active in the next row.)

j. With the insertion point positioned in the field in the *Title* column, complete steps similar to those in 6a through 6i to enter the information for the three other clients shown in Figure 6.2 (reading the records from left to right in each row).

7. After entering all the information for the last client in Figure 6.2 (Ms. Wanda Houston), click OK in the bottom right corner of the New Address List dialog box.
8. At the Save Address List dialog box, navigate to your WL2C6 folder, type 6-MFDS in the *File name* text box, and then click the Save button.

Figure 6.2 Activity 1a

Title	=	Mr.	Title	=	Ms.
First Name	=	Kenneth	First Name	=	Carolyn
Last Name	=	Porter	Last Name	=	Renquist
Address Line 1	=	7645 Tenth Street	Address Line 1	=	13255 Meridian Street
Address Line 2	=	Apt. 314	Address Line 2	=	(leave this blank)
City	=	New York	City	=	New York
State	=	NY	State	=	NY
Zip Code	=	10192	Zip Code	=	10435
Fund	=	Mutual Investment Fund	Fund	=	Quality Care Fund
Title	=	Dr.	Title	=	Ms.
First Name	=	Amil	First Name	=	Wanda
Last Name	=	Ranna	Last Name	=	Houston
Address Line 1	=	433 South 17th Street	Address Line 1	=	566 North 22nd Avenue
Address Line 2	=	Apt. 17-D	Address Line 2	=	(leave this blank)
City	=	New York	City	=	New York
State	=	NY	State	=	NY
Zip Code	=	10322	Zip Code	=	10634
Fund	=	Priority One Fund	Fund	=	Quality Care Fund

Tutorial

Creating a Main Document

Creating a Main Document

After creating and typing the records in the data source file, type the main document. Insert fields to identify where variable information will be added when the document is merged with the data source file. Use buttons in the Write & Insert Fields group to insert fields in the main document.

Quick Steps

Create Main Document

1. Click Mailings tab.
2. Click Start Mail Merge button.
3. Click document type at drop-down list.
4. Type main document text and insert fields as needed.

Address Block

Greeting Line

Insert Merge Field

Insert all the fields required for the inside address of a letter with the Address Block button in the Write & Insert Fields group. Click this button and the Insert Address Block dialog box displays with a preview of how the fields will be inserted in the document to create the inside address; the dialog box also contains buttons and options for customizing the fields. Click OK and the *«AddressBlock»* field is inserted in the document. The *«AddressBlock»* field is an example of a composite field, which groups a number of fields (such as *Title*, *First Name*, *Last Name*, *Address Line 1*, and so on).

Click the Greeting Line button and the Insert Greeting Line dialog box displays with options for customizing how the fields are inserted in the document to create the greeting line. Click OK at the dialog box and the *«GreetingLine»* composite field is inserted in the document.

To insert an individual field from the data source file, click the Insert Merge Field button. This displays the Insert Merge Field dialog box with a list of the fields from the data source file. Click the Insert Merge Field button arrow and a drop-down list displays containing the fields in the data source file.

A field or composite field is inserted in the main document surrounded by chevrons (« and »). The chevrons distinguish fields in the main document and do not display in the merged document. Formatting can be applied to merged data by formatting the merge field in the main document.

Activity 1b **Creating a Main Document** — Part 2 of 3

1. At the blank document, create the letter shown in Figure 6.3. Begin by clicking the *No Spacing* style in the styles gallery on the Home tab.
2. Press the Enter key six times and then type February 23, 2021.
3. Press the Enter key four times and then insert the *«AddressBlock»* composite field by completing the following steps:
   a. Click the Mailings tab and then click the Address Block button in the Write & Insert Fields group.
   b. At the Insert Address Block dialog box, click OK.
   c. Press the Enter key two times.
4. Insert the *«GreetingLine»* composite field by completing the following steps:
   a. Click the Greeting Line button in the Write & Insert Fields group.
   b. At the Insert Greeting Line dialog box, click the option box arrow for the option box containing the comma (the box at the right of the box containing *Mr. Randall*).
   c. At the drop-down list, click the colon.

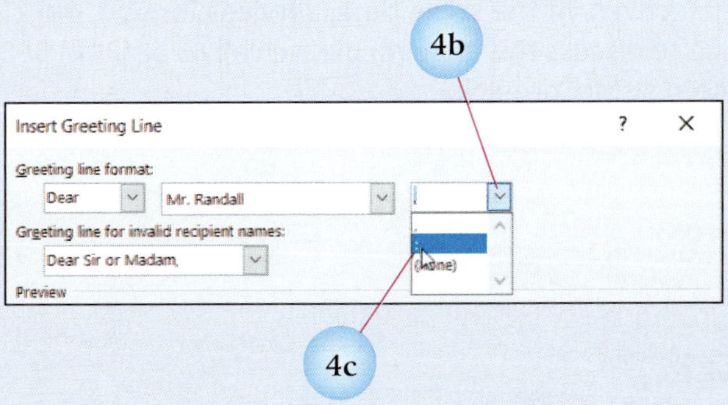

   d. Click OK to close the Insert Greeting Line dialog box.
   e. Press the Enter key two times.

5. Type the letter shown in Figure 6.3 to the point where *«Fund»* appears and then insert the *«Fund»* field by clicking the Insert Merge Field button arrow in the Write & Insert Fields group and then clicking *Fund* at the drop-down list.
6. Type the letter to the point where the *«Title»* field appears and then insert the *«Title»* field by clicking the Insert Merge Field button arrow and then clicking *Title* at the drop-down list.
7. Press the spacebar and then insert the *«Last_Name»* field by clicking the Insert Merge Field button arrow and then clicking *Last_Name* at the drop-down list.
8. Type the remainder of the letter shown in Figure 6.3. (Insert your initials instead of *XX* at the end of the letter.)
9. Save the document and name it **6-MFMD**.

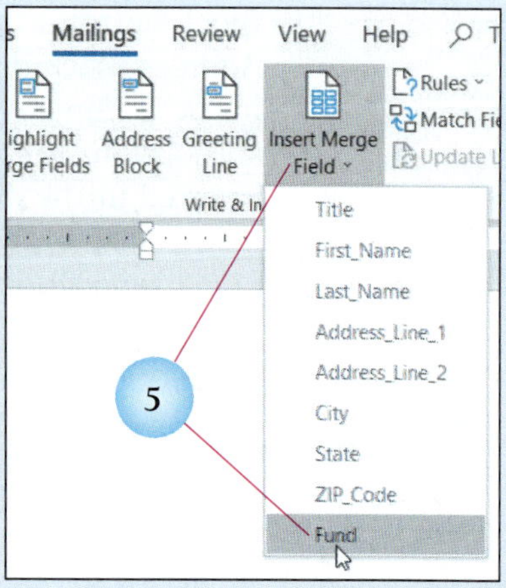

Check Your Work

Figure 6.3 Activity 1b

February 23, 2021

«AddressBlock»

«GreetingLine»

McCormack Funds is lowering its expense charges beginning May 1, 2021. The reduction in expense charges means that more of your account investment performance in the «Fund» is returned to you, «Title» «Last_Name». The reductions are worth your attention because most of our competitors' fees have gone up.

Lowering expense charges is noteworthy because before the reduction, McCormack expense deductions were already among the lowest, far below most mutual funds and variable annuity accounts with similar objectives. At the same time, services for you, our client, will continue to expand. If you would like to discuss this change, please call us at (212) 555-2277. Your financial future is our main concern at McCormack.

Sincerely,

Jodie Langstrom
Director, Financial Services

XX
6-MFMD

Tutorial

Previewing and Merging Documents

Preview Results

First Record

Previous Record

Next Record

Last Record

Find Recipient

Previewing a Merge

To view how the main document will appear when merged with the first record in the data source file, click the Preview Results button in the Preview Results group on the Mailings tab. View the main document merged with other records by using the navigation buttons in the Preview Results group. This group contains the First Record, Previous Record, Next Record, and Last Record buttons and the *Go to Record* text box. Click the button that will display the main document merged with the specific record. Viewing the merged document before printing is helpful to ensure that the merged data is correct. To use the *Go to Record* text box, click in the text box, type the number of the record, and then press the Enter key. Turn off the preview feature by clicking the Preview Results button.

The Preview Results group on the Mailings tab also includes a Find Recipient button. To search for and preview merged documents with specific entries, click the Preview Results button and then click the Find Recipient button. At the Find Entry dialog box, type the specific field entry in the *Find* text box and then click the Find Next button. Continue clicking the Find Next button until Word displays a message indicating that there are no more entries that contain the typed text.

Check for Errors

Checking for Errors

Before merging documents, check for errors using the Check for Errors button in the Preview Results group on the Mailings tab. Click this button and the Checking and Reporting Errors dialog box, shown in Figure 6.4, displays containing three options. Click the first option, *Simulate the merge and report errors in a new document,* and Word will test the merge, not make any changes, and report errors in a new document. Choose the second option, *Complete the merge, pausing to report each error as it occurs,* and Word will merge the documents and display errors as they occur during the merge. Choose the third option, *Complete the merge without pausing. Report errors in a new document,* and Word will complete the merge without pausing and insert any errors in a new document.

Finish & Merge

Merging Documents

To complete the merge, click the Finish & Merge button in the Finish group on the Mailings tab. At the drop-down list, merge the records and create a new document, send the merged documents directly to the printer, or send the merged documents by email.

Figure 6.4 Checking and Reporting Errors Dialog Box

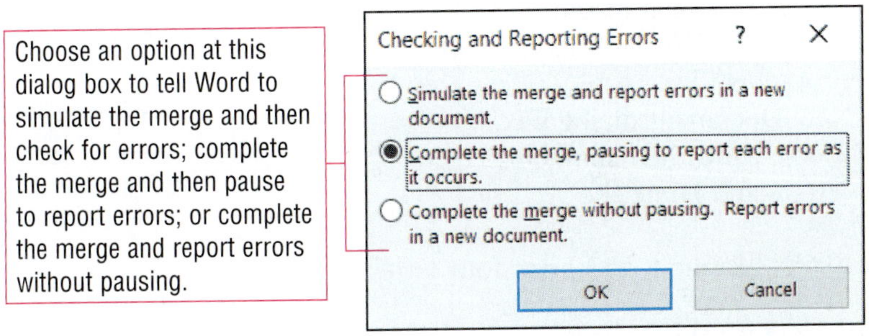

Quick Steps

Merge Documents

1. Click Finish & Merge button.
2. Click *Edit Individual Documents* at drop-down list.
3. Make sure *All* is selected in Merge to New Document dialog box.
4. Click OK.

Hint Press Alt + Shift + N to display the Merge to New Document dialog box and press Alt + Shift + M to display the Merge to Printer dialog box.

To merge the documents and create a new document with the merged records, click the Finish & Merge button and then click *Edit Individual Documents* at the drop-down list. At the Merge to New Document dialog box, make sure *All* is selected in the *Merge records* section and then click OK. This merges the records in the data source file with the main document and inserts the merged documents in a new document.

Identify specific records to be merged with options at the Merge to New Document dialog box. Display this dialog box by clicking the Finish & Merge button on the Mailings tab and then clicking the *Edit Individual Documents* option at the drop-down list. Click the *All* option in the Merge to New Document dialog box to merge all the records in the data source file and click the *Current record* option to merge only the current record. To merge specific adjacent records, click in the *From* text box, type the beginning record number, press the Tab key, and then type the ending record number in the *To* text box.

Activity 1c Merging the Main Document with the Data Source File

Part 3 of 3

1. With **6-MFMD** open, preview the main document merged with the first record in the data source file by clicking the Preview Results button on the Mailings tab.
2. Click the Next Record button to view the main document merged with the second record in the data source file.
3. Click the Preview Results button to turn off the preview feature.

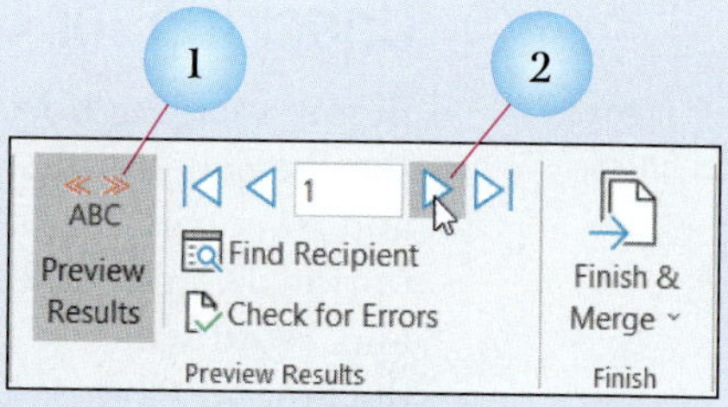

4. Automatically check for errors by completing the following steps:
   a. Click the Check for Errors button in the Preview Results group on the Mailings tab.
   b. At the Checking and Reporting Errors dialog box, click the first option, *Simulate the merge and report errors in a new document*.
   c. Click OK.
   d. If a new document displays with any errors, print the document, close it without saving it, and then correct the errors. If a message displays that no errors were found, click OK.

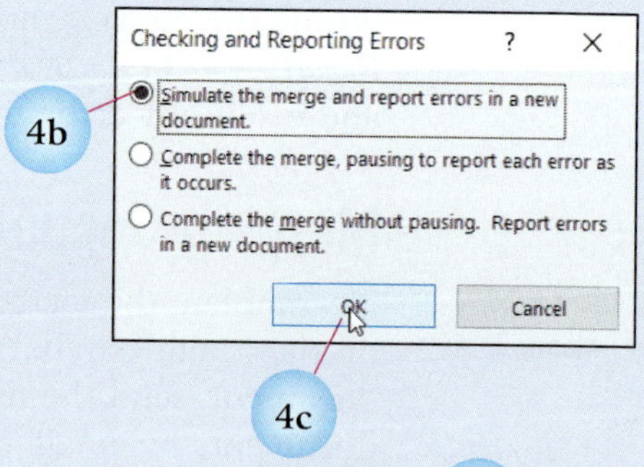

5. Click the Finish & Merge button in the Finish group and then click *Edit Individual Documents* at the drop-down list.
6. At the Merge to New Document dialog box, make sure *All* is selected and then click OK.
7. Save the merged letters and name the document **6-MFLtrs**.
8. Print **6-MFLtrs**. (This document will print four letters.)
9. Close **6-MFLtrs**.
10. Save and then close **6-MFMD**.

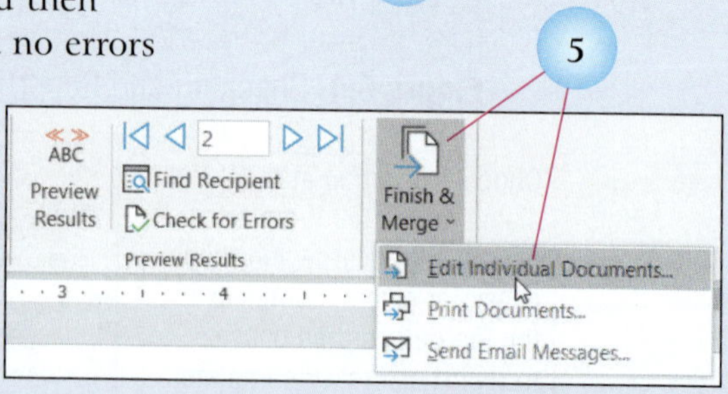

Check Your Work

Activity 2 Merge Envelopes

1 Part

You will use Mail Merge to prepare envelopes with customer names and addresses.

Merging with Other Main Documents

In addition to being merged with a letter, a data source file can be merged with an envelope, a label, or a directory main document. Create an envelope main document with the *Envelopes* option at the Start Mail Merge button drop-down list and create a label main document with the *Labels* option. Create a directory, which merges fields to the same page, with the *Directory* option at the Start Mail Merge button drop-down list.

Tutorial

Merging Envelopes

Merging Envelopes

To send out a letter created as a main document and then merged with a data source file will likely require creating properly addressed envelopes. To prepare an envelope main document that is merged with a data source file, click the Mailings tab, click the Start Mail Merge button, and then click *Envelopes* at the drop-down list. This displays the Envelope Options dialog box, as shown in Figure 6.5. At this dialog box, specify the envelope size, make any other changes, and then click OK.

The next step in the envelope merge process is to create the data source file or identify an existing data source file. To identify an existing data source file, click the Select Recipients button in the Start Mail Merge group and then click *Use an Existing List* at the drop-down list. At the Select Data Source dialog box, navigate to the folder containing the data source file and then double-click the file.

With the data source file attached to the envelope main document, the next step is to insert the appropriate fields. Click in the envelope in the approximate location the recipient's address will appear and a box with a dashed gray border displays. Click the Address Block button in the Write & Insert Fields group and then click OK at the Insert Address Block dialog box.

Figure 6.5 Envelope Options Dialog Box

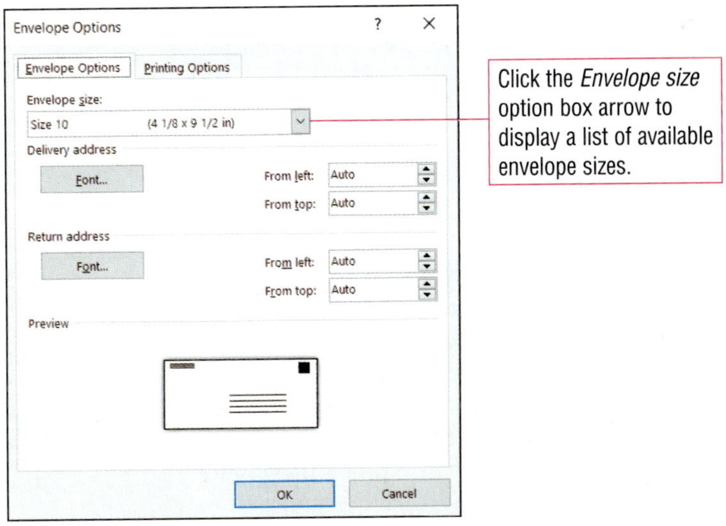

Activity 2 Merging Envelopes

Part 1 of 1

1. At a blank document, click the Mailings tab.
2. Click the Start Mail Merge button in the Start Mail Merge group and then click *Envelopes* at the drop-down list.

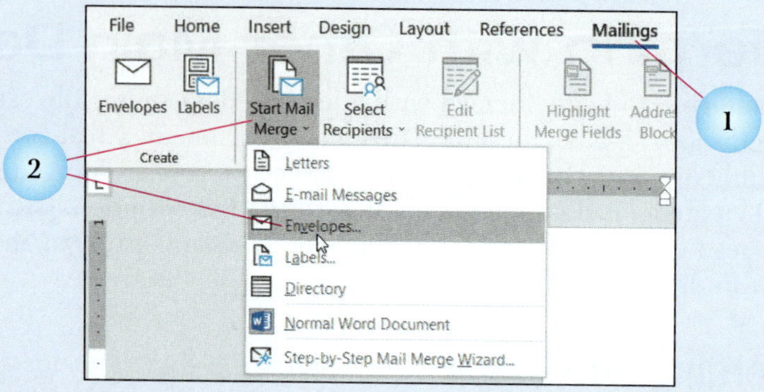

3. At the Envelope Options dialog box, make sure the envelope size is Size 10 and then click OK.
4. Click the Select Recipients button in the Start Mail Merge group and then click *Use an Existing List* at the drop-down list.

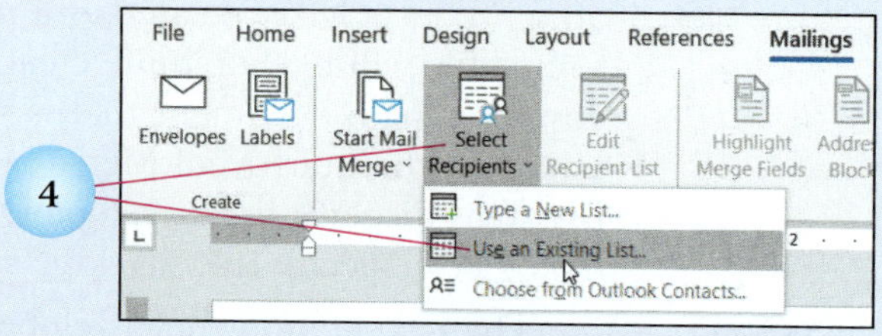

5. At the Select Data Source dialog box, navigate to your WL2C6 folder and then double-click the data source file named ***6-MFDS***. (Notice the Access icon that displays before the 6-MFDS file identifying it as an Access database file.)
6. Click in the approximate location in the envelope document where the recipient's address will appear. (This causes a box with a dashed gray border to display. If you do not see this box, try clicking in a different location on the envelope.)

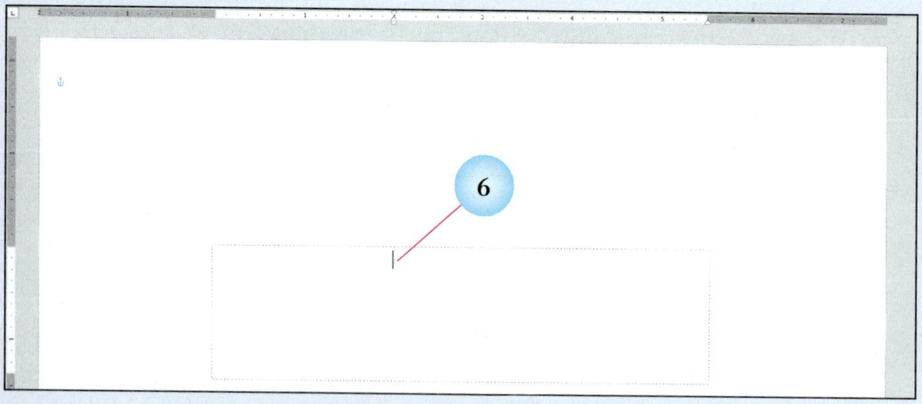

7. Click the Address Block button in the Write & Insert Fields group.
8. At the Insert Address Block dialog box, click OK.
9. Click the Preview Results button to see how the envelope appears merged with the first record in the data source file.
10. Click the Preview Results button to turn off the preview feature.
11. Click the Finish & Merge button in the Finish group and then click *Edit Individual Documents* at the drop-down list.

12. At the Merge to New Document dialog box, specify that you want only the first two records to merge by completing the following steps:
    a. Click in the *From* text box and then type 1.
    b. Click in the *To* text box and then type 2.
    c. Click OK. (This merges only the first two records and then opens a document with two merged envelopes.)
13. Save the merged envelopes and name the document **6-MFEnvs**.
14. Print **6-MFEnvs**. (This document will print two envelopes. Manual feeding of the envelopes may be required. Please check with your instructor.)
15. Close **6-MFEnvs**.
16. Save the envelope main document and name it **6-EnvMD**.
17. Close **6-EnvMD**.

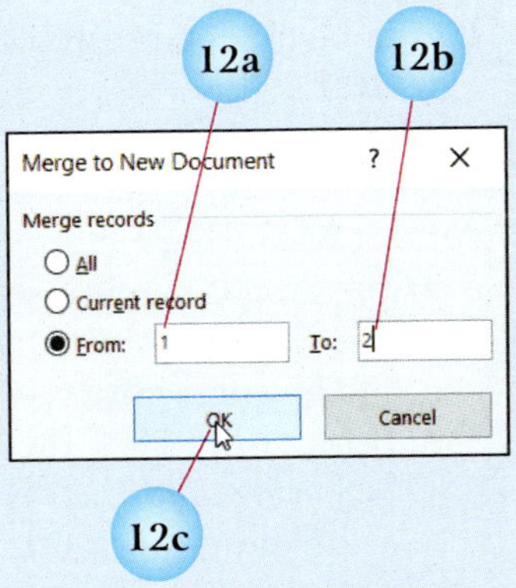

Check Your Work

Activity 3 Merge Mailing Labels — 1 Part

You will use Mail Merge to prepare mailing labels with customer names and addresses.

Tutorial

Merging Labels

Merging Labels

Mailing labels for records in a data source file are created in much the same way that envelopes are created. Click the Start Mail Merge button and then click *Labels* at the drop-down list. This displays the Label Options dialog box, as shown in Figure 6.6. Make sure the desired label is selected and then click OK to close the dialog box. The next step is to create the data source file or identify an existing data source file. With the data source file attached to the label main document, insert the appropriate fields and then complete the merge.

Figure 6.6 Label Options Dialog Box

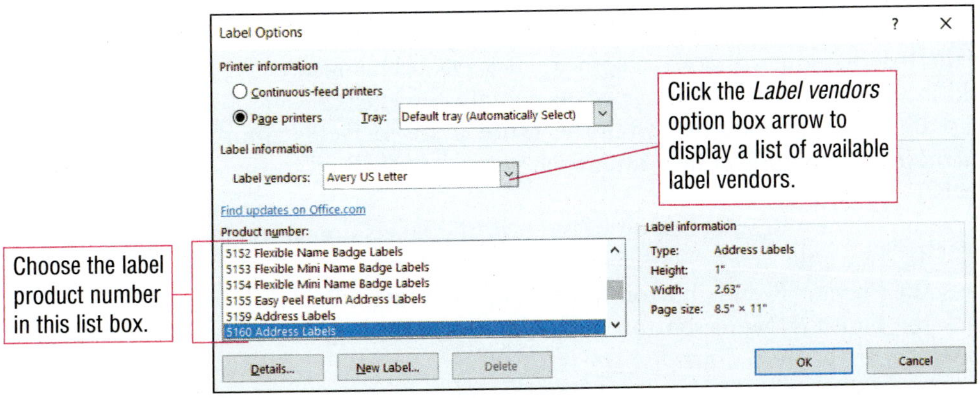

Activity 3 Merging Mailing Labels

Part 1 of 1

1. At a blank document, change the document zoom to 100%, if necessary, and then click the Mailings tab.
2. Click the Start Mail Merge button in the Start Mail Merge group and then click *Labels* at the drop-down list.

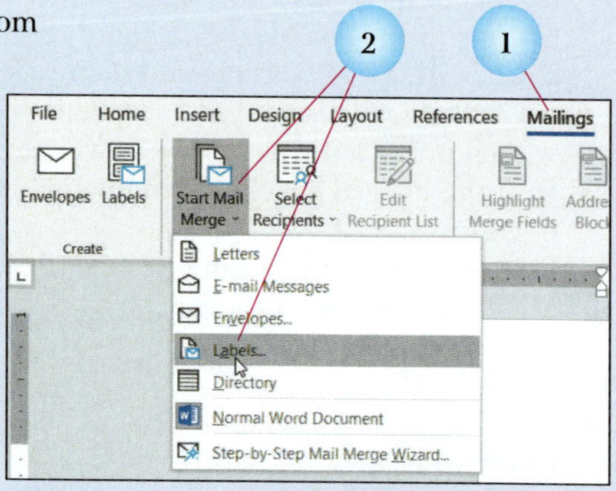

3. At the Label Options dialog box, complete the following steps:
   a. If necessary, click the *Label vendors* option box arrow and then click *Avery US Letter* at the drop-down list. (If this option is not available, choose a vendor that offers labels that print on a full page.)
   b. Scroll in the *Product number* list box and then, if necessary, click *5160 Address Labels*. (If this option is not available, choose a label number that prints labels in two or three columns down a full page.)
   c. Click OK to close the dialog box.

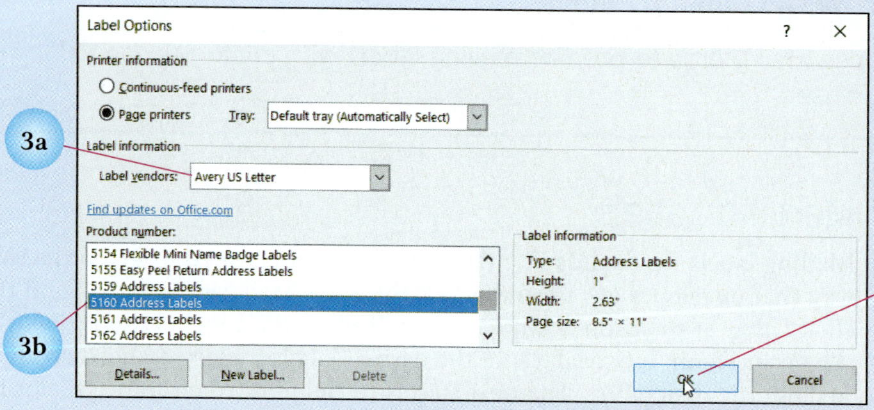

4. Click the Select Recipients button in the Start Mail Merge group and then click *Use an Existing List* at the drop-down list.
5. At the Select Data Source dialog box, navigate to your WL2C6 folder and then double-click the data source file named ***6-MFDS***.
6. At the label document, click the Address Block button in the Write & Insert Fields group.
7. At the Insert Address Block dialog box, click OK. (This inserts the *«AddressBlock»* composite field in the first label. The other labels contain the *«Next Record»* field.)
8. Click the Update Labels button in the Write & Insert Fields group. (This adds the *«AddressBlock»* composite field after each *«Next Record»* field in the second and subsequent labels.)
9. Click the Preview Results button to see how the labels appear merged with the records in the data source file.
10. Click the Preview Results button to turn off the preview feature.
11. Click the Finish & Merge button in the Finish group and then click *Edit Individual Documents* at the drop-down list.
12. At the Merge to New Document dialog box, make sure *All* is selected and then click OK.

13. Format the labels by completing the following steps:
   a. Click the Table Tools Layout tab.
   b. Click the Select button in the Table group and then click the *Select Table* option.
   c. Click the Align Center Left button in the Alignment group.
   d. Click the Home tab and then click the Paragraph group dialog box launcher.
   e. At the Paragraph dialog box, click the *Before* measurement box up arrow to change the measurement to 0 points.
   f. Click the *After* measurement box up arrow to change the measurement to 0 points.
   g. Click the *Inside* measurement box up arrow three times to change the measurement to 0.3 inch.
   h. Click OK.

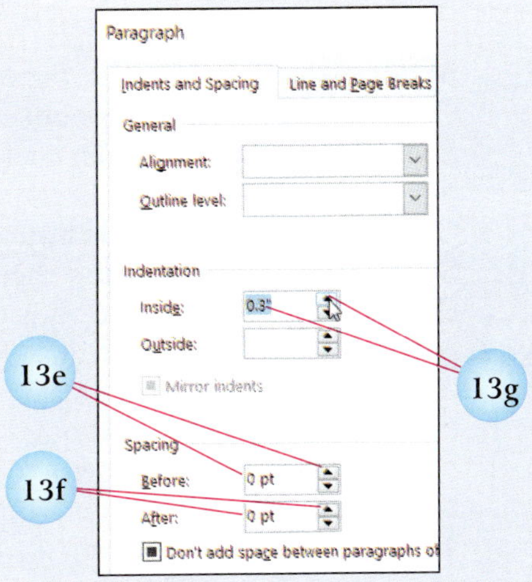

14. Save the merged labels and name the document **6-MFLabels**.
15. Print and then close **6-MFLabels**.
16. Save the label main document and name it **6-LabelsMD**.
17. Close **6-LabelsMD**.

Check Your Work

Activity 4 Merge a Directory

1 Part

You will use Mail Merge to prepare a directory list containing customer names and types of financial investment funds.

Tutorial

Merging a Directory

Merging a Directory

When merging letters, envelopes, or mailing labels, a new form is created for each record. For example, if the data source file merged with the letter contains eight records, eight letters are created, each on a separate page. In some situations, merged information should remain on the same page. This is useful, for example, when creating a list such as a directory or address list.

Begin creating a merged directory by clicking the Start Mail Merge button and then clicking *Directory* at the drop-down list. Create or identify an existing data source file and then insert the necessary fields in the directory document. To display the merged data in columns, set tabs for all the columns.

Activity 4 Merging a Directory

Part 1 of 1

1. At a blank document, click the Mailings tab.
2. Click the Start Mail Merge button in the Start Mail Merge group and then click *Directory* at the drop-down list.
3. Click the Select Recipients button in the Start Mail Merge group and then click *Use an Existing List* at the drop-down list.
4. At the Select Data Source dialog box, navigate to your WL2C6 folder and then double-click the data source file named ***6-MFDS***.
5. At the document screen, set left tabs at the 1-inch mark, the 2.5-inch mark, and the 4-inch mark on the horizontal ruler.

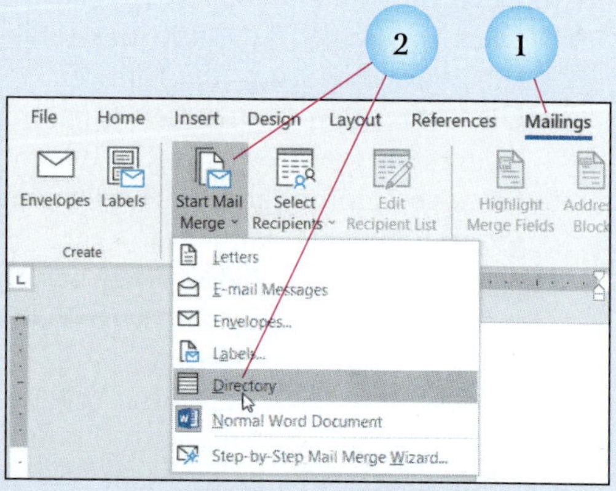

6. Press the Tab key. (This moves the insertion point to the tab set at the 1-inch mark.)
7. Click the Insert Merge Field button arrow and then click *Last_Name* at the drop-down list.
8. Press the Tab key to move the insertion point to the tab set at the 2.5-inch mark.
9. Click the Insert Merge Field button arrow and then click *First_Name* at the drop-down list.
10. Press the Tab key to move the insertion point to the tab set at the 4-inch mark.
11. Click the Insert Merge Field button arrow and then click *Fund* at the drop-down list.
12. Press the Enter key.
13. Click the Finish & Merge button in the Finish group and then click *Edit Individual Documents* at the drop-down list.
14. At the Merge to New Document dialog box, make sure *All* is selected and then click OK. (This merges the fields in the document.)
15. Press Ctrl + Home, press the Enter key, and then press the Up Arrow key.
16. Press the Tab key, turn on bold formatting, and then type Last Name.
17. Press the Tab key and then type First Name.
18. Press the Tab key and then type Fund.

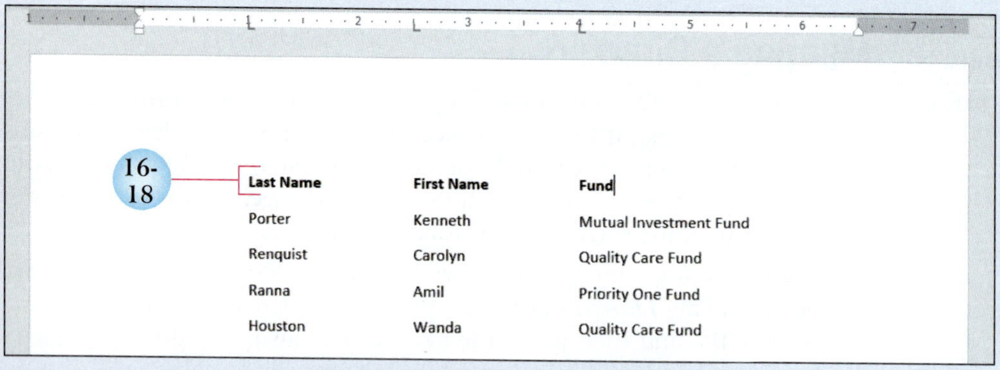

19. Save the directory document and name it **6-Directory**.
20. Print and then close the document.
21. Save the directory main document with the name **6-DirectoryMD** and then close the document.

Check Your Work

Activity 5 Select Records and Merge Mailing Labels **1 Part**

You will use Mail Merge to prepare mailing labels with the names and addresses of customers living in Baltimore.

Tutorial

Editing a Data Source File

Edit Recipient List

Editing a Data Source File

Edit a main document in the normal manner. Open the document, make the required changes, and then save the document. Since a data source file is actually an Access database file, it cannot be opened in the normal manner. Open a data source file for editing using the Edit Recipient List button in the Start Mail Merge group on the Mailings tab. Click the Edit Recipient List button and the Mail Merge Recipients dialog box displays, as shown in Figure 6.7. Select or edit records at this dialog box.

Selecting Specific Records

Each record in the Mail Merge Recipients dialog box contains a check mark before the first field. To select specific records for merging, remove the check marks from those records that should not be included in a merge. This way, only certain records in the data source file will be merged with the main document.

Figure 6.7 Mail Merge Recipients Dialog Box

Select specific records by removing the check marks from those records that should not be included in the merge.

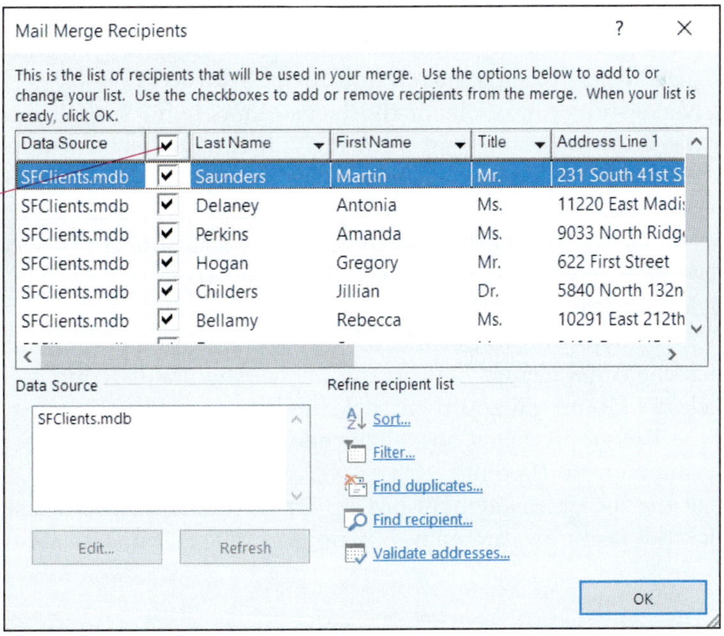

Activity 5 Selecting Records and Merging Mailing Labels

Part 1 of 1

1. At a blank document, create mailing labels for customers living in Baltimore. Begin by clicking the Mailings tab.
2. Click the Start Mail Merge button in the Start Mail Merge group and then click *Labels* at the drop-down list.
3. At the Label Options dialog box, make sure *Avery US Letter* displays in the *Label vendors* option box and *5160 Address Labels* is selected in the *Product number* list box and then click OK.
4. Click the Select Recipients button in the Start Mail Merge group and then click *Use an Existing List* at the drop-down list.
5. At the Select Data Source dialog box, navigate to your WL2C6 folder and then double-click the data source file named ***SFClients***.
6. Click the Edit Recipient List button in the Start Mail Merge group.
7. At the Mail Merge Recipients dialog box, complete the following steps:
   a. Click the check box immediately left of the *Last Name* field column heading to remove the check mark. (This removes all the check marks from the check boxes.)
   b. Insert check marks by clicking the check box immediately left of each of the following last names: *Saunders*, *Perkins*, *Dutton*, *Fernandez*, and *Stahl*. (These are the customers who live in Baltimore.)
   c. Click OK to close the dialog box.

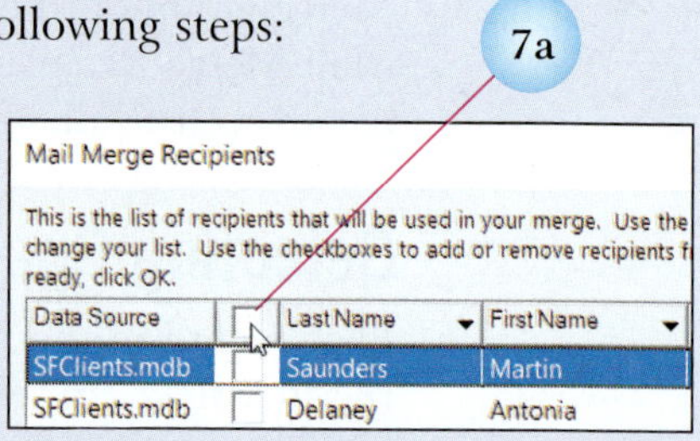

8. At the label document, click the Address Block button in the Write & Insert Fields group.
9. At the Insert Address Block dialog box, click OK.
10. Click the Update Labels button in the Write & Insert Fields group.
11. Click the Preview Results button and then click the Previous Record button to display each label. Make sure only labels for those customers living in Baltimore display.
12. Click the Preview Results button to turn off the preview feature.
13. Click the Finish & Merge button in the Finish group and then click *Edit Individual Documents* at the drop-down list.
14. At the Merge to New Document dialog box, make sure *All* is selected and then click OK.
15. Format the labels by completing the following steps:
   a. Click the Table Tools Layout tab.
   b. Click the Select button in the Table group and then click *Select Table*.
   c. Click the Align Center Left button in the Alignment group.
   d. Click the Home tab and then click the Paragraph group dialog box launcher.
   e. At the Paragraph dialog box, click the *Before* measurement box up arrow to change the measurement to 0 points.
   f. Click the *After* measurement box up arrow to change the measurement to 0 points.
   g. Click the *Inside* measurement box up arrow three times to change the measurement to 0.3 inch.
   h. Click OK.
16. Save the merged labels and name the document **6-SFLabels**.
17. Print and then close **6-SFLabels**.
18. Save the labels main document with the name **6-SFLabelsMD** and then close the document.

Check Your Work

Activity 6 Edit Records in a Data Source File — 1 Part

You will edit records in a data source file and then use Mail Merge to prepare a directory with the edited records that contains customer names, telephone numbers, and cell phone numbers.

Editing Records

Quick Steps

Edit Data Source File

1. Open main document.
2. Click Mailings tab.
3. Click Edit Recipient List button.
4. Click data source file name in *Data Source* list box.
5. Click Edit button.
6. Make changes at Edit Data Source dialog box.
7. Click OK.
8. Click OK.

A data source file may need editing on a periodic basis to add or delete customer names, update fields, insert new fields, or delete existing fields. To edit a data source file, click the Edit Recipient List button in the Start Mail Merge group. At the Mail Merge Recipients dialog box, click the data source file name in the *Data Source* list box and then click the Edit button below the list box. This displays the Edit Data Source dialog box, as shown in Figure 6.8. At this dialog box, add a new entry, delete an entry, find a particular entry, and customize columns.

Figure 6.8 Edit Data Source Dialog Box

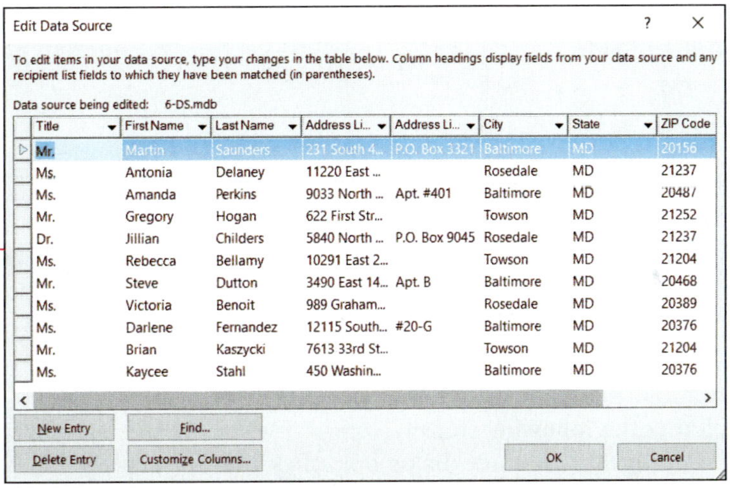

Edit text in fields in columns in the data source file at this dialog box.

Activity 6 Editing Records in a Data Source File — Part 1 of 1

1. Make a copy of the **SFClients** data source file by completing the following steps:
   a. Display the Open dialog box and make WL2C6 the active folder.
   b. If necessary, change the file type option to *All Files*.
   c. Right-click the ***SFClients*** data source file and then click *Copy* at the shortcut menu.
   d. Position the mouse pointer in a white portion of the Open dialog box Content pane (outside any file name), click the right mouse button, and then click *Paste* at the shortcut menu. (This inserts a copy of the file in the dialog box Content pane and names the file **SFClients - Copy**.)
   e. Right-click ***SFClients - Copy*** and then click *Rename* at the shortcut menu.
   f. Type 6-DS and then press the Enter key.
   g. Close the Open dialog box.

2. At a blank document, click the Mailings tab.
3. Click the Select Recipients button and then click *Use an Existing List* from the drop-down list.
4. At the Select Data Source dialog box, navigate to your WL2C6 folder and then double-click the data source file named ***6-DS***.
5. Click the Edit Recipient List button in the Start Mail Merge group.
6. At the Mail Merge Recipients dialog box, click *6-DS.mdb* in the *Data Source* list box and then click the Edit button.
7. Delete the record for Steve Dutton by completing the following steps:
   a. Click the square at the beginning of the row for *Mr. Steve Dutton*.
   b. Click the Delete Entry button.
   c. At the message asking if you want to delete the entry, click Yes.
8. Insert a new record by completing the following steps:
   a. Click the New Entry button in the dialog box.
   b. Type the following text in the new record in the specified fields:

Title	Ms.
First Name	Jennae
Last Name	Davis
Address Line 1	3120 South 21st
Address Line 2	(none)
City	Rosedale
State	MD
ZIP Code	20389
Home Phone	410-555-5774

9. Insert a new field and type text in the field by completing the following steps:
   a. At the Edit Data Source dialog box, click the Customize Columns button.
   b. At the message asking if you want to save the changes made to the data source file, click Yes.
   c. At the Customize Address List dialog box, click *ZIP Code* in the *Field Names* list box. (You will insert a new field below this field.)
   d. Click the Add button.
   e. At the Add Field dialog box, type Cell Phone and then click OK.
   f. You decide that you want the *Cell Phone* field to display after the *Home Phone* field. To move the *Cell Phone* field, make sure it is selected and then click the Move Down button.
   g. Click OK to close the Customize Address List dialog box.

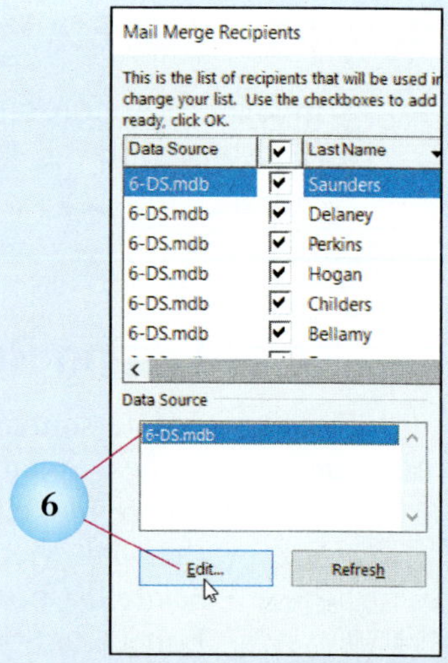

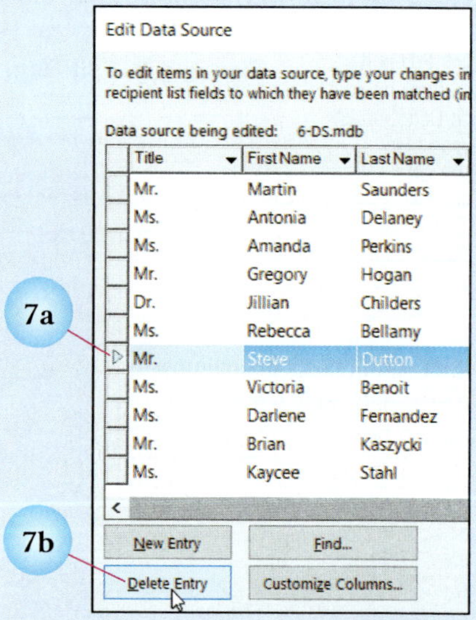

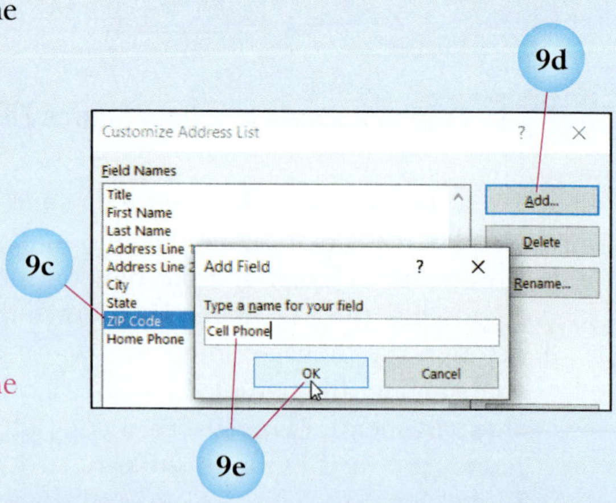

h. At the Edit Data Source dialog box, scroll right to display the *Cell Phone* field (the last field in the file) and then type the following cell phone numbers. (After typing each cell phone number except the last number, press the Down Arrow key to make the next field below active.)

Record 1	410-555-1249
Record 2	410-555-3443
Record 3	410-555-0695
Record 4	410-555-9488
Record 5	410-555-1200
Record 6	410-555-7522
Record 7	410-555-8833
Record 8	410-555-9378
Record 9	410-555-4261
Record 10	410-555-9944
Record 11	410-555-2321

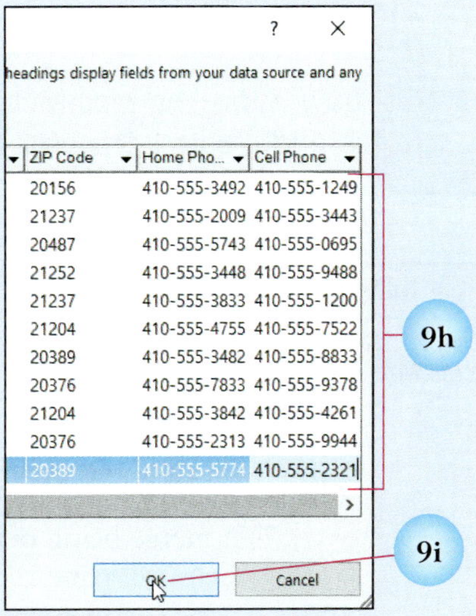

i. Click OK to close the Edit Data Source dialog box.
j. At the message asking if you want to update the recipient list and save changes, click Yes.
k. At the Mail Merge Recipients dialog box, click OK.

10. Create a directory by completing the following steps:
    a. Click the Start Mail Merge button and then click *Directory* at the drop-down list.
    b. At the blank document, set left tabs on the horizontal ruler at the 1-inch mark, the 3-inch mark, and the 4.5-inch mark.
    c. Press the Tab key. (This moves the insertion point to the first tab set at the 1-inch mark.)
    d. Click the Insert Merge Field button arrow and then click *Last_Name* at the drop-down list.
    e. Type a comma and then press the spacebar.
    f. Click the Insert Merge Field button arrow and then click *First_Name* at the drop-down list.
    g. Press the Tab key, click the Insert Merge Field button arrow, and then click *Home_Phone* at the drop-down list.
    h. Press the Tab key, click the Insert Merge Field button arrow, and then click *Cell_Phone* at the drop-down list.
    i. Press the Enter key.
    j. Click the Finish & Merge button and then click *Edit Individual Documents* at the drop-down list.
    k. At the Merge to New Document dialog box, make sure *All* is selected and then click OK.
11. Press Ctrl + Home, press the Enter key, and then press the Up Arrow key.
12. Press the Tab key, turn on bold formatting, and then type Name.
13. Press the Tab key and then type Home Phone.
14. Press the Tab key and then type Cell Phone.

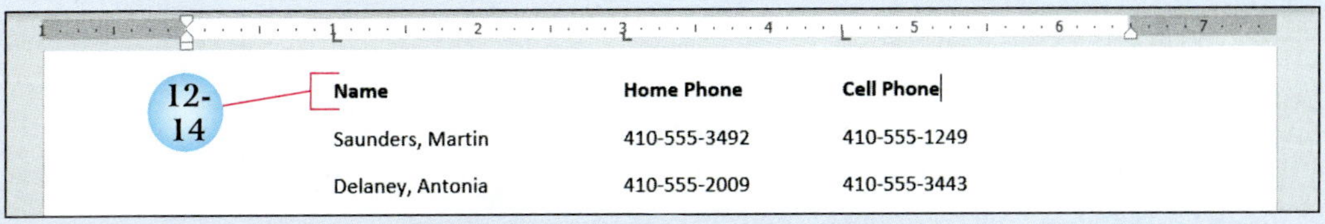

15. Save the directory document and name it **6-Directory-Act6**.
16. Print and then close the document.
17. Save the directory main document with the name **6-Directory-Act6-MD** and then close the document.

Check Your Work

Activity 7 Use Mail Merge Wizard — 1 Part

You will use the Mail Merge wizard to merge a main document with a data source file and create letters for clients of Sorenson Funds.

Tutorial

Using the Mail Merge Wizard

Merging Using the Mail Merge Wizard

The Mail Merge feature includes a Mail Merge wizard with steps for completing the merge process. To access the wizard, click the Mailings tab, click the Start Mail Merge button, and then click the *Step-by-Step Mail Merge Wizard* option at the drop-down list. The first of six Mail Merge task panes displays at the right side of the screen. The options in each task pane may vary depending on the type of merge being performed. Generally, one of the following steps is completed at each task pane:

- Step 1: Select the type of document to be created, such as a letter, email message, envelope, label, or directory.
- Step 2: Specify what is to be used to create the main document: the current document, a template, or an existing document.
- Step 3: Specify whether a new list will be created or an existing list or Outlook contacts list will be used.
- Step 4: Use the items in this task pane to help prepare the main document by performing tasks such as inserting fields.
- Step 5: Preview the merged documents.
- Step 6: Complete the merge.

Activity 7 Preparing Form Letters Using the Mail Merge Wizard — Part 1 of 1

1. At a blank document, click the Mailings tab, click the Start Mail Merge button in the Start Mail Merge group, and then click *Step-by-Step Mail Merge Wizard* at the drop-down list.
2. At the first Mail Merge task pane, make sure *Letters* is selected in the *Select document type* section and then click the Next: Starting document hyperlink at the bottom of the task pane.
3. At the second Mail Merge task pane, click the *Start from existing document* option in the *Select starting document* section.
4. Click the Open button in the *Start from existing* section of the task pane.
5. At the Open dialog box, navigate to your WL2C6 folder and then double-click ***SFLtrMD***.
6. Click the Next: Select recipients hyperlink at the bottom of the task pane.

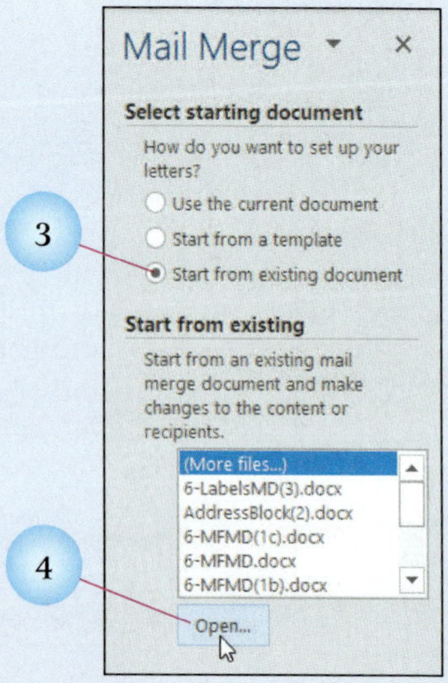

7. At the third Mail Merge task pane, click the Browse hyperlink in the *Use an existing list* section of the task pane.
8. At the Select Data Source dialog box, navigate to your WL2C6 folder and then double-click the ***SFClients*** data source file.
9. At the Mail Merge Recipients dialog box, click OK.
10. Click the Next: Write your letter hyperlink at the bottom of the task pane.
11. At the fourth Mail Merge task pane, enter fields in the form letter by completing the following steps:
    a. Position the insertion point a double space above the first paragraph of text in the letter.
    b. Click the Address block hyperlink in the *Write your letter* section of the task pane.
    c. At the Insert Address Block dialog box, click OK.
    d. Press the Enter key two times and then click the Greeting line hyperlink in the *Write your letter* section of the task pane.
    e. At the Insert Greeting Line dialog box, click the option box arrow at the right of the option box containing the comma (the box at the right of the box containing *Mr. Randall*).
    f. At the drop-down list, click the colon.
    g. Click OK to close the Insert Greeting Line dialog box.

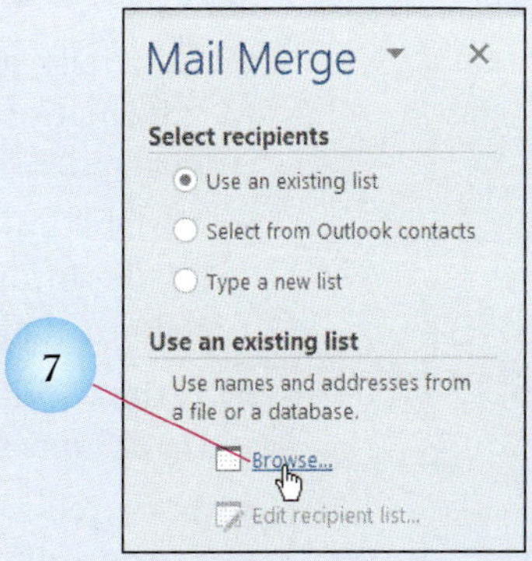

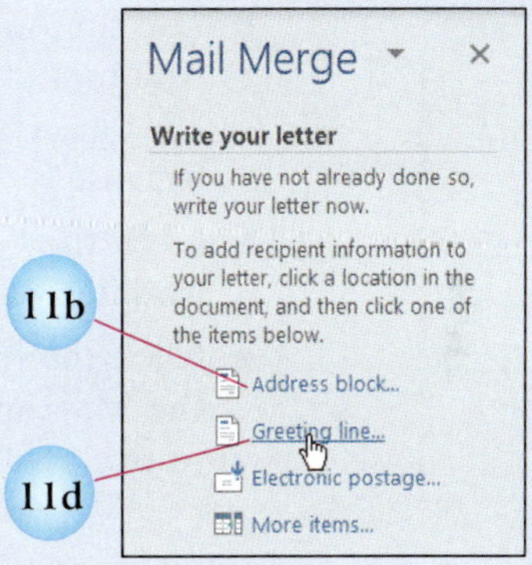

12. Click the Next: Preview your letters hyperlink at the bottom of the task pane.
13. At the fifth Mail Merge task pane, look over the letter in the document window and make sure the information is merged properly. If you want to see the letters for the other recipients, click the Next button (the button containing two right-pointing arrows) in the Mail Merge task pane.
14. Click the Preview Results button in the Preview Results group to turn off the preview feature.
15. Click the Next: Complete the merge hyperlink at the bottom of the task pane.
16. At the sixth Mail Merge task pane, click the Edit individual letters hyperlink in the *Merge* section of the task pane.
17. At the Merge to New Document dialog box, make sure *All* is selected and then click OK.
18. Save the merged letters document with the name **6-SFLtrs**.
19. Print only the first two pages of **6-SFLtrs**.
20. Close the document.
21. Save the main document with the name **6-SFLtrsMD** and then close the document.

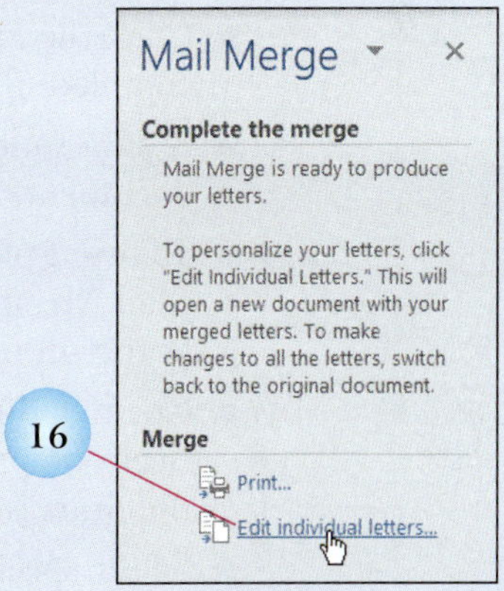

Check Your Work

Chapter Summary

- Generally, a merge takes two files: the data source file containing the variable information and the main document containing the standard text along with fields identifying where variable information is inserted during the merge process.
- Variable information in a data source file is saved as a record. A record contains all the information for one unit. A series of fields makes a record and a series of records makes a data source file.
- A data source file is saved as an Access database but having Access on the computer is not required to complete a merge with a data source file.
- Use predesigned fields when creating a data source file or create custom fields at the Customize Address List dialog box.
- Use the Address Block button in the Write & Insert Fields group on the Mailings tab to insert all the fields required for the inside address of a letter. This inserts the *«AddressBlock»* field, which is considered a composite field because it groups a number of fields.
- Click the Greeting Line button in the Write & Insert Fields group on the Mailings tab to insert the *«GreetingLine»* composite field in the document.
- Click the Insert Merge Field button arrow in the Write & Insert Fields group on the Mailings tab to display a drop-down list of the fields contained in the data source file.
- Click the Preview Results button in the Preview Results group on the Mailings tab to view the main document merged with the first record in the data source file. Use the navigation buttons in the Preview Results group on the Mailings tab to display the main document merged with specific records.
- Before merging documents, check for errors by clicking the Check for Errors button in the Preview Results group on the Mailings tab. This displays the Checking and Reporting Errors dialog box with three options for checking errors.
- Click the Finish & Merge button in the Finish group on the Mailings tab to complete the merge.
- A data source file can be merged with a letter, envelope, label, or directory main document.
- To begin preparing envelopes for merging, click the Mailings tab, click the Start Mail Merge button, and then click *Envelopes* at the drop-down list. Click *Labels* at the drop-down list to begin preparing labels for merging.
- Create a directory when merging records in a data source file on the same page. Begin preparing a directory for merging by clicking the Mailings tab, clicking the Start Mail Merge button, and then clicking *Directory* at the drop-down list.
- Select specific records for merging by inserting or removing check marks from the records in the Mail Merge Recipients dialog box. Display this dialog box by clicking the Edit Recipient List button in the Start Mail Merge group on the Mailings tab.
- Edit specific records in a data source file at the Edit Data Source dialog box. Display this dialog box by clicking the Edit Recipient List button on the Mailings tab, clicking the data source file name in the *Data Source* list box, and then clicking the Edit button.
- Word includes a Mail Merge wizard that provides guidance through the process of creating letters, envelopes, labels, directories, and email messages with personalized information.

Commands Review

FEATURE	RIBBON TAB, GROUP	BUTTON, OPTION
Address Block field	Mailings, Write & Insert Fields	
Checking and Reporting Errors dialog box	Mailings, Preview Results	
directory main document	Mailings, Start Mail Merge	, *Directory*
envelope main document	Mailings, Start Mail Merge	, *Envelopes*
finish merge	Mailings, Finish	
Greeting Line field	Mailings, Write & Insert Fields	
insert merge fields	Mailings, Write & Insert Fields	
label main document	Mailings, Start Mail Merge	, *Labels*
letter main document	Mailings, Start Mail Merge	, *Letters*
Mail Merge Recipients dialog box	Mailings, Start Mail Merge	
Mail Merge wizard	Mailings, Start Mail Merge	, *Step-by-Step Mail Merge Wizard*
New Address List dialog box	Mailings, Start Mail Merge	, *Type a New List*
preview merge results	Mailings, Preview Results	ABC

Microsoft®

Word

CHAPTER

7

Managing Building Blocks and Fields

Performance Objectives

Upon successful completion of Chapter 7, you will be able to:

1 Insert and sort building blocks
2 Save content as building blocks in specific galleries
3 Edit building block properties
4 Insert and modify custom building blocks
5 Create a building block gallery and save building blocks in a different template
6 Delete building blocks
7 Insert document property placeholders from Quick Parts
8 Insert and update fields from Quick Parts

Word contains a number of predesigned blocks of text and formatting referred to as *building blocks*. Building blocks are available in galleries throughout Word, most of them on the Insert tab, where they can be quickly and easily inserted into any document. You have been inserting building blocks such as predesigned headers, footers, page numbers, text boxes, cover pages, and so on. Predesigned building blocks can be customized to meet specific needs, or a new building block can be created and then saved in a gallery. In this chapter, you will learn how to build a document using building blocks; how to create, save, and edit your own building blocks; and how to create a button on the Quick Access Toolbar for faster access to a gallery. You will also learn how to insert fields in a document and to format and customize fields.

Data Files

Before beginning chapter work, copy the WL2C7 folder to your storage medium and then make WL2C7 the active folder.

The online course includes additional training and assessment resources.

Activity 1 Build a Document with Predesigned Building Blocks **1 Part**

You will open a report document and then add elements to it by sorting and then inserting predesigned building blocks.

Managing Building Blocks

Quick Parts

Word includes a variety of tools for inserting data such as text, fields, objects, and other items to help build a document. To view some of the tools available, click the Quick Parts button in the Text group on the Insert tab. This displays a drop-down list of choices for inserting document properties, fields, and building blocks. Building blocks are tools for developing a document. Word provides a number of predesigned building blocks that can be inserted in a document or custom building blocks can be created.

Inserting a Building Block

Tutorial

Inserting and Sorting Building Blocks

Quick Steps

Insert Building Block

1. Click Insert tab.
2. Click Quick Parts button.
3. Click *Building Blocks Organizer.*
4. Click building block.
5. Click Insert button.
6. Click Close.

To insert a building block into a document, click the Insert tab, click the Quick Parts button in the Text group, and then click *Building Blocks Organizer* at the drop-down list. This displays the Building Blocks Organizer dialog box, shown in Figure 7.1. The dialog box contains columns of information about each building block, including its name, the gallery that contains it, the template in which it is stored, its behavior, and a brief description of it.

The Building Blocks Organizer dialog box is a central location for viewing all the predesigned building blocks available in Word. Some of the building blocks were used in previous chapters when a predesigned header or footer, cover page, page number, or watermark was inserted in a document. Other galleries in the Building Blocks Organizer dialog box contain predesigned building blocks such as bibliographies, equations, tables of contents, tables, and text boxes. The Building Blocks Organizer dialog box provides a convenient location for viewing and inserting building blocks.

Sorting Building Blocks

Quick Steps

Sort Building Blocks

1. Click Insert tab.
2. Click Quick Parts button.
3. Click *Building Blocks Organizer.*
4. Click column heading.

The Building Blocks Organizer dialog box displays the building blocks in the list box sorted by the *Gallery* column. The building blocks can be sorted by another column by clicking that column heading. For example, to sort the building blocks alphabetically by name, click the *Name* column heading.

Figure 7.1 Building Blocks Organizer Dialog Box

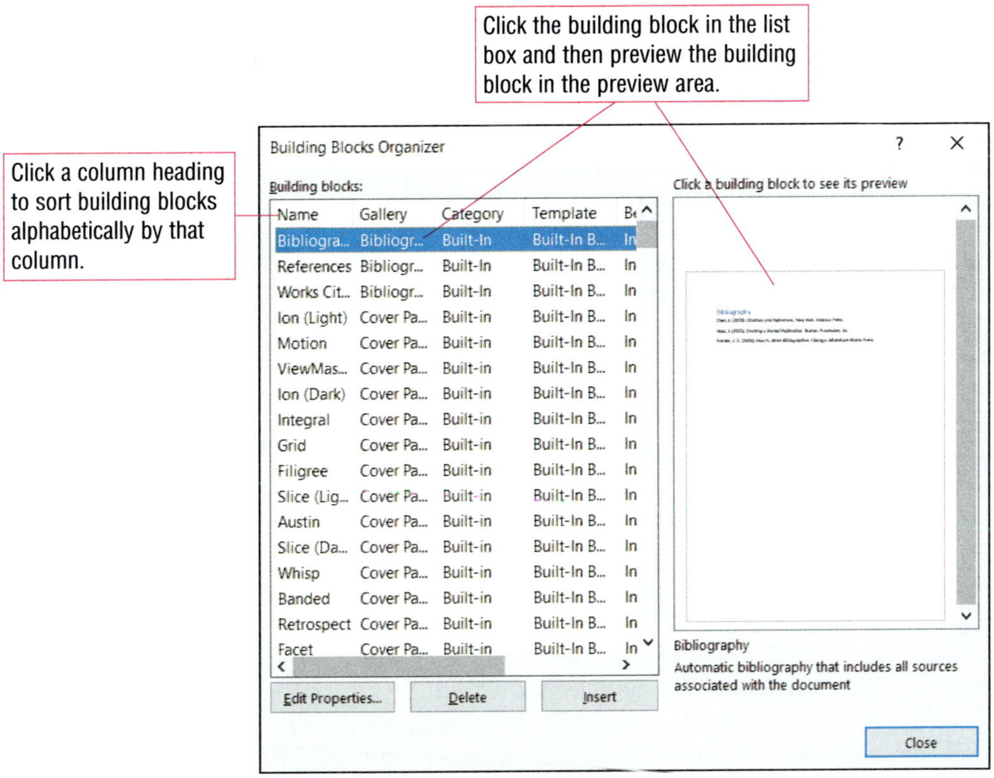

Activity 1 Sorting and Inserting Predesigned Building Blocks

Part 1 of 1

1. Open **CompViruses** and then save it with the name **7-CompViruses**.
2. Sort the building blocks and then insert a table of contents building block by completing the following steps:
   a. Press Ctrl + Home to move the insertion point to the beginning of the document, press Ctrl + Enter to insert a page break, and then press Ctrl + Home again.
   b. Click the Insert tab, click the Quick Parts button in the Text group, and then click *Building Blocks Organizer* at the drop-down list.
   c. At the Building Blocks Organizer dialog box, notice the arrangement of building blocks in the list box. (The building blocks are most likely organized alphabetically by the *Gallery* column.)
   d. Click the *Name* column heading. (This sorts the building blocks alphabetically by name. However, some blank building blocks may display at the beginning of the list box.)
   e. Scroll down the list box and then click *Automatic Table 1*. (You may see only a portion of the name. Click the name and the full name as well as a description display in the dialog box below the preview of the table of contents building block.)

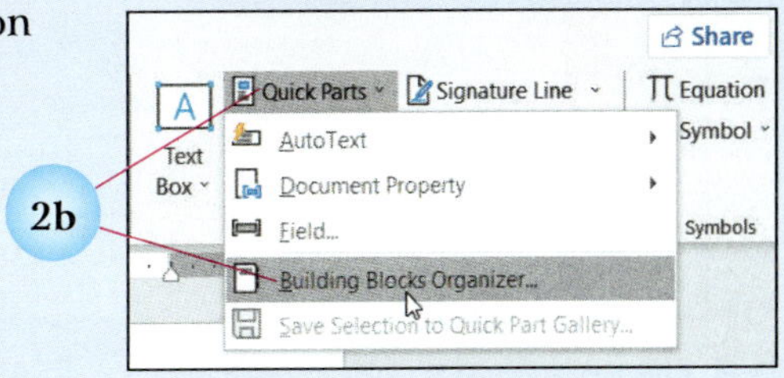

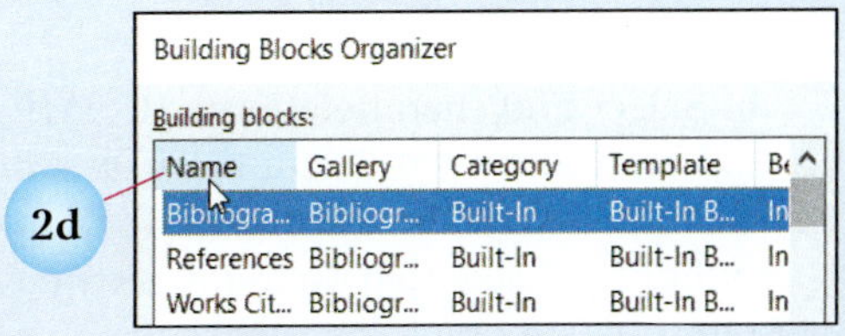

f. Click the Insert button at the bottom of the dialog box. (This inserts a contents page at the beginning of the document and creates a table of contents that includes the headings with styles applied.)

3. Insert a footer building block by completing the following steps:
   a. Click the Quick Parts button on the Insert tab and then click *Building Blocks Organizer*.
   b. Scroll down the Building Blocks Organizer list box, click the *Sempahore* footer, and then click the Insert button.
   c. Decrease the *Footer from Bottom* measurement to 0.3 inch (in the Position group on the Header & Footer Tools Design tab).
   d. Click the Close Header and Footer button.

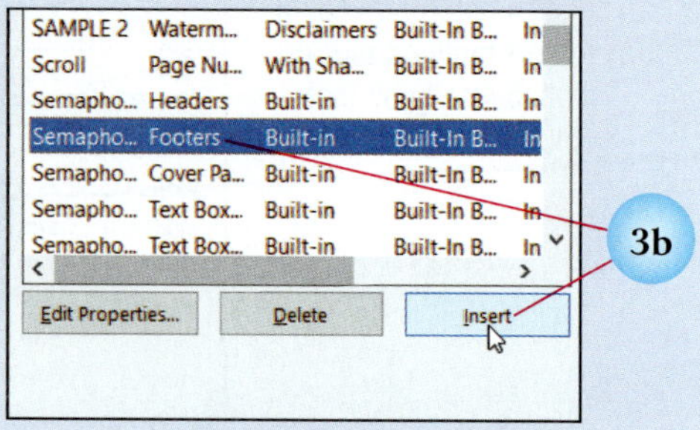

4. Insert a cover page building block by completing the following steps:
   a. Press Ctrl + Home to move the insertion point to the beginning of the document.
   b. Click the Insert tab, click the Quick Parts button, and then click *Building Blocks Organizer*.
   c. Scroll down the Building Blocks Organizer list box, click the *Semaphore* cover page, and then click the Insert button.
   d. Click the *[DATE]* placeholder and then type today's date.
   e. Click the *[DOCUMENT TITLE]* placeholder and then type Northland Security Systems. (The text will be converted to all uppercase letters.)
   f. Click the *[Document subtitle]* placeholder and then type Computer Viruses and Security Strategies. (The text will be converted to small caps.)
   g. Select the name above the *[COMPANY NAME]* placeholder and then type your first and last names.

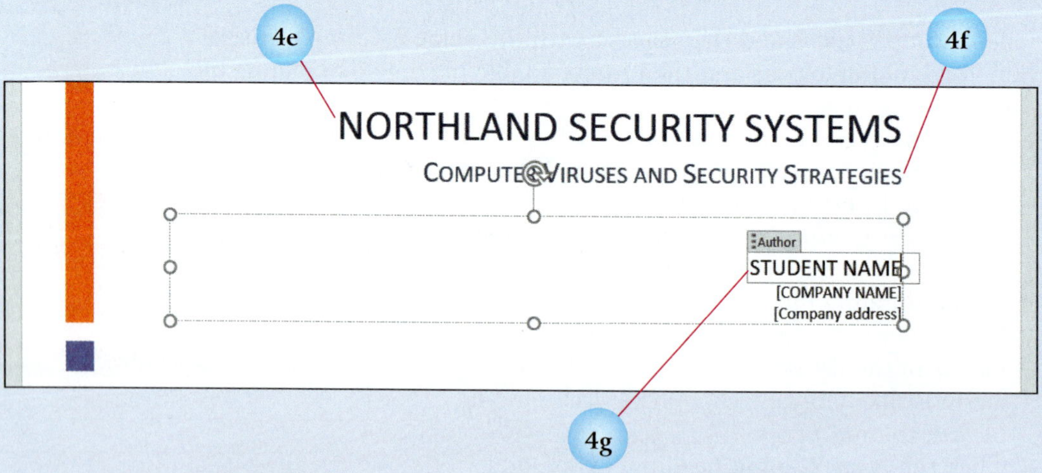

   h. Select and then delete the *[COMPANY NAME]* placeholder.
   i. Select and then delete the *[Company address]* placeholder.
5. Scroll through the document and look at each page. The Semaphore footer and cover page building blocks that were inserted have similar formatting and are part of the Semaphore group. Using building blocks from the same group provides consistency in the document and gives it a polished and professional appearance.
6. Save, print, and then close **7-CompViruses**.

Check Your Work

Activity 2 Create a Letter Document Using Custom Building Blocks 3 Parts

You will create custom building blocks and then use them to prepare a business letter.

Tutorial

Saving Content as a Building Block

Quick Steps

Save Content in Text Box Gallery
1. Select content.
2. Click Insert tab
3. Click Text Box button.
4. Click *Save Selection to Text Box Gallery.*

Save Content in Header Gallery
1. Select content.
2. Click Insert tab.
3. Click Header button.
4. Click *Save Selection to Header Gallery.*

Save Content in Footer Gallery
1. Select content.
2. Click Insert tab.
3. Click Footer button.
4. Click *Save Selection to Footer Gallery.*

Hint When selecting content to save as a building block, turn on the display of nonprinting characters by clicking the Show/Hide ¶ button in the Paragraph group on the Home tab.

Saving Content as a Building Block

Consider saving data that is typed and formatted on a regular basis as a building block. Saving commonly created data as a building block saves time and reduces errors that might occur each time the data is typed or formatting is applied. The data can be saved as a building block in a specific gallery, such as the Text Box, Header, or Footer gallery, or saved in the AutoText gallery or Quick Part gallery.

Saving Content in a Specific Gallery To save content in a specific gallery, use the button for the gallery. For example, to save a text box in the Text Box gallery, use the Text Box button. To do this, select the text box, click the Insert tab, click the Text Box button, and then click the *Save Selection to Text Box Gallery* option at the drop-down gallery. At the Create New Building Block dialog box as shown in Figure 7.2, type a name for the text box building block, type a description of it, and then click OK.

To save content in the Header gallery, select the content, click the Insert tab, click the Header button, and then click the *Save Selection to Header Gallery* option at the drop-down gallery. This displays the Create New Building Block dialog box, as shown in Figure 7.2 (except *Headers* displays in the *Gallery* option box). Complete similar steps to save content in the Footer gallery and Cover Page gallery.

When data is saved as a building block, it is available in the Building Blocks Organizer dialog box. If content is saved as a building block in a specific gallery, the building block is available at both the Building Blocks Organizer dialog box and the gallery. For example, if a building block is saved in the Footer gallery, it is available when the Footer button on the Insert tab is clicked.

Figure 7.2 Create New Building Block Dialog Box

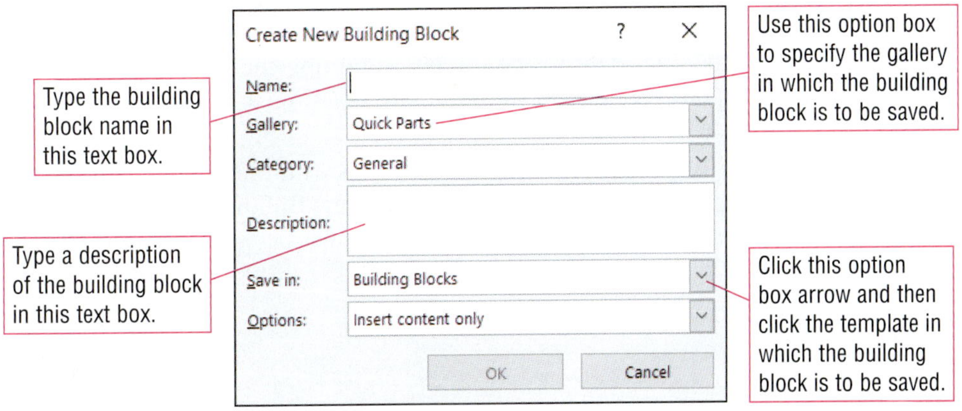

Quick Steps

Save Content in AutoText Gallery

1. Select content.
2. Click Insert tab.
3. Click Quick Parts button.
4. Point to *AutoText*.
5. Click *Save Selection to AutoText Gallery*.

Saving Content in the AutoText Gallery Content can be saved as a building block in the AutoText gallery. The building block can be inserted into a document by clicking the Insert tab, clicking the Quick Parts button, pointing to *AutoText*, and then clicking the AutoText building block at the side menu. To save content in the AutoText gallery, type and format the content and then select it. Click the Insert tab, click the Quick Parts button, point to *AutoText*, and then click the *Save Selection to AutoText Gallery* option at the side menu or use the keyboard shortcut Alt + F3. At the Create New Building Block dialog box, type a name for the building block, type a description of it, and then click OK.

Quick Steps

Save Content in Quick Part Gallery

1. Select content.
2. Click Insert tab.
3. Click Quick Parts button.
4. Click *Save Selection to Quick Part Gallery*.

Saving Content in the Quick Part Gallery Not only can content be saved in the AutoText gallery, but selected content can also be saved in the Quick Part gallery. To do this, select the content, click the Insert tab, click the Quick Parts button, and then click the *Save Selection to Quick Part Gallery* option at the drop-down gallery. This displays the Create New Building Block dialog box with *Quick Parts* specified in the *Gallery* option box and *Building Blocks* specified in the *Save in* option box. Type a name for the building block, type a description of it, and then click OK.

Quick Steps

Save as Template

1. Click File tab.
2. Click *Save As* option.
3. Click *Browse* option.
4. Click *Save as type* option.
5. Click *Word Template*.
6. Type name for template.
7. Click Save button.

Saving Building Blocks in a Specific Template By default, building block content is saved in one of two templates: *Building Blocks* or *Normal*. The template location depends on the gallery selected at the Create New Building Block dialog box. A building block saved in either of these templates is available each time a document is opened in Word. In a public environment, such as a school, saving to one of these templates may not be possible. To create a new personal template, display the Save As dialog box and then change the *Save as type* option to *Word Template*. Choosing this option automatically selects the Custom Office Templates folder. Type a name for the template and then click the Save button; the template is saved in the Custom Office Templates folder.

Quick Steps

Open Document Based on Template

1. Click File tab.
2. Click *New* option.
3. Click *Personal* option.
4. Click template thumbnail.

OR

1. Click File Explorer icon on taskbar.
2. Navigate to folder containing template.
3. Double-click template.

To open a document based on a personal template, click the File tab and then click the *New* option. At the New backstage area, click the *Personal* option below the search text box. This displays thumbnails of the templates saved in the Custom Office Templates folder. Click the thumbnail of a specific template and a blank document opens based on the selected template.

Another option for opening a document based on a template is to save a template to a location other than the Custom Office Templates folder, such as the WL2C7 folder on your storage medium, and then use File Explorer to open a document based on the template. To do this, click the File Explorer icon on the taskbar, navigate to the folder containing the template, and then double-click the template. Instead of the template opening, a blank document opens that is based on the template.

To specify the template in which a building block is to be saved, click the *Save in* option box arrow in the Create New Building Block dialog box and then click the specific template. A document must be opened based on a personal template for the template name to display in the drop-down list.

Activity 2a Saving a Template and Saving Content in the Text Box, Footer, AutoText, and Quick Part Galleries

Part 1 of 3

1. Press Ctrl + N to display a blank document and then save the document as a template by completing the following steps:
   a. Press the F12 function key to display the Save As dialog box.
   b. At the Save As dialog box, type 7-FAVTemplate in the *File name* text box.
   c. Click the *Save as type* option box and then click *Word Template* at the drop-down list.
   d. Navigate to your WL2C7 folder.
   e. Click the Save button.
2. Close **7-FAVTemplate**.
3. Open a document based on the template by completing the following steps:
   a. Click the File Explorer icon on the taskbar. (The taskbar displays along the bottom of the screen.)
   b. Navigate to your WL2C7 folder.
   c. Double-click ***7-FAVTemplate***.
4. Insert the document named **FAVContent** into the current document. (Do this with the Object button arrow on the Insert tab. This document is in your WL2C7 folder.)
5. Save the text box as a building block in the Text Box gallery by completing the following steps:
   a. Select the text box by clicking in it and then clicking its border.
   b. With the Insert tab active, click the Text Box button and then click *Save Selection to Text Box Gallery* at the drop-down list.
   c. At the Create New Building Block dialog box, type FAVTextBox in the *Name* text box.
   d. Click the *Save in* option box arrow and then click *7-FAVTemplate* at the drop-down list.
   e. Click OK to close the Create New Building Block dialog box.

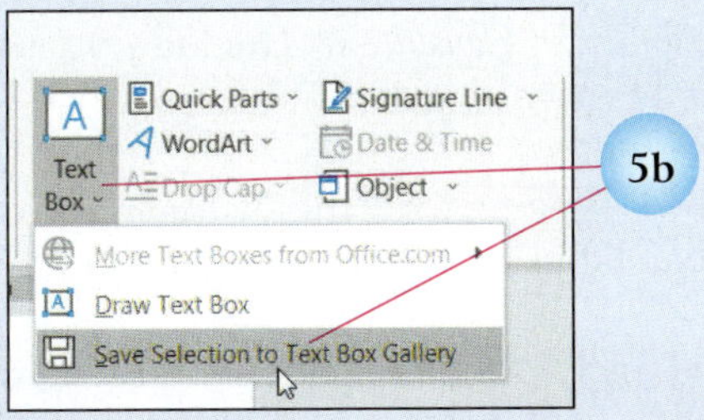

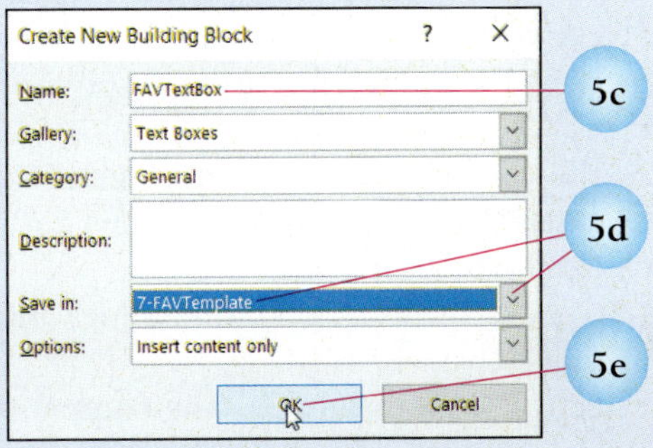

6. Save content as a building block in the Footer gallery by completing the following steps:
   a. Select the text *"Making your vacation dreams a reality"* below the text box. (Be sure to select the paragraph mark at the end of the text. If necessary, click the Show/Hide ¶ button in the Paragraph group on the Home tab to display the paragraph mark.)
   b. Click the Footer button in the Header & Footer group on the Insert tab and then click *Save Selection to Footer Gallery* at the drop-down list.
   c. At the Create New Building Block dialog box, type FAVFooter in the *Name* text box.
   d. Click the *Save in* option box and then click *7-FAVTemplate* at the drop-down list.
   e. Click OK to close the Create New Building Block dialog box.

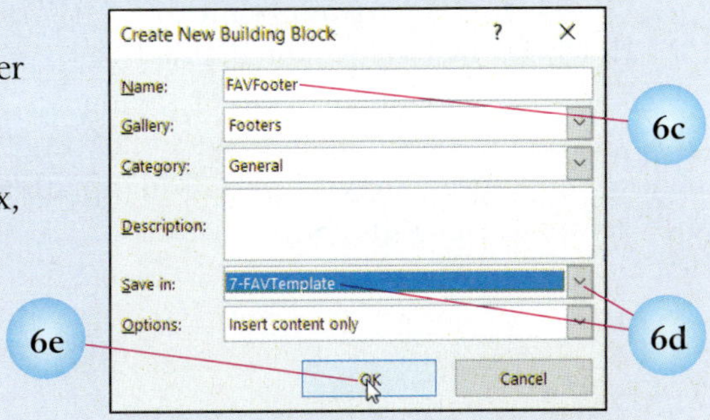

7. Save the company name *Pacific Sky Cruise Lines* and the address below it as a building block in the AutoText gallery by completing the following steps:
   a. Select the company name and address (the two lines below the company name). (Be sure to include the paragraph mark at the end of the last line of the address.)
   b. Click the Quick Parts button in the Text group on the Insert tab, point to *AutoText*, and then click *Save Selection to AutoText Gallery* at the side menu.

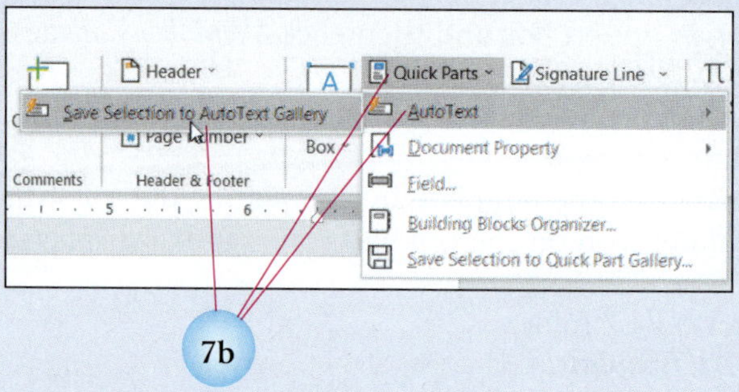

   c. At the Create New Building Block dialog box, type PacificSky in the *Name* text box.
   d. Click the *Save in* option box arrow and then click *7-FAVTemplate* at the drop-down list.
   e. Click OK to close the dialog box.
8. Type your name and company title and then save the text as a building block in the AutoText gallery by completing the following steps:
   a. Move the insertion point two lines below the address for Pacific Sky Cruise Lines.
   b. Type your first and last names and then press the spacebar.
   c. Press the Down Arrow key to move the insertion point to the next line and then type Travel Consultant. (Do not press the Enter key.)
   d. Select your first and last names and the title *Travel Consultant*. (Include the paragraph mark at the end of the title.)
   e. Press Alt + F3.
   f. At the Create New Building Block dialog box, type Title in the *Name* text box.
   g. Click the *Save in* option box arrow and then click *7-FAVTemplate* at the drop-down list.
   h. Click OK to close the dialog box.
9. Save the letterhead as a building block in the Quick Part gallery by completing the following steps:
   a. Select the letterhead text (the company name *FAMILY ADVENTURE VACATIONS*, the address and telephone number below the name, and the paragraph mark at the end of the address and telephone number).
   b. Click the Quick Parts button in the Text group on the Insert tab and then click *Save Selection to Quick Part Gallery* at the drop-down list.
   c. At the Create New Building Block dialog box, type FAV in the *Name* text box and then change the *Save in* option to *7-FAVTemplate*.
   d. Click OK to close the dialog box.
10. Close the document without saving it.
11. At the message that displays indicating that you have modified styles, building blocks, or other content stored in 7-FAVTemplate and asking if you want to save the changes to the template, click the Save button.

Tutorial

Editing Building Block Properties

Quick Steps

Edit Building Block

1. Click Insert tab.
2. Click Quick Parts button.
3. Click *Building Blocks Organizer.*
4. Click building block.
5. Click Edit Properties button.
6. Make changes.
7. Click OK.

OR

1. Click button.
2. Right-click custom building block.
3. Click *Edit Properties.*
4. Make changes.
5. Click OK.

Editing Building Block Properties

Changes can be made to the properties of a building block with options at the Modify Building Block dialog box. This dialog box contains the same options as the Create New Building Block dialog box.

Display the Modify Building Block dialog box by opening the Building Blocks Organizer dialog box, clicking the specific building block in the list box, and then clicking the Edit Properties button. The dialog box can also be displayed for a building block in the Quick Parts button drop-down gallery. To do this, click the Quick Parts button, right-click the building block in the drop-down gallery, and then click *Edit Properties* at the shortcut menu. Make changes to the Modify Building Block dialog box and then click OK. At the confirmation message, click Yes.

The dialog box can also be displayed for a custom building block in a button drop-down gallery by clicking the button, right-clicking the custom building block, and then clicking the *Edit Properties* option at the shortcut menu. For example, to modify a custom text box building block, click the Insert tab, click the Text Box button, and then scroll down the drop-down gallery to display the custom text box building block. Right-click the custom text box building block and then click *Edit Properties* at the shortcut menu.

Activity 2b **Editing Building Block Properties** Part 2 of 3

1. Open a blank document based on your template **7-FAVTemplate** by completing the following steps:
   a. Click the File Explorer icon on the taskbar.
   b. Navigate to your WL2C7 folder.
   c. Double-click ***7-FAVTemplate***.
2. Edit the PacificSky building block by completing the following steps:
   a. Click the Insert tab, click the Quick Parts button, and then click *Building Blocks Organizer* at the drop-down list.
   b. At the Building Blocks Organizer dialog box, click the *Gallery* heading to sort the building blocks by gallery. (This displays the AutoText galleries at the beginning of the list.)
   c. Using the horizontal scroll bar at the bottom of the *Building blocks* list box, scroll to the right and notice that the PacificSky building block does not contain a description.
   d. Click the *PacificSky* building block in the list box.
   e. Click the Edit Properties button at the bottom of the dialog box.

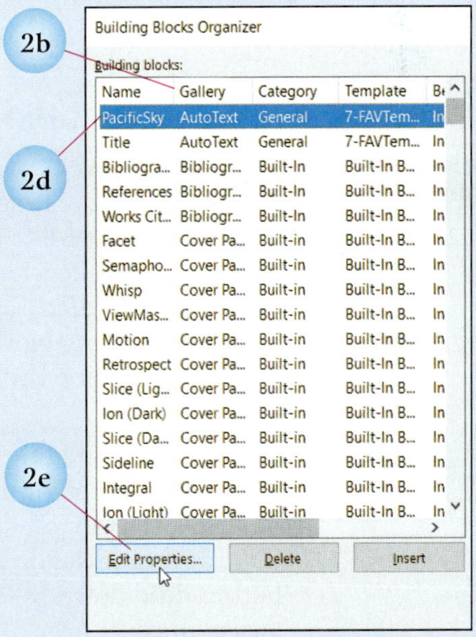

f. At the Modify Building Block dialog box, click in the *Name* text box and then type Address at the end of the name.
g. Click in the *Description* text box and then type Inserts the Pacific Sky name and address.
h. Click OK to close the dialog box.
i. At the message asking if you want to redefine the building block entry, click Yes.
j. Close the Building Blocks Organizer dialog box.

3. Edit the letterhead building block by completing the following steps:
   a. Click the Quick Parts button, right-click the *Family Adventure Vacations* letterhead building block, and then click *Edit Properties* at the shortcut menu.
   b. At the Modify Building Block dialog box, click in the *Name* text box and then type Letterhead at the end of the name.
   c. Click in the *Description* text box and then type Inserts the Family Adventure Vacations letterhead including the company name and address.
   d. Click OK to close the dialog box.
   e. At the message asking if you want to redefine the building block entry, click Yes.
4. Close the document.
5. At the message that displays, click the Save button.

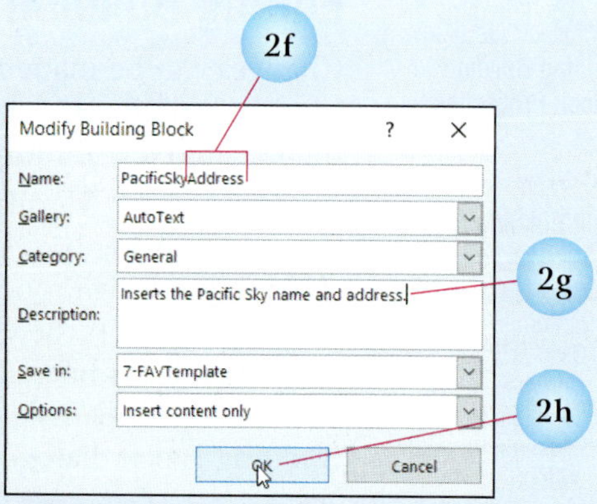

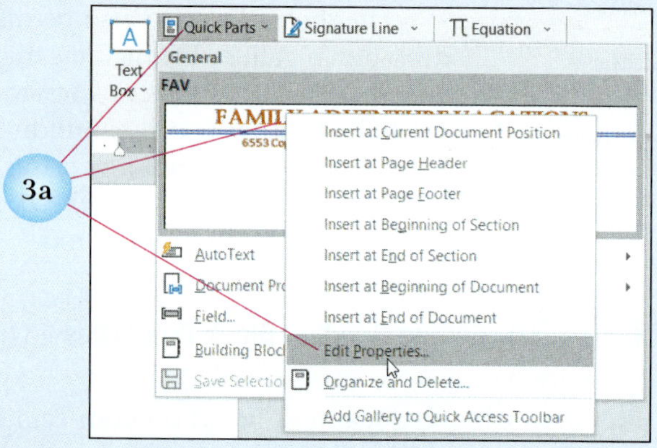

Tutorial

Inserting a Custom Building Block

Inserting a Custom Building Block

Any content saved as a building block can be inserted in a document using options at the Building Blocks Organizer dialog box. Some content can also be inserted using specific drop-down galleries. Insert a custom building block saved to the AutoText gallery by clicking the Insert tab, clicking the Quick Parts button, pointing to *AutoText*, and then clicking the building block at the side menu. Insert a custom building block saved to the Quick Part gallery by clicking the Insert tab, clicking the Quick Parts button, and then clicking the building block at the drop-down list.

A custom building block can also be inserted from a specific gallery such as the header, footer, or text box gallery. For example, insert a custom text box building block by clicking the Text Box button on the Insert tab and then clicking the text box at the drop-down gallery. Insert a custom header at the Header button drop-down gallery, a custom footer at the Footer button drop-down gallery, a custom cover page at the Cover Page button drop-down gallery, and so on.

Use the button drop-down gallery to specify where the custom building block content should be inserted in a document. To do this, display the button drop-down gallery, right-click the custom building block, and then click the location at the shortcut menu. For example, click the Insert tab, click the Quick Parts button, and then right-click the *FAVLetterhead* building block and a shortcut menu displays, as shown in Figure 7.3.

Figure 7.3 Quick Parts Button Drop-Down Gallery Shortcut Menu

Right-click the building block at the Quick Parts button drop-down gallery and then click the location for inserting the building block at the shortcut menu.

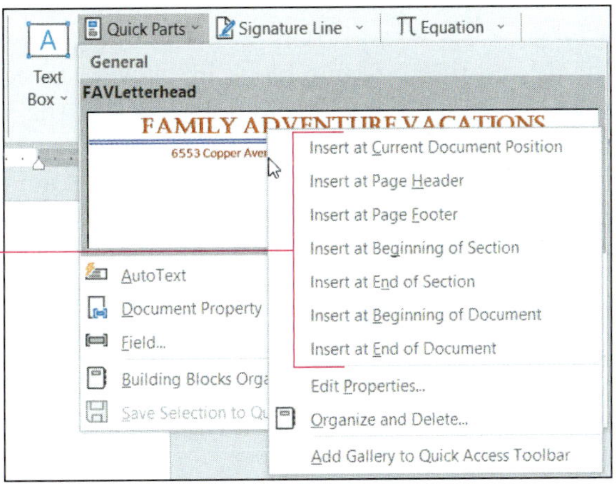

Activity 2c Inserting Custom Building Blocks

Part 3 of 3

1. Open File Explorer, navigate to your WL2C7 folder, and then double-click ***7-FAVTemplate***.
2. At the blank document, click the *No Spacing* style in the Styles group on the Home tab and then change the font to Candara.
3. Insert the letterhead building block as a header by completing the following steps:
   a. Click the Insert tab.
   b. Click the Quick Parts button, right-click the *FAVLetterhead* building block, and then click the *Insert at Page Header* option at the shortcut menu.

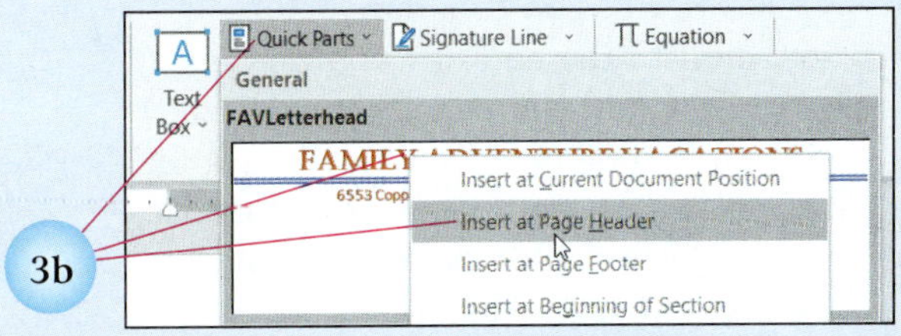

4. Press the Enter key two times, type the current date, and then press the Enter key five times.
5. Type Ms. Jody Lancaster and then press the Enter key.
6. Insert the Pacific Sky Cruise Lines name and address building block by clicking the Quick Parts button, pointing to *AutoText*, and then clicking the *PacificSkyAddress* building block at the side menu.

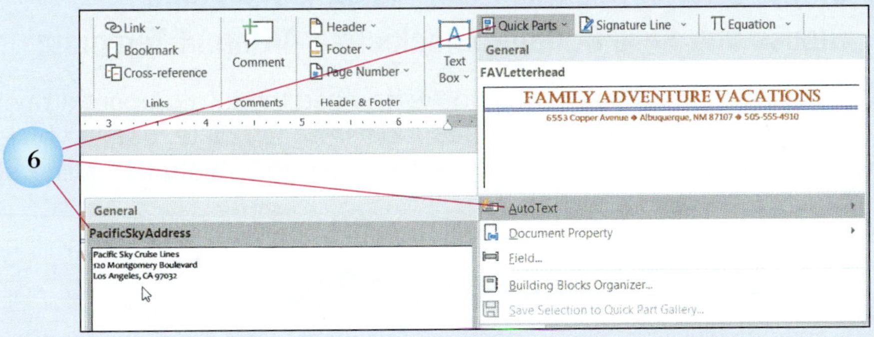

7. Press the Enter key and then insert a letter document by completing the following steps:
   a. Click the Object button arrow in the Text group on the Insert tab and then click *Text from File* at the drop-down list.
   b. At the Insert File dialog box, navigate to your WL2C7 folder and then double-click ***PSLetter01***.

8. With the insertion point positioned two lines below the last paragraph of text in the body of the letter, type Sincerely, and then press the Enter key four times.
9. Insert your name and title building block by clicking the Quick Parts button, pointing to *AutoText*, and then clicking the *Title* building block at the side menu.
10. Press the Enter key and then type 7-PSLtr01.
11. Press the Enter key five times and then insert the custom text box you saved as a building block by completing the following steps:
    a. Click the Text Box button in the Text group on the Insert tab.
    b. Scroll to the end of the drop-down gallery and then click the *FAVTextBox* building block. (Your custom text box will display in the *General* section of the drop-down gallery.)
    c. Click in the document to deselect the text box.
12. Insert the custom footer you created by completing the following steps:
    a. Click the Insert tab.
    b. Click the Footer button in the Header & Footer group.
    c. Scroll to the end of the drop-down gallery and then click the *FAVFooter* building block. (Your custom footer will display in the *General* section.)
    d. Close the footer pane by double-clicking in the document.
13. Save the completed letter and name it **7-PSLtr01**.
14. Print and then close **7-PSLtr01**.

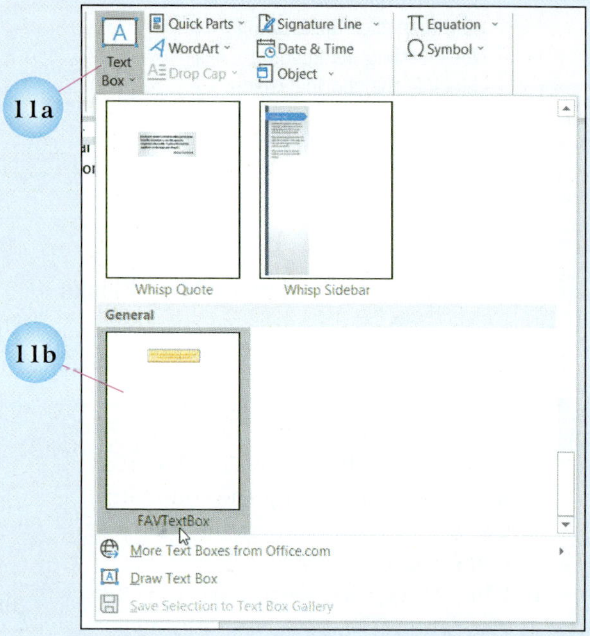

Check Your Work

Activity 3 Create a Letter Document with Modified Building Blocks and Save Building Blocks to a Different Template — 3 Parts

You will modify your custom building blocks and use them to prepare a business letter. You will also save building blocks to a different template, use the building blocks to format an announcement, and then delete your custom building blocks.

Tutorial

Modifying and Deleting Building Blocks

Modifying a Custom Building Block

A building block can be inserted in a document, corrections or changes can be made to the building block, and then the building block can be saved with the same name or a different name. Save a building block with the same name when updating the building block to reflect any changes. Save the building block with a new name when using an existing building block as the foundation for creating a new building block.

To save a modified building block with the same name, insert the building block into the document and then make modifications. Select the building block data and then specify the gallery. At the Create New Building Block dialog box, type the original name and description and then click OK. At the confirmation message that displays, click Yes.

Adding a Building Block Gallery as a Button on the Quick Access Toolbar

Quick Steps

Add Building Block Gallery as Button on Quick Access Toolbar

1. Click specific button.
2. Right-click building block.
3. Click *Add Gallery to Quick Access Toolbar*.

To make building blocks more accessible, add a building block gallery as a button on the Quick Access Toolbar. To do this, right-click a building block and then click *Add Gallery to Quick Access Toolbar*. For example, to add the *Quick Part* gallery to the Quick Access Toolbar, click the Quick Parts button on the Insert tab, right-click a building block at the drop-down gallery, and then click *Add Gallery to Quick Access Toolbar*.

To remove a button from the Quick Access Toolbar, right-click the button and then click *Remove from Quick Access Toolbar* at the shortcut menu. Removing a button containing a building block gallery does not delete the building block.

Activity 3a Modifying Building Blocks and Adding Custom Building Blocks as Buttons on the Quick Access Toolbar

Part 1 of 3

1. Open File Explorer, navigate to your WL2C7 folder, and then double-click ***7-FAVTemplate***.
2. Modify your name and title building block to reflect a title change by completing the following steps:
   a. At the blank document, click the Insert tab, click the Quick Parts button, point to *AutoText*, and then click the *Title* building block at the side menu.
   b. Edit your title so it displays as *Senior Travel Consultant*.
   c. Select your name and title, click the Quick Parts button, point to *AutoText*, and then click the *Save Selection to AutoText Gallery* option.
   d. At the Create New Building Block dialog box, type Title in the *Name* text box.
   e. Click the *Save in* option box arrow and then click *7-FAVTemplate* at the drop-down list.
   f. Click OK.

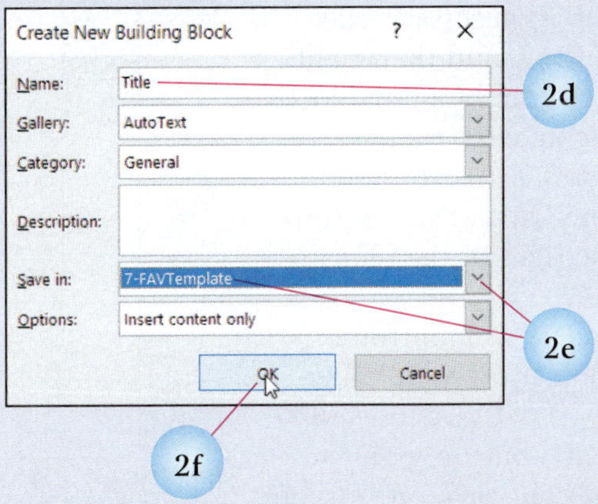

   g. At the message asking if you want to redefine the building block entry, click Yes.
   h. With your name and title selected, press the Delete key to remove them from the document.

3. Since most of the correspondence you send to Pacific Sky Cruise Lines is addressed to Jody Lancaster, you decide to include her name at the beginning of the company name and address by completing the following steps:
   a. With the Insert tab active, click the Quick Parts button, point to *AutoText*, and then click the *PacificSkyAddress* building block at the side menu.
   b. Type Ms. Jody Lancaster above the name of the cruise line.
   c. Select the name, company name, and address.
   d. Click the Quick Parts button, point to *AutoText*, and then click the *Save Selection to AutoText Gallery* option.
   e. At the Create New Building Block dialog box, type PacificSkyAddress (the original name) in the *Name* text box.
   f. Click the *Save in* option box arrow and then click *7-FAVTemplate* at the drop-down list.
   g. Click OK.
   h. At the message asking if you want to redefine the building block entry, click Yes.

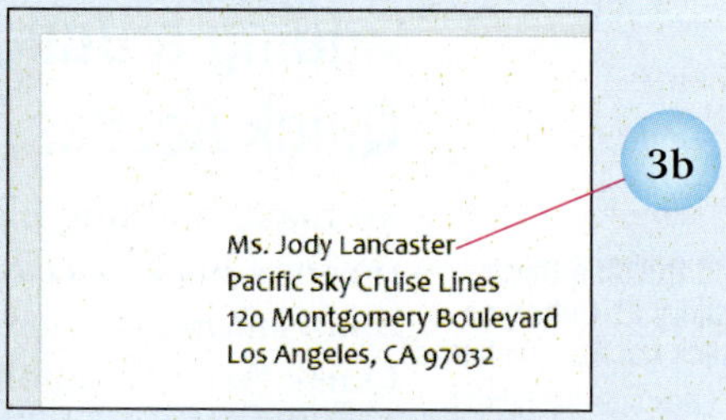

4. Press Ctrl + End and then add the FAVFooter building block in the Quick Part gallery by completing the following steps:
   a. Click the Footer button on the Insert tab, scroll down the drop-down gallery, and then click the *FAVFooter* custom building block.
   b. Press the Down Arrow key to move the insertion point to the blank line below the text in the footer and then press the Backspace key to delete the extra space below the footer text.
   c. Press Ctrl + A to select the footer.
   d. Click the Insert tab, click the Quick Parts button, and then click *Save Selection to Quick Part Gallery*.
   e. At the Create New Building Block dialog box, type FAVFooter in the *Name* text box.
   f. Click the *Save in* option box arrow and then click *7-FAVTemplate* at the drop-down list.
   g. Click OK to close the Create New Building Block dialog box. (You now have the footer saved in the Footer gallery and the Quick Part gallery.)
   h. Double-click in the document.
5. Add the Quick Part gallery as a button on the Quick Access Toolbar by completing the following steps:
   a. Click the Insert tab, if necessary, click the Quick Parts button, and then right-click one of your custom building blocks.
   b. At the shortcut menu, click the *Add Gallery to Quick Access Toolbar* option. (Notice the Explore Quick Parts button that appears at the right of the Quick Access Toolbar.)

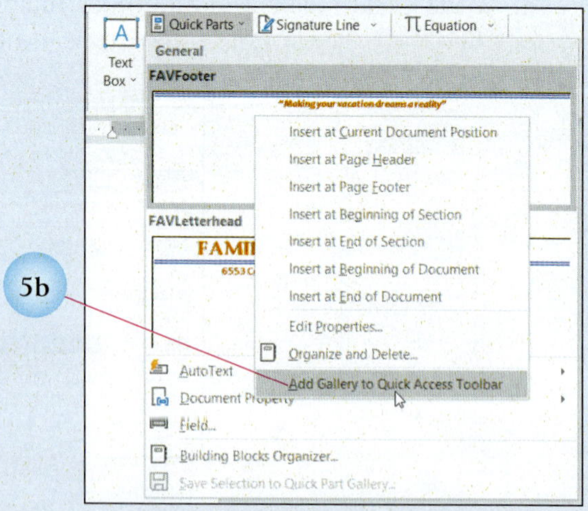

6. Add the AutoText gallery as a button on the Quick Access Toolbar by completing the following steps:
   a. Click the Quick Parts button, point to *AutoText*, and then right-click one of your custom building blocks.
   b. At the shortcut menu, click the *Add Gallery to Quick Access Toolbar* option. (Notice the AutoText button that appears at the right side of the Quick Access Toolbar.)

7. Close the document without saving it. At the message that displays indicating you have modified styles, building blocks, and other content, click the Save button.
8. Create a business letter by completing the following steps:
   a. Use File Explorer to open a blank document based on **7-FAVTemplate** in your WL2C7 folder.
   b. Click the *No Spacing* style in the Styles group on the Home tab and then change the font to Candara.
   c. Insert the FAVLetterhead building block as a page header.
   d. Press the Enter key two times, type today's date, and then press the Enter key four times.
   e. Insert the building block that includes Jody Lancaster's name and the cruise line name and address by clicking the AutoText button on the Quick Access Toolbar and then clicking the *PacificSkyAddress* building block at the drop-down list.
   f. Press the Enter key and then insert the file named **PSLetter02** in your WL2C7 folder. ***Hint: Do this with the Object button arrow in the Text group on the Insert tab.***
   g. Type Sincerely, and then press the Enter key four times.
   h. Click the AutoText button on the Quick Access Toolbar and then click the *Title* building block.
   i. Press the Enter key and then type 7-PSLtr02.
   j. Insert the footer building block by clicking the Explore Quick Parts button on the Quick Access Toolbar, right-clicking *FAVFooter*, and then clicking *Insert at Page Footer* at the shortcut menu.

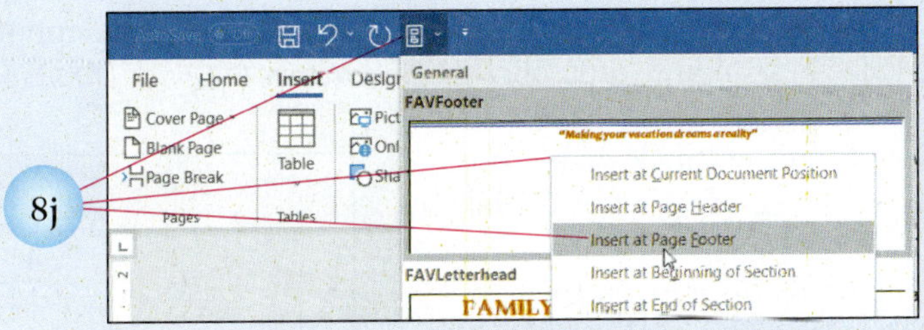

9. Save the completed letter and name it **7-PSLtr02**.
10. Print and then close **7-PSLtr02**.
11. Use File Explorer to open a blank document based on your template **7-FAVTemplate**.
12. Click the AutoText button on the Quick Access Toolbar, press the Print Screen button on your keyboard, and then click in the document to remove the drop-down list.
13. At the blank document, click the Paste button. (This pastes the screen capture in your document.)
14. Print the document and then close it without saving it.
15. Remove the Explore Quick Parts button you added to the Quick Access Toolbar by right-clicking the Explore Quick Parts button and then clicking *Remove from Quick Access Toolbar* at the shortcut menu. Complete similar steps to remove the AutoText button from the Quick Access Toolbar. (The buttons will display dimmed if no documents are open.)

Check Your Work

Saving Building Blocks in a Different Template

Building blocks saved to a personal template are available only when a document is opened based on the template. To make building blocks available for all documents, save them in the Building Block template or Normal template. Use the *Save in* option at the Create New Building Block or Modify Building Block dialog box to save building blocks to one of these two templates.

If an existing building block in a personal template is modified and saved in the Normal or Building Block template, the building block is no longer available in the personal template. It is available only in documents based on the default template Normal. To keep a building block in a personal template and also make it available for other documents, insert the building block content in the document, select the content, and then create a new building block.

Activity 3b Saving Building Blocks in a Different Template

Part 2 of 3

1. Use File Explorer to open a blank document based on your template **7-FAVTemplate**.
2. Create a new FAVLetterhead building block and save it in the Building Block template so it is available for all documents by completing the following steps:
   a. Click the Insert tab.
   b. Click the Quick Parts button and then click the *FAVLetterhead* building block to insert the content in the document.
   c. Select the letterhead (company name, address, and telephone number, including the paragraph mark at the end of the line containing the address and telephone number).
   d. Click the Quick Parts button and then click *Save Selection to Quick Part Gallery* at the drop-down list.
   e. At the Create New Building Block dialog box, type XXX-FAVLetterhead. (Type your initials in place of the *XXX*.)
   f. Make sure *Building Blocks* displays in the *Save in* option box and then click OK. (The *FAVLetterhead* building block is still available in your template 7-FAVTemplate, and the new *XXX-FAVLetterhead* building block is available in all documents, including documents based on your 7-FAVTemplate.)
   g. Delete the selected letterhead text.

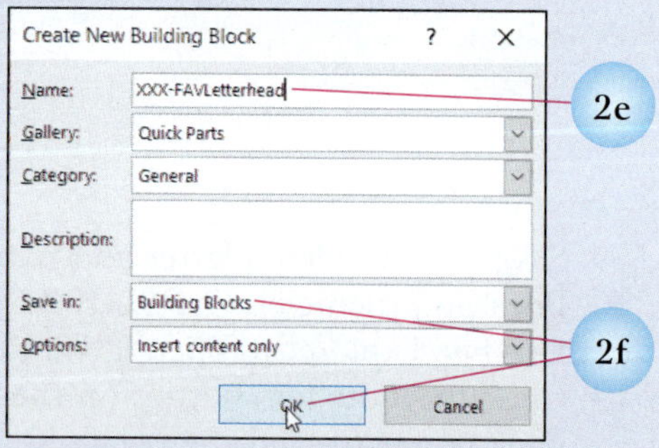

3. Create a new *FAVFooter* building block and then save it in the Building Blocks template so it is available for all documents by completing the following steps:
   a. Click the Quick Parts button and then click the *FAVFooter* building block to insert the content in the document.
   b. Select the footer text *"Making your travel dreams a reality"* (including the paragraph mark at the end of the text).
   c. Click the Quick Parts button and then click *Save Selection to Quick Part Gallery* at the drop-down list.
   d. At the Create New Building Block dialog box, type XXX-FAVFooter. (Type your initials in place of the *XXX*.)
   e. Make sure *Building Blocks* displays in the *Save in* option box and then click OK.
4. Close the document without saving it.
5. Open **FAVContent**.

6. Create a new *FAVTextBox* building block and save it in the Building Blocks template so it is available for all documents by completing the following steps:
   a. Select the text box by clicking the text box and then clicking the text box border.
   b. Click the Insert tab, click the Text Box button, and then click *Save Selection to Text Box Gallery* at the drop-down list.
   c. At the Create New Building Block dialog box, type XXX-FAVTextBox. (Type your initials in place of the *XXX*.)
   d. Make sure *Building Blocks* displays in the *Save in* option box and then click OK.
7. Close **FAVContent**.
8. Insert in a document the building blocks you created by completing the following steps:
   a. Open **PSAnnounce** and then save it with the name **7-PSAnnounce**.
   b. Insert the *XXX-FAVLetterhead* building block as a header by clicking the Insert tab, clicking the Quick Parts button, right-clicking *XXX-FAVLetterhead* (where your initials display in place of the *XXX*), and then clicking *Insert at Page Header* at the shortcut menu.

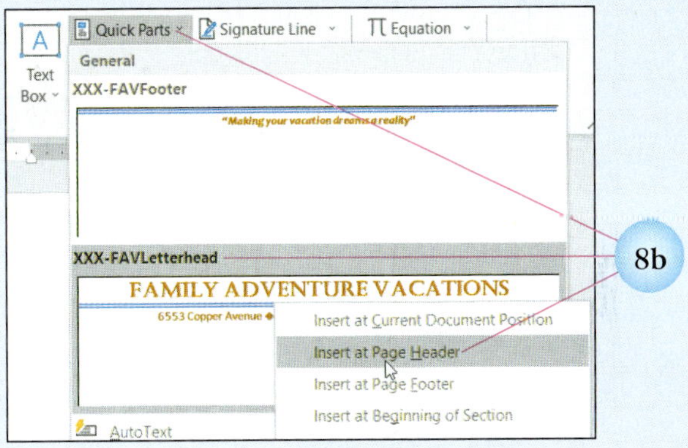

   c. Insert the *XXX-FAVFooter* building block by clicking the Quick Parts button, right-clicking *XXX-FAVFooter* (where your initials display in place of the *XXX*), and then clicking *Insert at Page Footer* at the shortcut menu.
   d. Press Ctrl + End to move the insertion point to the end of the document.
   e. Insert the *XXX-FAVTextBox* building block by clicking the Text Box button, scrolling down the drop-down gallery, and then clicking *XXX-FAVTextBox* (where your initials display in place of the *XXX*).
   f. Horizontally align the text box by clicking the Align button in the Arrange group on the Drawing Tools Format tab and then clicking *Distribute Horizontally* at the drop-down list.

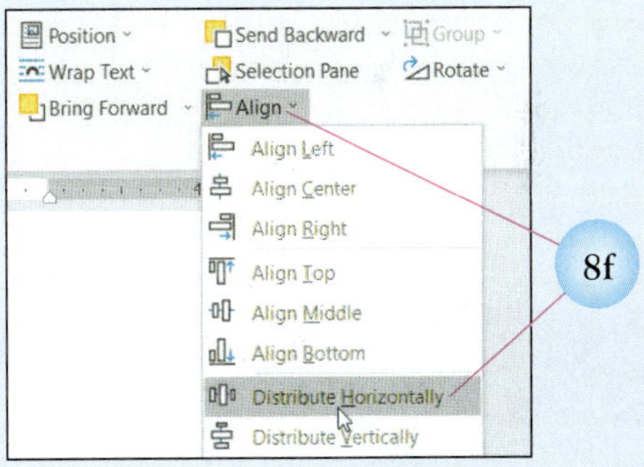

9. Save, print, and then close **7-PSAnnounce**.

Check Your Work

Quick Steps

Delete Building Block
1. Display Building Blocks Organizer dialog box.
2. Click building block.
3. Click Delete button.
4. Click Yes.

OR

1. Display button drop-down gallery.
2. Right-click building block.
3. Click *Organize and Delete* option.
4. Click Delete button.
5. Click Yes.

Deleting a Building Block

A custom building block that is no longer needed can be deleted by displaying the Building Blocks Organizer dialog box, clicking the building block, and then clicking the Delete button. At the confirmation message box, click Yes.

Another method for deleting a custom building block is to right-click the building block at the drop-down gallery and then click the *Organize and Delete* option at the shortcut menu. This displays the Building Blocks Organizer dialog box with the building block selected. Click the Delete button and then click Yes at the confirmation message box.

Activity 3c Deleting Building Blocks

1. At a blank document, delete the *XXX-FAVLetterhead* building block by completing the following steps:
   a. Click the Insert tab and then click the Quick Parts button in the Text group.
   b. Right-click the *XXX-FAVLetterhead* building block and then click *Organize and Delete* at the shortcut menu.

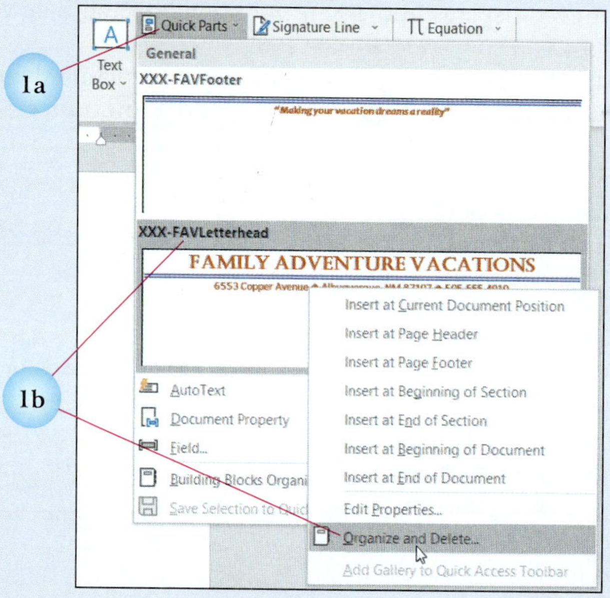

   c. At the Building Blocks Organizer dialog box with the building block selected, click the Delete button.
   d. At the message asking if you are sure you want to delete the selected building block, click Yes.
   e. Close the Building Blocks Organizer dialog box.
2. Complete steps similar to those in Steps 1a through 1e to delete the *XXXFAVFooter* building block.
3. Delete the *XXX-FAVTextBox* building block (in the Text Box gallery) by completing the following steps:
   a. Click the Text Box button in the Text group on the Insert tab.
   b. Scroll down the drop-down gallery to display your custom text box.
   c. Right-click your text box and then click *Organize and Delete* at the shortcut menu.
   d. At the Building Blocks Organizer dialog box with the building block selected, click the Delete button.
   e. At the message asking if you are sure you want to delete the selected building block, click Yes.
   f. Close the Building Blocks Organizer dialog box.
4. Close the document without saving it.

Activity 4 Insert Document Properties and Fields in a Testing Agreement Document

2 Parts

You will open a testing agreement document and then insert and update document properties and fields.

Inserting a Document Property Placeholder

Click the Quick Parts button on the Insert tab and then point to *Document Property* at the drop-down list and a side menu displays with document property options. Click an option at this side menu and a document property placeholder is inserted in the document. Text can be typed in the placeholder.

If a document property placeholder is inserted in multiple locations in a document, updating one occurrence of the placeholder will automatically update all occurrences of that placeholder in the document. For example, in Activity 4a, a Company document property placeholder is inserted in six locations in a document. The content of the first occurrence of the placeholder will be changed and the remaining placeholders will update to reflect the change.

Click the File tab and then click the *Info* option and the Info backstage area displays containing information about the document. Document properties display at the right side of the Info backstage area, including information such as the document size, number of pages, title, and comments.

Activity 4a Inserting Document Property Placeholders

Part 1 of 2

1. Open **TestAgrmnt** and then save it with the name **7-TestAgrmnt**.
2. Select the first occurrence of *FP* in the document (in the first line of text after the title) and then insert a document property placeholder by completing the following steps:
   a. Click the Insert tab, click the Quick Parts button in the Text group, point to *Document Property*, and then click *Company* at the side menu.
   b. Type Frontier Productions in the company placeholder.
   c. Press the Right Arrow key to move the insertion point outside the company placeholder.

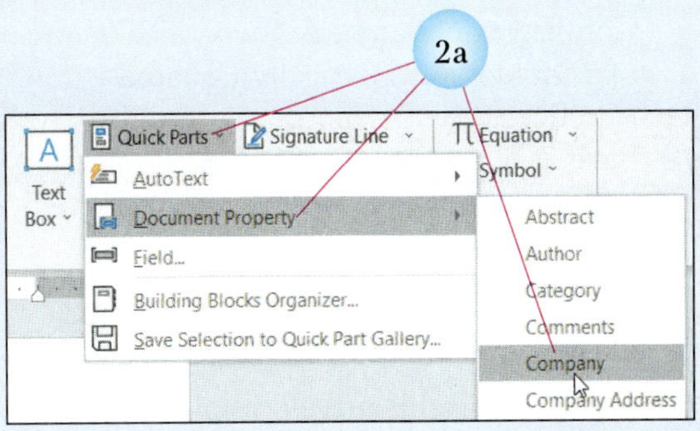

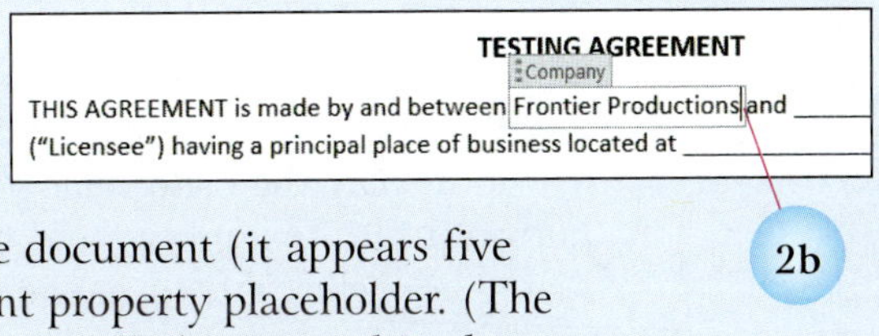

3. Select each remaining occurrence of *FP* in the document (it appears five more times) and insert the company document property placeholder. (The company name, *Frontier Productions,* will automatically be inserted in the placeholder.)

4. Press Ctrl + End to move the insertion point to the end of the document and then insert a comments document property placeholder by completing the following steps:
   a. Click the Quick Parts button, point to *Document Property*, and then click *Comments* at the side menu.
   b. Type First Draft in the comments placeholder.
   c. Press the Right Arrow key.
   d. Press Shift + Enter.
5. Click the File tab, click the *Info* option, if necessary, and notice that the comment typed in the comments document property placeholder displays at the right side of the Info backstage area. Click the Back button to display the document.

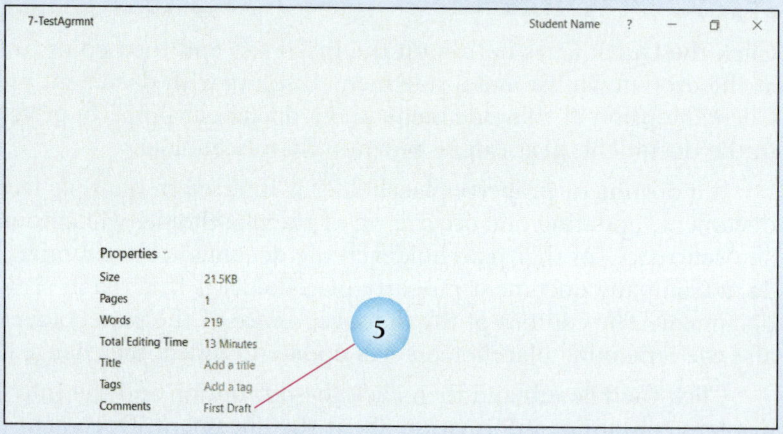

6. Save and then print **7-TestAgrmnt**.
7. Click in the first occurrence of the company name *Frontier Productions* and then click the company placeholder tab. (This selects the company placeholder.)
8. Type Frontier Video Productions.
9. Press the Right Arrow key. (Notice that the other occurrences of the Company document property placeholder automatically updated to reflect the new name.)
10. Save **7-TestAgrmnt**.

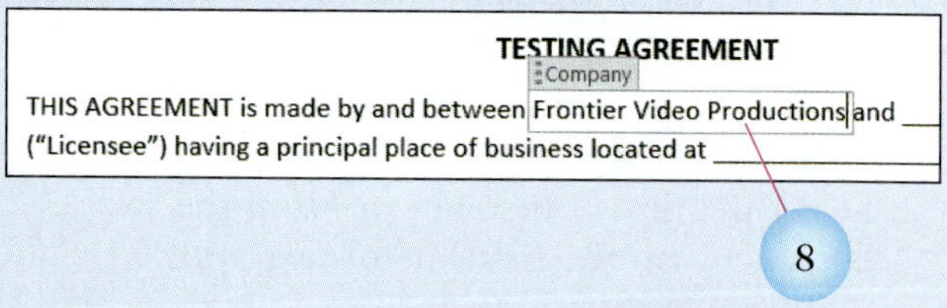

Check Your Work

Tutorial

Inserting and Updating Fields

Quick Steps

Insert Field

1. Click Insert tab.
2. Click Quick Parts button.
3. Click *Field* at drop-down list.
4. Click field.
5. Click OK.

Managing Fields

Fields are placeholders for data that varies. Word provides buttons for many of the types of fields that can be inserted in a document as well as options at the Field dialog box, shown in Figure 7.4. This dialog box contains a list of all the available fields. Just as the Building Blocks Organizer dialog box is a central location for building blocks, the Field dialog box is a central location for fields.

To display the Field dialog box, click the Insert tab, click the Quick Parts button in the Text group, and then click *Field* at the drop-down list. At the Field dialog box, click a field in the *Field names* list box and then click OK.

Figure 7.4 Field Dialog Box

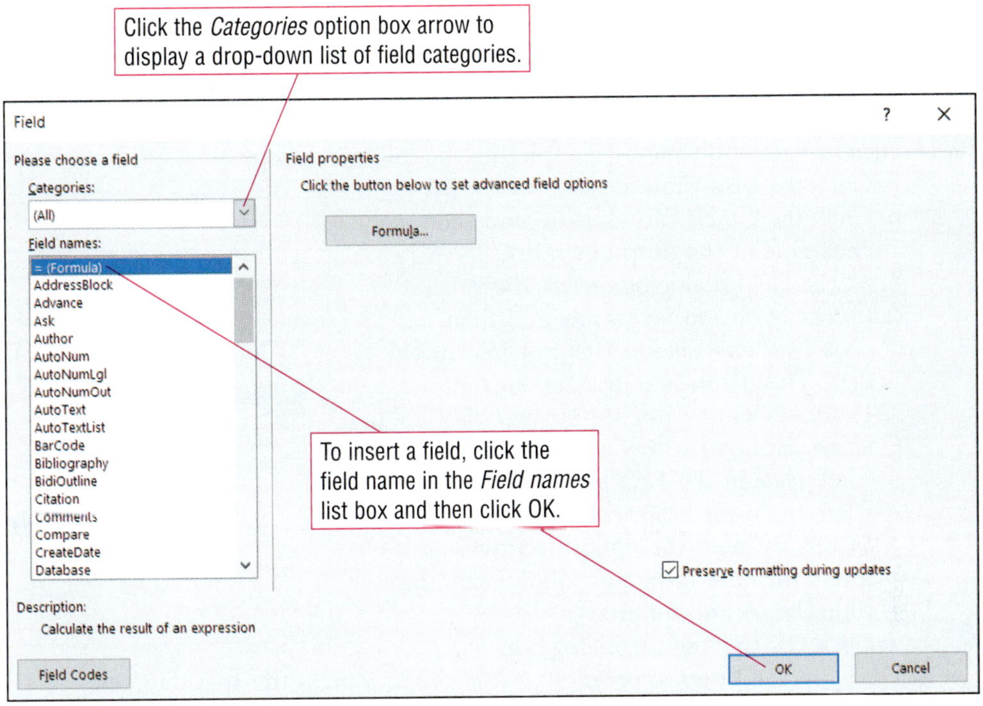

Choosing Field Categories

All the available fields display in the *Field names* list box at the Field dialog box. Narrow the list of fields to a specific category by clicking the *Categories* option box arrow and then clicking a specific category at the drop-down list. For example, to display only date and time fields, click the *Date and Time* category at the drop-down list.

Creating Custom Field Formats

Click a field in the *Field names* list box and a description of the field displays below the list box. Field properties related to the selected field also display in the dialog box. Custom field formats can be created for some fields. For example, click the *NumWords* field in the *Field names* list box and custom formatting options display in the *Format* list box and the *Numeric format* list box.

By default, the *Preserve formatting during updates* check box contains a check mark. With this option active, the custom formatting specified for a field will be preserved if the field is updated.

Updating Fields

Quick Steps

Update Field

1. Click field.
2. Click Update tab.

OR

1. Click field.
2. Press F9.

OR

1. Right-click field.
2. Click *Update Field*.

Some fields, such as the date and time field, update automatically when a document is opened. Other fields can be updated manually. A field can be updated manually by clicking the field and then clicking the Update tab; by clicking the field and then pressing the F9 function key; and by right-clicking the field and then clicking *Update Field* at the shortcut menu. Update all the fields in a document (except headers, footers, and text boxes) by pressing Ctrl + A to select the document and then pressing the F9 function key.

Activity 4b Inserting and Formatting Fields

Part 2 of 2

1. With **7-TestAgrmnt** open, press Ctrl + End to move the insertion point to the end of the document.
2. Type Current date and time:, press the spacebar, and then insert a field that inserts the current date and time by completing the following steps:
   a. Click the Insert tab, if necessary.
   b. Click the Quick Parts button and then click *Field* at the drop-down list.
   c. At the Field dialog box, click the *Categories* option box arrow and then click *Date and Time* at the drop-down list. (This displays only fields in the Date and Time category in the *Field names* list box.)
   d. Click *Date* in the *Field names* list box.
   e. Click the twelfth option in the *Date formats* list box (the option that will insert the date in figures followed by the time [hours and minutes]).
   f. Click OK to close the dialog box.

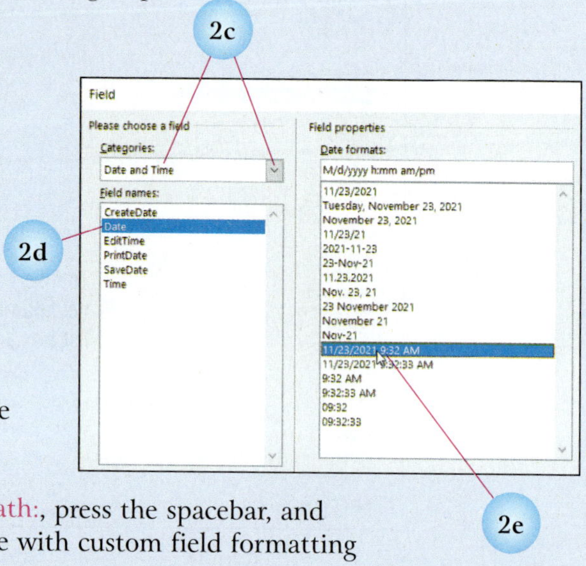

3. Press Shift + Enter, type File name and path:, press the spacebar, and then insert a field for the current file name with custom field formatting by completing the following steps:
   a. With the Insert tab active, click the Quick Parts button and then click *Field* at the drop-down list.
   b. At the Field dialog box, click the *Categories* option box arrow and then click *Document Information* at the drop-down list.
   c. Click *FileName* in the *Field names* list box.
   d. Click the *Uppercase* option in the *Format* list box.
   e. Click the *Add path to filename* check box to insert a check mark.

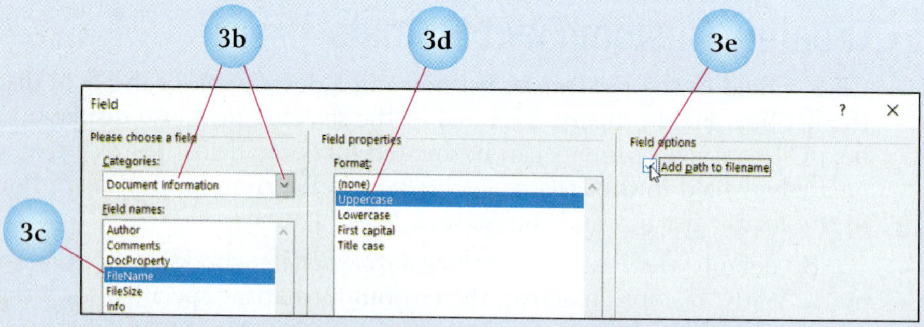

   f. Click OK to close the dialog box. (The current file name is inserted in the document in uppercase letters and includes the path to the file name.)
4. Insert a header and then insert a custom field in the header by completing the following steps:
   a. Click the Header button in the Header & Footer group and then click *Edit Header* at the drop-down list.
   b. In the Header pane, press the Tab key two times. (This moves the insertion point to the right tab at the right margin.)
   c. Click the Quick Parts button in the Insert group on the Header & Footer Tools Design tab and then click *Field* at the drop-down list.

d. At the Field dialog box, click the *Categories* option box arrow and then click *Date and Time* at the drop-down list.

e. Click in the *Date formats* text box and then type MMMM yyyy. (This tells Word to insert the month as text followed by the four-digit year.)

f. Click OK to close the dialog box.

g. Double-click in the document.

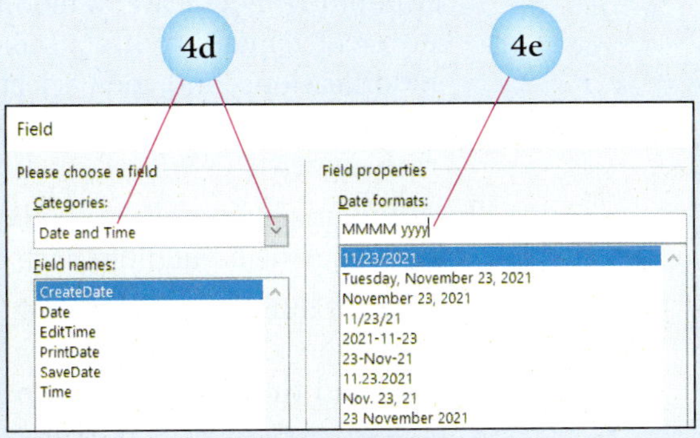

5. Update the time in the date and time field at the end of the document by clicking the date and time and then clicking the Update tab.
6. Save, print, and then close **7-TestAgrmnt**. (If a message displays asking if you want to save the changes to the template, click the Don't Save button.)

Check Your Work

Chapter Summary

- Word provides a number of predesigned building blocks that can be used to help build a document.
- Insert building blocks at the Building Blocks Organizer dialog box. Display the dialog box by clicking the Quick Parts button in the Text group on the Insert tab and then clicking *Building Blocks Organizer* at the drop-down list.
- Sort building blocks at the Building Blocks Organizer dialog box by clicking the column heading.
- Content can be saved as building blocks in specific galleries, such as the Text Box, Header, Footer, and Cover Page galleries.
- Save content to the AutoText gallery by selecting the content, clicking the Insert tab, clicking the Quick Parts button, pointing to *AutoText*, and then clicking the *Save Selection to AutoText Gallery* option.
- Save content to the Quick Part gallery by selecting the content, clicking the Insert tab, clicking the Quick Parts button, and then clicking *Save Selection to Quick Part Gallery*.
- Building block content is saved, by default, to the *Building Blocks* template or the *Normal* template. The template location depends on the gallery selected at the Create New Building Block dialog box. A personal template can be created and saved to the Custom Office Templates folder and then building blocks can be saved to the personal template using the *Save in* option at the Create New Building Block dialog box.
- Open a personal template saved to the Custom Office Templates folder at the New backstage area with the *Personal* option selected.
- A personal template can be created and saved to a specific location other than the Custom Office Templates folder and then File Explorer can be used to open a document based on the template.
- Edit building block properties with options at the Modify Building Block dialog box. Display this dialog box by displaying the Building Blocks Organizer dialog box, clicking the specific building block in the list box, and then clicking the Edit Properties button.

- A building block can be modified and then saved with the same name or a different name. Modify a building block by inserting the building block, making modifications, and then select the building block data and specify the gallery. At the Create New Building Block dialog box, type the original name or type a new name.
- A building block gallery can be added as a button on the Quick Access Toolbar by right-clicking a building block and then clicking *Add Gallery to Quick Access Toolbar*.
- Insert a building block at the Building Blocks Organizer dialog box by displaying the dialog box, clicking the building block in the *Building blocks* list box, and then clicking the Insert button.
- Insert a custom building block saved to the AutoText gallery by clicking the Insert tab, clicking the Quick Parts button, pointing to *AutoText*, and then clicking the building block at the side menu.
- Insert a custom building block saved to the Quick Part gallery by clicking the Insert tab, clicking the Quick Parts button, and then clicking the building block at the drop-down list.
- Insert a custom building block from a specific drop-down gallery using a button by clicking the specific button (such as the Text Box, Header, Footer, or Cover Page button), scrolling down the drop-down gallery, and then clicking the custom building block at the gallery.
- Delete a building block at the Building Blocks Organizer dialog box by clicking the building block, clicking the Delete button, and then clicking Yes at the confirmation message.
- Insert a document property placeholder by clicking the Insert tab, clicking the Quick Parts button, pointing to *Document Property*, and then clicking the document property placeholder at the side menu.
- Fields are placeholders for data that varies. They can be inserted with options at the Field dialog box, which is a central location for all the fields provided by Word. Display the Field dialog box by clicking the Quick Parts button and then clicking *Field* at the drop-down list.
- A custom field format can be created for some fields by clicking the field in the *Field names* list box at the Field dialog box and then customizing formatting options.
- Some fields in a document update automatically when a document is opened. Other fields can be manually updated by clicking the field and then clicking the Update tab, by clicking the field and then pressing the F9 function key, or by right-clicking the field and then clicking *Update Field* at the shortcut menu.

Commands Review

FEATURE	RIBBON TAB, GROUP	BUTTON, OPTION	KEYBOARD SHORTCUT
Building Blocks Organizer dialog box	Insert, Text	*Building Blocks Organizer*	
Create New Building Block dialog box	Insert, Text	*Save Selection to Quick Part Gallery*	Alt + F3
Document Property side menu	Insert, Text	*Document Property*	
Field dialog box	Insert, Text	*Field*	

Microsoft®

Word

CHAPTER 8

Managing Shared Documents

Performance Objectives

Upon successful completion of Chapter 8, you will be able to:

1. Insert, edit, show, reply to, print, resolve, and delete comments
2. Navigate between comments
3. Distinguish comments from different users
4. Edit a document using the Track Changes feature
5. Display changes, show markups, display tracked changed information, and change user information
6. Lock the Track Changes feature and customize tracked changes options
7. Navigate to and accept/reject changes
8. Restrict and enforce formatting and editing in a document and protect a document with a password
9. Protect a document by marking it as final, encrypting it, restricting editing, and adding a digital signature
10. Open a document in different views
11. Share a document electronically
12. Manage document versions

In a workplace environment, you may need to share documents with coworkers and associates. You may be part of a workgroup, which is a networked collection of computers that share files, printers, and other resources. As a member of a workgroup, you can collaborate with other members and distribute documents for their review and/or revision. Workgroup activities include inserting and managing comments and tracking the changes made to a document. Managing shared document might also include restricting the formatting and editing changes users can make to a document and protecting a document with a password. In this chapter, you will learn how to manage shared documents as well as how to open a document in different views, share a document electronically, and manage document versions.

Data Files

Before beginning chapter work, copy the WL2C8 folder to your storage medium and then make WL2C8 the active folder.

The online course includes additional training and assessment resources.

Activity 1 Insert Comments in a New Employees Document — 4 Parts

You will open a report containing company information for new employees and then insert and edit comments from multiple users.

Tutorial

Inserting Comments

Quick Steps

Insert Comment

1. Select text.
2. Click Review tab.
3. Click New Comment button.
4. Type comment.

New Comment

Hint Use comments to add notes, suggestions, and explanations and to communicate with members of your workgroup.

Inserting and Managing Comments

Use Word's comment feature to provide feedback on and suggest changes to a document that someone else has written. Similarly, get feedback on a document by distributing it electronically to others and having them insert comments in it.

To insert a comment in a document, select the text or item the comment pertains to or position the insertion point at the end of the text, click the Review tab, and then click the New Comment button in the Comments group. This displays a comment balloon in the right margin, as shown in Figure 8.1. Another method for displaying a comment balloon is to click the Comments button in the upper right corner of the screen and then click *New Comment* at the drop-down list.

Depending on what settings have been applied, clicking the New Comment button (or clicking the Comments button in the upper right corner of the screen and then clicking *New Comment* at the drop-down list) may cause the Reviewing pane to display, rather than the comment balloon. If this happens, click the Show Markup button in the Tracking group on the Review tab, point to *Balloons*, and then click *Show Only Comments and Formatting in Balloons* at the side menu. Also check to make sure the *Display for Review* option box in the Tracking group is set to *Simple Markup*. If it is not, click the *Display for Review* option box arrow and then click *Simple Markup* at the drop-down list.

Figure 8.1 Sample Comment Balloon

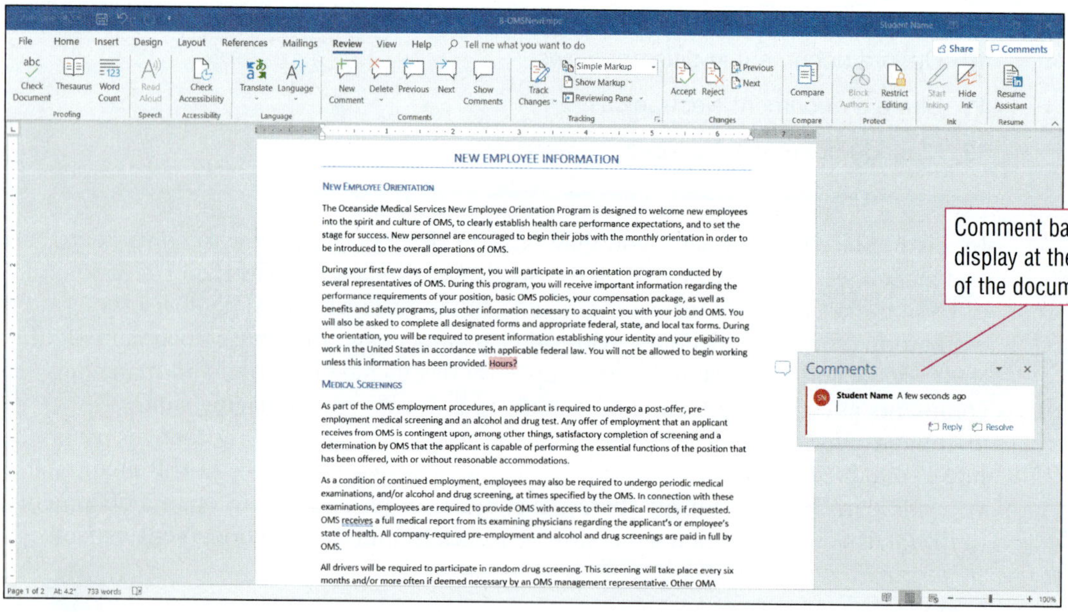

Activity 1a Inserting Comments

Part 1 of 4

1. Open **OMSNewEmps** and then save it with the name **8-OMSNewEmps**.
2. Insert a comment by completing the following steps:
   a. Position the insertion point at the end of the second paragraph in the *New Employee Orientation* section.
   b. Press the spacebar and then type Hours?.
   c. Select *Hours?*.
   d. Click the Review tab.
   e. Make sure *Simple Markup* displays in the *Display for Review* option box. If it does not, click the *Display for Review* option box arrow and then click *Simple Markup* at the drop-down list.
   f. If the Show Comments button in the Comments group is active (displays with a gray background), click the button to deactivate it.
   g. Click the New Comment button in the Comments group.
   h. Type Please include the total number of orientation hours. in the comment balloon.

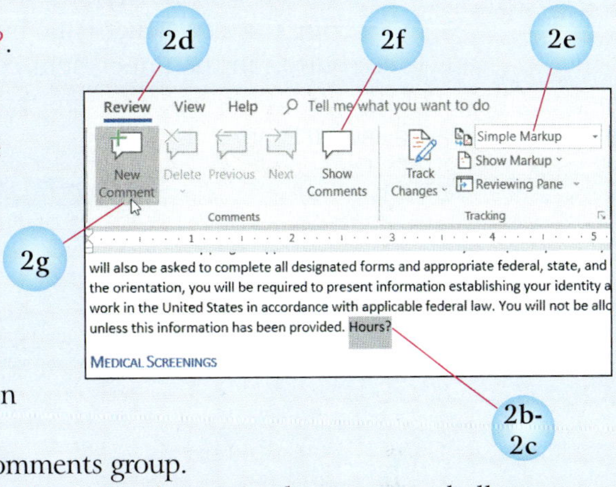

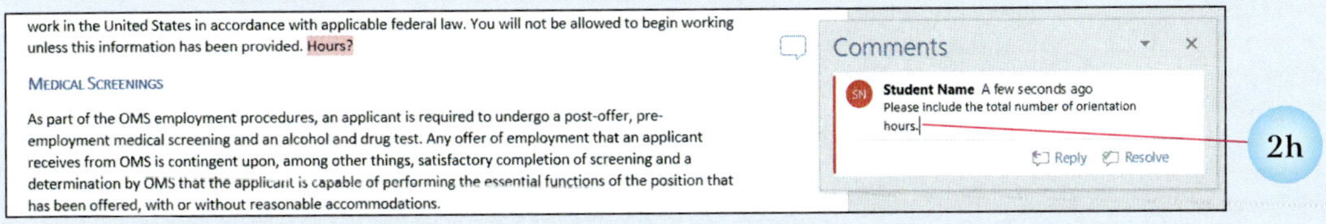

3. Insert another comment by completing the following steps:
   a. Move the insertion point to the end of the third (last) paragraph in the *Medical Screenings* section.
   b. Click the New Comment button in the Comments group.
   c. Type Specify the locations where drug tests are administered. in the comment balloon. (Since you did not select any text before clicking the New Comment button, Word selects the word immediately left of the insertion point.)
   d. Click in the document to close the comment balloons.
4. Save **8-OMSNewEmps**.

Check Your Work

Inserting Comments in the Reviewing Pane

Comments can also be inserted with the Reviewing pane open on the screen. The Reviewing pane displays both inserted comments and changes recorded with the Track Changes feature. (Track Changes is covered later in this chapter.)

Reviewing Pane

To open the Reviewing pane, click the Reviewing Pane button in the Tracking group on the Review tab. The Reviewing pane usually displays at the left side of the screen, as shown in Figure 8.2. Click the New Comment button in the Comments group and a comment icon and balloon displays in the right margin; the reviewer's name followed by "Commented" displays in the Reviewing pane. Type the comment and the text displays in the comment balloon and in the Reviewing pane. (The Reviewing pane might display along the bottom of the screen, rather than at the left side. To specify where the pane displays, click the Reviewing Pane button arrow in the Tracking group on the Review tab and then click *Reviewing Pane Vertical* or *Reviewing Pane Horizontal*.)

Hint If your computer has a sound card and microphone, you can record voice comments.

A summary displays at the top of the Reviewing pane and provides counts of the number of comments inserted and the types of changes that have been made to the document. After typing a comment in the Reviewing pane, close the pane by clicking the Reviewing Pane button in the Tracking group or by clicking the Close button in the upper right corner of the pane.

Figure 8.2 Vertical Reviewing Pane

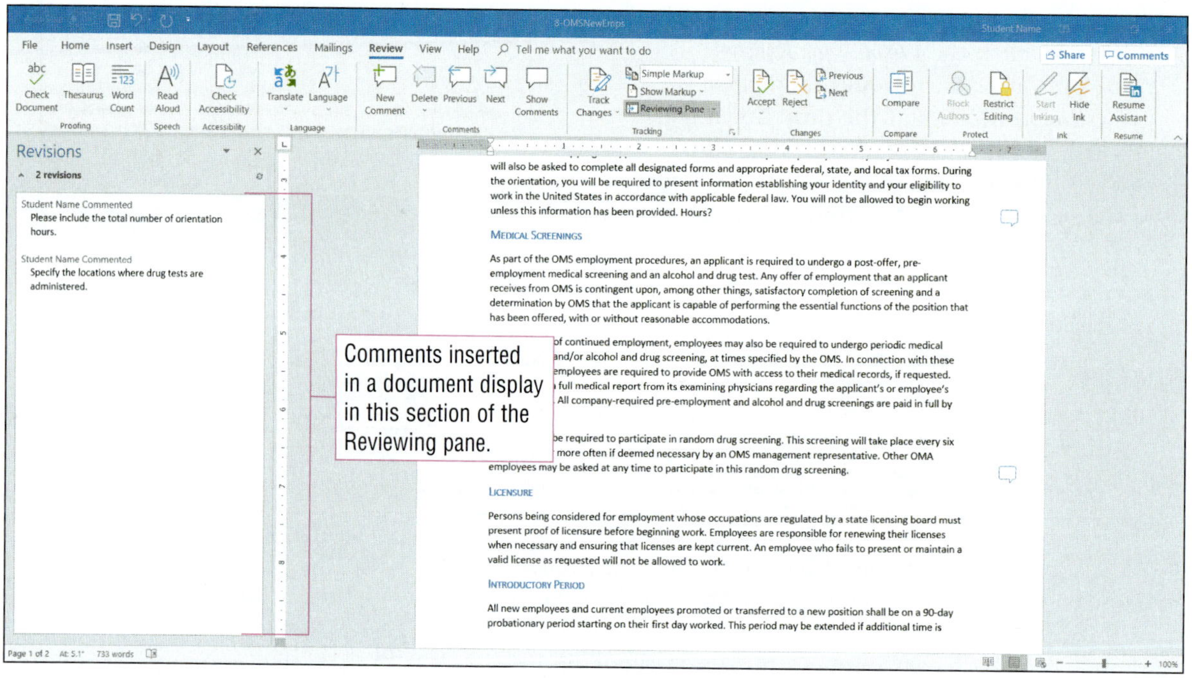

Activity 1b Inserting a Comment in the Reviewing Pane

Part 2 of 4

1. With **8-OMSNewEmps** open, show the comments in the Reviewing pane by completing the following steps:
   a. If necessary, click the Review tab.
   b. Click the Reviewing Pane button in the Tracking group.
   c. Click the Show Markup button in the Tracking group, point to *Balloons* at the drop-down list, and then click *Show All Revisions Inline* at the side menu.

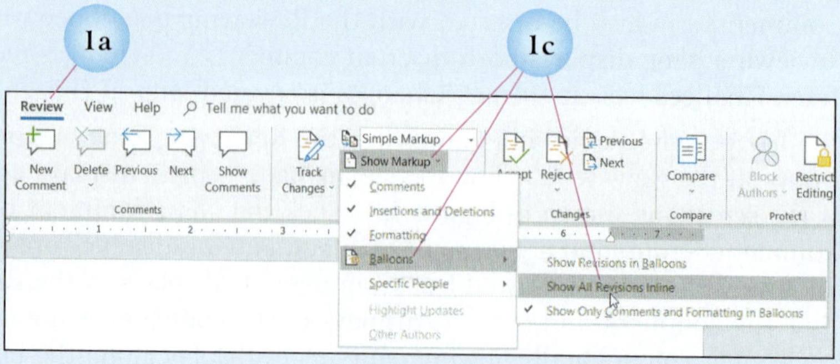

2. Insert a comment by completing the following steps:
   a. Move the insertion point to the end of the paragraph of text in the *INTRODUCTORY PERIOD* section.
   b. Press the spacebar once, type Maximum?, and then select *Maximum?*.
   c. Click the New Comment button in the Comments group.
   d. With the insertion point positioned in the Reviewing pane, type Please include in this section the maximum length of the probationary period.

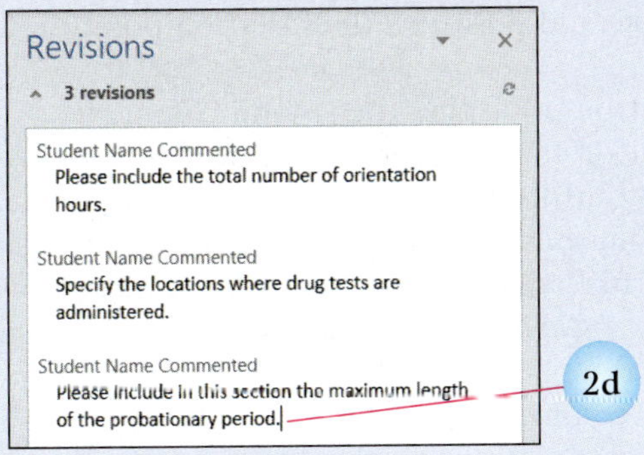

3. Click the Reviewing Pane button in the Tracking group to turn off the display of the Reviewing pane.
4. Save **8-OMSNewEmps**.

Check Your Work

Navigating between Comments

Previous

Next

When working in a long document with many comments, use the Previous and Next buttons in the Comments group on the Review tab to move easily from comment to comment. Click the Next button to move the insertion point to the next comment or click the Previous button to move the insertion point to the previous comment.

Tutorial

Managing Comments

Quick Steps

Edit Comment
1. Click Review tab.
2. Click Reviewing Pane button.
3. Click in comment in pane.
4. Make changes.

OR

1. Click Review tab.
2. Turn on display of comment balloons.
3. Click in comment balloon.
4. Make changes.

Editing Comments

Edit a comment in the Reviewing pane or in a comment balloon. To edit a comment in the Reviewing pane, click the Reviewing Pane button to turn on the pane and then click in the comment to be edited. Make changes to the comment and then close the Reviewing pane. To edit a comment in a comment balloon, turn on the display of comment balloons, click in the comment balloon, and then make changes.

Showing Comments

The Comments group on the Review tab contains a Show Comments button. Click this button and comments display at the right of the document. The Show Comments button is available only when the *Display for Review* option in the Tracking group is set to *Simple Markup*.

Activity 1c Editing Comments

Part 3 of 4

1. With **8-OMSNewEmps** open, navigate from one comment to another by completing the following steps:
   a. Press Ctrl + Home to move the insertion point to the beginning of the document.
   b. If necessary, click the Review tab.
   c. Click the Next button in the Comments group. (This moves the insertion point to the first comment, opens the Reviewing pane, and positions the insertion point in the pane.)
   d. Click the Next button to display the second comment.
   e. Click the Next button to display the third comment.
   f. Click the Previous button to display the second comment.

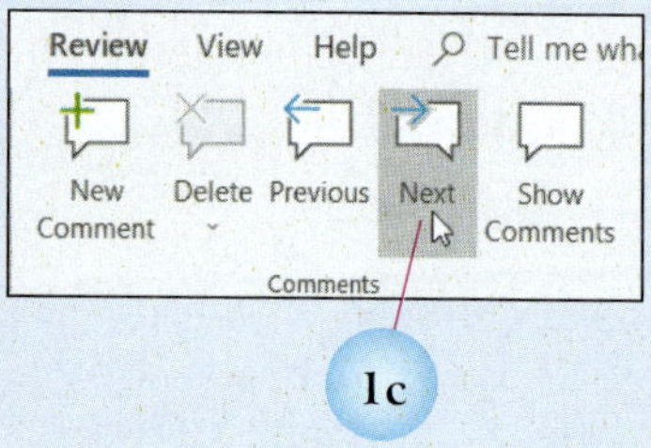

2. With the insertion point positioned in the Reviewing pane, edit the second comment to read as follows: *Specify the locations within OMS where drug tests are administered as well as any off-site locations.*
3. Click the Reviewing Pane button to close the pane.
4. Edit a comment in a comment balloon by completing the following steps:
   a. Click the Show Markup button in the Tracking group, point to *Balloons*, and then click *Show Only Comments and Formatting in Balloons* at the side menu.
   b. Click the Show Comments button in the Comments group to display the balloons at the right of the document.
   c. Display the paragraph of text in the *Introductory Period* section and then click in the comment balloon at the right.
   d. Edit the comment to read as follows: *Please include in this section the maximum probationary period, if any.*

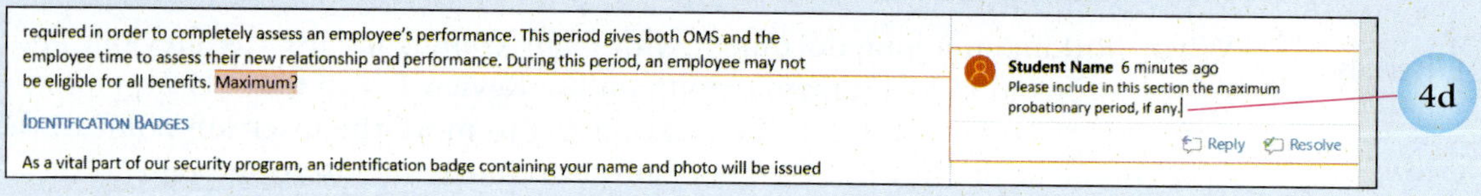

   e. Click in the document and then click the Show Comments button to turn off the display of comment balloons.
   f. Click the Show Markup button, point to *Balloons*, and then click *Show All Revisions Inline*.
5. Save **8-OMSNewEmps**.

Check Your Work

Replying to Comments

Quick Steps

Reply to Comment

1. Open comment balloon.
2. Hover mouse pointer over comment text.
3. Click Reply button.
4. Type reply in reply window.

During the review of a document, a reply can be made to a comment. To reply to a comment, open the comment balloon, hover the mouse pointer over the comment text, click the Reply button in the comment balloon, and then type the reply. Other methods of replying to a comment are to click in a comment and then click the New Comment button in the Comments group and to right-click in a comment (in either a comment balloon or the Reviewing pane) and then click *Reply To Comment* at the shortcut menu.

Printing Comments

Quick Steps

Print Document with Comments

1. Click File tab.
2. Click *Print* option.
3. Click first gallery in *Settings* category.
4. If necessary, click *Print Markup* to insert check mark.
5. Click Print button.

Print Only Comments

1. Click File tab.
2. Click *Print* option.
3. Click first gallery in *Settings* category.
4. Click *List of Markup*.
5. Click Print button.

Delete

A document containing comments can be printed one of three ways: the document and the comments, the document without the comments, or only the comments. By default, a document will print with the comments. To print the document without the comments, display the Print backstage area and then click the first gallery in the *Settings* category (the gallery that contains the text *Print All Pages*). At the drop-down list, click the *Print Markup* option to remove the check mark, and then click the Print button. To print only the comments, display the Print backstage area, click the first gallery in the *Settings* category, and then click the *List of Markup* option at the drop-down list.

Deleting and Resolving Comments

Delete a comment by clicking the Next button in the Comments group on the Review tab until the specific comment is selected and then clicking the Delete button in the Comments group. To delete all the comments in a document, click the Delete button arrow and then click *Delete All Comments in Document* at the drop-down list. To leave a comment in a document but identify that it has been resolved, right-click the comment and then click *Resolve Comment* at the shortcut menu. The resolved comment remains in the document and is dimmed.

Distinguishing Comments from Different Users

More than one user can insert comments in the same document. Word uses different colors to distinguish comments inserted by different users, generally displaying the first user's comments in red and the second user's comments in blue. (These colors may vary.)

The user name and initials can be changed at the Word Options dialog box with *General* selected, as shown in Figure 8.3. To change the user name, select the name that displays in the *User name* text box and then type the new name. Complete similar steps to change the user initials in the *Initials* text box. A check mark may need to be inserted in the *Always use these values regardless of sign in to Office* check box.

Figure 8.3 Word Options Dialog Box with *General* Selected

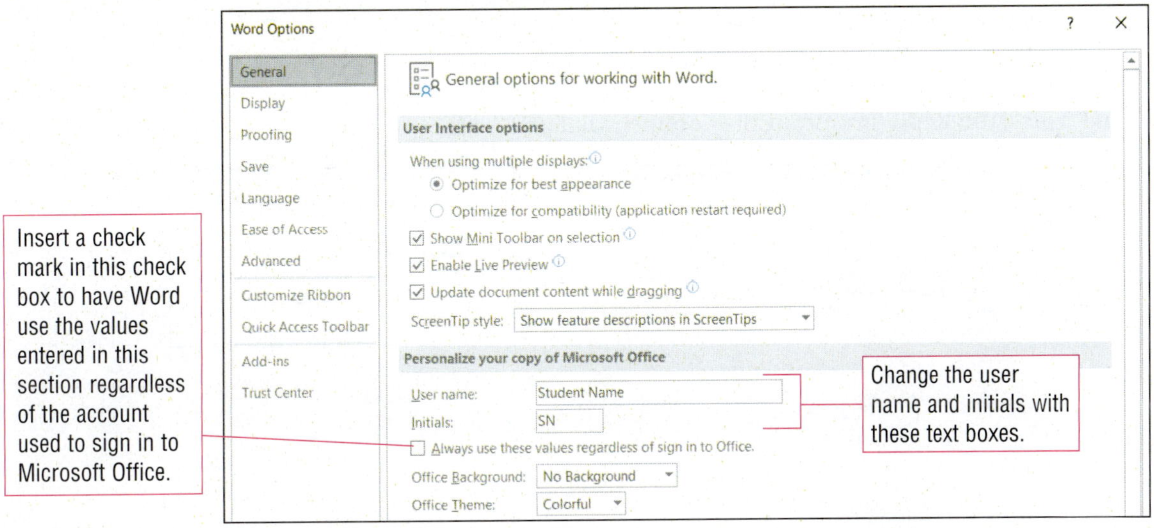

Activity 1d Changing User Information and Inserting, Resolving, and Deleting Comments

1. With **8-OMSNewEmps** open, change the user information by completing the following steps:
   a. Click the File tab.
   b. Click *Options*.
   c. At the Word Options dialog box, make sure *General* is selected in the left panel.
   d. Make a note of the current name and initials in the *Personalize your copy of Microsoft Office* section.
   e. Select the name displayed in the *User name* text box and then type Taylor Stanton.
   f. Select the initials displayed in the *Initials* text box and then type TS.
   g. Click the *Always use these values regardless of sign in to Office* check box to insert a check mark.
   h. Click OK to close the Word Options dialog box.

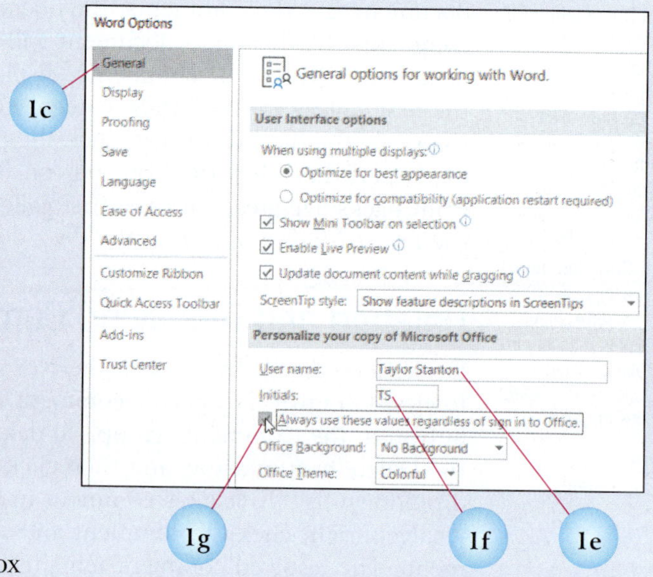

2. Insert a comment by completing the following steps:
   a. Move the insertion point to the end of the first paragraph of text in the section PERFORMANCE REVIEW.
   b. Click the New Comment button in the Comments group.
   c. Type Provide additional information on performance evaluation documentation. in the Reviewing pane.
   d. Click the Reviewing Pane button to close the pane.

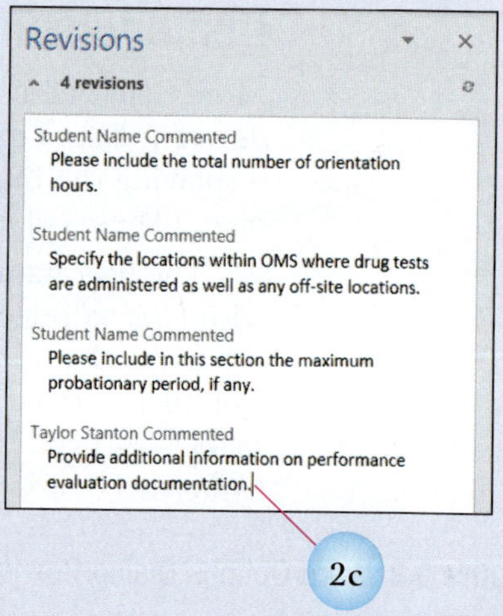

3. Respond to a comment by completing the following steps:
   a. Press Ctrl + Home to move the insertion point to the beginning of the document.
   b. Click the Show Markup button, point to *Balloons*, and then click *Show Only Comments and Formatting in Balloons* at the drop-down list.
   c. Click the Next button in the Comments group. (This opens the comment balloon for the first comment.)
   d. Click the Reply button in the comment balloon.

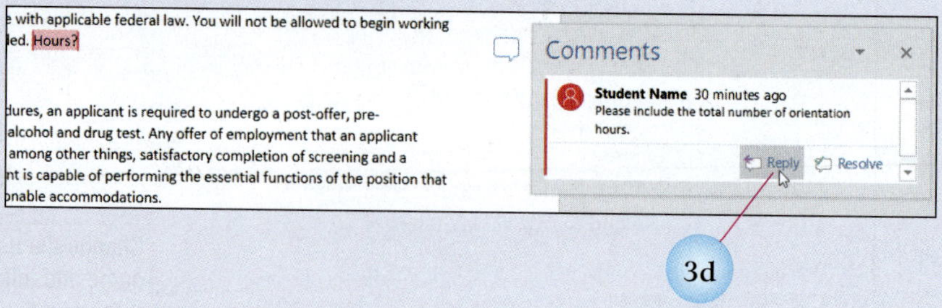

e. Type Check with Barb on the total number of orientation hours.

f. Click in the document to close the comment balloon.

4. Print only the information in the Reviewing pane by completing the following steps:
   a. Click the File tab and then click the *Print* option.
   b. At the Print backstage area, click the first gallery in the *Settings* category and then click *List of Markup* in the *Document Info* section of the drop-down list.
   c. Click the Print button.

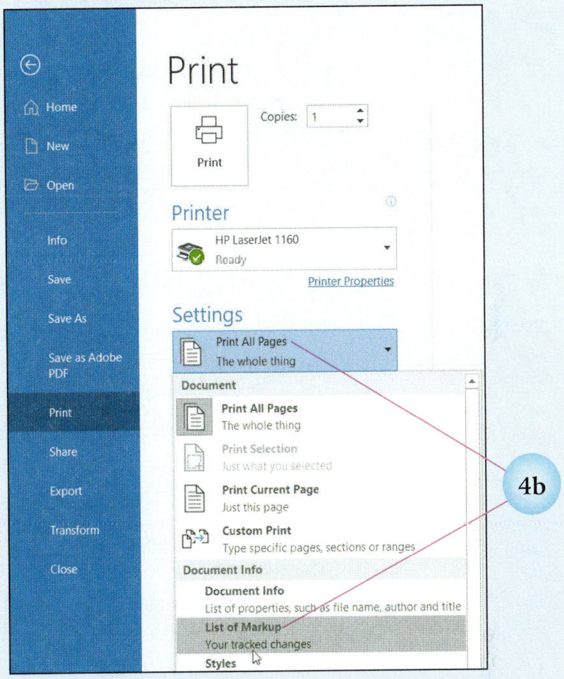

5. Resolve and delete a comment by completing the following steps:
   a. Press Ctrl + Home.
   b. If necessary, click the Review tab.
   c. Click the Next button.
   d. Hover the mouse pointer over the first comment balloon and then click the Resolve button.
   e. Click the Next button again.
   f. Click the Next button again.
   g. Click the Delete button in the Comments group.

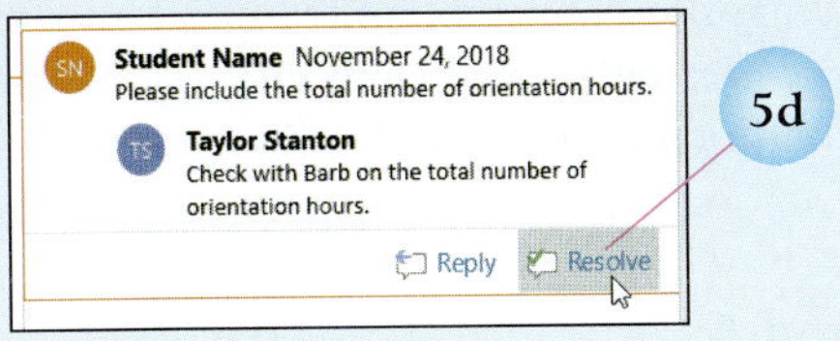

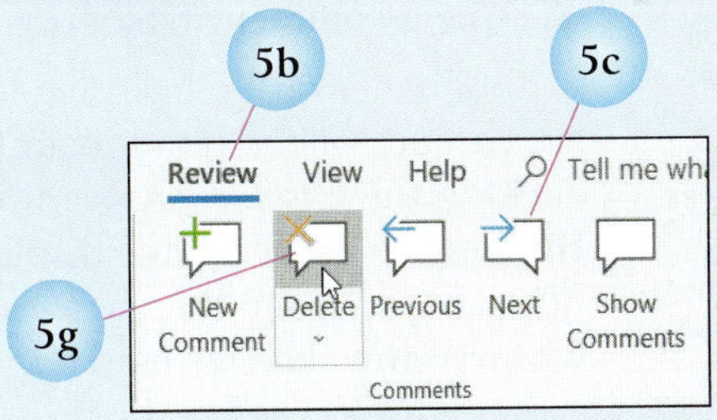

6. Print only the information in the Reviewing pane by completing Step 4.
7. Change the user information back to the default settings by completing the following steps:
   a. Click the File tab and then click *Options*.
   b. At the Word Options dialog box with *General* selected, select *Taylor Stanton* in the *User name* text box and then type the original name.
   c. Select the initials *TS* in the *Initials* text box and then type the original initials.
   d. Click the *Always use these values regardless of sign in to Office* check box to remove the check mark.
   e. Click OK to close the dialog box.
8. Save and then close **8-OMSNewEmps**.

Check Your Work

Activity 2 Track Changes in a Building Construction Agreement — 4 Parts

You will open a building construction agreement, turn on Track Changes, and then make changes to the document. You will also customize Track Changes and accept and reject changes.

Tutorial
Tracking Changes in a Document

Track Changes

Tracking Changes in a Document

If more than one person in a workgroup needs to review and edit a document, consider using Word's Track Changes feature. When Track Changes is turned on, Word tracks each deletion, insertion, and formatting change made in a document. Turn on Track Changes by clicking the Review tab and then clicking the Track Changes button in the Tracking group or by using the keyboard shortcut Ctrl + Shift + E. Turn off Track Changes by completing the same steps.

Tutorial
Displaying Changes for Review and Showing Markup

Quick Steps

Turn on Track Changes

1. Click Review tab.
2. Click Track Changes button.

OR

Press Ctrl + Shift + E.

Hint Each of the four options at the *Display for Review* option drop-down list displays a document at various stages in the editing process.

Displaying Changes for Review

The *Display for Review* option box in the Tracking group on the Review tab has a default setting of *Simple Markup*. With this setting applied, each change made to the document displays in it and a vertical change line displays in the left margin next to the line of text in which the change was made. To see the changes along with the original text, click the *Display for Review* option box arrow and then click the *All Markup* option.

With *All Markup* selected, all the changes display in the document along with the original text. For example, if text is deleted, it stays in the document but displays in a different color and with strikethrough characters through it. The display of all markups can be turned on by clicking one of the vertical change lines that display in the left margin next to changes that have been made or by clicking a comment balloon.

If changes have been made to a document with Track Changes turned on, the appearance of the final document with the changes applied can be previewed by clicking the *Display for Review* option box arrow and then clicking *No Markup* at the drop-down list. This displays the document with the changes made but does not actually make the changes to the document. To view the original document without any changes marked, click the *Display for Review* option box arrow and then click *Original* at the drop-down list.

Showing Markups

Show Markup

With the display of all markups turned on, specify what tracking information displays in the body of the document with options at the Balloons side menu. To show all the changes in balloons in the right margin, click the Show Markup button, point to *Balloons*, and then click *Show Revisions in Balloons* at the side menu. Click *Show All Revisions Inline* to display all the changes in the document with vertical change lines in the left margin next to the affected lines of text. Click the *Show Only Comments and Formatting in Balloons* option at the side menu and insertions and deletions display in the text while comments and formatting changes display in balloons in the right margin.

Activity 2a Tracking Changes in a Document

1. Open **Agreement** and then save it with the name **8-Agreement**.
2. Turn on Track Changes by clicking the Review tab and then clicking the Track Changes button in the Tracking group.

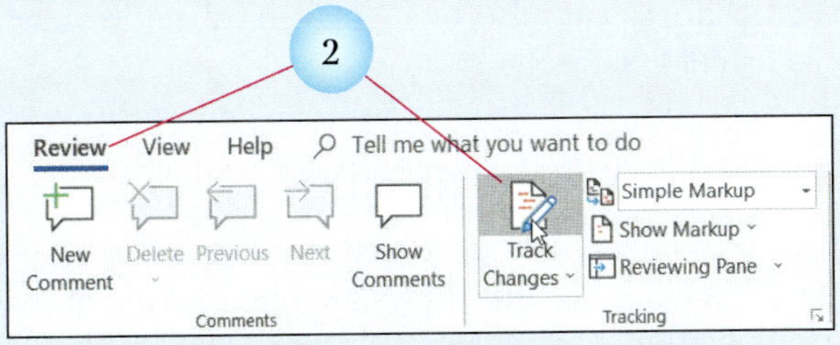

3. Type the word BUILDING between the words *THIS* and *AGREEMENT* in the first paragraph of the document.

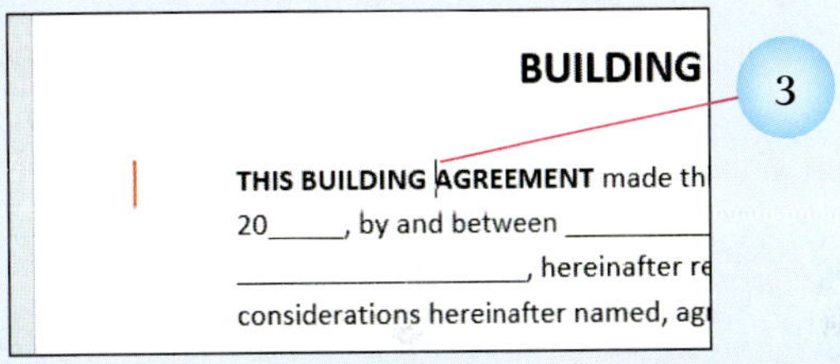

4. Show all markups by clicking the *Display for Review* option box arrow in the Tracking group and then clicking *All Markup* at the drop-down list. (Notice that the text *BUILDING* is underlined and displays in red in the document [the color may vary].)

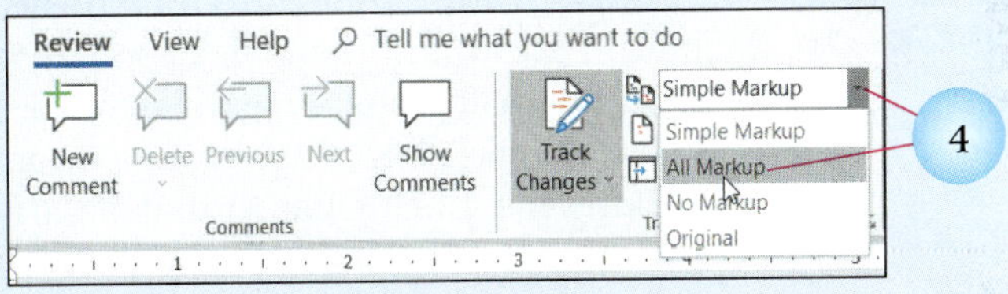

5. Select and then delete *thirty (30)* in the second paragraph. (The deleted text displays in the document with strikethrough characters through it.)
6. Type sixty (60).
7. Move a paragraph of text by completing the following steps:
   a. Select the paragraph that begins *Supervision of Work* (including the paragraph mark that ends the paragraph).
   b. Press Ctrl + X to cut the text. (The text stays in the document and displays in red with strikethrough characters through it.)
   c. Position the insertion point immediately before the word *Start* (in the paragraph that begins *Start of Construction and Completion:*).
   d. Press Ctrl + V to paste the cut text in the new location. The inserted text displays in green and has a double underline below it. Notice that the text in the original location changes to green and has double-strikethrough characters through it.)
8. Turn off Track Changes by clicking the Track Changes button in the Tracking group.
9. Display revisions in balloons by clicking the Show Markup button, pointing to *Balloons*, and then clicking *Show Revisions in Balloons* at the side menu.

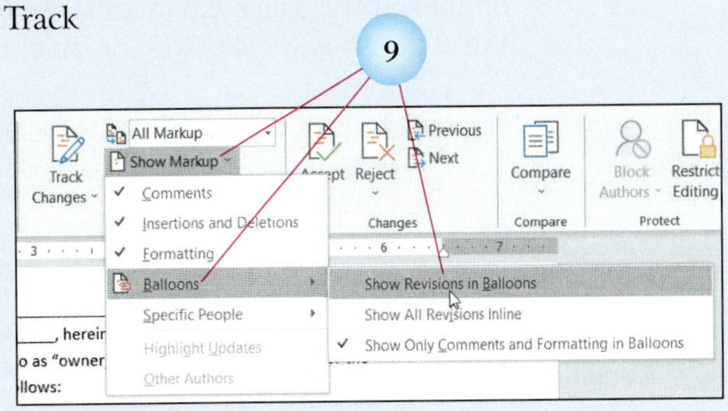

10. After looking at the revisions in balloons, click the Show Markup button, point to *Balloons*, and then click *Show All Revisions Inline* at the side menu.
11. Save **8-Agreement**.

Check Your Work

Displaying Information about Tracked Changes

Display information about a specific tracked change by hovering the mouse pointer over it. After approximately one second, a box displays above the change that contains the author's name, the date and time the change was made, and the type of change (for example, whether it was a deletion or insertion). Information on tracked changes can also be displayed in the Reviewing pane, where each change is listed separately.

Changing User Information

Word uses different colors to record the changes made by different people (up to eight). This color coding allows anyone looking at the document to identify which users made which changes. How to change the user name and initials at the Word Options dialog box was covered earlier in the chapter (see the section *Distinguishing Comments from Different Users*). In Activity 2b, the user name and initials will be changed and then additional tracked changes will be made.

Locking and Unlocking Track Changes

Quick Steps

Lock Track Changes

1. Click Review tab.
2. Click Track Changes button arrow.
3. Click *Lock Tracking.*
4. Type password.
5. Press Tab.
6. Type password.
7. Click OK.

To ensure that all the changes made to a document will be tracked, lock the Track Changes feature so it cannot be turned off. To do this, click the Track Changes button arrow and then click *Lock Tracking* at the drop-down list. At the Lock Tracking dialog box, type a password, press the Tab key, type the password again, and then click OK. (Typing a password is optional.) Unlock Track Changes by clicking the Track Changes button arrow and then clicking *Lock Tracking*. At the Unlock Tracking dialog box, type the password and then click OK. If track changes was locked without a password, unlock track changes by clicking the Track Changes button arrow and then clicking *Lock Tracking* at the drop-down list.

Tutorial

Customizing Track Changes Options

Customizing Track Changes Options

Customize how tracked changes display in a document with options at the Show Markup button drop-down list. To show only one particular type of tracked change, remove the check marks before all the options except the specific one. For example, to view only formatting changes and not other types of changes, such as insertions and deletions, remove the check mark before each option except *Formatting*. Another method of customizing which tracked changes display is to use options at the Track Changes Options dialog box, shown in Figure 8.4. Display this dialog box by clicking the Tracking group dialog box launcher.

Figure 8.4 Track Changes Options Dialog Box

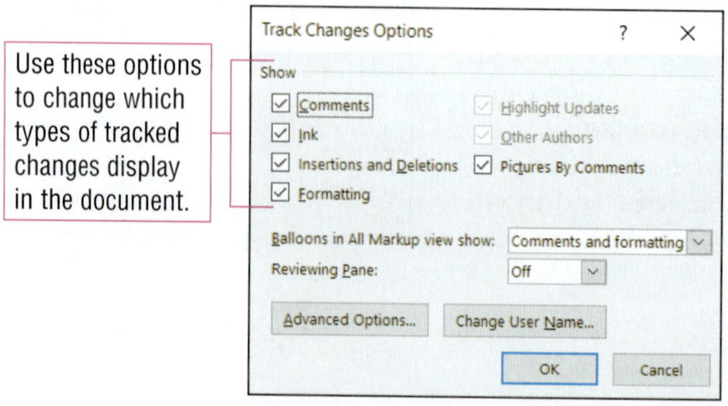

If the changes made by multiple reviewers have been tracked in a document, the changes made by a particular reviewer can be displayed. To do this, click the Show Markup button, point to *Specific People* at the drop-down list, and then click the *All Reviewers* check box to remove the check mark. Click the Show Markup button, point to *Reviewers*, and then click the check box of the specific reviewer.

Printing Markups

A document, by default, will print with all markups including comments, tracked changes, and changes to headers, footers, text boxes, footnotes and endnotes. To print a document without markups, display the Print backstage area, click the first gallery in the *Settings* category (contains the text *Print All Pages*) and then click the *Print Markup* option to remove the check mark. To print only the markups, display the Print backstage area, click the first gallery in the *Settings* category, and then click the *List of Markup* option at the drop-down list.

Activity 2b Changing User Information, Tracking Changes, and Locking Track Changes — Part 2 of 4

1. With **8-Agreement** open, change the user information by completing the following steps:
   a. Click the File tab and then click *Options*.
   b. At the Word Options dialog box with *General* selected, select the current name in the *User name* text box and then type Julia Moore.
   c. Select the initials in the *Initials* text box and then type JM.
   d. Click the *Always use these values regardless of sign in to Office* check box to insert a check mark.
   e. Click OK to close the dialog box.
2. Make additional changes to the contract and track the changes by completing the following steps:
   a. Click the Track Changes button in the Tracking group to turn on tracking.
   b. Select the title *BUILDING CONSTRUCTION AGREEMENT* and then change the font size to 14 points.
   c. Delete the text *at his option* (located in the second sentence in the second paragraph).
   d. Delete the text *and Completion* (located near the beginning of the fourth paragraph).

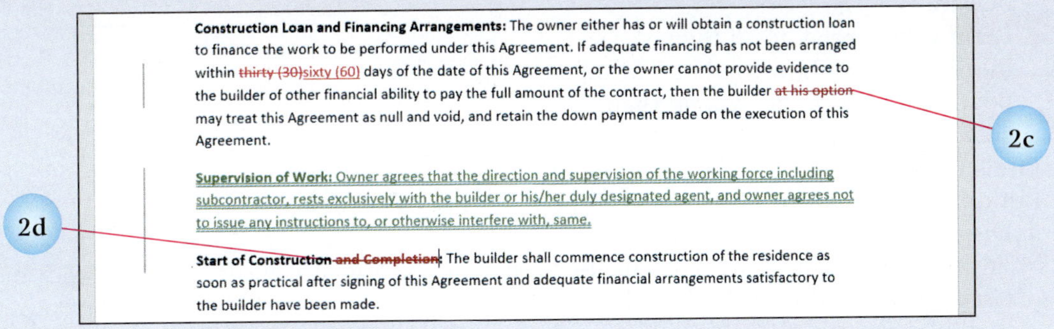
Construction Loan and Financing Arrangements: The owner either has or will obtain a construction loan to finance the work to be performed under this Agreement. If adequate financing has not been arranged within ~~thirty (30)~~sixty (60) days of the date of this Agreement, or the owner cannot provide evidence to the builder of other financial ability to pay the full amount of the contract, then the builder ~~at his option~~ may treat this Agreement as null and void, and retain the down payment made on the execution of this Agreement.

Supervision of Work: Owner agrees that the direction and supervision of the working force including subcontractor, rests exclusively with the builder or his/her duly designated agent, and owner agrees not to issue any instructions to, or otherwise interfere with, same.

Start of Construction ~~and Completion~~: The builder shall commence construction of the residence as soon as practical after signing of this Agreement and adequate financial arrangements satisfactory to the builder have been made.

   e. Delete *thirty (30)* in the paragraph that begins *Builder's Right to Terminate the Contract:* (located on the second page).
   f. Type sixty (60).
   g. Select the text *IN WITNESS WHEREOF* (located near the bottom of the document) and then apply bold formatting.

3. Click the Review tab and then click the Track Changes button to turn off Track Changes.
4. Click the Reviewing Pane button to turn on the display of the Reviewing pane and then use the vertical scroll bar at the right of the Reviewing pane to review the changes.

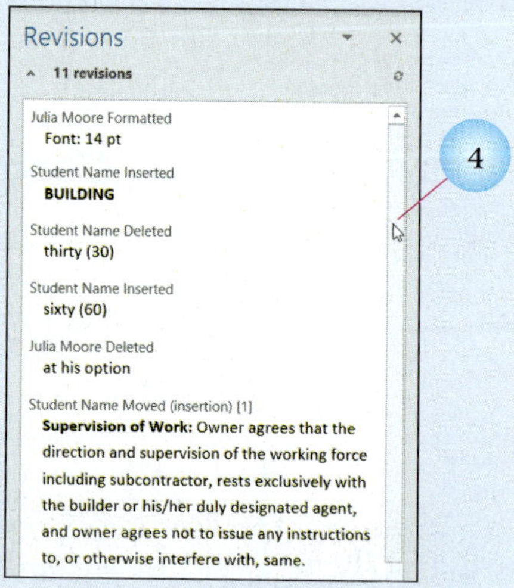

5. View the changes in balloons by clicking the Show Markup button, pointing to *Balloons*, and then clicking *Show Revisions in Balloons*.
6. Click the Reviewing Pane button to turn off the display of the pane.
7. Scroll through the document and view the changes in the balloons.
8. Click the Show Markup button, point to *Balloons*, and then click *Show All Revisions Inline* at the side menu.
9. Change the user information back to the original information by completing the following steps:
   a. Click the File tab and then click *Options*.
   b. At the Word Options dialog box, select *Julia Moore* in the *User name* text box and then type the original name.
   c. Select the initials *JM* in the *Initials* text box and then type the original initials.
   d. Click the *Always use these values regardless of sign in to Office* check box to remove the check mark.
   e. Click OK to close the dialog box.
10. Display only those changes made by Julia Moore by completing the following steps:
   a. Click the Show Markup button in the Tracking group and then point to *Specific People* at the drop-down list.
   b. Click *All Reviewers* at the side menu.
   c. Click the Show Markup button, point to *Specific People*, and then click *Julia Moore*.
   d. Scroll through the document and notice that only changes made by Julia Moore display.
   e. Return the display to all the reviewers by clicking the Show Markup button, pointing to *Specific People*, and then clicking *All Reviewers*.

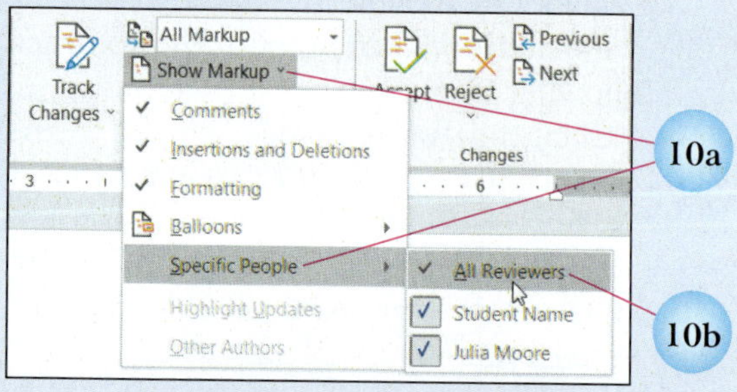

11. Print the document. (The document will print with the markups.)
12. Print only the markups by completing the following steps:
   a. Display the Print backstage area.
   b. At the Print backstage area, click the first gallery in the *Settings* category and then click the *List of Markup* option at the drop-down list. (You may need to scroll down the drop-down list to display this option.)
   c. Click the Print button.
13. Lock track changes by completing the following steps:
   a. Click the Track Changes button arrow and then click *Lock Tracking* at the drop-down list.

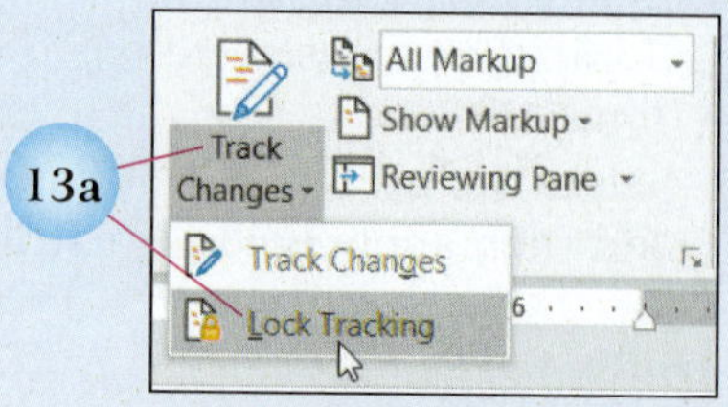

b. At the Lock Tracking dialog box, type agreement in the *Enter password (optional)* text box, press the Tab key, and then type agreement again in the *Reenter to confirm* text box.
c. Click OK.

14. Save **8-Agreement**.

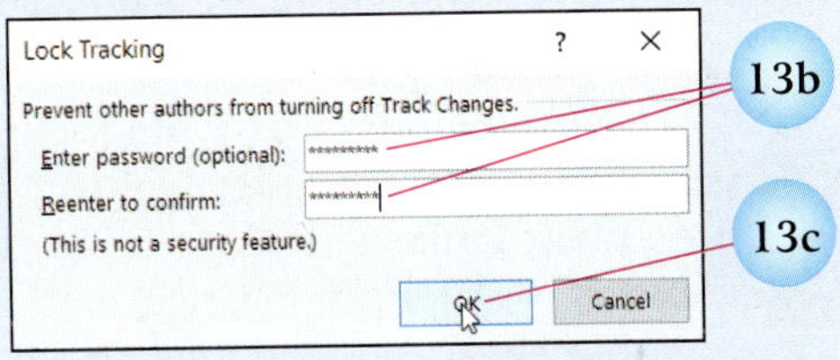

Check Your Work

Tutorial

Customizing Advanced Track Changes Options

Customizing Advanced Track Changes Options

How tracked changes display in a document is determined by default settings. For example, with all the markups showing, inserted text displays in red with an underline below it and deleted text displays in red with strikethrough characters through it. Moved text displays in the original location in green with double-strikethrough characters through it and in the new location in green with double-underlining below it.

Customize these options, along with others, at the Advanced Track Changes Options dialog box, shown in Figure 8.5. Use options at this dialog box to customize the display of markup text, moved text, table cell highlighting, formatting, and balloons. Display the dialog box by clicking the Tracking group dialog box launcher. At the Track Changes Options dialog box, click the Advanced Options button.

Figure 8.5 Advanced Track Changes Options Dialog Box

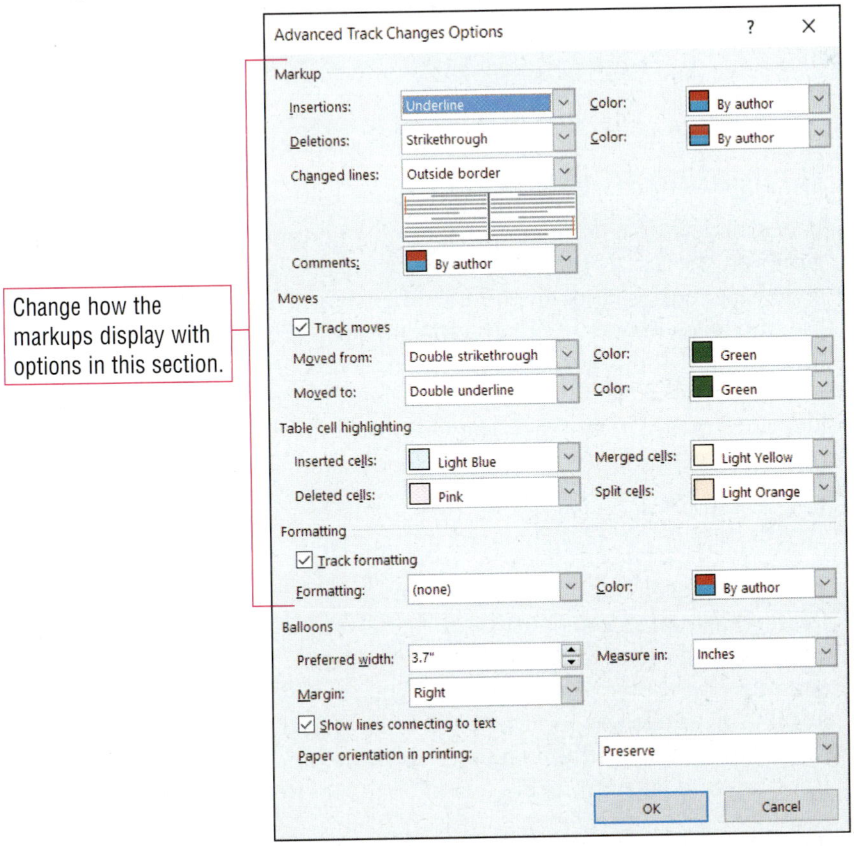

Activity 2c Customizing Track Changes Options

Part 3 of 4

1. With **8-Agreement** open, unlock track changes by clicking the Review tab (if necessary), clicking the Track Changes button arrow, and then clicking *Lock Tracking* at the drop-down list. At the Unlock Tracking dialog box, type agreement and then press the Enter key.
2. Customize the Track Changes options by completing the following steps:
   a. If necessary, click the Review tab.
   b. Click the Tracking group dialog box launcher.
   c. Click the Advanced Options button at the Track Changes Options dialog box.
   d. At the Advanced Track Changes Options dialog box, click the *Insertions* option box arrow and then click *Double underline* at the drop-down list.
   e. Click the *Insertions Color* option box arrow and then click *Green* at the drop-down list. (You will need to scroll down the list to display this color.)
   f. Click the *Moved from Color* option box arrow and then click *Dark Blue* at the drop-down list.
   g. Click the *Moved to Color* option box arrow and then click *Violet* at the drop-down list. (You will need to scroll down the list to display this color.)
   h. Click OK to close the dialog box.
   i. Click OK to close the Track Changes Options dialog box.
3. Save **8-Agreement**.

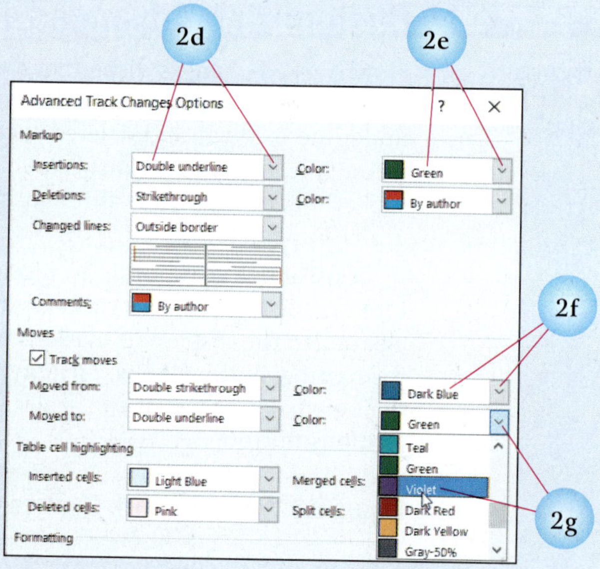

Check Your Work

Tutorial

Navigating, Accepting, and Rejecting Tracked Changes

Next

Previous

Navigating to Changes

When reviewing a document, use the Next and Previous buttons in the Changes group on the Review tab to navigate to changes. Click the Next button to review the next change in the document and click the Previous button to review the previous change. If the Track Changes feature is turned on, move text and then turn on the display of revision balloons and a small Go button (a blue right-pointing arrow) will display in the lower right corner of any balloon that identifies moved text. Click the Go button in the balloon identifying the original text to move the insertion point to the balloon identifying the moved text.

Accept

Reject

Accepting or Rejecting Changes

Tracked changes can be removed from a document only by accepting or rejecting them. Click the Accept button in the Changes group on the Review tab to accept a change and move to the next change or click the Reject button to reject a change and move to the next change. Click the Accept button arrow and a drop-down list displays with options to accept the change and move to the next change, accept the change, accept all the changes showing, and accept all the changes and stop tracking. Similar options are available at the Reject button drop-down list.

Activity 2d Accepting or Rejecting Changes

1. With **8-Agreement** open, show all the tracked changes *except* formatting changes by completing the following steps:
   a. Click the Show Markup button in the Tracking group and then click *Formatting* at the drop-down list. (This removes the check mark before the option.)
   b. Scroll through the document and notice that the vertical change lines in the left margin next to the two formatting changes have been removed.
   c. Click the Show Markup button and then click *Formatting* at the drop-down list. (This inserts a check mark before the option.)
2. Navigate to review tracked changes by completing the following steps:
   a. Press Ctrl + Home to move the insertion point to the beginning of the document.
   b. Click the Next button in the Changes group to select the first change.
   c. Click the Next button again to select the second change.
   d. Click the Previous button to select the first change.
3. Navigate between the original and new locations of the moved text by completing the following steps:
   a. Press Ctrl + Home to move the insertion point to the beginning of the document.
   b. Click the Show Markup button, point to *Balloons*, and then click *Show Revisions in Balloons*.
   c. Click the Go button (a blue right-pointing arrow) in the lower right corner of the Moved balloon. (This selects the text in the *Moved up* balloon.)
   d. Click the Go button in the lower right corner of the *Moved up* balloon. (This selects the moved text in the document.)
   e. Click the Show Markup button, point to *Balloons*, and then click *Show All Revisions Inline*.

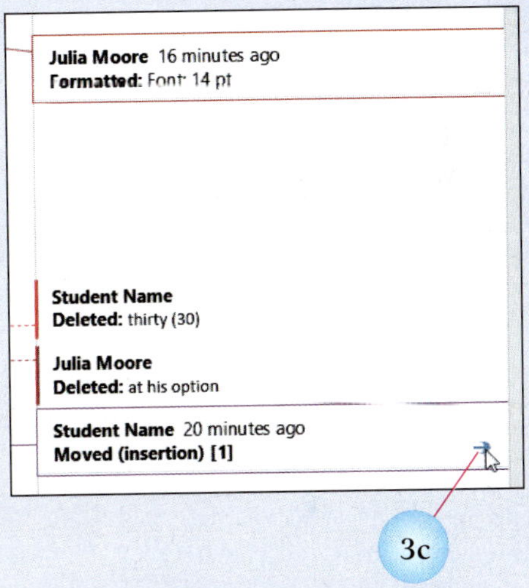

4. Press Ctrl + Home to move the insertion point to the beginning of the document.
5. Display and then accept only formatting changes by completing the following steps:
   a. Click the Tracking group dialog box launcher.
   b. At the Track Changes Options dialog box, click the *Comments* check box to remove the check mark.
   c. Click the *Ink* check box to remove the check mark.
   d. Click the *Insertions and Deletions* check box to remove the check mark.
   e. Click OK to close the Track Changes Options dialog box.

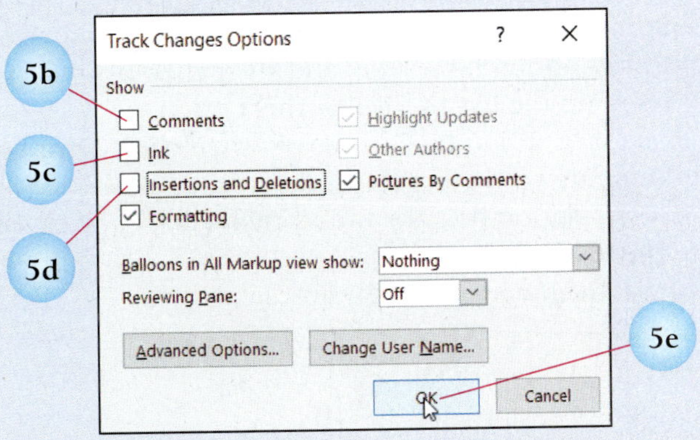

f. Click the Accept button arrow and then click *Accept All Changes Shown* at the drop-down list. (This accepts only the formatting changes in the document because those are the only changes showing.)

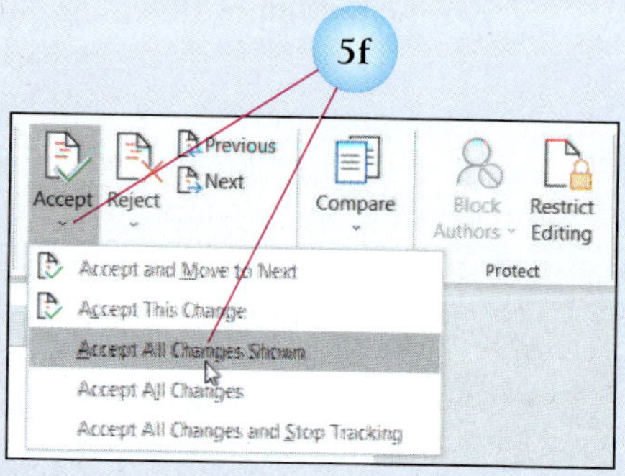

6. Redisplay all the changes by completing the following steps:
   a. Click the Tracking group dialog box launcher.
   b. Click the *Comments* check box to insert a check mark.
   c. Click the *Ink* check box to insert a check mark.
   d. Click the *Insertions and Deletions* check box to insert a check mark.
   e. Click OK to close the Track Changes Options dialog box.
7. Press Ctrl + Home to move the insertion point to the beginning of the document.

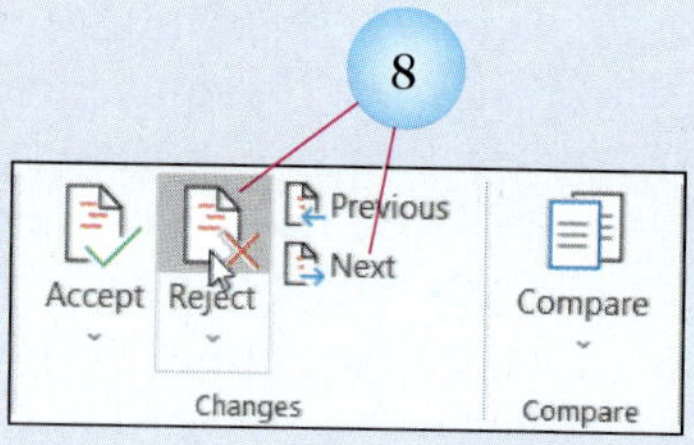

8. Reject the change that inserts the word *BUILDING* by clicking the Next button in the Changes group and then clicking the Reject button. (This rejects the change and moves to the next revision in the document.)
9. Click the Accept button to accept the change that deletes *thirty (30)*.
10. Click the Accept button to accept the change that inserts *sixty (60)*.
11. Click the Reject button to reject the change that deletes the words *at his option*.
12. Accept all the remaining changes by clicking the Accept button arrow and then clicking *Accept All Changes* at the drop-down list.

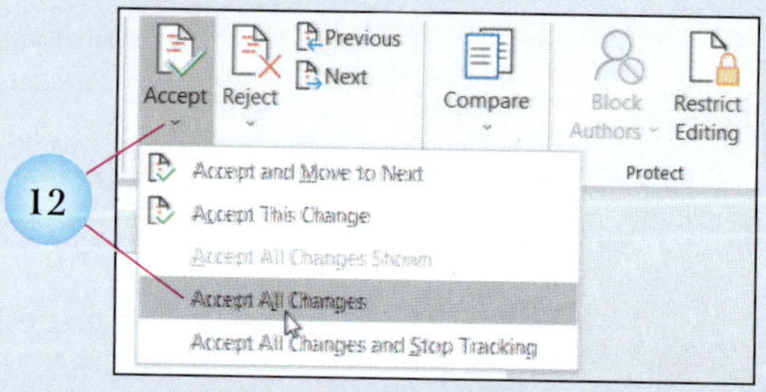

13. Return the track changes options to the default settings by completing the following steps:
   a. If necessary, click the Review tab.
   b. Click the Tracking group dialog box launcher.
   c. At the Track Changes Options dialog box, click the Advanced Options button.
   d. At the Advanced Track Changes Options dialog box, click the *Insertions* option box arrow and then click *Underline* at the drop-down list.
   e. Click the *Insertions Color* option box arrow and then click *By author* at the drop-down list. (You will need to scroll up the list to display this option.)
   f. Click the *Moved from Color* option box arrow and then click *Green* at the drop-down list. (You may need to scroll down the list to display this color.)
   g. Click the *Moved to Color* option box arrow and then click *Green* at the drop-down list.
   h. Click OK to close the dialog box.
   i. Click OK to close the Track Changes Options dialog box.

14. Check to make sure all the tracked changes are accepted or rejected by completing the following steps:
   a. Click the Reviewing Pane button in the Tracking group.
   b. Check the summary information at the top of the Reviewing pane and make sure that each option is followed by a 0. (You may need to click the up arrow at the right of *0 revisions* to show all the options.)
   c. Close the Reviewing pane.
15. Save, print, and then close **8-Agreement**.

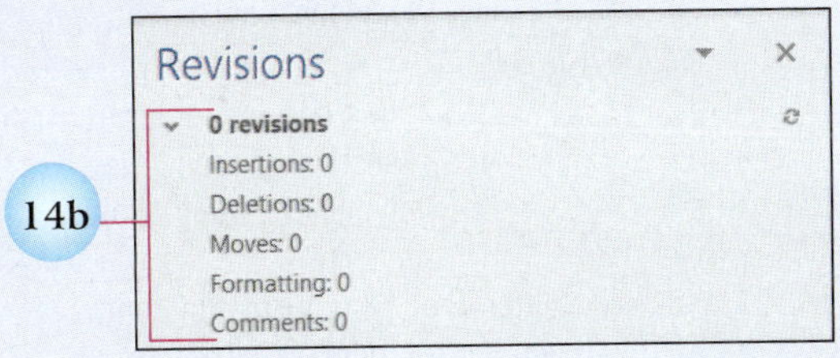

Check Your Work

Activity 3 Restrict Formatting and Editing in a Company Report — 4 Parts

You will open a company report document, restrict formatting and editing in the document, enforce protection, and protect the document with a password.

Tutorial

Restricting Formatting and Editing

Restricting a Document

Within an organization, copies of a document may be distributed among members of a group. In some situations, the document may need to be protected and the changes that can be made to it need to be limited. If a document contains sensitive, restricted, or private information, consider protecting it by saving it as a read-only document or securing it with a password.

Use options in the Restrict Editing task pane to limit what formatting and editing users can perform on a document. Limiting formatting and editing is especially useful in a workgroup environment, in which a number of people review and edit the same document.

For example, suppose a company's annual report is being prepared and it contains information from a variety of departments, such as Finance, Human Resources, and Sales and Marketing. Access to the report can be restricted so only certain employees are allowed to edit specific parts of the document. For instance, the part of the report pertaining to finance can be restricted to allow only someone in the Finance Department to make edits. Similarly, the part of the report on employees can be restricted so only someone in Human Resources can make edits. By limiting options for editing, the integrity of the document can be protected.

Restrict Editing

To protect a document, display the Restrict Editing task pane, shown in Figure 8.6, by clicking the Review tab and then clicking the Restrict Editing button in the Protect group. Use options in the *Formatting restrictions* section to limit formatting to specific styles and use options in the *Editing restrictions* section to specify the types of editing allowed in the document.

Figure 8.6 Restrict Editing Task Pane

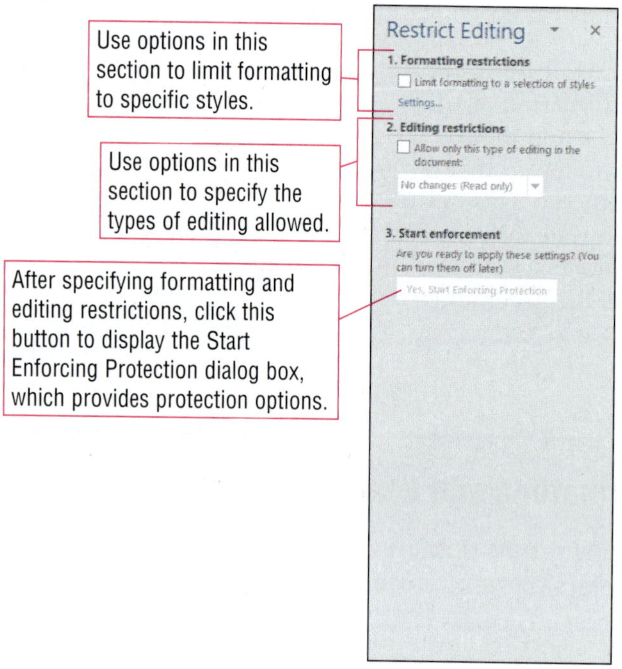

The Protect group on the Review tab contains a Block Authors button when a document is saved to a Microsoft SharePoint site that supports workspaces. If the button is active, select the portion of the document to block from editing and then click the Block Authors button. To unblock authors, click in the locked section of the document and then click the Block Authors button.

Applying Formatting Restrictions

Quick Steps

Display Formatting Restrictions Dialog Box

1. Click Review tab.
2. Click Restrict Editing button.
3. Click Settings hyperlink.

Use options in the *Formatting restrictions* section of the Restrict Editing task pane to lock specific styles used in a document, thus allowing the use of only those styles and prohibiting users from making other formatting changes. Click the Settings hyperlink in the *Formatting restrictions* section and the Formatting Restrictions dialog box displays, as shown in Figure 8.7.

Insert a check mark in the *Limit formatting to a selection of styles* check box and the styles become available in the *Checked styles are currently allowed* list box. In this list box, insert check marks in the check boxes preceding the styles that are allowed and remove check marks from the check boxes preceding the styles that are not allowed. Limit formatting to a minimum number of styles by clicking the Recommended Minimum button. This allows formatting with styles that Word uses for certain features, such as bulleted and numbered lists. Click the None button to remove all the check marks and prevent all the styles from being used in the document. Click the All button to insert check marks in all the check boxes and allow all the styles to be used in the document.

Use options in the *Formatting* section of the dialog box to allow or not allow AutoFormat to make changes in a document. Also use options in this section of the dialog box to allow or not allow users to switch themes or style sets.

Figure 8.7 Formatting Restrictions Dialog Box

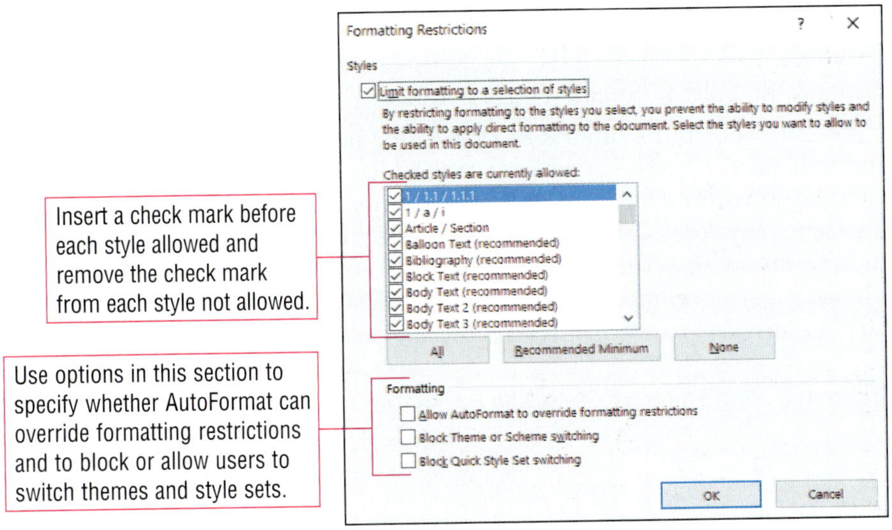

Activity 3a Restricting Formatting of a Document

Part 1 of 4

1. Open **TECRpt** and then save it with the name **8-TECRpt**.
2. Restrict formatting to the Heading 1 and Heading 2 styles by completing the following steps:
   a. Click the Review tab.
   b. Click the Restrict Editing button in the Protect group.

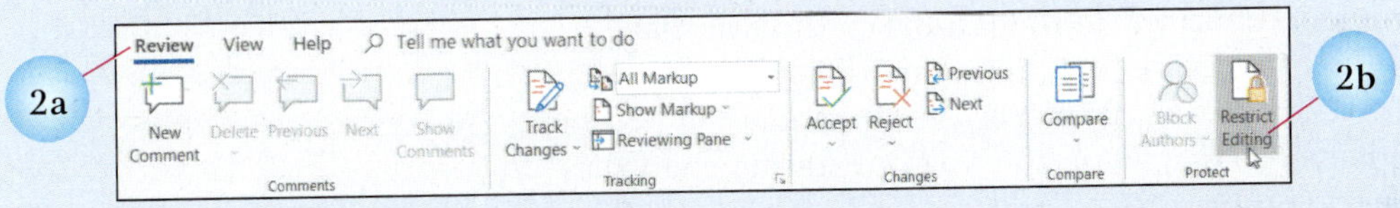

   c. At the Restrict Editing task pane, click the *Limit formatting to a selection of styles* check box to insert a check mark. (Skip this step if the check box already contains a check mark.)
   d. Click the Settings hyperlink.
   e. At the Formatting Restrictions dialog box, click the None button.
   f. Scroll down the *Checked styles are currently allowed* list box and then click to insert check marks in the *Heading 1* and *Heading 2* check boxes.
   g. Click OK.
   h. At the message stating that the document may contain formatting or styles that are not allowed and asking about removing them, click Yes.
3. Save **8-TECRpt**.

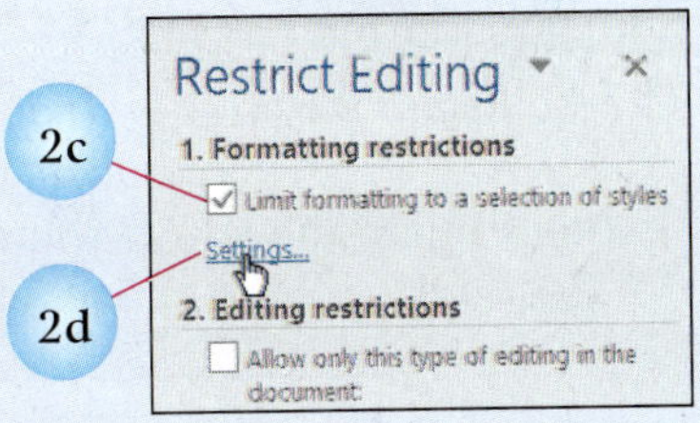

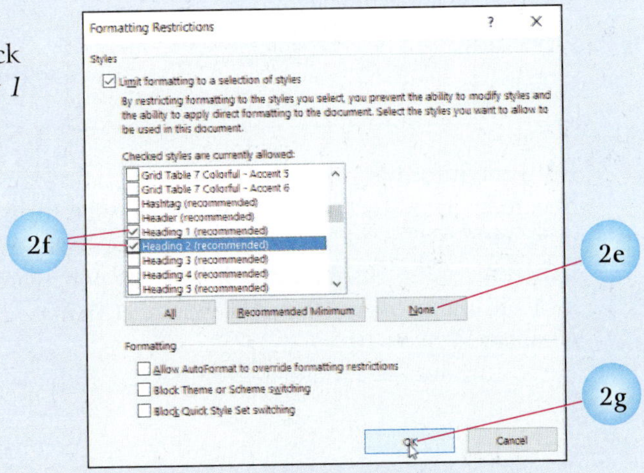

Enforcing Protection

Quick Steps

Display Start Enforcing Protection Dialog Box

1. Click Review tab.
2. Click Restrict Editing button.
3. Specify formatting and/or editing options.
4. Click Yes, Start Enforcing Protection button.

When restrictions have been specified in the Restrict Editing task pane, enforce the restrictions by clicking the Yes, Start Enforcing Protection button. This displays the Start Enforcing Protection dialog box shown in Figure 8.8.

At the Start Enforcing Protection dialog box, the *Password* option is automatically selected. To add a password, type it in the *Enter new password (optional)* text box. Click in the *Reenter password to confirm* text box and then type the same password again. Choose the *User authentication* option to use encryption to prevent any unauthorized changes. If Word does not recognize the password when a password-protected document is being opened, check to make sure Caps Lock is turned off and then try typing the password again.

Figure 8.8 Start Enforcing Protection Dialog Box

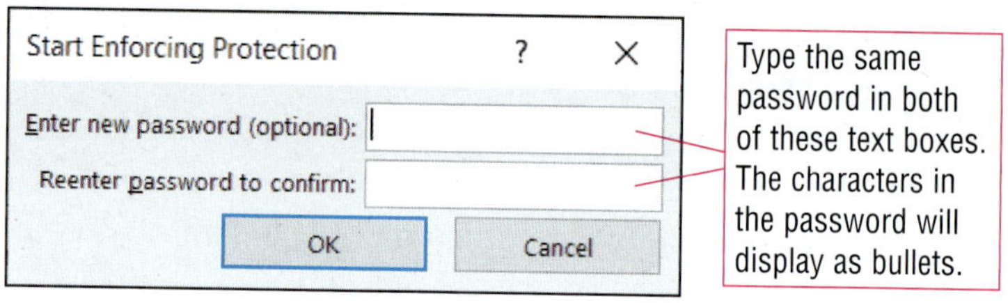

Activity 3b Enforcing Protection in a Document

Part 2 of 4

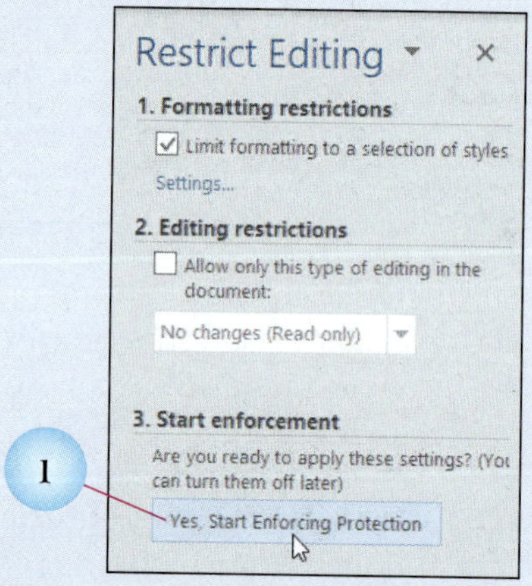

1. With **8-TECRpt** open, click the Yes, Start Enforcing Protection button (in the middle of the task pane).
2. At the Start Enforcing Protection dialog box, type formatting in the *Enter new password (optional)* text box. (Bullets will display in the text box, rather than the letters you type.)
3. Press the Tab key (which moves the insertion point to the *Reenter password to confirm* text box) and then type formatting. (Again, bullets will display in the text box, rather than the letters you type.)
4. Click OK to close the dialog box.

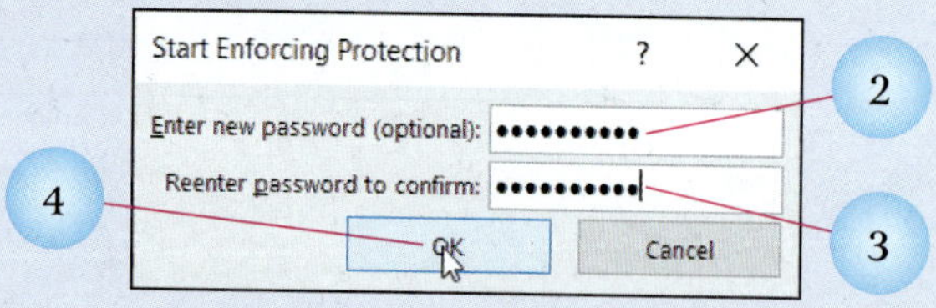

5. Read the information in the task pane stating that the document is protected and that text may be formatted only with certain styles. Click the Available styles hyperlink. (This displays the Styles task pane with four styles in the list box: *Clear All*, *Normal*, *Heading 1*, and *Heading 2*.)

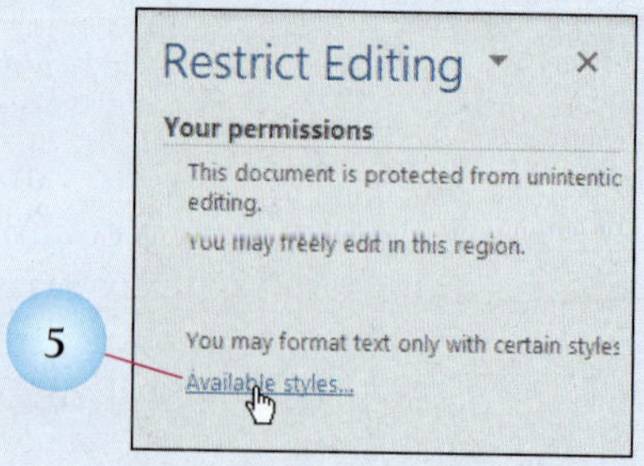

6. Close the Styles task pane.
7. Apply the Heading 1 style to the title *TANDEM ENERGY CORPORATION* and apply the Heading 2 style to the following headings: *Overview*, *Research and Development*, *Manufacturing*, and *Sales and Marketing*.
8. Apply the Lines (Simple) style set. (This style set is in the Document Formatting group on the Design tab.)
9. At the message stating that some of the styles could not be updated, click OK.
10. Save the document.
11. Remove the password protection from the document by completing the following steps:
    a. Click the Stop Protection button at the bottom of the Restrict Editing task pane.
    b. At the Unprotect Document dialog box, type formatting in the *Password* text box.
    c. Click OK.
12. Save **8-TECRpt**.

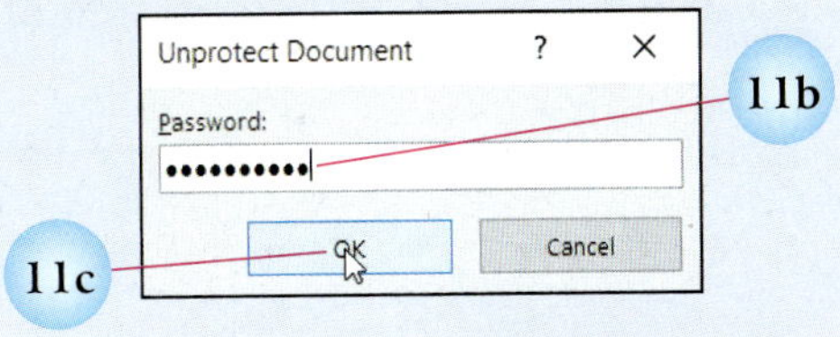

Check Your Work

Applying Editing Restrictions

Use the *Editing restrictions* option in the Restrict Editing task pane to limit the types of changes users can make to a document. Insert a check mark in the *Allow only this type of editing in the document* check box and the drop-down list below the option becomes active. Click the option box arrow and the following options become available: *Tracked changes*, *Comments*, *Filling in forms*, and *No changes (Read only)*.

To restrict users from making changes to a document, choose the *No changes (Read only)* option. Choose the *Tracked changes* option to allow users to make tracked changes in a document and choose the *Comments* option to allow users to insert comments in a document. These two options are useful in a workgroup environment, in which a document is routed to various individuals for review. Choose the *Filling in forms* option and users will be able to fill in the fields in a form but not make any other changes.

Activity 3c Restricting Editing of and Enforcing Protection in a Document

Part 3 of 4

1. With **8-TECRpt** open, restrict editing to inserting comments by completing the following steps:
    a. Make sure the Restrict Editing task pane displays.
    b. Click the *Allow only this type of editing in the document* check box to insert a check mark.
    c. Click the option box arrow below *Allow only this type of editing in the document* and then click *Comments* at the drop-down list.
2. Click the Yes, Start Enforcing Protection button at the bottom of the task pane.
3. At the Start Enforcing Protection dialog box, click OK. (Adding a password is optional.)
4. Read the information in the task pane stating that the document is protected and that editing is restricted to inserting comments.

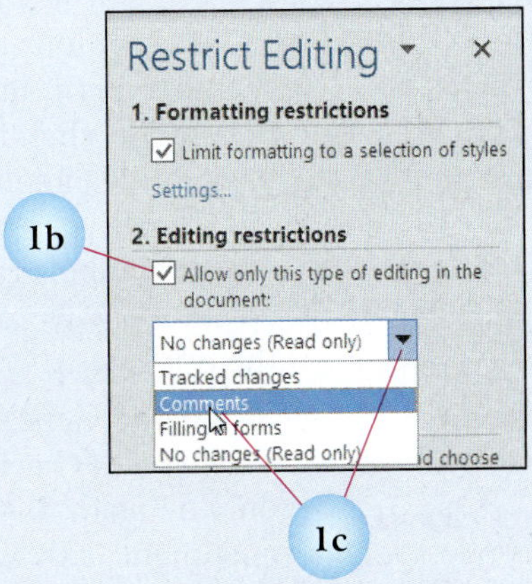

5. Click each ribbon tab and notice the buttons and options that are dimmed and unavailable.
6. Insert a comment by completing the following steps:
   a. Move the insertion point immediately to the right of the period that ends the last sentence in the second paragraph of the *Overview* section.
   b. Click the Review tab, if necessary; click the Show Markup button in the Tracking group; point to *Balloons*; and then click the *Show All Revisions Inline* option if necessary.
   c. Click the Reviewing Pane button to turn on the display of the Reviewing pane.
   d. Click the New Comment button in the Comments group on the Review tab.
   e. Type the following text in the Reviewing pane: Include additional information on the impact of this purchase.

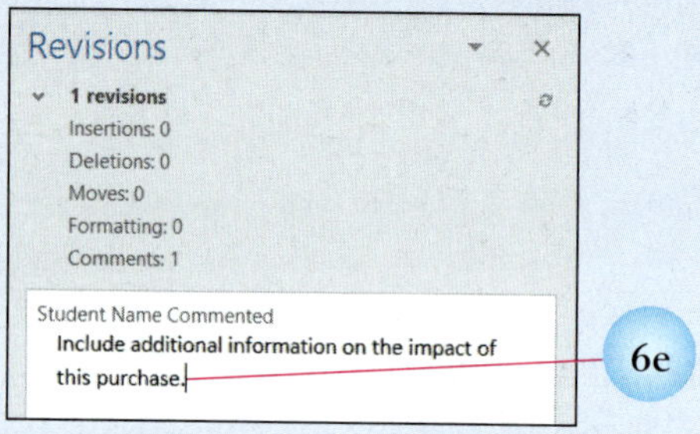

   f. Close the Reviewing pane.
   g. Click the Stop Protection button at the bottom of the Restrict Editing task pane.
   h. Close the Restrict Editing task pane.
7. Save the document and then print only page 1.
8. Print only the comment. (To do this, display the Print backstage area, click the first gallery in the *Settings* category, click the *List of Markup* option, and then click the Print button.)

Check Your Work

Tutorial

Protecting a Document with a Password

Quick Steps

Protect Document with Password

1. Press F12.
2. Click Tools button.
3. Click *General Options.*
4. Type password in *Password to modify* text box.
5. Press Enter key.
6. Type same password again.
7. Press Enter key.

Hint A strong password contains a mix of uppercase and lowercase letters as well as numbers and symbols.

Protecting a Document with a Password

In addition to protecting a document with a password using options at the Start Enforcing Protection dialog box, a document can be protected with a password using options at the General Options dialog box, shown in Figure 8.9. Display this dialog box by pressing the F12 function key to display the Save As dialog box, clicking the Tools button at the bottom of the dialog box next to the Save button, and then clicking *General Options* at the drop-down list.

Use options at the General Options dialog box to assign a password to open the document, modify the document, or both. To insert a password to open the document, click in the *Password to open* text box and then type the password. A password can contain up to 15 characters, should be at least 8 characters, and is case sensitive. Consider combining uppercase letters, lowercase letters, numbers, and/or symbols to make a password secure. Use the *Password to modify* option to create a password that someone must enter before being allowed to make edits to the document.

At the General Options dialog box, insert a check mark in the *Read-only recommended* check box to save a document as a read-only file. A read-only file can only be read, not modified. If changes are made, they must be saved into a new document with a new name. Use this option if the contents of the original document should not be changed.

Figure 8.9 General Options Dialog Box

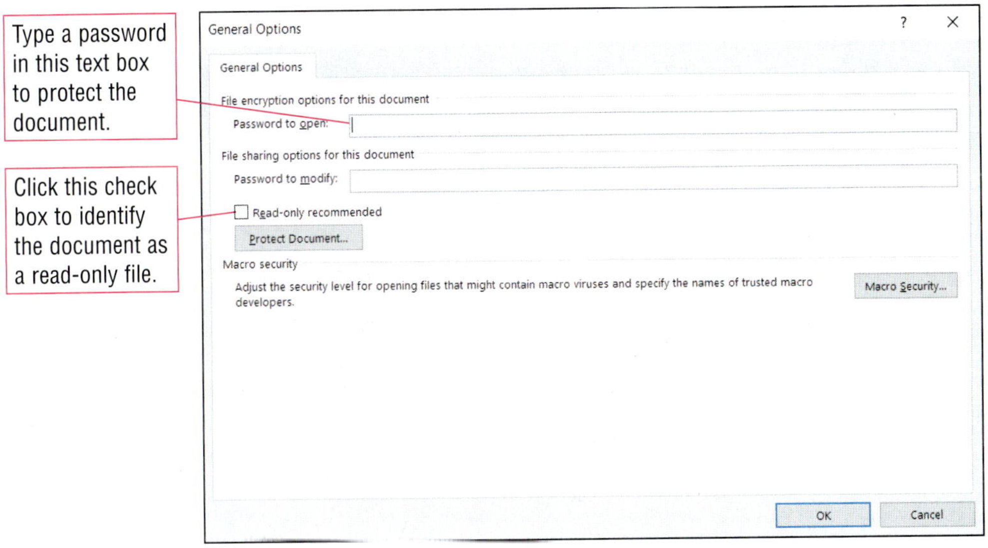

Activity 3d **Protecting a Document with a Password** Part 4 of 4

1. With **8-TECRpt** open, save the document and protect it with a password by completing the following steps:
   a. Press the F12 function key to display the Save As dialog box.
   b. Click the Tools button at the bottom of the dialog box (next to the Save button) and then click *General Options* at the drop-down list.
   c. At the General Options dialog box, type your first name in the *Password to open* text box. (If your name is longer than 15 characters, abbreviate it. You will not see your name; Word inserts bullets in place of the letters.)
   d. After typing your name, press the Enter key.
   e. At the Confirm Password dialog box, type your name again in the *Reenter password to open* text box. (Be sure to type it exactly as you did in the *Password to open* text box, including the same uppercase and lowercase letters.) Press the Enter key.
   f. Click the Save button at the Save As dialog box.

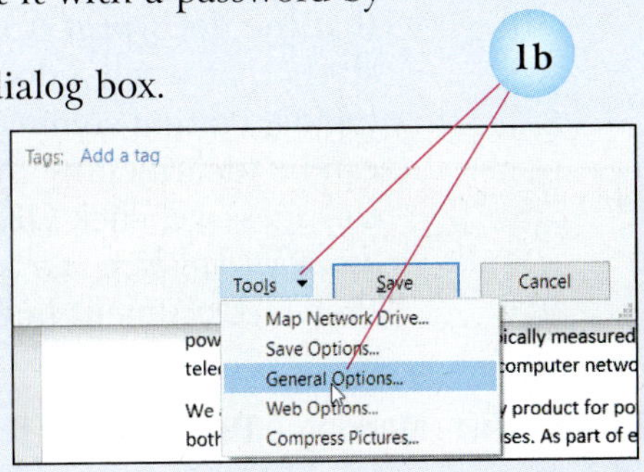

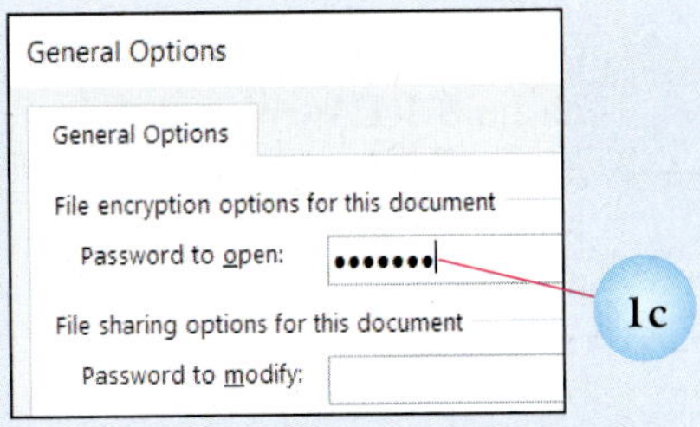

2. Close **8-TECRpt**.
3. Open **8-TECRpt** and type your password when prompted in the *Enter password to open file* text box and then press the Enter key.

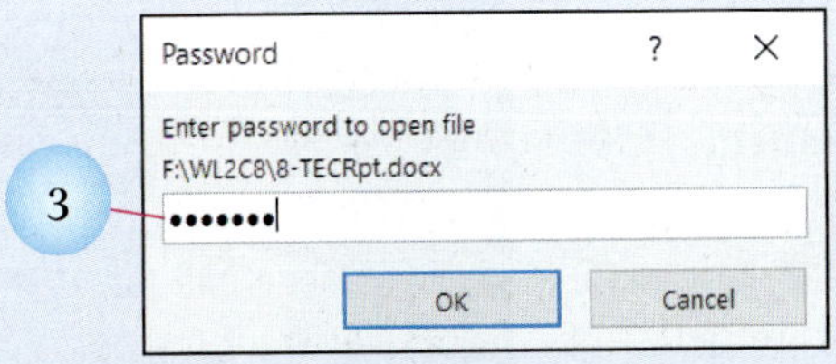

4. Close the document.

Activity 4 Prepare a Document for Distribution

4 Parts

You will open a real estate document and prepare it for distribution by marking it as final and encrypting it with a password. You will also open the document in different views and share a document electronically.

Protecting a Document

Protect Document

The middle panel of the Info backstage area contains buttons for protecting a document, checking for issues in a document such as personal data and accessibility, and managing versions of a document. Click the Protect Document button in the middle panel and a drop-down list displays with options for opening a document as a read-only file, encrypting the document with a password, restricting editing and access, adding a digital signature, and marking a document as final.

Marking a Document as Final

Click the *Mark as Final* option to save the document as a read-only document. Click this option and a message displays stating that the document will be marked and then saved. At this message, click OK. This displays another message stating that the document is the final version of the document. The message further states that when a document is marked as final, the status property is set to *Final*; typing, editing commands, and proofing marks are turned off; and the document can be identified by the Mark as Final icon, which displays on the Status bar. At this message, click OK. After a document is marked as final, the message *This document has been marked as final to discourage editing* displays at the right of the Protect Document button at the Info backstage area.

Activity 4a Marking a Document as Final

Part 1 of 4

1. Open **REAgrmnt** and then save it with the name **8-REAgrmnt**.
2. Mark the document as final by completing the following steps:
   a. Click the File tab and then, if necessary, click the *Info* option.
   b. Click the Protect Document button at the Info backstage area and then click *Mark as Final* at the drop-down list.
   c. At the message stating that the document will be marked and saved, click OK.
   d. At the next message that displays, click OK. Notice the message at the right of the Protect Document button.
   e. Click the Back button to return to the document.

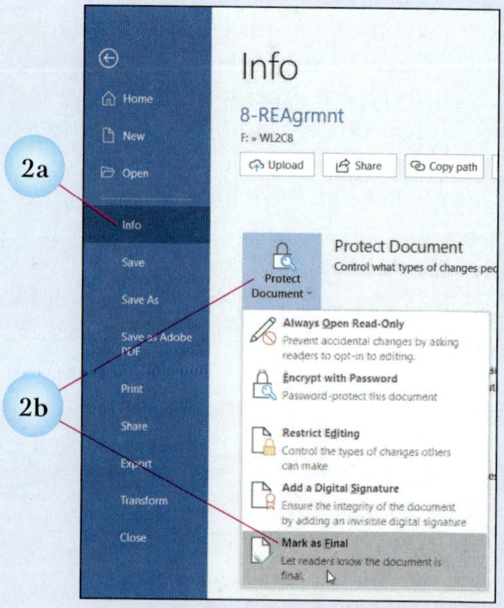

3. In the document window, notice the message bar at the top of the screen and then close the document.
4. Open **8-REAgrmnt** and then click the Edit Anyway button on the yellow message bar.

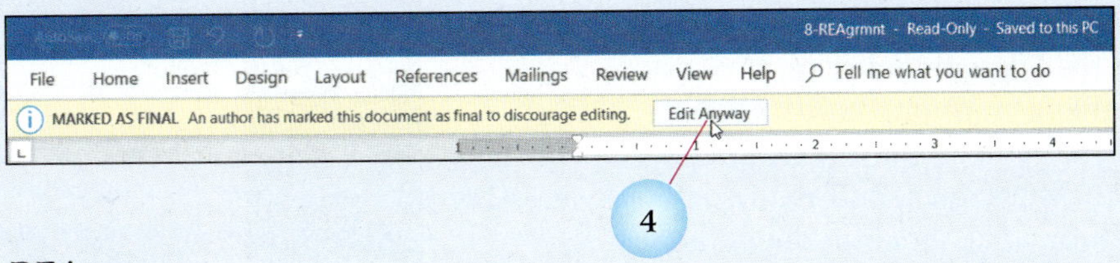

5. Save **8-REAgrmnt.**

Encrypting a Document

Quick Steps

Encrypt Document

1. Click File tab.
2. Click *Info* option.
3. Click Protect Document button.
4. Click *Encrypt with Password.*
5. Type password and then press Enter key.
6. Type password again and then press Enter key.

Word provides a number of methods for protecting a document with a password. As previously discussed in this chapter, a document can be protected with a password using options at the Start Enforcing Protection dialog box and the General Options dialog box.

In addition to these two methods, a document can be protected with a password by clicking the Protect Document button at the Info backstage area and then clicking the *Encrypt with Password* option at the drop-down list. At the Encrypt Document dialog box, type a password in the text box (the text will display as bullets) and then press the Enter key or click OK. At the Confirm Password dialog box, type the password again (the text will display as bullets) and then press the Enter key or click OK. When a password is applied to a document, the message *A password is required to open this document* displays at the right of the Protect Document button.

Restricting Editing

Click the Protect Document button at the Info backstage area and then click the *Restrict Editing* option at the drop-down list and the document displays with the Restrict Editing task pane open. This is the same task pane discussed previously in this chapter.

Adding a Digital Signature

Use the *Add a Digital Signature* option at the Protect Document button drop-down list to insert an invisible digital signature in a document. A digital signature is an electronic stamp that verifies the authenticity of the document. Before a digital signature can be added, it must be obtained. A digital signature can be obtained from a commercial certification authority.

Activity 4b Encrypting a Document with a Password

Part 2 of 4

1. With **8-REAgrmnt** open, encrypt the document with a password by completing the following steps:
   a. Click the File tab and then, if necessary, click the *Info* option.
   b. Click the Protect Document button at the Info backstage area, and then click *Encrypt with Password* at the drop-down list.
   c. At the Encrypt Document dialog box, type your initials in uppercase letters in the *Password* text box. (The text will display as bullets.)

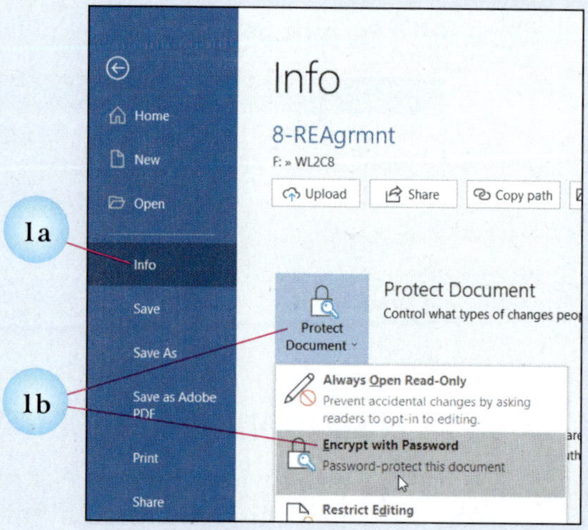

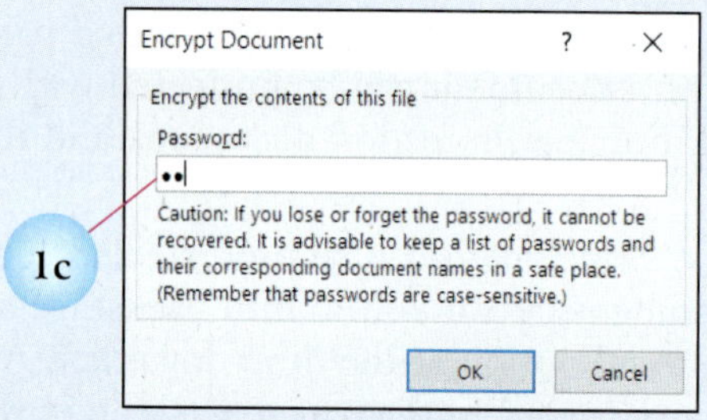

   d. Press the Enter key.
   e. At the Confirm Password dialog box, type your initials again in uppercase letters in the *Reenter password* text box (the text will display as bullets) and then press the Enter key.
2. Click the Back button to return to the document.
3. Save and then close the document.
4. Open **8-REAgrmnt**.
5. At the Password dialog box, type your initials in uppercase letters in the *Enter password to open file* text box and then press the Enter key.
6. Save **8-REAgrmnt**.
7. Remove the password from the document by completing the following steps:
   a. Click the File tab and then click the *Info* option.
   b. Click the Protect Document button and then click *Encrypt with Password*.
   c. Delete the circles in the *Password* text box.
   d. Click OK.
   e. Click the Back button to return to the document.
8. Save and then close **8-REAgrmnt**.

Check Your Work

Quick Steps

Open Document in Different Views

1. Display Open dialog box.
2. Click document name.
3. Click Open button arrow.
4. Click option at drop-down list.

Opening a Document in Different Views

Use the Open button at the Open dialog box to open a document in different views. At the Open dialog box, click the Open button arrow and a drop-down list of options displays. Click the *Open Read-Only* option and the document opens in Read-Only mode. In Read-Only mode, changes can be made to the document but the document cannot be saved with the same name.

Click the *Open as Copy* option and a copy of the document opens with the text *Copy (1)* before the document name in the Title bar. Click the *Open in Protected View* option and the document opens with the text *(Protected View)* after the document name in the Title bar. A message bar displays above the document indicating that the file was opened in Protected view. To edit the document, click the Enable Editing button in the message bar. Open a document with the *Open and Repair* option and Word will open a new version of the document and attempt to resolve any issues.

Activity 4c Opening a Document in Different Views

Part 3 of 4

1. Open a document as a read-only document by completing the following steps:
   a. Press Ctrl + F12 to display the Open dialog box and then navigate to your WL2C8 folder.
   b. Click the document name ***8-REAgrmnt***. (Click only one time.)
   c. Click the Open button arrow (in the bottom right corner of the dialog box) and then click *Open Read-Only* at the drop-down list.
   d. The document opens as a read-only document. Notice that *Read-Only* displays after the name of the document in the Title bar.
   e. Close the document.

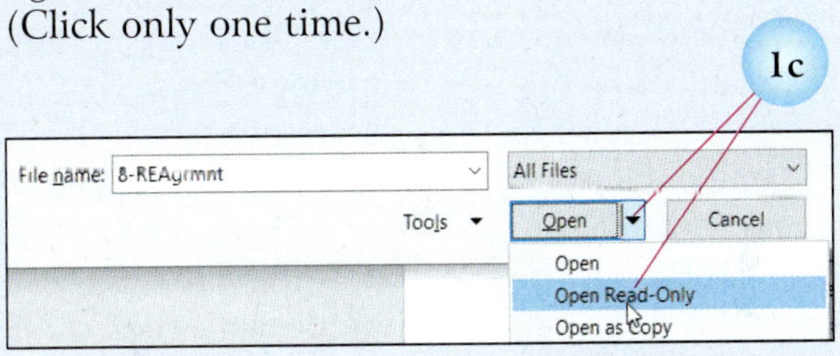

2. Open a document in Protected view by completing the following steps:
   a. Press Ctrl + F12 to display the Open dialog box.
   b. Click the document name ***PremProduce***.
   c. Click the Open button arrow and then click *Open in Protected View* at the drop-down list.
   d. Notice the message bar stating that the file was opened in Protected view.
   e. Click each tab and notice that most of the formatting options are dimmed.
   f. Click in the document and then click the Enable Editing button in the message bar. This removes *Protected View* after the document name in the Title bar and makes available the options on the tabs.

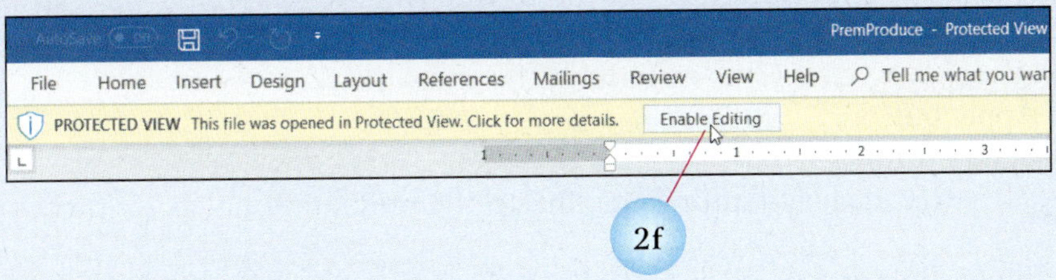

3. Close the document.

Sharing a Document Electronically

When collaborating with others in a workplace environment, being able to share files electronically may be useful. To share a document electronically with others, the document must be saved to a OneDrive account or a shared location such as a website. Share a document saved to a OneDrive account or other shared location by clicking the Share button in the upper right corner of the screen; clicking the File tab and then clicking the *Share* option; or by clicking the File tab, clicking the *Info* option, and then clicking the Share button below the document name.

At the Share window or task pane that displays, follow the instructions to send a link and invite others to view the document by typing in the email addresses of people to be invited. By default, anyone who is invited to view the document can also make edits to it. This option can be changed so that people can only view, but not edit, the document.

Activity 4d Sharing a Document Electronically

Part 4 of 4

Note: To complete this optional activity, you need to be connected to the internet and have a OneDrive account. Depending on your version of Word, the activity steps may vary. Activity 4d assumes that a Share window will display. If a Share task pane displays, check with your instructor to determine the steps to follow to share your document.

1. Open **8-REAgrmnt**.
2. Save **8-REAgrmnt** to your OneDrive account folder and name it **8-REAgrmnt-Shared** by completing the following steps:
   a. Click the File tab and then click the *Save As* option.
   b. Double-click the OneDrive account in the middle panel.
   c. At the Save As dialog box with the OneDrive account folder active, type **8-REAgrmnt-Shared** in the *File name* text box and then click the Save button.
3. With **8-REAgrmnt-Shared** open, click the Share button in the upper right corner of the screen.

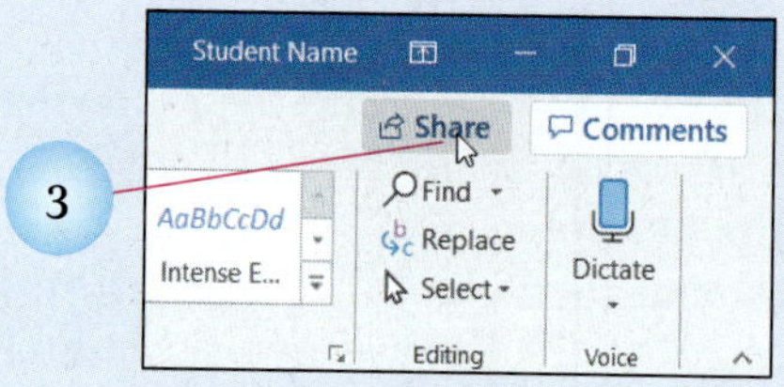

4. With the insertion point positioned in the *Enter a name or email address* text box (displays above the blue line) in the Share window, type the email address for your instructor and/or the email of a classmate or friend.
5. Click the Link settings option near the top of the window to specify who can edit the presentation.
6. Click the *Allow editing* check box to remove the check mark.
7. Click the Apply button.
8. Click the Send button.
9. At the message that displays stating the link to the presentation was sent, click the Close button.
10. Check with your instructor, classmate, and/or friend to determine if he or she was able to open the email containing the link to your document.
11. Close **8-REAgrmnt-Shared** saved to your OneDrive account folder.

Activity 5 Manage Versions of a Document 1 Part

You will decrease the autorecovery time to 1 minute, open a document containing an advertising flyer for a produce market, and make changes to it without saving the file. You will then review autorecovered versions of the document created automatically by Word.

Tutorial

Managing Document Versions

Manage Document

Quick Steps

Display UnsavedFiles Folder

1. Click File tab.
2. Click *Info* option.
3. Click Manage Document button.
4. Click *Recover Unsaved Documents*.

OR

1. Click File tab.
2. Click *Open* option.
3. Click Recover Unsaved Documents button.

Delete Autorecover Backup File

1. Click File tab.
2. Click *Info* option.
3. Right-click autorecover backup file.
4. Click *Delete This Version* at shortcut menu.

Delete All Unsaved Files

1. Click File tab.
2. Click *Info* option.
3. Click Manage Document button.
4. Click *Delete All Unsaved Documents*.
5. Click Yes.

Managing Document Versions

When working in an open document, Word automatically saves it every 10 minutes. This automatic backup feature can be very helpful if the document is closed accidentally without saving it or the power to the computer is disrupted. As backups of the open document are automatically saved, they are listed at the right of the Manage Document button at the Info backstage area, as shown in Figure 8.10. Each autorecovered document displays with *Today* followed by the time and *(autorecovery)*. When the document is saved and then closed, the autorecover backup documents are deleted.

To open an autorecover backup document, click the File tab, click the *Info* option, and then click the autorecover document. (Backup documents display at the right of the Manage Document button.) The document opens as a read-only document and a message bar displays with a Compare button and Restore button. Click the Compare button and the autorecover document is compared to the original document. Review the comparison to decide which changes to accept and reject. Click the Restore button and a message displays stating that the selected version will overwrite the saved version. At this message, click OK.

When a document is saved, the autorecover backup documents are deleted. However, if a document is closed without being saved (after 10 minutes) or the power is disrupted, Word keeps the autorecover backup files in the UnsavedFiles

Figure 8.10 Autorecover Documents at the Info Backstage Area

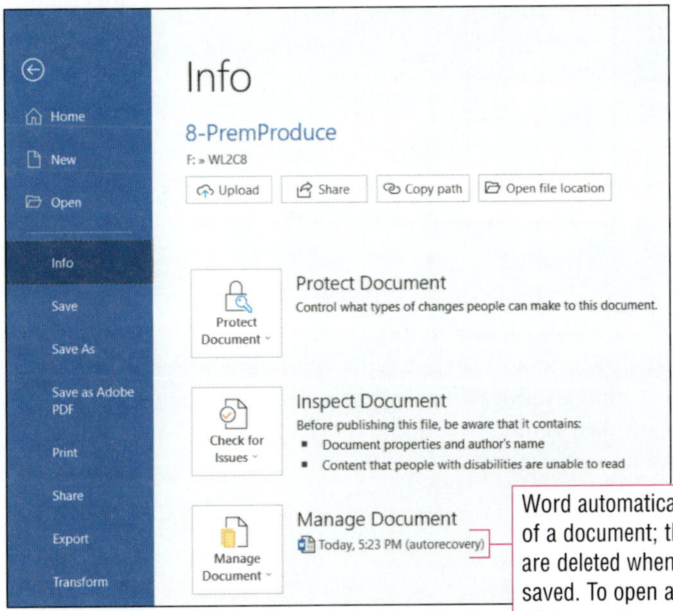

Word automatically creates backups of a document; these backups are deleted when the document is saved. To open a backup document, click an autorecover version.

folder on the hard drive. Access this folder by clicking the Manage Document button at the Info backstage area and then clicking *Recover Unsaved Documents*. At the Open dialog box, double-click the backup file to be opened. The UnsavedFiles folder can also be displayed by clicking the File tab, clicking the *Open* option, and then clicking the Recover Unsaved Documents button below the *Recent* option list. Files in the UnsavedFiles folder are kept for four days after a document is created. After that, they are automatically deleted.

Delete an autorecover backup file by displaying the Info backstage area, right-clicking the autorecover file (at the right of the Manage Document button), and then clicking *Delete This Version* at the shortcut menu. At the confirmation message, click the Yes button. To delete all unsaved files from the UnsavedFiles folder, display a blank document, click the File tab, click the *Info* option, click the Manage Document button, and then click the *Delete All Unsaved Documents* option at the drop-down list. At the confirmation message, click Yes.

Quick Steps

Change AutoRecover Time

1. Click File tab.
2. Click *Options*.
3. Click *Save*.
4. Type minutes in *Save AutoRecover information every* measurement box.
5. Click OK.

As mentioned previously, Word automatically saves a backup of an unsaved document every 10 minutes. To change this default setting, click the File tab and then click *Options*. At the Word Options dialog box, click *Save* in the left panel. Notice that the *Save AutoRecover information every* measurement box is set at 10 minutes. To change this number, click the measurement box up arrow to increase the number of minutes between autorecovers or click the down arrow to decrease the number of minutes.

Activity 5 Opening and Deleting an Autorecover Document

Part 1 of 1

1. At a blank screen, decrease the autorecover time to 1 minute by completing the following steps:
   a. Click the File tab and then click *Options*.
   b. At the Word Options dialog box, click *Save* in the left panel.
   c. Click the *Save AutoRecover information every* measurement box down arrow until *1* displays.

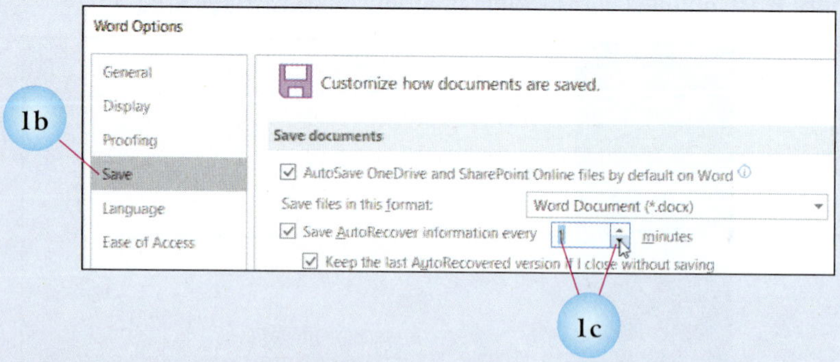

   d. Click OK to close the dialog box.
2. Open **PremProduce** and save it with the name **8-PremProduce**.
3. Press Ctrl + End to move the insertion point to the end of the document and then type your first and last names.

4. Leave the document open for more than one minute without making any further changes. After at least one minute has passed, click the File tab and then, if necessary, click the *Info* option. Check to see if an autorecover document displays at the right of the Manage Document button. (If not, click the Back button to return to the document and wait a few more minutes.)
5. When an autorecover document displays at the Info backstage area, click the Back button to return to the document.
6. Scroll down the document, select the SmartArt graphic, and then delete it.
7. Click the File tab, click the *Info* option if necessary, and then click the autorecover document at the right of the Manage Document button. If more than one autorecover document displays, click the one at the top of the list (the most recent autorecover document). This opens the autorecover document as a read-only file.

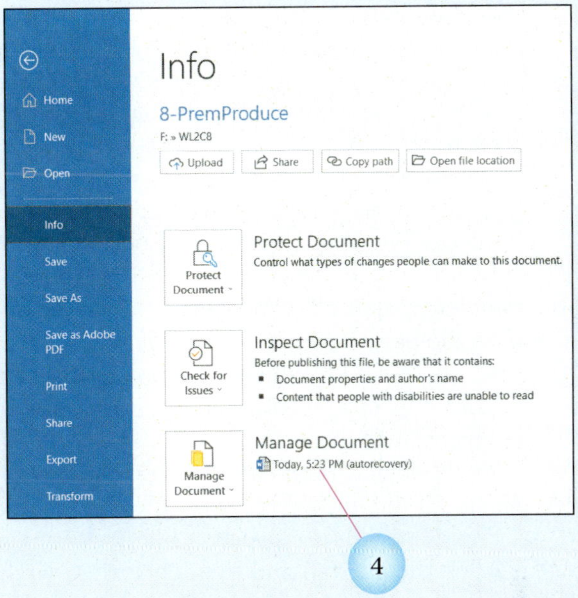

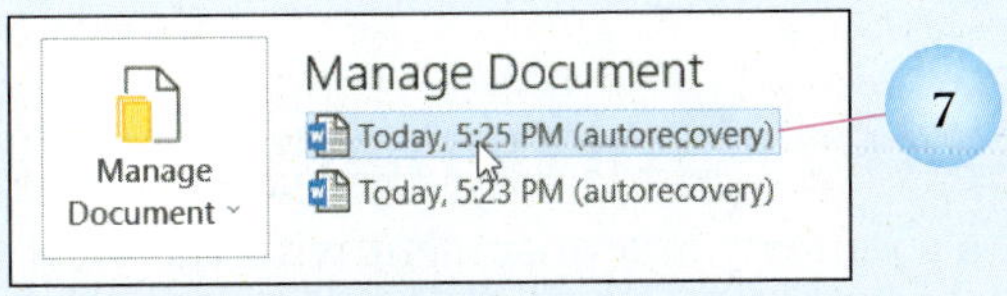

8. Restore the document to the autorecovered version by clicking the Restore button in the message bar.

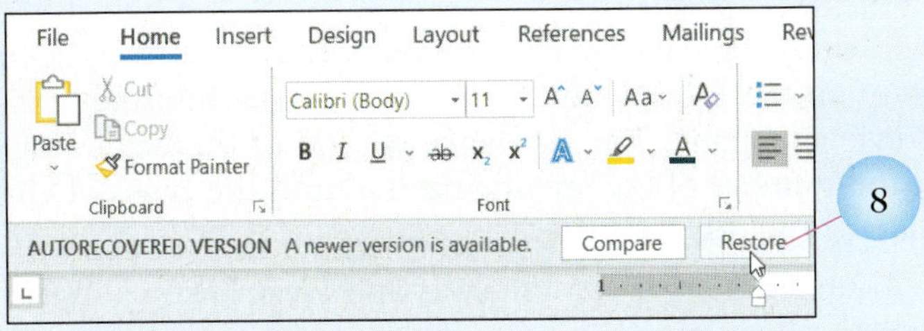

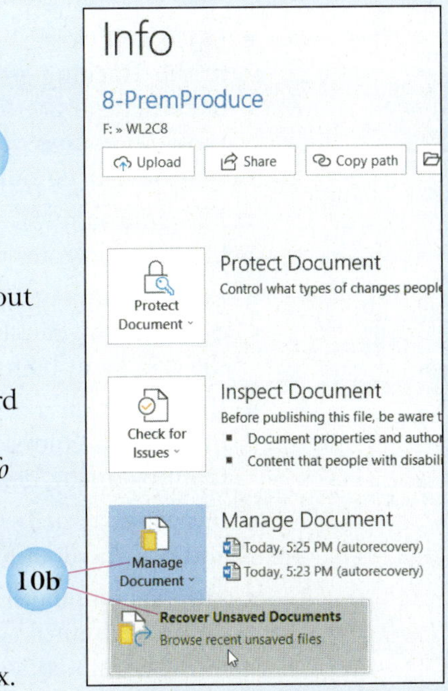

9. At the message stating that the last saved version is about to be overwritten with the selected version, click OK. (This saves the document with the SmartArt.)
10. Check to see what versions of previous documents Word has saved by completing the following steps:
    a. Click the File tab and then, if necessary, click the *Info* option.
    b. Click the Manage Document button and then click *Recover Unsaved Documents* at the drop-down list.
    c. At the Open dialog box, check the documents that display in the content pane.
    d. Click the Cancel button to close the Open dialog box.

11. Delete an autorecover backup file by completing the following steps:
    a. Click the File tab and then click the *Info* option.
    b. Right-click the first autorecover backup file name at the right of the Manage Document button.
    c. Click *Delete This Version* at the shortcut menu.
    d. At the message asking whether to delete the selected version, click the Yes button.

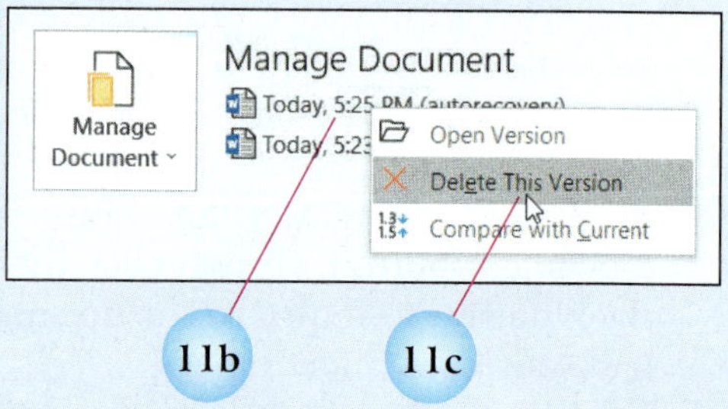

12. Return the autorecovery time to 10 minutes by completing the following steps:
    a. At the backstage area, click *Options*.
    b. At the Word Options dialog box, click *Save* in the left panel.
    c. Click the *Save AutoRecover information every* measurement box up arrow until *10* displays.
    d. Click OK to close the dialog box.
13. Save, print, and then close **8-PremProduce**.
14. Delete all the unsaved backup files by completing the following steps:
    a. Press Ctrl + N to display a blank document.
    b. Click the File tab and then click the *Info* option.
    c. Click the Manage Document button and then click *Delete All Unsaved Documents*.
    d. At the message that displays, click Yes.
15. Click the Back button to return to the blank document.

Check Your Work

Chapter Summary

- Insert a comment in a document with the New Comment button in the Comments group on the Review tab or the Comment button in the upper right corner of the screen. A comment balloon opens and displays in the right margin. If any previous settings have been applied, the Reviewing pane, rather than a comment balloon, may open.
- Open and close the Reviewing pane by clicking the Reviewing Pane button in the Tracking group on the Review tab. Comments can be inserted in a document in the Reviewing pane. The summary section of the Reviewing pane provides counts of the number of comments inserted and the types of changes that have been made to the document.
- Navigate to review comments using the Previous and Next buttons in the Comments group on the Review tab.
- Edit a comment in the Reviewing pane or in a comment balloon. Reply to a comment by clicking the Reply button at the right of the reviewer's name in the comment balloon and then typing the reply.
- If changes are made to a document by different users, the changes display in different colors. The user name and initials can be changed at the Word Options dialog box with *General* selected.
- Print a document with or without the comments or print only the comments and not the document.
- Delete a comment by clicking the Next button in the Comments group on the Review tab until the comment is selected and then clicking the Delete button in the Comments group.

- Use the Track Changes feature when more than one person is reviewing and editing a document. Turn on Track Changes by clicking the Track Changes button in the Tracking group on the Review tab.
- The *Display for Review* option box in the Tracking group on the Review tab has a default setting of *Simple Markup*, which shows changes in the document and a vertical change line at the left margin where the change was made. This setting can be changed to *All Markup*, showing all changes in the document along with the original text or *No Markup*, showing the document with all of the changes applied.
- With the *Display for Review* option box set at *All Markup*, specify what tracking information displays in document with options at the Balloon side menu. Display this side menu by clicking the Show Markup button in the Tracking group on the Review tab and then pointing to *Balloons*.
- Display information about tracked changes—such as the author's name, date and time, and type of change—by hovering the mouse pointer over a change. After approximately one second, a box displays with the information. Another method for displaying information about tracked changes is to display the Reviewing pane.
- To ensure that all changes made to a document are tracked, lock the Track Changes feature by clicking the Track Changes button arrow in the Tracking group on the Review tab, clicking *Lock Tracking*, and then typing a password at the Lock Tracking dialog box.
- Customize what tracked changes display in a document with options at the Show Markup button drop-down list. At the drop-down list, remove check marks from those options that should not display and specify what reviewer changes should display.
- Change Track Changes default settings with options at the Advanced Track Changes Options dialog box. Display this dialog box by clicking the Tracking group dialog box launcher and then clicking the Advanced Options button at the Track Changes Options dialog box.
- When reviewing a document, move to the next change by clicking the Next button in the Changes group on the Review tab and move to the previous change by clicking the Previous button.
- Use the Accept and Reject buttons in the Changes group on the Review tab to accept and reject changes made in a document.
- Restrict formatting and editing in a document and apply a password to protect it with options in the Restrict Editing task pane. Display this task pane by clicking the Review tab and then clicking the Restrict Editing button in the Protect group.
- Apply formatting restrictions in a document by specifying what styles are and are not allowed at the Formatting Restrictions dialog box. Display this dialog box by clicking the Settings hyperlink in the *Formatting restrictions* section of the Restrict Editing task pane.
- Enforce restrictions to a document by clicking the Yes, Start Enforcing Protection button at the Restrict Editing task pane and then entering a password at the Start Enforcing Protection dialog box.
- Apply editing restrictions in a document using options in the *Editing restrictions* section of the Restrict Editing task pane.

- Mark a document as final, which saves it as a read-only document, by clicking the Protect Document button at the Info backstage area and then clicking *Mark as Final* at the drop-down list. Typing, editing commands, and proofing marks are turned off when a document is marked as final.
- Protect a document with a password by clicking the Protect Document button, click the *Encrypt with Password* option, and then specify a password at the Encrypt Document dialog box.
- Another method for displaying the Restrict Editing task pane is to click the Protect Document button at the Info backstage area and then click *Restrict Editing* at the drop-down list.
- Open a document in different views with options at the Open button drop-down list at the Open dialog box.
- Share a document that has been saved to a OneDrive account or a shared location such as a website with options at the Share window or Share task pane. Use options at the Share window or task pane to identify who will receive the shared document and to specify whether or not the shared document can be viewed only or viewed and edited.
- By default, Word automatically saves a backup of an unsaved document every 10 minutes. A list of autorecover backup documents of an open document displays at the right of the Manage Document button at the Info backstage area. To open an autorecover backup document, click the File tab, click the Info option, and then click the name of the document.
- When a document is saved, Word automatically deletes the autorecover backup documents. However, if a document is closed without saving it or the power to the computer is disrupted, Word keeps a backup document in the UnsavedFiles folder on the hard drive. Access this folder by clicking the Manage Document button at the Info backstage area and then clicking *Recover Unsaved Documents* at the drop-down list.
- Delete an autorecover backup file by displaying the Info backstage area, right-clicking the autorecover backup file, and then clicking *Delete This Version* at the shortcut menu.
- Delete all the unsaved documents from the UnsavedFiles folder by displaying a blank document, clicking the File tab, clicking the Manage Document button, and then clicking *Delete All Unsaved Documents*. At the message that displays, click Yes.
- Change the 10-minute autorecover default setting with the *Save AutoRecover information every* measurement at the Word Options dialog box with *Save* selected in the left panel.

Commands Review

FEATURE	RIBBON TAB, GROUP	BUTTON, OPTION	KEYBOARD SHORTCUT
accept changes	Review, Changes		
Advanced Track Changes Options dialog box	Review, Tracking	, Advanced Options	
balloons	Review, Tracking	, *Balloons*	
delete comment	Review, Comments		
display for review	Review, Tracking		
Encrypt Document dialog box	File, *Info*	, *Encrypt with Password*	
Formatting Restrictions dialog box	Review, Protect	, *Settings*	
new comment	Review, Comments		
next comment	Review, Comments		
next revision	Review, Changes		
previous comment	Review, Comments		
previous revision	Review, Changes		
reject changes	Review, Changes		
Restrict Editing task pane	Review, Protect		
Reviewing pane	Review, Tracking		
Share window or task pane			
show markup	Review, Tracking		
Track Changes	Review, Tracking		Ctrl + Shift + E
Track Changes Options dialog box	Review, Tracking		
UnsavedFiles folder	File, *Info*	, *Recover Unsaved Documents*	

Index

A

Absolute position option, 130
Accept button, 226
Accessibility Checker, 30–32
Add Gallery to Quick Access Toolbar, 199–201
Address Block button, 167
Add Text button, 106
Advanced Track Changes Options dialog box, 225–226
Alignment option, 130–131
Allow overlap option, 131
alphanumeric sort, punctuation and symbols in, 58
American Psychological Association (APA) style, 83–84, 94
antonyms, 49—50
Artistic Effects button, 133–135
AutoCaption button, 113
AutoCorrect Options button, 151
AutoExpansion feature, 151
autosave backup document, 241–244
AutoText gallery, saving to content to, 192–194

B

bibliography
- creating, 83–95
- formatting, 94–95
- inserting, 92–93
- managing sources, 89–92
- modifying and updating, 93–94

Bibliography button, 92
Block Authors button, 230
body fonts, finding and replacing, 21–23
Book layout option, 130
Bookmark button, 116
Bookmark dialog box, 117
bookmarks
- deleting, 117
- displaying, 116–117
- inserting and navigating with, 116–118
- for insertion point at specific location, 117
- naming, 116
- for selected text, 117

Break Link button, 142
Building Block Organizer dialog box, 203
building blocks
- defined, 187
- deleting, 203–204
- editing building block properties, 195–196
- inserting, 188–204
  - as buttons on Quick Access toolbar, 199–201
  - custom, 196–201
- modifying custom, 198–201
- saving
  - content as, 191–194
  - content to Quick Part gallery, 192–194
  - in different template, 202–203
- sorting, 188–190

Building Blocks Organizer dialog box, 188–189, 191

C

Caption dialog box, 110, 113
captions
- creating, 110, 114–115
- customizing, 113–115

changes, tracking, 220–229
character formatting, 4–13
- adjusting character spacing, 4–5
- applying OpenType features, 6–9
- applying Text Effects, 9–11
- changing default font, 12–13
- finding and replacing
  - characters and fonts, 17–24
  - special characters, 19–20
  - using wildcard characters, 23–24
- kerning, 5

character spacing, adjusting, 4–5
Chart button, 151
Chart Elements button, 153
Chart Filters button, 153–154
charts, 151–160
- changing
  - color in, 153
  - design of, 155–156
- creating
  - column chart, 152
  - pie chart, 158–160
- entering data in Excel worksheet to create, 151
- formatting
  - changing, 156–158
  - with chart buttons, 153–155
  - with Chart Tools Format tab buttons, 155–158
  - with task pane options, 158–160

Chart Styles button, 153
Chart Tools Design tab, 155
Chart Tools Format tab, 155–156
Check Document button, 38
Check for Errors button, 169
Check for Issues button, 28
Checking and Reporting Errors dialog box, 169
Chicago Manual of Style (Chicago), 83, 94
chronologic sort, 58
citations
- choosing style for, 83, 95
- creating, 83–95
- editing sources, 88
- inserting

with existing source, 88
pages number in, 89
sources and citation placeholder, 85–87
managing sources, 89–92
color
changing in charts, 153
customizing track changes options and, 225–226
to distinguish comments from different users, 217
column chart, creating, 152
columns, sorting text in, 59–60
comment balloon, 212–213
comments, 212–219
comment balloon, 212–213
deleting, 217–218
distinguishing comments from different users, 217
editing, 215–216
inserting, 212–219
navigating between, 215
printing, 217
replying to, 216
resolving, 217–219
showing, 215
Compare button, 241
Compatibility Check, 32–33
contextual alternates, 8–9
copyrighted intellectual property, 13–14
Cover Page gallery, saving content to, 191
Create Custom Dictionary dialog box, 46
Create Link button, 142
Create New Building Block dialog box, 191
Create New Document button, 120
Create Source dialog box, 85, 86
Cross-reference button, 123
Cross-reference dialog box, 123–124
cross-references
defined, 123
inserting and navigating with, 123–124
Custom Dictionaries dialog box, 46
customizing
building blocks, 196–201
captions in table of figures, 113–115
dictionary, 45–47
field formats, 207–209
icons, 145–146
images, 130–135
markup display, 222–225
objects, 130–150
page numbering, 74–75
photograph, 134–135
shapes, 137–139
spelling checker, 38–39
table of contents, 103–105
text box, 135–144
3D models, 147–150
track changes options, 225–226

D

data source file
creating, 164–166
editing
records, 179–181
specific records, 177–178
main document merging with, 169–170
Date & Time button, 66
Delete button, 217
deleting
autosave backup file, 242–244
bookmark, 117
building blocks, 203–204
comments, 217–218
footnotes and endnotes, 81
table of figures, 113
dictionary
changing default, 45–47
creating custom, 45–47
removing, 46
digital signature, adding, 237
directory, merging, 175–176
Display for Review option, 220
Document Info button, 66
document inspector, 28–30
Document Inspector dialog box, 28–29
document properties
inserting, 27
into header or footer, 66
placeholders, 205–206
managing, 25–27
document property information, 25–26
documents
accessibility check, 30–32
comments, inserting and managing, 212–219
compatibility check, 32–33
encrypting, 237–238
grammar check, 41–43
inserting property placeholder, 205–206
linking
to new, 120–122
to place in, 119
managing
properties for, 25–27
versions of, 241–244
marking as final, 236–237
merging, 163–183
navigating in, 115–124
opening in different views, 238–239
protecting, 236–239
readability statistics for, 43–44
restricting, 229–235
spell check, 38–40
track changes, 220–229
word count for, 48, 50
Drawing Tools Format tab, 135, 137

E

Edit Data Source dialog box, 179
editing
building block properties, 195–196
citations and sources, 88
comments, 215–216

data source file, 177–181
footnotes and endnotes, 81–83
hyperlinks, 122–123
points in a shape, 140–141
Restrict Editing task pane, 229–230
restricting, 229, 233–234, 237
during spelling and grammar check, 38
wrap points in shape, 141–142
Editor feature, 38
Editor task pane, reading feature, 38
Edit Points option, 140–141
Edit Recipient List button, 177
Edit Shape button, 140
Edit Wrap Points option, 141–142
email address, linking to, 120
E-Mail Address button, 120
em dash, 15
Encrypt Document dialog box, 237–238
en dash, 15
endnotes
converting to footnotes, 82–83
creating, 78, 80
defined, 78
deleting, 81
inserting, 78–83
note reference number, 78–79
printing, 80
viewing and editing, 81–83
Envelope Options dialog box, 171
envelopes, merging, 171–173
Excel
entering data in worksheet to create chart, 151
linking to file in, from Word, 120–122

F

Field dialog box, 206–207
fields
choosing, 207
creating custom formats, 207–209
defined, 206
inserting, 206–209
marking table of contents entries as, 106–108
sorting on more than one, 59–60
updating, 207
figures. *See* table of figures
files, linking to file in another program, 120–122
finding and replacing
body and heading fonts, 21–23
characters and fonts, 17–24
font formatting, 17–18
paragraph formatting, 17–18
special characters, 19–20
styles, 20–21
using wildcard characters, 23–24
Find Recipient button, 169
Finish & Merge button, 169
First Record button, 169
Flesch-Kincaid Grade Level score, 43
Flesch Reading Ease score, 43
Font dialog box, advanced tab selected, 4–5
fonts
adjusting character spacing, 4–5
changing default, 12–13
contextual alternates, 8–9
finding and replacing
body and heading fonts, 21–23
formatting, 14–15
styles, 20–21
ligatures, 6, 7
stylistic sets, 8–9
Text Effects, 9–11
footers
default margins for, 68
defined, 66
for different sections, 72–73
first page footer, 70
inserting elements in, 66–67
for odd and even pages, 71–72
positioning, 68–69
Footer button, 66
Footer gallery, saving content to, 191, 193–194
Footnote and Endnote dialog box, 81
footnotes
converting to endnotes, 82–83
creating, 78–79
defined, 78
deleting, 81
inserting, 78–83
note reference number, 78–79
printing, 80
viewing and editing, 81–83
Format Picture task pane, 133
Format Selection button, 158
Format Shapes task pane, 135, 137
Format Text Effects dialog box, 9–10
formatting
bibliography or works cited page, 94–95
character formatting, 4–13
adjusting character spacing, 4–5
applying OpenType features, 6–9
applying Text Effects, 9–11
changing default font, 12–13
charts, 151–160
fields, 206–209
finding/replacing
body and heading fonts, 21–23

characters and fonts, 17–24
font formatting, 17–18
paragraph formatting, 17–18
special characters, 19–20
styles, 20–21
using wildcard characters, 23–24
inserting symbols and special characters
hyphens, 14–15
intellectual property symbols, 13–14
restricting, 230–231
shapes, 138–139
3D models, 150
Formatting Restrictions dialog box, 231

G

General Options dialog box, password options, 234–235
Go To button, 117
grammar checker, 38
changing options, 41–43
editing while using, 38
setting proofing language, 43
graphic, linking to, 120–122
Graphic Tools Format tab, 145
Greeting Line button, 167
grouping
images, text boxes, shapes, 137–138
objects, 137–138

H

headers
default margins for, 68
defined, 66
for different sections, 72–73
first page header, 70
inserting elements in, 66–67
not including in table sort, 61
for odd and even pages, 71–72
positioning, 68–69
Header button, 66
Header & Footer Tools Design tab, 66, 67, 68, 69
Header gallery, saving content to, 191
heading fonts, finding and replacing, 21–23
Headings tab, 115
Hyperlink button, 118
hyperlinks
editing, 122–123
inserting, 118–122
linking to
email address, 120
file in another program, 120–122
new document, 120–122
place in document, 119
using graphic, 120–122
navigating using, 119–120
purpose of, 118
removing, 122–123
in table of contents, 101, 104
hyphenation, 14-15
em and en dashes, 15
nonbreaking hyphens, 14–15
optional, 14
Hyphenation button, 14

I

icons, inserting and customizing, 145–146
Icons button, 145–146
images
applying artistic effects to, 133–135
applying formatting at Format Picture task pane, 133
customizing image layout, 130–150
grouping and ungrouping, 137–138
inserting and customizing clip art image, 131–133
Info backstage area, 25, 241–242
Insert Alignment Tab button, 68
Insert Caption button, 110
Insert Chart dialog box, 151
Insert Citation button, 85
Insert Endnote button, 78
Insert Footnote button, 78
Insert Hyperlink dialog box, 118
Insert Icons window, 145–146
inserting
bibliography, 92–93
bookmarks, 116–118
building blocks, 188–204
citations, 85–87
comments, 212–219
cross-references, 123–124
custom building blocks, 196–198
document properties, 27
placeholders, 205–206
endnotes, 78–83
fields, 206–209
footers, 66–75
footnotes, 78–83
headers, 66–75
hyperlinks, 118–123
icons, 145–146
line numbers, 48, 50–51
photograph, 134–135
Quick Parts, 188–204
source list, 92–93
table of contents, 100–103
table of figures, 111–112, 114–115
3D models, 147–150
works cited page, 92–93
insertion point, creating bookmark for desired location, 117
Insert Merge Field button, 167
Insert tab, 66, 188
Insert Table of Figures button, 110
intellectual property symbols, inserting, 13–14

K

Keep lines together option, 77–78
Keep with next option, 77–78
kerning, 5
keyboard shortcuts
  Insert Hyperlink dialog box, 118
  inserting intellectual property symbols, 13–14
  spelling and grammar check, 38
  thesaurus, 49
  update fields, 207

L

Label dialog box, 113
Label Options dialog box, 173
labels, merging, 173–175, 178
Language button, 43
Language group, 55
languages
  language option in thesaurus, 49
  translating text to/from different, 55–57
Last Record button, 169
Layout dialog box, 130–131
Layout Options button, 153
letters
  merge letters to customers, 164–170
  using Mail Merge wizard, 182–183
ligatures
  applying, 6, 7
  categories of, 6
line numbers, inserting, 48, 50–51
Line Numbers button, 48, 50
Line Numbers dialog box, 48, 51
lining number form, 6–7
linking
  breaking section link, 72–73
  hyperlinks
    to email address, 120
    to file in another program, 120–122
    to new document, 120–122
    to place in document, 119
    using graphics, 120–122
  text boxes, 142–144
Link to Previous button, 72
Lock anchor option, 131
Lock aspect ratio check box, 131
Lock Tracking dialog box, 222

M

mailing labels, merging, 173–175, 178
mail merge. *See* merging documents
Mail Merge Recipients dialog box, 177
Mail Merge wizard, 182–183
main document
  creating, 166–168
  merging with data source file, 169–170
Manage Sources button, 89
Manage Versions button, 241
Mark Table of Contents Entry dialog box, 106–107
markup in track changes
  customizing display of, 222–225
  printing, 223
  showing, 220–221
Master List list box, 89
merging documents, 163–183
  checking for errors, 169
  data source file
    creating, 164–166
    editing, 177–181
  directory, 175–176
  envelopes, 171–173
  labels, 173–175
  main document
    creating, 166–168
    merging with data source file, 169–170
  previewing merge, 169
  using Mail Merge wizard, 182–183
metadata, 28
Modern Language Association (MLA) style, 83–84, 94
Modify Building Block dialog box, 195
Move object with text option, 131

N

navigation
  with bookmarks, 116–118
  between comments, 215
  with cross-references, 123–124
  with hyperlinks, 118–123
  with Navigation pane, 115–116
  table of contents for, 101
  track changes, 226–229
Navigation pane, 115–116
New Address List dialog box, 164–165
New Comment button, 212
New Label button, 113
Next button, 215, 226
Next Footnote button, 81
Next Record button, 169
Nonbreaking Hyphen option, 14–15
nonbreaking spaces, inserting, 16
note reference number, 78–79
Numbering button, 113
numbers/numbering
  changing page numbering, 74–75
  changing section numbering, 75–76
  number forms, 6–7
  spacing, 6–7
Number spacing option, 6–7
numeric sort, 58

O

objects
  customizing, 130–150
  grouping and ungrouping, 137–138
old-style number form, 6–7
Online Pictures button, 67

Online 3D Models window, 147
Open button, 238
opening
autosaved backup version, 241–244
document in different views, 238–239
OpenType font file format
applying ligatures and number forms, 6, 7
applying stylistic set and contextual alternates, 8–9
ligature categories, 6
overview of, 6
orphan, defined, 77

P

page break, soft, 77
Page break before option, 77–78
Page Number button, 74, 100
Page Number Format dialog box, 74, 100–101
page numbers
changing numbering, 74–75
customizing, 74–75
inserting in citations, 89
for table of contents, 100–101
Pages tab, 115
Pan & Zoom button, 147
Paragraph dialog box, 77–78
paragraphs
finding and replacing formatting, 14–15
sorting text in, 58–59
password
encrypting document with, 237–238
protecting document with, 234–235
photograph, inserting and customizing, 134–135
Picture Tools Format tab, 130, 133, 137
pie chart, creating and formatting, 158–160
plagiarism, 83
positioning, header and footer, 68–69
PowerPoint, linking to file in, from Word, 120–122
Preview Results button, 169
Previous button, 215, 226
Previous Record button, 169
printing
comments, 217
endnotes, 80
footnotes, 80
markup in track changes, 223
sections, 75–76
pronunciation feature, 49
proofing documents
displaying word count, 48
inserting line numbers, 48
Smart Lookup feature, 52–54
spelling and grammar check, 38–47
thesaurus and, 49–52
translating text to/from different languages, 55–57
Proofing option, 38–39
properties
inserting document property placeholder, 205–206
managing for documents, 25–27
Properties button, 26
Properties dialog box, 26
Protect Document button, 236
protecting documents, 236–239
adding digital signature, 237
encrypting document, 237–238
enforcing restrictions, 232–233
marking document as final, 236–237
opening document in different views, 238–239
with password, 234–235
restricting editing, 233–234
restricting formatting, 230–231
punctuation, in alphanumeric sort, 58

Q

Quick Access toolbar
adding building block gallery as button, 199–201
Quick Part gallery, saving content to, 192–194
Quick Parts, 188–204
Building Blocks Organizer dialog box, 188–189
deleting building blocks, 203–204
drop-down list shortcut menu, 196–197
editing building block properties, 195–196
inserting
building blocks, 188–204
custom building blocks, 196–198
document property placeholders, 205–206
saving
building blocks in different templates, 202–203
saving content
to AutoText gallery, 192–194
as building blocks, 191–194
to Quick Part gallery, 192–194
to specific gallery, 193–194
sorting building blocks, 188–190
Quick Parts button, 67, 188

R

readability statistics, 4344
reading feature, Editor task pane, 38
Read-Only mode, 238
Reference tab, 81
registered trademark symbol, 13–14
Reject button, 226
Replace button, 17
Reply button, 216

replying, to comments, 216
research paper/reports
citations and bibliographies, 83–95
first page formatting, 84–85
footnotes and endnotes, 78–83
formatting guidelines, 83–84
resolving, comments, 217–219
Restore button, 241
Restrict Editing button, 229, 237
Restrict Editing task pane, 229–230
restricting
adding digital signature, 237
editing, 229, 233–234, 237
encrypting document, 237–238
enforcing restrictions, 232–233
formatting, 230–231
marking document as final, 236–237
Results tab, 115
review, displaying changes for, 220–221
Reviewing pane, inserting comments in, 213–215
Reviewing Pane button, 213
Review tab, 38, 49, 55
revisions
accepting or rejecting, 226–229
navigating, 226–229
RoamingCustom.dic, 45
Rotation option, 131

S

saving
building blocks in different template, 202–203
content as building blocks, 191–194
content to AutoText gallery, 192–194
content to Quick Part gallery, 192–194
Scale options, 4–5
Screen Tip button, 118
Screen Tips, hyperlinks, 118, 119
sections
breaking section link, 72–73
changing section numbering, 75–76
creating headers/footers for different, 72–73
printing, 75–76
Select Recipients button, 164
Set As Default button, 12
shapes
customizing, 137–139
editing points in, 140–141
editing wrap points in, 141–142
formatting, 138–139
grouping and ungrouping, 137–138
inserting text box on, 142
Shape Styles group, 158
shared documents, 211–244
inserting and managing comments, 212–219
sharing electronically, 239–240
tracking changes, 220–229
Share task pane, 239–240
Show Comments button, 215
Show Markup button, 220
Show Notes button, 81
Smart Lookup button, 52
Smart Lookup feature, 52–54
Smart Lookup task pane, 52–53
soft page break, 77
Sort button, 58
sorting
alphanumeric, numeric and chronologic, 58
building blocks, 188–190
on more than one field, 59–60
text
in columns, 59–60
in paragraphs, 58–59
in tables, 61
Sort Options dialog box, 58–59
Sort Text dialog box, 58
Source Manager dialog box, 89–90
sources
editing, 88
inserting, 85–87
existing, 88
source list, 92–93
managing, 89–92
placeholders for, 85–87
spacing
adjusting character spacing and kerning, 4–5
inserting nonbreaking spaces, 16
special characters. *See* symbols and special characters
spelling checker
creating custom dictionary for, 45–47
customizing, 38–39
editing during, 38
errors found by, 38
setting proofing language, 43
with words in uppercase, 39–40
Start Enforcing Protection dialog box, 232–233
Start Mail Merge button, 164
styles
finding and replacing, 20–21
for table of contents, 100
stylistic set, 8–9
symbols and special characters
in alphanumeric sort, 58
finding and replacing, 19–20
using wildcard characters, 23–24
inserting
hyphens, 14–15
intellectual property symbols, 13–14
nonbreaking spaces, 16
synonyms, 49–50
replacing with shortcut menu, 52

T

table of contents, 100–109
applying styles, 100
assigning levels to, 106
customizing, 103–105
inserting, 100–103
marking entries as fields, 106–108
navigating using, 101
numbering pages of, 100–101
removing, 104
updating, 104–105, 109
Table of Contents button, 100
Table of Contents dialog box, 103
Table of Figures dialog box, 111
table of figures, 110–115
creating captions, 110, 114–115
customizing captions, 113–115
deleting, 113
inserting, 111, 114–115
updating, 113
tables, sorting text in, 61
Tell Me feature
Smart Lookup feature and, 52
template, saving
building blocks in different, 202–203
content as building blocks, 192–194
text
page breaks and keeping text together, 77–78
sorting
in columns, 59–60
in paragraphs, 58–59
in tables, 61
translating to/from different languages, 55–57
text box
customizing, 135–144
grouping and ungrouping, 137–138
inserting on shape, 142
linking and unlinking, 142–144
Text Box gallery, saving content to, 191, 193–194
Text effects, applying, 9–11
Text Effects and Typography button, 6
Text Effects button, 9
Text Fill, 9–10
Text Outline, 9–10
Text Wrapping tab, 131
thesaurus
language option, 49
pronunciation feature, 49
using, 49–52
Thesaurus button, 49
Thesaurus task pane, 49
3D models
inserting and customizing, 147–150
3D Models button, 147
Track Changes button, 220
Track Changes feature, 220–229
accepting or rejecting revisions, 226–229
changing user information, 222–225
customizing
change options, 225–226
markup display, 222–225
displaying
changes for review, 220–221
information about, 222
locking, 222
navigating revisions, 226–229
showing markup, 220–221
Track Changes Options dialog box, 222–223
trademark symbol, 13–14
Translate button, 55
translation, to/from different languages, 55–57
choosing translation language, 55
preparing documents for, 57

U

ungrouping
images, text boxes, shapes, 137–138
objects, 137–138
unlinking
breaking section link, 72–73
text boxes, 142–144
Update Table button, 104, 113
updating
bibliography, 93–94
table of contents, 104–105, 109
table of figures, 113
users
changing information of, 222–225
distinguishing comments from different, 217

V

views, opening document in different, 238–239
View tab, 115

W

widow, defined, 77
Widow/Orphan control option, 77–78
wildcard characters
finding and replacing using, 23–24
functions of common, 23
WordArt Styles group task pane, 135, 158
word count, displaying, 48, 50
Word Count button, 48
Word Count dialog box, 48
Word Options dialog box
general selected, 217
workgroup, 211
works cited page
formatting, 94–95
inserting, 92–93
modifying and updating, 93–94
wrap points, 141–142
Wrap Text button, 141

Interior Photo Credits

Page GS-1 (banner image) © lowball-jack/GettyImages; *page GS-1, (in Figure G.1)* all images courtesy of Paradigm Education Solutions; *page GS-2*, © irbis picture/Shutterstock.com; *page GS-3*, © th3fisa/Shutterstock.com; *page GS-4*, © goldyg/Shutterstock.com; *page GS-5*, © Pressmaster/Shutterstock.com.

Contents

Unit 1
Formatting and Customizing Documents 1

Chapter 1 Applying Advanced Formatting 3

Chapter 2 Proofing Documents 7

Chapter 3 Inserting Headers, Footers, and References 13

Chapter 4 Creating Specialized Tables and Navigating in a Document 19

Unit 1 Performance Assessment 25

Unit 2
Editing and Formatting Documents 31

Chapter 5 Customizing Objects and Creating Charts 33

Chapter 6 Merging Documents 41

Chapter 7 Managing Building Blocks and Fields 47

Chapter 8 Managing Shared Documents 53

Unit 2 Performance Assessment 59

Microsoft®

Word Level 2

Unit 1

Formatting and Customizing Documents

Chapter 1 Applying Advanced Formatting

Chapter 2 Proofing Documents

Chapter 3 Inserting Headers, Footers, and References

Chapter 4 Creating Specialized Tables and Navigating in a Document

Unit 1 Performance Assessment

Applying Advanced Formatting

CHAPTER 1

The online course includes additional review and assessment resources.

Skills Assessment

Assessment 1
Apply Character Spacing and OpenType Features to a Donations Document

1. Open **PRDonations** and then save it with the name **1-PRDonations**.
2. Select the quote text *"In every community there is work to be done. In every nation there are wounds to heal. In every heart there is the power to do it."* and then apply stylistic set 4. (Do this at the Font dialog box with the Advanced tab selected.)
3. Select the heading *Domestic Donations* and change the scale to 90% and the spacing to Expanded. (Do this at the Font dialog box with the Advanced tab selected.)
4. Apply the same formatting in Step 3 to the heading *International Donations*.
5. Select the numbers in the *Domestic Donations* section. ***Hint: To select only the numbers, position the mouse pointer at the beginning of $450,000, press and hold down the Alt key, use the mouse pointer to drag down and select the four numbers in the second column, and then release the Alt key.***
6. With the numbers selected, change the number spacing to Tabular spacing. (Do this at the Font dialog box with the Advanced tab selected.)
7. Select the numbers in the *International Donations* section and then change the number spacing to Tabular spacing.
8. Select the text *We are dedicated to working toward a more just and peaceful world.* and then insert a check mark in the *Use Contextual Alternates* check box at the Font dialog box with the Advanced tab selected.
9. Save, print, and then close **1-PRDonations**.

Assessment 2
Find and Replace Formatting and Use a Wildcard Character in an Employee Guide Document

1. Open **EmpGuide** and then save it with the name **1-EmpGuide**.
2. Find text set in the +Headings font and replace the font with Candara.
3. Find text set in the +Body font and replace the font with Constantia.
4. Find text set in 11-point Candara and replace it with 12-point Candara italic.
5. Using a wildcard charcter, find all occurrences of *Ne?land?Davis* and replace them with *Newland-Davis*.
6. Select the title *Newland-Davis Medical* and then change the scale option to 150% and the spacing option to Expanded. (Do this at the Font dialog box with the Advanced tab selected.)
7. Save, print, and then close **1-EmpGuide**.

Assessment 3

Replace Special Characters, Insert Document Properties, and Inspect and Check the Accessibility of a First Aid Training Flyer

1. Open **FirstAidTraining** and then save it with the name **1-FirstAidTraining**.
2. Move the insertion point immediately right of *Health* in the subtitle *Sponsored by Frontline Health* and then insert a trademark symbol.
3. Search for all occurrences of hyphens and replace them with nonbreaking hyphens.
4. Search for all occurrences of em dashes and replace them with en dashes.
5. Display the Info backstage area and then type First Aid Training in the *Title* document property text box.
6. Display the 1-FirstAidTraining Properties dialog box and then type the following in each specified document property:
   a. Subject: Training
   b. Company: Tri-State Products
   c. Keywords: first aid, training, CPR
7. Save the document and then inspect the document and remove headers, footers, and watermarks.
8. Complete an accessibility check and then insert alternate text for the picture image by typing Stethoscope image in the text box in the Alt Text task pane. Position the picture image inline with text and then close all open task panes.
9. Print only the document properties.
10. Save, print, and then close **1-FirstAidTraining**.

Assessment 4

Check a Travel Document for Accessibility Issues

1. Open **TTSAdventures** and then save it with the name **1-TTSAdventures**.
2. Using the Help feature, learn more about the rules for the Accessibility Checker.
3. After reading the information, complete an accessibility check on the document. Look at the errors that appear in the Accessibility Checker task pane and then correct each error.
4. Save, print, and then close **1-TTSAdventures**.
5. Open a blank document and then type text explaining the errors that were found in **1-TTSAdventures** by the Accessibility Checker and what you did to correct the errors.
6. Save the completed document and name it **1-TTSAccessibility**.
7. Print and then close **1-TTSAccessibility**.

Visual Benchmark

Format a Travel Document

1. Open **Hawaii** and then save it with the name **1-Hawaii**.
2. Apply the following formatting so your document appears similar to the document shown in Figure 1.1:
   - Inspect the document and remove the watermark (the watermark is in the footer) and the header.
   - Expand the spacing (by increasing the spacing point size) for the title and apply a stylistic set so your title appears similar to the title in the figure.
   - Expand the spacing (by increasing the spacing point size) and apply a stylistic set to the two headings in the document so the headings appear similar to the headings in the figure.

- Apply a stylistic set to the quote and the author of the quote near the bottom of the page.
- Select the tabbed text and then use the Text Effects and Typography button in the Font group on the Home tab to apply the tabular lining number style.
- Search for all occurrences of em dashes and replace each with a colon followed by a space.
- Search for all occurrences of hyphens and replace each with an en dash.
- Insert the trademark symbol as shown in the figure.

3. Save, print, and then close **1-Hawaii**.

Figure 1.1 Visual Benchmark

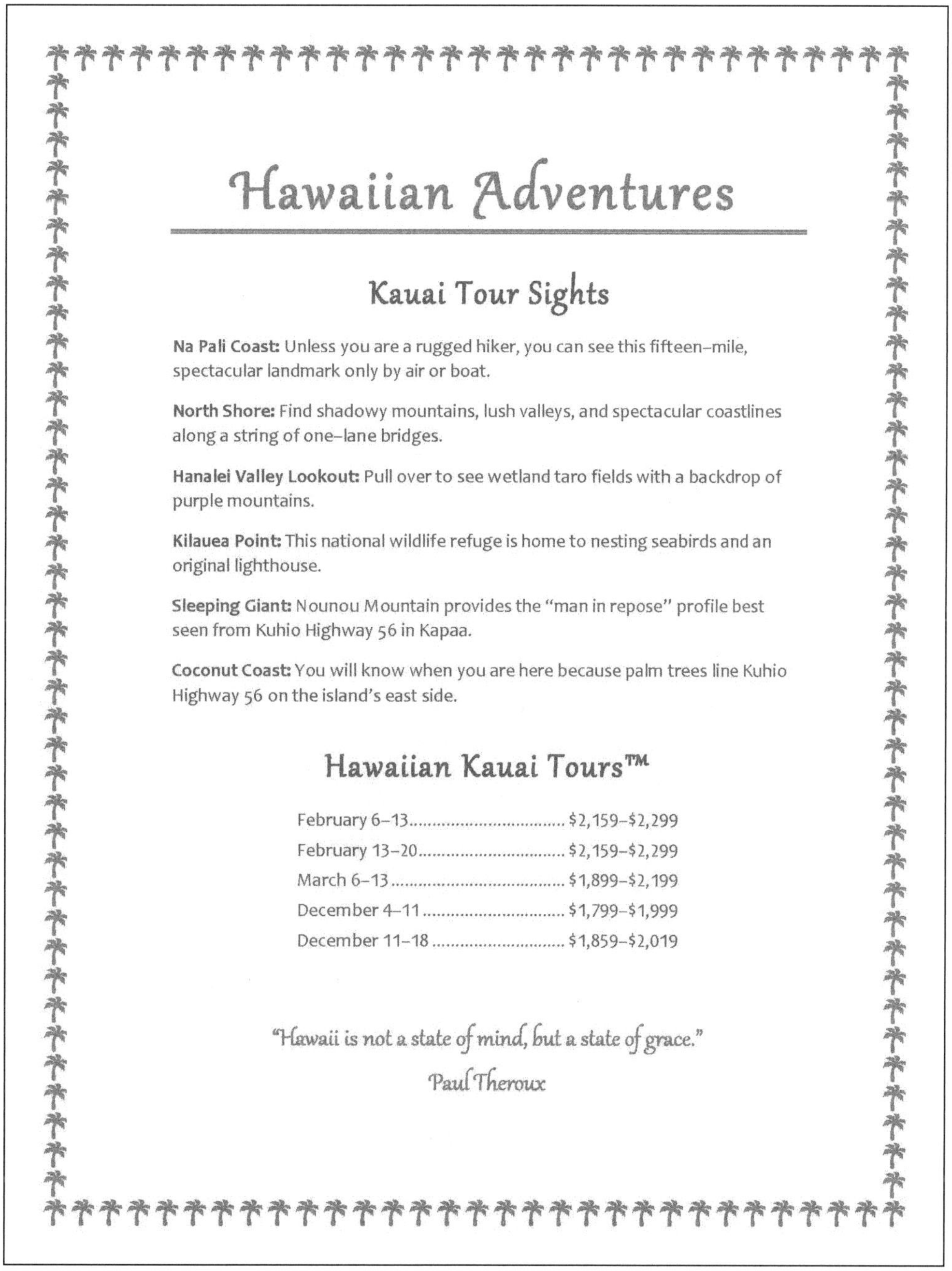

Hawaiian Adventures

Kauai Tour Sights

Na Pali Coast: Unless you are a rugged hiker, you can see this fifteen–mile, spectacular landmark only by air or boat.

North Shore: Find shadowy mountains, lush valleys, and spectacular coastlines along a string of one–lane bridges.

Hanalei Valley Lookout: Pull over to see wetland taro fields with a backdrop of purple mountains.

Kilauea Point: This national wildlife refuge is home to nesting seabirds and an original lighthouse.

Sleeping Giant: Nounou Mountain provides the "man in repose" profile best seen from Kuhio Highway 56 in Kapaa.

Coconut Coast: You will know when you are here because palm trees line Kuhio Highway 56 on the island's east side.

Hawaiian Kauai Tours™

February 6–13	$2,159–$2,299
February 13–20	$2,159–$2,299
March 6–13	$1,899–$2,199
December 4–11	$1,799–$1,999
December 11–18	$1,859–$2,019

"Hawaii is not a state of mind, but a state of grace."

Paul Theroux

Case Study

Part 1

You are the assistant to the executive director of Phoenix Rising, a nonprofit organization. Phoenix Rising is sponsoring an affordable housing forum and you need to format a flyer for the event. Open **PRForum** and then save it with the name **1-PRForum**. The information about the forum is provided in the document and your responsibility is to apply attractive and appealing formatting to the information. To provide a frame of reference for formatting, open **1-PRDonations** and **1-PRDonorApp** to see how those documents are formatted and then apply similar formatting to **1-PRForum**. Replace any regular hyphens with en dashes and consider whether you want to have an em dash or other punctuation after *Date*, *Time*, and *Location*. Save, print, and then close **1-PRForum**.

Part 2

The executive director of Phoenix Rising needs a new organizational chart. Open **PRLtrhd** and then save it with the name **1-PROrgChart**. Look at the information in Figure 1.2 below and then create a SmartArt organizational chart to display the information. Provide a title for the organizational chart and apply formatting so the title and organizational chart appear similar to the other documents you prepared in this case study. Save, print, and then close **1-PROrgChart**.

Figure 1.2 Case Study, Part 2

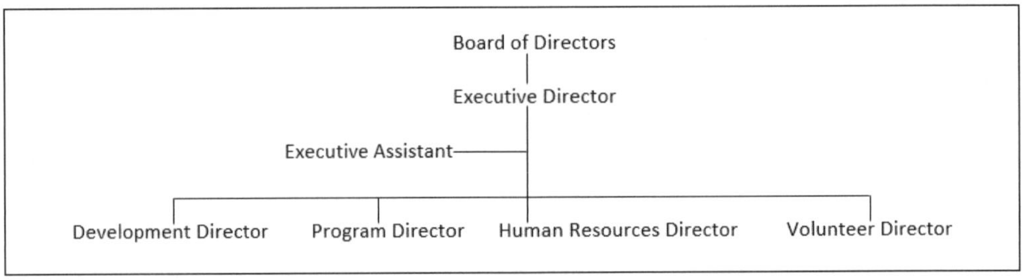

Part 3

The executive director wants to ensure that all documents you prepare for Phoenix Rising are checked for accessibility issues and has asked you to check two documents. Open **1-PRForum**, run an accessibility check on the document, and fix any errors identified by the Accessibility Checker. Save and then close **1-PRForum**. Open **1-PROrgChart**, run an accessibility check, and fix any errors identified by the Accessibility Checker. Save and then close **1-PROrgChart**. Open **PRLtrhd** and then save it with the name **1-PRAccessibility**. Write a letter to the executive director explaining any accessibility issues found in each document by the Accessibility Checker and the steps you took to correct them. Save, print, and then close **1-PRAccessibility**.

Part 4

To further identify a document and its contents, the executive director has asked you to provide document properties for **1-PROrgChart**. Open **1-PROrgChart** and then insert at least the following document properties:

- Title
- Author (use your name)
- Company
- Keywords

After inserting the document properties, save **1-PROrgChart**, print only the document properties, and then close the document.

Microsoft® Word
Review and Assessment

CHAPTER 2

Proofing Documents

The online course includes additional review and assessment resources.

Skills Assessment

Assessment 1 — Check Spelling in a Document

1. Open **QuoteMarks** and then save it with the name **2-QuoteMarks**.
2. Complete a spelling and grammar check on the document.
3. Apply the Heading 1 style to the title of the document and the Heading 2 style to the headings in the document (which currently display with bold formatting).
4. Apply the Parallax theme.
5. Center the document title.
6. Save, print, and then close **2-QuoteMarks**.

Assessment 2 — Check Spelling and Grammar and Proofread a Letter

1. Open **AirMiles** and then save it with the name **2-AirMiles**.
2. Complete a spelling and grammar check on the document. (Proper names are spelled correctly.)
3. After completing the spelling and grammar check, proofread the letter and make any necessary changes. (The letter contains mistakes that the grammar checker will not select.) Replace the *XX* near the end of the document with your initials.
4. Select the entire document and then change the font to 12-point Candara.
5. Save, print, and then close **2-AirMiles**.

Assessment 3 — Check Spelling and Grammar and Display Readability Statistics and Word Count in a Document

1. Open **Ethics** and then save it with the name **2-Ethics**.
2. Turn on the display of readability statistics and then complete a spelling and grammar check on the document.
3. Make a note of the Flesch Reading Ease score and the Flesch-Kincaid Grade Level score and then type that information in the appropriate locations at the end of the document.
4. Turn off the display of readability statistics.
5. Determine the number of words in the document and then type that information in the appropriate location at the end of the document.
6. Insert continuous line numbering.
7. Apply formatting to enhance the appearance of the document.
8. Save, print, and then close **2-Ethics**.

Assessment 4

Translate Selected Text in a Document

1. Open **PRConference** and then save it with the name **2-PRConference**.
2. Select all the text in the first cell in the table (begins with *Annual Conference*).
3. Display the Translator task pane with the *Selection* option selected.
4. Specify that the text is to be translated into Spanish.
5. Click in the empty row at the bottom of the table and then insert the translated text.
6. Close the Translator task pane.
7. Save, print, and then close **2-PRConference**.

Assessment 5

Translate an Entire Document

1. Open **Announcement** and then save it with the name **2-Announcement**.
2. Translate the entire document into French.
3. Save the translated document and name it **2-Announce-French**.
4. Print and then close **2-Announce-French**.
5. Close the Translator task pane and then close **2-Announcement**.

Assessment 6

Sort Text in a Document

1. Open **SFSSorting** and then save it with the name **2-SFSSorting**.
2. Select the nine lines of text below the heading *Executive Team* and then sort the text alphabetically by last name.
3. Sort the three columns of text below the title *New Employees* by date of hire in ascending order.
4. Sort the text in the *First Qtr.* column in the table numerically in descending order.
5. Save, print, and then close **2-SFSSorting**.

Visual Benchmark

Activity 1

Sort Data in a Document

1. Open **Natura** and then save it with the name **2-Natura**.
2. Complete sorts so your text appears as shown in Figure 2.1. ***Hint: Sort the text in the table first by the country and then by the customer name***.
3. Save, print, and then close **2-Natura**.

Activity 2

Translate Text

1. Open **CCDonations** and then save it with the name **2-CCDonations**.
2. Type the paragraph of text below the heading *English*: as shown in Figure 2.2 on page 10 and then complete a spelling and grammar check on the text.
3. Select the paragraph of text below the heading *English:* and then translate the paragraph into Spanish and then into French. Insert the translated text into the document, as shown in Figure 2.2 (Your translations may vary from those shown in the figure.)
4. Use the Curlz MT font to format the heading at the beginning of each paragraph and the quote that displays near the end of the letter. Center the quote and apply the Blue font color to the quote and then apply paragraph shading as shown in the figure.
5. Save, print, and then close **2-CCDonations**.

Figure 2.1 Visual Benchmark 1

Natura

Natural products for natural beauty...

Natura Representatives

Denise Beaulieu	206-555-3901
Marcus Brown	347-555-2389
Charles Collins	202-555-9954
Dallas Conway	305-555-3492
Midori Fujita	504-555-7384
Isaac Hill	520-555-4366
Finn McDougal	312-444-0394
Paulina Menzel	346-555-2348
Hamilton Pierce	410-555-2384
Genevieve Salinger	602-555-4392

Natura Customers

Customer	Street Address	City	State/ Province	Postal Code	Country
Flying Queen	478 River Ave.	Winnipeg	MB	V4B 4A9	Canada
Rose	467 Seventh St. E.	Saskatoon	SK	S7H1A3	Canada
Swan	347 Park St.	Halifax	NS	B3H 2W2	Canada
Wave Rider	342 W. Georgia	Vancouver	BC	V6E 3H7	Canada
Beauty	89 Kiefer Creek Rd.	Ballwin	MO	63021	USA
Belle	P.O. Box 359	Belt	MT	59412	USA
Blue Fairy	307 Gold Hill Dr.	Grass Valley	CA	95945	USA
Maiden	345 Polk St.	San Francisco	CA	94109	USA
Melody	P.O. Box 789	Stromsburg	NE	68666	USA
Nautilus	45 Scarborough St.	Hartford	CT	06105	USA
Nina's Gift	784 Arizona Ave.	Santa Monica	CA	90401	USA
Red Coral	67 N. 73rd St.	Omaha	NE	68114	USA
Sailing Beauty	358 Fifth Ave.	Anchorage	AK	99501	USA
Sea Princess	876 N. Roxboro St.	Durham	NC	27701	USA
Suzanna	2331 S. Pioneer St.	Abilene	TX	79605	USA
The Dolphin	478 Dodson Dr.	East Point	GA	30344	USA
The Mermaid	782 West Fairway Pl.	Chandler	AZ	85224	USA
The Picasso	784 Parks St.	Duxbury	MA	02331	USA
Water Spirit	215 Vine St.	Cincinnati	OH	45202	USA
Woodwinds	34 Downey Ave.	Modesto	CA	95354	USA

Figure 2.2 Visual Benchmark 2

Cordova Children's Community Center

Support Your Local Community Center

English:

As you consider your donation contributions for the coming year, we ask that you consider your community by supporting the Cordova Children's Community Center. The center is a nonprofit agency providing educational and recreational activities for children. Please stop by for a visit. Our dedicated staff will be available to discuss with you the services offered by the center, how your donation dollars are spent, and provide information on current and future activities and services.

Spanish:

Al considerar sus contribuciones de donación para el próximo año, le pedimos que considere a su comunidad apoyando el Cordova Children's Community Center. El centro es una agencia sin fines de lucro que ofrece actividades educativas y recreativas para los niños. Por favor, visítanos. Nuestro personal dedicado estará disponible para discutir con usted los servicios ofrecidos por el centro, cómo se gastan sus dólares de donación, y proporcionar información sobre las actividades y servicios actuales y futuros.

French:

Comme vous considérez vos contributions de don pour l'année à venir, nous vous demandons de considérer votre communauté en soutenant le centre communautaire des enfants de Cordova. Le centre est une Agence à but non lucratif offrant des activités éducatives et récréatives pour les enfants. Veuillez vous arrêter pour une visite. Notre personnel dévoué sera disponible pour discuter avec vous des services offerts par le centre, comment vos dollars de Don sont dépensés, et fournir des informations sur les activités et les services actuels et futurs.

"Children are our most valuable natural resource." ~ Herbert Hoover

770 Sunrise Terrace ◆ Santa Fe, NM 87509 ◆ 505-555-7700

Case Study

Part 1

You work in the executive offices at Nickell Industries and have been asked to develop a writing manual for employees. The company has not used a consistent theme when formatting documents, so you decide to choose a theme and use it when formatting all Nickell documents. Open **NIManual** and then save the document and name it **2-NIManual**. Check the spelling and grammar in the document and then make the following changes to it:

- Insert a section break at the beginning of the title *Editing and Proofreading*.
- Apply styles of your choosing to the titles and headings in the document.
- Apply the theme you have chosen for company documents.
- Insert headers and/or footers.
- Create a cover page.
- Save the document.

Part 2

As you review the writing manual document you have created for Nickell Industries, you decide to highlight the points for developing sections of documents. You decide that a vertical block list SmartArt graphic will present the ideas in an easy-to-read format and provide some visual interest to the manual. Insert a page break at the end of the text in **2-NIManual**, type the title *Developing a Document*, and then insert the following in the appropriate shapes:

Beginning
- Introduce main idea.
- Get reader's attention.
- Establish a positive tone.

Middle
- Provide detail for main idea.
- Lead reader to intended conclusion.

End
- State conclusion.
- State action reader should take.

Apply colors that follow the theme you have chosen for company documents. Save the document.

Part 3

Nickell Industries does business in other countries, including Mexico. One of the executives in the Finance Department has asked you to translate into Spanish some terms that will be used to develop an invoice. Create a document that translates the following terms from English to Spanish and also include in the document the steps for translating text. Your reason for doing this is that if the executives know the steps, they can translate the text at their own computers.

- city
- telephone
- invoice
- product
- description
- total

Format the document with the theme you have chosen for company documents and add any other enhancements to improve the appearance of the document. Save the completed document and name it **2-NITranslations**. Print and then close **2-NITranslations**.

Part 4

While working on the writing manual for Nickell Industries, you decide to purchase some reference books on grammar and punctuation. Using the internet, search for books that provide information on grammar and punctuation and then choose three books. You know that the books will be purchased soon, so you decide to add the information in the writing manual document, telling readers what reference books are available. Include this information on a separate page at the end of the text in **2-NIManual**. Save, print, and then close the document.

Microsoft® Word
Review and Assessment

CHAPTER 3

Inserting Headers, Footers, and References

The online course includes additional review and assessment resources.

Skills Assessment

Assessment 1
Insert Specialized Footers in a Report

1. Open **Robots** and then save it with the name **3-Robots**.
2. Keep the heading *NAVIGATION* together with the paragraph of text that follows it.
3. Move the insertion point to the beginning of the document and then create an odd page footer that includes the following:
   a. Insert the current date at the left margin. (Choose the date option that displays the month spelled out, such as *January 1, 2021*.)
   b. Using the Pictures button in the Insert group on the Header & Footer Tools Design tab, insert the **Robot** image file in the middle of the footer. Change the height of the robot image to 0.5 inch and the text wrapping to Behind Text. Drag the robot image below the footer pane border.
   c. At the right margin, type Page, press the spacebar, and then insert a plain page number at the current position.
4. Create an even page footer that includes the following:
   a. At the left margin, type Page, press the spacebar, and then insert a plain page number at the current position.
   b. Insert the **Robot** image file in the middle of the footer and apply the same formatting as you did to the image in the odd page footer.
   c. Insert the current date at the right margin in the same format you chose for the odd page footer.
5. Save, print, and then close **3-Robots**.

Assessment 2
Insert a Header and Footer in a Report on All Pages Except the First Page

1. Open **Volcanoes** and then save it with the name **3-Volcanoes**.
2. Create a header for all pages except the first page and type Volcano Report at the right margin of the Header pane. (Make sure the First Page Header pane is blank.)
3. Create a footer for all pages except the first page and insert the Banded predesigned footer in the Footer pane. (Make sure the First Page Footer pane is blank.)
4. Save, print, and then close **3-Volcanoes**.

Assessment 3

Insert a Section Break and Format and Print Sections

1. Open **CompViruses** and then save it with the name **3-CompViruses**.
2. Insert a section break that begins a new page at the beginning of the title *CHAPTER 2 SECURITY RISKS*.
3. Move the insertion point to the beginning of the document and then create a footer for the first section in the document with *Chapter 1* at the left margin, the page number in the middle, and your first and last names at the right margin.
4. Edit the footer for the second section to Chapter 2 instead of Chapter 1. ***Hint: Make sure you break the link.***
5. Print only the pages in section 2.
6. Save and then close **3-CompViruses**.

Assessment 4

Insert Footnotes in a Newsletter

1. Open **DesignNwsltr** and then save it with the name **3-DesignNwsltr**.
2. Create the first footnote shown in Figure 3.1 at the end of the first paragraph in the *Applying Guidelines* section.
3. Create the second footnote shown in the figure at the end of the last paragraph in the *Applying Guidelines* section.
4. Create the third footnote shown in the figure at the end of the only paragraph in the *Choosing Paper Size and Type* section.
5. Create the fourth footnote shown in the figure at the end of the only paragraph in the *Choosing Paper Weight* section.
6. Save and then print **3-DesignNwsltr**.
7. Select the entire document and then change the font to Constantia.
8. Select all the footnotes and then change the font to Constantia. ***Note: Pressing Ctrl + A will select all the footnotes in the document.***
9. Delete the second footnote (*Maddock*).
10. Save, print, and then close **3-DesignNwsltr**.

Figure 3.1 Assessment 4

James Haberman, "Designing a Newsletter," *Desktop Designs* (2021): 23-29.

Arlita Maddock, "Guidelines for a Better Newsletter," *Desktop Publisher* (2020): 32-38.

Monica Alverso, "Paper Styles for Newsletters," *Design Technologies* (2021): 45-51.

Keith Sutton, "Choosing Paper Styles," *Design Techniques* (2021): 8-11.

Assessment 5

Insert Sources and Citations in a Privacy Rights Document

1. Open **PrivRights** and then save it with the name **3-PrivRights**.
2. Make sure that MLA style is selected in the Citations & Bibliography group on the References tab.
3. With the insertion point positioned at the beginning of the document, type your name, press the Enter key, type your instructor's name, press the Enter key, type the title of your course, press the Enter key, type the current date, and then press the Enter key. Type the title Privacy Rights and then center the title.
4. The text in the document is set in 12-point Cambria. Make this the default font for the document. ***Hint: Do this with the Set As Default button at the Font dialog box.***

5. Insert a header that displays your last name and the page number at the right margin.
6. Select and then delete the text *(Hartley)* that appears in the second paragraph.
7. With the insertion point positioned between the word *policy* and the period that ends the third sentence in the second paragraph, press the spacebar and then insert the source information for a journal article written by Kenneth Hartley using the following information:

Author	Kenneth Hartley
Title	Privacy Laws
Journal Name	Business World
Year	2021
Pages	24-46
Volume	XII

8. Select and then delete the text *(Ferraro)* that appears in the second paragraph.
9. With the insertion point positioned between the word *place* and the period that ends the fourth sentence in the second paragraph, press the spacebar and then insert the following source information for a book:

Author	Ramona Ferraro
Title	Business Employee Rights
Year	2021
City	Tallahassee
Publisher	Everglades Publishing House

10. Select and then delete the text *(Aldrich)* that appears in the last paragraph.
11. With the insertion point positioned between the word *limit"* and the period that ends the second sentence in the last paragraph, press the spacebar and then insert the following information for an article in a periodical:

Author	Kelly Aldrich
Title	What Rights Do Employees Have?
Periodical Title	Great Plains Times
Year	2021
Month	May
Day	6
Pages	18-22

12. Insert page number 20 in the Kelly Aldrich citation using the Edit Citation dialog box.
13. Edit the Kenneth Hartley source title to read *Small Business Privacy Laws* in the *Master List* section of the Source Manager dialog box. (Update both the Master List and the Current List.)
14. Select and delete the last two sentences in the second paragraph and then delete the Ramona Ferraro source in the *Current List* section of the Source Manager dialog box.
15. Insert a works cited page on a separate page at the end of the document.
16. Create a new source in the document using the Source Manager dialog box and include the following source information for a website:

Author	Harold Davidson
Name of Web Page	Small Business Policies and Procedures
Year	2020
Month	December
Day	12
Year Accessed	2021
Month Accessed	February
Day Accessed	23
URL	https://ppi-edu.net/policies

17. Insert a citation for Harold Davidson at the end of the last sentence in the first paragraph.
18. Update the works cited page.
19. Format the works cited page to meet MLA requirements with the following changes:
    a. Select the *Works Cited* heading and all the entries and then click the *No Spacing* style.
    b. Change the spacing to 2.0.
    c. Format the works cited entries with a hanging indent.
    d. Center the title *Works Cited*.
20. Save and then print **3-PrivRights**.
21. Change the document and works cited page from MLA style to APA style. Make sure you change the title of the sources list to *References*. Select the references in the list and then change the line spacing to double spacing.
22. Save the document **3-PrivRights**, print page 2, and then close **3-PrivRights**.

Visual Benchmark

Format a Report in MLA Style

1. Open **SecurityDefenses** and then save it with the name **3-SecurityDefenses**.
2. Format the document so it displays as shown in Figure 3.2 with the following specifications:
    a. Change the document font to 12-point Cambria and then set 12-point Cambria as the default.
    b. Use the information from the works cited page when inserting citations into the document. The Hollingsworth citation is for a journal article, the Montoya citation is for a book, and the Gillespie citation is for a website.
    c. Format the works cited page to meet MLA requirements.
3. Save, print, and then close **3-SecurityDefenses**.

Figure 3.2 Visual Benchmark

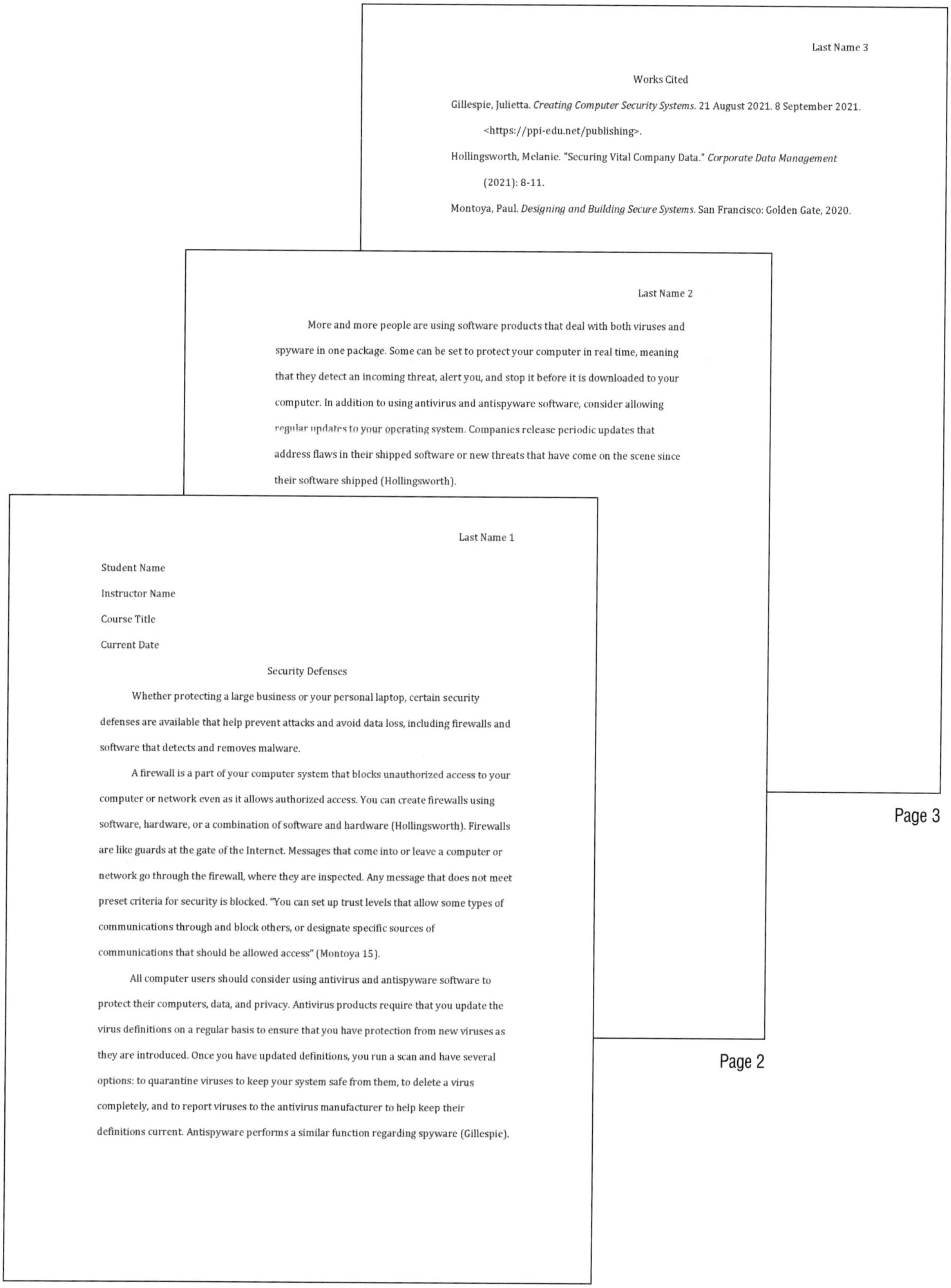

Last Name 1

Student Name

Instructor Name

Course Title

Current Date

Security Defenses

Whether protecting a large business or your personal laptop, certain security defenses are available that help prevent attacks and avoid data loss, including firewalls and software that detects and removes malware.

A firewall is a part of your computer system that blocks unauthorized access to your computer or network even as it allows authorized access. You can create firewalls using software, hardware, or a combination of software and hardware (Hollingsworth). Firewalls are like guards at the gate of the Internet. Messages that come into or leave a computer or network go through the firewall, where they are inspected. Any message that does not meet preset criteria for security is blocked. "You can set up trust levels that allow some types of communications through and block others, or designate specific sources of communications that should be allowed access" (Montoya 15).

All computer users should consider using antivirus and antispyware software to protect their computers, data, and privacy. Antivirus products require that you update the virus definitions on a regular basis to ensure that you have protection from new viruses as they are introduced. Once you have updated definitions, you run a scan and have several options: to quarantine viruses to keep your system safe from them, to delete a virus completely, and to report viruses to the antivirus manufacturer to help keep their definitions current. Antispyware performs a similar function regarding spyware (Gillespie).

Page 1

Last Name 2

More and more people are using software products that deal with both viruses and spyware in one package. Some can be set to protect your computer in real time, meaning that they detect an incoming threat, alert you, and stop it before it is downloaded to your computer. In addition to using antivirus and antispyware software, consider allowing regular updates to your operating system. Companies release periodic updates that address flaws in their shipped software or new threats that have come on the scene since their software shipped (Hollingsworth).

Page 2

Last Name 3

Works Cited

Gillespie, Julietta. *Creating Computer Security Systems.* 21 August 2021. 8 September 2021. <https://ppi-edu.net/publishing>.

Hollingsworth, Melanie. "Securing Vital Company Data." *Corporate Data Management* (2021): 8-11.

Montoya, Paul. *Designing and Building Secure Systems.* San Francisco: Golden Gate, 2020.

Page 3

Case Study

Part 1

You just opened a new company, Chrysalis Media, that helps businesses creatively communicate with customers. Some of the media design services you offer are business letterhead, logos, flyers, newsletters, signage, and business cards. Create a company letterhead document by opening a blank document and then inserting the **CMHdr** image file as a first page header. Change the height of the image to 1.4" and change the header position from the top to 0.3". Insert the **CMFtr** image file as a first page footer. Save the completed letterhead document and name it **3-CMLtrhd**. Print and then close the document.

Part 2

You have a document on defining newsletter elements that you want to make available to clients. Open **Nwsltr-Define** and then save it with the name **3-Nwsltr-Define**. Create a header for all the pages except the first page and insert the **CMHdr** image file in the Header pane. Change the width of the image to 2" and change the header position from the top to 0.3". Insert a footer with the page number at the bottom center of each page. Save, print, and then close **3-Nwsltr-Define**.

Part 3

You want to provide information for employees on designing newsletters and have a report on newsletter design that needs to be formatted into the APA style. Open **CM-DesignNwsltr** and then save it with the name **3-CM-DesignNwsltr-APA**. Look at the information in Figure 3.1 (on page 14) and then insert the information as in-text journal article citations in the locations indicated in Steps 2 through 5 in Assessment 4. However, position the insertion point inside the period before inserting the citation. Add a reference page on a separate page at the end of the document. Center the title *References* and change the title to all uppercase letters. Select the entire document and change the font to 12-point Cambria. Apply any other formatting to follow APA guidelines. Save **3-CM-DesignNwsltr-APA**.

Part 4

You want to include some additional information on newsletter guidelines. Using the internet, look for websites that provide information on desktop publishing and/or newsletter design. Include in the **3-CM-DesignNwsltr-APA** report document at least one additional paragraph with information you found on the internet and include a citation for each source from which you have borrowed information. Save, print, and then close the report.

Microsoft® Word
Review and Assessment

CHAPTER 4

Creating Specialized Tables and Navigating in a Document

The online course includes additional review and assessment resources.

Skills Assessment

Assessment 1

Create and Update a Table of Contents for a Photography Report

1. Open **PhotoRpt** and then save it with the name **4-PhotoRpt**.
2. Move the insertion point to the beginning of the heading *Photography* and then insert a section break that begins a new page.
3. With the insertion point positioned below the section break, insert a page number at the bottom center of each page and change the beginning number to *1*.
4. Press Ctrl + Home to move the insertion point to the beginning of the document (on the blank page) and then create a table of contents with the *Automatic Table 1* option at the Table of Contents button drop-down list.
5. Display the Table of Contents dialog box, change the *Formats* option to *Distinctive*, and make sure a *3* displays in the *Show levels* measurement box.
6. Change the page number format of the table of contents page to lowercase roman numerals.
7. Save the document and then print only the table of contents page.
8. Insert a page break at the beginning of the heading *Camera Basics*.
9. Update the table of contents.
10. Save the document and then print only the table of contents page.
11. Close **4-PhotoRpt**.

Assessment 2

Insert Captions and a Table of Figures in a Report

1. Open **InputDevices** and then save it with the name **4-InputDevices**.
2. Insert a caption for each of the three images in the document that uses *Figure* as the label, uses an arabic number (1, 2, 3) as the figure number, and displays centered below the image. Use *Keyboard* for the first figure caption, *Mouse* for the second, and *Laptop* for the third.
3. Move the insertion point to the beginning of the title *Computer Input Devices* and then insert a section break that begins a new page.
4. Press Ctrl + Home, type Table of Figures, press the Enter key, and then insert a table of figures with the Formal format applied.
5. Apply the Heading 1 style to the title *Table of Figures*.
6. Move the insertion point to the title *Computer Input Devices*. Insert a page number at the bottom center of each page and change the starting number to *1*.
7. Move the insertion point to the title *Table of Figures* and then change the page numbering style to lowercase roman numerals.
8. Insert a page break at the beginning of the heading *Mouse*.
9. Update the table of figures.
10. Save, print, and then close **4-InputDevices**.

Assessment 3

Format and Navigate in a Corporate Report

1. Open **DIReport** and then save it with the name **4-DIReport**.
2. Turn on the display of bookmarks.
3. Move the insertion point to the end of the third paragraph (the paragraph that begins *The audit committee selects*) and then insert a bookmark named *Audit*.
4. Move the insertion point to the end of the first paragraph in the section *FEES TO INDEPENDENT AUDITOR*, following the *(Excel worksheet)* text, and then insert a bookmark named *Audit_Fees*.
5. Move the insertion point to the end of the last paragraph and then insert a bookmark named *Compensation*.
6. Navigate in the document using the bookmarks.
7. Move the insertion point to the end of the first paragraph in the section *COMMITTEE RESPONSIBILITIES*, press the spacebar, and then insert a hyperlink to the Audit_Fees bookmark.
8. Select the text *(Excel worksheet)* at the end of the first paragraph in the section *FEES TO INDEPENDENT AUDITOR* and then insert a hyperlink to the Excel file **AuditorFees**.
9. Move the insertion point to the end of the document, click the image, and then insert a hyperlink to the Word document **DIGraphic**. At the Insert Hyperlink dialog box, create a ScreenTip with the text *Click to view a long-term incentives graphic*.
10. Press and hold down the Ctrl key, click the *(Excel worksheet)* hyperlink, and then release the Ctrl key. Print the Excel worksheet that displays by clicking the File tab, clicking the *Print* option, and then clicking the Print button in the Print backstage area.
11. Close the Excel program without saving the file.
12. Press and hold down the Ctrl key, click the image to display the Word document containing the graphic, and then release the Ctrl key. Print and then close the graphic document.
13. Save, print, and then close **4-DIReport**.

Assessment 4

Customize a Table of Contents

1. Open **DIInformation** and then save it with the name **4-DIInformation**.
2. By default, an automatic table of contents is created using text with the Heading 1, Heading 2, and Heading 3 styles applied. The **4-DIInformation** document contains text with Heading 4 applied. Display the Table of Contents Options dialog box and determine how to specify that the table of contents should include text with the Heading 4 style applied. Replace the existing table of contents.
3. Save **4-DIInformation** and then print only section 1 (the two pages of the table of contents).
4. Close **4-DIInformation**.

Visual Benchmark

Create a Table of Contents and a Table of Figures

1. Open **Networks** and then save it with the name **4-Networks**.
2. Format the document so it appears as shown in Figure 4.1 with the following specifications:
   a. Insert the captions for the figures as shown (see Page 3 of the figure).

   b. Insert the table of figures as shown (see Page 2 of the figure) using the *From template* format option with period leaders. Apply the Heading 1 style to the *FIGURES* heading.
   c. Insert the table of contents as shown (see Page 1 of the figure) using the *From template* format option with period leaders. Apply the Heading 1 style to the *TABLE OF CONTENTS* heading.
   d. Insert page numbers at the right margins as shown (see Pages 2, 3, and 4 of the figure).
3. Save, print, and then close **4-Networks**.

Figure 4.1 Visual Benchmark

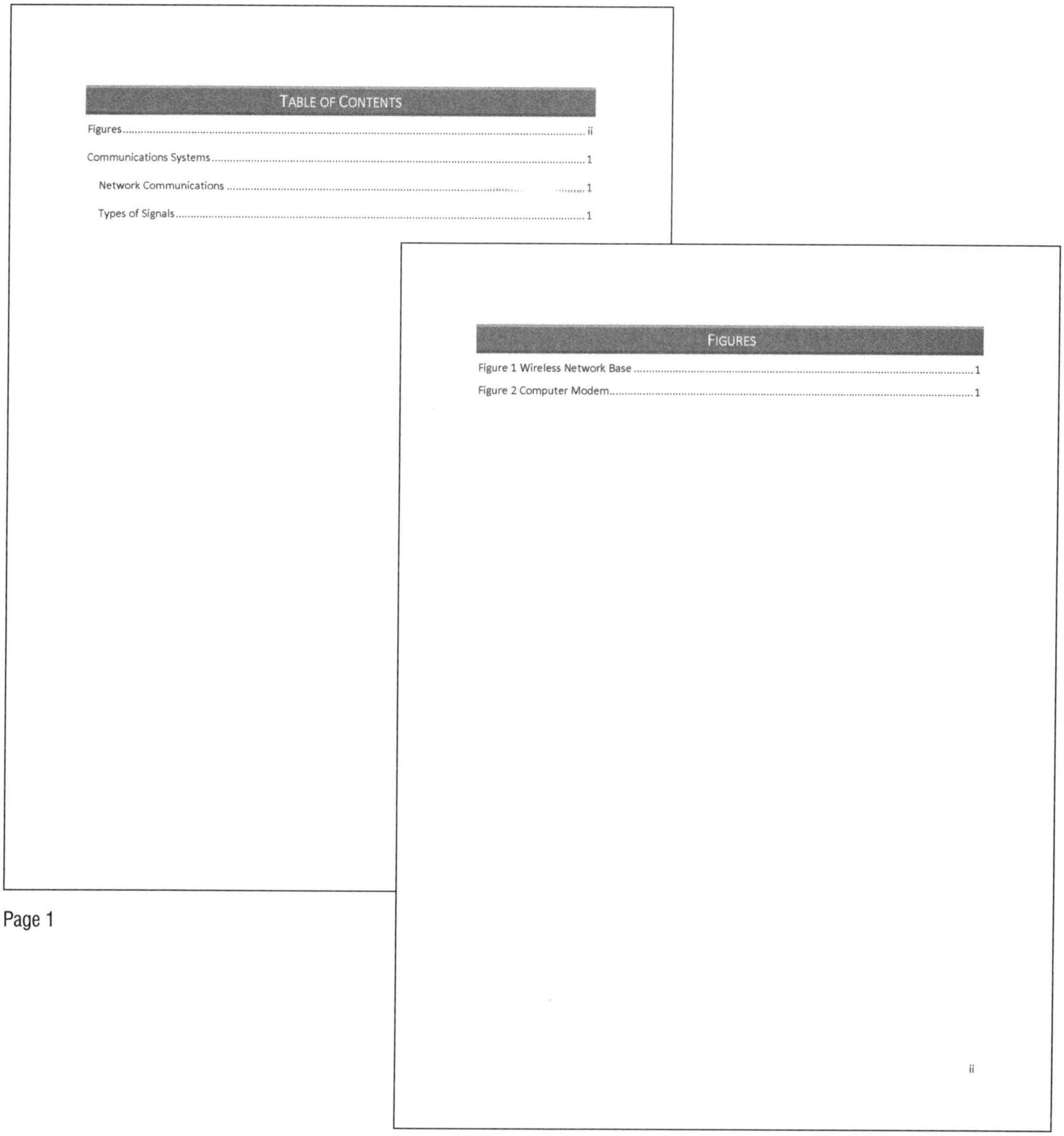

TABLE OF CONTENTS

Figures ii
Communications Systems 1
Network Communications 1
Types of Signals 1

FIGURES

Figure 1 Wireless Network Base 1
Figure 2 Computer Modem 1

ii

Page 1

Page 2

continues

Figure 4.1 Visual Benchmark—*continued*

COMMUNICATIONS SYSTEMS

A computer network is one kind of communications system. This system includes sending and receiving hardware, transmission and relay systems, common sets of standards so all the equipment can "talk" to each other, and communications software.

NETWORK COMMUNICATIONS

You use such a networked communications system whenever you send/receive IM or email messages, pay a bill online, shop at an Internet store, send a document to a shared printer at work or at home, or download a file.

The world of computer network communications systems is made up of:

- Transmission media upon which the data travels to/from its destination.
- A set of standards and network protocols (rules for how data is handled as it travels along a communications channel). Devices use these to send and receive data to and from each other.
- Hardware and software to connect to a communications pathway from the sending and receiving ends.

Figure 1 Wireless Network Base

The first step in understanding a communications system is to learn the basics about transmission signals and transmission speeds when communicating over a network.

TYPES OF SIGNALS

Two types of signals are used to transmit voices and other sc
digital. An analog signal is formed by continuous sound wave
voice is transmitted as an analog signal over traditional telep
signal uses a discrete signal that is either high or low. In com
1, and low represents the digital bit 0. These are the only tw

Telephone lines carry your voice using an analog signal. How

Figure 2 Computer Modem

rather, they use a binary system of
signals. If you send data between c
phone line, the signal has to be tra
(modulated) and back again to digi
computer on the receiving end. Th

Page 3

data from a transmission source such as your telephone line or cable television connection is a modem. The word modem comes from the combination of the words *mod*ulate and *dem*odulate.

Today, most new communications technologies simply use a digital signal, saving the trouble of converting transmissions. An example of this trend is the demise in 2009 of analog television transmissions as the industry switched to digital signals. Many people were sent scrambling to either buy a newer television set or buy a converter to convert digital transmissions back to analog to work with their older equipment. Newer computer networks, too, use a pure digital signal method of sending and receiving data over a network.

2

Page 4

Case Study

Part 1

You work in the Human Resources Department at Brennan Distributors and are responsible for preparing an employee handbook. Open **BDEmpHandbook** and then save it with the name **4-BDEmpHandbook**. Apply the following specifications to the document:

- Insert a page break before each centered title (except the first title, *Introduction*).
- Apply the Heading 1 style to the titles and the Heading 2 style to the headings.
- Apply a style set of your choosing.
- Apply a theme that makes the handbook easy to read.
- Insert a table of contents.
- Insert appropriate page numbering. ***Hint: Insert a* Next Page *section break at the beginning of the title* Introduction.**
- Insert a cover page and insert the appropriate text in the placeholders. Delete any extra placeholders.
- Add any other elements that will improve the appearance of the document.

Save, print, and then close **4-BDEmpHandbook**.

Part 2

Open **NavigateWeb** and then save it with the name **4-NavigateWeb**. Apply the following specifications to the document:

- Position the insertion point in the first table and then use the caption feature to create the caption *Table 1: Common Top-Level Domain Suffixes* above the table.
- Position the insertion point in the second table and then create the caption *Table 2: Common Search Tools*.
- Position the insertion point in the third table and then create the caption *Table 3: Advanced Search Parameters*.
- Insert a table of contents. (Apply the Heading 1 style to the Table of Contents heading.)
- Insert a table of figures on the page following the table of contents. (Apply the Heading 1 style to the Table of Figures heading and then update the table of contents to include a reference to the Table of Figures.)
- Insert appropriate page numbers.
- Check the page breaks in the document. If a heading displays at the bottom of a page and the paragraph of text that follows displays at the top of the next page, format the heading so it stays with the paragraph. ***Hint: Do this at the Paragraph dialog box with the Line and Page Breaks tab selected.***
- If necessary, update the table of contents and the table of figures.

Save, print, and then close **4-NavigateWeb**.

Part 3

Send an email to your instructor detailing the steps you followed to create the table captions. Attach **4-NavigateWeb** to the email.

Microsoft®

Word Level 2

Unit 1 Performance Assessment

Data Files

Before beginning unit work, copy the WL2U1 folder to your storage medium and then make WL2U1 the active folder.

Assessing Proficiency

In this unit, you have learned to apply advanced character formatting; insert symbols and special characters; find and replace formatting, special characters, styles, and using wildcard characters; manage, inspect, and proof documents; and insert custom headers, footers, and references. You have also learned to create a table of contents and a table of figures and to navigate in a document with the Navigation pane as well as bookmarks, hyperlinks, and cross-references.

Assessment 1

Apply Character Spacing and OpenType Features

1. Open **CVTakeoutMenu** and then save it with the name **U1-CVTakeoutMenu**.
2. Select the title *Take Out Menu*, change the character spacing to Expanded by 1.5 points, turn on kerning, apply Stylistic Set 5, and use contextual alternates.
3. Select the heading *Soups*, change the font size to 22 points, change the character spacing to Expanded, turn on kerning, and apply Stylistic Set 5.
4. Apply the same formatting applied to the heading *Soups* in Step 3 to the other headings (*Salads*, *Main Dishes*, and *Desserts*).
5. Select the last sentence in the document (the sentence that begins *Enjoy the tastes*) and then turn on kerning and apply Stylistic Set 5.
6. Save, print, and then close **U1-CVTakeoutMenu**.

Assessment 2

Find and Replace Formatting and Use a Wildcard Character

1. Open **Agreement** and then save it with the name **U1-Agreement**.
2. Find text set in the *+Headings* font and replace the font with Corbel.
3. Find text set in the *+Body* font and replace the font with Candara.
4. Using a wildcard character, find all occurrences of *Pin?h?rst?Mad?s?n Builders* and replace them with *Pinehurst-Madison Builders*. (Make sure you remove the formatting option from the *Find what* and *Replace with* text boxes.)

5. Using a wildcard character, find all occurrences of *?erry L?w?ndowsk?* and replace them with *Gerry Lewandowski*.
6. Save, print, and then close **U1-Agreement**.

Assessment 3 Sort Text

1. Open **SHSSort** and then save it with the name **U1-SHSSort**.
2. Select the five clinic names, addresses, and telephone numbers below the heading *SUMMIT HEALTH SERVICES* and then sort the text alphabetically in ascending order by clinic name.
3. Sort the three columns of text below the heading *EXECUTIVE TEAM* by the extension number in ascending order.
4. Sort the text in the table in the *First Half Expenses* column numerically in descending order.
5. Save, print, and then close **U1-SHSSort**.

Assessment 4 Insert Document Properties and Inspect a Health Plan Document

1. Open **KLHPlan** and then save it with the name **U1-KLHPlan**.
2. Display the U1-KLHPlan Properties dialog box, type the following in the specified text boxes, and then close the dialog box:

Title	Key Life Health Plan
Subject	Company Health Plan
Author	(Insert your first and last names)
Category	Health Plan
Keywords	health, plan, network
Comments	This document describes highlights of the Key Life Health Plan.

3. Save the document and then print only the document properties.
4. Inspect the document and remove any hidden text.
5. Check the accessibility of the document. Type the alternate text Key Life Logo for the image (a key with *KEY LIFE* on the key) and the alternate text KLHP SmartArt including Compassion, Quality, and Commitment for the SmartArt diagram.
6. Save, print, and then close **U1-KLHPlan**.

Assessment 5 Proof and Insert Custom Footers for a Building Website Document

1. Open **BuildWebsite** and then save it with the name **U1-BuildWebsite**.
2. Display the Word Options dialog box with *Proofing* selected in the left panel, remove the check mark in the *Ignore words in UPPERCASE* check box, insert a check mark in the *Show readability statistics* check box, and then close the dialog box.
3. Complete a spelling and grammar check on the document.
4. Create a custom odd page footer that prints the document title, *Building a Website*, at the left margin and the page number at the right margin. Also create a custom even page footer that prints the page number at the left margin and the document title at the right margin.
5. Display the Word Options dialog box with *Proofing* selected in the left panel, insert a check mark in the *Ignore words in UPPERCASE* check box, remove the check mark in the *Show readability statistics* check box, and then close the dialog box.
6. Save, print, and then close **U1-BuildWebsite**.

Assessment 6 Insert Footnotes in a Desktop Publishing Report

1. Open **DTP** and then save it with the name **U1-DTP**.
2. Insert the first footnote shown in Figure U1.1 at the end of the second paragraph in the section *Defining Desktop Publishing*.
3. Insert the second footnote shown in the figure at the end of the fourth paragraph in the section *Defining Desktop Publishing*.
4. Insert the third footnote shown in the figure at the end of the second paragraph in the section *Planning the Publication*.
5. Insert the fourth footnote shown in the figure at the end of the last paragraph in the document.
6. Keep the heading *Planning the Publication* together with the paragraph of text that follows it.
7. Save and then print **U1-DTP**.
8. Select the entire document and then change the font to Constantia.
9. Select all the footnotes and then change the font to Constantia.
10. Delete the third footnote.
11. Save, print, and then close **U1-DTP**.

Figure U1.1 Assessment 6

Laurie Fellers, *Desktop Publishing Design* (Dallas: Cornwall & Lewis, 2021), 67-72.

Joel Moriarity, "The Desktop Publishing Approach," *Desktop Publishing* (2021): 3-6.

Jin Loh, *Desktop Publishing with Style* (Los Angeles: Monroe-Ackerman, 2020), 89-93.

Andrew Rushton, *Desktop Publishing Tips and Tricks* (Minneapolis: Aurora, 2021), 103-106.

Assessment 7 Create Citations and Prepare a Works Cited Page for a Report

1. Open **DesignWebsite** and then save it with the name **U1-DesignWebsite**.
2. Format the title page to meet Modern Language Association (MLA) style requirements with the following changes:
   a. Make sure that MLA style is selected in the Citations & Bibliography group on the References tab.
   b. With the insertion point positioned at the beginning of the document, type your name, press the Enter key, type your instructor's name, press the Enter key, type the title of your course, press the Enter key, type the current date, and then press the Enter key. Type the title Designing a Website and then center the title.
   c. The text in the document is set in 12-point Cambria. Make this the default font for the document.
   d. Insert a header that displays your last name and the page number at the right margin.

3. Select and then delete the text *(Mercado)* in the second paragraph of text. With the insertion point positioned between the word *users* and the period that ends the sentence, press the spacebar and then insert the source information from a journal article using the following information:

Author	Claudia Mercado
Title	Connecting a Web Page
Journal Name	Connections
Year	2021
Pages	12-21
Volume	4

4. Select and then delete the text *(Holmes)* in the second paragraph of text. With the insertion point positioned between the word *routing* and the period that ends the sentence, press the spacebar and then insert the source information from a website using the following information:

Author	Brent Holmes
Name of Web Page	Hosting Your Web Page
Year	2020
Month	September
Day	20
Year Accessed	(type current year)
Month Accessed	(type current month)
Day Accessed	(type current day)
URL	https://ppi-edu.net/webhosting

5. Select and then delete the text *(Vukovich)* in the last paragraph of text. With the insertion point positioned between the word *hyperlinks"* and the period that ends the sentence, press the spacebar and then insert the source information from a book using the following information:

Author	Ivan Vukovich
Title	Computer Technology in the Business Environment
Year	2021
City	San Francisco
Publisher	Gold Coast

6. Insert the page number *20* in the citation by Ivan Vukovich using the Edit Citation dialog box.
7. Edit the Ivan Vukovich source by changing the last name to *Vulkovich* in the *Master List* section of the Source Manager dialog box. Click Yes at the message asking about updating the source in both the *Master List* and the *Current List* sections.
8. Create a new source in the document using the Source Manager dialog box and include the following source information for a journal article:

Author	Sonia Jaquez
Title	Organizing a Web Page
Journal Name	Design Techniques
Year	2021
Pages	32-44
Volume	9

9. Type the following sentence at the end of the last paragraph in the document: Browsers look for pages with these names first when a specific file at a website is requested, and index pages display by default if no other page is specified.
10. Insert a citation for Sonia Jaquez at the end of the sentence you just typed.
11. Insert a citation for Claudia Mercado following the second sentence in the first paragraph of the document.

12. Insert a works cited page at the end of the document on a separate page.
13. Format the works cited page as follows to meet MLA requirements:
    a. Select the *Works Cited* title and all the entries and then click the *No Spacing* style.
    b. Change the line spacing to double spacing.
    c. Center the title *Works Cited*.
    d. Format the works cited entries with a hanging indent. ***Hint: Use Ctrl + T to create a hanging indent***.
14. Save and then print **U1-DesignWebsite**.
15. Change the document and works cited page from MLA style to APA style. Change the title *Works Cited* to *References*. Select the references in the list and then change the line spacing to double spacing with 0 points of spacing after paragraphs.
16. Save **U1-DesignWebsite**, print page 3, and then close the document.

Assessment 8 Create Captions and Insert a Table of Figures in a Report

1. Open **SoftwareCareers** and then save it with the name **U1-SoftwareCareers**.
2. Click in the first table and then insert the caption *Table 1 Software Development Careers* above the table. (Change the paragraph spacing after the caption to 3 points.)
3. Click in the second table and then insert the caption *Table 2 Application Development Careers* above the table. (Change the paragraph spacing after the caption to 3 points.)
4. Move the insertion point to the beginning of the heading *SOFTWARE DEVELOPMENT CAREERS* and then insert a section break that begins a new page.
5. With the insertion point below the section break, insert a page number at the bottom center of each page and change the starting page number to *1*.
6. Move the insertion point to the beginning of the document and then insert the *Automatic Table 1* table of contents.
7. Press Ctrl + Enter to insert a page break.
8. Type Tables, press the Enter key, and then insert a table of figures using the Formal format.
9. Apply the Heading 1 style to the title *Tables*.
10. Move the insertion point to the beginning of the document and then change the number format to lowercase roman numerals.
11. Update the entire table of contents.
12. Save, print, and then close **U1-SoftwareCareers**.

Writing Activities

Activity 1 Prepare an APA Guidelines Document

You work for a psychiatric medical facility and many of the psychiatrists and psychiatric nurses you work with submit papers to journals that require formatting in APA style. Your supervisor has asked you to prepare a document that describes the APA guidelines and provides the steps for formatting a Word document in APA style. Find a website that provides information on APA style and include the hyperlink in your document. (Consider websites for writing labs at colleges and universities.) Apply formatting to enhance the appearance of the document. Save the document and name it **U1-APA**. Print and then close **U1-APA**.

Activity 2

Create a Rental Form Template

You work in a real estate management company that manages rental houses. You decide to automate the standard rental form that is normally filled in by hand. Open **LeaseAgreement** and then save the document and name it **U1-LeaseAgreement**. Look at the lease agreement document and determine how to automate it so it can be filled in using the Find and Replace feature in Word. Change the current *Lessor* and *Lessee* names to *LESSOR* and *LESSEE*. Save the document as a template named **LeaseForm** in your WL2U1 folder. Use File Explorer to open a document based on the **LeaseForm** template. Find and replace the following text (use your judgment about which occurrences should be changed and which should not):

DAY	22nd
MONTH	February
YEAR	2021
RENT	$950
DEPOSIT	$500
LESSOR	Samantha Herrera
LESSEE	Daniel Miller

Save the document and name it **U1-Lease1**. Print and then close **U1-Lease1**. Use File Explorer to open a document based on the **LeaseForm** template and then create another rental document. You determine the text to replace with the standard text. Save the completed rental document and name it **U1-Lease2**. Print and then close **U1-Lease2**.

Internet Research

Create a Job Search Report

Use a search engine to locate companies that offer jobs in a field in which you are interested in working. Locate at least three websites that identify employment opportunities and then create a report in Word that includes the following information about each site:

- Name and URL
- A brief description
- Employment opportunities available

Create a hyperlink from your report to each site and include any additional information pertinent to the site. Apply formatting to enhance the document. Save the document and name it **U1-JobSearch**. Print and then close **U1-JobSearch**.

Microsoft®

Word Level 2

Unit 2

Editing and Formatting Documents

Chapter 5 Customizing Objects and Creating Charts

Chapter 6 Merging Documents

Chapter 7 Managing Building Blocks and Fields

Chapter 8 Managing Shared Documents

Unit 2 Performance Assessment

Microsoft® Word
Review and Assessment

CHAPTER 5

Customizing Objects and Creating Charts

The online course includes additional review and assessment resources.

Skills Assessment

Assessment 1

Insert and Customize an Image and Text Box in a Timeline Document

1. Open **Timeline** and then save it with the name **5-Timeline**.
2. Move the insertion point to the right of the text *Electronic Commerce* (item 2).
3. Display the Insert Picture dialog box, navigate to your WL2C5 folder, and then double-click the ***CreditCard*** image file.
4. Customize the image so it appears as shown in Figure 5.1 by completing the following steps:
   a. Change the height of the image to 1.8 inches.
   b. Change the text wrapping to Square.
   c. Display the Layout dialog box with the Position tab selected.
   d. Precisely position the image on the page with an absolute horizontal measurement of 4.5 inches to the right of the left margin and an absolute vertical measurement of 5.3 inches below the page.
   e. Display the Format Picture task pane with the Effects icon active.
   f. Click *Shadow* to expand the shadow options.
   g. Apply the Offset: Top Left shadow effect (last option in the *Outer* section).
   h. Change the shadow color to Dark Blue (ninth option in the *Standard Colors* section). (Do this with the Color button in the *Shadow* section of the Format Picture task pane.)
   i. Click *Artistic Effects* to expand the options and then apply the Paint Strokes artistic effect (second column, second row in the drop-down gallery). (Do this with the Artistic Effects button in the *Artistic Effects* section of the task pane.)
   j. Close the Format Picture task pane.
5. Move the insertion point to the end of the document and then insert the text *Cell phones* and *Apple Pay* in text boxes as shown in Figure 5.2 with the following specifications:
   a. Insert a text box below the arrow line on page 2 and then type Cell phones in the text box.
   b. Use the Text Direction button to rotate the text in the text box 270 degrees.
   c. Remove the outline from the text box. (Do this with the Shape Outline button in the Shape Styles group.)
   d. Change the text wrapping to Behind Text.
   e. Drag the text box so it is positioned as shown in Figure 5.2.
   f. Complete similar steps to create the text box with the text *Apple Pay* and position the text box as shown in the figure.
6. Save, print, and then close **5-Timeline**.

Figure 5.1 Assessment 1, Step 4

ELECTRONIC TECHNOLOGY

Information Systems and Commerce

1. Information Systems
   A. Information System Classifications
      1) Distribution Management Systems
      2) Office Information Systems
      3) Management Information Systems
      4) Decision Support Systems
      5) Executive Support Systems
   B. Choosing an Information System
      1) User Interface Design
      2) Niche Information Systems
      3) Turnkey Solutions
      4) System Support
2. Electronic Commerce
   A. Transaction Payment Methods
      1) Check or Credit Card by Phone
      2) Credit Accounts
      3) Credit Cards
      4) Smart Cards
      5) Digital Cash
      6) Electronic Wallets
      7) Apple Pay
   B. Business-to-Business Software
      1) Electronic Data Exchange
      2) Payment and Transaction Systems
      3) Security Technologies
      4) Customer Relationship Management

Figure 5.2 Assessment 1, Step 5

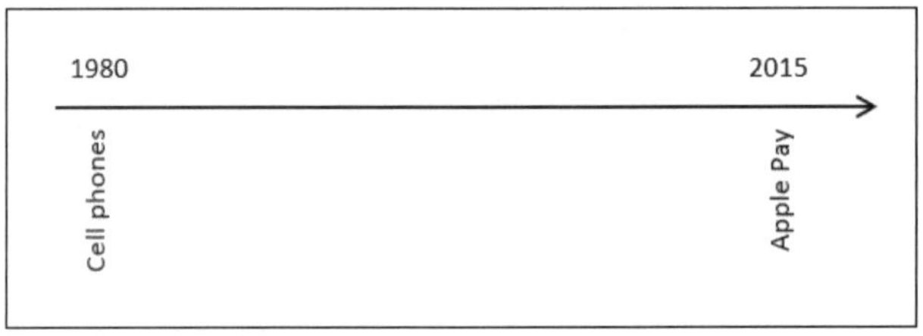

Assessment 2

Format a Shape and Edit Points and Wrap Points

1. Open **CedarMeadows** and then save it with the name **5-CedarMeadows**.
2. Select the shape in the document, display the Format Shape task pane (click the Shape Styles group task pane launcher on the Drawing Tools Format tab), and then apply the following formatting:
   a. Apply the Bottom Spotlight - Accent 5 gradient fill (fifth column, fourth row).
   b. Apply the Inside: Bottom shadow effect (second column, third row in the *Inner* section).
   c. Close the Format Shape task pane.
3. Display editing points around the shape and then adjust the points so they display in a manner similar to what is shown in Figure 5.3. (Click outside the shape after adjusting the editing points.)
4. Select the shape, display the wrap points, and then adjust the wrap points so they display in a manner similar to what is shown in Figure 5.3. (Click outside the shape after adjusting the wrap points.)
5. Save, print, and then close **5-CedarMeadows**.

Figure 5.3 Assessment 2

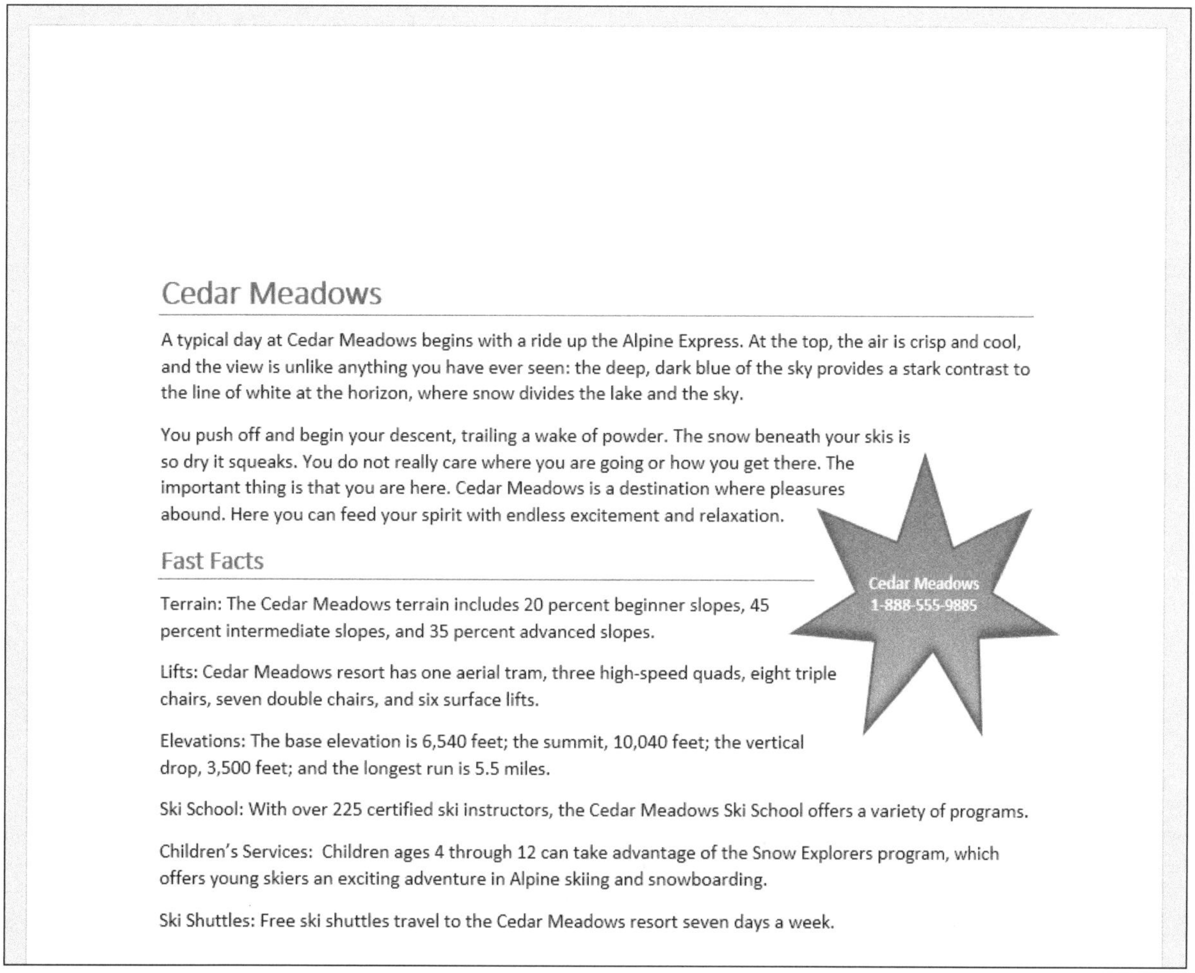

Cedar Meadows

A typical day at Cedar Meadows begins with a ride up the Alpine Express. At the top, the air is crisp and cool, and the view is unlike anything you have ever seen: the deep, dark blue of the sky provides a stark contrast to the line of white at the horizon, where snow divides the lake and the sky.

You push off and begin your descent, trailing a wake of powder. The snow beneath your skis is so dry it squeaks. You do not really care where you are going or how you get there. The important thing is that you are here. Cedar Meadows is a destination where pleasures abound. Here you can feed your spirit with endless excitement and relaxation.

Cedar Meadows
1-888-555-9885

Fast Facts

Terrain: The Cedar Meadows terrain includes 20 percent beginner slopes, 45 percent intermediate slopes, and 35 percent advanced slopes.

Lifts: Cedar Meadows resort has one aerial tram, three high-speed quads, eight triple chairs, seven double chairs, and six surface lifts.

Elevations: The base elevation is 6,540 feet; the summit, 10,040 feet; the vertical drop, 3,500 feet; and the longest run is 5.5 miles.

Ski School: With over 225 certified ski instructors, the Cedar Meadows Ski School offers a variety of programs.

Children's Services: Children ages 4 through 12 can take advantage of the Snow Explorers program, which offers young skiers an exciting adventure in Alpine skiing and snowboarding.

Ski Shuttles: Free ski shuttles travel to the Cedar Meadows resort seven days a week.

Assessment 3 Link Text Boxes

1. Open **ProtectIssues** and then save it with the name **5-ProtectIssues**.
2. Select the text box at the left and link it to the text box at the right.
3. With the insertion point positioned in the text box at the left, insert the file named **ProIssues**. ***Hint: Click the Insert tab, click the Object button arrow, and then click the*** **Text from File** ***option.***
4. Adjust the columns so all the text fits in the two columns by changing the height of both text boxes to 8.4 inches and the width of both to 3.1 inches.
5. Save, print, and then close **5-ProtectIssues**.

Assessment 4 Customize a 3D Model

1. Open **Announcement** and then save it with the name **5-Announcement**.
2. Select the 3D model (a red square with a cross) and then apply the following formatting:
   a. Apply the Above Front Right 3D model view. (You will need to click the More 3D Model Views button in the 3D Model Views group to display additional views. The Above Front Right view is in the fifth column, second row.)
   b. Change the height of the model to 2.7 inches.
   c. Apply Tight text wrapping.

d. Precisely position the model on the page with an absolute horizontal measurement of 4.7 inches to the right of the left margin and an absolute vertical measurement of 4.8 inches below the page.
e. Display the Format 3D Model task pane and then apply the Perspective: Upper Right shadow effect. (To do this, click the Effects icon, click *Shadow* to expand the options, click the Presets button in the *Shadow* section, and then click the *Perspective: Upper Right* option, in the second column, first row in the *Perspective* section.)

3. Select the icon in the upper left corner of the document (a cross in a circle) and then apply the following formatting:
   a. Change the height of the icon to 1.7 inches.
   b. Apply the Light 1 Fill, Colored Outline - Accent 4 graphic style (fifth graphic style in the Graphics Styles gallery).
   c. Change the position of the icon to Position in Top Left with Square Text Wrapping.
   d. Apply the In Front of Text text wrapping.
4. Save, print, and close **5-Announcement**.

Assessment 5

Create and Format a Column Chart and a Pie Chart

1. At a blank document, use the data in Figure 5.4 to create a column chart (using the default chart style at the Insert Chart dialog box) with the following specifications:
   a. Use the Chart Elements button outside the upper right border of the chart to add a data table and remove the legend.
   b. Apply the Style 4 chart style.
   c. Change the chart title to *Units Sold First Quarter*.
   d. Apply the first WordArt style to the chart area.
   e. Change the chart height to 4 inches.
   f. Change the position of the chart to Position in Top Center with Square Text Wrapping.
2. Move the insertion point to the end of the document, press the Enter key two times, and then create a pie chart (using the default pie chart style at the Insert Chart dialog box) with the data shown in Figure 5.5 and with the following specifications:
   a. Apply the Style 3 chart style.
   b. Move the data labels to the inside end of the pie pieces. ***Hint: Click the Chart Elements button that displays outside the upper right corner of the chart, click the arrow at the right of* Data Labels*, and then click* Inside End.**
   c. Change the chart title to *Expense Distribution*.
   d. Apply the Colored Outline - Orange, Accent 2 shape style to the title (third shape style).
   e. Change the chart height to 3 inches and the width to 5.5 inches.
   f. Change the position of the chart to Position in Bottom Center with Square Text Wrapping.
3. Save the document and name it **5-ColumnPieCharts**.
4. Print and then close **5-ColumnPieCharts**.

Figure 5.4 Assessment 5, Step 1, Data for Column Chart

Salesperson	January	February	March
Barnett	55	60	42
Carson	20	24	31
Fanning	15	30	13
Han	52	62	58
Mahoney	49	52	39

Figure 5.5 Assessment 5, Step 2, Data for Pie Chart

Category	Percentage
Salaries	67%
Travel	15%
Equipment	11%
Supplies	7%

Assessment 6

Insert a Horizontal Line in a Footer

1. Open a blank document and then insert a horizontal line by clicking the Borders button arrow in the Paragraph group on the Home tab and then clicking *Horizontal Line* at the drop-down list. Click the horizontal line to select it and then right-click the line. Click *Picture* at the shortcut menu and the Format Horizontal Line dialog box displays. Look at the formatting options that are available at the dialog box and then click the Cancel button to close the dialog box. Close the document without saving it.
2. Open **ShopOnline** and then save it with the name **5-ShopOnline**.
3. Keep the heading *ONLINE SHOPPING MALLS* together with the paragraph that follows it.
4. Create a footer that contains a horizontal line in the standard blue color (eighth color option in the *Standard Colors* section) with a height of 3 points.
5. Save, print, and then close **5-ShopOnline**.

Visual Benchmark

Create a Company Chart

1. Open **Blueline** and then save it with the name **5-Blueline**.
2. Select the gears icon and then customize the icon so it appears as shown in Figure 5.6 with the following specifications:
   - Flip the gears icon horizontally.
   - Apply the Colored Fill - Accent 1, Dark 1 Outline graphic style (second column, third row in the Graphics Styles group gallery).
   - Apply text wrapping that moves the icon behind text.
   - Size and move the gears icon so it is positioned as shown in Figure 5.6.
3. Create the column chart shown in Figure 5.6 with the following specifications:
   - Choose the 3-D Clustered Column Chart at the Insert Chart dialog box.
   - Use the information shown in the chart in the figure to create the data for the chart. (You will need to decrease the size of the data range by one column.)
   - Add a data table to the chart.
   - Change the color of the 2021 series to Dark Blue.
   - Make any other changes so your chart appears similar to the chart in the figure.
4. Save, print, and then close **5-Blueline**.

Figure 5.6 Visual Benchmark

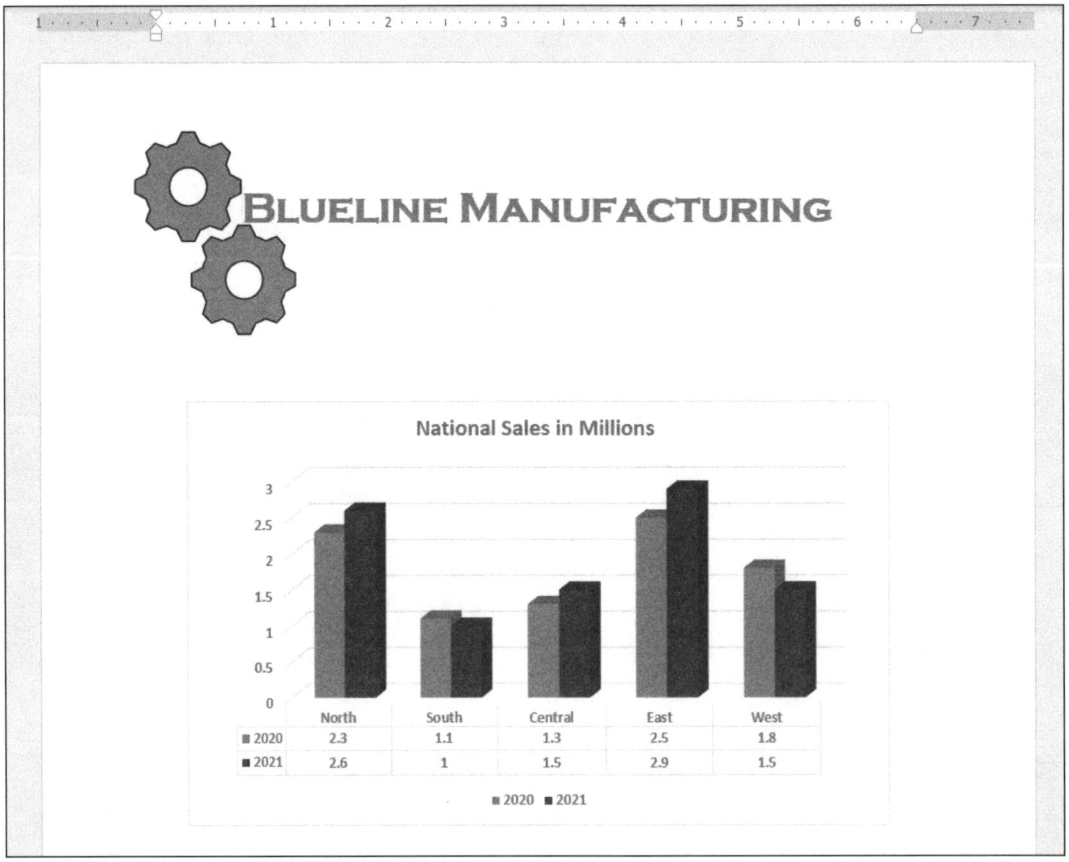

Case Study

Part
1

You are the office manager for Hometown Music, a music store in your town. You have been asked by the owner to create a new letterhead for the music store. Open a blank document, create a custom first page header, and then create a letterhead for the store in the First Page Header pane. Use an image in the letterhead. Some possible images are available in your WL2C5 folder and begin with *Music*. Include an address for the music store and use your town, state, and zip code in the letterhead; also include a telephone number. (The address and phone number can be inserted in the First Page Footer pane rather than the First Page Header pane.) In the First Page Footer pane, insert three icons in the footer, including the eye icon (in the *Analytics* category), the heart icon (in the *Signs and Symbols* category), and the music note icon (in the *Arts* category). (These icons represent the saying "I love music.") Customize, size, and position the icons in the First Page Footer pane. Save the completed letterhead document and name it **5-HMLtrhd**. Save **5-HMLtrhd** as a template in your WL2C5 folder and name the template **5-HMLtrhd-Template**. Close **5-HMLtrhd-Template**.

Part
2

The owner of Hometown Music would like to have a chart of the percentage breakdown of income for the year. Open **HMIncome**, print the document, and then close it. Use File Explorer to open a document based on the **HMLtrhd-Template** you created in Part 1. Use the information you printed to create a pie chart. Apply formatting and customize the pie chart so it is attractive and easy to understand. Save the completed document and name it **5-HMPieChart**. Print and then close **5-HMPieChart**.

Part
3

You have created an invitation for an upcoming piano recital at Hometown Music. You inserted a 3D model in the invitation and need to customize it so it has more visual impact. Open **HMPianoRecital** and then save it with the name **5-HMPianoRecital**. Select the grand piano 3D model, rotate the image so that the keyboard is facing to the right, increase the size, apply a text wrapping option, and move the piano image into the lower left corner of the invitation. Save, print, and then close **5-HMPianoRecital**.

Part
4

The owner would like to have a flyer describing Hometown Music's instrument rental program that can be distributed at recitals and at local schools. Open **HMRentals**, look at the information, and then create a flyer that includes some of the information in the document. Include visual interest in the flyer by inserting a photograph, picture, icon, and/or 3D model. Format the flyer so it appears similar to other Hometown Music documents you have created. Save the completed flyer and name it **5-HMRentalFlyer**. Print and then close **5-HMRentalFlyer**.

Microsoft® Word
Review and Assessment

CHAPTER
6

Merging Documents

The online course includes additional review and assessment resources.

Skills Assessment

Assessment 1

Create a Data Source File

1. At a blank document, display the New Address List dialog box and then display the Customize Address List dialog box. (To do this, click the Mailings tab, click the Select Recipients button, click the *Type a New List* option, and then click the Customize Columns button.)
2. At the Customize Address List dialog box, delete the following fields—*Company Name*, *Country or Region*, *Work Phone*, and *E-mail Address*—and then add a custom field named *Cell Phone*. (Position the *Cell Phone* field after the *Home Phone* field.)
3. Close the Customize Address List dialog box and then type the following information in the New Address List dialog box as the first record:

Title	Mr.
First Name	Tony
Last Name	Benedetti
Address Line 1	1315 Cordova Road
Address Line 2	Apt. 402
City	Santa Fe
State	NM
ZIP Code	87505
Home Phone	(505) 555-0489
Cell Phone	(505) 555-0551

4. Type the following information as the second record:

Title	Ms.
First Name	Theresa
Last Name	Dusek
Address Line 1	12044 Ridgeway Drive
Address Line 2	(leave blank)
City	Santa Fe
State	NM
ZIP Code	87504
Home Phone	(505) 555-1120
Cell Phone	(505) 555-6890

5. Type the following information as the third record:

Title	Ms.
First Name	Mary
Last Name	Arguello
Address Line 1	2554 Country Drive
Address Line 2	#105
City	Santa Fe
State	NM
ZIP Code	87504
Home Phone	(505) 555-7663
Cell Phone	(505) 555-5472

6. Type the following information as the fourth record:

Title	Mr.
First Name	Preston
Last Name	Miller
Address Line 1	120 Second Street
Address Line 2	(leave blank)
City	Santa Fe
State	NM
ZIP Code	87505
Home Phone	(505) 555-3551
Cell Phone	(505) 555-9630

7. Save the data source file and name it **6-CCDS**.
8. Close the blank document without saving changes.

Assessment 2

Create a Letter Main Document and Merge with a Data Source File

1. Open **CCVolunteerLtr** and then save it with the name **6-CCMD**.
2. Select the **6-CCDS** data source file you created in Assessment 1.
3. Move the insertion point to the beginning of the first paragraph of text in the body of the letter, insert the *«AddressBlock»* field, and then press the Enter key two times.
4. Insert the *«GreetingLine»* field specifying a colon rather than a comma as the greeting line format and then press the Enter key two times.
5. Move the insertion point one space to the right of the period that ends the second paragraph of text in the body of the letter and then type the following text inserting the *«Title»*, *«Last_Name»*, *«Home_Phone»*, and *«Cell_Phone»* fields where indicated:

   Currently, *«Title»* *«Last_Name»*, our records indicate your home telephone number is *«Home_Phone»* and your cell phone number is *«Cell_Phone»*. If this information is not accurate, please contact our office with the correct numbers.

6. Merge the main document with all the records in the data source file.
7. Save the merged letters document as **6-CCLetters**.
8. Print and then close **6-CCLetters**.
9. Save and then close **6-CCMD**.

Assessment 3 — Create an Envelope Main Document and Merge with a Data Source File

1. Create an envelope main document using the Size 10 envelope size.
2. Select **6-CCDS** as the data source file.
3. Insert the *«AddressBlock»* field in the appropriate location in the envelope document.
4. Merge the envelope main document with all the records in the data source file.
5. Save the merged envelopes document and name it **6-CCEnvs**.
6. Print and then close the envelopes document. (Check with your instructor before printing the envelopes.)
7. Save the envelope main document with the name **6-CCEnvsMD** and then close the document.

Assessment 4 — Create a Label Main Document and Merge with a Data Source File

1. Create a label main document using the option *Avery US Letter 5160 Address Labels*.
2. Select **6-CCDS** as the data source file.
3. Insert the *«AddressBlock»* field.
4. Update the labels.
5. Merge the label main document with all the records in the data source file.
6. Select the entire document and then apply the No Spacing style.
7. Save the merged labels document and name it **6-CCLabels**.
8. Print and then close the labels document.
9. Save the label main document with the name **6-CCLabelsMD** and then close the document.

Assessment 5 — Edit a Data Source File

1. Open **6-CCMD**. (At the message asking if you want to continue, click Yes.) Save the main document with the name **6-CCMD-A5**.
2. Edit the **6-CCDS** data source file by making the following changes:
   a. Change the address for Ms. Theresa Dusek from *12044 Ridgeway Drive* to *1390 Fourth Avenue*.
   b. Delete the record for Ms. Mary Arguello.
   c. Insert a new record with the following information:
      Mr. Cesar Rivera
      3201 East Third Street
      Santa Fe, NM 87505
      Home Phone: (505) 555-6675
      Cell Phone: (505) 555-3528
3. Merge the main document with all the records in the data source file.
4. Save the merged letters document as **6-CCLtrsEdited**.
5. Print and then close **6-CCLtrsEdited**.
6. Save and then close **6-CCMD-A5**.

Visual Benchmark

Prepare and Merge Letters

1. Open **FPLtrhd** and then save it with the name **6-FPMD**.
2. Look at the information in Figure 6.1 and Figure 6.2 and then use Mail Merge to prepare four letters. (When creating the main document, as shown in Figure 6.2, insert the appropriate fields where you see the text *Title*; *First Name*; *Last Name*; *Street Address*; and *City, State ZIP*. Insert the appropriate fields where you see the text *Title* and *Last Name* in the first paragraph of text.) Create the data source file with customized field names using the information in Figure 6.1 and then save the file and name it **6-FPDS**.
3. Merge the **6-FPMD** main document with the **6-FPDS** data source file and then save the merged letters document and name it **6-FPLtrs**.
4. Print and then close **6-FPLtrs**.
5. Save and then close **6-FPMD**.

Figure 6.1 Visual Benchmark Data Source Records

Mr. Chris Gallagher
17034 234th Avenue
Newport, VT 05855

Mr. Gene Goodrich
831 Cromwell Lane
Newport, VT 05855

Ms. Heather Segarra
4103 Thompson Drive
Newport, VT 05855

Ms. Sonya Kraus
15933 Ninth Street
Newport, VT 05855

Figure 6.2 Visual Benchmark Main Document

FRONTLINE
PHOTOGRAPHY

Current Date

Title First Name Last Name
Street Address
City, State ZIP

Dear Title Last Name:

We have enjoyed being a part of the Newport business community for the past two years. Our success has been thanks to you, Title Last Name, and all our other loyal customers. Thank you for shopping at our store for all of your photography equipment and supply needs.

To show our appreciation for your business, we are enclosing a coupon for 20 percent off any item in our store, including our incredibly low-priced clearance items. Through the end of the month, all camera accessories are on sale. Use your coupon and take advantage of additional savings on items such as camera lenses, tripods, cleaning supplies, and camera bags.

To accommodate our customers' schedules, we have extended our weekend hours. Our store will be open Saturdays until 7:00 p.m. and Sundays, until 5:00 p.m. Come by and let our sales associates find the right camera and accessories for you.

Sincerely,

Student Name

XX
6-FPMD

Enclosure

559 Tenth Street, Suite A, Newport, VT 05855
802.555.4411 ⦿ https://ppi-edu.net/frontline

Case Study

Part 1

You are the office manager for Freestyle Extreme, a sporting goods store that specializes in snowboarding and snow skiing equipment and supplies. The store has two branches: one on the east side of town and the other on the west side. One of your job responsibilities is to send letters to customers letting them know about sales, new equipment, and upcoming events. Next month, both stores are having a sale and all snowboarding and snow skiing supplies will be 15 percent off the last marked price.

Create a data source file that contains the following customer information: first name, last name, address, city, state, zip code, and branch. Add six customers to the data source file. Indicate that three usually shop at the East branch and three usually shop at the West branch.

Create a letter as a main document that includes information about the upcoming sale. The letter should contain at least two paragraphs and in addition to the information on the sale, it might include information about the store, snowboarding, and/or snow skiing.

Save the data source file with the name **6-FEDS**, save the main document with the name **6-FEMD**, and save the merged document with the name **6-FELtrs**. Create envelopes for the six merged letters and name the merged envelope document **6-FEEnvs**. Save the envelope main document with the name **6-FEEnvsMD**. Print the merged letters document and the merged envelopes document.

Part 2

A well-known extreme snowboarder will be visiting both branches of Freestyle Extreme to meet with customers and sign autographs. Use the Help feature to learn how to insert an *If...Then...Else...* merge field in a document and then create a letter that includes the name of the extreme snowboarder (you determine the name), the times of the visits to the two branches (1:00 p.m. to 4:30 p.m.), and any additional information that might interest customers. Also include in the letter an *If...Then...Else...* merge field that will insert *Wednesday, September 22* if the customer's branch is *East* and *Thursday, September 23* if the customer's branch is *West*. Add visual interest to the letter by inserting an image, WordArt, or other feature that will attract readers' attention. Save the letter main document and name it **6-SnowMD**. Merge the letter main document with the **6-FEDS** data source file. Save the merged letters document and name it **6-SnowLtrs**. Print the merged letters document.

Part 3

The owner of Freestyle Extreme wants to try selling short skis known as "snow blades" or "skiboards." He has asked you to research these skis and identify one type and model to sell only at the West branch of the store. If the model sells well, the owner will consider selling it at the East branch at a future time. Prepare a main document letter that describes the new snow blade or skiboard that the West branch is going to sell. Include information about pricing and tell customers that they can save 40 percent if they purchase the new item within the next week. Merge the letter main document with the **6-FEDS** data source file and include only those customers that shop at the West branch. Save the merged letters document and name it **6-SBLtrs**. Print the merged letters document. Save the letter main document and name it **6-SBMD**. Save and then close the main document.

Microsoft® Word
Review and Assessment

CHAPTER 7

Managing Building Blocks and Fields

The online course includes additional review and assessment resources.

Skills Assessment

Assessment 1 Create Building Blocks

1. Press Ctrl + N to open a blank document and then save the blank document as a template in your WL2C7 folder and name it **7-WLTemplate**. (Make sure you change the *Save as type* option at the Save As dialog box to *Word Template*.)
2. Close **7-WLTemplate**.
3. Use File Explorer to open a document based on **7-WLTemplate** in your WL2C7 folder.
4. Insert **WLFooter** into the document. ***Hint: Use the Object button arrow on the Insert tab.***
5. Select the line of text containing the address and telephone number (including the paragraph mark that ends the line). Save the selected text in a custom building block in the Footer gallery; name the building block *WLFooter* and save it in **7-WLTemplate**. ***Hint: Use the Footer button to save the content to the Footer gallery.***
6. Select the entire document, press the Delete key, and then insert **WLHeading** into the current document. ***Hint: Use the Object button arrow on the Insert tab.***
7. Select the two lines of text (including the paragraph mark at the end of the second line). Save the selected text in a custom building block in the Quick Part gallery; name the building block *WLHeading* and save it in **7-WLTemplate**.
8. Select the entire document and press the Delete key, and then type the text shown in Figure 7.1. (Make sure you apply bold formatting to *Fees:*. If autocorrect superscripts the *th* in *1/6th*, undo the correction.)
9. Select the entire document, save the selected text in a custom building block in the AutoText gallery and name the building block *WLFeesPara* and save it in **7-WLTemplate**.
10. Close the document without saving it. At the message asking if you want to save changes to the template, click the Save button.

Figure 7.1 Assessment 1

Fees: My hourly rate is $350, billed in one-sixth (1/6th) of an hour increments. All time spent on work performed, including meetings, telephone calls, correspondences, and emails, will be billed at the hourly rate set forth in this paragraph. Additional expenses, such as out-of-pocket expenses for postage, courier fees, photocopying charges, and search fees, will be charged at the hourly rate set forth in this paragraph.

Assessment 2 — Use Building Blocks to Prepare an Agreement

1. Use File Explorer to open a blank document based on **7-WLTemplate** in your WL2C7 folder.
2. At the blank document, create an agreement with the following specifications:
   a. Insert the *WLHeading* custom building block in the Quick Part gallery.
   b. Press the Enter key and then insert the *WLFeesPara* custom building block in the AutoText gallery.
   c. Insert **WLRepAgrmnt**. ***Hint: Use the Object button arrow on the Insert tab.***
   d. Insert the *WLFooter* custom building block. ***Hint: Do this with the Footer button.***
3. Click the Close Header and Footer button and then save the completed agreement and name it **7-WLRepAgrmnt**.
4. Print and then close **7-WLRepAgrmnt**.
5. Use File Explorer to open a document based on **7-WLTemplate**.
6. Click the Insert tab, click the Quick Parts button, and then point to *AutoText*.
7. Press the Print Screen button on your keyboard and then click in the document.
8. At the blank document, click the Paste button.
9. Print the document and then close it without saving it.

Assessment 3 — Format a Property Protection Report

1. Open **ProtectIssues** and then save it with the name **7-ProtectIssues**.
2. With the insertion point positioned at the beginning of the document, insert the *Automatic Table 2* table of contents building block.
3. Insert the *Banded* header building block, click the *[DOCUMENT TITLE]* placeholder and then type property protection issues.
4. Insert the *Banded* footer building block and then make the document active.
5. Press Ctrl + End to move the insertion point to the end of the document and then insert a field that will insert the file name (without any formatting).
6. Press Shift + Enter and then insert a field that will insert the current date and time (you choose the format).
7. Save, print, and then close **7-ProtectIssues**.

Assessment 4 — Insert an Equation Building Block

1. The Building Blocks Organizer dialog box contains a number of predesigned equations that you can insert in a document. At a blank document, display the Building Blocks Organizer dialog box and then insert one of the predesigned equations.
2. Select the equation and then click the Equation Tools Design tab. Notice the groups of commands available for editing an equation.
3. Type the steps you followed to insert the equation and then type a list of the groups available on the Equation Tools Design tab.
4. Save the document and name it **7-Equation**. Print and then close the document.

Visual Benchmark

Create an Agreement with Building Blocks and AutoCorrect Text

1. Use File Explorer to open a document based on **7-WLTemplate**.
2. Create the document shown in Figure 7.2 with the following specifications:
   a. Insert **WLAgreement** into the open document.
   b. At the AutoCorrect dialog box with the AutoCorrect tab selected, create AutoCorrect entries for the text *Woodland Legal Services* (use *wls*) and *Till-Harris Management* (use *thm*).

c. Press Ctrl + Home and then type the first three paragraphs of text shown in Figure 7.2 using the AutoCorrect entries you created.
d. Insert the *WLHeading* building block at the beginning of the document and insert the *WLFooter* building block as a footer.
e. Justify the six paragraphs of text in the document.

3. Save the completed document and name it **7-THMAgrmnt**.
4. Print and then close **7-THMAgrmnt**.
5. Display the AutoCorrect dialog box, delete the *wls* and *thm* entries, and then close the dialog box.

Figure 7.2 Visual Benchmark

REPRESENTATION AGREEMENT

Carlos Sawyer, Attorney at Law

This agreement is made between Carlos Sawyer of Woodland Legal Services and Till-Harris Management for legal services to be provided by Woodland Legal Services.

Legal Representation: Woodland Legal Services will perform the legal services required by Till-Harris Management, keep Till-Harris Management informed of progress and developments, and respond promptly to Till-Harris Management's inquiries and communications.

Attorney's Fees and Costs: Till-Harris Management will pay Woodland Legal Services for attorney's fees for legal services provided under this agreement at the hourly rate of the individuals providing the services. Under this agreement, Till-Harris Management will pay all costs incurred by Woodland Legal Services for representation of Till-Harris Management. Costs will be advanced by Woodland Legal Services and then billed to Till-Harris Management unless the costs can be met from deposits.

Deposit for Fees: Till-Harris Management will pay to Woodland Legal Services an initial deposit of $5,000, to be received by Woodland Legal Services on or before November 1, 2021. Twenty percent of the deposit is nonrefundable and will be applied against attorney's fees. The refundable portion will be deposited by Woodland Legal Services in an interest-bearing trust account. Till-Harris Management authorizes Woodland Legal Services to withdraw the principal from the trust account to pay attorney's fees in excess of the nonrefundable portion.

Statement and Payments: Woodland Legal Services will send Till-Harris Management monthly statements indicating attorney's fees and costs incurred, amounts applied from deposits, and current balance owed. If no attorney's fees or costs are incurred for a month, the statement may be held and combined with that for the following month. Any balance will be paid in full within 30 days after the statement is mailed.

Effective Date of Agreement: The effective date of this agreement will be the date when it is executed by both parties.

Client: ______________________________ Date: ______________

Attorney: ____________________________ Date: ______________

7110 FIFTH STREET ◆ SUITE 200 ◆ OMAHA NE 68207 ◆ 402-555-7110

Case Study

Part 1

You have been hired as the office manager for Highland Construction Company. The address of the company is 9025 Palmer Park Boulevard, Colorado Springs, CO 80904 and the telephone number is (719) 555-4575. You are responsible for designing business documents that have a consistent visual style and formatting. You decide that your first task is to create a letterhead document. Press Ctrl + N to open a blank document and then save the document as a template named **7-HCCTemplate** in your WL2C7 folder. Close the template document. Use File Explorer to open a document based on **7-HCCTemplate**. At the blank document based on the template, create a letterhead that includes the company name, address, and telephone number, along with an image and/or any other elements to add visual interest. Select the letterhead text and element(s) and then create a building block in the Quick Part gallery named **HCCLtrhd** that is saved in **7-HCCTemplate**. Create the following additional building blocks for your company. (You decide on the names and save the building blocks in **7-HCCTemplate**.)

- Create a building block footer that contains a border line (in a color matching the colors in the letterhead) and the company slogan:

  Colorado Business Since 1985

- Create the following complimentary close building block:

  Sincerely,

  Your Name
  Office Manager

- Create the following company name and address building block:

  Mr. Eric Rashad
  Roswell Industries
  1020 Wasatch Street
  Colorado Springs, CO 80902

- Create the following company name and address building block:

  Ms. Claudia Sanborn
  S & S Supplies
  537 Constitution Avenue
  Colorado Springs, CO 80911

Select and then delete the contents of the document. Close the document without saving it. At the message asking if you want to save changes to the template, click the Save button.

Part 2

Use File Explorer to open a document based on **7-HCCTemplate**. Apply the No Spacing style and then create a letter to Eric Rashad by inserting the Highland Construction Company letterhead (the *HCCLtrhd* building block). Press the Enter key, type today's date, press the Enter key four times, and then insert the *Eric Rashad* building block. Press the Enter key, type an appropriate salutation (such as *Dear Mr. Rashad:*), insert the file named **HCCLetter**, and then insert your complimentary close building block. Finally, insert the footer building block you created for the company. Check the letter and modify the spacing as needed. Save the letter and name it **7-RashadLtr**. Print and then close the letter. Complete similar steps to create a letter to Claudia Sanborn. Save the completed letter and name it **7-SanbornLtr**. Print and then close the letter.

Part 3

Use File Explorer to open a document based on **7-HCCTemplate**. Insert the Highland Construction Company letterhead building block you created in Part 1, type the title *Company Services*, and then insert a SmartArt graphic of your choosing that contains the following text:

Residential Construction
Commercial Construction
Design Consultation
Site Preparation

Apply a heading style to the *Company Services* title, insert the company footer building block, and then save the document and name it **7-CoServices**. Print and then close the document.

Microsoft® Word
Review and Assessment

CHAPTER 8

Managing Shared Documents

The online course includes additional review and assessment resources.

Skills Assessment

Assessment 1
Insert Comments in a Web Report

1. Open **NavigateWeb** and then save it with the name **8-NavigateWeb**.
2. Delete the only comment in the document.
3. Position the insertion point at the end of the first paragraph in the section *IPs and URLs* and then insert a comment and type the following comment text: Please identify what the letters ICANN stand for.
4. Position the insertion point at the end of the third paragraph in the section *IPs and URLs* and then insert a comment and type the following comment text: Insert a caption for the following table and the two other tables in the document.
5. Position the insertion point at the end of the last paragraph in the document (above the last table) and insert a comment and type the following comment text: Include in the following table additional examples of methods for narrowing a search.
6. Save the document and then print only the comments.
7. Close **8-NavigateWeb**.

Assessment 2
Track Changes in a Computer Viruses Report

1. Open **CompChapters** and then save it with the name **8-CompChapters**.
2. Turn on Track Changes and then make the following changes:
   a. Edit the first sentence in the document so it displays as follows: *The computer virus is one of the most familiar forms of risk to computer security.*
   b. Type computer's between *the* and *motherboard* in the last sentence in the first paragraph of the document.
   c. Delete the word *real* in the second sentence in the section *Types of Viruses* and then type significant.
   d. Select and then delete the last sentence in the section *Methods of Virus Operation* (which begins *A well-known example of the logic bomb was the*).
   e. Turn off Track Changes.
3. Display the Word Options dialog box with *General* selected and then change the user name to *Stanley Phillips* and the initials to *SP*. Insert a check mark in the *Always use these values regardless of sign in to Office* check box.

4. Turn on Track Changes and then make the following changes:
   a. Delete the words *or cracker* in the seventh sentence in the section *Types of Viruses*.
   b. Delete the word *garner* in the first sentence in the section *CHAPTER 2: SECURITY RISKS* and then type generate.
   c. Select and then move the section *Employee Theft* after the section *Cracking Software for Copying*.
   d. Turn off Track Changes.
5. Display the Word Options dialog box with *General* selected. Change the user name back to the original name and the initials back to the original initials. Also remove the check mark from the *Always use these values regardless of sign in to Office* check box.
6. Print the document. (The document will print with the markups.)
7. Accept all the changes in the document *except* the change moving the section *Employee Theft* after the section *Cracking Software for Copying*; reject this change.
8. Save, print, and then close **8-CompChapters**.

Assessment 3

Restrict Formatting and Editing of a Writing Report

1. Open **WritingProcess** and then save it with the name **8-WritingProcess**.
2. Display the Restrict Editing task pane and then restrict formatting to the Heading 2 and Heading 3 styles. (At the message asking about removing formatting or styles that are not allowed, click No.)
3. Enforce the protection and include the password *writing*.
4. Click the Available styles hyperlink.
5. Apply the Heading 2 style to the two titles *THE WRITING PROCESS* and *REFERENCES*.
6. Apply the Heading 3 style to the seven remaining headings in the document. (The Heading 3 style may not display until the Heading 2 style is applied to the first title.)
7. Close the Styles task pane and then close the Restrict Editing task pane.
8. Save the document and then print only page 1.
9. Close **8-WritingProcess**.

Assessment 4

Insert Comments in a Software Life Cycle Document

1. Open **CommCycle** and then save it with the name **8-CommCycle**.
2. Display the Restrict Editing task pane, restrict editing to comments only, and then start enforcing the protection. (Do not include a password.)
3. At the end of the first paragraph in the document, type the comment Create a SmartArt graphic that illustrates the software life cycle.
4. At the end of the paragraph in the *Design* section, type the comment Include the problem-solving steps.
5. At the end of the paragraph in the *Testing* section, type the comment Describe a typical beta testing cycle.
6. Print only the comments.
7. Close the Restrict Editing task pane.
8. Save and then close **8-CommCycle**.

Assessment 5

Track Changes in a Table

1. Open **SalesTable** and then save it with the name **8-SalesTable**.
2. Display the Advanced Track Changes Options dialog box, look at the options for customizing tracked changes in a table, and then make the following changes:
   a. Change the color for inserted cells to Light Purple.
   b. Change the color for deleted cells to Light Green.
3. Turn on Track Changes and then make the following changes:
   a. Insert a new row at the beginning of the table.
   b. Merge the cells in the new row. (At the message stating that the action will not be marked as a change, click OK.)
   c. Type Clearline Manufacturing in the merged cell.
   d. Delete the *Fanning, Andrew* row.
   e. Insert a new row below *Barnet, Jacqueline* and then type Montano, Neil in the first cell, $530,678 in the second cell, and $550,377 in the third cell.
   f. Turn off Track Changes.
4. Save and then print the document. (The document will print with the markups.)
5. Accept all the changes.
6. Display the Advanced Track Changes Options dialog box and then return the color of the inserted cells to Light Blue and the color of the deleted cells to Pink.
7. Save, print, and then close **8-SalesTable**.

Visual Benchmark

Track Changes in an Employee Performance Document

1. Open **NSSEmpPerf** and then save it with the name **8-NSSEmpPerf**.
2. Turn on Track Changes and then make the changes shown in Figure 8.1. (Make the editing changes before moving the *Employment Records* section after the *Performance Evaluation* section.)
3. Turn off Track Changes and then print only the list of markups. ***Hint: Do this by displaying the Print backstage area, clicking the first gallery in the Settings category, and then clicking the* List of Markup *option.***
4. Accept all the changes to the document.
5. Save, print, and then close **8-NSSEmpPerf**.

Figure 8.1 Visual Benchmark

N

Northland Security Systems

3200 North 22nd Street ✦ Springfield ✦ IL ✦ 62102

EMPLOYEE PERFORMANCE

Work Performance Standards

~~Some~~ work performance standards are written statements of the results [and/or behavior] expected of an employee when his or her job elements are satisfactorily performed under existing working conditions. Each employee in a permanent position must be provided with a current set of work performance standards for his or her position.

cap

Employment Records

Your personnel file is maintained in the human resources department. ~~at the main office of Northland Security Systems.~~ The human resources department maintains a [working] file with copies of the documentation in your specific department. Your file includes personnel action documents, mandatory employment forms, your performance evaluations, and documentation of disciplinary action. Your file may include letters of commendation, training certificates, or other work-related documents that your supervisor has requested to be included in your file.

Performance Evaluation

If you are serving a six-month [(full-time equivalent)] probationary period, your supervisor will evaluate your performance at the end of the second and fifth months. If you are completing a one-year probationary period, your evaluations will be conducted at the end of the third, seventh, and eleventh month. You will receive a copy of each performance report. Once you have attained permanent employee status, your performance will be evaluated annually during the month prior to your pay progression date. Each evaluation will include a discussion between you and your supervisor to review and clarify goals and methods to achieve them. The evaluation will also include a [written] report of your progress on the job. Evaluations will be made with reference to established work performance standards.

1-888-555-2200 ✦ https://ppi-edu.net/nss

Case Study

Part 1

You work for Premier Associates, a career development company that provides career placement, transition, and outplacement for clients. Some of the company's materials need formatting to reflect the company's brand. Open **PALtrhd** and look at the first page header and first page footer. Notice the colors and images used in the header and footer and then close the document. Open **PAResume** and then save it with the name **8-PAResume**. This document has been reviewed by your supervisor, who made her edits as tracked changes. Accept the editing changes to the document and turn off tracked changes. Look at the one comment in the document, make the change mentioned in the comment and then delete the comment. Format the document so it is attractive and easy to read. Consider using the **PAHead** image as a header and **PAFoot** as a footer. Add any additional information to the header or footer that you think is needed. Save, print, and then close **8-PAResume**.

Part 2

Your supervisor has given you another document that she has edited and wants you to format. Open **PAResumeStyles** and then save it with the name **8-PAResumeStyles**. Accept or reject the edits made by your supervisor and then turn off tracked changes. (The document contains two edits that should be rejected.) Make the change suggested by her comment. Apply formatting to the document similar to what you applied to **8-PAResume**. Save, print, and then close **8-PAResumeStyles**.

Part 3

Your company provides a sample chonological resume to clients. Your supervisor wants you to open the sample resume and apply formatting to the resume so it has the look and branding of the other Premier Associates documents. Open **PAChronoResume** and then save it with the name **8-PAChronoResume**. Apply formatting so the document has the look of other Premier Associates documents. Save, print, and then close **8-PAChronoResume**.

Part 4

Your supervisor has asked you to search for a resume template and then download and print it to make it available for clients. Display the New backstage area and search for resumes. Download a resume that looks interesting to you. Apply formatting to the resume so it has the look of the other Premier Associates documents. Save the resume and name it **8-PAWordResume**. Print and then close **8-PAWordResume**.

Unit 2 Performance Assessment

Data Files

Before beginning unit work, copy the WL2U2 folder to your storage medium and then make WL2U2 the active folder.

Assessing Proficiency

In this unit, you have learned to customize objects, create and format charts, merge documents, apply and customize building blocks, and insert and update fields. You have also learned to insert and manage comments, track changes, and restrict and protect documents.

Assessment 1 Insert and Format Objects

1. Open **HMConcert** and then save it with the name **U2-HMConcert**.
2. The border is a drawn image that is positioned in the First Page Header pane. Double-click in the header, select the border image, apply the following formatting, and then close the First Page Header pane:
   - Apply the Light Gray, Background 2, Darker 10% shape fill (third column, second row in the *Theme Colors* section).
   - Apply the Offset: Center shape shadow effect (second column, second row in the *Outer* section).
3. Select the image of the music notes and then apply the following formatting:
   - Change the height of the image to 2.5 inches and the width to 4.5 inches.
   - Precisely position the image on the page with an absolute horizontal measurement of 0.46 inch to the right of the left margin and an absolute vertical measurement of 0.9 inch below the page.
4. Click in the table cell immediately left of the telephone number 253.555.4500 (you may want to turn on the display of table gridlines), insert the telephone icon ☎ (located in the *Communication* category in the Insert Icons window), and then apply the following formatting:
   - Change the height of the image to 0.3 inch.
   - Apply the Light 1 Fill, Colored Outline - Accent 3 graphic style (fourth style in the Graphic Styles gallery).

5. Click in the table cell immediately left of the email address, insert the envelope icon 🖂 (located in the *Communication* category), and then apply the same formatting to the envelope icon that you applied to the telephone icon.
6. Save, print, and then close **U2-HMConcert**.

Assessment 2 Customize a 3D Model

1. Open **OpenHouse** and then save it with the name **U2-OpenHouse**.
2. Insert a 3D model of a person in a spacesuit located in the Space category at the Online 3D Models window. (Insert the 3D model that does not contain a "runner" badge.) ***Note: If you do not have access to the internet, open the OpenHouse-3D document from your WL2U2 folder and then save it with the name U2-OpenHouse.***
3. Select the 3D model of the person in a spacesuit and then apply the following formatting:
   - Rotate the image so the person in the spacesuit is looking more toward his or her right.
   - Increase the height of the image to 4.4 inches.
   - Move the image so it is positioned to the right of *25!* (The image can overlap a portion of the *25!*)
4. Save, print, and then close **U2-OpenHouse**.

Assessment 3 Create and Format a Column Chart

1. At a blank document, use the data in Figure U2.1 to create a column chart with the following specifications:
   a. Choose the 3-D Clustered Column chart type.
   b. Apply the Layout 3 quick layout.
   c. Apply the Style 5 chart style.
   d. Change the chart title to *Yearly Sales*.
   e. Insert a data table with legend keys.

Figure U2.1 Assessment 3

Salesperson	First Half	Second Half
Bratton	$235,500	$285,450
Daniels	$300,570	$250,700
Hughes	$170,200	$180,210
Marez	$308,520	$346,400

f. Select the chart area, apply the Subtle Effect - Green, Accent 6 shape style (last column, fourth row in the *Theme Styles* section), and then apply the Offset: Bottom shadow shape effect (second column, first row in the *Outer* section).
g. Select the series *Second Half* and then apply the standard dark red shape fill (first option in the *Standard Colors* section).
h. Change the chart height to 4 inches and the chart width to 6.25 inches.
i. Use the Position button in the Arrange group to position the chart in the middle center of the page with square text wrapping.

2. Save the document with the name **U2-SalesChart**.
3. Print **U2-SalesChart**.
4. With the chart selected, display the Excel worksheet and then edit the data in the worksheet by changing the following:
   a. Change the amount in cell C2 from *$285,450* to *$302,500.*
   b. Change the amount in cell C4 from *$180,210* to *$190,150.*
5. Save, print, and then close **U2-SalesChart**.

Assessment 4 Create and Format a Pie Chart

1. At a blank document, use the data in Figure U2.2 to create a pie chart with the following specifications:
   a. Apply the Layout 6 quick layout.
   b. Apply the Style 3 chart style.
   c. Change the chart title to *District Expenditures*.
   d. Move the legend to the left side of the chart.
   e. Select the chart area, apply the Gold, Accent 4, Lighter 80% shape fill (eighth column, second row in the *Theme Colors* section), and then apply the Glow: 11 point; Gray, Accent color 3 glow shape effect (third column, third row in the *Glow Variations* section).
   f. Select the legend and apply the Blue color shape outline (eighth option in the *Standard Colors* section).
   g. Move the data labels to the inside ends of the pie pieces.
   h. Select the legend and center it between the left edge of the chart border and the pie.
   i. Use the Position button to center the chart at the top of the page with square text wrapping.
2. Save the document with the name **U2-ExpendChart**.
3. Print and then close **U2-ExpendChart**.

Figure U2.2 Assessment 4

	Percentage
Basic Education	42%
Special Needs	20%
Support Services	19%
Vocational	11%
Compensatory	8%

Assessment 5

Merge and Print Letters

1. Look at the information shown in Figure U2.3 and Figure U2.4. Use the Mail Merge feature to prepare six letters using the information shown in the figures. When creating the letter main document, open **SoundLtrhd** and then save it with the name **U2-SoundMD**. (Change the punctuation in the greeting line from a comma to a colon.) Create the data source file with the text shown in Figure U2.3 and name the file **U2-SoundDS**. (When creating the data source, customize the columns to accommodate the text in the figure.)
2. Type the text in the main document as shown in Figure U2.4. Insert the *Title* and *Last_Name* fields in the last paragraph as indicated.
3. Merge the document with the **U2-SoundDS** data source file.
4. Save the merged letters document and name it **U2-SoundLtrs**. Print and then close the document.
5. Save and then close the main document.

Assessment 6

Merge and Print Envelopes

1. Use the Mail Merge feature to prepare Size 10 envelopes for the letters created in Assessment 5.
2. Specify **U2-SoundDS** as the data source document.
3. Save the merged envelopes document and name the document **U2-SoundEnvs**.
4. Print and then close **U2-SoundEnvs**.
5. Save the envelope main document with the name **U2-SoundEnvMD** and then close the document.

Figure U2.3 Assessment 5

Mr. Antonio Mercado
3241 Court G
Tampa, FL 33623

Ms. Kristina Vukovich
1120 South Monroe
Tampa, FL 33655

Ms. Alexandria Remick
909 Wheeler South
Tampa, FL 33620

Mr. Minh Vu
9302 Lawndale Southwest
Tampa, FL 33623

Mr. Curtis Iverson
10139 93rd Court South
Tampa, FL 33654

Ms. Holly Bernard
8904 Emerson Road
Tampa, FL 33620

Figure U2.4 Assessment 5

December 14, 2021

«AddressBlock»

«GreetingLine»

Sound Medical is switching hospital care in Tampa to Bayshore Hospital beginning January 1, 2022. As mentioned in last month's letter, Bayshore Hospital was selected because it meets our requirements for high-quality, patient-centered care that is also affordable and accessible. Our physicians look forward to caring for you in this new environment.

Over the past month, staff members at Sound Medical have been working to make this transition as smooth as possible. Surgeries planned after January 1 are being scheduled at Bayshore Hospital. Mothers delivering babies after January 1 are receiving information about delivery room tours and prenatal classes available at Bayshore Hospital. Your Sound Medical doctor will have privileges at Bayshore Hospital and will continue to care for you if you need to be hospitalized.

You are a very important part of our patient family, «Title» «Last_Name», and we hope this information is helpful. If you have any additional questions or concerns, please call our health coordinator at (813) 555-9886 between 8:00 a.m. and 4:30 p.m.

Sincerely,

Jody Tiemann
District Administrator

XX
U2-SoundMD

Assessment 7 Create and Insert Custom Building Blocks

1. Using the Open dialog box in Word, open the template **CPTemplate** and then save it as a template with the name **U2-CPTemplate**.
2. This template contains three custom building blocks for Capital Properties. Add two more custom building blocks with the following specifications:
   a. Select the heading *Attorney's Fees* and the paragraph of text below the heading and then save the selected text in a custom building block in the Quick Part gallery with the name *Fees*.
   b. Select the image (the horizontal line and house with *Est. 1990*) and then save the image as a custom building block in the Footer gallery with the name *CPFooter*.
3. Select and then delete the entire document.
4. Save and then close **U2-CPTemplate**.
5. Use File Explorer to open a blank document based on **U2-CPTemplate**.
6. Build a real estate agreement by completing the following steps:
   a. Insert the *CPHeader* building block located in the Header gallery. Close the Header pane.
   b. Insert the *CPFooter* building block located in the Footer gallery. Close the Footer pane.
   c. Insert the *REAgreement* building block located in the Quick Part gallery.
7. Save the document and name it **U2-CPAgreement**.
8. Print and then close **U2-CPAgreement**.
9. Use File Explorer to open a blank document based on **U2-CPTemplate**.
10. Build a lease agreement by completing the following steps:
    a. Insert the *CPHeader* building block located in the Header gallery. Close the Header pane.
    b. Insert the *CPFooter* building block located in the Footer gallery. Close the Footer pane.
    c. Insert the *LeaseAgreement* building block located in the Quick Part gallery.
    d. Move the insertion point to the beginning of the heading *Use of Premises* and then insert the *Fees* building block in the Quick Part gallery. (If necessary, press the Enter key to start a new paragraph at the *Use of Premises* heading.)
11. Save the document and name it **U2-CPLease**.
12. Print and then close **U2-CPLease**.

Assessment 8 Insert Comments and Track Changes in an Online Shopping Report

1. Open **OnlineShop** and then save it with the name **U2-OnlineShop**.
2. Move the insertion point to end of the first paragraph in the report and then insert a comment and type the following comment text: Include the source where you found this definition.
3. Move the insertion point to the end of the paragraph in the *Online Shopping Venues* section and then insert a comment and type the following comment text: Include at least two of the most popular online shopping stores.
4. Click the *Display for Review* option box arrow and then click *All Markup* at the drop-down list, if necessary.
5. Turn on Track Changes and then make the following changes:
   a. Delete the comma and the words *and most are eliminating paper tickets altogether*, which display at the end of the last sentence in the second paragraph. (Do not delete the period that ends the sentence.)
   b. Edit the heading *Advantages of Online Shopping* so it displays as *Online Shopping Advantages.*

c. Apply bold formatting to the first sentence of each bulleted paragraph on the first page.
d. Turn off Track Changes.

6. Display the Word Options dialog box with *General* selected and then type Trudy Holmquist as the user name and TH as the user initials. (Make sure you insert a check mark in the *Always use these values regardless of sign in to Office* check box.)
7. Turn on Track Changes and then make the following changes:
   a. Delete the words *the following* in the first paragraph in the *Online Shopping Advantages* section.
   b. Type the following bulleted text between the third and fourth bulleted paragraphs on the second page: Keep thorough records of all transactions.
   c. Turn off Track Changes.
8. Print the document with markups.
9. Display the Word Options dialog box with *General* selected and then change the user name back to the original name and the initials back to the original initials. (Remove the check mark from the *Always use these values regardless of sign in to Office* check box.)
10. Accept all the changes in the document *except* reject the change deleting the comma and the text *and most are eliminating paper tickets altogether*. (Leave the comments in the document.)
11. Save, print, and then close **U2-OnlineShop**.

Assessment 9 Restrict Formatting in a Report

1. Open **CompPioneers** and then save it with the name **U2-CompPioneers**.
2. Display the Restrict Editing task pane and then restrict formatting to the Heading 1 and Heading 2 styles. (At the message that displays asking if you want to remove formatting or styles that are not allowed, click No.)
3. Enforce the protection and include the password *report*.
4. Click the Available styles hyperlink in the Restrict Editing task pane.
5. Apply the Heading 1 style to the title of the report (*PIONEERS OF COMPUTING*) and apply the Heading 2 style to the two headings in the report (*Konrad Zuse* and *William Hewlett and David Packard*).
6. Close the Styles task pane.
7. Close the Restrict Editing task pane.
8. Save, print, and then close **U2-CompPioneers**.

Writing Activities

Activity 1

Create Building Blocks and Compose a Letter

You are the executive assistant to the vice president of Clearline Manufacturing. You are responsible for preparing company documents and decide to create building blocks to increase the efficiency of and consistency in the documents. Press Ctrl + N to open a blank document and then save the document as a template named **U2-CMTemplate** in your WL2U2 folder. Create the following building blocks in the template:

- Create a letterhead that includes the company name and any other enhancements to improve the appearance. Save the letterhead as a building block in the Header gallery.
- Create a building block footer that inserts the company address and telephone number. (You determine the address and telephone number.) Include a visual element in the footer, such as a border. Save the footer building block in the Footer gallery.
- You send documents to the board of directors and decide to include the board members' names and addresses as building blocks. Save each board member's name and address as a building block in the Quick Part gallery.

Ms. Nancy Logan
12301 132nd Avenue East
Warminster, PA 18974

Mr. Dion Jarvis
567 Federal Street
Philadelphia, PA 19093

Dr. Austin Svoboda
9823 South 112th Street
Norristown, PA 18974

- Create a complimentary close building block that includes *Sincerely yours,* your name, and the title *Executive Assistant*. Save the building block in the Quick Part gallery.

Delete the contents of **U2-CMTemplate** and then save the template. (This saves the building blocks you created in the template.)

At a blank document, write the body of a letter to a member of the board of directors and include at least the following information:

- Explain that the director of the Human Resources Department has created a new employee handbook and that it will be made available to all new employees. Also mention that the attorney for Clearline Manufacturing has reviewed the handbook and approved its content.
- Open **CMHandbook** and then use the headings to summarize the contents of the handbook in a paragraph in the letter. Explain in the letter that a draft of the handbook is enclosed.
- Include any additional information you feel the directors may want to know.

Save the body of the letter as a separate document named **U2-CMLtr** and then close **U2-CMLtr**. Use File Explorer to open a blank document based on **U2-CMTemplate** and then create a letter to Nancy Logan with the following specifications:

- Insert the letterhead building block you created for Clearline Manufacturing.
- Insert the footer building block.
- Insert the building block containing Nancy Logan's name and address.
- Insert into the document the file named **U2-CMLtr**.

- Insert the complimentary close building block.
- Insert any other text or make any changes to complete the letter.

Save the completed letter and name it **U2-CMLtrNL**. Print and then close the letter. Complete similar steps to create a letter to Dion Jarvis. Save the letter and name it **U2-CMLtrDJ**. Print and then close the letter. Complete similar steps to create a letter to Austin Svoboda. Save the letter and name it **U2-CMLtrAS**. Print and then close the letter.

Activity 2

Create a Slogan Building Block

You decide to create a building block for the company slogan and save it in **U2-CMTemplate**. Open **U2-CMTemplate** from your WL2U2 folder. In the template, create a text box with the slogan *Where innovation and production come together.* inside the text box. Enhance the appearance of the text box by applying formatting similar to that applied to the company letterhead. After creating the text box, select it and then save it in the Text Box gallery with the name **CMSlogan**. After saving the text box as a building block, delete the text box and then save and close **U2-CMTemplate**. Use File Explorer to open a document based on **U2-CMTemplate**. Insert the letterhead header building block and the footer building block you created in Activity 1 and then insert the text box building block you created in this activity. Save the document and name it **U2-CMDocument**. Print and then close **U2-CMDocument**.

Internet Research

Create a Population Chart

Use a search engine to determine the population of the country in which you currently live for the years 1970, 1980, 1990, 2000, and 2010. Create a line chart with the information you find. Apply formatting to the chart to make the data easy to interpret and to improve the visual interest of the chart.

Save the document and name it **U2-Population**. Print and then close **U2-Population**.

Job Study

Format a Guidelines Report

As a staff member of a computer e-tailer, you are required to maintain cutting-edge technology skills, including being well versed in the use of new software applications, such as those in the Microsoft Office suite. Recently, your supervisor asked you to develop and distribute a set of strategies for reading technical and computer manuals that staff members will use as they learn new applications. Use the concepts and techniques you learned in this textbook to edit the guidelines report as follows:

1. Open **Strategies** and then save it with the name **U2-Strategies**.
2. Turn on Track Changes and then make the following changes:
   a. Change all the occurrences of *computer manuals* to *technical and computer manuals*.
   b. Format the document with appropriate heading styles.
   c. Turn off Track Changes.
   d. Insert at least two comments about the content and/or formatting of the document.
   e. Print the list of markups.
   f. Accept all the Tracked Changes.
3. Insert a table of contents.
4. Number the pages in the document.
5. Insert a cover page.
6. Save, print, and then close **U2-Strategies**.

Level 2

BENCHMARK SERIES

Microsoft® Word 365

2019 Edition

Review and Assessment

Nita Rutkosky

Audrey Roggenkamp
Pierce College Puyallup
Puyallup, Washington

Ian Rutkosky
Pierce College Puyallup
Puyallup, Washington

PARADIGM
EDUCATION SOLUTIONS
St. Paul

Vice President, Content and Digital Solutions: Christine Hurney
Director of Content Development: Carley Fruzzetti
Developmental Editor: Jennifer Joline Anderson
Director of Production: Timothy W. Larson
Production Editor/Project Manager: Jen Weaverling
Senior Design and Production Specialist: Jack Ross
Cover and Interior Design: Valerie King
Copy Editor: Communicáto, Ltd.
Testers: Janet Blum, Traci Post
Indexer: Terry Casey
Vice President, Director of Digital Products: Chuck Bratton
Digital Projects Manager: Tom Modl
Digital Solutions Manager: Gerry Yumul
Senior Director of Digital Products and Onboarding: Christopher Johnson
Supervisor of Digital Products and Onboarding: Ryan Isdahl
Vice President, Marketing: Lara Weber McLellan
Marketing and Communications Manager: Selena Hicks

Cover Photo Credit: © lowball-jack/GettyImages

ISBN 978-0-76388-719-3 (print)
ISBN 978-0-76388-708-7 (digital)

875 Montreal Way
St. Paul, MN 55102
Email: CustomerService@ParadigmEducation.com
Website: ParadigmEducation.com

Printed in the United States of America

28 27 26 25 24 23 22 21 20 19   1 2 3 4 5 6 7 8 9 10 11 12